D1216816

Writing
Matters

A Handbook for Writing and Research

Rebecca Moore Howard
Syracuse University

McGraw Hill

Connect
Learn
Succeed™

The *McGraw·Hill* Companies

Connect
Learn
Succeed™

Published by McGraw-Hill, an imprint of The McGraw-Hill Companies, Inc., 1221 Avenue of the Americas, New York, NY 10020. Copyright © 2010. All rights reserved. No part of this publication may be reproduced or distributed in any form or by any means, or stored in a database or retrieval system, without the prior written consent of The McGraw-Hill Companies, Inc., including, but not limited to, in any network or other electronic storage or transmission, or broadcast for distance learning.

This book is printed on acid-free paper.

1 2 3 4 5 6 7 8 9 0 WCT/WCT 0 9

ISBN: 978-0-07-241875-0
MHID: 0-07-241875-3

Editor in Chief: *Michael Ryan*
Editorial Director: *Beth Mejia*
Publisher: *David S. Patterson*
Director of Development: *Dawn Groundwater*
Sponsoring Editor: *John Kindler*
Developmental Editors: *Jane Carter and David Chodoff*
Executive Market Development Manager: *Nanette Giles*
Editorial Coordinators: *Jesse Hassenger, Patrick Brown*
Executive Marketing Manager: *Allison Jones*
Senior Digital Sponsoring Editor: *Paul R. Banks*
Digital Product Manager: *Andrea Pasquarelli*

Media Project Manager: *Thomas Brierly*
Production Editor: *Alison Meier*
Art Director: *Jeanne Schreiber*
Cover Design: *Gearbox*
Interior Design: *Elise Lansdon*
Photo Research Coordinator: *Nora Agbayani*
Photo Research: *Deborah Bull and Deborah Anderson*
Art Editor: *Ayelet Arbel*
Production Supervisor: *Louis Swaim*
Composition: *9.5/11 ITC Garamond Light by Thompson Type*
Printing: *45# New Era Matte Thin Plus, Quebecor World Color*

Cover image: Howard Sokol/Index Stock Imagery/Photolibrary
The credits section for this book begins on page C1 and is considered an extension of the copyright page.

Library of Congress Cataloging-in-Publication Data

Howard, Rebecca Moore.
   Writing matters : a handbook for writing and research / Rebecca Moore Howard. — 1st ed.
      p.   cm.
   Includes bibliographical references and indexes.
   ISBN-13: 978-0-07-241875-0 (acid-free)
   ISBN-10: 0-07-241875-3 (acid-free)
   1. English language—Rhetoric—Handbooks, manuals, etc. 2. Academic writing—Handbooks, manuals, etc. I. Title.
   PE1408.H68524 2009
   808'.042—dc22   2009019989

The Internet addresses listed in the text were accurate at the time of publication. The inclusion of a Web site does not indicate an endorsement by the authors or McGraw-Hill, and McGraw-Hill does not guarantee the accuracy of the information presented at these sites.

www.mhhe.com

The love, support, and patience of Tom Howard, Mike Moore, Jack Richardson, and Melisa Richardson have made it possible for me to write this book. *Writing Matters* is dedicated to the memory of my sister, Sandy.

Dear Colleague:

Thank you for taking the time to consider *Writing Matters*! As I look back on a decade's worth of teaching, writing, and research, I ask myself, "Becky, what have you been doing that makes you think it would be a good idea to create a new handbook program for composition?" Since this seems like a question you also might ask, I'll answer.

In *Writing Matters*, I draw on my teaching experience and my research to focus sustained attention on issues of responsibility, specifically the responsibilities writers have to other writers, to their readers, to their topic, and, most especially, to themselves. The result is a teaching and learning framework that unites research, rhetoric, documentation, grammar, and style into a cohesive whole, helping students to find consistency in rules that might otherwise confound them. Students experience responsible writing not only by using conventions appropriate to their audience—an academic readership, for example, as opposed to readers of an informal blog—but also by writing clearly and providing readers with the information and interpretation they need to make sense of a topic. Students demonstrate responsible writing not only by citing the work of other writers accurately but also by treating those writers' ideas fairly. They practice responsible writing by providing reliable information about a topic at a depth that does the topic justice. Most importantly, they embrace responsible writing by taking their writing seriously and approaching writing assignments as opportunities to learn about new topics and to expand their scope as writers.

Rebecca Moore Howard has researched and published extensively on literacy education and plagiarism. She has been driven by a concern that plagiarism circumvents the education that she regards as instrumental in individual development and essential for a democratic society. She is Associate Professor of Writing and Rhetoric at Syracuse University.

Students are more likely to write well when they think of themselves as writers rather than as error-makers. By explaining rules in the context of responsibility, I address composition students respectfully as mature and capable fellow participants in the research and writing process.

Sincerely,

Rebecca Moore Howard

Writing Matters helps students recognize and respect their role in their own writing by focusing on four key areas of responsibility:

1. **Responsibility to other writers**
2. **Responsibility to audience**
3. **Responsibility to topic**
4. **Responsibility to self**

Getting It Across

Incorporating Visual Evidence

Visuals can offer crucial support in college research projects as examples, explanations of processes, or presentations of factual or statistical data. When including visuals, place a figure number in the text and in the figure caption, so readers can identify immediately the visual to which you are referring. Also include the following in the figure caption:

■ A title or brief description of the illustration.

■ The point you are making with the visual without repeating information from the text.

■ Source information, if the visual or data in the visual is borrowed.

Remember that, in academic essays, all visuals must contribute to your argument, not merely ornament the text.

3. Introduce and contextualize borrowed material with signal phrases.

To incorporate borrowed material smoothly, use a ***signal phrase*** to identify sources. A signal phrase couples the name of the writer from whom you are borrowing words or ideas with a verb that conveys your sense of the writer's intent.

In choosing a verb, consider the attitude or position of the writer you are citing. Is the writer making a claim? Is she or he agreeing or disagreeing, or even conceding a point? Or is the writer's position neutral? You will often choose a neutral verb, such as *writes, says,* or *comments.* (In the example paragraph on pp. 289–90, Nichols uses "argues" and "agrees.") Where possible, though, go beyond these neutral verbs to indicate the writer's attitude:

Oscar Wilde quipped, "A poet can survive everything but a misprint."

For the Wilde quotation above, *quipped* ("uttered a witty remark") is clearly appropriate, given the cleverness of the sentence quoted. *Snarled,* on the other hand, would not be appropriate: Wilde's quip may have an edge to it, but most would disagree that the anger or viciousness associated with the verb *snar-* ing signal verbs, avoid implying an intention that ca determined by a dispassionate reading of the source.

To hold your audience's interest, vary the signal and your placement of the signal phrase. (A list of signa in the Quick Reference box on p. 292.) In most cases, contextualize borrowed information the first time you

Writing Matters teaches students to recognize and respect other authors, not only by citing their work accurately but also by treating their ideas fairly.

Writing Matters demonstrates that writers must be responsible to their audience, for example, by using conventions appropriate to their readership, by writing clearly and providing readers with the information and interpretation they need to make sense of a topic, and by considering feedback to drafts by others through processes such as peer review.

2. Regionalisms, colloquialisms, and slang

Regionalisms are expressions that are characteristic of particular areas. Saying the car "needs washed" is acceptable in Pittsburgh but not in Boston. The expression "I might could do it" might be acceptable in Pikeville, Kentucky, but not in Des Moines, Iowa. Regionalisms can be appropriate in conversation or informal writing but are usually out of place in formal academic writing.

▶ Many scientists believe that we might ~~could~~ *be able to* slow global warming if

   we can reduce carbon emissions.

Colloquialisms are informal expressions common in speech but usually out of place in formal writing.

▶ An R rating designates a movie that is not appropriate for ~~kids~~ *children*

   under 17 who are not accompanied by ~~a grown-up~~ *an adult.*

Used judiciously, however, the occasional colloquialism can add verve to your writing.

▶ The musicians were only kids, none of them more than ten years old,

   but they played like seasoned professionals.

Slang is the extremely informal, inventive, often colorful (and off-color) vocabulary of a particular group. People in the group may use it as a badge of membership, a way to distinguish themselves from outsiders. Slang is often ephemeral, passing rapidly in and out of fashion. Some terms endure, however, and, like *jazz*, enter the ranks of widely accepted vocabulary. In general, slang is inappropriate in formal writing, but as with colloquial language, when used sparingly and judiciously, it can enliven a sentence and help emphasize an important point.

connect
mhconnectcomposition.com
Additional resources: QL29001

Writing Responsibly **Online Shortcuts**

Users of text messaging, instant messaging, and social networking sites have developed a host of acronyms and abbreviations—like *BTW* for "by the way" and *LOL* for "laughing out loud"—that save typing time and space on the tiny screens of mobile phones. With the possible exception of informal email, these expressions are almost never appropriate in other contexts, particularly not in academic or business writing. The same applies to emoticons like :-) and :-(and to other shortcuts such as writing entirely in lowercase without punctuation, as in *i saw her this am.*

Responsibility to Audience

Make It Your Own!

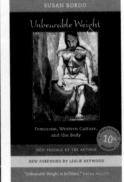

FIGURE 14.1 Popular versus scholarly books *The South Beach Diet* (Rodale) is a popular-press book aimed at a general audience: people wanting to lose weight. *Unbearable Weight: Feminism, Western Culture, and the Body* (University of California Press), on the other hand, is a scholarly book about our culture's obsession with women's weight; its target audience is scholars in fields such as women's studies and cultural studies.

those in scholarly publications are likely to be the most reliable of all.

■ **Is the author an expert on the topic?** Does the author have special knowledge of or experience with the subject? You can determine this by reading about the author in a biographical ~~finding~~ other works the author has pub-~~lish~~ing the author's academic background, and ~~whet~~her the author has been cited in the foot-~~not~~es of other reliable sources.

~~Is th~~e~~m objective?~~ Does the author use an ~~argu~~reasonable claims supported by logical ~~evi~~dence, recognize alternative perspectives, ~~wit~~h respect? Or does the author use emo-~~tional langu~~age, make exaggerated claims, or sup-~~port wit~~h faulty logic and questionable or scanty ~~evidence? ...~~may care deeply and write passionately ~~about a topic. I~~f he or she ~~characterizes groups unfairly~~ ~~or attacks the indivi~~~~...one, then you~~

> **More about ▶▶▶**
> Biographical reference works,
> 236–37

connect
mhconnectcomposition.com
Additional resources: QL14002

> **More about ▶▶▶**
> Tone, 16–17, 143,
> 567, 573–75
> Opinion vs. belief,
> 154–56
> Types of evidence,
> 46–47
> Bias, 568–71

Writing Responsibly **Choosing a Fresh Topic**

In addition to making sure your topic is arguable, you should also ask yourself the following questions:

1. Is my topic fresh?
2. Do I have something to add?
3. Is it worth reading (and writing) about?

Thinking critically about saturated topics (such as abortion and gun control) is difficult. Instead of articulating your own reasons, you can easily wind up offering a rehash of other people's.

The topics about which you can write most interestingly are those on which you have a distinctive perspective. Almost any eighteen-year-old can write passionately about the drinking age, for example, but to justify resuscitating tired topics, you have to have something original to add. Whatever topic you choose, you will have your best shot at engaging your readers and doing justice to your topic when you write about something you and your readers will find compelling.

Writing Matters helps students recognize their responsibility to provide reliable information about their topic at a depth that does the topic justice.

Writing Matters emphasizes the responsibility writers have to themselves to take their writing seriously and to approach writing tasks as an opportunity to learn about a topic and to expand their scope as writers.

Part Four

Research
Matters

Writing
↑ Responsibly   Voice and Responsibility

Because the passive voice allows the agent of an action to remain unnamed, it lends itself to misuse by people evading responsibility for their own or others' mistakes and misdeeds. Consider, for example, the classic dodge of the cornered politician or bureaucrat: "Mistakes were made."

Be on the lookout for this evasive use of the passive voice in the statements and writing of others and, of course, in your own. It is a usage that comes all too readily to hand when we need to convey unflattering or damaging information about ourselves or others whom we represent.

Writing Matters Makes Responsible Writing Easier!

Writing Matters empowers students to own their ideas and to view their writing as consequential, and it equips them with a powerful set of tools that can help put responsible writing into practice. Developed by studying the workflow of students and their instructors through hours of ethnographic, qualitative, and quantitative research, *Writing Matters* offers:

- a flexible, powerful toolkit
- a familiar, web-based interface including an authority-based keyword search
- proven course architecture
- market-tested content
- additional learning, writing, editing, and research resources

The Tools for Writing Responsibly

Writing Matters includes a web-based assignment and assessment platform that connects students with their coursework, their classmates, and their instructors.

- **Customized Learning Plans.** *Writing Matters* promotes original thinking and writing by giving instructors a system for individualizing content, assignments, and learning plans. *Writing Matters* recognizes that different students need different plans to become responsible writers.

- **Documentation Tools.** Students can practice being responsible to other writers and to their sources and learn to meet the documentation requirements of an assignment through numerous interactive, step-by-step citation activities for a wide range of print and electronic sources.

Students: Visit **ShopMcGraw-Hill.com** to purchase registration codes for this exciting new product. Instructors: Contact **English@mcgraw-hill.com**.

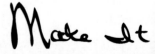

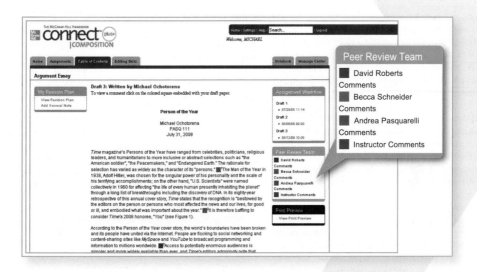

Superior Peer Reviewing Capability

Writing Matters provides superior peer review capability, allowing students not only to see and consider the comments of others but also to create a roadmap for revision based on the feedback they receive. The *Writing Matters* peer review system embraces the idea of a writer's responsibility to audience and self, providing a better way for writers to understand their readers, to recognize the impact of their writing on others, and to revise their work in a way that honors the contributions of their peers. Instructors can use the technology to organize peer groups that reflect classroom dynamics, improving the peer review experience for their students.

your Own!

Acknowledgments

The creation and evolution of *Writing Matters* has been an exciting and humbling experience. I began in the belief that I knew what I was doing, but I quickly realized that I had launched myself on the path not only of sharing what I know but also of learning what I should know. *Writing Matters* lists a single author, Rebecca Moore Howard, but that author is actually the central figure in a collaboration of hundreds of students, teachers, and editors.

Students from all over the country have generously contributed their ideas and their writing to *Writing Matters*: Abrams Conrad from American University; Betsy Smith, Barnard College; Lynn Holmlund and Joe Olinto, Bentley College; Robyn Worthington, Bristol Community College; Leyla Abdul-Mesih, Broward Community College; Cassie Neary, Cazenovia College; Charlie Eichacker, Lauren Harding, Judith Murphy, and Richard Waterman, Colby College; Billy Archer, Emily Braseth, Lauren Cohen, Elizabeth Harbison, Derek Hom, Michelle LeRoux, Molly Patterson, Alicia Regina, and Hollie Young, Colgate University; Shona Sequeira, Connecticut College; Yuen Yuen Lim and Amy Snyder, Cornell University; Darlery Franco and Sonu Ray, Drew University; Rita McMahan, Eastern Oregon University; Christina Huey, Georgia Southern University; Michael Conrad, Hampden-Sydney College; Amy Ehret, Illinois State University; Kathryn Betz, Heather DeGroot, and Brandon White, James Madison University; Stephanie Warnekros, Jefferson County Community College; Mary Bennett, Johnson County Community College; Amanda Godfrey, Mike Parr, and Stephanie Traub, McHenry County College; Isaiah Samson, New York University; Heidi Johnson, Jeff Loken, and Erika Schuler, North Dakota State University; Caitlin Cairns, Mike Haxton, and Ideen Tabatabai, Oklahoma City University; Stephen Scotti, Pepperdine University; Jeremy Van Keuren, Portland State University; Alea Wratten, SUNY–Geneseo; Jonathan Adler, Jana Barnello, Erin Buksbaum, Milissa Carter, Kelly Concannon, Tom Hackman, Rachana Ky, Dave Marsteller, Lydia Nichols, Jia Shin, Jessica Toro, and Joe Vogel, Syracuse University; Adrianne Anderson, Texas Christian University; Rachel Bateman and Aura Whitcomb, University of Kansas; Alicia Keefe, University of Maryland; Alyssa Laferrera and Frances Freire, University of Miami; Leonard Lin, University of Southern California; Leah Rabinowitz, Wellesley College; and Michael Bosomworth, Western Illinois University. Many students at Syracuse, Binghamton, and Colgate Universities have responded to my ideas and drafts; in particular, I thank Katie Garman, Laura Grimm, and Kelsea Loveless.

I would like to thank the instructors who have provided invaluable insights and suggestions as reviewers and members of the board of advisors. Talking with instructors at all sorts of institutions and learning from them about the teaching of writing has been an unparalleled experience. As a result of this project, I have many new colleagues, people who care deeply about teaching writing and who are experts at doing so.

Writing Matters Board of Advisors

Sonja Andrus, *Collin County Community College*
Steve Brahlek, *Palm Beach Community College, Lake Worth*
Richard Carpenter, *Valdosta State University*
April Childress, *Greenville Technical College*
Darren DeFrain, *Wichita State University*
Jason DePolo, *North Carolina A&T State University*
Heather Eaton, *Daytona State College*
Nancy Enright, *Seton Hall University*
Stacha Floyd, *Wayne County Community College*
Cathy Gorvine, *Delgado Community College*
Steffen Guenzel, *University of Alabama*
Lynda Haas, *University of California—Irvine*
Brandy James, *University of West Georgia*
Susan Lang, *Texas Tech University*
Heidi Marie Magoon Connor, *Aims Community College*
Caroline Mains, *Palo Alto College*
Sarah Mallonee, *Indian River State College*
Randall McClure, *Florida Gulf Coast University*
Janice McIntire-Strasburg, *St. Louis University*
Shellie Michael, *Volunteer State Community College*
Irv Peckham, *Louisiana State University*
K. J. Peters, *Loyola Marymount University*
Sharon Prince, *Wharton County Junior College*
Shelley Rodrigo, *Mesa Community College*
John Ross, *Fort Hays State University*
Michelle Sidler, *Auburn University*
James Suderman, *Northwest Florida State College*
Judith Szerdaelyi, *Western Kentucky University*

Manuscript Reviewers

Allan Hancock College: Kate Adams
Angelina College: Howard Cox, Patty Rogers
Anne Arundel Community College: Sandra Goettel, Jacquelyn Lyman, Grace Sikorski
Baltimore City Community College: Paul Long
Barton College: Michael Fukuchi
Benedictine University: Jean-Marie Kauth, Elizabeth Kubek
Black Hills State University: David Cremean, Vincent King, Ronda Mehrer
Boston University: Matthew Parfitt
Bowie State University: Stephanie Johnson

> ❝ This is a contemporary, student-focused text that offers sound, practical advice for any college writer. It is so much more than a first-year handbook—in fact, this is the type of text students can invest in and use their entire college career. It is an excellent and engaging guide to communicating effectively and ethically. ❞
>
> —Caroline Mains, *Palo Alto College*

Bowling Green State University: Dawn Hubbell-Staeble, Erica Messenger
Calhoun Community College: Stephen Calatrello
California State University—Chico: David Martins
Capital University: Kevin Griffith
Catawba Valley Community College: Jimmy Rumple
Cecil College: Craig Frischkorn
Central New Mexico Community College: Rosemary Day
Central Piedmont Community College: Barbara Urban
Central Texas College: Joshua Everett
Centralia College: Linda Foss, Susanne Weil
Clark Atlanta University: Constance Chapman
Clark State Community College: Laurie Buchanan, Cecilia Kennedy, Kathryn Ward
Collin County Community College: Susan Grimland
County College of Morris: Janet Eber, Mary Anne Garbowsky
Cuyahoga Community College: Ashlee Brand
Darton College: Elizabeth Gassel
East Mississippi Community College: Elizabeth Stringer

East Tennessee State University: Thomas Holmes
Eastern Arizona College: Tracy Lassiter
Florida Community College at Jacksonville: Amanda Bauch, Susan Brackin, Carol Grimes, Laura Jeffries, Daniel Powell, Susan Slavicz, Christopher Twiggs
Frank Phillips College: Shannon Carroll
Gadsden State Community College: Melia Gagliardo
Georgetown College: Stacy Cartledge, Carrie Cook
Georgia Gwinnett College: Thomas Clancy
Greenville Technical College: April Childress, Susan Perry, Tom Treffinger
Indian River State College: Donald Skinner, April Van Camp
Jackson State Community College: Powell Franklin
Joliet Junior College: James Baskin, Tamara Brattoli
Jones County Junior College: David Lowery, Patti Smith, Tammy Townsend, Cheryl Windham
Kishwaukee College: Nate Gordon, Tina Hultgren, Todd West
Lake-Sumter Community College: Jacklyn Pierce
Lamar State College—Orange: Andrew Preslar, Arlene Turkel, Gwen Whitehead
Lamar University: Daniel Bartlett, Nancy Staub

> ❝ *Writing Matters* breathes new life into old topics with its real-world focus and reader-friendly approach. It gives students an identity as writers, and encourages them to be responsible for their writing reputations and to acknowledge intellectual property. ❞
>
> —Susan D. Aguila, *Palm Beach Community College, Lake Worth*

Lambuth University: Ann Ecoff
Lee College: Michael Gos, Gordon Lee, Debbie Smart, Al Zucha
Lincoln University: William Donohue
Lorain County Community College: Kimberly Greenfield, Suzanne Owens
Louisiana State University: Michael Alleman
Loyola University Chicago: Margaret Loweth
Macomb Community College: Donna Marino
Marist College: Joseph Zeppetello
Mercy College—Dobbs Ferry: Sean Dugan
Miami Dade College: Robert Hach
Middle Tennessee State University: Jean Rhodes

Midland College: Pamela Howell, Mary Williams
Montgomery College—Takoma Park/Silver Spring: Robert Giron
Morgan State University: Helen Madry, Adam Mekler
Nicholls State University: Keri Turner
North Carolina A&T State University: Jason DePolo
Northern Illinois University: Kathleen Turner
Northern Virginia Community College—Alexandria: Brian Delaney
Northern Virginia Community College—Annandale: Christina Wells
Northwest Florida State College: Beverly Holmes, James Suderman, Patrice Williams
Palm Beach Community College: Susan Aguila, Diane Bifano, Steve Brahlek, Regina Dilgen, John Kadela, Shelly Hedstrom, Patricia McDonald, Vicki Scheurer
Palo Alto College: Ruth Ann Gambino, Caroline Mains, Diana Nystedt
Pensacola Junior College: Marian Wernicke
Piedmont College: Stephanie Almagno
Pitt Community College: Patricia Baldwin
Point Park University: Robert Alexander, P. K. Weston
Polk Community College: Rebecca Heintz
Roanoke College: Jennifer Maclean, Jennifer Rosti
Santa Fe College: Naana Banyiwa Horne, Marcy Carbajal-Van Horn, Gail Ellyson
Seton Hall University: Nancy Enright, Ed Jones
South Arkansas Community College: Jennifer Baine
Southeast Community College: Carolee Ritter
Southern University—Baton Rouge: Kendric Coleman
Southern University—Shreveport: Joyce Cottonham
Southwestern Illinois College: Steve Moiles
St. Clair Community College: John Lusk
St. Johns River Community College: Paul Andrews, Melody Hargraves, Elise McClain, Jeannine Morgan, Rebecca Sullivan
St. Louis Community College—Meramec: Richard Peraud
SUNY New Paltz: Pauline Uchmanowicz
Tarrant County College: Kirk Adams, Jeanette Adkins, Pamela Bensons, Dixil Rodriguez, Vicki Sapp

Tennessee State University: Samantha Morgan-Curtis
Texas Tech University: Susan Lang
The College of New Jersey: Nina Ringer
Tulsa Community College: Mary Cantrell, Ken Claney
University of Arkansas: Carole Lane
University of Arkansas Community College—Morrilton: Gretchen Schol
University of Central Arkansas: Donna Bowman
University of Houston—Downtown: Michael Dressman, Catherine Howard, Daniel Shea
University of Illinois at Urbana-Champaign: Cara Finnegan, Grace Giorgio
University of Maryland—University College: Andrew Cavanaugh
University of South Florida: Elizabeth Metzger
University of St. Thomas: Suzanne Donsky
University of Texas—Arlington: Jennifer Cooper, Ruth Gerik, Luke Tesdal
University of Texas—El Paso: Amanda Cuellar
University of Texas—San Antonio: Marguerite Newcomb
University of the Cumberlands: Tom Frazier, Jolly Sharp
University of Toledo: Michelle Davidson, Anthony Edgington
Valdosta State University: Richard Carpenter, Jane Kinney, Chere Peguesse
Vance-Granville Community College: Crystal Brantley, Tanya Olson
Walters State, The Great Smoky Mountains Community College: Chris Morelock, Carla Todaro
Wesley College: Linda De Roche, Jeffrey Gibson
West Liberty State College: William Clough
West Virginia Wesleyan College: Eric Waggoner
Westminster College: Susan Gunter
Wharton County Junior College: Mary Lang, Jennifer Mooney, Sharon Prince
Wichita State University: Darren DeFrain

> From the open to the close of the text, it charges [students] with being critical thinkers and responsible writers. One of the most effective aspects of this text is the concurrent theme of what 'matters.'
>
> —Carla Todaro, *Walters State, The Great Smoky Mountains Community College*

Design Reviewers

Angelina College: Howard Cox, Patty Rogers
Boston University: Matthew Parfitt
Bowie State University: Stephanie Johnson
Capital University: Kevin Griffith
Cecil College: Craig Frischkorn
Clark State Community College: Laurie Buchanan, Cecilia Kennedy
Georgia Gwinnett College: Thomas Clancy
Greenville Technical College: April Childress
Indian River State College: April Van Camp
Jones County Junior College: Cheryl Windham
Loyola University Chicago: Margaret Loweth
Northern Virginia Community College—Alexandria: Brian Delaney
Northwest Florida State College: James Suderman, Patrice Williams
Palm Beach Community College: Patricia McDonald, Vicki Scheurer
Palo Alto College: Ruth Ann Gambino, Caroline Mains, Diana Nystedt
Seton Hall University: Nancy Enright
Southwestern Illinois College: Steve Moiles
St. Clair County Community College: John Lusk
St. Johns River Community College: Melody Hargraves, Elise McClain, Jeannine Morgan, Rebecca Sullivan
Tennessee State University: Samantha Morgan-Curtis
University of Illinois at Urbana-Champaign: Grace Giorgio
University of Maryland—University College: Andrew Cavanaugh
University of Texas—San Antonio: Marguerite Newcomb
Valdosta State University: Richard Carpenter, Jane Kinney, Chere Peguesse
Wesley College: Linda De Roche
Westminster College: Susan Gunter
Wharton County Junior College: Mary Lang, Sharon Prince
Wichita State University: Darren DeFrain

Symposia Attendees

Every year McGraw-Hill conducts several writing symposia for instructors from across the country. These events offer a forum for instructors to exchange ideas and experiences with colleagues they might not have the chance to meet otherwise.

They also provide an opportunity for members of the McGraw-Hill team to learn about the needs and challenges of writing program instructors and students. The feedback we have received has been invaluable and has contributed—directly and indirectly—to the development of *Writing Matters*.

Alabama State University: Kevin Hicks
Angelina College: Howard Cox, Edith Miller
Anne Arundel Community College: Rebecca Kajs
Arizona State University: Duku Anokye, Sherry Cisler, Katherine Heenan, Christine Helfers, Camille Newton, Sherry Robertson, Shirley Rose
Arizona Western College—Yuma: Steve Moore
Auburn University: John Hagerty, Victoria Lisle, Michelle Sidler
Auburn University at Montgomery: Elizabeth Woodworth
Bergen Community College: Lou Ethel Roliston
Bowie State University: Sidney Walker
Brevard Community College: Beverly Slaughter
Bridgewater State College: Ann Doyle
Broward College: Carolyn Barr
Bucks County Community College: Lois Gilmore
Butte College: Molly Emmons
Calhoun Community College: Stephen Calatrello
Capella University: Stone Shiflet
Central Florida Community College: Sandra Cooper, Chuck Gonzalez
Central New Mexico Community College: Rosemary Day
Central Piedmont Community College: Lynn Kirk
Central Texas College: Mike Matthews
Clark State Community College: Laurie Buchanan, Cecilia Kennedy
Coastal Carolina University: Ellen Arnold
College of DuPage: Jim Allen, Karin Evans, Sheryl Mylan, Beverly Reed, Cathy Stablein
Columbia College of Chicago: Jennie Fauls, Matthew Killian McCurrie
Columbus State Community College: Lisa Gordon
Cuyahoga Community College: Colleen Lloyd, Beverly Thornton
Darton College: Elizabeth Gassel
Daytona State College: Evan Rivers
Delgado Community College: Janet McArthur
El Camino College: Bruce Peppard
El Paso Community College: Mauricio Rodriguez
Florida Atlantic University—Boca Raton: Barclay Barrios

Florida International University—Biscayne:
Michael Creeden

Gadsden State Community College: Charles Hill

George Washington University: Cayo Gambler,
Michael Svoboda

Georgia State University: Baotong Gu

Glendale Community College: Carmela Arnoldt,
Marla Desoto, Claire Englehart, Casey Furlong, Kay
Grosso, Johnnie May

Houston Community College: Alan Ainsworth,
Rob Blain, Sandy Jordan, Michael Ronan,
Syble Simon

Hudson Valley Community College:
Anne Dearing

Indian River State College: Ray Considine,
April Van Camp

Ivy Tech Community College: Carol Schuck

Jackson State Community College: Mark Walls

James Madison University: Elizabeth Gumnior

Joliet Junior College: Laura Basso

Jones County Junior College: Cheryl Windham

Keiser University: Mara Rainwater

Kennedy-King College: Terry Clark

Lakeland Community College: Jayne Magee

Lamar State College—Orange: Arlene Turkel

Loyola University Chicago: Victoria Anderson,
Margaret Loweth

Marshall University: Roxanne Kirkwood

Mesa Community College: Shelley Rodrigo

Metropolitan State College of Denver: Jane
Chapman Vigil

Mississippi State University: Ann Spurlock

Montgomery County Community College: Bonnie
Finkelstein

Moraine Valley Community College: Erika Dieters,
Shelita Shaw

New York University: Denise Martone

Nicholls State University: Keri Turner

North Carolina Central University: Regina Alston

North Lake College: D'Ann Madewell

Northeast State Technical Community College:
Victoria Houser, William Wilson

Northern Arizona University: Bruce Fox

Northern Virginia Community College:
Christina Wells

Northwest Arkansas State Community College:
Audley Hall

Northwest Florida State College: Beverly Holmes

Palm Beach Community College—Lake Worth:
Steve Brahlek, Roberta Proctor

Palo Alto College: Ruth Ann Gambino

Pima Community College: Meg Files

Polk Community College: Rebecca Heintz,
Sherry Siler

Pulaski Technical College: Joey Cole

Sacred Heart University: Sandra Young

Samford University: Charlotte Brammer

San Antonio College: Irma Luna

Scottsdale Community College: Julie Knapp

Seton Hall University: Nancy Enright

Shawnee Community College: Judy Strickland

South Mountain Community College:
Alisa Cooper

Southern University—Shreveport: Joyce
Cottonham

Southwest Tennessee Community College:
Loretta McBride

Southwestern Illinois College: Tom Lovin,
Steve Moiles

St. John's River Community College:
Jeannine Morgan

St. Louis Community College: Jim Sodon

SUNY—New Paltz: Pauline Uchmanowicz

Tarrant County College: Jeannette Adkins, Ruth
McAdams

Towson University: Cheryl Brown

University of Akron: William Thelin

University of Alabama: Karen Gardiner, Steffen
Guenzel, Jessica Kidd, Denise Millstein,
Kevin Waltman

University of Alabama at Birmingham: Peggy Jolly

University of Delaware: Melissa Ianetta

University of Maryland: Elizabeth Colson

University of Miami: Andrew Green, Gina Maranto

University of Texas—Arlington: Jennifer Cooper

University of Texas—San Antonio:
Marguerite Newcomb

University of West Georgia: Maren Henry,
Brandy James

Valdosta State University: Richard Carpenter,
Chere Peguesse

Valencia Community College: Susan Dauer

Volunteer State Community College:
Shellie Michael

**Walters State, The Great Smoky Mountains
Community College:** Chris Morelock, Carla
Todaro

Weatherford College: Beau Black

Western Connecticut State University:
Anam Govardhan

Wharton County Junior College: Sharon Prince

Components of *Writing Matters*

Writing Matters includes a tightly crafted array of components for instructors and students. As a first step in the authoring process, the author team met in New York for an all-day workshop dedicated to exchanging ideas and developing a plan to build a thoroughly integrated course solution. Under the leadership of Rebecca Moore Howard, the team established a supplements strategy, situating each resource in relation to the project's overarching emphasis on writing responsibly.

Writing Matters includes the following resources: *Instruction Matters, Assessment Matters, Practice Matters* (Application, ESL, Grammar), and *Presentation Matters*.

Instruction Matters

Andrew Preslar, *Lamar State College*
The Instructor's Manual includes teaching tips and learning outcomes. This manual connects each component to the core material and ensures that the exercises are relevant to the handbook and to the student.

Assessment Matters

Elizabeth Kubek, *Benedictine University*
This flexible assessment tool offers twenty to thirty exercises or questions per chapter.

Practice Matters

Writing Matters offers students a wealth of grammar and ESL activities and exercises to practice writing well. Included are:

Exercises for ESL Students
by Jason DePolo, *North Carolina A&T State University*

Exercises for Students
by Jacqueline Lyman, *Anne Arundel Community College*

Grammar Exercises for Students
by Mary Lang, *Wharton County Junior College*

Presentation Matters

Marguerite Newcomb, *University of Texas–San Antonio*
This *PowerPoint* deck is designed to give new teachers confidence in the classroom and can be used as a teaching support tool by all instructors. The *PowerPoint* slides emphasize key ideas and help students take useful notes. Instructors can alter the slides to meet their own needs.

The *Writing Matters* Team
Jason DePolo, *North Carolina A&T State University;* Elizabeth Kubek, *Benedictine University;* Andrew Preslar, *Lamar State College;* Mary Lang, *Wharton County Junior College;* Rebecca Moore Howard, *Syracuse University;* Jacquelyn Lyman, *Anne Arundel Community College;* Marguerite Newcomb, *University of Texas–San Antonio.*

Additional Resources

MLA Quick Reference Guide

(ISBN: 0-07-730080-7)

Preston Allen, *Miami Dade College*

This handy card features the basic guidelines for MLA citation in a convenient, portable format.

APA Quick Reference Guide

(ISBN: 0-07-730076-9)

Carol Schuck, *Ivy Tech Community College*

This handy card features the basic guidelines for APA citation in a convenient, portable format.

CourseSmart
Learn Smart. Choose Smart.

Visit coursesmart.com to purchase registration codes for this exciting new product.

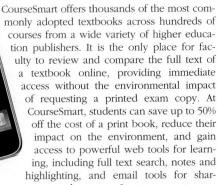

CourseSmart offers thousands of the most commonly adopted textbooks across hundreds of courses from a wide variety of higher education publishers. It is the only place for faculty to review and compare the full text of a textbook online, providing immediate access without the environmental impact of requesting a printed exam copy. At CourseSmart, students can save up to 50% off the cost of a print book, reduce their impact on the environment, and gain access to powerful web tools for learning, including full text search, notes and highlighting, and email tools for sharing notes among classmates. Learn more at www.coursesmart.com.

Personal Acknowledgments

Writing Matters is the result of rich collaboration with a creative, supportive, knowledgeable team who have a deep understanding of both teaching and publishing: Tom Howard, senior lecturer in University Studies at Colgate University, has worked with me from the beginning to the end, and his intelligence and ingenuity are evident everywhere in this project. Colleagues have also drafted sections of *Writing Matters:* Amy Rupiper Taggart from North Dakota State, Chapter 24, "Writing in Business and as a Citizen"; Ted Johnston, El Paso Community College, and Maggie Sokolik, University of California–Berkeley, Part 9, "ESL Matters," and the ESL boxes that appear throughout *Writing Matters;* and Sandra Jamieson, Drew University, and Bruce R. Thaler, many of the exercises. McGraw-Hill has supported the project from beginning to end. My thanks go out to David Patterson, publisher for English; Dawn Groundwater, director of development; Lisa Moore, now the publisher for literature, who signed this book and helped me develop its early structure; Christopher Bennem, who shepherded *Writing*

Matters to full draft; John Kindler; Nanette Giles; and Allison Jones. My special thanks go to David Chodoff, senior development editor, whose wit and attention to detail have made Parts 7, 8, and 9 and the project as a whole both lively and compact; and to Jane Carter, senior development editor, who has been my collaborator and mentor, teaching me how to develop a new writing handbook.

In addition, *Writing Matters* has benefited greatly from the efforts of an extended editorial team: Anne Stameshkin; Joshua Feldman; Leslie Taggart; Judy Voss; Jesse Hassenger; Patrick Brown; Jen Nelson; Denise Wright; Paul Banks; and Andrea Pasquarelli. It has been a pleasure to work with an outstanding production team: Alison Meier; Jeanne Schreiber; Elise Lansdon; Nora Agbayani; Deborah Bull; Deborah Anderson; Ayelet Arbel; Marty Moga; Elsa Peterson; Louis Swaim; Tom Brierly; Margaret Moore; and Nancy Ball. In particular, I would like to thank Joan Pendleton, the copyeditor, whose careful eye saved me from many embarrassing errors, and Alison Meier, our production editor, who juggled schedules and personalities with aplomb.

Contents

Part Two   Reasoning Matters   Reading, Thinking, and Arguing   115

Part Five   Documentation Matters 297

Part Six Genre Matters Writing in and beyond College 447

Part Seven Style Matters 515

Part Eight Grammar Matters 599

Part One

Writing Matters

Planning, Drafting, Revising, Editing, Proofreading, Formatting

Writing Responsibly: A Checklist

Audience

- ❑ Have you chosen a topic that is appropriate and interesting to your reader?

- ❑ Does your title prepare your reader for what follows?

- ❑ Does your thesis focus your reader's attention on your main point?

- ❑ Will your reader find the reasons you supply logical and compelling?

- ❑ Have you supplied enough relevant evidence to persuade your reader to accept (or at least to consider) your position?

- ❑ Will your reader find your project logically organized?

- ❑ Will your reader find your paragraphs clearly organized and tightly focused?

- ❑ Have you provided transitions to guide your reader?

- ❑ Is your project written at an appropriate level for your reader?

- ❑ Is your tone appropriate to your reader?

- ❑ Have you revised, edited, and proofread your project so that your reader will find the writing clear, correct, and powerful?

Writing Responsibly: A Checklist

Other Writers

❏ Have you given credit to those from whom you have borrowed words or ideas, whether you have summarized, paraphrased, or quoted material or whether your source is printed or online?

❏ Have you avoided patchwriting by paraphrasing borrowed material fully, putting the text into your own words and sentence structures?

❏ Have you represented the ideas of other writers accurately and fairly?

❏ Have you treated other writers respectfully, even when you disagree with them?

❏ Have you considered alternative viewpoints?

❏ Have you addressed alternative perspectives that conflict with your own position?

Topic

❑ Have you explored your topic thoroughly and creatively?

❑ Have you conducted research (when needed), using the most in-depth and reliable sources available to you?

❑ Have you provided logical reasons that support your thesis?

❑ Have you provided sufficient evidence to support your claims?

❑ Have you used visuals when they are the most effective way of presenting supporting evidence or when they provide a visual example (and only when they are appropriate to your context and genre)?

❑ Have you assessed your sources carefully and presented evidence from reliable sources?

❑ Have you represented ideas borrowed from sources accurately and fully?

Lydia Nichols

Ms. Concannon

Writing 205

6 April 2009

Holy Underground Comics, Batman! Moving Away from the Mainstream

When most people think of comic books, predictable images usually come to mind: caped heroes, maniacal villains, deeds of incredible strength, and other typical elements of super-powered adventures. Undeniably, characters like Batman, Superman, and Spider-Man are the most prominent features of the comic book landscape, in terms of both popularity and of revenue (Wright xiv). However, there is more to comic books than superpowers and secret identities. Underground comics (also known as *comix*), printed by small publishers or by individual artists, are very different from what is usually expected in the genre. While far less well-known than their superhero counterparts, underground comics often offer an innovative and more sophisticated alternative to mainstream titles.

Almost from the beginning, comic books were associated with superheroes. The first comic books appeared in the early 1930s, nearly four decades after comic strips such as *Yellow Boy* began appearing in the major newspapers. Yet comic books did not gain widespread popularity until June of 1938, when writer Jerry Siegel and artist Joe Shuster debuted their character Superman in *Action Comics* #1 (Daniels 9). Superman was an immediate success, and he quickly inspired the creation of copycat superheroes in other comic books. The protagonists

This paper appears in full on pp. 346–57.

Audience/Topic: Nichols chooses a title that reflects her topic and draws the reader in.

Topic: Nichols uses reliable sources, including scholarly books (see list of works cited, pp. 356–57).

Audience: Nichols writes at a level appropriate for college-level readers, and writes clearly and correctly.

Audience: Nichols uses a transition ("Yet") to prepare readers for a contrasting idea.

Audience: Nichols chooses a topic that engages both the writer and her reader.

Audience: Nichols starts the paragraph with a topic sentence to focus the reader's attention.

Topic: Nichols provides an accurate summary of information borrowed from Daniels.

of these comics each had their own strengths and vulnerabilities, but the stories all shared a basic formula: individuals with extraordinary abilities battling against evil and struggling to maintain a secret identity. These superhero comics, though similar to each other, set the comic book industry on its feet, paving the way to profits and sustained success (Daniels 9). Over the decades and even today, the best-selling comics have typically been in the superhero genre.

> **Other writers:** Nichols paraphrases fully to avoid "patchwriting."

While artists and writers over the years have certainly done inventive work in superhero comics, some similarity in mainstream titles was for many years unavoidable. This was due to the creation in 1954 of the Comics Code Authority (CCA), an organization formed by a number of the leading comic publishers to regulate the content of comics (Heller 101). It set very explicit standards, dictating what content was allowed in comic books and what content was expected. Some parts of the code are incredibly specific and controlling:

> **Self:** Nichols writes in a voice that is true to herself and appropriate to her audience, context, and genre.

> **Self:** Nichols has revised, edited, and proofread to make the essay the best reflection of herself that it can be.

> **Other writers:** Nichols represents the ideas of others accurately and fairly.

> The letters of the word "crime" on a comics magazine shall never be ap-
> preciably greater in dimension than the other words contained in the title.
> The word "crime" shall never appear alone on a cover. . . . Restraint in
> the use of the word "crime" in titles or subtitles shall be exercised. (qtd. in
> "Good Shall Triumph over Evil")

> **Other writers:** Nichols uses quotations as support and cites sources.

Other rules were more general—vague enough to allow the CCA a free hand in shaping content. One read, "Respect for parents, the moral code, and for honorable behavior shall be fostered" (qtd. in "Good Shall Triumph over Evil"). The CCA also regulated the presentation of criminals and criminal acts, themes of religion and race, and dialogue, especially profanity. While the CCA had no legal authority,

> **Self:** Nichols synthesizes information from a variety of sources to provide the reader with something original.

This paper appears in full on pp. 346–57.

Yourself

❑ Have you used the writing assignment to learn something new and to expand your scope as a writer?

❑ Have you represented your ideas clearly, powerfully, and accurately?

❑ Have you integrated your own ideas or your own synthesis of sources to provide a text that is original and interesting?

❑ Have you used language inclusively, avoiding bias and representing yourself as a respectful person?

❑ Have you written in a voice that is true to yourself and in keeping with your context (academic, business, public, personal) and genre (college essay, PowerPoint presentation, newsletter)?

❑ Have you revised, edited, and proofread your project to make sure your presentation reflects the effort you have put into the writing?

❑ Is your project the best representation of yourself that you can make it?

1 Writing Responsibly in the Information Age

In 2004, the National Commission on Writing published a report called "Writing: A Ticket to Work . . . Or a Ticket Out,"[1] surveying 120 of the largest corporations in America. Among the results: American corporations expect their salaried employees to be able to write clearly, correctly, and logically. Eighty percent of finance, insurance, and real estate employers take writing skills into consideration when hiring salaried employees. "The survey reveals that good writing is . . . a 'threshold skill' for salaried employment and promotion" (5). These employers regard writing clearly, logically, and accurately; for the appropriate audience; and with the necessary level of support and documentation as core business skills (12).

But writing well is more than a ticket to a good job. Whether drafting business emails or making *PowerPoint* presentations, texting friends or tweaking a *Facebook* page, updating a blog or even composing a paper for a college course, we write to develop and evaluate beliefs and ideas, to move others, to express ourselves, and to explore possibilities. For all these reasons and more, writing matters!

---

[1] For a copy of the report (as a PDF file), visit <http://www.collegeboard.com/prod_downloads/writingcom/writing-ticket-to-work.pdf>.

1a Writing Today

Since Johannes Gutenberg's invention of the printing press in about 1440, a *page* has been a sheet of paper covered with text, and *literacy* has been the ability to read and write the text on that page. But as the internet revolution changes our understanding of what a page is, it also expands our concept of literacy (Figure 1.1). Today, a page can be a sheet of paper, but it can also be a screen in a website or an email message on a BlackBerry; it can include not only words, but also images and sound files, links to other web pages, and flash animations. The ability to exploit these new kinds of pages requires not one literacy but multiple literacies.

Like most people reading this book, you are probably already multi-literate: You read and produce "texts" in a variety of media. You shift from medium to medium easily because the "literacies" of each medium are not entirely separate. Whether penning a thank-you note, searching a library database, interpreting an advertisement, composing a college paper, or texting your best friend, you analyze and interpret, adjusting your message in response to your purpose, audience, and context.

More about ▶▶▶
Writing business
  memos, 501–03
Creating *Power-
  Points*, 204–5
Creating websites,
  191–98
Writing in literature
  and other humani-
  ties, 448–71 (ch. 21)
Writing in the sci-
  ences, and social
  sciences, 472–86
  (ch. 22)
Reading critically,
  116–40 (ch. 7)
Interpreting visuals,
  129, 131, 135
Incorporating
  visuals, 105,
  314–15, 336–37,
  342–44, 387

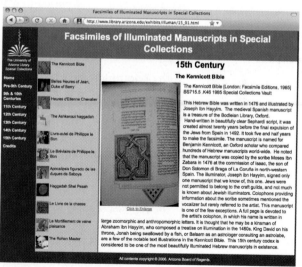

FIGURE 1.1 The Kennicott Bible The Kennicott Bible (left) was handwritten in Hebrew in 1476, nearly fifty years after Gutenberg invented the printing press. The original is housed in the Bodleian Library at Oxford University. Today, images of the Kennicott Bible are available in a facsimile edition and online (right).

This handbook, *Writing Matters,* focuses on the ability to read and write, which remains the central literacy. This literacy is so important that years of education are devoted to it, and it is so complex that books such as *Writing Matters* are essential tools. Yet *Writing Matters* also addresses digital, visual, oral, and information literacies because these literacies have become impossible to separate from one another and from traditional literacy. They can be as important as the ability to read and write. As a reader, you must be able not only to decipher written language but also to interpret visuals. As a writer, you may incorporate graphics into papers in economics and psychology courses; contribute to class blogs or discussion boards; search online databases; or create presentations using *PowerPoint* and *WebEx*. As both a reader and a writer, you will be expected to manage all the information you receive and transmit. Being multiliterate *means* being information literate.

Getting It
Across   "Code-Switching" between Media

"Code-switching" is the ability to adjust your language to your context. Bilingual speakers code-switch, or alternate between languages, depending on the audience they are addressing. Writers code-switch in response to the medium in which they are communicating: in print or online; in person, over the internet, and on the telephone; in words, sounds, and images. However you are communicating with others, think carefully about how you can best use the medium to convey your message, and tailor your message to your audience.

connect
mhconnectcomposition.com
Additional resources: QL1001

1b The Writer's Responsibilities

With opportunities to express and even create yourself in words come responsibilities to your readers, to the topics you address, to the other writers from whom you borrow and to whom you respond, and perhaps especially to yourself.

1. Your responsibilities to your readers

If audience members are to spend their time reading your work, then you must make it worth their while:

- Choose a topic that they will find interesting and about which you have something fresh to say.

- Make a claim that will focus their reading.

- Provide thoughtful, logical, even creative supporting reasons and evidence.

- Consider carefully the credibility of your sources.

- Write clearly: The reader (even if that reader is your composition teacher) should not have to struggle to understand what you are trying to say. Do this by building a logical structure, using transitional techniques to guide readers, and correcting errors of grammar, punctuation, and spelling.

- Write appropriately by adopting a tone and vocabulary that are in keeping with your topic, audience, context, and genre.

- Write engagingly by varying sentence structures and word choices, avoiding wordiness, and using repetition only for effect.

2. Your responsibilities to your topic

Examples of writers who did not take seriously their responsibility to their topic are everywhere. Here are three:

- A six-year-old child who won tickets to a Hannah Montana concert with an essay about her father's Iraq War death; her father had *not* been killed in Iraq. She lost those tickets.

- Jayson Blair, a *New York Times* reporter who concocted stories without leaving his apartment; he was forced to resign.

- The president of Raytheon Company, who plagiarized large sections of his book *Swanson's Unwritten Rules of Management* from a book published in 1944; he was fined one million dollars by the company's shareholders.

You show respect for your topic when you explore it thoroughly and creatively and when you offer supporting evidence that is accurate, relevant, and reliable. Offering adequate support means not making up evidence or relying on untrustworthy sources. Showing responsibility toward your topic also means not suppressing evidence that does not support your position. In a college essay, hiding evidence might lead merely to a bad grade; in the workplace, it could have life-and-death consequences: The Merck pharmaceutical company is accused of suppressing evidence that its drug Vioxx could cause heart attacks and strokes. Many patients may have suffered, and the company faces a host of lawsuits.

More about ▶▶▶
Writing responsibly, foldout following p. 1
List of Writing Responsibly boxes, page facing inside back cover
Devising a topic, 22–29
Finding information, 222–47 (ch. 13)
Using supporting evidence, 46–48
Evaluating sources, 248–62 (ch. 14)
Organizing, 37–42
Providing transitions, 61–62
Correcting grammar, 600–736 (part 8, Grammar Matters)
Correcting punctuation, 782–867 (part 10, Details Matter)
Writing with flair, 515–98 (part 7, Style Matters)

connect
mhconnectcomposition.com
Additional resources: QL1002

More about ▶▶▶
Avoiding hypothetical "evidence," 47
Avoiding altering images inappropriately, 86–89

Quick **Reference** ➡ **Your Responsibilities as a Writer**

Four areas of responsibility:

1. To your readers
2. To your topic
3. To other writers
4. To yourself

3. Your responsibilities to other writers

You have several responsibilities to other writers whose work you may be using.

More about ▶▶▶
Using a search
  engine, 223–26
Using an online
  database, 228–33
Using an electronic
  library catalog,
  238–41

More about ▶▶▶
When to quote, para-
  phrase, or summa-
  rize, 269–79, 290
Using quotation
  marks, 814–23
  (ch. 50)
Formatting block
  quotations, 342,
  386, 897
Adjusting quotations
  using brackets and
  ellipses, 820–21,
  832, 835–36

More about ▶▶▶
Citing and docu-
  menting sources,
  298–446 (chs.
  17–20)
Avoiding plagiarism
  and "patchwriting,"
  267–68, 271–75
Common knowl-
  edge, 265–67

Acknowledge Your Sources Writing circulates easily today, and unfathomable quantities of it are available online, readily accessible through search engines such as *Google* and databases such as *JSTOR*. It may seem natural, then, simply to copy the information you need from a source and paste it into your own text, as you might if you were collecting information about a disease you were facing or a concert you hoped to attend. But when you provide readers with information, ideas, language, or images that others have collected or created, you also have a responsibility to *acknowledge* those sources. Such acknowledgment gives credit to those who contributed to your thinking, and it allows your readers to read your sources for themselves. Acknowledging your sources also protects you from charges of plagiarism, and it builds your authority and credibility as a writer by establishing that you have reviewed key sources on a topic and taken other writers' views into consideration.

To acknowledge sources in academic writing, you must do *all three* of the following:

1. When quoting, copy accurately and use quotation marks or block indention to signal the beginning and end of the copied passage; when paraphrasing or summarizing, put the ideas fully into your own words and sentences.
2. Include an in-text citation to the source, whether you are quoting, paraphrasing, or summarizing.
3. Document the source, providing enough information for your readers to locate the source and to identify the type of source you used. This documentation usually appears in a bibliography at the end of college research papers.

You need not, however, acknowledge sources of *common knowledge,* widely known information such as the chemical composition of water (H_2O) or the capital of Nebraska (Lincoln).

 Writing Responsibly around the World Concepts of plagiarism vary from culture to culture. Where one culture may see cooperation, another may see plagiarism. Even if borrowing ideas and language without acknowledgment is the custom in your home culture, writers in the United States (especially in academic contexts) must acknowledge all ideas and information borrowed from another source.

Writing
↑ Responsibly   **Your College's Plagiarism Policy**

Most colleges publish their plagiarism policies in their student handbook, which is often available online. Consult the handbook's table of contents or index, or search your college's website, using key terms such as *plagiarism, academic honesty,* or *academic integrity*. Before writing a research project, read your school's plagiarism policy carefully. If you are unsure what the policy means, talk with your adviser or instructor. In addition to the general policy for your college, read your course syllabi carefully to see what specific guidelines your instructors may provide there.

Obtain Copyright Clearance While plagiarism is concerned with acknowledging sources of ideas or language, copyright focuses on the right to compensation for the use of writers' words and ideas in a public context. When writers use a substantial portion of another writer's text, they must not only acknowledge the source but also obtain the original author's permission, often in exchange for a fee.

As a student, your use of sources is covered under the *fair use* provision of copyright law, which allows you to include copyrighted material without permission in projects for a class. If, however, you were to publish a project for readers beyond your class (and a web page is a publication), your text would no longer be exclusively for educational purposes, and you would have to obtain permission for extensive use of the borrowed material.

How long a work is covered by copyright varies from one country to another and changes over time. Even after copyright expires, however, you would still have to acknowledge quotations, paraphrases, or summaries to avoid plagiarizing.

Copyright protections also apply to you as a writer: Anything you write is protected by U.S. copyright law, and other writers must obtain your permission before reusing substantial portions of your work in a public context.

Treat Other Writers Fairly Your responsibility to other writers does not stop with the need to acknowledge your use of their ideas or language. You must also represent *accurately* and *fairly* what your sources say: Quoting selectively to distort meaning or taking a comment out of context is irresponsible. So is treating other writers with scorn. After radio talk-show host Bill Cunningham made disparaging remarks about Democratic presidential candidate Barack Obama at a McCain rally, John McCain demonstrated his sense of responsibility by denouncing

Cunningham's remarks and calling Obama an "honorable American" with whom he has "strong philosophical differences." McCain drew a distinction between ideas and the person espousing the ideas. This distinction is as important in academic writing as it is in politics: It is perfectly acceptable to criticize the ideas of others; in fact, a large part of the academic endeavor is to examine ideas under the bright light of careful scrutiny. But treating the people who developed the ideas with derision is not. Avoid ad hominem (or personal) attack, and focus your attention on the ideas and expression of these ideas by other writers.

More about ▶▶▶
Bias, 568–71
Ad hominem, 152

4. Your responsibilities to yourself

Your final responsibility is to yourself as a writer. Writers represent themselves on paper and screen through the words and images (and even sounds) they create and borrow, so submitting a paper as your own that someone else has written is a form of impersonation—it does not represent you. Make sure that the writing "avatar," or **persona,** you create is the best representation of yourself it can be. Encourage readers to view you with respect by treating others—not only other writers but also other people and groups—respectfully and without bias. Engender respect by synthesizing information from sources to produce new, fresh, and compelling ideas and by using language clearly, correctly, logically, and with flair. In short, gain respect by producing the best writing you can.

More about ▶▶▶
Synthesis, 132–34
Common sentence
  problems, foldout
  following p. 599
Style, 515–98 (part 7,
  Style Matters)
Grammar, 600–736
  (part 8, Grammar
  Matters)
Punctuation and me-
  chanics, 782–867
  (part 10, Detail
  Matters)

This chapter began by reporting on the importance that some of the largest employers in the United States attach to good writing—clear, logical, correct, and persuasive writing. If you graduate from college having learned to be an effective writer, you will have learned something employers value highly. More importantly, though, you will have fulfilled a key responsibility to yourself.

Writing Responsibly   **Taking Yourself Seriously as a Writer**

Many students enter writing classes thinking of themselves as "bad writers." This belief can be a self-fulfilling prophecy—students fail to engage because they already believe they are doomed to fail. You can escape from this vicious circle by remembering that writing is not an inborn tal-

ent but a skill to be learned. Instead of thinking of yourself as a bad writer, think of yourself as a writer-in-progress, someone who has something to say and who is learning how to say it effectively.

⟶ EXERCISE **1.1** Assessing the writer's responsibilities

Read "Plagiarism Cheats Students," written by Salt Lake Community College student Jeff Gurney for his college newspaper, *The Globe*. To what extent do you agree with Gurney's argument? What reservations do you have about it? What other issues of writers' responsibilities might a revision of the article take into account?

Plagiarism Cheats Students

By JEFF GURNEY (23 Nov. 2005)

In the world of higher education, your growth as a student comes with a heavy price. Many hours are spent reading, researching and writing for required reports in most of your classes. This means staying up many nights until almost dawn and drinking a lot of coffee.

Or at least this is how it should be. Unfortunately, an amazing number of students are getting into buying ready-made reports. There are many places that you can go online and pick the type of paper you want. For a fee they will send you the paper and all you have to do is change a few sentences. Once that part is done all you need to do is turn it in.

This is the way some students have made it through college. Then the professors got smart and noticed that there were a lot of papers that sounded pretty much the same or had just about the same content.

Along come services like Turnitin .com where the professor tells you to first send the report online, and for a fee, usually paid for by the school, your paper is compared to many different papers and texts that are in a massive data base. The service can tell in percentages how much content in your paper was gleaned from other sources.

This service also provides [instructors] with the results of the scan and tells them what your scores are in each of several categories.

Over the past few years there have been several writers working for very prominent media services that have been caught plagiarizing, and surprisingly they were using quite a bit of other people's stuff. The most amazing thing about this misuse is that they worked for trusted publications and broke that trust for money.

In a recent study reported by Mark Edmundson in the *New York Times* (September 9, 2003, p. A29), 38 percent of American college students admitted to committing "cut and paste" plagiarism. This percentage is up 10 percent from 2000.

These numbers pose a question. What is the reason we go to college? Are you attending SLCC merely to get a better job, or to learn something in the process for that job? An unknown author once said, "If it were easy then everybody would have done it." This is the ideal that those that started higher education probably had in mind. It is much more valuable, that diploma in hand, when you earn it yourself.

2 Planning Your Project

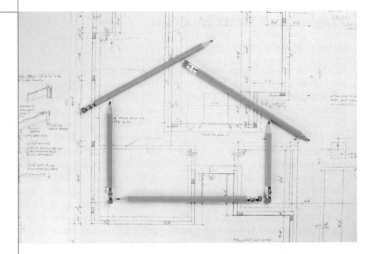

connect

mhconnectcomposition.com

Additional resources: QL2004

Just as an architect creates a blueprint to show how to fit together the concrete footings, steel beams, and electrical wiring of a building, so, too, does a writer create a plan that takes into account the project's purpose, audience, context, and genre. As an architect must choose the right materials (wood or tile? granite or soapstone?) and devise plans to complete the project on budget and on schedule, a writer must select an engaging topic, devise ideas that will resonate with the reader, fulfill the terms of the assignment, and do it all on time.

2a Analyzing Your Writing Situation

The first step in planning a writing project is analyzing the **writing situation:**

- What is your ***purpose***? What do you hope to accomplish with the text?

- Who is your ***audience***? Who will be reading the text you produce and why?

- What are the ***context*** (academic, business, personal) and ***genre*** (or type) of writing you will produce, and what are the conventions governing this context and genre?

Throughout the writing process—planning, drafting, revising, and editing—you will have opportunities to refine or reconsider the decisions you make at the outset to make sure that you are fulfilling your responsibilities as a writer.

66 Believing that I could just sit down and bang out a paper caused me many difficulties. Learning to make a plan and stick to it really helped. 99

—Michael Bosomworth, Western Illinois University

1. Establish a purpose.

The classical reasons, or *purposes,* for writing are to entertain, to express your feelings or impressions, to inform, or to persuade your audience.

- **To entertain.** Entertaining your readers (in the sense of providing them with an engaging reading experience) is a goal all writers share, but it is unlikely to be your primary purpose in academic or business writing.

- **To express thoughts, feelings, or impressions.** In ***expressive*** writing, an experience is often conveyed through *description,* and the language is richly evocative. The purpose of the following paragraph is expressive; the writer's goal is to convey the feelings and experiences of a small would-be ballerina.

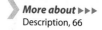

connect
mhconnectcomposition.com
Additional resources: QL2001

> **More about** ▶▶▶
> Description, 66

She stood in the doorframe shivering. She was a tiny girl, about four years old, and her wispy blonde hair was tied back with a pink satin ribbon. Leaning against her mother's leg, she gazed into the unfamiliar room. Other girls her age were twirling and jumping with confidence, laughing at their reflections in the mirrors, spinning on the slippery wooden floors. The girl's mother handed her the ballet shoes, gave her a quick peck on the cheek, and stepped back into the snowstorm. Alone now, the girl retreated to the wall and slid into a dark corner. She bent her knees against her chest and wrapped her arms around her legs. There she sat.

—Amanda Godfrey, McHenry County College, "Ballet Blues"

In most college courses, an expressive purpose is unlikely to be primary, but it may well play a secondary role, as you draw on your own experiences to illustrate a point.

 Writing about Personal Experiences In many cultures, writing about personal issues and experiences is discouraged. Instructors at U.S. colleges and universities, however, sometimes assign expressive essays as a way to get their students to write about something they already know. If you are uncomfortable writing on a personal topic, discuss the issue with your instructor.

connect
mhconnectcomposition.com
Additional resources: QL2002

▶▶▶Sample informative student projects:
   "The Risks of Online Networking," Erin Buksbaum, 106–11
   "The Power of Wardrobe," Heather De-Groot, 389–400
   "Nature vs. Nurture," Robyn Worthington, 479–86

connect
mhconnectcomposition.com
Additional resources: QL2003

More about ▶▶▶
Analyzing and crafting arguments, 141–74 (ch. 8)

■ **To inform.** An *informative* (or *expository*) text may explain a concept, describe a sequence of events or a process, or analyze a relationship. Scientific, technical, journalistic, and business writing are typically informative. The abstract below, which comes from a psychology research paper, is expository because it informs the reader of the results of a psychological study:

> This study explores the potential influence of stereotypical appearances on male subjects' stated opinions regarding entertainment perceived as "feminine." The findings show that participants were more likely to give a favorable ranking of a "chick-flick" in the presence of a counter-stereotypical male than in the presence of a stereotypical male. The discussion focuses on possible explanations for participant behavior, with a theoretical basis in gender role conflict.
>
> —Heather DeGroot, James Madison University,
> "The Power of Wardrobe: Male Stereotype Influences"

■ **To persuade or argue.** Texts that try to convince readers to adopt beliefs or opinions or to take action have a *persuasive* (or *argumentative*) purpose. Editorials, book and movie reviews, and grant proposals all have a persuasive purpose. The paragraph below comes from an editorial. It draws on evidence from studies to support its claim that Head Start is a worthwhile program:

> Head Start, the federally funded pre-kindergarten program, has been under attack recently as a waste of money, because some say the effects don't last long enough to make a difference later in life. I beg to differ. Studies show that eighth graders who were

in Head Start do as well as kids who received education from a private pre-school. Poor children who do not attend Head Start do no better than their parents. To raise our population out of poverty, children must learn at an early age to have confidence, have goals and strive for them, and receive the best education they can. Head Start provides a good start.

—Lynn Holmlund, Bentley College, "Going Public: Head Start"

EXERCISE **2.1** **Analyzing purpose**

Read the passages below and determine whether the primary purpose of each passage is expressive, informative, or persuasive:

connect
mhconnectcomposition.com
Online exercise: QL2101

Camels do not store water in their humps. They drink furiously, up to twenty-eight gallons in a ten-minute session, then distribute the water evenly throughout their bodies. Afterward, they use the water stingily. They have viscous urine and dry feces. They breathe through their noses, and keep their mouths shut. They do sweat, but only as a last resort, after first allowing their body temperatures to rise 10 degrees Fahrenheit. As they begin to dehydrate, the volume of their blood plasma does not at first diminish. They can survive a water loss of up to one-third of their body weight, then drink up and feel fine. Left alone, unhurried and unburdened, they can live two weeks between drinks.

—William Langewiesche, *Sahara Unveiled*

Gentlemen, I want you to suppose a case for a moment. Suppose that all the property you were worth was in gold, and you had to put it in the hands of Blondin, the famous rope-walker, to carry across the Niagara Falls on a tight rope. Would you shake the rope while he was passing over it, or keep shouting to him, "Blondin, stop a little more! Go a little faster!"? No. I am sure you would not. You would hold your breath as well as your tongue and keep your hand off until he was safely over. Now the Government is in the same situation. It is carrying an immense weight across a stormy ocean. Untold treasures are in its hands. It is doing the best it can. Don't badger it! Just keep still, and it will get you safely over.

—Abraham Lincoln, "Reply to Critics of His Administration"

Have you ever had to ask for help, knowing your children will suffer unless you get it? Think about asking for a loan from a relative, if this is the only way you can imagine asking for help. I will tell you how it feels. You find out where the office is that you are supposed to visit.

You circle that block four or five times. Thinking of your children, you go in. Everybody is very busy. Finally, someone comes out and you tell her that you need help. That never is the person you need to see. You go see another person, and after spilling the whole shame of your poverty all over the desk between you, you find that this isn't the right office after all—you might repeat the whole process, and it never is any easier at the next place.

—Jo Goodwin Parker, "What Is Poverty?"

2. Identify and address your audience.

A text is seldom written for the writer alone. Rather, it is intended for an *audience,* and this fact shapes the text in large and small ways. That is why, for a piece of writing to be effective, the writer must make a careful analysis of the intended reader (or readers).

Before putting fingers to keyboard, consider the characteristics of your audience, such as age and gender, occupation and interests, educational background, political or cultural affiliations, and ethnic or religious background. Next, consider the audience's expectations:

- Do your readers already possess a good deal of information about the topic, or are they reading your text to learn about something new?

- Are your readers eager to learn about your topic, or do they have only a passing interest?

- Do readers hold strong opinions about your topic, or are they likely to be open-minded?

Next, consider what will make your writing most effective for this audience:

- **What information will your audience need in order to understand and appreciate what you are saying?** A general audience will need you to define all specialized terms as you use them as well as to provide any background information necessary for them to understand the topic. A specialist audience, on the other hand, may be bored by too much

Writing Responsibly　**Your Audience and You**

Putting yourself in the shoes of your reader is challenging. But as a writer, you have a responsibility to look beyond your own slice of the community, beyond your own experiences and beliefs, beyond your own self-interest. Try adopting a perspective on the issue that contradicts or conflicts with the position you actually hold to see what motivates the supporters of that position. Then, as you write, no matter which position you support in your text, let alternative and opposing viewpoints infuse your writing.

explanation, but they will still need you to define any terms you are using in an unusual sense and to provide background information about aspects of the topic likely to fall outside of their area of expertise. An instructor, while an expert, may expect you to write for a nonspecialist reader.

- **What kinds of language, examples, evidence, or reasons will be most effective?** Someone arguing for the legalization of marijuana in front of a group of college students will make very different choices than will someone arguing the same position in front of an audience filled with police officers and state troopers or with the speaker's parents and relatives.

One way to write for an audience is, first, to picture a few specific people (representative of your audience) and then to think about what each of them will need in order to understand and appreciate what you are saying.

ESL **Getting Help in Understanding Your Audience** When you do not share your readers' cultural experiences, you can turn to your classmates, a writing tutor, or your instructor to help you determine how much background information your readers will need and what kinds of evidence they will find most effective.

The excerpt below shows a writer crafting a text with her audience in mind:

Dear Governor:

Your effort to improve education has been quite extensive. Throughout these past few years the creation of after-school programs that have offered tutoring for students has been possible because of your involvement. You have also formed the National Teachers Academy in Illinois, which works to improve the quality of teaching in schools. In addition, you secured several hundred million dollars that gave libraries the ability to replace many outdated books. Although you have made some great accomplishments for education, the conditions of our schools still call for much improvement. By striving to implement a voucher system, you could cause a nationwide education reform, and give every child a chance at a quality education. . . .

—Amanda Godfrey, McHenry County College

By imagining the governor's reactions, what he might appreciate and what he might resist, Godfrey knows to start her letter by listing the

connect

mhconnectcomposition.com
Additional resources: QL2012

> *More about* ▶▶▶
> Writing letters,
> 496–501 (ch. 24)

actions he has already taken to improve the state's schools. *Then* Godfrey argues for a new school voucher program.

In much of your college writing, you will have an audience of one—your instructor. To satisfy that audience, begin with a careful analysis of what the instructor hopes you will learn from the assignment. These objectives may be specified in the assignment or in the course syllabus, but sometimes you will simply need to ask. Generally, your instructor will be a specialist reader who wants to be reassured that you have done the reading, understood the issues, and synthesized the information from classroom lectures, discussions, and assigned reading. In addition, most instructors want to see that you can express yourself clearly and correctly in writing. To accomplish these goals, provide the following:

- Important background information

- Definitions of key terms

- Explanations of key concepts

- Analysis of the issues

- Synthesis of evidence from assigned reading and classroom discussion to support claims

- Citations and a list of works cited or references for source-based writing

A good way to get a sense of what your instructor expects is to read sample papers or exams from a previous class or sample essays in your discipline. (Ask your instructor if she or he can supply good examples, or read the sample essays in this book.)

3. Match your tone to your purpose and your audience.

When you speak, your tone of voice, gestures, facial expressions, and body language all convey your attitude. Are you patient, annoyed, angry, pleasantly surprised? All of these attitudes are conveyed in a moment by the pitch of your voice or the look on your face. Writers also convey their attitude toward their readers and their subject through their ***tone.*** In writing, tone is conveyed primarily through ***level of diction*** (formal or informal) and the ***connotation*** (emotional resonance) of the words you choose. To write at a formal level of diction, use standard American English; avoid regionalisms (such as *y'all*), colloquial language (such as *what up*), and slang (such as *hot* rather than

More about ▶▶▶
Reading to comprehend, 116–21
Reading to reflect, 124–29
Reading to write, 129–35
Analysis, 129–31
Synthesis, 132–34

More about ▶▶▶
Citing and documenting sources, 298–357 (MLA style, ch. 17), 358–400 (APA style, ch. 18), 401–28 (*Chicago* style, ch. 19), 429–46 (CSE style, ch. 20)

More about ▶▶▶
Developing a thesis, 33–37
Level of diction, 567
Connotation and denotation, 573–75

good or *exciting*); and write in complete sentences (*Are you coming?* rather than just *Coming?*).

Although most college instructors will expect you to adopt a fairly formal level of diction, the individual decisions you make will vary from course to course and discipline to discipline. In some courses, using the first-person pronoun *I* might be perfectly acceptable or even required, but for others (economics, sociology) it might be considered too informal.

 Recognizing Differences in Connotation A word in your first language may share a literal meaning with an English word but have a very different connotation. The word *ambitious* ("eager for success"), for example, can be positive or negative in English; in Spanish, *ambición* is generally negative. If you are not sure how a word is used in American English, consult a dictionary written especially for second-language learners, or check with classmates, a writing tutor, or your instructor.

 ESL *More about*
▶ ▶ ▶
Dictionaries for second-language learners, 585

Whatever the particular demands of your course, all disciplines expect you to adopt a measured tone. In general, opt for connotatively neutral language: Shrill or sarcastic prose will suggest to your audience that your opinions spring from your heart and not your head. This does not mean that emotional topics are off limits or that you may not express your beliefs, but temperance (moderation, self-restraint) is highly valued in academic discourse. Your instructor will expect you to have looked at all sides of an issue carefully before drawing a conclusion and to exhibit respect for those with whom you disagree.

More about ▶ ▶ ▶
Writing in literature and the other humanities, 448–71 (ch. 21)
Writing in the sciences and social sciences, 472–86 (ch. 22)
Exploratory arguments, 142–43
Considering alternative viewpoints, 163–64

→ EXERCISE 2.2 Addressing an audience

Draft a paragraph on one of the topics below as if you were writing to knowledgeable adults (perhaps even college professors). Next, revise the paragraph to address an audience of high school students. Finally, revise it to appeal to a general audience.

1. The importance of participating in local government
2. Restrictions on language, dress, and behavior in public schools
3. Cell phone etiquette
4. Campus parking regulations
5. Individual participation in recycling projects

connect
mhconnectcomposition.com
Online exercise: QL2102

Work **Together**

Working in pairs or small groups, compare your work on Exercise 2.2 with that of your classmate(s). What tone did you each adopt? Point to specific words and discuss their connotations, assess the level of formality of each sample paragraph, and point to words or sentences that make the diction more or less formal. Then discuss the similarities and differences you observed among the paragraphs for each audience.

More about ▶▶▶
Business writing,
498–514
Public writing,
499–501

connect

mhconnectcomposition.com
Additional resources: QL2013

Writing samples
▶▶▶
Essay (academic),
49, 106, 137, 168,
460, 465
Research project
(academic), 168,
346, 389, 422
Essay exam (aca-
demic), 493–95
Letter (business), 500
Memo (business),
502
Résumé (business),
508, 510
Press release (pub-
lic), 513
Editorial (public),
125–27
Article (public), 9,
76, 121
Review (public), 469

4. Consider context and genre.

As earlier sections on addressing an academic audience have implied, the ***context*** (or setting) in which your text is to be read will affect all your writing decisions. So, too, will the ***genre*** (or type) of writing you produce.

The contexts in which you are likely to write, now and in the future, are *academic, business, public,* and *personal.* Like academic writing, business writing generally adopts a formal level of diction and uses words with neutral connotations. Public writing, which ranges from letters to the editor to press releases and reports, generally maintains a fairly formal level of diction (it is directed to a wide-ranging audience), but its tone may be more impassioned than would be appropriate in an academic or business context. An informal tone is most appropriate in a personal context, but even then, the audience makes a difference: A casual, bantering tone and highly informal level of diction might be appropriate in a text message to a friend, while a warm but slightly more formal tone might be appropriate for an email to a grandparent. Whenever you write in an unfamiliar context, consulting examples can help you hit the right note.

In literature classes, you may have learned that poetry, drama, fiction, and nonfiction were the four major literary genres, but genre extends beyond literature. If you are unfamiliar with the genre in which you will be writing, read several examples to determine what they have in common. This handbook contains sample documents in a variety of genres. Your instructor may also be able to provide examples, or you could locate examples in your library or on the internet. Whether you are writing a business email, a scientific report, a grant proposal, or a letter to the editor, the expectations readers have for this type of writing will affect every choice you make.

2b Analyzing an Assignment

Recognizing the purpose of an assignment is crucial to success. If you are asked to *argue* for or against the goals of the plain speech movement of the 1920s, for example, and, instead, you *describe* those goals, you will probably not get an *A*. When analyzing an assignment, look for words that indicate purpose.

The audience for an assignment is, of course, your instructor, and the instructor's goal in assigning the project is to assess your knowledge of the facts, to gauge how well you have synthesized this information with other knowledge, and to assess your ability to express your understanding in writing. Occasionally, your instructor may ask you to imagine another audience—the readership of a particular magazine, for example.

Frequently, an assignment will specify the approach you should take. If you are asked to analyze, for example, your instructor will expect you to break a topic, issue, or text into its component parts and, perhaps, evaluate each one. If your instructor asks you to summarize a reading assignment, you will be expected to write the main idea and key supporting points briefly, in your own words and using your own sentence structures.

> **More about ▶▶▶**
> Analyzing, 129–31, 290–92
> Summarizing, 119–20, 292

Quick Reference ➡ Analyzing the Purpose of an Assignment

If the assignment asks you to . . .	The purpose is . . .	The approach is . . .
describe, explain	informative (expository)	to put into words *what* something looks, sounds, feels, smells, or tastes like; to discuss *how* something functions
assess, evaluate, argue	persuasive	to make a judgment based on evidence or offer an interpretation based on close reading, and to explain *why*
analyze, consider, discuss	informative or persuasive	to break a topic, reading assignment, or issue into its component parts and explain *how* it works; to reflect critically on the pros and cons of an issue, offer an interpretation based on a close reading, and sometimes explain *why* you have reached this conclusion

→ **Tech**

Using Alarms in an Electronic Calendar

Setting an alarm in an electronic calendar on your PDA, cell phone, or computer (in *iCal* or *Outlook, Yahoo!* or *Google*) can remind you of approaching deadlines. These "alarms" can be sounds, pop-ups, or emails.

Sometimes, an assignment will specify the genre, although the genre may be taken for granted. A biology instructor teaching a laboratory class may assume that you understand that a laboratory report is required. If you are not sure what the genre of the assignment is, or what it requires, ask your instructor.

Finally, an assignment will generally include a due date. In order to meet that date, you will have to create a realistic schedule. Start by listing the steps in the writing process in reverse order on a sheet of paper or in a new computer file so that you can work back from the due date. Next, list all your other obligations: other assignments, studying for exams, work, rehearsals or team practices, family and social obligations. Then work backward to figure out how much time you can allot to each task. The more obligations you have, the more time you will need to leave between steps. Finally, write the intermediate due dates on a calendar—a date book, the calendar on your computer, or your PDA. For each of these due dates, write down not just the name of the project ("English paper") but also the specific action that you need to have taken by that date ("outline English paper"). A schedule for a five-page paper that does not require research might look like that shown in Figure 2.1 (p. 21).

▶ More about ▶▶▶
Time management,
212–13
Online assignment
calendar, 213

→ EXERCISE **2.3** **Analyzing an assignment**

Read the assignments below; indicate whether their purpose is informative, persuasive, or both; and underline the words that indicate purpose.

1. Describe two or three medical services available to families in your community, and explain how a family nurse-practitioner could use these services.

2. Evaluate the constitutionality of judicial review, explaining its origins and offering several examples from U.S. Supreme Court decisions.

SEPTEMBER						
Sunday	Monday	Tuesday	Wednesday	Thursday	Friday	Saturday
		19 Track meet	20	21 Comp. assignment distributed	22 Analyze Comp. assignment and writing situation	23 Work Date with the "girls"
24 Generate ideas, develop topic, draft thesis for comp. paper	25 Review notes, draft outline for comp. paper	26 Study for Econ quiz	27 Write first draft, make appt. at Writing Center	28 Econ quiz	29 Bring draft to class for peer review	30 Work

OCTOBER						
Sunday	Monday	Tuesday	Wednesday	Thursday	Friday	Saturday
1 Lunch with Mom & Dad	2 Bring essay to Writing Center	3 Revise comp. essay	4	5	6 → Revise comp. essay	7 Work Proofread & edit comp. paper
8 Format & print comp. paper	9 Comp. paper due	10 Study for psych midterm	11	12	13 → Psych midterm!	14 Work

FIGURE 2.1 A sample calendar Your calendar will differ depending on the complexity of the assignment, the time you have to complete it, and your other obligations.

3. Analyze the impact an increase in the price of higher education in the United States would have on the market for higher education in India.

4. Assess the main arguments of Handlin's *Boston's Immigrants* (1941) in light of the other assigned course reading. Are they still persuasive? Why or why not?

Make It **Your Own**

For an upcoming writing assignment (or one already under way), analyze the assignment and set up a schedule that takes into account all your other obligations.

connect
mhconnectcomposition.com
Additional resources: QL2006,
QL2007

More about ▶▶▶
Finding information,
    222–47 (ch. 13)
Reading and think-
    ing critically,
    116–40 (ch. 7)

2c   Generating Ideas

For some writing projects, especially in college or business, your topic will often be assigned. When you are required to come up with a topic on your own, ask yourself these questions:

- What topics are appropriate to the assignment?
- What topics will interest, exasperate, or intrigue me *and* my reader?
- What topics do I have special access to or knowledge about?

You will be most engaged when you choose a topic that interests you, but your reader will be most engaged when you offer some special knowledge or insight into what you are writing about. You can create that special knowledge by doing research, but you can also create special knowledge by thinking critically about your topic.

Invention techniques, like those outlined below, can help you devise and develop a topic. No single strategy works for everyone, and most writers use several methods. If you have tried some of these before, experiment with the others. Drawing on new techniques may increase your creativity.

ESL **Generating Ideas in English or Your First Language?** Keeping a journal, freewriting, or brainstorming in English can be excellent practice, but if you get stuck, try using words and phrases from your first language. But be careful when returning to your notes to translate not merely your *words* but also your *ideas* into idiomatic English.

1.   Keep an idea journal or commonplace book.

In the nineteenth century, the philosopher Ralph Waldo Emerson wrote his essays from ideas he had jotted down in a notebook. In the twenty-first century, writers often use PDAs, smartphones, or online tools like *Google Docs* to store ideas. Whatever medium you use, you may find that keeping an ***idea journal*** or a ***commonplace book*** (or both) is an effective part of the creative process.

Like a diary, an idea journal is something to write in every day. Unlike a diary, it is not a record of your life but rather of your thoughts. A commonplace book records the ideas (quotations, summaries, paraphrases) of others that you might find useful in the future. You can also use your commonplace book to record your reactions to those ideas. As you jot notes in your commonplace book, record your

More about ▶▶▶
Keeping a reading
    journal, 127–28
Keeping a research
    journal, 217–18

Getting It **Across**   Using an Image to Capture an Idea

Not all ideas need to be written down. Some, in fact, might be easier to capture with a sketch or a photograph (or even a sound or video recording). Ted Salizar included this photograph of a 9/11 memorial in his online idea journal to capture his sense of sadness when visiting the site.

Writing **Responsibly**   Note Taking and Plagiarism

Many people accused of plagiarism have blamed their note-taking system, saying that they did not record the source when taking notes or that they failed to put quotation marks around passages they copied. To avoid finding yourself in such a situation, consider putting all quotations, summaries, and paraphrases in one column of your journal or commonplace book and your own comments and reactions in another. That way, even if you forget to put quotation marks around a quotation or to record a page number, you will not be lulled into believing the words or ideas were your own.

sources and use quotation marks to separate carefully the words of others from your own.

The commonplace book entries shown in Figure 2.2 provided useful material for Erin Buksbaum's essay on social networking sites, the first draft of which appears in chapter 3.

> **More about ▶▶▶**
> Avoiding accidental plagiarism,
> 267–68, 271–75

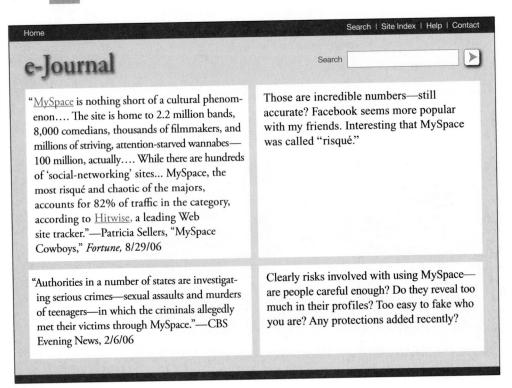

FIGURE 2.2 **Sample entries in an online commonplace book**

Home　　　　　　　　　　　　　　　Search | Site Index | Help | Contact

e-Journal　　　　　　　　　　Search [   ] ▶

"MySpace is nothing short of a cultural phenomenon.... The site is home to 2.2 million bands, 8,000 comedians, thousands of filmmakers, and millions of striving, attention-starved wannabes—100 million, actually.... While there are hundreds of 'social-networking' sites... MySpace, the most risqué and chaotic of the majors, accounts for 82% of traffic in the category, according to Hitwise, a leading Web site tracker."—Patricia Sellers, "MySpace Cowboys," *Fortune*, 8/29/06

Those are incredible numbers—still accurate? Facebook seems more popular with my friends. Interesting that MySpace was called "risqué."

"Authorities in a number of states are investigating serious crimes—sexual assaults and murders of teenagers—in which the criminals allegedly met their victims through MySpace."—CBS Evening News, 2/6/06

Clearly risks involved with using MySpace—are people careful enough? Do they reveal too much in their profiles? Too easy to fake who you are? Any protections added recently?

◤ Make It **Your Own**

Keep an idea journal for one week. Write in it daily about the topics discussed in your classes, and at the end of the week, read through your notes. What topics have arisen repeatedly? Which are most engaging? What ideas might you use in a writing assignment?

2. Freewrite.

Have you ever found yourself sitting in front of a blank screen, knowing you had to begin writing but just not being able to get started? Try *freewriting:* writing the first thing that enters your head and then continuing to write nonstop for ten to fifteen minutes (or for a set number of pages). What you write about does not matter; if you draw a blank, just write (or type) the same word over and over again until something comes to you.

To be useful, freewriting must be fast and spontaneous. If you find that you cannot resist correcting and revising, turn the brightness down until your screen is very dim or even black. Here is a sample of freewriting for Erin Buksbaum's essay:

> Not sure what I want to write not sure what I want to say would rather be at the gym or just catching up on sleep. Stayed up too late last night futzing with my Facebook page. Finally managed to get that video to play when it opens. Prob. should take down that pic of Hannah from Friday night, but it's really, really funny. Maybe she shld just put it on her page, but she hardly ever updates. I hope my mother--or Hannah's mother--doesn't look at it! LOL!

Once the time has elapsed, read through what you wrote. You might find a usable idea. Buksbaum's essay topic—social networking sites like *Facebook*—appears in this freewriting snippet, for example. But the exercise is also beneficial for freeing the mind and exorcising writer's block.

A variation of freewriting is **_focused freewriting._** Instead of starting from the first idea to pop into your head, start from something specific: your topic, a quotation, a memory, an image. If you stray from the topic, just keep writing, trying to circle back to it.

connect
mhconnectcomposition.com
Additional resources: QL2008

3. Brainstorm.

Brainstorming (or **_listing_**) is writing down everything you can think of on a topic. Brainstorming helps get ideas percolating and provides a record of that percolation. Here is a snippet of brainstorming on Erin Buksbaum's topic, social networking sites:

connect
mhconnectcomposition.com
Additional resources: QL2009

> Anyone with an email address can use a social networking site
>
> Lots of networking sites: Facebook, Friendster, Bebo . . .
>
> People post tons of pictures, not only of themselves, of friends, too
>
> Other things they post: name, school, job, fave bands, books, movies, etc.
>
> Easy for friends to stay in touch and meet friends of friends
>
> Easy for people to track down other people—old classmates, people with shared interests, etc.
>
> Do criminals take advantage of networking sites? Are people aware of this?

If you brainstorm with friends, classmates, or colleagues, work to make all participants comfortable: Everyone should feel free to shout out any idea, no matter how zany it seems at the time. Otherwise, the creative energy gets stifled, and the ideas stop flowing.

After you have amassed a useful number of items, sort through the material to make connections: Move items around or draw lines to connect related items. Then brainstorm about the idea groups that seem most important, interesting, or challenging.

connect

mhconnectcomposition.com
Additional resources: QL2010

4. Cluster.

Clustering (or ***mapping***) is a visual method for identifying and developing ideas. To create a cluster or idea map, follow these steps:

1. Write your topic in the middle of the page, and draw a circle around it.
2. Write other ideas related to your topic around the central idea bubble, and draw a circle around each of those.
3. Draw connecting lines from the word bubbles to the central topic or to the other word bubbles to show the relationships among the ideas.

When creating a cluster, keep two things in mind:

1. Your topic and idea notes should be brief—if you write more than a word or two, the diagram will quickly become difficult to read.
2. You will probably make many changes as you work, so use a pencil.

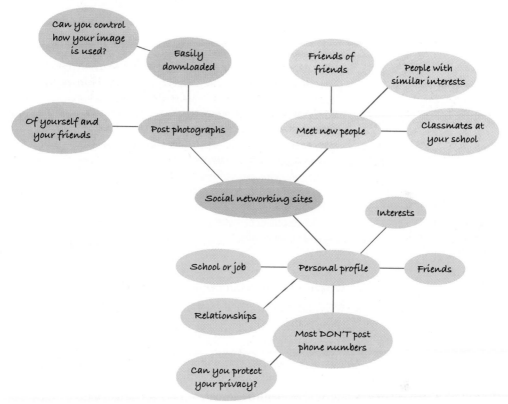

FIGURE 2.3 A sample cluster diagram

The cluster diagram above (Figure 2.3) shows some of Erin Buksbaum's ideas for her paper on social networking sites.

5. Answer the journalists' questions plus two.

The *journalists' questions*—*who, what, where, when, why,* and *how*—not only can help you generate ideas about your topic but also can help you figure out what you need to learn in order to write the paper. When considering a topic, ask yourself questions like these:

- **Who** are the key figures?
- **What** did they accomplish, or what are the issues?

	Who uses social networking sites?
	What do social networking sites allow you to do? What forms of communication do they allow?
	When did social networking sites become popular?
	Where can one find information on users of social networking sites (statistics)?
	Why do people use social networking sites? Why do they post information about themselves?
	How might social networking sites be abused?
	What social significance does the popularity of social networking sites have?
	What consequences might result from posting too much personal information?

FIGURE 2.4 The journalists' questions, plus two

- **Where** and **when** did the main events occur?
- **Why** did they do what they did, or why did these events transpire as they did?
- **How** did it happen?

As a college student, you will also benefit from adding two additional questions to the journalists' list:

- What is the **significance?**
- What are the **consequences?**

The journalists' questions tailored to Erin Buksbaum's topic are shown in Figure 2.4.

6. Discuss your topics with friends and classmates.

Sometimes just batting ideas around with friends or classmates can help you generate ideas. This can be as casual as a late-night chat with your roommate or texting with a friend ("What do you think about . . . ?"), or it can be as formal as a scheduled brainstorming session with a collaborative writing group. Whatever approach you take, keep the discussion open enough that people feel free to speak their minds but focused enough that your discussion does not drift too far from your topic, and always be ready to record ideas.

7. Use the internet, the library, and classroom tools.

Surfing the internet can provide direction and stimulate ideas when you are faced with a new topic. Start by searching a ***subject directory,*** a collection of websites organized into groups by topic and arranged hierarchically from most general to most specific to get a sense of the range of related subtopics. Subject directories are useful for narrowing or expanding your topic. For very current topics, searching a news site or locating a specialized blog can also be useful.

More about ▸ ▸ ▸
Subject directories, 225–26
Blogs, 227
Evaluating online sources, 254–57

The reference sources provided by your college library are another resource for generating ideas. Browse through general encyclopedias and dictionaries to get a sense of how your topic is usually discussed, or turn to specialized dictionaries or encyclopedias to get a more detailed introduction. Some reference sources may be available online through your college library's website.

Finally, because you will often be writing about topics that were introduced in class, you can get ideas by reading (or rereading) course materials, such as your textbook, class notes, and any handouts your instructor has distributed. All can provide context or help you identify a topic that interests you.

More about ▸ ▸ ▸
Reference sources, 234–37

⬆ Make It **Your Own**

Use focused freewriting, brainstorming, or clustering to develop one of the ideas that came out of your weeklong experiment with keeping an idea journal (p. 24) or an idea from the reading in one of your classes.

More about ▸ ▸ ▸
Note taking, 129–35, 267–69
Annotating, 124–27

2d Narrowing or Broadening a Topic

Once you have devised a topic, consider whether you can do justice to it in the assigned length. In most cases, you will need to narrow your topic further; occasionally, you may have to broaden it.

1. Narrow your topic.

To narrow an overly general topic, use brainstorming or one of the other idea-generating techniques to develop a list of subtopics. Erin Buksbaum wanted to write about social networking sites, and she had personal experience with *Facebook* that her instructor lacked. But the topic was so big, she could not cover it in a three- to five-page paper;

she had to narrow it. Some of her possible subtopics are listed in the brainstorming example below.

	Social networking sites form a "virtual" community.
	Social networking sites allow friendships across distances, help people stay in touch.
	How people create a "virtual identity" in their profiles
	Stories of romances found via social networking sites
	Risks of social networking sites—how they can be abused, mistakes users make in posting information
	Social networking sites as new form of advertising for bands and movies

Buksbaum chose to focus on the risks of social networking sites, something that would be important to both her and her instructor.

2. Broaden your topic.

While you are much more likely to have to narrow your topic, you may occasionally find yourself struggling to come up with something to say about the topic you have selected, in which case your topic may be too narrow. If, for example, you were thinking about exploring whether social workers in your town are pressured to overreport their contact hours with Medicare patients but you were finding too little research on this topic, you could broaden your topic by expanding the region (from social workers in your town to social workers throughout the country), or you could broaden the type of caregivers you studied by including medical personnel (doctors, nurses, and technicians) and social workers. The idea-generating techniques discussed above can help you broaden, as well as narrow, your topic.

connect

mhconnectcomposition.com
Additional resources: QL2016

2e   ## Working with Others: Planning a Collaborative Project

In academic and professional contexts, collaborative work is common. Working in a group can be challenging, but there are several steps you can take to make collaborative work more satisfying and less frustrating.

1. Form a cohesive group.

Start group projects by establishing rapport. A few small steps taken at the outset can help:

- Meet face-to-face, at least at the start.

- Start your first meeting by having group members introduce themselves and mention some detail—hometown, favorite book, a special interest or talent—to help everyone get to know each other.

- Make an effort to learn everyone's name.

- At the end of the first session, distribute the contact information, such as email address and mobile and home telephone numbers (with best times to call) for every group member.

- Send a friendly message to everyone the next day.

2. Anticipate pitfalls.

Anyone who has participated in a collaborative project knows that pitfalls abound: One person is consistently late, another lets other team members do all the work, a third dominates the proceedings, and a fourth is resentful but never says a word. Before starting a project, work together to figure out the likely pitfalls and to decide in advance how the group will respond:

- What will you do if someone does not complete assigned work?

- What will you do if someone does assigned work badly?

- If it is a class assignment, how will you want the instructor to grade the completed project?

> In a committee reporting on student concerns to the Board of Trustees, two of the members had one idea of what they wanted to focus on, another had a different idea, and I was caught in the middle. I wish we had resolved this at the beginning.
>
> —Adrianne Anderson, Texas Christian University

Once you have developed a list of potential problems and how the group will resolve them, put it in writing, have everybody sign the document, and distribute copies to all members. This written agreement not only will provide a record but also will remind everyone of their responsibilities to the group. If something does go wrong, address the problem immediately; do not let it fester.

Reference ➞   **What the Group Should Do Together**

Everyone needs to participate in the following:

- Deciding on a topic
- Drafting a thesis statement
- Brainstorming ideas
- Organizing the project
- Assigning tasks

3. Devise a schedule and assign tasks.

The writing process for individual projects applies to collaborative projects as well. Some additional steps include the following:

> **More about ▶▶▶**
> Analyzing the writing situation, 10–18
> Devising a topic, 22–29
> Drafting, 43–48
> Revising globally and locally, 90–99
> Drafting and revising visuals, 80–89 (ch. 5)
> Proofreading and formatting, 102–5

- Select a secretary. That role can be performed by one person or can rotate among group members.

- Brainstorm project ideas, making sure everyone participates.

- List component tasks (such as coordinating the group; researching the topic; drafting, revising, and editing the text; identifying or creating appropriate visuals).

- Establish dates by which each task needs to be completed, and construct a timetable.

- Divide the work among group members, taking into account people's talents, interests, and schedules and the difficulty of each task. Keep in mind that some phases of the project should be done by the entire group. (See the Quick Reference box above.)

- Plan periodic meetings to discuss progress and problems.

- Distribute a schedule of meetings and due dates.

Work **Together** ◀

With a group of two to five classmates, choose a topic for a collaborative project, and plan how the group would work together to fulfill the assignment. Be sure to list the problems that might arise and to discuss how the group would resolve them.

3

Organizing and Drafting Your Project

connect

mhconnectcomposition.com
Additional resources: QL3001, QL3002

Before producing a new line of clothing or automobile, designers sketch the product, drafting and arranging the shapes before dressing them in colors and textures. Writers, too, begin with a draft: They sketch their ideas in words and arrange them in sentences and paragraphs. Both designers and writers sometimes erase initial ideas and revise early efforts. For both, until that first sketch is penned, the finished work is merely an idea.

3a Crafting an Effective Thesis

A preliminary *thesis statement* is an important part of a writer's draft. A thesis is a brief statement (one or two sentences) indicating the topic you will explore, your focus on the topic, and your attitude toward the topic. An effective thesis statement establishes your main point and gives readers something against which to measure the project's success.

Stating the Main Idea In some cultures, the main idea is often implied, but readers in the United States, especially in academic and business contexts, will usually expect you to state your main idea clearly and directly, usually at the beginning of your writing project.

1. Devise a thesis statement.

Before you begin to draft a thesis, review your notes. Do any ideas jump out? If not, return to the idea-generating stage. If so, focus on an aspect of your topic that will engage you and your reader and that is appropriate to your purpose, context, and genre. Next, ask and answer a question about your topic. The answer to your question should specify your topic and make a claim about it. Your answer will become your preliminary thesis statement. Here are some sample questions and answers, with the claim highlighted in yellow and the topic underlined:

More about ▶▶▶
Generating ideas,
22–29

Questions	Answers
Should members of political parties be barred from overseeing presidential elections?	Members of political parties should be barred from overseeing presidential elections to avoid even the suspicion of electoral manipulation such as occurred in Florida in 2000 and Ohio in 2004.
What drove the ivory-billed woodpecker to near-extinction in the United States?	The direct effects of the two world wars led to the near-extinction of the ivory-billed woodpecker.
What kinds of privacy violations or other social mischief occur with social networking sites like *MySpace* and *Facebook*?	Social networking sites open new avenues for privacy violations and other social dangers, such as publication of incriminating photographs, stalking, and contact with inappropriate new "friends."
What motivates students to plagiarize, and what can we do to reduce the number of incidents?	Reducing the incidents of plagiarism among college students requires understanding its causes, which include late-night desperation, fear of a bad grade, lack of interest in a course, ignorance of citation requirements, and societal norms.

▶▶▶ Sample informative essay: "The Risks of Online Networking," Erin Buksbaum, 106–10

▶▶▶ Sample exploratory argument essay: "Why Students Cheat," Tom Hackman, 168–74

If you are not sure how to answer your question, use idea-generating techniques to develop an answer.

EXERCISE **3.1** Drafting a thesis statement

Draft a thesis statement for two of the following topics:

1. Violence in college sports
2. The social significance of reality TV
3. Compulsory military service
4. National academic standards
5. Internet restrictions in the People's Republic of China
6. Credit cards for college students
7. Taking a year off after high school
8. Passenger screening in airports
9. Cell phone use
10. Shopping

connect
mhconnectcomposition.com
Online exercise: QL3101

Underline your topic, and circle your claim.

2. Revise a thesis statement.

A well-crafted thesis statement should indicate your topic and make a claim that is appropriate to your purpose, and it should do so in language that will engage the reader. Only rarely does a writer accomplish all of these in the first draft of the thesis. Most writers need to revise the thesis statement repeatedly as they draft.

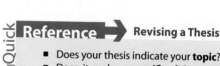

Quick Reference ➡ Revising a Thesis

- Does your thesis indicate your **topic**?
- Does it make a **specific claim**—a claim of **fact** for an informative project, a **claim of judgment** or **value** for a persuasive project?
- Does it convey your **attitude**?
- Will it **engage** readers?

Purpose: Informative The thesis of an informative essay makes a claim of fact, a claim that can be verified. To be engaging, an informative thesis must make a claim of fact that is not yet widely known to or accepted by the audience, and it must be specific enough that the writer can explore it fully.

More about ▶▶▶
Claims of fact, 154

DRAFT THESIS

This paper is about using social networking sites.

This draft thesis establishes a topic but does not make a claim of fact, and it is far too general to explore fully.

REVISION 1

While social networking sites allow for new forms of social communication, they can also be dangerous.

This thesis statement establishes the topic and makes a claim of fact, but the claim is too broad: By not specifying the types of dangers social networking sites represent, it commits the writer to discussing *all* the ways in which social networking sites can be dangerous (physically, psychologically, financially).

REVISION 2

While social networking sites allow for new forms of communication, they also open new avenues for privacy violations and other social dangers.

The thesis statement now narrows the claim to one the writer can explore fully, and it makes a claim of fact, focusing on an issue that will inform her instructor, who knows little about social networking sites.

More about ▶▶▶
Claims of value,
154–55
Claims of judgment,
155–56

Purpose: Argumentative/Persuasive The thesis of a *persuasive* text must make a claim of value or judgment, an opinion or a provisional judgment that is not widely shared and that can be defended with reasons and evidence.

DRAFT THESIS

There are many types of plagiarism.

This thesis makes a claim of fact, which is not appropriate for a persuasive essay, and is too broad to develop fully.

REVISION 1

Plagiarism has many motivations, which makes a single punishment inappropriate.

This revision makes a claim of judgment, but the first half of the statement remains overly general (it would take many pages to discuss the motivations of *all* writers).

REVISION 2

Reducing the incidents of plagiarism among college students will be difficult without understanding its causes. This requires going beyond the simplistic explanations that are frequently offered.

The thesis makes a claim of judgment and narrows its focus to a much smaller group (college students).

You can revise your thesis statement at any stage of the writing process, but you are most likely to revise it at two points:

- At the beginning, as you draft your thesis statement
- As you revise your first draft

When drafting your thesis statement, make sure it focuses on a claim you can defend and that will engage your reader. When revising your thesis statement, focus on making sure your reasons and evidence actually support your claim. If not, either replace the irrelevant reasons and evidence or revise your thesis so that the support you offer is pertinent.

↑ Make It **Your Own**

For an essay that you are working on, draft and revise a thesis statement so that it makes a claim you can defend fully.

EXERCISE **3.2** Revising a thesis statement

Revise the thesis statements you drafted in Exercise 3.1 (p. 35), and explain why you made your revisions.

connect
mhconnectcomposition.com
Online exercise: QL3102

3b Organizing Your Ideas

Most essays benefit from attention to organization both *before* and *after* the essay is drafted. Organizing beforehand makes the essay easier to write; reviewing the structure after you have written a draft can show you where you need more support, whether the essay is logically organized, and whether any of the evidence is irrelevant.

More about ▶▶▶
Reorganizing a draft,
93–95

1. Review your prewriting and make a list of ideas.

Start organizing by reviewing all the preparatory writing you have done. Then write your preliminary thesis statement at the top of a clean sheet of paper or in a new electronic document. Below the thesis statement, list all the ideas that might be relevant to it.

More about ▶▶▶
Keeping a journal,
22–24
Freewriting, 24–25
Brainstorming,
25–26
Clustering, 26–27
Journalists' questions, 27–28

2. Arrange your ideas into logical groupings.

Read through your list of ideas. How are they related? Create a cluster diagram or table to group ideas by topic.

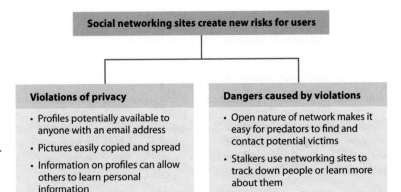

FIGURE 3.1 A tree diagram A tree diagram can help you organize your thoughts before you begin writing.

3. Arrange your ideas from general to specific.

More about ▶▶▶
Organizing para-
graphs, 56–58,
60–61

Arrange ideas within each group from most general to most specific. A **tree diagram** can help. To create a tree diagram, write your main idea at the top of the page and let subsequent ideas branch off below it. The tree diagram in Figure 3.1 above provides preliminary organization for Erin Buksbaum's essay.

4. Consider your essay's overall shape.

The typical essay has three basic parts:

- Introduction
- Body
- Conclusion

In its simplest form, this becomes a "five-paragraph theme": one paragraph for the introduction, three for the body, and one for the conclusion. Of course, college writing seldom takes such a tidy form. Instead, it is more likely to unfold in this manner:

More about ▶▶▶
Writing the introduc-
tion, 70-72

Introduction The introduction is typically brief (one to three paragraphs, depending on the length of the essay). Often, the thesis statement appears in the introduction, where it can shape the reader's expectations of the essay. What goes into the introduction depends on the essay's purpose, audience, context, and genre, but it should entice readers to carry on and should prepare them for what follows.

Body The body is the longest portion of the essay, with length depending on the complexity of ideas being conveyed and the quantity of support needed to convince the audience. Each paragraph in the body should make one main point, expressed in a topic sentence; the body paragraphs should supply reasons and evidence that support the topic sentence; and each topic sentence should support the thesis.

More about ▶▶▶
Relevance, 53, 249
Unity, 54–59
Coherence, 59–64
Development, 66–70
Reasons and evi-
    dence, 46–48
Conclusion, 72–74

Conclusion Like the introduction, the conclusion is usually rather brief (one to three paragraphs, depending on the length of the essay). Just as the introduction should entice readers, so the conclusion should convince them that they have spent their time well.

5. Choose an organizational strategy.

Once you have collected and organized your notes, choose the order in which to present your ideas that best fits your thesis and supporting materials. Some organizational patterns include the following:

Chronological Organization Use *chronological* (or *time*) order to tell a story (narrative) or explain a process (process analysis).

More about ▶▶▶
Description, 66
Narration, 67
Exemplification, 68
Comparison-
    contrast, 68–69
Cause-effect, 69
Analysis, 69
Definition, 69–70

Spatial Organization Organize your essay spatially, from left to right, inside to outside, top to bottom when describing a scene or structure.

Logical Organization This is probably the most common organizational scheme for academic essays: Begin with an introduction that includes a general statement—the thesis—and then proceed to the body of the essay, where specific reasons and evidence are provided. With indifferent or even hostile readers consider reversing this order: Begin with something specific—an engaging anecdote, some dramatic statistics, a provocative illustration—that will gain your audience's interest, attention, or sympathy, and then move on to the general conclusion.

If you are writing for an audience likely to balk when faced with new ideas or ideas that challenge their beliefs, organize your essay from *familiar to unfamiliar*. To startle your readers into seeing a familiar issue in a new light, use *unfamiliar-to-familiar order*.

You may choose to organize your body paragraphs in *climactic order*, from least to most exciting. You might even save your thesis until the end of the essay.

↟ Make It **Your Own**

Revisit a paper that you wrote recently. What organizational strategy or strategies does it use? What organizational changes would you make now?

6. Choose an outlining technique that is appropriate for you.

Outlines, whether formal or "scratch," not only guide you as you draft, but also allow you to experiment with ways of sequencing your supporting paragraphs.

connect

mhconnectcomposition.com
Additional resources: QL3003, QL3004

An Informal (Scratch) Outline An *informal,* or *scratch, outline* is simply a list of the ideas in your essay in the order you want to present them. You can jot down your ideas in words, phrases, complete sentences, even pictures—whatever you need to jog your memory about what to put next. Here is a sample scratch outline for Erin Buksbaum's essay on social networking sites:

▶▶▶Sample student essay by Erin Buksbaum:
First draft, "Is Social Networking a Serious Danger?" 49–50
Final draft, "The Risks of Online Networking," 106–10

Intro

Social networking sites = new pathways of communication.

Benefits: Way to communicate with friends, make new friends, promote movies, shows, bands.

Thesis: While social networking sites allow for exciting new forms of communication, they also open new avenues for privacy violations and even danger.

Body

Background: User profiles and the kind of information/elements they include, how information is accessed

Privacy violations: Pictures—some inappropriate or misused (ruin reputation, lose jobs); Profiles—information available too widely (teachers, parents, criminals, perverts), lying about who you are

Conclusion

Be cautious; don't post info you wouldn't want in the newspaper

connect

mhconnectcomposition.com
Additional resources: QL3005

A Formal Outline (Topic or Sentence) A formal outline uses roman numerals (I, II, III), capital letters (A, B, C), arabic numerals (1, 2, 3), lowercase letters (a, b, c), and indentions of five spaces (or half an inch) to indicate level of generality, with roman numeral headings being most general and lowercase letters most specific. Each level of your outline should include at least two entries.

Each subsidiary point must support the idea at the level above it, and each heading must unify the subsidiary points in the level below. To use a simple example, if the first-level heading was *I. Types of Cheese,* the next-level headings could be

A. Muenster

B. Swiss

C. Cheddar

They could not be

A. Methods of Making Cheese

B. Aging the Cheese

C. Using the Right Feed Grain

All the headings at each level must be ***parallel,*** following the same pattern. Thus, the sequence

More about ▶▶▶
Parallelism, 539–48
(ch. 27)

A. Muenster

B. Swiss

C. Cheddar

is fine (all are adjectives describing a type of cheese), whereas the sequence

A. Methods of Making Cheese

B. Aging the Cheese

C. Using the Right Feed Grain

is not. (You would have to change *Methods of Making Cheese* to *Making the Cheese* for this heading to be parallel with the others.)

The examples above are from a ***topic outline:*** They use words and phrases to indicate the ideas to be discussed. Some writers prefer to create a ***sentence outline*** because it provides a starting point from which to draft. Compare the first section of a topic outline and a sentence outline for Erin Buksbaum's essay:

Thesis: While social networking sites allow for exciting new forms of communication, they also open new avenues for privacy violations and other social dangers.

Topic Outline

I. User profiles

    A. Typical Components

        1. Basic personal information: name, age, school

        2. Favorite music, movies, books

        3. Animations, videos, *Flash* movies, banners

    B. Dangers they create

        1. Personal info available to anyone with an account

        2. Children posting details that make them easy to find and harm

Sentence Outline

I. The center of the social networking experience is the user's profile.

    A. These profiles can be thought of as personalized web pages.

        1. Profiles usually include basic personal information such as a user's name, age, and school.

        2. Most users also post lists of their favorite books, bands, and songs.

        3. More sophisticated users post animations, videos, and *Flash* movies.

    B. While it sounds like harmless fun, what people post in their profiles can be extremely dangerous.

        1. User profiles allow any other member of the social network to learn user's personal details.

        2. Many children may foolishly post details that make it easy for others to track them down off-line.

Which type of outline you choose depends entirely on your own preferences, the complexity of your essay, and your instructor's expectations.

7. Check your outline for unity and coherence.

> **More about ▶▶▶**
> Coherence, 60–64
> Unity, 54–59

Once you have completed your outline, review it critically for **unity** and **coherence.** Unity is achieved when all the supporting paragraphs are relevant to the thesis and when all the examples, reasons, and evidence are relevant to the main idea of the supporting paragraph. Coherence is achieved when the supporting paragraphs, with all their reasons, evidence, and examples, are organized logically so that readers can move from idea to idea without having to pause to consider the relationships among the parts.

→ EXERCISE **3.3** Creating an informal outline

connect
mhconnectcomposition.com
Online exercise: QL3103

Using the thesis statement below, arrange the ideas in the list that follows into an informal (or scratch) outline for an essay.

Thesis (informative): The first modern people lived in Africa.

List of ideas:

- Populations with the greatest genetic diversity have been established for the longest time.

- Scientists today can study genetic code—the "genome"—of people alive today to learn about where their ancestors lived.

- All humans alive today share 99.9% of their genetic code with all other humans.

- Until the last twenty-five years, scientists could learn about humans only from bones and cultural artifacts.

- When random mutations occur in the remaining 0.01% of a person's genetic code, they are passed on to his or her descendants.

- Mutations occur at a fairly steady rate.

- The greatest genetic diversity occurs in women of African descent.

EXERCISE 3.4 Creating a topic outline

Using the ideas in Exercise 3.3, create a formal topic outline.

connect

mhconnectcomposition.com
Online exercise: QL3104

Work **Together**

Exchange your outline from Exercise 3.3 or 3.4 with a classmate, and assess your classmate's outline for unity and coherence. Explain your observations to your classmate. Then, using whatever useful ideas you gained from your classmate's response, revise your outline.

3c **Preparing to Draft**

When the moment comes to combine words and sentences into paragraphs and paragraphs into an essay, set aside some time and find a place where you can concentrate. Even in the best circumstances, you may encounter writer's block, but by using the appropriate techniques, you will be able to get past it.

❝ My ideas flow best when I'm alone—locked up in my room. Too many distractions and the last thing I will do is think about writing the paper. ❞

—Frances Freire, University of Miami

1. Get ready: Allocate enough time and find a good place to write.

Ideally, allocate a substantial block of time to writing your first draft. How you define *substantial* depends on how long or complex your essay will be: An hour or two might be enough for a three- to five-page essay; a longer text will require more. If you are unable to find a block of time, work in smaller chunks over several days. Do not delay starting just because you can cobble together only a half hour at a time.

Next, consider what place is best for you: a study carrel in the library or a table for one at a noisy streetside café? Whatever your preference, focus on the task at hand by turning off your cell phone and email and closing your internet browser.

2. Start writing.

The writing you have done while analyzing your writing situation and devising your topic, drafting your thesis, and organizing your ideas will provide you with a starting point. Begin by reviewing this material, and then try one of the following methods (or a combination of them):

- **Method 1: Fill in your outline.** Use your outline as scaffolding, filling it in and fleshing it out until it becomes a first draft.

- **Method 2: Start with what you have.** Instead of beginning at the beginning, start writing whatever parts of the essay you feel confident about—an engaging example, a descriptive passage in support of one of your ideas, or even just a sentence or a phrase that captures a relevant thought. Continue writing out-of-order thoughts until you can stitch them together and fill in the gaps.

- **Method 3: Write straight from your brain.** Type your thesis statement at the top of a computer file, and then just start writing. This may produce a very brief, general first draft, but it will be one that actually speaks from what you have to say. You can supplement it later.

Make It **Your Own**

For a paper that you are working on, produce a first draft using one of the drafting methods described above.

Whatever method you choose, do not worry about the language you use to present your ideas. Just get words on paper. You can smooth out the kinks later, when you revise and edit.

3. Overcome writer's block.

Gene Fowler, a newspaper columnist, novelist, and screenwriter, once said, "Writing is easy: All you do is sit staring at a blank sheet of paper until drops of blood form on your forehead." Fortunately, there are techniques to help you avoid writing trauma.

66 I usually have writer's block—my thoughts dam up in my brain. One technique I find really helpful is talking about the topic with an unsuspecting bystander, like a friend or a professor. As I begin talking, I hear what it is I am trying to get across, and this gives me a springboard for writing. 99

—Milissa Carter, Syracuse University

Quick Reference ➡ **Overcoming Writer's Block**

- **Write something else.** Just the act of writing can help unblock you.
- **Write what you can.** You do not have to start at the beginning and keep writing until you get to the conclusion. Instead, write the parts you *can* write, even if you cannot yet string them together.
- **Do not start from scratch.** Use your outline, brainstorming, and other notes to jump-start your writing.
- **Write a message to yourself.** For some writers, the idea of an audience can be inhibiting, so write a note to yourself: "What I want to say is . . . ," and then finish the sentence.
- **Talk.** Tell a tutor, instructor, classmate, or friend what your paper will be about. Get your listener to take notes as you talk. Then use these notes as a starting point for writing.
- **Use technology.** Instead of talking with someone face-to-face, use web communication tools such as instant messaging or *Facebook*. This will force you to start writing.
- **Return to research.** Perhaps you are stuck because you do not yet know enough to continue writing. If this is the case, return to your research, but be alert for when you do know enough to return to the writing.
- **Change your situation.** Switch media—from pencil and paper to word processor, or vice versa—or change the setting in which you are writing.
- **Avoid perfection.** It is the rare writer who produces a masterpiece on the first try. If you cannot avoid focusing on problems, turn off your computer screen so that you cannot see what you have written until it is time to start revising.

> *More about* ▶▶▶
> Finding information,
> 222–47 (ch. 13)

Tech

Protecting Your Work

You have just spent a lovely Saturday afternoon indoors in front of the computer. After several hours of hard work, you reward yourself with a snack. You return to your desk just as your cat steps onto the keyboard, deleting everything you have spent all day writing. Because terrible things happen to computer files all the time, it is important to take these steps:

- **Save early and often.** Adjust the options for your word processing program so that it will save your file automatically every five or ten minutes. Each time you pause, manually save your file.
- **Save your file in multiple locations.** Each time you finish a writing session, make a

backup of your file, and store it someplace other than where the original is stored. Burn it to a CD or DVD; save it on a USB flash drive, or send a copy to your email account.

- **Do not delete.** When you cut something you have written, no matter how goofy or off the mark, paste it into a file for discards.
- **Use the Undo command in your word processor.** Almost all word processors today have an "undo" function that will enable you to revert back a step in your draft if you delete a paragraph by mistake or make a change you do not like.

3d Drafting: Explaining and Supporting Your Ideas

To draft a thesis statement for your paper, you asked yourself a question and devised a tentative answer. The body of your essay will explain *why* you believe that the answer included in your thesis statement is true and why your readers should agree with you. The topic sentence (or main idea) in each supporting paragraph will form the backbone of your essay, and the reasons and evidence you supply will be the flesh that covers the skeleton.

Specific evidence is needed to make your writing convincing and interesting. Some kinds of evidence you can draw on include the following:

- facts and statistics
- expert opinion

Writing
Responsibly   Made-up "Evidence"

In May 2005, a stem cell expert resigned his position at Seoul National University following revelations by the journal *Nature* that his lab had falsified data. Hwang Woo Suk's case is not an isolated one: In 2002, for example, Bell Laboratories fired star researcher Jan Hendrik Schon for falsifying data. Commentators have noted that competition was a factor in these cases: The desire for acclaim had become more important than the desire for truth.

The highly competitive academic environment may tempt you, too, to make up "facts" to support a thesis in a paper. It is easy to alter data, invent statistics or quotations, or manipulate an image so that it "shows" what you want it to. Resist the temptation: The short-term benefits are not worth it. Not only are you likely to get caught—fabricated evidence often *sounds* fake—but you are also sacrificing the opportunity to learn something about your topic and about the writing process.

- examples
- observations
- case studies
- anecdotes
- passages from the text you are studying

The paragraph below uses facts and examples:

> The physical demands on competitive cyclists are immense. One day, they will have to ride two hundred kilometres through the mountains; the next day there might be a long, flat sprint lasting seven hours. Because cyclists have such a low percentage of body fat, they are more susceptible to infections than other people. (At the beginning of the Tour, Armstrong's body fat is around four or five per cent; this season Shaquille O'Neal, the most powerful player in the N.B.A., boasted that his body-fat level was sixteen percent.)
>
> —Michael Specter, "The Long Ride," *New Yorker*

Topic sentence

Support: Facts/ Examples

This paragraph uses facts and statistics:

> One of the most important, if often unnoticed, features of American life in the late twentieth century was the aging of the American population. After decades of steady growth, the nation's birth rate began to decline in the 1970s and remained low through the 1980s and 1990s. In 1970,

Topic sentence

Support: Facts and statistics

there were 18.4 births for every 1,000 people in the population. By 1996, the rate had dropped to 14.8 births. The declining birth rate and a significant rise in life expectancy produced a substantial increase in the proportion of elderly citizens. Almost 13 percent of the population was more than sixty-five years old in 2000, as compared with 8 percent in 1970. The median age in 2000 was 35.3, the highest in the nation's history. In 1970, it was 28.0.

—Alan Brinkley, *American History: A Survey*

> ***More about*** ▶▶▶
> Relevance, 53, 249

As you draft, ask yourself: Have I supplied *enough* reasons and evidence to persuade my reader? Is the evidence I've supplied relevant?

connect
mhconnectcomposition.com
Online exercise: QL3105

EXERCISE **3.5** Analyzing evidence

Analyze the evidence in one of the sample paragraphs on pp. 56–57. What types of evidence are provided? Is there enough evidence to support the topic sentence? Why or why not?

Make It **Your Own**

Analyze an essay you are writing or have recently written. First, identify the essay's thesis statement (or main idea). Then check each supporting paragraph. Does each support the essay's main idea? Does the evidence in each support the paragraph's main point? If so, write a paragraph explaining how; if not, revise the paragraph.

> ▶▶▶Additional
> samples:
> Draft thesis, 34
> Revised thesis,
>   35–36
> Outlines, 40, 41
> Final draft, 106–10

Student Essay: First Draft

The first draft of Erin Buksbaum's essay on social networking appears on pp. 49–50. Note that in this draft she does not worry about polished writing or even perfect grammar and spelling. She knows she can make changes as she revises. For now, her focus is on getting her ideas down in a logical order and on supporting her thesis with evidence. Note, too, that Buksbaum includes a place for a screen capture from a social networking site. Although she has not selected the particular image she will use, she is wise to build a place for this major element into her earliest draft.

Is Social Networking a Serious Danger?

The internet has changed the way people communicate and interact with each other forever. Social networking sites let users create a personalized Web profile, meet new people with common interests, organize clubs, plan gatherings, promote bands or movies—the possibilities for communication are nearly endless. But there are risks involved. The immediate access of these sites are easily exploited. (Remember the teenage girl who killed herself because of a mean message from a boy she liked— really from a friend's mom?) While social networking sites allow for new forms of communication, they can also be dangerous.

The center of the social networking experience is the user's profile. The user's profile can be thought of as personalized Web pages. Profiles usually include basic personal information such as a user's name, age, current school, and Zodiac sign. They also usually include lists of the user's "favorites": favorite books, songs, bands, and movies. More sophisticated users also post animations, videos, and Flash movies on their profiles. People really push the technical envelope in their profiles, and it's very impressive.

[INSERT SCREENCAPTURE HERE.]

While it sounds like harmless fun, what people post in their profiles can be extremely dangerous. User profiles allow any other member of the social network to learn personal details of that user. In other words: If you have a profile, anyone else in the network can see what you are like. That's fine for users who are experienced using the Internet, and know to keep certain key details hidden. However, many children post details that make it easy for others to track them down off-line. Considering how open a site like MySpace.com is, this is a serious problem.

Photographs are another key feature of social networking sites. Photographs are an extremely popular element in most user profiles. The Internet is a visual medium, after all. Hence, most profiles include many, many pictures. Usually, users post photographs of themselves, their friends, or their pets. But the prevalence of photographs creates its own set of problems. Children may see images that are not appropriate for their age group. Also, photographs can be easily downloaded and hence easily misused. When you post your face on the internet, you lose all control over what happens to it.

Perhaps the most powerful part of social networking sites, though, is their capacity for user interaction. Using a "Search" feature, you can find a user who likes the same band, or who lives in the same area, or who is the same age. Then you can send them a message or post a note on their profile. It's that easy. But while most users are just looking for new friends, some might have darker purposes. Criminals like stalkers and pedophiles have been known to use social networking sites to track down targets.

There is no way to reverse the internet revolution, even if we wanted to. MySpace, Facebook, and other such sites are here to stay. So, users need to be careful. A good rule of thumb is to never post something online you wouldn't want in a major newspaper. While you might not realize it, the internet offers that level of access to the outside world. While social networking sites offer exciting new paths of communication between people the world over, these new rewards also come with new risks.

connect
mhconnectcomposition.com
Online exercise: QL3106

EXERCISE 3.6 Analyzing a draft

Create a topic outline for Erin Buksbaum's draft above. (Hint: An outline of the first part of her draft appears on pp. 40, 42.) Based on your outline, how unified is her draft? How cohesive is it? Now consider the evidence she provides: Is there enough? Is it specific enough?

3e   Writing with Others: Collaborative Projects

The work of many academic courses is conducted collaboratively, as are many workplace writing projects. Collaboration may mean that each team member is responsible for a separate part of the project, but often projects are ***coauthored:*** Group members work together to draft a thesis, devise an outline, and even write the text.

Drafting collaboratively can be a difficult process to manage, but it can also be rewarding and creative. The following principles will help keep the experience a happy one:

More about ▶▶▶
Planning a collaborative project, 30–32
Peer response, 100–101

- If possible, keep groups small (three to four participants); smaller groups can reach the "critical mass" needed for creativity without the many management difficulties (such as finding a time to meet) that larger groups face.

- As with planning, it is important to the drafting process that each member of the group has an opportunity to contribute. Make an effort to restrain overbearing members and to encourage reluctant participants.

- Treat everyone's writing respectfully. Some group members may be more skilled than others, but insightful ideas can be coaxed from initially unimpressive material.

- Whether your group is collaborating over email or courseware such as *Blackboard,* in a *Facebook* group, or in face-to-face meetings, make sure everyone has a copy of the latest draft and the current schedule following each session.

4 Crafting and Connecting Paragraphs

American architect Frank Lloyd Wright claimed that "[t]rue ornament is not a matter of prettifying externals. It is organic with the structure it adorns. . . ." He designed furniture and stained glass windows (like the one here) that were as much a part of the structure as the walls that surrounded them.

Similarly, a paragraph is effective not when it is adorned with lofty sounding words or prettified with extraneous turns of phrase, but when it is an organic part of the text to which it belongs. A paragraph will be an organic part of the whole when it is all of the following:

- **Relevant.** It must support the main idea of the paper (your *thesis*) and, when possible, remind readers of what that thesis is.

- **Unified.** It should have a clear point (*topic*) and include only the material that explains that point.

- **Coherent.** It should include connections that make relationships among sentences clear to readers.

- **Well developed.** It should supply the information your readers need to be persuaded of your point.

- **Connected.** It should begin and end so that your readers can see how it relates to the paragraphs that precede and follow it.

- **Interesting.** It should make your readers want to move on to the next paragraph.

4a Writing Relevant Paragraphs

A *relevant* paragraph not only addresses the general topic of your paper but also contributes to the reader's understanding of or belief in the main idea of the paper (the *thesis*). Compare this paragraph to the essay's thesis:

Second, by calling hip-hop a "lethal genre," Staples places it into a category separate from other works of art that are not as "virulent." Yes, many hip-hop lyrics are violent, but that does not distinguish the songs from many other artistic works. Edgar Allan Poe, considered one of America's greatest writers, wrote numerous stories about murder and death, including "The Tell-Tale Heart," whose narrator is a confessed killer. *The Talented Mr. Ripley,* a novel by Patricia Highsmith, and the movie based on this novel, make Tom Ripley, an unrepentant murderer, a sympathetic character. Sculptor Kiki Smith depicts mutilated or deformed bodies in her art (see fig. 1) and, instead of being criticized, she is considered one of today's most important sculptors. No one would claim, I think, that Kiki Smith influences her viewers to commit mayhem. Clearly, hip-hop artists are not alone in depicting horrible people and events; they should not be singled out for doing so, and it should not be assumed that their audience will blindly follow suit.

Fig. 1 Kiki Smith, *Untitled* (1993).

Thesis:
... [Staples's] argument fails to be persuasive for several reasons: he doesn't account for the influence positive role models have, he ignores the fact that art frequently depicts violence without dire consequences to its consumers, and he overlooks the broad spectrum of hip-hop to focus on only a single strand.

Topic Sentence

Concession/rebuttal

Example 1

Example 2

Example 3

Concluding sentence (also recalls thesis)

—Alea Wratten, SUNY–Geneseo, "Reflecting on Brant Staples's Editorial 'How Hip-Hop Music Lost Its Way and Betrayed Its Fans'"

▶▶▶ Complete student essay, 137–39

⬆ Make It **Your Own**

Analyze an essay you are writing or have recently written. First, identify the essay's thesis statement (or main idea). Then check to see whether each body paragraph supports the essay's main idea. If not, revise the paragraph.

4b   Writing Unified Paragraphs

Paragraphs are most effective when they are *unified*—when the information and ideas in the paragraph are closely related to each other and to a single idea, a single *topic,* that controls the paragraph.

connect
mhconnectcomposition.com
Additional resources: QL4001, QL4002

1. Focus the paragraph on a central idea and delete irrelevant details.

All the sentences in a supporting paragraph should support or explain the paragraph's main idea or topic, and each supporting paragraph should provide evidence for or develop further the text's main idea.

Topic Sentence

Irrelevant: Focus of ¶ is on how writer came to inherit, not writer's or city attorney's reaction or library's location—cut

Relevant: Explains why writer inherited library

Last year I inherited a library—not just the books, but the whole building. I didn't see it as a boon at first; I saw it only as a legal nuisance. In the 1950s, my grandfather, I discovered, had donated the library to the town. Fifty years later, when the townspeople built a new library and decided to sell the old building, they discovered that they couldn't: The deed specified that if they ceased to use the building as a library, it would revert to the owner or his heirs. When the city attorney found the deed, he called every member of the town council. I was that heir. So now I owned the library in which I had spent so many hours as a girl. The building stands on a shady corner in what was once a quiet town.

When revising, hone your paragraphs until they focus on a single supporting idea: No matter how much you may like a certain sentence, if it does not support the main idea of the paragraph, it must be cut.

Unifying a paragraph is easiest when it includes a ***topic sentence,*** a single sentence (sometimes two) that clearly states the main idea of the paragraph. That way, you can check each supporting sentence against this main idea and eliminate all those that are not relevant.

connect
mhconnectcomposition.com
Online exercise: QL4101

→ **EXERCISE 4.1 Unifying a paragraph**

First, underline the topic sentence of the sample paragraph below. Then cross through any sentences that do not support that main idea.

The more exercise the better, right? It turns out that many people who are now fifty and older would answer "It depends."

These are the people who literally jumped into the fitness craze when it first became popular in the 1980s. Once, gyms were primarily the province of men. Beginning around 1980, working out, or "aerobics," gradually became fashionable, and it was common for large groups of people, especially women, to exercise together. These exercises often consisted of jumping jacks, high knee lifts, twirling one's arms, kicking, running in place, and punching the sky while hopping on one foot, all done in time to throbbing popular music. In those days, gyms were filled with the pounding rhythms from the movies *Footloose* and *Flashdance*. The problem was that people often did these lengthy, repetitive, high-impact exercises on unforgiving concrete floors in bad tennis shoes. The result? Today, many of these aerobics exercisers, now in their fifties and sixties, suffer from osteoarthritis and other severe joint problems. Most would still attest to the benefits of exercising, with the qualification that "it depends" on good flooring in gyms, proper shoes, moderation, variety, and common sense: quality, not quantity. For instance, swimming is great exercise, but too much swimming can cause shoulder problems. The answer: Do not swim too much.

→ EXERCISE 4.2 Writing unified paragraphs

Using the topic sentence and some of the supporting details given below, write a unified paragraph. Be selective: Not all the supporting details provided may be relevant.

connect
mhconnectcomposition.com
Online exercise: QL4102

Topic sentence: Over the last three and a half decades, the average American has increased the amount of food eaten from 16.4 pounds to 18.2 pounds per week while Americans' obesity rate has doubled.

Possible supporting details:

1. From 1970 to 2006, the average American's consumption of dairy products decreased by 20 percent, primarily due to less milk drinking.
2. These consumption figures were compiled by the U.S. Department of Agriculture.
3. Milk is a good source of calcium, animal protein, vitamin E, omega-3 essential fatty acids, and important minerals, including magnesium, zinc, and potassium.

4. Americans are eating 15 percent more vegetables and 26 percent more fruit.
5. Almost half of the increased fruit consumption is in the form of juice, some of which is used as a food sweetener.
6. There was a 42 percent increase in consumption of grains, a 17 percent increase of sugar and sweeteners, and a 59 percent increase of oils and animal fats.
7. The popularity of fast-food restaurants has seriously accelerated this trend.
8. The Centers for Disease Control and Prevention compiles obesity statistics.
9. In 1980, 15 percent of American adults aged 20 to 74 were obese; by 2007, that number had more than doubled.

Make It **Your Own**

Analyze a paragraph you have written for a recent or current writing project. First, identify the paragraph's topic sentence or main idea. Then check the supporting details, and eliminate any that are not relevant.

2. Place the topic sentence appropriately.

Topic sentences can appear at the beginning, middle, or end of a paragraph, but most commonly they appear at the beginning or end of the paragraph.

Topic Sentence at Beginning of Paragraph The most common placement for a topic sentence is at the beginning of the paragraph:

Topic sentence

Environmentalists paint a bleak picture of aquaculture. The David Suzuki Foundation, for example, maintains that fish waste contained in the fishery pens kills organisms living in the seabed. Yvon Gesinghaus, a manager of a tribal council in British Columbia, Canada, also notes that the scummy foam from the farms collects on the beaches, smothering the clams that provide the natives with food and money. George K. Iwama, Biksham Gujja, and Andrea Finger-Stich point to the destruction of coastal habitats in Africa and Southeast Asia to make room for shrimp ponds.

—Adrianne Anderson, Texas Christian University

In the paragraph above, the main idea is spelled out in the first sentence, so readers can easily see the relationship between the main idea and the supporting reasons and evidence that follow.

Topic Sentence at End of Paragraph Writers may place the topic sentence at the end of a paragraph to draw a conclusion based on the evidence presented and to enhance dramatic effect.

> When I was a little girl, Walt Disney's *The Little Mermaid* was my favorite movie, and Ariel (the title character) was my favorite character. I watched this movie three times a day, repeating Ariel's lines word for word. I wanted to be like her—cute and little and sweet and lovable, with big eyes and a tiny waist. But when I watched *The Little Mermaid* for the first time in more than seven years, I noticed things I had overlooked as a child. Was Ariel unhealthily thin? Was she more childlike than a full-grown woman should be? Was Ariel too willing to make sacrifices for Prince Charming? Maybe *The Little Mermaid* wasn't the innocent entertainment I had once thought.

> Topic sentence

> —Heidi Johnson, North Dakota State University

Holding the topic sentence until the end of the paragraph and starting with dramatic statistics or (as in the example above) a provocative anecdote may stimulate interest before you draw your conclusion. Remember, though: The relationship between evidence and main point must be clear, or you might leave your readers puzzled.

Topic Sentence in Middle of Paragraph Occasionally writers will place the topic sentence somewhere in the middle of the paragraph:

> Biology is destiny—or at least more and more people seem ready to believe that it is. Perhaps this is because recent scientific advances—gene splicing, in vitro fertilization, DNA identification of criminals, mapping the human genome—have been repeatedly echoed and amplified by popular culture. From science fact to science fiction (and back again), the gene has become a pervasive cultural symbol. It crops up not just in staid scientific journals and PBS documentaries, but also with increasing regularity in political discourse, popular entertainment, and advertising.

> Topic sentence

> —Jeff Reid, "The DNA-ing of America," *Utne Reader*

In cases where the main idea appears in the middle of the paragraph, it acts as a linchpin: In the example above, the paragraph begins with examples of genetic advances, and it ends with a sentence supporting the widespread cultural importance of these genetic tests. The topic sentence links these two different kinds of support.

3. In some paragraphs, leave the main idea unstated.

Some paragraphs (especially descriptive and narrative ones) may leave the main idea unstated. The main idea of the paragraph below, for example, is implied by the details and the word choices. The words and phrases that suggest the main idea are highlighted.

> The sound of discreet footsteps echoed in my ears as our choir followed a monk through one of the dark, damp archways into a grand hall furnished with ancient tables and chairs; it had been immaculately preserved by the family that had inhabited the old palace, which now served as a monastery, school, and museum. From the hall we passed into a room filled with religious relics that had belonged to the old prince. In another room, brown music manuscripts in Beethoven's and Haydn's own handwriting lay in crystal cases. In a third, bright tapestries woven from gold thread hung from the shiny stone walls, and sparkling crown jewels bedecked glass cabinets. We passed quickly through room after room filled with rusty (or bloodstained?) torture devices. Just before we reached an open-air walkway, we passed doors that seemed to belong to dwarves: They were entrances to the rooms of children who attended school here.
>
> —Christina Huey, Georgia Southern University

In this paragraph, the implied main idea—something like "Everything in the monastery seemed strange and remarkable"—comes through without Huey's having to state it explicitly. But be careful: Including just one irrelevant idea in a paragraph without an explicit topic sentence can confuse your readers.

connect
mhconnectcomposition.com
Online exercise: QL4103

→ EXERCISE 4.3 Identifying the topic sentence

Identify the topic sentence (main idea) in the following paragraphs:

1. Rock music had always been a vehicle to express frustration, rebellion, and obloquy, but as the 1970s proceeded, these themes were often softened to achieve mass acceptance. The notion of rock as mainstream entertainment was gaining ground steadily. David Bowie, for example, who in an earlier era might have been considered too inaccessible a figure for television audiences, turned up as a smiling guest on Cher's variety show in 1975. Rock was becoming a common language, the reference point for a splintered culture. In March 1976, presidential candidate Jimmy Carter told a lecture audience that Bob Dylan, Led Zeppelin, and the Grateful Dead

were among the artists who had inspired him to work hard as governor of Georgia, and once he won the election, Carter continued to court rock by inviting numerous musicians to the White House. —Ken Tucker, "The Seventies and Beyond," in *Rock of Ages: The Rolling Stone History of Rock & Roll,* p. 520

2. Straddling the top of the world, one foot in China and the other in Nepal, I cleared the ice from my oxygen mask, hunched a shoulder against the wind, and stared absently down at the vastness of Tibet. I understood on some dim, detached level that the sweep of earth beneath my feet was a spectacular sight. I'd been fantasizing about this moment, and the release of emotion that would accompany it, for many months. But now that I was finally here, actually standing on the summit of Mount Everest, I just couldn't summon the energy to care. —Jon Krakauer, *Into Thin Air,* p. 5

EXERCISE 4.4 Developing a unified paragraph

connect
mhconnectcomposition.com
Online exercise: QL4104

Choose one of the following topic sentences and develop it into a unified paragraph, placing the topic sentence at the beginning of the paragraph.

1. Rock and roll is no longer a useful term for describing popular music.
2. Asian religions seem to differ significantly from Western ones.
3. The best of the Star Wars movies is _____.
4. Central governments all over the world are more powerful than ever.
5. Formula One racing is/is not a sport.

Now revise the paragraph, moving the topic sentence to the middle or to the end of the paragraph and changing the other sentences as needed.

4c Writing Coherent Paragraphs

connect
mhconnectcomposition.com
Additional resources: QL4003

A paragraph is *coherent* when readers can understand the relationships among the sentences without having to pause or ponder. Readers are most likely to find a paragraph coherent when all the sentences in the paragraph are relevant, when the paragraph is clearly organized, and when transitional strategies link sentences.

1. Organize your paragraphs logically.

connect

mhconnectcomposition.com
Additional resources: QL4004,
QL4005

There are many ways to organize a paragraph logically. Most paragraphs follow deductive order: They begin with a topic sentence, the most general statement in the paragraph, and the supporting evidence follows:

Topic sentence

Supporting evidence

The handbags in the museum exhibition were hardly Murakami's only contribution to the Roppongi Hills complex of glass-and-steel towers. Cute cartoonlike characters that he had created as branding elements for the center—Barney-like brontosaurs, droopy-eared rabbits and smiling aliens—grinned down on me from pennants and from express buses to Roppongi Hills. In the same development, at a large Vuitton store, new handbags in a cherry design by Murakami would soon be introduced, along with a couple of the artist's sculptures of a red, smiling cherry. Last year at another Vuitton shop in Tokyo, Murakami displayed a large fiberglass sculpture and a four-panel screen painted in his LV monogram design.

—Arthur Lubow, "The Murakami Method," *New York Times*

connect

mhconnectcomposition.com
Additional resources: QL4006

A less common option is to organize the paragraph inductively, so that it begins with the supporting details and concludes with the topic sentence:

Supporting evidence

Topic sentence

His trademark character Mr. DOB (who appears in the sculpture *DOB in the Strange Forest*) is reminiscent of both Mickey Mouse and Sonic the Hedgehog. But there's something heavier going on here. It's hinted at in the manic eyes of Murakami's characters. It's unleashed fully in the show's centerpiece painting *Tan Tan Bo Puking,* aka *Geo Tan,* where the cartoon character subject is bearing fearsome jagged teeth, and the whole lot is melting. It's like cartoon Dali, sure, but it's also another reminder that Japan experienced the flesh-melting horror of atomic attack.

—Daniel Etherington, "Nasty Cartoons from Japan," bbc.co.uk

The painting referred to in the paragraph above is shown in Figure 4.1 on the next page.

connect

mhconnectcomposition.com
Additional resources: QL4007

A third option is to organize the paragraph by increasing order of emphasis or interest:

Least emphatic

Most emphatic

Monotonously the trucks sway, monotonously come the calls, monotonously falls the rain. It falls on our heads and on the heads of the dead up the line, on the body of the little recruit with the wound that is so much too big for his hip; it falls on Kemmerich's grave; it falls in our hearts.

—Erich Maria Remarque, *All Quiet on the Western Front*

FIGURE 4.1 *Tan Tan Bo Puking—a.k.a. Gero Tan*, 2002, by artist Takashi Murakami. © 2002 Takashi Murakami/Kaikai Kiki Co., Ltd. All Rights Reserved.

connect

mhconnectcomposition.com
Additional resources: QL4008

A fourth option is to organize the paragraph by posing a problem or question and then resolving it:

> So why exactly is the protagonist drawn to the dreams of the past? It may be because those dreams are not the trivialities of modern times. They are not about realizing suddenly that you are standing at your locker naked or unable to get to the airport in time for your flight. Instead, the dreams of the past are dreams of death, of unknown gods, of devouring monsters.
>
> —Michael Parr, McHenry Community College, "The Importance of Dreaming in Sylvia Plath's 'Johnny Panic and the Bible of Dreams'"

Question

Answer

2. Use transitions within (and between) paragraphs.

In addition to omitting irrelevancies and being well organized, a coherent paragraph provides guideposts that point readers from one sentence to the next. These are ***transitional words and phrases.*** They alert readers to the significance of what you are saying and point up the relationships among your ideas. The following paragraph uses transitional words and phrases to guide readers through a comparison of two books:

> Baron's book, which is written in the relentlessly melodramatic style of *Jaws,* describes cougars spreading inexorably eastward. By contrast, Elizabeth Marshall Thomas, in *The Tribe of Tiger: Cats and Their Culture,* argues that cougars were never fully exterminated in the East and instead survived in remote areas by being especially stealthy around

Contrast

Quick Reference ➡ **Sample Transitional Expressions**

To add to an idea: again, also, and, and then, besides, further, furthermore, in addition, incidentally, likewise, moreover, next, still, too

To indicate cause or effect: accordingly, as a result, because, consequently, hence, since, then, therefore, thus

To indicate chronology (time sequence): after, afterward, as long as, as soon as, at last, before, earlier, finally, first, formerly, immediately, in the first place, in the interval, in the meantime, in the next place, in the last place, later, latter, meanwhile, next, now, often, once, previously, second, shortly, simultaneously, since, sometime later, subsequently, suddenly, then, third, today, tomorrow, until, until now, when, years ago, yesterday

To compare: alike, also, in the same way, like, likewise, resembling, similarly

To conclude: all in all, finally, in brief, in conclusion, in other words, in short, in sum, in summary, that is, to summarize

To contrast: after all, and yet, although, but, conversely, despite, difference, dissimilar,

even so, even though, granted, however, in contrast, in spite of, instead, nevertheless, nonetheless, notwithstanding, on the contrary, on the other hand, otherwise, regardless, still, though, unlike, while this may be true, yet

To concede: certainly, granted, of course

To emphasize: after all, certainly, clearly, even, indeed, in fact, in other words, in truth, it is true, moreover, of course, undoubtedly

To offer an example: as an example, for example, for instance, in other words, namely, specifically, that is, thus, to exemplify, to illustrate

To indicate spatial relationships: above, adjacent to, against, alongside, around, at a distance from, behind, below, beside, beyond, encircling, far off, farther along, forward, here, in front of, inside, near the back, near the end, nearly, next to, on, over, surrounding, there, through, to the left, to the right, to the north, to the south, up front

Cause-effect
Emphasis
Time

humans. The difference is significant. If you accept Marshall Thomas's argument, then the eastern seaboard sounds a great deal like pre–cougar-resurgence Colorado. Indeed, the herds of deer plaguing the unbroken strip of Eastern suburbs makes a replay of the Boulder situation likely—but on a far larger scale. Already, bears and coyotes are invading the Eastern suburbs. Can cougars and wolves be far behind?

—Peter Canby, "The Cat Came Back," *Harper's*

More about ▶▶▶
Avoiding repetition, 519–20

Make sure you choose the appropriate transition for the situation, and vary your selection to avoid ineffective repetition.

3. Repeat words, phrases, and sentence structures.

Repetition—especially repetition used for padding—can annoy readers, but repetition used consciously, to knit sentences into a cohesive paragraph or to call attention to an idea, can be an asset. The paragraph below repeats words and phrases (*deer hunting, hunting, deer season*) to emphasize the point made in the final sentence, where the writer uses the word *deer* on its own.

More about ▶▶▶
Developing without
padding, 99
Effective repetition,
599

> I don't object to deer hunting: let everyone have his sport, I say. I don't for a moment doubt the value, importance, and dignity of hunting for those who do it. Deer hunting teaches skill, discipline, and patience. More than that, it teaches the moral lesson of seriousness—that certain things must be entered into advisedly, done with care, and done right. That hunting provides an education I am very willing to believe. And yet deer season is for me a sad couple of weeks. Because with all its profound advantages for the hunter, the fact remains that deer season is a little tough on the deer.
>
> —Castle Freeman, "Surviving Deer Season:
> A Lesson in Ambiguity," *Atlantic*

Repeated structure

Repeated words

Key concept

The paragraph above repeats sentence structures ("I don't object," "I don't . . . doubt"; "Deer hunting teaches," "It teaches") but largely relies on the repetition of words (*deer, hunting, season*) for emphasis. The paragraph below uses related concepts (the word *gangster,* the names of gangsters and others from the FBI's most wanted list), but it mainly relies on repetition of phrase and sentence structures to lend emphasis.

> When he said he'd been a gangster, they smiled. Sure you were, pops. When he said he'd been Public Enemy Number One—right after John Dillinger, Pretty Boy Floyd and his old protégé Baby Face Nelson—people turned away and rolled their eyes. When he said he and his confederates had single-handedly "created" J. Edgar Hoover and the modern FBI, well, then he would get bitter and people would get up and move to another table. He was obviously unstable. How could you believe anyone who claimed he was the only man in history to have met Charles Manson, Al Capone, and Bonnie and Clyde?
>
> —Bryan Burrough, *Public Enemies*

Key concept

Repeated structure

Examples of concept

4. Use pronouns, synonyms, and equivalent expressions.

Pronouns (I, you, he, she, it, we, they), synonyms (words that mean the same thing), and equivalent expressions not only help writers avoid having to repeat the same word over and over (unintentional repetition) but also create coherence by establishing links to words and phrases that appeared earlier. The following paragraph, for example,

Writing Responsibly   **Guiding the Reader**

As a writer, you have a responsibility to guide your reader from point to point, highlighting the relationships among your words, sentences, and paragraphs. Do not leave readers to puzzle out the relationships among your ideas for themselves.

uses several equivalent expressions for the word *gossip* as well as the pronoun *it* to refer to this concept:

Key concept

Repeated structure

Pronouns

Equivalent expressions

The first law of gossip is that you never know how many people are talking about you behind your back. The second law is thank God. The third—and most important—law is that as gossip spreads from friends to acquaintances to people you've never met, it grows more garbled, vivid, and definitive. Out of stray factoids and hesitant impressions emerges a hard mass of what everyone knows to be true. Imagination supplies the missing pieces, and repetition turns these pieces into facts; gossip achieves its shape and amplitude only in the continual retelling. The best stories about us are told by perfect strangers.

—Tad Friend, "The Harriet-the-Spy Club," *New Yorker*

5. Combine techniques.

The example paragraphs above used more than one technique to achieve coherence. When revising your own paragraphs, draw on a variety of techniques to make your paragraphs cohere.

connect

mhconnectcomposition.com
Online exercise: QL4105

EXERCISE **4.5** Analyzing coherence

For each of the following paragraphs, identify how the paragraph is organized, underline the transitional words and phrases, and circle the words that are repeated or the pronouns or synonyms that replace them.

1. Readers of this novel can attribute multiple meanings to the word *paradise* depending on whose point of view they are looking from. The founders of Ruby consider *paradise* to consist of preserving the history of the Old Fathers and remaining isolated from outsiders, but this view proves faulty and falls apart. On their journey toward seeking comfort, the women of the convent realize that *paradise* means coming to terms with one's past instead of running from it or letting it deter-

mine who they are, and this understanding leads them to show compassion and mercy toward those who have harmed them.—Sonu Ray, Drew University, "Journey to *Paradise:* Discovering Its Gateway"

2. The group worshipped unharassed until 1667. At that time, the Court acted on the complaints of the orthodox churches of the area against Myles and his followers. In an order from the Plymouth Court dated July 2, 1667, the members were fined five pounds each for "setting up of a public meeting without the knowledge and approbation of the Court to the disturbance of the peace of the place" (King 30–31). The Court offered them three alternatives: They could discontinue their worship services, leave the town, or petition the Court for an alternate site of worship. Mr. Myles moved his church to New Meadow Neck, just south of Rehoboth, which is today in Barrington, Rhode Island.—Robyn Worthington, Bristol Community College, "The Covenant between Church and Town in Swansea, Massachusetts"

3. First, use the cork borer to cut 2 cylinders out of the potato and then slice the cores into pieces 2 cm long. It is a good idea to place the slices in a beaker to prevent them from drying out. There should be two potato cylinders for each treatment. Weigh the two cylinders for each treatment and record the weight in grams: that is your initial weight. Next, blot the cylinders with a paper towel and put each of the sets of cylinders into 100 ml beakers (there should be five) and place 50 ml of each solution in the beakers.—Stephanie Warnekros, Johnson County Community College, "Osmosis in Potato Cubes"

→ **EXERCISE 4.6 Unscrambling the Gettysburg Address**

The sentences below make up the final paragraph of Abraham Lincoln's "Gettysburg Address," but they have been scrambled. Without checking the original, use the clues within the paragraph to restore Lincoln's sentences to their proper order. Then list the coherence techniques that helped you put the paragraph back together again.

connect
mhconnectcomposition.com
Online exercise: QL4106

1. It is rather for us to be here dedicated to the great task remaining before us—that from these honored dead we take increased devotion to that cause for which they gave the last full measure of devotion—that we here highly resolve that these dead shall not have died in vain—that this nation, under God, shall have a new birth of freedom—and that government of

the people, by the people, for the people, shall not perish from the earth.

2. The world will little note, nor long remember, what we say here, but it can never forget what they did here.

3. But, in a larger sense, we cannot dedicate—we cannot consecrate—we cannot hallow—this ground.

4. The brave men, living and dead, who struggled here, have consecrated it, far above our poor power to add or detract.

5. It is for us the living, rather, to be dedicated here to the unfinished work which they who fought here have thus far so nobly advanced.

↑ Make It **Your Own**

Assess the coherence of a paragraph you wrote recently. List the techniques you used to weave the sentences together into a paragraph. What would you change now to make it even more coherent?

connect

mhconnectcomposition.com
Additional resources: QL4009

4d Developing Paragraphs Using Patterns

Using *patterns*—description, narration or process analysis, exemplification, comparison and contrast, cause and effect, analysis, and definition—can help you develop your paragraphs (and your essay) into a cohesive and unified whole.

connect

mhconnectcomposition.com
Additional resources: QL4010

Description When describing, include details that appeal to the senses (sight, sound, taste, smell, touch) and organize them spatially (from left to right, top to bottom, near to middle to far) to mimic how we normally take in a scene. Spatially organized paragraphs rely on indications of place or location to guide the reader by the mind's eye (or ear or nose).

Sensory description

Indications of place
or location

A few moments later French announces, "Bottom contact on sonar." The seafloor rolls out like a soft, beige carpet. Robison points to tiny purple jellies floating just above the floor. Beyond them, lying on the floor itself, are several bumpy sea cucumbers, sea stars with skinny legs, pink anemones, and tube worms, which quickly retract their feathery feeding arms at *Tiburon*'s approach. A single rattail fish hangs inches above the bottom, shoving its snout into the sediments in search of a meal.

—Virginia Morell, "OK, There It Is—Our Mystery Mollusk,"
National Geographic

connect

mhconnectcomposition.com
Additional resources: QL4011,
QL4012

Narration, Process Analysis A paragraph that tells a story or describes a process unrolls over time. Include each step or key moment, and describe it in enough detail that readers can envision it.

The very first trick ever performed by Houdini on the professional stage was a simple but effective illusion known generally as the "Substitution Trunk," though he preferred to call it "Metamorphosis." Houdini and his partner would bring a large trunk onto the stage. It was opened and a sack or bag produced from inside it. Houdini, bound and handcuffed, would get into the sack, which was then sealed or tied around the neck. The trunk was closed over the bag and its occupant. It was locked, strapped and chained. Then a screen was drawn around it. The partner (after they married, this was always Mrs. Houdini) stepped behind the screen which, next moment, was thrown aside—by Houdini himself. The partner had meanwhile disappeared. A committee of the audience was called onstage to verify that the ties, straps, etc. around the trunk had not been tampered with. These were then laboriously loosened; the trunk was opened and there, inside the securely fastened bag, was—Mrs. Houdini!

| Step 1 |
| Step 2 |
| Step 3 |
| Step 4 |
| Step 5 |
| Step 6 |
| Step 7 |

—Ruth Brandon, *The Life and Many Deaths of Harry Houdini*

The sequence of events in the Substitution, or Metamorphosis, trick is depicted in Figure 4.2.

Exemplification: Explaining through Example Exemplification works by providing examples to make a general point specific:

For many years I believed that women had only one thing to learn from men: how to get the attention of a waiter by some means short of kicking over the table and shrieking. Never in my life have I gotten the attention of a waiter, unless it was an off-duty waiter whose car I'd accidentally scraped in a parking lot somewhere. Men, however, can summon a maître d' just by thinking the word "coffee," and this is a power women would be well-advised to study. What else would we possibly want to learn from them? How to interrupt someone in midsentence as if you were performing an act of conversational euthanasia? How to drop a pair of socks three feet from an open hamper and keep right on walking? How to make those weird guttural gargling sounds in the bathroom?

FIGURE 4.2 A visual process analysis

| Example 1 |
| Example 2 |
| Example 3 |

—Barbara Ehrenreich, "What I've learned from Men: Lessons for a Full-Grown Feminist," *Ms.*

connect

mhconnectcomposition.com
Additional resources: QL4013

Comparison-Contrast: Showing Similarities and Differences A paragraph that is developed using comparison-contrast points out similarities or differences (sometimes both). A comparison-contrast paragraph can proceed by either the ***block method*** or the ***alternating method.*** In the block method, the writer groups all the traits of the first item together before discussing the second item. In the alternating method, the writer proceeds point by point, discussing each common or divergent trait of both items before moving to the next trait. In the block method, readers must remember everything you have said about item A while they read about item B, so the more complex your material, the more your readers are likely to need the alternating method.

Block Method	**Alternating Method**
A	A
A	B
A	
	A
B	B
B	
B	A
	B

The first paragraph below uses the alternating method; the second uses the block method.

At first glance, it would appear that surgery and writing have little in common, but I think that is not so. For one thing, they are both sub-celestial arts; as far as I know, the angels disdain to perform either one. In each of them you hold a slender instrument that leaves a trail wherever it is applied. In one, there is the shedding of blood; in the other it is ink that is spilled upon a page. In one, the scalpel is restrained; in the other, the pen is given rein. The surgeon sutures together the tissues of the body to make whole what is sick or injured; the writer sews words into sentences to fashion a new version of human experience. A surgical operation is rather like a short story. You make the incision, rummage around inside for a bit, then stitch up. It has a beginning, a middle and an end. If I were to choose a medical specialist to write a novel, it would be a psychiatrist. They tend to go on and on. And on.

Surgery

Writing

—Richard Selzer, "The Pen and the Scalpel," *New York Times*

Europeans interpreted the simplicity of Indian dress in two different ways. Some saw the lack of clothing as evidence of "barbarism." André Thevet, a shocked French visitor to Brazil in 1557, voiced this point of view when he attributed nakedness to simple lust. If the Indians could weave hammocks, he sniffed, why not shirts? But other Europeans viewed unashamed nakedness as the Indians' badge of innocence. As remnants of a bygone "golden age," they believed, Indians needed clothing no more than government, laws, regular employment, or other corruptions of civilization.

—James West Davidson et al., *Nation of Nations,* 5th ed.

"Barbarism"

"Innocence"

Cause-and-Effect: Reasons and Consequences A cause-and-effect paragraph explains why something happened or what its consequences are:

When we exhibit these [positive] emotions, society showers us with positive reinforcement; we learn this even before we get out of diapers. When, as children, we hug our rotten little puke of a sister and give her a kiss, all the aunts and uncles smile and twit and cry, "Isn't he the sweetest little thing?" Such coveted treats as chocolate-covered graham crackers often follow. But if we deliberately slam the rotten little puke of a sister's fingers in the door, sanctions follow—angry remonstrance from parents, aunts and uncles; instead of a chocolate-covered graham cracker, a spanking.

—Stephen King, "Why We Crave Horror Movies," *Playboy*

connect
mhconnectcomposition.com
Additional resources: QL4014

Causes

Effects

Analysis: Dividing a Whole into Its Parts Analysis divides a single entity into its component parts:

The central United States is divided into two geographical zones: the Great Plains in the west and the prairie in the east. Though both are more or less flat, the Great Plains—extending south from eastern Montana and western North Dakota to eastern New Mexico and western Texas—are the drier of the two regions and are distinguished by short grasses, while the more populous prairie to the east (surrounding Omaha, St. Louis, and Fort Leavenworth) is tall-grass country. The Great Plains are the "West"; the prairie, the "Midwest."

—Robert D. Kaplan, *An Empire of Wilderness*

connect
mhconnectcomposition.com
Additional resources: QL4015

United States

Great Plains

Prairie

Definition: Explaining the Meaning of a Word or Concept Like those in a dictionary, a definition explains the meaning of a word or concept by grouping it into a class and then providing the distinguishing characteristics that set it apart from other members of that class:

connect
mhconnectcomposition.com
Additional resources: QL4016

Term to Be Defined	Class	Distinguishing Characteristics
Argument is	a way to discover truth	by examining all sides of the issue.

Extended definitions (definitions that run to a paragraph or more) analyze in detail what a term does or does not mean. They go beyond a desktop dictionary, often using anecdotes, examples, or reasons for using the word in this particular way:

Term to be defined

Class

Distinguishing characteristics

The international movement known as *theater of the absurd* so vividly captured the anguish of modern society that late twentieth-century critics called it "the true theater of our time." Abandoning classical theater from Sophocles and Shakespeare through Ibsen and Miller, absurdist playwrights rejected traditional dramatic structure (in which action moves from conflict to resolution), along with traditional modes of character development. The absurdist play, which drew stylistic inspiration from dada performance art and surrealist film, usually lacks dramatic progression, direction, and resolution. Its characters undergo little or no change, dialogue contradicts actions, and events follow no logical order. Dramatic action, leavened with gallows humor, may consist of irrational and grotesque situations that remain unresolved at the end of the performance—as is often the case in real life.

—Gloria Fiero, *The Humanistic Tradition,* 5th ed.

connect
mhconnectcomposition.com
Online exercise: QL4107

→ **EXERCISE 4.7 Using the patterns of development**

Write two paragraphs, each of which uses one of the patterns of development. Check to make sure that they are unified and that they use appropriate transitions to guide the reader.

Work **Together**

Exchange with a classmate the paragraphs you wrote for Exercise 4.7. Study your classmate's revisions. What techniques did your classmate use to develop the paragraph and to create coherence? Suggest one or more ways your classmate could improve the paragraph.

connect
mhconnectcomposition.com
Additional resources: QL4018, QL4019

4e   Writing Introductory Paragraphs

Introductory paragraphs shape readers' attitudes toward the rest of the text. Yet writers often have a hard time producing these paragraphs.

Many writers find it helpful to draft the body of the essay before tackling the introduction.

 Avoid Praising the Reader in Your Introduction In some cultures, writers win the approval of readers by praising their taste, character, or intelligence. Generally, however, U.S. writers avoid referring directly to the reader and occasionally will actually challenge the reader's beliefs.

Whether you write the introduction first or last, it should prepare the reader for what follows. In many cases, this means including the thesis in the introduction. A common placement for the thesis statement is at the end of the introduction—this is the *funnel* introduction.

Regardless of whether you include your thesis in your introduction, hold it until your conclusion, or merely imply your main idea, your introduction should identify and convey your stance toward your topic, establish your purpose, and engage readers to make them want to read on. One or more of the following strategies can help you write an effective introduction:

- Begin with a vivid quotation, a compelling question, or some interesting data.
- Start with an engaging—and relevant—anecdote.
- Offer a surprising but apt definition of a key term.
- Provide background information.
- State a commonly held belief and then challenge it.
- Explain what interesting, conflicting, difficult, or misunderstood territory the essay will explore.

(For some opening gambits to avoid, see the Quick Reference box on p. 72.)

In the introductory paragraph that follows, the writer uses several effective strategies: She begins with a question that challenges the audience to examine some common assumptions about the topic, she provides background information that her readers may lack, and she concludes with a thesis statement that explains why reading her text should be important to the audience.

Many people enjoy sitting down to a nice seafood dinner, but how many of those people actually stop to think about where the fish on their plate came from? With many species of wild fish disappearing because of overfishing, increasingly the answer will be a fish farm. But

Opening question

Answer that provides background information

Quick Reference ➡ Five Don'ts for Introductions

Avoid common problems that can undermine your introduction's success:

1. **"In my paper I will do. . . ."** While announcing your topic is acceptable in some academic disciplines (in the sciences, for example), announcing what your paper is or will do is usually unnecessary and boring. Also avoid referring to your own text by its title.

2. **"In this paper I hope to . . ." or "In this paper I will try to. . . ."** These openers share the shortcomings of "In my paper I will do . . ."; they also state something your instructor already assumes, and they undermine your credibility by emphasizing your lack of confidence.

3. **"I don't know much about this topic, but. . . ."** Introductions that apologize for your amateur status undermine your credibility as a writer and give readers an excuse to stop reading.

4. **"My expertise on this topic is legendary."** Refrain from claiming more prestige or credit than is your due.

5. **"According to *Merriam-Webster's Third Unabridged Dictionary*. . . ."** While starting with a definition can be an effective opening gambit, merely providing readers with a definition they could easily find for themselves is tedious.

Thesis

while fish farming can help to supply the demand, it can threaten the environment and cause problems with wild fish. It can also threaten the health of consumers by increasing the risk of disease and increasing the quantity of antibiotics consumed. In fact, as a careful and conscientious consumer, you would do well to learn the risks involved in buying and eating farm-raised fish before one winds up on your dinner plate.

—Adrianne Anderson, Texas Christian University

While brief essays may require only a one-paragraph introduction, longer texts often need more. A text of twenty pages may have an introduction that runs several paragraphs, and introductions to books generally run to the length of a short chapter. While there are no firm rules about the length of the introduction, they should be in proportion to the essay's length.

connect

mhconnectcomposition.com
Additional resources: QL4020, QL4021

4f Writing Concluding Paragraphs

As with the introduction, the conclusion is a part of the essay that readers are likely to remember. In fact, because it is the last thing the audience will read, it is what they will probably remember best. Thus, it demands a writer's best work.

The shape of the conclusion is often what might be called an **inverted funnel:** While the introduction often starts at a general level and then narrows down to the thesis, a common strategy for the conclusion is to start out specific—with a restatement of the thesis (in different words)—and then to broaden out.

The purpose of the conclusion is to provide readers with a sense of closure and also to provide them with a sense that reading the text was worthwhile. To achieve closure and convey the importance of the essay, try one or more of the following strategies:

- Recur to the anecdote, question, or quotation with which you began.

- Summarize your findings (especially in long or technical projects).

- Discuss how what you have learned has changed your thinking.

- Suggest a possible solution (or solutions) to the problems raised in the text.

- Indicate additional research that needs to be conducted or what the reader can do to help solve the problem.

- Leave readers with a vivid and pertinent image, quotation, or anecdote.

(For some strategies to avoid when writing your conclusion, see the Quick Reference box on the next page.)

The concluding paragraph below provides an example of an effective conclusion.

> The farmers of nineteenth-century America could afford to do here what they had not dared to do in the Old World: hope. This hope—for greater economic security, for more opportunity for themselves, their children, and their grandchildren—is the optimism and idealism that has carried our country forward and that, indeed, still carries us forward. Although the American dream has evolved across the centuries, it survives today and is a cornerstone of American philosophy. It is what underlies our Constitution and our laws, and it is a testimony to the vision of the farmers who founded this nation.
>
> —Leonard Lin, University of Southern California, "The Middle Class Farmers and the American Philosophy"

Makes reader feel time reading was well spent by showing importance of American dream

Restates thesis (American dream = hope for greater security, opportunity)

Achieves closure by recurring to introduction with mention of American dream

Quick **Reference** ➔ **Five Don'ts for Conclusions**

1. **Do not offer additional support for your thesis in your conclusion.** Such conclusions undermine the feeling of closure and leave readers wanting and expecting more.

2. **Do not end with a generality or a cliché.** Almost nothing will undermine the readers' sense that they have spent their time well than ending with something trite.

3. **Do not apologize for the shortcomings of your paper.** Such an ending will leave readers feeling they have wasted their time. If your paper is truly bad, you should have revised your draft, not passed it on to readers; if it is not, you have nothing to apologize for.

4. **Do not repeat your introduction.** It may be useful to recur to the anecdote or statistics with which you began, but a mere rehash of your introduction or word-for-word repetition of your thesis will not work. Your readers will not want to read the same text a second time.

5. **Do not announce what your essay has done or shown ("In my paper, I have shown . . .").** In a long or complicated text, a summary can be useful to readers, but your readers will be reminded of what your text has done when they read your summary; there is no need to announce it.

---

connect

mhconnectcomposition.com
Online exercise: QL4108

➔ **EXERCISE 4.8** **Writing introductory paragraphs**

Revise the following introductory paragraph to make it more effective:

> People aged 50 and older cannot see as well at night as younger people. The small muscles that control the size of the pupil get weaker with age, and with age there may be a loss of rods, which are crucial for night vision. This affects older people's ability to adapt to the dark. This can cause problems when driving at night after the bright headlights of a car pass or just walking from well-lit to dark parts of a home. Older people need to recognize their decreased ability to see at night and to take measures that will help them be safe in the dark, whether driving, walking outdoors, or getting around the home. This paper presents the reasons why night vision is weaker in older people and some methods of compensating for this problem.

connect

mhconnectcomposition.com
Online exercise: QL4109

➔ **EXERCISE 4.9** **Writing concluding paragraphs**

Revise the following concluding paragraph to make it more effective:

> To summarize the point of this essay, the majority of experts acknowledge that every one of the world's seven species

of marine turtles is threatened by extinction. At present humans are causing more turtle deaths than natural forces. A key cause is habitat destruction and alteration. Coastal development is rapidly eliminating access to beaches for female turtles to nest and lay eggs. Another important cause is predation for turtle meat, eggs, hides, and shells. Incidental capture in fisheries increases the loss of turtles. Masking the threat is the slow maturation of turtles, which can hide the effect of overexploitation for many years. We need to greatly expand our knowledge of marine turtle life history patterns and the true conservation status of turtle populations, as well as the level and types of exploitation. With this knowledge we need to formulate and implement effective management and conservation strategies to preserve viable marine turtle populations. If we do not, time will run out for one of the most intriguing creatures on the face of the earth.

Make It **Your Own**

Revisit the introduction and conclusion of a paper you wrote recently. What strategies did you use? Referring to the Quick Reference boxes (pp. 72, 74) and the strategies discussed in the sections above, revise your introduction and conclusion.

Work **Together**

Exchange your revised introduction and conclusion with a classmate. What strategies did your classmate use? What strategies might make these paragraphs more powerful?

4g Connecting Paragraphs

Readers need to know not only how sentences connect to one another but also how paragraphs connect to one another. One way to connect paragraphs is by using one of the patterns of development (pp. 67–70) for the essay, just as you would do with individual paragraphs; you can also link paragraphs using the techniques for linking sentences:

- Providing transitional expressions (and sentences)
- Repeating words and phrases strategically

- Using pronouns and synonyms to refer back to words and ideas

- Creating parallel sentence structures

A final way to create coherence among paragraphs is by referring back to the essay's main idea.

The essay excerpted below, by former vice president and 2007 Nobel Peace Prize recipient Al Gore, uses all of these strategies to create a unified and cohesive text:

An Inconvenient Truth

By AL GORE

Some experiences are so intense while they are happening that time seems to stop altogether. When it begins again and our lives resume their normal course, those intense experiences remain vivid, refusing to stay in the past, remaining always and forever with us.

Seventeen years ago my youngest child was badly—almost fatally—injured. This is a story I have told before, but its meaning for me continues to change and to deepen.

That is also true of the story I have tried to tell for many years about the global environment. It was during that interlude 17 years ago when I started writing my first book, *Earth in the Balance*. It was because of my son's accident and the way it abruptly interrupted the flow of my days and hours that I began to rethink everything, especially what my priorities had been. Thankfully, my son has long since recovered completely. But it was during that traumatic period that I made at least two enduring changes: I vowed always to put my family first, and I also vowed to make the climate crisis the top priority of my professional life.

Unfortunately, in the intervening years, time has not stood still for the global environment. The pace of destruction has worsened and the urgent need for a response has grown more acute.

. . . I also want to convey my strong feeling that what we are facing is not just a cause for alarm, it is paradoxically also a cause for hope. The Chinese expression for "crisis" consists of two characters side by side. The first is the symbol for "danger," the second the symbol for "opportunity."

The climate crisis is, indeed, extremely dangerous. In fact it is a true planetary emergency. Two thousand scientists, in a hundred countries, working for more than twenty years in the most elaborate

Key words, phrases (highlighted on first use)

¶ 2 provides an example of the intense experiences mentioned in ¶ 1.

Transitional words, expressions

Adjective *that* in "that interlude 17 years ago," "that traumatic period" refers back to period of child's injury, introduced in ¶ 2.

"abruptly . . . hours" refers back to "time seems to stand still" (¶ 1).

"Time has not stood still" refers back to "time seems to stop" (¶ 1).

¶ 5 sets up logical (problem-solution) structure of essay: Global warming is a crisis that is dangerous but also presents opportunities. The words *danger* and *opportunity* and synonyms for these words appear throughout.

This section elaborates on the idea that global warming puts the earth in *danger*.

and well-organized scientific collaboration in the history of humankind, have forged an exceptionally strong consensus that all the nations on Earth must work together to solve the crisis of global warming. . . .

So the message is unmistakably clear. This crisis means "danger!"

Why do our leaders seem not to hear such a clear warning? Is it simply that it is inconvenient for them to hear the truth?

If the truth is unwelcome, it may seem easier just to ignore it. But we know from bitter experience that the consequences of doing so can be dire. For example, when we were first warned that the levees were about to break in New Orleans because of Hurricane Katrina, those warnings were ignored. Later, a bipartisan group of members of Congress chaired by Rep. Tom Davis (R-Va.) said in an official report, "The White House failed to act on the massive amounts of information at its disposal," and that a "blinding lack of situational awareness and disjointed decision-making needlessly compounded and prolonged Katrina's horror."

Today, we are hearing and seeing dire warnings of the worst potential catastrophe in the history of human civilization: a global climate crisis that is deepening and rapidly becoming more dangerous than anything we have ever faced.

And yet these dire warnings are also being met with a "blinding lack of situational awareness"—in this case, by the Congress, as well as the president.

As Martin Luther King Jr. said in a speech not long before his assassination: "We are now faced with the fact, my friends, that tomorrow is today. We are confronted with the fierce urgency of now. In this unfolding conundrum of life and history, there is such a thing as being too late."

But along with the danger we face from global warming, this crisis also brings unprecedented opportunities. There will be plenty of new jobs and new profits—we can build clean engines; we can harness the sun and the wind; we can stop wasting energy; we can use our planet's plentiful coal resources without heating the planet. . . .

But there's something even more precious to be gained if we do the right thing. The climate crisis also offers us the chance to experience what very few generations in history have had the privilege of knowing: a generational mission; the exhilaration of a compelling moral purpose, a shared and unifying cause; the thrill of being forced by circumstances to put aside the pettiness and conflict that so often stifle the restless human need for transcendence; the opportunity to rise.

When we do rise, it will fill our spirits and bind us together.

Sidebar annotations:

"Unwelcome" is a synonym for "inconvenient" in previous ¶.

"Today" contrasts with "when we were first warned . . ." in previous ¶.

Repetition of "blinding lack of situational awareness" connects this ¶ to the previous one.

This section elaborates on the *opportunities* global warming presents.

Transitional sentence refers to list of opportunities in previous ¶.

Uses *chance* as synonym for *opportunity.*

Repetition of *rise* and sentence structure ("When we . . .") ties these 3 ¶s together.

Those who are now suffocating in cynicism and despair will be able to breathe freely. Those who are now suffering from a loss of meaning in their lives will find hope.

When we rise, we will experience an epiphany as we discover that this crisis is not really about politics at all. It is a moral and spiritual challenge. At stake is the survival of our civilization and the habitability of the Earth. . . .

This too is a moral moment, a crossroads. This is not ultimately about any scientific discussion or political dialogue. It is about who we are as human beings. It is about our capacity to transcend our own limitations, to rise to this new occasion. To see with our hearts, as well as our heads, the response that is now called for. This is a moral, ethical and spiritual challenge.

We should not fear this challenge. We should welcome it. We must not wait. In the words of Dr. King, "Tomorrow is today."

I began with a description of an experience 17 years ago that, for me, stopped time. During that painful period I gained an ability I hadn't had

before to feel the preciousness of our connection in our children and the solemnity of our obligation to safeguard their future and protect the Earth we are bequeathing to them.

Imagine with me now that once again, time has stopped—for all of us—and before it starts again, we have the chance to use our moral imaginations and to project ourselves across the expanse of time, 17 years into the future, and share a brief conversation with our children and grandchildren as they are living in the year 2023.

Will they feel bitterness toward us because we failed in our obligation to care for the Earth that is their home and ours? Will the Earth have been irreversibly scarred by us? Imagine now that they are asking us: "What were you thinking? Didn't you care about our future? Were you really so self-absorbed that you couldn't—or wouldn't—stop the destruction of Earth's environment?" What would our answer be?

We can answer their questions now by our actions, not merely with our promises. In the process, we can choose a future for which our children will thank us.

Side annotations:

"This too is a moral moment" and "This is a moral, ethical, and spiritual challenge" hearken back to "moral and spiritual challenge" in previous ¶.

Reference to Dr. King and repetition of "Tomorrow is today" connect this ¶ to earlier ¶ above.

Emphasis on pronouns, contrast, connects final ¶ with previous ¶s.

---

connect

mhconnectcomposition.com
Online exercise: QL4110

> **EXERCISE 4.10 Identifying introductions and conclusions**
>
> Identify the introductory and concluding paragraphs in the excerpt from "An Inconvenient Truth." What techniques does Al Gore use to begin and end this essay?

> EXERCISE **4.11** **Identifying techniques of unity and cohesion**

Find an essay of three or more pages in a magazine or collection of essays. Identify the techniques used to weave the paragraphs into a unified and cohesive whole: Highlight the repeated words, circle the transitional expressions, and underline the pronouns and synonyms that refer back to earlier passages. Identify the patterns the writer used to develop paragraphs. (Patterns may be mixed.)

connect

mhconnectcomposition.com
Online exercise: QL4111

Make It **Your Own**

Revisit a text you have written recently. Identify the transitional devices that you used to link paragraphs. Identify, too, any links back to the thesis. What revisions would you make now to connect the paragraphs to each other and to the thesis more effectively? What techniques would you use to develop your ideas more fully?

5 Drafting and Revising Visuals

connect

mhconnectcomposition.com
Additional resources: QL5001

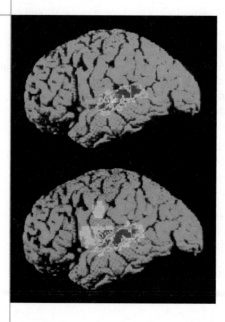

Visuals can add pizzazz to a written text: A *Facebook* page, a political ad, a website—all would be boring without images. Visuals play a much more important role than mere decoration, however; they help us understand the world. The colors in these PET scans, for example, inform researchers about the portions of the brain that are activated while a subject is listening to words (top) or repeating them (bottom). Images from the Hubble Space Telescope (p. 282) inform viewers about the universe that surrounds our home planet.

5a Deciding Whether to Illustrate College Writing Projects

In personal writing, visuals are often used to entertain or express the writer's thoughts or feelings. In business and public writing, visuals can make an arguable claim and provide evidence for it. In academic writing, visuals may help to engage or persuade readers, but their primary role is to aid understanding. A photograph of a painting you are analyzing for an art history course, a graph comparing voter turnout among age groups for a political science project, a video or animation that describes the course of a disease for a biology assignment—all these would be appropriate illustrations in an academic text.

To determine whether a visual is appropriate in a college project, ask yourself these questions:

More about ▶▶▶
Purpose, 11–13
Audience, 14–16
Context and genre, 18

- **Does this visual reinforce my purpose?** The primary purpose of visuals in academic writing is to inform. They may have a secondary persuasive purpose—evidence should be chosen that the reader will find convincing—but the primary purpose will be informative.

- **Is this visual appropriate to my audience, context, and genre?** To determine whether illustrations are appropriate, look at articles from journals in your field or ask your instructor.

▶▶▶ Visual support
in sample student essays, 107, 138, 169, 349, 351, 353, 395, 423, 483

ESL **Photographs in Job Applications** In Europe and Asia it is common to include a personal photograph with a job application. In the United States, however, it is generally considered inappropriate for a résumé to include a photograph (or a description of the job candidate), and employers are barred from asking applicants personal questions, such as their age, marital status, race, religion, or sexual orientation.

- **Does the "tone" of the visual match that of the text?** While a caricature might be appropriate in a political magazine like the *Nation,* it would not be appropriate in most college projects (Figure 5.1).

5b Using Visuals as Evidence

In academic writing, visuals are used primarily as evidence. Choose the right type of illustration for the information you wish to convey.

1. Information graphics

Information graphics, such as tables, bar graphs, line graphs, and pie charts, convey and depict relationships among data.

FIGURE 5.1 Caricature vs photograph Unless you were analyzing the political content of such an image, a caricature like this one of former president George W. Bush would not be appropriate in a college project.

Quick

Reference ➡ **Matching Visual Evidence to Claims**

- **Tables.** Use to display large amounts of data, data that include decimals, or data on multiple variables that are difficult to convey in a graph.
- **Pie charts.** Use to convey significant divisions in a single entity that add up to 100 percent.
- **Bar graphs.** Use to compare two or more variables.
- **Line graphs.** Use to show changes among variables over time.
- **Diagrams.** Use to model processes or locations.

- **Maps.** Use to represent geographical locations; may also include data.
- **Photographs.** Provide readers with a reference point or example, or depict a process (two or more photographs needed).
- **Movie stills.** Provide a reference point, offer an example, show a process (two or more stills needed).
- **Screenshots.** Provide a reference point or example from an electronic resource, such as a website.

connect

mhconnectcomposition.com
Additional resources: QL5002

TABLE 5.1 | **CHILDREN 3 TO 21 YEARS OLD SERVED IN FEDERALLY SUPPORTED PROGRAMS FOR THE DISABLED, BY TYPE OF DISABILITY (2001–04)**

Type of Disability	2000–01	2001–02	2002–03	2003–04
Specific learning disabilities	45.2	44.4	43.7	42.7
Speech or language impairments	17.2	16.9	21.6	21.7
Mental retardation	9.5	9.2	9.2	8.9
Emotional disturbance	7.5	7.4	7.4	7.4
Hearing impairments	1.1	1.1	1.2	1.2
Orthopedic impairments	1.1	1.1	1.3	1.2
Other health impairments	4.6	5.3	6.2	7.0
Visual impairments	0.4	0.4	0.4	0.4
Multiple disabilities	1.9	2.0	2.1	2.1
Autism and traumatic brain injury	1.5	1.8	2.4	2.8
Developmental delay	0.4	0.7	4.3	4.6

Source: U.S. Dept. of Educ., Inst. of Educ. Sciences, Natl. Center for Educ. Statistics, *Digest of Education Statistics,* U.S. Dept. of Educ., Sept. 2006; Print; table 48.

Tables Tables, such as Table 5.1 (above), organize large amounts of information in rows and columns for easy scanning. The information in a table can be textual, graphic, or numeric, but it is usually numeric. Tables are frequently the best choice for presenting data on more than four variables or data that include decimals.

Bar Graphs and Pie Charts Bar graphs and pie charts allow comparison of data in two or more categories. A bar graph (Figure 5.2) uses bars of different colors and heights (or lengths). A pie chart (Figure 5.3) uses segments of a circle to depict portions of a whole. Choose a pie chart

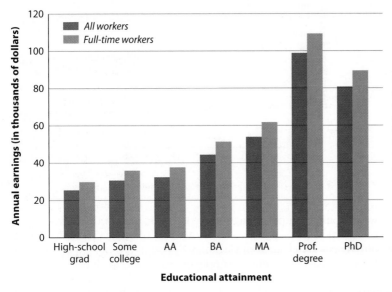

FIGURE 5.2 Work experience and average annual earnings of workers 25–62 by educational attainment The bar graph shown here uses bars of different colors to compare earnings of full-time workers against all workers (both full-time and part-time) by education level. (U.S. Census Bureau, *Current Population Surveys,* Mar. 1998, 1999, 2000; Print.)

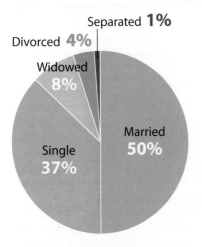

FIGURE 5.3 Who reads romance? This pie chart breaks down the total number of romance readers (100 percent) into groups. Because the information to be conveyed is relatively simple and all of one type (marital status of romance readers), it can readily be conveyed by a pie chart. (Data from "About the Romance Genre," *The Voice of Romance,* Romance Writers of America. 2008. Web.)

FIGURE 5.4. Smoking, overweight, and seatbelt use, trends 1983–2007 This line graph allows readers to see at a glance the trend in these behaviors and to compare the trends for the three variables: The graph shows that, while the number of smokers has declined slightly over the period, the number of overweight Americans has increased, and the number of Americans wearing seatbelts has skyrocketed. (Data from the Harris Poll, 1983–2007 <www.harrisinteractive.com>.)

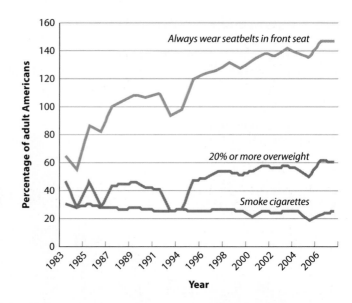

▶▶▶Student samples:
"Why Students Cheat," Tom Hackman, 168–74
"Nature versus Nurture," Robyn Worthington, 479–86
"The Power of Wardrobe: Male Stereotype Influences," Heather DeGroot, 389–400

when comparing percentages that add up to 100. Both bar graphs and pie charts work best with a small number of categories among which differences are clear. Tom Hackman, Robyn Worthington, and Heather DeGroot use bar graphs to supply evidence succinctly.

Line Graphs Line graphs (such as Figure 5.4) are especially useful in illustrating change over time. The more lines, the more types of data can be compared (but the more complex the graphic). As with bar graphs and pie charts, line graphs work best when you are comparing a few variables—the more variables, the more difficult it will be to convey the information clearly.

2. Images

Academic writers use images (photographs, screenshots, film stills, architectural renderings, and the like) as references, as when writing about a work of art or a scene from a movie, and they use them as examples. The photograph in Figure 5.5 would provide an effective example in a project discussing the connections between the women's movement of the 1970s and Vietnam War protests.

Erin Buksbaum includes a screenshot of a *MySpace* profile as a reference for readers unfamiliar with social networking sites. Alea

FIGURE 5.5 Photographs in history Photographs are frequently used in history to supply visual evidence.

 Tech

Consider the Size of Your Document

Submitting an illustrated document brings with it certain concerns:

- If you will be submitting your project on paper, make sure you have access to a printer of sufficiently high quality that it can handle your graphics.
- If you will be submitting your project electronically, think about how large a file your

email program—and that of your recipient—can handle. Image files dramatically increase the size of a document file.

- If you will be delivering your project online, make sure to optimize your graphics for the Web so that they load quickly into the reader's web browser.

▶▶▶ Student samples:
"The Risks of On-line Networking," Erin Buksbaum, 106–10
"Reflecting on Brent Staples's Editorial, . . ." Alea Wratten, 137–39
"Holy Underground Comics, Batman!" Lydia Nichols, 346–57

Wratten uses a photograph of a sculpture as a visual example. Lydia Nichols uses illustrations from superhero and underground comics to demonstrate the differences between these two types of comic books. Heather DeGroot shows photographs of the proctor in stereotypical, counterstereotypical, and "control" outfits.

 EXERCISE 5.1 Using visuals as evidence

For one of the thesis statements you revised in Exercise 3.2 (p. 37), describe the type of visuals you might use as support.

connect
mhconnectcomposition.com
Online exercise: QL5101

Writing Responsibly

Exploitative Images

When using images in your academic work, keep in mind that scholarly essays refrain from including images that may be seen as emotionally manipulative of the reader, as well as those that might be emotionally exploitative of those whom they depict. As you review your selection of images, think about how much respect you are extending to the people depicted and how they might feel about the use of the image.

More about ▶▶▶
Placing visuals on
the page,
343–44 (MLA),
387 (APA)

5c Deciding Whether to Copy Visuals or to Create Them

Original artwork, like original thoughts, can often be more effective than material "quoted" from others. Some illustrations, however, must come from an outside source, either because the subject is inaccessible (as with a historical photograph) or because the software needed to create the visual is beyond the writer's ability.

Whenever you borrow images from an outside source, be sure to indicate your source, either in the figure caption (for most illustrations) or in a source note (for tables). While you are not required to obtain permission to use a visual in an unpublished academic work, you will need permission if you plan to publish your project, even on the Web.

5d Revising Visuals

As with the words you have written, reconsider your supporting visuals while revising to make sure that they are clear, that they are accurate, and that they avoid distortion.

1. Avoid visual clutter.

Your readers will understand your information graphics best when they are clean and simple. Omit lines around cells in a table; use them only to set off headings or to indicate major divisions (Table 5.2). Leave space between columns, and align numbers to make graphics easier to read. Avoid using special views or shading that could make your visual more difficult to interpret (Figure 5.6, p. 88).

Johnsville Boxers, Batting Statistics

NAME	AB	R	H	SO	BA
Tammy	12	2	5	7	.416
Alyssa	14	0	1	13	.071
Travis	12	5	7	5	.583
Jose	15	3	5	10	.333
Akira	13	6	8	5	.615
Walt	14	7	7	7	.500
Taylor	5	4	1	4	.200
Leslie	11	2	4	7	.363
Chloe	9	3	5	4	.555
Derek	8	7	6	2	.250
Maria	14	4	6	8	.571
Lance	12	5	3	9	.250
Carlos	12	4	4	8	.333
Antoine	14	6	5	9	.357
B.J.	5	2	2	3	.400
Sasha	15	7	6	9	.400

NAME	AT BATS	RUNS	HITS	STRIKE OUTS	BATTING AVERAGE
Tammy	12	2	5	7	.416
Alyssa	14	0	1	13	.071
Travis	12	5	7	5	.583
Jose	15	3	5	10	.333
Akira	13	6	8	5	.615
Walt	14	7	7	7	.500
Taylor	5	4	1	4	.200
Leslie	11	2	4	7	.363
Chloe	9	3	5	4	.555
Derek	8	7	6	2	.250
Maria	14	4	6	8	.571
Lance	12	5	3	9	.250
Carlos	12	4	4	8	.333
Antoine	14	6	5	9	.357
B.J.	5	2	2	3	.400
Sasha	15	7	6	9	.400

TABLE 5.2 Less is more Instead of enhancing clarity, lines around cells and abbreviations in headings in the table on the left make the visual more difficult to read.

2. Keep visuals clear and accurate.

Double-check the numbers in tables and figures to make sure totals are accurate and that percentages in a pie chart total 100. (If rounding the numbers up or down has caused inaccuracy, indicate this in a note.) Label all parts of your tables and figures (columns, rows, vertical and horizontal axes, "slices" of a pie chart) so that readers can understand them without having to read the text. Avoid abbreviations that might be unfamiliar or confusing (Figure 5.6, p. 88).

3. Avoid distortion.

Make sure the information supplied in visuals is complete. The graph on the left in Figure 5.7 distorts the disparity in number of Democratic and Republican voters by starting the scale at 104. Changing the vertical axis in the revised graph on the right more accurately reflects the difference. Cropping photographs to eliminate background or to focus on the main action is acceptable, but cropping to distort information is unethical, as is using image processing programs to change or distort an image.

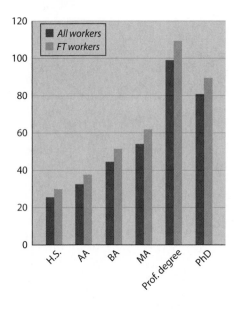

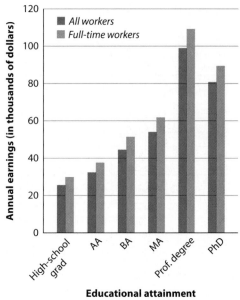

Educational attainment

FIGURE 5.6 Clarity and precision The bar graph at left will be more difficult for readers to interpret than the graph at right: "Full-time" is abbreviated to FT and "high-school" to HS, which could be confusing; no indication is given that the dollar amounts are in thousands; and the shading and the box around the legend make the figure unnecessarily busy.

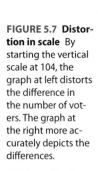

FIGURE 5.7 Distortion in scale By starting the vertical scale at 104, the graph at left distorts the difference in the number of voters. The graph at the right more accurately depicts the differences.

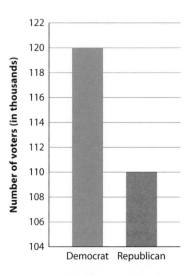

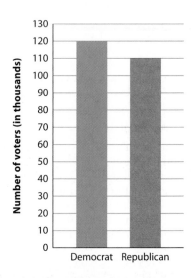

FIGURE 5.8 Manipulative images in advertising This famous advertisement, showing a tearful Iron Eyes Cody, makes a powerful emotional argument in favor of protecting the environment, but it does not offer a reasoned position that would be expected in an academic or business context. <www.adcouncil.org/files/pollution_historic_cody.gif>

4. Do not manipulate.

Advertisements may use photographs that tug on readers' heartstrings (see Figure 5.8). An academic audience, however, will expect images that stir the emotion to be supported by arguments grounded in logic.

> *More about* ▶▶▶
> Logical appeals
>   (logos), 160–61
> Emotional appeals
>   (pathos), 162–63

6 Revising, Editing, Proofreading, and Formatting

As writers chisel meaning from their first words and sentences, they erase and redraw parts of the broad outline, they carve out details to craft meaning, and they refine their work by sanding down rough edges. Only through revising and editing carefully can a writer transform a rough-hewn draft into a polished work.

REVISING GLOBALLY: LEARNING TO RE-SEE

Revising globally means looking at the big picture to address issues like purpose, audience, context, genre, and ethical responsibilities. The first step toward assessing these aspects of your writing is to take a step backward to gain distance. The second is to dive in, adjusting focus and organization, making changes to address your audience more effectively, and developing your ideas more fully.

6a Gaining Perspective

Writers generally feel a sense of "ownership" toward the texts they compose. This helps them produce an authentic voice and a commitment toward the ideas they express. But that sense of ownership can be an impediment to revising; it can hold a writer back from making core changes. To gain the objectivity they need, writers can draw on a wide range of techniques, such as those described in the Quick Reference box below.

6b Revising Your Draft

connect
mhconnectcomposition.com
Additional resources: QL6001,
QL6002, QL6003

Once you have gained some distance, you are ready to start revising, which begins with rereading the text. Read your project through to the end before making any changes. Then reread with a pencil in your hand. Work through each paragraph, considering issues of focus, audience, organization, and development.

1. Is your thesis the true focus of your draft, and does it fulfill your purpose and assignment?

Because writers often discover and develop their ideas as they draft, the draft thesis may not capture the project's main idea. (Often, the

Quick **Reference** ➔ **Seven Ways to Gain Perspective**

1. **Allow time between drafts.** A few days or even a few hours between drafts can provide the distance you need.
2. **Clear your mind.** Do something to get your mind off your paper, such as go for a run or play a quick game of *Guitar Hero*.
3. **Learn from other readers.** Having others read and react to your draft will give you a sense of what your text is (and is not) communicating.
4. **Analyze the work of a fellow writer.** Most tutors and teachers will tell you that they learn as much from the coaching experience as do the people whom they coach.
5. **Listen to your draft being read aloud.** Every time your reader stumbles, pauses, or has to reread a passage, mark the spot. Then figure out what caused the interruption, and revise accordingly.
6. **Outline your draft.** Once your outline is complete, read it through carefully. If any sections seem unconnected to the thesis or to the sections before or after, reorganize.
7. **Compare your text to others in the target context and genre.** When writing in an unfamiliar context or genre, consider reading professional texts to help you see what does and does not work in your own writing.

More about ▶ ▶ ▶
Peer revising,
100–101

➜ **Tech**

Revision Tools

To preserve your original text when revising (in case you change your mind), use the Track Changes feature on your word processor.

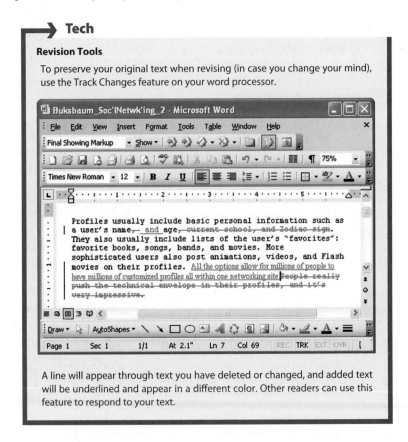

A line will appear through text you have deleted or changed, and added text will be underlined and appear in a different color. Other readers can use this feature to respond to your text.

> **More about ▶▶▶**
> Drafting a thesis,
> 34–35
> Revising a thesis,
> 35–37

true thesis appears in the conclusion of the first draft.) This might mean you should adjust your reasons and evidence to your thesis. More frequently it means you should revise your thesis to match the reasons and evidence offered in your draft.

When revising, make sure, too, that your draft fulfills your purpose and assignment. If you were asked to analyze a work of literature, check to see that you have not merely summarized it; if you were instructed to argue for or against corporal punishment in elementary school, be sure you have not merely explained the arguments on both sides.

2. Is your draft appropriate for your readers?

After rereading your text, consider how your readers will react. Have you won them over? Think about your introduction: Does it draw your readers into your text? Next, consider the reasons and evidence you supply in your body paragraphs. Will they persuade your readers, given their background, interest level, and attitude toward your topic? Is the language appropriate to your audience? An academic or business audience will expect a more formal tone but will not need you to define specialized terms; a general audience may be more engaged by an informal tone and may need specialized terms clearly defined. Finally, consider your conclusion. Does it provide readers with a feeling of closure? The number of possibilities for creating this sense of closure is great. Tailor the conclusion to your readers. For a long or complex text, readers may need a summary; for a persuasive essay, readers may want to take action, so offer them a plan.

> *More about ►►►*
> Audience, 14–16
> Introduction, 70–72
> Development,
>   46–48, 66–70
> Connotation, 16, 575
> Level of formality, 16,
>   576
> Conclusions, 72–74

3. Is your draft coherent and unified?

Rereading your text may have alerted you to problems with organization. When revising, make sure that your essay is both unified and coherent. In a unified essay, all the paragraphs support the thesis, and all the details in each paragraph support the paragraph's main idea. When revising, be prepared to delete ideas, facts, and even whole paragraphs—no matter how much you like them—if you notice that they do not support your thesis.

> *More about ►►►*
> Unity, 54–58
> Coherence, 59–64

Writing
▲ Responsibly   The Big Picture

Another way to think about revising is to focus on your responsibilities to your audience, your topic, other writers, and yourself:

- Have you provided your audience with a worthwhile reading experience?
- Have you covered your topic fully and creatively?
- Have you represented borrowed ideas accurately and acknowledged all your

sources, whether you have quoted, summarized, or paraphrased?

- Have you developed a voice that readers will find credible, represented your ideas clearly and powerfully, and written in a voice that is a reflection of your best self?

	Focus (unity)	**Audience**
Introduction	Does my introduction identify my topic? Does it suggest that my topic is worth reading about? Does it indicate my purpose and attitude toward my topic? Does it convey the essay's main claim?	Does my introduction provide needed background information? Will my readers find my introduction engaging or compelling?
Body Paragraphs	Is each body paragraph relevant to my thesis? Is the evidence in each paragraph relevant to the paragraph's topic?	Will my readers need more (or less) information? Will my readers be sympathetic, or, if not, can I soften their response? Is my language at the right level?
Conclusion	Is my conclusion focused on a relevant issue that shows the importance of my topic? Does it reinforce my purpose?	Does my conclusion provide something to think about or supply a necessary summary? Does my conclusion provide readers with a feeling of completion?

In a coherent essay, the relationship among the paragraphs is clear and logical. Sometimes a text lacks coherence because the writer has not included transitional words and phrases that signal the relationships among ideas. Sometimes a text lacks coherence because a step in the argument has been omitted. Also, be sure to clarify the relationships among your paragraphs, by adding or changing transitions or by tightening the logic of your argument or both.

> I've revised the paper I'm working on twice already. I'll revise again to smooth out my transitions and to make sure each point relates directly to my thesis. (I know I drift, especially when writing on a subject that interests me.)
>
> —Christina Huey,
> Georgia Southern University

4. Did you explore and support your ideas fully?

In rereading your text, you may have had concerns about the reasons or evidence you offered in support of your thesis. Perhaps you noticed that a reason you offered was weak or irrelevant, that you did not offer enough reasons, that the evidence you supplied was overly general, or that you just did not supply enough evidence. If you need more or better reasons, or more relevant, more specific, or just more evidence, go back to the idea-generating stage or return to the library to do additional research.

	Organization (cohesion/unity)	Development (reasons/support)
Introduction	Does my thesis state my main claim? Does my introduction prepare readers for what follows?	Does my introduction provide necessary background, a relevant anecdote, or compelling statistics related to my thesis or main idea?
Body Paragraphs	Does my organizational pattern suit my reasons and evidence? Does each paragraph lead logically to the next? Have I provided transitions between paragraphs?	Are the reasons and evidence I supply relevant? Do I supply enough evidence? Is the evidence compelling? Do I credit my sources?
Conclusion	Does my conclusion grow logically out of my body paragraphs?	Does my conclusion avoid introducing new supporting evidence?

You may find it possible to revise for focus, audience, organization, and development simultaneously; most writers, though, focus on only one issue at a time.

> **More about** ▶▶▶
> Relevance, 53, 249
> Generating ideas, 22–29
> Developing paragraphs, 66–70
> Finding information, 222–47 (ch. 13)

6c Reconsidering Your Title

Once you have revised your draft globally, revisit your title. Your title should prepare the audience for what they will read in your essay. In most college projects, your title should accurately reflect not only the topic but also your approach to the topic:

- The Power of Wardrobe: An Analysis of Male Stereotype Influences

- Transcending Stereotypes in Hurston's *Their Eyes Were Watching God*

> Note how many of these titles use a descriptive phrase (underlined) to make their titles more specific.

You might also use a clever turn of phrase, a quotation, or a question to intrigue your readers and draw them into your project:

- Holy Underground Comics, Batman! Moving Away from the Mainstream

> Note how many of these titles indicate their approach in their titles (highlighted).

- My View from the Sidelines: <u>A Close Reading of Gary Snyder's</u> <u>"Front Lines"</u>

A question in your title can also suggest your approach (analysis, comparison-contrast, cause-effect).

- Differing Intentions? <u>Comparing Raphael's Painting with a Print of Raphael's *Saint Cecilia*</u>

↑ Make It **Your Own**

For a writing project you have gotten back from an instructor, write a paragraph explaining how you fulfilled your responsibilities as a writer, or what global issues you would revise now if you had the opportunity.

REVISING LOCALLY: EDITING WORDS AND SENTENCES

Your writing is a reflection of you—your ideas and your attitude toward your topic and audience. Revise locally to make sure that your

Getting It
Across   The Importance of a Title

The title plays an important role in guiding the viewer. Consider this painting. Without knowing the title, a viewer might have seen this as a painting of trees. By titling it *Farmhouse in Normandy* (1882), the painter, Paul Cézanne (1839–1906), shifts the viewer's focus from the dense foliage in the foreground to the small building in the background.

words and sentences reflect your meaning and that together they create a ***persona*** that is appropriate for your purpose, audience, context, and genre.

> **Persona** The apparent personality of the writer as conveyed through tone and style (8)

6d Choosing Your Words with Care

When revising, reconsider your word choices. Each word should reflect your intended meaning; it should have the right ***denotation***. Be very careful to use the word that expresses your exact meaning: Readers may sometimes guess your intent, but you cannot count on this, and you should not expect readers to be charitable.

In addition to denotations, words carry emotional associations that color meaning and indicate the writer's attitude. Compare *freedom fighter* with *terrorist*. Both words have roughly the same denotation; both refer to people who use violence to achieve political ends. But the connotative difference is enormous.

Next, consider the level of formality that is appropriate to your audience, context, and genre: A text message to a friend may be filled with slang and acronyms, but this informality is rarely appropriate in business or academic writing. Writers who intend to sound sophisticated by trotting out a word like *progenitor* to mean *parent* or even *mom* or *dad* may instead make themselves sound pompous. All writing, though, benefits from avoiding biased language—language that unfairly or offensively characterizes groups or individuals.

Finally, consider whether you have combined general, abstract language with specific, concrete words; explaining broad issues requires abstract language, but specific words will make your writing more compelling.

> **connect**
> mhconnectcomposition.com
> Additional resources: QL6004

> ▶ **More about** ▶▶▶
> Denotation, 16, 573–74
> Connotation, 16, 575
> Levels of formality, 16, 576
> Biased language, 568–71
> General and specific language, 567–77

6e Editing Your Sentences

When revising, reconsider the structure of your sentences:

1. Are they grammatically correct?
2. Are they varied, and do they emphasize the most important information?
3. Are they as concise as they can be without losing meaning or affecting style?

In most contexts (academic and business, in particular), readers expect sentences to be formed according to the conventions of English grammar. Nongrammatical sentences may confuse, distract, or even

> ▶ **More about** ▶▶▶
> Common sentence problems, foldout following p. 599
> Sentence types, 623–24
> Sentence variety, 550–56
> Writing concisely, 515–25 (ch. 25)
> Generating ideas, 22–29
> Finding information, 222–47 (ch. 13)
> Style, 515–98 (part 7)
> Grammar, 599–736 (part 8)
> Punctuation and mechanics, 781–867 (part 10)

annoy readers. Edit your prose to conform to standard written English. Nine of the most common sentence problems are listed in the Quick Reference box on the left.

Once you are sure that your sentences are clear and correct, shape them to reflect your emphases. A good way to begin editing for style is to read your draft out loud—or better still, get a friend to read it to you. Listen to the rhythm of your sentences. Do they all sound alike? If so, your sentences probably use the same sentence structure or they all begin the same way.

To correct this problem, consider the information in your sentences. Combine related information in a single sentence by putting the most important information in the independent clause and additional information in the subordinate, or dependent, clause. If the information is of equal weight, use compound sentences and parallel structures to emphasize this balance. Where appropriate, use questions, commands, and exclamations for variety or emphasis.

In addition to writing varied sentences, hone them to eliminate clutter and polish them to add luster to your ideas. Try these strategies to revise for wordiness:

More about ▶▶▶
Writing concisely, 515–25 (ch. 25)
Coordination and subordination, 526–38 (ch. 26)
Parallelism, 539–48 (ch. 27)
Variety and emphasis, 549–62 (ch. 28)

- Eliminate empty expressions, intensifiers, roundabout expressions, and redundancies.

- Eliminate ineffective repetition.

- Favor the active voice.

Writing concisely for the Web is particularly important, as most users prefer pages that are easy to scan.

Because not every writer makes the same kinds of mistakes, a personalized editing checklist can come in handy. To create one, try the following:

More about ▶▶▶
Empty phrases, 518
Roundabout expressions, 518–19
Ineffective repetition, 519–20
Using the active voice, 560–61

1. Review the last five texts that you have produced, looking for the kinds of errors noted in the Quick Reference box above.
2. Make a list of the issues you find (or that your instructor marked).
3. Reorganize the list so that the type of mistake you make most frequently is at the top.

Writing
↑ Responsibly   **Making an Essay Long Enough without Wordiness**

When your paper is not long enough, you may be tempted to pad, but that might make it hard (and boring) to read. Instead, try these tips:

- Revisit your thesis: Is it too narrow? If so, explore strategies for broadening it.
- Reconsider your reasons: Have you offered enough reasons for you to believe that your thesis is true? If not, try freewriting on the topic *I believe my thesis is true because.* . . . Also consider whether you can unpack the reasons you already have by breaking them

down into their component parts or considering the assumptions that underlie them.

- Check your evidence: Have you offered facts, statistics, expert testimony, and examples to support your reasons? If not, return to the library or its website to search for more information. Also consider whether you have explained the significance of your evidence fully. Do not leave it to your readers to analyze the importance of your evidence.

The next time you have to write an essay, paper, letter, website, or *PowerPoint* presentation, use the top five items on your checklist to guide your local revision. Over time, you are likely to find that you make fewer of these errors and can add some of your less common mistakes.

NOTE Instructors often use symbols to indicate the most common mistakes.

▶▶▶List of editing symbols, inside back cover

REVISING WITH OTHERS

As writers we can be touchy. We pour ourselves into our texts and feel hurt that others might not understand or appreciate what we have written. Little wonder, then, that we often feel defensive when others read our work before it is finished. Yet paradoxically, getting feedback from a real, live audience is one of the best ways to make sure readers who do not have you standing by to explain will understand your writing, will be convinced by your evidence, will be persuaded by your conclusion, and will form a high opinion of you as a responsible, authoritative writer.

❝❝ If someone says something that I don't agree with in peer review, I try not to get my back up. I've learned to step back and try to figure out why the person said what he or she did. ❞❞

—Christina Huey, Georgia Southern University

6f Peer Revising

One common way to get feedback from readers is to solicit comments from your peers. In business, this might mean sharing your text with co-workers online or via email. In school, this usually means sharing your draft with your classmates face-to-face, through a class blog or wiki, or in an online writing environment like the *Connect Composition* website that accompanies this book (mhconnectcomposition .com). Whether in a business or academic context, the role of writer and peer editor carries its own responsibilities.

connect

mhconnectcomposition.com

Online exercise

1. The writer's role

When readers respond to your text, adopt a stance that is both engaged and receptive:

- **Talk.** Before readers begin to comment, explain what you are trying to accomplish and what you would like help with.

ESL **Peer Revising with Native Speakers** If you are a non-native speaker of English, you may be nervous about participating in peer groups. But participation can reduce your fears by showing that native speakers also make mistakes. Working with peers can also help you resolve issues of idiom and word choice you struggle with.

- **Listen.** As others respond to your draft, listen instead of arguing or defending. If readers seem clueless or careless, figure out how you can revise the text so that even a clueless or careless reader can understand what you are trying to say.

- **Question.** If your readers are not addressing your concerns or are speaking in generalities, ask them to point to specific passages. Ask yourself what underlying issue they are trying to get at. Do not settle for a disappointing response.

- **Write.** Take notes as your readers talk. What they say may be vivid at the time, but you will be surprised by how quickly you will forget the details.

- **Evaluate.** You are the person who must make the final decision. Be open to advice, but consider whether there may be a better way of solving the problem.

2. The peer editor's role

As a reader of a classmate's paper, keep the following guidelines in mind:

- **Stay positive.** Tell the writer what is working well, along with what could be improved (see Figure 6.1).

- **Talk to the writer.** Listen and respond to the writer's concerns, whether conducting the session face-to-face or electronically.

- **Look at the big picture, but be specific.** Focus on what the writer is trying to achieve, but back up general comments by pointing to specific passages in the text and explaining as best you can why they do not work for you.

- **Be a reader and a fellow writer—not a teacher, editor, or critic.** Your job is not to judge the text or to rewrite it, but to participate in its composition by helping the writer recognize and resolve issues.

> 66 My advice to peer revisers is simple: Keep your comments positive but be honest. 99
> —Michael Bosomworth, Western Illinois University

6g Working with a Tutor or an Instructor

Many colleges sponsor a writing center that offers free tutoring or on-line services such as *NetTutor* or *Smarthinking*. Many instructors also allow students to submit a rough draft of their papers for comment.

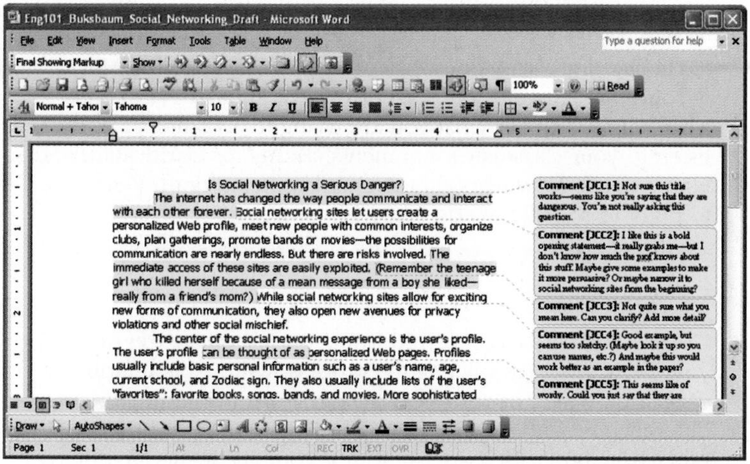

FIGURE 6.1 Electronic peer review If conducting peer review electronically, remember that there is a person on the receiving end of your comments. Stay positive, helpful, and friendly, and link each comment to something specific in the text.

More about ▶▶▶
Time management,
20–21, 212–13

" If you are going to the writing center, don't come in three hours before your paper is due and expect miracles—good writing takes time. Also be willing to do the hard work of revising; don't expect the peer tutor to do it for you. "

—Adrianne Anderson, Texas Christian University

Take full advantage of these opportunities, and when you do, follow these guidelines:

- **Be prepared.** Never come into a session empty-handed (or empty-headed) and expect the tutor or instructor to do your thinking or writing for you.

- **Be open to advice.** Bring your own list of issues or concerns about the text or project, but also be receptive to broader issues or suggestions. Your tutor or instructor may have concerns that go beyond your list and that require you to rethink your assumptions, revise your thesis, or revisit the library for additional research.

- **Be an active participant.** If the tutor or instructor makes a suggestion that you do not understand, ask for an explanation (and take notes). If you do not agree with a suggestion, consider the underlying issue and offer an alternative resolution. Then revise thoughtfully and fully.

Work **Together** ◄

Exchange drafts (the one you wrote in response to the Make It Your Own exercise on p. 44 or one for another class) with a classmate. Explain what you are trying to accomplish, and listen to your classmate's comments, asking for clarification and taking notes. Now respond to your classmate's draft. Remember to point to specific words, sentences, and paragraphs.

Make It **Your Own**

Using comments you received from your classmate, revise your draft. After completing the process, write a paragraph discussing which of your peer's suggestions made the biggest difference in your revision, and why. If you did not find the process helpful, discuss what you or your classmate might have done to make it more productive.

PROOFREADING AND FORMATTING

6h Proofreading

When revising, you concentrate on your ideas and how you express them; when you proofread, you pull back from the content of the essay to concentrate on correcting errors.

Writing Responsibly

Beware the Spelling Checker!

While spell-check software can be very helpful in catching typos, it cannot distinguish between homonyms (*they're, their*) or other frequently confused words (*lay, lie; affect, effect*). Spelling checkers may even lead you astray, suggesting words that are close to the word you mistyped (*defiant* for the misspelled *definate*) but worlds away from the word you intended (*definite*). As a writer, you have a responsibility not to leave your reader guessing. Do not merely run your computer's spell-check software; also use a dictionary to double-check the spelling checker's suggestions, check usage in the usage glossary, and proofread your text carefully yourself. Only you can know what you *meant* to say!

> **More about ▶▶▶**
> Using a dictionary,
> 586–87
> Usage glossary,
> G15–G21
> Homonyms and
> near homonyms,
> 589–91

Quick Reference ➡ A Checklist for Proofreading

Spelling

- Spell-check your project using your word processing software.
- Read through the text carefully, looking for misused words.
- Check specifically for words you frequently confuse or misspell.

Punctuation

- Check sentence punctuation, especially use of the comma and the apostrophe.
- In a text with dialogue or in a research project, double-check that all quotations have quotation marks and that end punctuation and in-text citations are correctly placed.

- Check specifically for errors you regularly make (for example, comma splices or fused sentences).

Other errors

- Check to make sure that remnants of previous corrections—an extra word, letter, or punctuation mark—do not remain.
- For a research project, check that you have included all in-text citations where needed (for summaries, paraphrases, quotations, or ideas you have borrowed).
- Check that all in-text citations are included in the reference list or list of works cited, and make sure that all formats are correct and consistent.

To proofread effectively, divorce yourself from the content you know so well, so that you can see the text as it appears on the page. An effective way to achieve this distance is to print out your draft and read the hard copy line by line from the bottom up. Mark each correction on the printout as you read; enter them one by one, and then check to make sure that you have made each correction without introducing additional errors. Another option for proofreading is to work in teams: One person reads the text (including punctuation marks) out loud, while the other person marks errors on the printout.

ESL **Proofreading When English Is Not Your First Language** If you have difficulty proofreading a project, try reading it aloud; this may help you recognize errors. Also, ask your instructor if you can have a friend or classmate help you proofread. A visit to the writing center may help, too.

Make It **Your Own**

Customize the proofreading checklist (p. 103) to reflect your own needs by adding the errors you have made on your last two or three writing projects.

More about ▶▶▶
Visual design,
176–85 (ch. 9)
MLA format, 340–44
APA format, 385–88

Work **Together**

Working in pairs, trade printed copies of a writing project. Have the other student read the text out loud while you mark corrections. When the process is complete for one text, trade roles with your partner and repeat the process.

▶▶▶Prewriting
and earlier drafts of
"The Risks of Online
Networking":
e-Journal, 24
Freewriting, 25
Brainstorming, 26
Cluster diagram-
ming, 27
Journalists' ques-
tions, 28
Thesis, 34–36
Outline, 42
Early draft, 49–50
Peer revising, 101
(Figure 6.1)

6i   **Formatting an Academic Text**

The Quick Reference box on the next page provides guidelines for formatting and incorporating visuals in an academic text. More coverage of formatting appears elsewhere in this book.

Student Essay: Final Draft

You have seen Erin Buksbaum's essay as it developed, from journal and freewriting entry, to draft thesis statement and outline, to initial draft. Now consider her final draft (pp. 106–10). If you compare this to Buksbaum's earlier draft, you will see how she has revised globally and locally to tighten her thesis, develop her reasons and evidence, and make her introduction and conclusion more compelling.

Quick Reference → Formatting Academic Texts

- Leave 1- to 1.5-inch margins.
- Indent the first line of each paragraph by half an inch.
- Use a standard font, such as Times New Roman or Cambria, in 12-point size.
- Use headings, headers, page numbers, and paragraph indents to help readers navigate the text easily.

- Format headings of the same level the same way throughout the project.
- Use figure and table numbers to guide the reader from text to visual.
- Use a style guide that is appropriate to your discipline.
- Keep your design simple; focus on content.

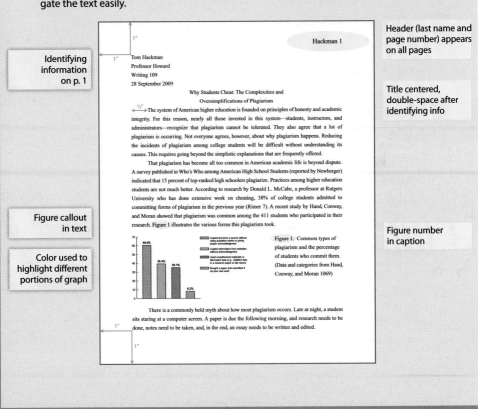

Header (last name and page number) appears on all pages

Identifying information on p. 1

Title centered, double-space after identifying info

Figure callout in text

Color used to highlight different portions of graph

Figure number in caption

Header (last name and page number)

Erin Buksbaum

Identifying information

Professor Locke

Composition 102

10 Oct. 2010

The Risks of Online Networking

Descriptive title (centered)

Introduction: Background and thesis

The internet has changed forever the ways people communicate and interact with each other. Personal letters have largely been replaced by emails. The water cooler chat is now less common than the exchange of instant messages (IMs). Even the vast, complex web of friendships and gossip represented by the high school hallway has been reborn on the computer screen in the form of social networking sites such as *MySpace* and *Facebook*. These sites allow users to create personalized profiles, which they can customize in a multitude of ways. The sites also allow users to view the profiles of others, designate their "friends," organize clubs, plan gatherings, promote bands or movies—the possibilities for communication are nearly endless. But for all the benefits of social networking sites, there are risks involved. The immediate access these sites offer—to tens of thousands of people—is easily exploited. While social networking sites allow for exciting new forms of communication, they also open new avenues for privacy violations and other social mischief.

Thesis: Claim of fact (informative)

Topic sentences

The center of the social networking experience is the user's profile (fig. 1). These profiles can be thought of as personalized web pages. Users include personal information on their profiles such as descriptions of themselves and their relationships; lists of their favorite music, books, and movies, sometimes even

Figure reference

Support: Facts, example

106

Visual example

Fig. 1. A *Facebook* profile

contact information such as an email address or instant messenger screen name. A profile can be piled high with photos, animations, soundtracks, videos, colors, pictures, and text. There is also an abundance of websites catering to users of social networking sites, allowing even more profile innovation in the form of *Flash* movies, unique color schemes, banners, slide shows, and more. All the options allow for millions of people to have millions of customized profiles all within one networking site.

Topic sentence

While creating a profile sounds like harmless, creative fun, what people post in their profiles can be extremely dangerous. Many people post information that would make them easy to track down in the "real world," such as where they work or go to school. Unless the profile is secured, anyone else with an account on the social networking site can access the profile. Although in the past two years *MySpace* has banned 90,000 (Honan, 2009), stalkers remain. Often, users do not realize the risks

Support: Reasons, facts

they are running. Many young teenagers naïvely post their age, grade, and school location. *MySpace* and *Facebook* have taken some precautions, allowing users to make their profiles "private," but even non-friends can still see the name and default picture of a "private" user.

Topic sentence

Another popular feature of social networking sites is the ability to post photographs on profiles. The prevalence of captured images on social networking sites creates its own set of complications. Most users post harmless photographs of themselves, their friends, and their pets. However, some profiles feature pornographic pictures or photos showing drug abuse, children with guns, and other images that could potentially be inappropriate for young social network users. Even posting pictures of a party, where underage friends are shown drinking or smoking pot, can cause problems with parents or school administrators. Students at the University of Oxford have been punished for violating school policies based on photographs posted on *Facebook* (Panja 2007). Additionally, once a photo is posted, it is easily downloaded by anyone viewing it. Although many users of social networking sites assume their photos will never be used beyond their profile, they can never be sure where their pictures end up.

Support: Facts, examples

Topic sentence

Perhaps the most powerful application of social networking sites, though, is their capacity for user interaction. On *MySpace,* for example, users can not only engage in all the conventional forms of internet communication, such as sending emails and instant messages, but they can also take advantage of networking site–specific features as well. Users can post messages on other users' profiles. They can post bulletins to all their designated "friends," announcing an upcoming

Support: Facts

concert or another event of interest. Users can create groups around common interests, such as favorite games or types of music. The "search" function on *MySpace* and other social networking sites also makes it very easy to find people of a certain age, who live in a particular place, or who like a particular band, movie, or book. In short, social networking sites provide users with quick access to thousands and thousands of other people who share their interests.

[Topic sentence]   With all these open doors to communication, abuse is almost inevitable. There are countless examples of stalkers and pedophiles using the internet to track and lure their victims. In 2006, MSNBC reported two cases, one in Connecticut and another in Long Island, in which sex offenders attacked victims they "met" through a social networking site (Williams 2006). In 2009, a newspaper in Tennessee **[Support: Facts, examples]** reported that a fourteen-year-old was targeted by a forty-year-old man for sex ("Girls' Softball Coach" 2009). Social networking sites, with their huge reach and vast amounts of data, only make such crimes easier to perpetrate. In a way, social networking sites are like an index of people who are easy to learn about, easy to contact, and easy to find. It is a wonderful resource for those who are simply looking to make a new friend or check in with an old one. But an ill-intentioned user can easily take advantage of social networking resources. There is even a website, *MyCrimeSpace.com,* which documents misuses of social networking sites and other internet resources.

     Now that the internet revolution has begun, it can never be reversed. Sites like *MySpace* and *Facebook* are unlikely to fade from the social scene. The best **[Conclusion: Highlights importance of caution]** course of action is for users of such sites to be cautious. The fact is that once something is posted on a social networking site, it is potentially available to anyone with an internet connection and nearly impossible to remove completely. One should never reveal too much in a profile or share pictures one would not want printed in a national newspaper or shown on a major television network. The beauty of social networking sites is that they are an open forum for communication, but people need to be aware that not all users have good intentions. While social networking sites offer exciting new paths of communication between people the world over, these new rewards also come with new risks.

Restates thesis

Works Cited

Honan, Edith. "MySpace: 90,000 Sex Offenders Removed in Two Years." *Reuters.com*. Reuters, 3 Feb. 2009. Web. 6 Oct. 2010.

"Girls' Softball Coach." *Knoxville News Sentinel* 31 Mar. 2009, Local sec.: n.p. Web.

Panja, Tariq. "Oxford Using Facebook to Snoop." *MSNBC.com*. MSNBC, 17 July 2007. Web.

Williams, Pete. "MySpace, Facebook Attract Online Predators." *NBC Nightly News*. NBC. WSYR, Syracuse, 3 Feb. 2006. Television.

➜ **EXERCISE 6.1 Assessing a revision**

Compare the final version of Erin Buksbaum's essay (above) with the earlier version (pp. 49–50). Which of her changes are global, and which are local? Is there anything more that you would suggest she do with this essay before submitting it? Explain.

connect

mhconnectcomposition.com
Online exercise: QL6101

6j Creating and Submitting a Portfolio

Some instructors (and prospective employers) may ask you to submit a writing portfolio. A portfolio may contain any of the following:

- A collection of texts that show your best work

- A collection of texts (such as a proposal, a formal report, a set of instructions, a website) that demonstrate the range of work you have produced

- A collection of texts from a single project (such as journal entries, freewriting and brainstorming, outline, first draft, revised draft) that show your writing process

What you include depends on the portfolio's purpose, audience, and context: You may create a portfolio of your best work to demonstrate your writing skills for admission to a course (a creative writing course, for example); you may create a portfolio showing the range of writing you have done to apply for a job; or you may create a portfolio to demonstrate the process you followed for a composition class.

As you select the contents, consider your audience:

- What kinds of writing projects will your readers be interested in?

- How many examples will your readers expect you to include? Will they want to see multiple examples of the same type of work, or is one example sufficient? Will they be interested in work you have created in electronic media, or will they focus exclusively on your writing?

- How will they want you to submit the portfolio, electronically or in print?

Once you have selected the items to be included, think about how you want to arrange the contents. A portfolio that shows your writing process should be arranged chronologically; a portfolio that includes a range of your work might be arranged from strongest to weakest; and a portfolio that includes your best work might be arranged in order of interest to your audience. While the contents of a portfolio will vary, in general, include the following:

Title Page or Home Page For a printed portfolio, include a title page with the following information:

- Title (for example, "One Writer's Journey through Sophomore Composition" or "Portfolio for Application to Stockbridge Writers' Group")
- Identifying information (name, course, contact information)
- Date of submission

For an electronic portfolio, include this information in a separate document or on the home page.

Table of Contents or Menu with Hyperlinks For a printed portfolio, include a table of contents listing the items in the order in which they are arranged, number the pages sequentially, and provide page references in your table of contents. An electronic portfolio should include a menu with hyperlinks to the contents.

▶▶▶Sample personal statement, 113–14

Personal Statement Whether submitted electronically or in print, a portfolio should include a personal statement that describes the contents of the portfolio and explains your choice and arrangement of selections and what the selections demonstrate about you as a writer. For portfolios submitted electronically, consider embedding links to your writing selections from your personal statement as well as from the menu.

⬆ Make It **Your Own**

Review three recent texts that you have written. What do they reveal about you as a writer? Compose a two-page reflective essay about these pieces.

connect
mhconnectcomposition.com
Additional resources: QL6005

Submission Submitting a printed portfolio is straightforward: You assemble the contents, make sure each page is clearly labeled with your name and a brief title, place the contents in a folder or three-ring binder with your identifying information on the front, double-check the contents against the table of contents, and hand it in.

Submitting an electronic portfolio offers more options: You might create an electronic folder that contains your documents and either save the documents to a CD-ROM or DVD and mail it or attach the folder to an email message. Alternatively, you might create a website, post the contents to a server, and send the URL to recipients. Consult your recipient in advance to determine the best method of electronic submission.

▶ **More about** ▶▶▶
Creating a website, 191–98

Dear Professor Howard:

Here is my writing portfolio, the culmination of the semester's work. The selections I have included are the literacy development essay and ethnography from Writing 205 (Sophomore Composition) and a paper on the Parthenon from Architecture 133 (History of Architecture). The purpose of including these papers is to show how I write on a range of assignments, from the personal to the purely academic. The literacy development essay was based on my own life experience. The ethnography describes my observations in the weight room but is more objective than the literacy development essay. The Parthenon essay is the most objective of the three, focusing on a topic about which I have no personal knowledge.

Each of these three pieces of work reflects different qualities or characteristics that reveal me as a writer. The literacy development essay describes my intellectual growth. This piece was written for a broad audience. To show my own growth, I used simple, direct language in the early parts of the essay and more sophisticated language later. My development is best reflected through the verb choices: From simple forms of "to be" and "learned," I moved on to "flogged," "balked," and "superseded."

My ethnography strives to capture the mood of the weight room, and I used descriptive language to convey the smell of body odor, the feel of extreme exertion, and the look of the sweaty, muscular bodies. I also tried to capture the different mind-sets of those using the weight room, from steroidal bodybuilders to svelte women striving for better abs.

The paper on the Parthenon shows my writing when it is limited to the language of architecture. It describes the Parthenon, what it meant to the people who built it, and the history of the building (what remains and how pieces of it were dispersed across the Western world). I notice that in this essay, my word choices were fairly simple, but I was still able to get my point across without using all the fancy words used by architecture critics.

I believe the introduction to each paper is strong. In general, when I cannot come up with a good start to a paper, I notice that I have problems developing the rest of the essay, so I work hard to develop an introduction that creates a sense of what my paper will discuss and how. The first two samples in particular, where I was not limited to following a certain style, have particularly engaging introductions that, I hope, have captured the reader's imagination.

I look forward to hearing your thoughts about the enclosed.

Rachana

Rachana Ky

Part Two

Reasoning
Matters
Reading, Thinking, and Arguing

7 Thinking and Reading Critically

connect
mhconnectcomposition.com
Additional resources: QL7001

When you think or read critically, you peel back layer after layer, going deeper and deeper to uncover meaning. You begin with comprehension, just getting the gist of a text. At the next stage, you reflect, considering how the parts work together and assessing the claims and evidence presented. As you think and read again and again, often in preparation for writing, you delve not only into what is written but also into what is left unstated, arguing with the text and drawing on your own experience and other texts to hone your appreciation and evaluation. That process of peeling a text, as you would an onion, is what drives engagement and deepens the pleasure you derive from the intellectual process.

7a Comprehending

In our day-to-day lives, we read constantly, and the texts range from instant messages to thousand-page books. Some texts, like street signs (Figure 7.1), are simple messages of just a few words or images; they are designed to communicate information quickly, simply, and clearly.

Reading
Responsibly **Engaging with What You Read**

As a reader and as a student, you have a responsibility to engage with the texts you read. If you are struggling, begin by determining what barrier is keeping you from making a connection with the text: Is the language too challenging? Is the topic unfamiliar or too familiar? Is your concentration poor because you forgot to eat lunch? Then try to overcome the barrier: Use a dictionary to acquaint yourself with the unfamiliar vocabulary; consider the material as a primer or a recapitulation of an important topic; eat a sandwich.

Most texts you read in college were also written to communicate information. But they have a different objective: to engage you in the complexities—not the simplicities—of an issue. They require careful thought. They may also have a second purpose: to persuade. You will get the most out of complex texts if you prepare to read, preview the text, read through it quickly to get the gist, write a brief summary, and, most importantly, enjoy what you read!

ESL **Reading for Comprehension** Many non-native speakers think the key to better reading is to read more slowly. In fact, research shows that reading *more quickly* can help increase your comprehension, because you associate ideas more easily.

FIGURE 7.1 Everyday texts Street signs convey information through words, shapes, and images. They are simple, so we can act on them immediately, almost without thinking.

1. Prepare.

Reading a complex text carefully and actively requires concentration. You will be able to concentrate best when you create the ideal conditions. But what are they? For some people, concentration is easiest first thing in the morning; for others, it is late at night, when everyone else is asleep. Some people focus best at a carrel in the library; for others, the white noise of a crowded dining hall helps. Of course, sometimes life intervenes, and you must grab time when and where you can— during lunch, on the bus, in the dentist's waiting room. But whenever you can, create the ideal conditions for yourself so that you can make the most of your time.

Also, set aside ample time. After each class, make note of assigned reading and estimate how long it might take you to complete it.

Consider not only the length of the assignment but also how difficult it is, how accessible it is, and how much you are likely to be engaged by it: A brief text full of specialized terminology may take you longer to read than a lengthy chapter from an engaging novel.

2. Preview.

connect
mhconnectcomposition.com
Additional resources: QL7003, QL7006

The more you know about a text before you begin reading, the more efficiently you will be able to read. Unless you are reading a work of literature—a novel, a poem, or a play—resist the urge to dive in and read the text from beginning to end. Instead, start by *previewing:*

- **Note the title and subtitle.** The title sets the stage for the work and may reveal its topic, approach, and even tone.

- **Read the abstract, introduction, conclusion, and sidebars.** Many scholarly journals place an *abstract,* or summary, at the beginning of each article; abstracts also appear in article database entries. Other texts may offer overviews of main ideas and important questions in introductions, prologues, conclusions, boxes, or sidebars. Textbook chapters often conclude with study questions that provide a framework for thinking about key topics.

- **Note the key terms.** In textbooks, important terms are often indicated in italic or boldfaced type and may also be listed at the end of the chapter or in a glossary. Terms are generally defined in the body or margins of a text; the text may also have a glossary.

- **Read the headings and subheadings.** If the text is organized into sections with headings, skim them for an outline.

- **Scan figures and illustrations.** Figures may signal important ideas. Visuals convey complex processes quickly and are often accompanied by a succinct explanation (Figure 7.2).

3. Get the gist.

More about ▶▶▶
Paraphrasing and patchwriting, 271–74

After surveying the text, you are ready to read it once through from beginning to end to get the *gist,* or basic idea. As you read, circle words or phrases you have questions about, but press on without looking them up—yet. When you have finished, close the book and write down what you remember. Try to *paraphrase,* to state the

Ancestor to whales. *Ambulocetus,* an ancestor to modern whales dated to 50 MYA. The presence of limbs is evidence that land-based mammals gave rise to whales.

FIGURE 7.2 Preview figures Previewing the figures can also provide insight. This figure, for example, emphasizes the descent of whales, pointing to an emphasis on evolution. (From Mader, *Biology,* 9th ed., New York, McGraw-Hill, 2007, p. 297)

ideas in your own words, rather than reproducing the language of the text. If you can accurately paraphrase the text's major points without *patchwriting,* you have grasped its literal meaning. If you cannot, read the text again, close the book, and try to paraphrase once more.

> **Patchwriting** Using the language or sentence structure of the source; not putting the content into fresh words (271)

4. Summarize.

When you feel you have a good (though not necessarily perfect) grasp of the text, *summarize* it. Whereas a paraphrase may be as long as (or longer than) the passage it restates, a summary only restates the main idea and major supporting points of a text. To qualify as a summary, what you write should be at least 50 percent shorter than the text it restates; many summaries are only 10 percent (or less) as long as the original. The summary on the next page captures the main idea and major supporting points of the Brent Staples editorial that Alea Wratten writes about later in this chapter. The original editorial, which starts on p. 125, is about 730 words; this summary is about 140, a bit less than a quarter of the original.

mhconnectcomposition.com
Additional resources: QL7002

▶▶▶Sample student essay:
"Reflecting on Brent Staples's Editorial 'How Hip-Hop Music Lost Its Way and Betrayed Its Fans,'" Alea Wratten, 137–39

Summary of "How Hip-Hop Music
Lost Its Way and Betrayed Its Fans"

In this editorial, *New York Times* writer Brent Staples claims that both rap music and the way it is marketed perpetuate racial stereotypes and glorify violence, materialism, and sexism. Citing the example of an actual gang war in the 1990s, Staples argues that rival rappers use their music to insult each other and initiate violence. 50 Cent, for instance, timed a post–radio-interview gun battle to coincide with the release of his album *Massacre*. Staples worries that rap will influence inner-city kids, who already face poverty and violence, to adopt the glamorous "gangsta" lifestyle and maybe even wind up in prison. He also blames producers like Jimmy Iovine and Dr. Dre for the direction hip-hop has taken. Staples ends by saying that he feels the public will not stand for much more of this; if hip-hop continues in this vein, he thinks, it won't last.

For any complex reading assignment, writing a summary will help you to remember the main points of the text, and the summary you create will also provide a useful reference. As with paraphrasing, avoid patchwriting: The more you can write about a reading in your own words, the better you will understand it.

5. Enjoy.

You are most likely to comprehend a text when you enjoy it, and you are far more likely to do so if you *think* about the text as you read. Engage with it as you would with a message from a friend or with a new movie you have been anticipating. Pleasure often lies in the details: a nice turn of phrase, a subtle joke, or a clever comparison. Enjoyment does not require total agreement with—or even a complete understanding of—every word on the page. It requires only active engagement and an open mind. You will find that this approach yields results, too: an improved academic performance and an increased ability to connect (or *synthesize*) what you learn with material from other classes and your own life.

> **More about ▶▶▶**
> Synthesis, 132–134,
> 279–80

Getting It
Across **Recording First Impressions of a Visual**

We will do whatever it takes.

A cyclone in Myanmar. A civil war in Darfur. A worldwide food crisis. In emergencies, UNICEF doesn't just get there fast. UNICEF is there already. UNICEF operates in 150 countries around the globe. And when disaster strikes, we are able to bring immediate lifesaving relief to children and their families.

No matter how treacherous the locale, or how great the catastrophe, UNICEF is there for children. UNICEF provides clean water, medicines, nutrition, and emergency supplies. We do whatever it takes to save children before, during, and after a crisis.

With more than 60 years of results, UNICEF has saved more children than any humanitarian organization in the world.

Join us. Visit unicefusa.org.

unicef
united states fund
Whatever it takes to save a child.

Understanding visuals starts with first impressions. Take a look at the advertisement at left.

What grabs your attention first? What do you notice next? What is your overall reaction? Write down your first impression as soon after looking at an image as possible. Ask yourself questions like these:

- What is the subject of the image?
- What colors does it use, or is the image black and white (as here)?
- What is in the foreground? background?
- Can you identify the location in which the image is set?
- If the image includes words, what impact do they have on you? What do they make you feel or want to do?
- What parts or aspects of the image grabbed your attention immediately? What took a few seconds to understand or focus on?
- How did you react to the image overall?

➤ EXERCISE 7.1 Comprehending the text

Look at the title of the article below, and then write a sentence indicating what you think the essay will be about, based on the title alone. Next, read the essay and summarize the text. Finally, write one or two sentences explaining what you found surprising, interesting, or challenging about this essay, and why.

connect
mhconnectcomposition.com
Online exercise: QL7101

Why Uncertainty May Be Bad for Your Health
By Wray Herbert

I recall sitting once before an open window, listening to the radio. Outside it was pouring rain. I mean horizontal monsoon, umbrellas buckling in people's hands. But on the radio, the DJ was calmly announcing "a chance of showers today." He's right, I remember thinking, an excellent chance.

The English language is not very helpful when it comes to talking about uncertainty. What does it really mean when a report forecasts "a possibility" of rain or snow today or a friend assures you that there's "not much chance" of dying in a plane crash? And when it comes to personal health, the vocabulary of likelihood is often even foggier because it's so laden with emotion. How do you respond if you're told that it's "possible" your breast cancer will recur, or that a serious side effect of treatment is "unlikely"?

According to a new study, there's a good chance you end up misinformed and make unwise health decisions as a result. That's not only because language is inexact, but also because quirks of our psychology make it very difficult to convey probabilities as simply that: probabilities. Instead, because of a deep-seated motivation to be polite and tactful, we clumsily try to make things seem better than they are and often end up making them worse.

Much of this miscommunication has to do with what social scientists call "face work.". . . When we are forced by circumstance to do things that threaten someone—disagreeing with a colleague, for example—we resort to strategies that we hope will dampen the threat and help them save face. One strategy is to fall back on words like "possibly."

Doctor-patient conversation is an example of such a face-threatening situation, because doctors often have to tell people unwanted news. They often resort to qualifiers when speaking with patients about the risks of developing certain medical conditions or about potential side effects to a drug or a procedure. Psychologist Jean-François Bonnefon of the University of Toulouse in France wanted to explore whether misuse of probability language might have untoward health consequences. Specifically, he wanted to know: when delivering bad news to a patient, do physicians help unfortunate patients save face by using words like "possibly" just to be polite? And if they do, are they more apt to use face-saving language if the health threat is more severe? How do patients interpret such polite euphemisms? Do they work, or backfire?

To explore this idea in the laboratory, Bonnefon had several hundred people imagine that they were patients and that their family doctor had given them some bad news: for some the news was that they would "possibly" develop insomnia within the year. Others were told that they would "possibly" go deaf inside a year. The psychologist then asked the participants if the doctor meant "possibly" to mean 10 percent, 20 percent and so on up to 100 percent. They were also asked whether they thought the doctor was actually making a medical risk assessment, or just being nice.

The results, as reported in the September issue of the journal *Psychological Science,* were unambiguous. When the "doctor" talked about the possibility of deafness, patients believed he was describing a much greater likelihood than when he discussed the possibility of insomnia. Bonnefon labels this phenomenon the "severity bias," meaning that "possibly" is taken as an actual prediction of modest risk when the subject is something like insomnia—a condition that is unpleasant, certainly, but not devastating. But with deafness, the same probability word is taken as diplomatic finessing of dire news. In other words, the "patients" didn't believe the doctor when the threat was serious. They knew intuitively that he was not being forthcoming, and they gave the news the worst possible spin. . . .

These findings have some serious implications for personal health choices and for health policy. Doctors are encouraged to be direct about potential side effects of treatments. They use qualifiers like "possibly" and "likely" all the time, as do package inserts that accompany prescription drugs. Such terms are nebulous enough. If a side effect or medical condition is "possible," should a patient take precautions—or seek potential treatment to lower their perceived risk? But the confusion only grows if patients don't know a phrase's true intended purpose—if they're unsure whether the doctor is being kind to save face or is serious about the risk assessment. That patient could easily end up reading the remark as tactfulness and so assume that the news is far worse than it is. Treatment choices made as a result of such misunderstandings would be at best uninformed, and at worst life-threatening.

Though it may go against all of our natural impulses, physicians need to forget about tact and social niceties when talking to patients about risk, Bonnefon concludes. This means avoiding vague words like "possibly" and stating explicitly the known risk (whether it's one in 100 or one in 10) whenever possible. It may not seem nice. But it's better than taking the risk of killing a patient with kindness.

—*Newsweek*, 19 Sept. 2006. Web. 15 Mar. 2007.

▲ Make It **Your Own**

Find a photograph in a printed or online newspaper, and write a one- or two-paragraph description of it. Be sure to indicate your first impression and what the photo depicts. Then photocopy the image, but place it behind your description so that readers will see the description *before* they see the image.

Work **Together**

In groups of two or three, trade descriptions from the Make It Your Own exercise above. Without looking at the photograph, try to form a mental picture of the image. Now look at the photograph. Discuss how well the description captured the image and what you would change. Did the description change what you noticed or the impact the image had on you?

7b Reflecting

Reflecting refers to the important transition between getting the gist and fully coming to terms with a text. Steps in reflecting on a text may include annotating it or writing about it in your reading journal.

> **Tech**
>
> **Annotating Online Texts**
>
> When you read from a screen instead of a page, consider saving the text to your hard drive, USB drive, or network drive and using Track Changes or footnoting options to comment on a text or the highlighting function to mark key ideas.

> **More about ▶▶▶**
> Tone, 16–17, 143,
>   567, 573–74
> Bias, 568–71
> Note taking, 159–71,
>   267–80
> Working bibliogra-
>   phy, 219–20

> connect
> mhconnectcomposition.com
> Additional resources: QL7007,
> QL7008

1. Annotate.

A first step in reflecting upon a text is to reread it with a pencil or pen in hand (or a computer at the ready). Careful annotations can be useful when it comes time to study for a test or to respond to a text in writing. As you annotate, focus on some or all of the following:

- **Definitions.** Look up and write down definitions of unfamiliar words.

- **Concepts.** Underline the most important, interesting, or difficult concepts.

- **Tone.** Note the writer's tone—sarcastic, sincere, witty, shrill.

- **Biases.** Look out for the writer's biases and unstated assumptions (and your own).

- **Responses.** Ask questions and note your own reactions and insights.

- **Connections.** Make connections with other texts you have read or your own experiences.

Read footnotes and any text in parentheses: They seldom contain the main claims or supporting evidence, but they can provide key background information, references to additional scholarship on a topic, and juicy tidbits the writer felt compelled to share.

Getting It
Across   Annotating an Image

Annotating an image can help you come to grips with it, just as annotating a text does. Although you may not find unfamiliar vocabulary and the concepts may not be spelled out clearly, you can still focus on the following:

- **Tone.** Does it strike you as warm, amused, angry, dispassionate? Point to specific parts of the image that convey the tone.
- **Responses.** What responses does the image elicit from you, and why? Again, tie your responses directly to the image.
- **Biases.** Do you detect any assumptions or biases? If so, what are they, and how does the visual indicate them?
- **Connections.** Does this image remind you of another visual or printed text? If so, in what ways? (Be specific.) Can you make any connections between the visual and your own experience?

The annotations to this editorial by Brent Staples, which appeared in the *New York Times,* reflect Alea Wratten's thoughts, insights, and struggles with a text she would later write about. The annotations define unfamiliar vocabulary, note reflections, and make connections.

I loved "Just Walk on By" (same author)

There are certainly negative images out there, but there are many positive African American role models, too (including Staples).

virulent—extremely infectious or damaging. Why is rap the most "virulent" music?

How Hip-Hop Music Lost Its Way and Betrayed Its Fans

By BRENT STAPLES

(12 May 2005)

African-American teenagers are beset on all sides by dangerous myths about race. The most poisonous one defines middle-class normalcy and achievement as "white," while embracing violence, illiteracy and drug dealing as "authentically" black. This fiction rears its head from time to time in films and literature. But it finds its most virulent

expression in rap music, which started out with a broad palette of themes but has increasingly evolved into a medium for worshiping misogyny, materialism and murder.

This dangerous narrowing of hip-hop music would be reason for concern in any case. But it is especially troubling against the backdrop of the 1990's, when rappers provoked a real-world gang war by using recordings and music videos to

Too strong? Rap sometimes glamorizes, but it can raise awareness, too.

Central argument—raises an important issue but overgeneralizes.

"palette" compares music to painting

misogyny—hatred of women

Have things changed since then?

Is this logic backwards? Sometimes gangsta rappers are violent, but does their music describe the violence or cause it?

The "rap community" isn't entirely gangsta rap; there are other kinds of rap/hip-hop out there.

Many people "learned" or were not involved in the violence: Kanye West, Chuck D., Public Enemy, etc.

True—recording labels are marketing an image.

Example: 50 Cent and the release/marketing of "The Massacre"

insult and threaten rivals. Two of the music's biggest stars—Tupac Shakur and the Notorious B.I.G.—were eventually shot to death.

People who pay only minimal attention to the rap world may have thought the killings would sober up the rap community. Not quite. The May cover of the hip-hop magazine *Vibe* was on the mark when it depicted fallen rappers standing among tombstones under the headline: "Hip-Hop Murders: Why Haven't We Learned Anything?"

The cover may have been prompted in part by a rivalry between two rappers that culminated in a shootout at a New York radio station, Hot 97, earlier this spring. The events that led up to the shooting show how recording labels now exploit violence to make and sell recordings.

At the center of that Hot 97 shootout was none other than 50 Cent, whose given name is Curtis Jackson III. Mr. Jackson is a confessed former drug dealer who seems to revel in the fact that he was shot several times while dealing in Queens. He has also made a career of "beef" recordings, in which he whips up controversy and heightens tension by insulting rival artists.

He was following this pattern in a radio interview in March when a rival showed up at the station. The story's murky, but it appears that the rival's entourage met Mr. Jackson's on the street, resulting in gunfire.

Mr. Jackson's on-air agitation was clearly timed to coincide with the release of "The Massacre," his grotesquely violent and misogynist compact disc. The CD cover depicts the artist standing before a wall adorned with weapons, pointing what appears to be a shotgun at the camera. The photographs in the liner notes depict every ghetto stereotype—the artist selling drugs, the artist in a gunfight—and includes a mock autopsy report that has been seen as a covert threat aimed at some of his critics.

The "Massacre" promotion raises the ante in a most destructive way. New artists, desperate for stardom, will say or do anything to win notice—and buzz—for their next projects. As the trend escalates, inner-city listeners who are already at risk of dying prematurely are being fed a toxic diet of rap cuts that glorify murder and make it seem perfectly normal to spend your life in prison.

Critics who have been angered by this trend have pointed at Jimmy Iovine, the music impresario whose Interscope Records reaped millions on gangster rap in the 90's. Mr. Iovine makes a convenient target as a white man who is lording over an essentially black art form. But also listed on "The Massacre" as an executive producer is the

No concrete proof that 50 Cent planned a gunfight to promote his album. Is the inference fair? I think so.

Is it the marketing or the art itself that is "misogynistic" and "supremely violent"? Note: Listen to this song.

In many neighborhoods, kids grow up seeing people going to prison all the time, so for them it is normal.

I wonder who these other critics are?

impresario—entertainment manager or promoter

legendary rapper Dr. Dre, a black man who happens to be one of the most powerful people in the business. Dr. Dre has a unique vantage point on rap-related violence. He was co-founder of <u>Death Row Records</u>, an infamous California company that marketed West Coast rap in the 1990's and had a front-row seat for the feud that led to so much bloodshed back then.

The music business hopes to make a <u>financial killing</u> on a recently announced summer concert tour that is set to feature 50 Cent and the mega-selling rap star Eminem. But promoters will need to make heavy use of metal detectors to suppress the kind of gun-related violence that gangster artists celebrate. <u>That this lethal genre of art has grown speaks volumes about the industry's greed and lack of self-control.</u>

But trends like this reach a <u>tipping point,</u> when business as usual <u>becomes unacceptable to the public as a whole.</u> Judging from the rising hue and cry, <u>hip-hop is just about there.</u>

> *Good example of author's point— even in the name of the record company.*

> *A pun?*

> *Can art be "lethal"?*

> *tipping point— the moment when something rare becomes much more common*

> *Hip-hop is still popular. Does he just mean against gangsta rap?*

2. Keep a journal.

Articulating your responses in a ***journal*** is a good way to build a deeper understanding and a sense of taking part in—not just taking in—what you read. A journal entry can do any of the following:

- Assess the writer's purpose: Is it to entertain, inform, persuade?

- Develop insights through freewriting

- Brainstorm reasons to support or oppose the writer's claims

- Organize your ideas through clustering or outlining

- Synthesize ideas from the text with ideas of your own or ideas from other sources

> **More about ▶▶▶**
> Purpose, 11–13
> Generating ideas, 22–29
> Outlining, 40–42
> Synthesizing, 132–34, 279–80

A double-entry reading journal provides a column for quotations, summaries, or paraphrases and a column for your responses. This technique can help you avoid plagiarism by keeping your own ideas separate from the ideas you have found in the text.

The entries from a reading journal on the next page reflect one writer's thoughts about the Wray Herbert article that appears in Exercise 7.1 (pp. 121–23).

> ❝ Whenever I come across unfamiliar vocabulary or specialized terms, I write them in my reading journal. My instructor always tells us to consider the context in which a word is used, so I usually write down the definition plus the sentence or phrase the word appeared in. This helps me learn the word, so I can use it correctly later. ❞
>
> —Derek Hom, Colgate University

Quotation/Summary/Paraphrase	Response
"I recall sitting once before an open window, listening to the radio. Outside it was pouring rain. I mean horizontal monsoon, umbrellas buckling in people's hands. But on the radio, the DJ was calmly announcing 'a chance of showers today.' He's right, I remember thinking, an excellent chance." (par 1)	This opening story made me laugh. It was a great way to introduce a key point: language can often confuse what we mean instead of making it clearer.
Doctors try to avoid hurting patients' feelings in what Herbert calls "face-threatening situations" (par 5), which means they often use "euphemisms" (par 5) when they have to deliver bad news.	"Saving face" applies to the classroom, too. When we peer edit papers, we don't want to hurt anyone's feelings; I definitely hold back and say "you might need a better example" because the word "might" makes it sound nicer.
What Dr. Bonnefon calls a "severity bias" made more (fake) patients overestimate the likelihood they'd go deaf (a worse outcome) than that they'd develop insomnia (a less bad result). (par 6–7)	I learned about confirmation bias (the tendency to look for supporting evidence) and the representativeness bias (the tendency to overestimate the likelihood of things that seem common) in my psychology class; this severity bias must be a tendency to overestimate the likelihood that something bad will happen.

connect

mhconnectcomposition.com
Online exercise: QL7102

→ **EXERCISE 7.2 Writing a journal entry**

Using the journal entry above as a model, make a journal entry on the Staples editorial (pp. 125–27) or an article, essay, or textbook chapter you have read recently. For any quoted passages, make sure to note where it comes from, in case you have to cite it later.

connect

mhconnectcomposition.com
Online exercise: QL7103

→ **EXERCISE 7.3 Writing about an image**

Find a striking photograph online or in a magazine, newspaper, or textbook. Using the sample at the top of p. 129 as a model, write a journal entry about the image, relating your thoughts, feelings, and reactions to the photograph as a whole or to specific parts of it.

The colors in this photo are vibrant; robe concealing the woman in the foreground is almost the same shade of blue as the blue blouse that Preety Zinta is wearing.

Is the subject the woman in the foreground, covered head to toe, or the glamour shots of models and actresses (especially Preety Zinta) in the background? Preety Zinta almost looks like the woman's reflection. Her set expression reveals very little, almost as little as the covered woman's.

It's interesting to wonder what the woman in the foreground is thinking. Does she want to uncover her head (like Preety Zinta) or is she shocked by Zinta's flowing hair and red lipstick?

The contrast here makes me think about what these photos say about the way women are perceived and treated by their society (and ours).

7c Preparing to Write

Often, critical readers are readying themselves for the next step: writing. Having something interesting to say about a reading selection will come from *analyzing* the text carefully; *interpreting* the text to find or create a new, deeper meaning; *synthesizing* what you have learned from the text with what you have learned elsewhere; and *critiquing*, or evaluating, the text.

1. Analyze.

To understand how a text works, you must **_analyze_** it: Take it apart, consider its components, and figure out what each part means and how the parts fit together. When thinking about a text, consider the following:

- The major claims a text makes and the evidence (such as examples, facts, and expert testimony) offered to support them
- The organizational or rhetorical patterns (such as comparison-contrast or cause-effect) it employs

connect

mhconnectcomposition.com
Additional resources: QL7004

▶ **More about** ▶▶▶
Analysis, 67
Evaluating claims,
153–56
Evidence, 46–48
Analyzing works of
literature, 448–71
(ch. 21)

More about ▶ ▶ ▶
Purpose, 11–13
Audience, 14–16
Tone, 16–18, 143,
   567, 573–74
Style, 515–98 (part 7,
   Style Matters)

- The author's purpose in writing this piece and how this is reflected in the style or tone it uses

- The intended audience and how that might have influenced decisions about content, style, and tone

In analyzing the Staples editorial (pp. 125–27), Alea Wratten identified its main claim and the reasons and evidence provided to support that claim:

Major claims:
1. Today's hip-hop music spreads a dangerous myth that an authentic black experience is violent.
2. This has serious consequences for listeners.

Evidence:
- Lyrics promote racism, sexism, violence
- Behavior of hip-hop artists promotes violence: Deaths of Tupac Shakur, Notorious B.I.G.
- 50 Cent's insulting rivals and shootout at Hot 97 to promote record
- Violent imagery on cover of The Massacre and in liner notes
- Dr Dre—co-founder of Death Row Records, executive producer of 50 Cent's record
- Need for metal detectors at concerts

An analysis of an advertisement, focusing on the claims it makes, the relation between image and text, and the reaction the advertisement is trying to elicit from the reader appears on the next page.

Quick Reference ➡ **Steps in Developing Critical Understanding**

- **Analyze:** Break down a text into its component parts to study its meanings and mechanisms.
- **Interpret:** Dig below the surface to draw conclusions based on the author's assumptions and motives, omissions, and the circumstances in which the text was written.

- **Synthesize:** Connect ideas in a text to relevant ideas in other texts or experiences; analyze the relationships among ideas or draw comparisons and contrasts.
- **Critique:** Evaluate based on evidence accumulated through careful reading, analysis, interpretation, and synthesis.

This advertisement for Adopt Us Kids, sponsored by the Ad Council, appeared in a variety of magazines. It makes two explicit claims: "You don't have to be perfect to be a perfect parent" and "There are thousands of teens in foster care who would love to put up with you." These two claims suggest a third: *Readers should consider adopting a child in foster care.* The ad relies on the assumption that people don't adopt because they worry they won't be good parents.

You don't have to be perfect to be a perfect parent.
There are thousands of teens in foster care who would love to put up with you.
1 888 200 4005 · adoptuskids.org

The image of a flawed but still inviting birthday cake illustrates the first claim. This cake may sag a bit, but it's been placed in an elegant serving dish and lit up with polkadotted candles. Atop the cake is the number "sixteen"—a milestone age that people associate with sweet sixteen parties and driver's licenses.

The specificity of this age implies a particular person, and an engaged reader can't help but wonder about all the kids in foster care who turn sixteen without this rite of passage, the luxury of a birthday cake, or the love of a parent who'd buy or make one. The image elicits our emotional response, but the written text articulates and clarifies its message: What matters in parenthood is effort and love, not perfection. Omission is also used powerfully here; what is *missing* from the photograph—a child—might be missing from a reader's life, too.

2. Interpret.

After analyzing the text to determine how it works, consider the significance or meaning of the elements you have identified, and draw inferences about what may be below the surface of the text. Use the following questions to help guide your **interpretation** of a text:

- What assumptions does the writer make about the subject or audience? Why are such assumptions significant?

- What does the text omit (evidence, opposing views), and what might these omissions indicate?

> *More about* ▶▶▶
> Identifying assumptions, 162–63
> Identifying stakeholders, 253
> Interpreting, 279–80, 288–90

- What conclusions can you draw about the author's attitude from the tone? What motives can you infer from the author's background?

- Who published this text or sponsored the research, and what influence might these sponsors have upon the way the information, arguments, or evidence is presented?

- In what context was the text written—place, time, cultural environment—and how might this context have influenced the writer?

In prewriting for her critical response essay, Alea Wratten considered Staples's assumptions, omissions, and possible motivations:

Staples treats hip-hop and rap as synonyms. He refers to the "dangerous narrowing" of this kind of music, but there is no discussion of what this narrowed from. He gives examples of rappers whose albums glorify violence, but not of hip-hop artists with other themes. Also, while Staples states twice that rap is misogynistic, he doesn't provide any lyrics or examples to prove it. Is he relying on his readers to know enough about rap to know this is true? I don't think so—people who read the *New York Times* editorial page are probably mostly white, middle-aged, and well off, not the kind of folks who are usually into hip-hop. And he mustn't think his readers really know about hip-hop because he has to tell them what *Vibe* is ("the hip-hop magazine"). So are these gaps typical of editorials? They do have to be short, so not a lot of room for examples. And since they're directed toward a general audience, they're more likely to use this kind of dramatic language. Or is this an indication of a blind spot about hip-hop? This is something I think a lot of people from the Beatles or Motown generation—like my mom!—share.

connect

mhconnectcomposition.com
Additional resources: QL7009

3. Synthesize.

College assignments often ask you to **synthesize**—to connect what you have read to ideas in other texts or to the world around you. You may begin to synthesize early on, as you read and annotate the text. You will probably develop these connections in your reading journal and as you draft and revise your essay.

To synthesize, ask yourself the following questions:

- What else have you read or experienced that this text may explain, illustrate, clarify, complicate, or contradict?

- How do the author's other writings amplify, clarify, complicate, or contradict the selection you are writing about?

- What outside forces (historical events, socioeconomic forces, cultural shifts) might influence or underlie the text?

- What claims or points in each text do you find especially compelling? How do compelling points in one text connect to ideas in the other(s)?

- What claims could these texts, taken together, provide evidence for?

- How is your understanding of a topic enhanced or your thinking changed by putting these texts together? What might others gain by seeing these texts together?

> **More about ▶▶▶**
Synthesizing, 279–80
Comparing and contrasting, 66–67

An excerpt from prewriting for Alea Wratten's essay draws connections between Brent Staples's editorial "How Hip-Hop Music Lost Its Way and Betrayed Its Fans" and the hip-hop music she listens to.

Writing
↑ **Responsibly**   **Drawing Inferences**

An inference is only as good as what it is based on. Inferences based on facts are fair; those based on personal values and beliefs or on a faulty understanding of the text are apt to be one-sided and unfair. Aim for the former and avoid the latter.

Staples uses examples of gangsta rappers like 50 Cent and Eminem to support his claim that hip-hop promotes negative stereotypes and violence. Sure, 50 Cent's music may try to make violence look cool, but not all hip-hop is ultra-violent. Kanye West is a big star, and he has gone platinum with positive, even spiritual messages. Lauren Hill, Kam, KRS One, Arrested Development, Chuck D, and Public Enemy are just a few of the artists on my iPod who set positive examples for listeners.

Wratten's inferences are fair: They are based on facts (other hip-hop stars who are successful without violence) and on her analysis of Staples's omissions.

connect
mhconnectcomposition.com
Additional resources: QL7005

4. Critique.

A *critique* is a well-informed evaluation. It may be positive, negative, or a bit of both. A movie review, for example, is a critique; it provides readers with an evaluation to help them decide whether or not to see the film. A reviewer's opinion alone is usually not enough to sway a would-be audience member. The reviewer must also provide evidence for the judgment by describing the performances, the screenplay, or the director's vision. Similarly, critiques written for college courses offer judgments based on careful analysis of the text's component parts. They may also be informed by other texts, your own knowledge and experience, or both.

Writing
Responsibly   **Understanding *Criticism***

In everyday speech, *criticism* is often used simply to mean "finding fault." But in academic disciplines, *criticizing* means "evaluating a work's merits based on a careful and fair analysis." The ideal critic approaches a text skeptically yet with an open mind and provides evidence for the judgments she makes.

▶▶▶ Sample professional review, 469–71

More about ▶▶▶
Claims, 153–56
Evidence, 46–48
Authority, 159–60, 251
Relevance, 249–50
Reliability, 250–54
Audience, 14–15

As you prepare to write a critique, consider the following issues:

- **The writer's aims.** What are the author's goals? Does she or he achieve them? Are they worth achieving?

- **The writer's claims.** What are the writer's claims? Are you persuaded by them? Why or why not?

- **The writer's evidence.** How credible is the evidence? Is the evidence verifiable and relevant? Is the author's reasoning sound?

- **The writer's authority.** What expertise or life experience does the writer bring to the topic, and is it relevant?

Also consider your own goals and position:

- **Your aims, claims, and evidence.** Why are you writing the critique? What claims are you making? What evidence will you use to support those claims?

- **Your authority.** What authority do you have, and why might readers value your judgment and evaluation? You may not be an expert, but your opinion can be valid and interesting if it is based on thoughtful analysis.

Getting It Across

Preparing to Write about a Visual

When exploring a visual, especially if you will be writing about it, ask yourself the following questions:

Analysis

- **Parts and patterns.** What are the relationships among the parts? Does the image include or imply a comparison or contrast, a cause or effect?
- **Purpose.** Is the visual's purpose to inform, persuade, entertain, or express emotion? If the visual is persuasive, what does it claim and how does it support this claim?
- **Attitude.** What is the artist's attitude toward the subject or audience? On what basis can you make this inference?
- **Context.** Where is the image set? When was it created? Who produced or sponsored it, and why? How do accompanying words inform your reading?

Interpretation

- **Assumptions.** What values does the image assume or promote? How do those values match, contrast with, or challenge those of its audience?
- **Omissions.** Is something missing? Has the visual been cropped to eliminate background? If so, how does this affect your understanding?
- **Audience.** Who is the intended audience? Where was the visual originally published, or where did you find it? How was the image received by its original audience?

Synthesis

- **Other sources.** How is this image similar to or different from others that you know? Have you read or studied anything that could help you understand this visual?
- **Background.** What knowledge or personal experiences do you have that might deepen your understanding?

Critique

- **Aims.** Based on your analysis, what were the artist's aims, and were they achieved?
- **Claims.** What claims is the artist making, and are you persuaded?
- **Authority.** What expertise or experience does the artist bring?

- **Your audience.** What are your readers' interests and knowledge about the subject? What background information will you need to provide? Will they be sympathetic to your claims, or will you have to work hard to persuade them?

EXERCISE 7.4 Analyzing an article

Analyze the Al Gore essay on pp. 76–78. In two or three paragraphs, describe the author's assumptions and attitude. Also consider how circumstances (Hurricane Katrina, the 2000 presidential election) might have affected its reception.

connect
mhconnectcomposition.com
Online exercise: QL7104

→ **EXERCISE 7.5 Writing a synthesis**

Using the questions on p. 133 as a guide, write a 350- to 500-word synthesis of "Why Uncertainty May Be Bad for Your Health" (Exercise 7.1, pp. 121–23) with the information below and any other texts or experiences that are relevant.

How we state propositions can influence how we try to solve a problem, reason through a decision, or make a judgment (Anderson, 1991). For example, in one study college students who were told that a cancer treatment had a 50 percent success rate judged the treatment to be significantly more effective and expressed a greater willingness to have it administered to a family member than did participants who were told it had a 50 percent failure rate (Kahneman & Tversky, 1979). Representing outcomes in terms of positives or negatives has this effect because people tend to assign greater costs to negative outcomes (such as losing $100) than they assign value to an equivalent positive outcome (finding $100). The proposition that "there is a 50 percent chance of failure" evokes thoughts about the patient's dying and causes the "50-50" treatment to appear more risky (Slovic et al., 1988). Thus differences in how we verbally represent choices and goals can make a difference in our perceptions and decisions.

—Michael W. Passer and Ronald E. Smith,
Psychology: The Science of Mind and Behavior, 2nd ed.

⬆ Make It **Your Own**

Using the questions on p. 133 as a guide, write a brief essay (350–500 words) synthesizing information from texts in two or more of your classes.

Work **Together** ⬅

In groups of three or more, compare the syntheses you wrote in Exercise 7.5. In what ways are your classmates' syntheses similar to and different from your own? Discuss.

Student Project: Critique

In the essay that follows, Alea Wratten (SUNY–Geneseo) analyzes Brent Staples's essay "How Hip-Hop Music Lost Its Way and Betrayed Its Fans" and draws on her knowledge of hip-hop to create this critical response.

Reflecting on Brent Staples's Editorial "How Hip-Hop
Music Lost Its Way and Betrayed Its Fans"

Hip-hop is among today's most popular forms of American music. You can
hear it walking through the mall, during TV commercials, and on nearly anyone's
iPod (including mine). Despite, or perhaps because of, this popularity, Brent Staples,
in his *New York Times* editorial, "How Hip-Hop Music Lost Its Way and Betrayed
Its Fans," calls hip-hop a "lethal genre of art" (26), claiming the music brainwashes
and endangers black kids, who will identify blackness with the criminal underworld
depicted in these songs. He claims that hip-hop "has evolved into a medium for
worshiping misogyny, materialism, and murder" (26) and that it is only getting worse.

> Introduction:
> Brief summary
> of editorial
> to which it is
> responding

Staples raises some excellent concerns about the dangers of marketing violence to
young people, but ultimately his argument fails to be persuasive for several reasons:
He does not account for the influence positive role models have, he ignores the fact
that art frequently depicts violence without dire consequences to its consumers, and
he overlooks the broad spectrum of hip-hop to focus on only a single strand.

> Thesis: Acknowl-
> edges strengths
> of Staples's
> editorial but
> also lists three
> problems

First, it is distressing that Staples, who himself presents a positive role
model for black teens, would assume that black teens would be likely to identify
with violent, misogynistic lyrics, associating success and respect for the law with
whiteness and poverty, crime, and sexism with blackness. Staples, who grew up
poor and black, was likely smarter than this, and so are today's black teens. They
see successful black men and women all around them—our president, the nation's
wealthiest and most popular talk show host, an influential editorial writer for the
New York Times, not to mention scores of business men and women, actors,

> Topic sentence:
> Analyzes as-
> sumption that
> black teens
> use rap stars as
> models

> Counterevidence

comedians, and sports figures—all of whom are role models that black teens might identify with and aspire to become. With this range of possible models before them, it is unlikely that many black teens would be deluded about the world because they had listened to offensive hip-hop lyrics.

Second, by calling hip-hop a "lethal genre," Staples places it into a category separate from other works of art that are not as "virulent." Yes, many hip-hop lyrics are violent, but that does not distinguish them from many other artistic works.

Edgar Allan Poe, considered one of America's greatest writers, wrote numerous stories about murder and death, including "The Tell-Tale Heart," whose narrator is a confessed killer. *The Talented Mr. Ripley,* a novel by Patricia Highsmith, and

the movie based on this novel, make Tom Ripley, an unrepentant murderer, a sympathetic character. Sculptor Kiki Smith depicts mutilated bodies in her art (see fig. 1), and, instead of being criticized, she is considered one of today's most important sculptors. No one would claim, I think, that Kiki Smith influences her viewers to commit mayhem. Clearly, hip-hop artists are not alone in depicting horrible people and events; they should not be singled out for doing so, and it should not be assumed that their audience will blindly follow suit.

Fig. 1. Kiki Smith, *Untitled,* 1993. Paper and papier-mâché. Pace Wildenstein Gallery, New York.

Finally, tarring all of hip-hop with one brush is a mistake. While gangsta rap continues to be very popular, hip-hop includes many bands and artists who write uplifting and socially aware lyrics. Kanye West, for instance, currently among hip-hop's biggest stars, offers a positive, spiritual message in his music, a message of which Staples would likely approve. In his song "Family Business," West explains, "I woke up early this mornin' with a new state of mind / A creative way to rhyme without usin' nines and guns / keep your nose out the sky, keep your heart to God / and keep your face to the risin' sun" (West). And West is not alone: Lauren Hill, Kam, KRS One, Arrested Development, Chuck D, and Public Enemy are just a few of the musicians and bands on my iPod that explore hip-hop's more socially responsible side. These artists show that the strand of hip-hop that Staples accuses of providing a "toxic diet" (25) for listeners is just one of many.

Some of the most popular hip-hop songs do revolve around violent or sexist themes. It is important to remember, though, that these themes draw attention to conditions in the communities out of which hip-hop developed. They bring important social problems of poor communities to the attention of a wide audience—black and white. So hip-hop may offer more than just a catchy beat; it is also a way for artists to express themselves and a form of art that tells their stories.

Topic sentence: Challenges assumption that all hip-hop is *gangsta*

Counterexamples

Conclusion: Acknowledges violent and misogynistic lyrics in hip-hop but offers different interpretation

Works Cited

Staples, Brent. "How Hip-Hop Music Lost Its Way and Betrayed Its Fans." Editorial. *New York Times* 12 May 2005: A25. Print.

West, Kanye. "Family Business." *The College Dropout.* Roc-a-Fella, 2004. CD.

→ **EXERCISE 7.6** **Writing a critique**

Find an editorial in a printed or online newspaper. First, read the editorial using the techniques discussed in this chapter and write a summary noting the editorial's main idea and major supporting points. Then, write a paragraph-long critical response to it using analysis, interpretation, synthesis, and critique.

→ **EXERCISE 7.7** **Interpreting a graphic**

The bar graph below appeared on the front page of the newspaper *USA Today* with no accompanying story. Based on the graphic alone, write a one- to two-paragraph story to accompany it. What is the main claim of the graphic? What evidence does it use to support its main claim?

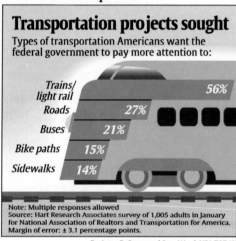

USA TODAY Snapshots®

Transportation projects sought

Types of transportation Americans want the federal government to pay more attention to:

Trains/light rail 56%
Roads 27%
Buses 21%
Bike paths 15%
Sidewalks 14%

Note: Multiple responses allowed
Source: Hart Research Associates survey of 1,005 adults in January for National Association of Realtors and Transportation for America. Margin of error: ± 3.1 percentage points.

By Anne R. Carey and Sam Ward, USA TODAY

8

Analyzing and Crafting Arguments

The advertisement on the back of this bus stop bench uses text and a visual to argue that drinking and driving is wrong because of the harm drunk drivers may cause to others. Visually, the ad is powerful because the symbol, a broken heart, is created using a red and a black profile, which suggests the absence of a loved one. The white type on a stark black background adds drama and highlights the message. The placement of the advertisement is also persuasive: That it is on the back of a bus bench suggests an alternative to driving under the influence—people who have been drinking can take the bus instead of getting behind the wheel.

The advertisement on the back of this bus bench is advocating for a social good, but many ads merely advocate that we eat fast food, drive an SUV, or buy a new cell phone. As consumers and as citizens, we have a responsibility to "read" critically the arguments that surround us and not just to respond blindly.

As writers, when we seek to persuade others, we must also take responsibility. We must take on positions that we can defend with good reasons and evidence; explore all perspectives on an issue with an open mind; and craft arguments that are carefully reasoned, treat conflicting perspectives fairly, and avoid manipulation.

More about ▶▶▶
Crafting a thesis, 33–37, 154, 283–84
Claims of judgment, 155–56
Tone, 16–17, 143, 567, 573–74
Diction, 16–17, 573–75

8a   Persuading and Exploring

Arguments may be **persuasive** (thesis-driven, claim-based) or **exploratory** (thesis-seeking, inquiry-based). In a persuasive (or claim-based) argument, the writer's purpose is to convince readers to agree with or at least to respect a position on a debatable issue. A persuasive argument articulates and advocates for a *claim of judgment*. It will be most effective when it provides compelling reasons and evidence in support of the claim and when the writer's tone is reasonable. The advertisement in Figure 8.1 makes a persuasive argument.

In an exploratory (or thesis-seeking) argument, the writer's purpose is to consider a wide range of evidence and eventually to arrive at the most plausible position. An exploratory argument begins by examining the evidence, which it then uses to arrive at a conclusion—its thesis. Exploratory arguments are useful for assessing complex issues and developing well-informed opinions about them, even if such opinions are provisional, subject to change when new information or a better interpretation becomes available. They can also be a useful way to convince those who disagree to reconsider the evidence.

In this excerpt from his journal, student William Archer explores two possible ways to understand the Vietnam War in the context of a class discussion of tragedy; he begins with a question, considers the evidence, and weighs his findings to arrive at a tentative position:

FIGURE 8.1 Arguing to persuade This advertisement argues that talking prevents alcohol abuse; it first asserts this claim, then backs it up with evidence.

My name is Peter,
and in eight years I'll be an alcoholic.

I'll start drinking in middle school, just at parties. But my parents won't start talking to me about it until high school. And by then, I'll already be in some trouble. The thing is, my parents won't even see it coming.

START TALKING BEFORE THEY START DRINKING
Kids who drink before age 15 are 5 times more likely to have alcohol problems when they're adults.
To learn more, go to www.stopalcoholabuse.gov or call 1 800 729 6686

Ad Council

Should the Vietnam War be viewed more as a Greek or Christian tragedy? Viewing the war as a Christian tragedy would suggest that

Writing
↑ Responsibly   The Well-Tempered Tone

In public discourse, especially in public blogs, the "zinger," or clever put-down, is often used to trump an opponent. Sarcasm also thrives: Many bloggers take a sarcastic tone toward whatever they disapprove of. But if you want your argument (and yourself) to be taken seriously (especially in academic and business circles) and if you want to persuade people who do not already agree with you, establishing a fair, even-tempered tone and avoiding sarcasm are crucial. Use logic and sound evidence, not snide comments, to make your point.

if certain things had been done differently, a more positive outcome might have resulted; officials made mistakes (moral and strategic) that led to their downfall (and the deaths of soldiers), and those mistakes could have been avoided. Viewing the war as a Greek tragedy would imply that nothing those involved did could have made any difference; officials had character flaws and destinies that ultimately led to their downfall.

There is valid evidence to support either claim. Someone could take the Christian tragedy outlook and argue that had the United States chosen to maintain democratic principles instead of overthrowing President Diem, then we might have avoided the war altogether. Others could take the Greek tragedy outlook and claim that under our government's built-in fear of the spread of communism, war in Southeast Asia was inevitable.

For now, I view the war more as a Greek tragedy; given the historical context following World War II, a proxy war between key powers was bound to happen somewhere in the region. I wonder what would have happened if the United States had chosen a different Southeast Asian nation to "draw the line" with?

—William Archer, Colgate University

Academic writing like Archer's is frequently exploratory in its early stages and becomes persuasive as the essay develops. Working this way often yields a more thoughtful, considered position than does beginning from a predetermined position.

ESL **Exploratory versus Persuasive Approaches to Argument** If members of your home culture are more likely to seek consensus than to assert their own opinion, you may be more comfortable writing an exploratory argument. Check with your instructor to be sure this approach is acceptable.

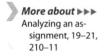

mhconnectcomposition.com
Online exercise: QL8101

> **More about ▶▶▶**
> Analyzing an as-
> signment, 19–21,
> 210–11

→ **EXERCISE 8.1 Choosing an approach to argument**

Consider the assignments below and decide whether each calls for a persuasive or exploratory argument; be prepared to defend your position.

1. Drawing on ideas and issues raised in lecture, discussion, and readings throughout the term, find, read, and critically analyze one or two newspaper articles on a controversial topic, focusing on the different points of view and assumptions underlying the press coverage. . . . (Anthropology 300, Portland State University)

2. Present a health promotion or nursing intervention that can be applied to a specific risk behavior or health problem. Include material from professional journals and clinical experiences about the risk behavior or health problem and information about the group of people at risk. Then identify and analyze a nursing intervention that can lead to risk reduction or that promotes improved health. (Nursing 224, University of Rhode Island)

3. Darwin, Marx, Nietzsche: Which one of the three was the most important "challenge" to the orthodoxy of his day? Why? Do you feel that the impact of the three was largely the same or significantly different? Why? (CORE 152, Colgate University)

Work **Together** ◀━━━━━━━

In small groups, discuss your analysis of the assignments in Exercise 8.1. Come to a consensus about each assignment and present your conclusions to the class. Finally, consider the process by which your group reached consensus: Was the debate more persuasive or exploratory, and why?

8b Reasoning Logically

Exploratory arguments, since they are thesis seeking, are likely to use **_inductive logic:_** They cite particular examples or specific instances and then draw a conclusion. Persuasive arguments, on the other hand, are thesis-driven, so they are likely to use **_deductive logic,_** offering premises from which conclusions can be drawn about specific instances. Both are susceptible to logical **_fallacies._**

1. Induction

Imagine that, over a period of months or years, you discover that you get better test grades after sleeping for a full eight hours before an exam. From this evidence, you might reasonably conclude that you perform better on tests when you get eight hours of sleep. This is inductive logic: You create a reasonable hypothesis based on a number of specific instances. But it is not a certainty—the weaker the evidence, the less likely the conclusion is to hold true.

A question central to inductive reasoning is "How much evidence is enough?" There is no definite answer, but the person who offers an inductive argument must supply enough to convince a reasonable audience that the conclusion is more likely than its denial. *Counterevidence* (evidence that undermines your claim), on the other hand, can weaken a conclusion reached inductively. When analyzing an argument based on inductive logic (or drawing your own inductive conclusions), consider not only the supporting evidence but also the counterevidence: Have I done well on a test I have taken with less than eight hours' sleep? Then explain why you find the evidence more persuasive than the counterevidence.

Writing Responsibly — Considering Counterevidence

When arguing inductively, considering the counterevidence will not only help you test your own assumptions, but it will also enhance your credibility by showing your audience that you have considered all the possibilities.

> **EXERCISE 8.2 Assessing the strength of a conclusion**
>
> Reread the student essay by Alea Wratten that appears at the end of chapter 7 (pp. 137–39). Does the writer include enough evidence to persuade you of her claim? Does she consider evidence that undermines her claim? How reasonable is her tone? Write a paragraph discussing these issues. Draw specific evidence from the essay to support your claims.

connect
mhconnectcomposition.com
Online exercise: QL8102

2. Deduction

Deduction is a form of reasoning that moves from a general principle (major premise) to a specific case (minor premise) to draw a conclusion (Figure 8.2A, p. 146). One form of deductive reasoning is the *syllogism:*

1. **Major premise.** All people are mortal.
2. **Minor premise.** Socrates is a person.
3. **Conclusion.** Socrates is mortal.

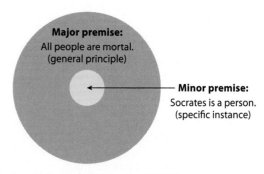

(A) *Conclusion:* **Socrates is mortal.** *VALID*

FIGURE 8.2 Visual analysis of a syllogism In (A), since all people are mortal and Socrates is a specific example of a person, then it follows logically that Socrates is mortal. But in (B), the two groups of gray things, rhinoceroses and battleships, are separate units; since the groups do not overlap, then the conclusion does not follow logically from the premises.

(B) *Conclusion:* **Some rhinoceroses are battleships.** *INVALID*

In a syllogism, if the premises are true, and if the conclusion follows logically from the premises, then the conclusion is inescapable—deduction leads to certainty. But these are big *if*s! Sometimes the conclusion does not follow because the minor premise is not, in fact, a specific case of the general principle stated in the major premise; sometimes the conclusion does not follow because one of the premises is false.

Consider the following syllogism:

1. **Major premise.** Some teenagers are motorists.
2. **Minor premise.** Some motorists are incompetent.
3. **Conclusion.** Some teenage motorists are incompetent.

Both premises are true, so the conclusion is inescapable, right? Wrong! Both premises are true: It is a fact that some teenagers drive, and we have all seen some very incompetent motorists behind the wheel.

The conclusion, too, is true: Teenage drivers *are* more likely to get into accidents than older, more experienced drivers—that is why insurance carriers charge drivers under 25 much higher premiums. But the conclusion here does not follow from the premises because the minor premise is not a specific instance of the major premise. Thus, the argument is ***invalid.*** This is easier to see if the conclusion is preposterous:

1. **Major premise.** Some rhinoceroses are gray.
2. **Minor premise.** Some gray things are battleships.
3. **Conclusion.** Some rhinoceroses are battleships.

The conclusion does not follow because the major premise does not state a principle that applies to the minor premise (Figure 8.2B).

Now consider the following:

1. **Major premise.** Test-takers do their best work if they have had a good night's sleep.
2. **Minor premise.** Ahmad will be taking a biology exam tomorrow.
3. **Conclusion.** Ahmad will do his best work on the biology exam if he gets a good night's sleep.

This syllogism is valid (the minor premise is a specific instance of the major premise, so the conclusion follows logically). The conclusion is inescapable—or is it? For the conclusion of a syllogism to be true, the syllogism must be valid *and* the premises on which it is based must be true. Since the minor premise is a specific instance, it is usually easy to determine whether that premise is true. Not so for the major premise—the general principle on which the conclusion rests. In the example above, a majority of instructors might accept the major premise *Test-takers do their best work if they have had a good night's sleep,* but students might argue that studying all night is more effective. In any case, the major premise would need to be established through careful research. In other words, it would need to be established *inductively;* it cannot be assumed.

In a syllogism, both premises are clearly stated. But in real-life deductive arguments, one or both of the premises, and sometimes even the conclusion, are often unstated. Consider the following example:

Bart to Milhouse: How can someone with glasses so thick be so stupid?

The argument here could be translated as follows:

1. **Major premise.** People who wear thick glasses are supposed to be smart.

2. Minor premise. Milhouse wears thick glasses.

3. Conclusion. Milhouse is supposed to be smart.

In this case, the premises are obvious, so they are left out. (They are rooted in a widely shared, childish prejudice, which is also obvious—and part of the joke.) Leaving the premises unstated can draw the audience in by asking them to supply what is missing. (They are not only witnesses to, but also participants in, the joke.) But often premises are left unstated because they are controversial. Teasing out the unstated premises allows you to evaluate them before accepting the conclusions on which they are based.

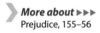

More about ▶▶▶
Prejudice, 155–56

connect

mhconnectcomposition.com
Online exercise: QL8103

↱ EXERCISE **8.3** Assessing the conclusion

Examine each of the following syllogisms. Then decide whether the conclusion follows logically from the premises and whether the premises are true. Be prepared to explain your answer.

1. Everyone who joins the gym gets one free session with a personal trainer.
   Ellen joined the gym.
   Ellen got one free session with a personal trainer.
2. All towns in Lincoln County have a 35-mph speed limit.
   Bentwood is a town in Lincoln County.
   It is not legal to drive 40 mph in Bentwood.
3. People who care about their community read local newspapers.
   Nayda reads her local newspaper.
   Nayda cares about her community.
4. Baseball, unlike football, is an untimed game.
   Richard likes baseball much more than he likes football.
   Richard does not like time limits in sports.

connect

mhconnectcomposition.com
Online exercise: QL8104

↱ EXERCISE **8.4** Identifying the missing premise

Each of the following passages leaves at least one premise unstated. Identify it.

1. "Robbery had not been the object of the murder, for nothing was taken."—Sir Arthur Conan Doyle, *Study in Scarlet.*
2. "The glove didn't fit. If it doesn't fit, you must acquit."—Attorney Johnnie Cochran, closing statement during the trial of O. J. Simpson for the murder of Nicole Brown Simpson and Ron Goldman, 1995.

3. "Now, I don't know or have never met my candidate; and for that reason I am more apt to say something good of him than anyone else."—Will Rogers

8c Avoiding Logical Fallacies

When assessing an argument that seems persuasive, keep an eye out for logical *fallacies.* Because inductive arguments depend on examples and the conclusions you draw from them, fallacies like the following can creep in:

- **Hasty generalization (jumping to conclusions).** Look at her, running that stop sign! She's a terrible driver!

  A hasty generalization occurs when a general conclusion is based on insufficient evidence: Since even the best drivers occasionally make mistakes, this one piece of evidence is not enough to incriminate this driver.

- **Sweeping generalization.** Women are terrible drivers! My girlfriend ran a stop sign the other day and almost got us both killed!

  Sweeping generalizations apply a claim to *all* cases when it actually applies to only a few or maybe to none. Stereotypes

> ❝ Even if someone cites loads of statistics, they might nevertheless be misleading. And even people who have tons of degrees may still allow beliefs to undermine the quality of their work. ❞
>
> —Leah Rabinowitz, Wellesley College

Writing Responsibly

Visual Claims and Visual Fallacies

In academic writing, you might use a visual to *support* a claim, but you should be cautious about using a visual to *make* a claim. Visual claims are effective sales tools (they are common in advertisements), but they are likely to commit a visual fallacy, such as *overgeneralization*—drawing a conclusion based on too little evidence. (Is it reasonable to assume that *all* men wearing a certain brand of cologne will drive women wild simply because actor Clive Owen is likely to?) This ad may also commit the fallacy of false authority. (Is the actor Clive Owen an authority on whose expertise we can rely when buying cologne?)

are often based on a sweeping generalization. (Whenever words like *all, every,* and *none* are used in an argument, take a closer look; these often signal that a sweeping generalization is coming.)

- **False analogy.** Our candidate's victories over his enemies during the war will ensure his victory over his political opponents in the election.

A false analogy draws a connection between two items or events that have few or no relevant common characteristics. This false analogy does not explain how the two things resemble each other: Why would a military victory guarantee a political victory? Is the political process really like a military campaign? Are opposition candidates really like enemy soldiers?

- **Stacking the deck (special pleading).** Got dandruff? Our shampoo contains MarvEll, guaranteed to end your dandruff problems!

An argument that stacks the deck focuses only on supporting evidence and ignores counterevidence that casts reasonable doubt upon it. In this case, the dandruff-killing properties of the shampoo may also make your hair brittle, but the ad would not mention that fact.

- **False authority.** My mother says that ice cream is more nourishing than a bowl of oatmeal.

Unless your mother is a nutritionist, her word alone is insufficient. An argument that appeals to a false authority draws evidence from someone who is *not* an expert on the topic.

- **Bandwagon appeal.** Teenager to parents: "You *have* to buy me an SUV; all my friends have one!"

The bandwagon appeal implies that the majority opinion is the right opinion and invites you to climb aboard. Some bandwagon appeals may be based on poll results, lending them the impression of reliability. But poll results merely report what the majority of respondents *believe* to be true. Many Americans in 1860 might have believed that holding other people in slavery was perfectly acceptable, which goes to show that the majority can be wrong.

The power of deductive arguments depends on the validity of the conclusion or the appeal of the premises, so watch out for arguments based on dubious logic or hidden or missing premises:

- **Begging the question (circular reasoning).** You must believe me because I never lie.

  An argument that begs the question uses the conclusion (in a disguised form) as one of the premises in the argument. In this example, the second half of the sentence repeats the conclusion rather than offering a premise from which it can be derived.

- **Non sequitur (irrelevant argument).** You can solve a lot of problems with money, so the rich must be much happier than we are.

  A non sequitur (which means "it does not follow" in Latin) draws a conclusion from a premise that does not follow logically. The conclusion in the statement above equates money with happiness, but anyone with money will tell you that the two do not go hand in hand.

- **Post hoc, ergo propter hoc (false cause).** This ring must be lucky: I wore it for the first time today, and I pitched a perfect game.

  Post hoc, ergo propter hoc means "after this, therefore, because of this" in Latin. In a *post hoc* fallacy, the speaker wrongly assumes that the first event caused the second: Just because the player wore a ring while pitching a perfect game does not mean that the ring is "lucky"; maybe he was just having a good day, or maybe the other team's hitters were weak.

- **Either-or fallacy (false dilemma).** You're either for us or against us!

  The either-or fallacy allows, misleadingly, for only two choices or sides in an argument, never allowing for other options, never acknowledging compromise or complexity. (A visual false dilemma occurs in the image shown in Figure 8.3, p. 152.)

- **Red herring.** Reporter: "Mayor, what do you have to say about the dangerous decay of the city's flood walls?" Mayor: "I'm proud of the accomplishments in my administration: We have a much larger, better-equipped police force than when I took office."

  According to the *Oxford English Dictionary,* a red herring is a smoked fish with a distinctive odor used to train dogs to follow

FIGURE 8.3 Either-or fallacy on a website This image from an anti–gun control website suggests that there are only two ways to protect yourself. A third option might be to call the police. (Source: <www.a-human-right.com> accessed 15 May 2007)

a scent. As early as 1884, it was used to mean an irrelevance used to distract attention from the real issue. In the example above, the mayor is trying to dodge a difficult question by changing the subject.

- **Ad hominem (personal attack).** His views on how to resolve the parking problem on campus are ridiculous! What would you expect from a member of a frat that has its own parking lot?

  An ad hominem (personal) attack attempts to undermine an opposing viewpoint by criticizing the motives or character of the individual offering the alternative view. When writers use ad hominem attacks, they focus their critiques on aspects of a person's character without connecting character flaws to the issues in question.

- **Guilt by association.** Tiffany is the most treacherous person I ever met. If Makoto is Tiffany's friend, he can't be trusted.

  Guilt by association dismisses or condemns people because of the relationships they have. Just because Tiffany is untrustworthy (if indeed she is) does not mean that everyone who befriends her is also untrustworthy.

- **Slippery slope.** If we exempt one person from the physical education requirement, everybody will want an exemption.

  The slippery slope fallacy implies that one event will initiate an unstoppable sequence of events. But as any skier can tell you, a slippery slope does not always mean that you will slide uncontrollably to the bottom of the hill. It is not impossible to exempt some students (those with a good excuse) while requiring the rest to take gym.

connect
mhconnectcomposition.com
Online exercise: QL8105

→ **EXERCISE 8.5 Locating logical fallacies in political websites**

Locate three logical fallacies in the websites of political figures—the president, your city's mayor, a senator from your home state, a candidate running for an upcoming election. (Go beyond the home page, deeper into the site, at least twice.) In a paragraph, name the fallacy and explain how the text (or visual) commits it.

Work **Together** ←

Working with two or more classmates, find a current editorial or opinion piece in a newspaper (in print or online). Read the editorial carefully. Does it commit any of the fallacies listed on pp. 149–52? If so, list them. If the editorial is fallacy-free, explain why its claims are logical.

8d Making a Claim

Just about every text—speeches, advertisements, websites, journal or magazine articles—has a main point or thesis that makes a claim (see Figure 8.4). When faced with any kind of text, begin your critical evaluation by determining whether the thesis makes a claim of *fact, opinion,* or *belief* or whether it simply expresses a *superstition* or *prejudice.*

FIGURE 8.4 *Adoriction Lifevest* by Erik Adigaard Claims can be advanced visually as well as in writing. This visual makes a claim about the relationship between junk food and obesity. Bring the same critical acumen to assessing the claims made through visuals that you bring to assessing print texts.

Quick

Reference ➜ **Devising an Arguable Thesis**

In an argumentative essay, make sure your thesis makes a claim of judgment or value:

Claim of Judgment (Opinion)
The use of email in the workplace reduces personal interactions among colleagues.

Claim of Value (Personal Belief)
Electronic communications ruin interpersonal relationships.

Claim of Fact
Email has surpassed the telephone as the most popular way to communicate in the workplace.

Also, consider qualifying your position with words like *often, sometimes, some,* and *most* to avoid committing yourself to a stronger position than you can effectively defend. Do not, however, use these qualifiers as a way of making claims that cannot be supported.

1. A fact is something that can be verified.

A text whose main claim is a statement of fact is *informative* (or *expository*):

> Susan B. Anthony and Martha Carey Thomas worked for women's voting rights in the United States.
>
> Denmark became a constitutional monarchy in 1849.
>
> The square root of 4 is 2.

> *More about* ▶▶▶
> Informative purpose,
> 12, 35–36

A **claim of fact** is not debatable and *cannot* be the central claim in an argument. For this reason, claims of fact are sometimes called *weak claims*.

> *More about* ▶▶▶
> Warrants, 166

Superstitions are claims with no basis in fact:

> A wish made on a falling star will come true.
>
> The Chicago Cubs will never win a World Series because of the Billy Goat Curse.
>
> If you don't forward this email to five friends, you'll suffer ten years of bad luck.

2. A belief is a conviction based on values.

Beliefs are something that an individual or a group holds to be true; they are based on a moral or religious value system:

> Humans should not eat animals.

All people should be treated fairly under the law.

Slavery is never justifiable.

People tend to defend their beliefs with great passion, and **claims of value,** like the three statements above, are frequently at the heart of argumentative (or persuasive) texts. As you craft your own argument or read others', carefully assess the relationship between a claim of value and the assumptions (or warrants) underlying it, whether you are assessing an argument or crafting one.

3. An opinion is a provisional judgment.

The holder of an opinion regards it as the most plausible answer *for now,* based on an evaluation of the available facts:

Graduates with engineering degrees are likely to find high-paying jobs.

The healthiest diet is low in carbohydrates.

The band Clap Your Hands and Say Yeah is better off without a record label.

Supplied with identical facts, not everyone will hold the same opinion. For this reason, the main claim of an argumentative text is often based on an opinion, or **claim of judgment.** Sometimes it makes a **claim of policy** (a claim about what we should do or how we should solve a problem). Sometimes it makes a **claim of causation** (a claim about the causes or effects of a problem).

When opinions are not provisional or temporary, they become **prejudices,** usually expressed in stereotypes:

Athletes are poor students.

Women are too emotional to be president.

Blondes are dumb.

Prejudice is by its very nature unfair because it ascribes qualities to an individual based on generalities about a group, generalities that are themselves often inaccurate. Whenever you suspect that a prejudice is operating as a claim, examine the evidence—and more importantly, the counterevidence—for the claim. Often a prejudice is based on an overgeneralization, and counterexamples are easy to come by. A claim based on prejudice never makes an effective thesis in an argumentative essay.

> **More about ▶▶▶**
> Counterevidence, 145
> Sweeping generalizations, 149–50

Writing
Responsibly Choosing a Fresh Topic

In addition to making sure your topic is arguable, you should also ask yourself the following questions:

1. Is my topic fresh?
2. Do I have something to add?
3. Is it worth reading (and writing) about?

Thinking critically about saturated topics (such as abortion and gun control) is difficult. Instead of articulating your own reasons, you can easily wind up offering a rehash of other people's.

The topics about which you can write most interestingly are those on which you have a distinctive perspective. Almost any eighteen-year-old can write passionately about the drinking age, for example, but to justify resuscitating tired topics, you must have something original to add. Whatever topic you choose, you will have your best shot at engaging your readers and doing justice to your topic when you write about something you and your readers will find compelling.

When writing an argumentative essay, ask yourself the following question: Do I take an arguable position on which reasonable people could disagree? A claim of fact (or a widely held opinion) is not debatable; reasonable people would not disagree about the number of Electoral College votes needed to win a U.S. presidential election (270) or about the temperature at which water boils at sea level (212 degrees Fahrenheit).

A claim of value (personal conviction or belief) is often difficult to support with objective evidence, as such claims rest on shared assumptions. Writers often find it difficult, if not impossible, to conduct an open-minded exploration of such issues. Writing about claims of value is an important way of exploring and sharing your beliefs, but if your assignment is to craft a persuasive argument, focusing on a claim of value can make your task extremely difficult.

connect

mhconnectcomposition.com
Online exercise: QL8106

EXERCISE 8.6 Assessing claims

Determine whether each of the following topics makes a claim of judgment, a claim of fact, or a claim of value. Explain each of your answers in a sentence or two.

EXAMPLE

It is illegal in this town for grocery stores to use plastic bags.

This is a claim of fact because it can be verified.

1. Grocery stores should charge customers for plastic bags to encourage people to recycle their old bags or to use canvas sacks instead.

2. Expecting customers to provide their own bags is ridiculous.

3. In some areas of the country, subsidizing solar energy is a waste of government money.

4. Solar panels have become much less expensive over the last ten years.

5. It is too difficult to be a vegetarian.

→ **EXERCISE 8.7 Assessing thesis statements**

Determine whether the following thesis statements are arguable or not, and explain why.

connect

mhconnectcomposition.com
Online exercise: QL8107

EXAMPLE

Theodore Roosevelt's sickly and weak physical condition as a child had a critical influence on many of his later personal and political decisions.

This is arguable because we have extensive factual information about Roosevelt's childhood physical condition as well as his later personal and political decisions, and a writer can form a knowledgeable and defensible opinion about the importance of the connection between them.

1. Using animals for drug experimentation is barbaric, cruel, and immoral.

2. Exposure to secondhand smoke significantly increases the risk of lung cancer and heart disease in nonsmokers, as well as several respiratory illnesses in young children.

3. Bilingual education is not effective in areas with large non-English-speaking populations of the United States.

4. Advertisements cause significant harm to people and our society as a whole.

5. Many invasive plants now threatening native species in the United States were deliberately planted by home gardeners.

⬆ Make It **Your Own**

Draft an arguable thesis for one of the topics in Exercise 3.1 (p. 35) or a topic of your own.

Work **Together** ←

In small groups, discuss the thesis statements you drafted in the Make It Your Own exercise above. Does each thesis make a claim of judgment or value? If not, what could be changed to make it an arguable claim?

8e Appealing to Readers: Intellect, Authority, and Emotions

An argument will be only as persuasive as the reasons and evidence, or **grounds,** that support the claim. When devising reasons and choosing evidence, ask yourself not only why you hold this opinion but also what your reader will find persuasive in this context. Support can appeal to your readers' intellect, it can draw on the authority of a figure they respect, or it can appeal to their emotions. The ancient Greeks called these approaches **logos, ethos,** and **pathos.** Each has a place in responsible writing.

1. Appeal to your readers' intellect (*logos*).

Logos refers to evidence that is rational and consistent; it appeals to readers by engaging their logical powers. Academic writing, such as the excerpt from Rachel Bateman's essay below, relies heavily on reasoned support and concrete evidence:

> Research suggests that violence in the media adversely affects a particularly vulnerable subset of children (usually males): those with Attention Deficit Disorder or information-processing disorders. These children have a hard time understanding the moral context of violence when it is used as entertainment; they may not differentiate enough between an action sequence in a movie and a face-to-face interaction in their daily lives (Gerteis 1993). Television viewing of children with these disorders should be carefully monitored, and role-models—parents, doctors, and teachers—should work with these kids to help them better understand the meaning and consequences of real-life violence.
>
> —Rachel Bateman, University of Kansas, "A Closer Look at the Causes of Violence"

A logical appeal can effectively reach a wide range of readers—from sympathetic to hostile—by reinforcing or challenging opinions with reasoned support.

Visuals that provide strong, quantifiable evidence—facts, data, statistics—appeal to the reader's intellect. This evidence may be displayed in a graph, chart, or map or in a before-after photo pair (Figure 8.5). They are effective for convincing a skeptical audience and are appropriate in all types of texts, especially academic texts, where logical reasoning is highly valued.

 Logos and Ethos in the United States In academic and business writing in the United States, argument relies primarily on rational appeals. Mentioning highly revered traditional authorities or sources (important political figures or religious works) is not considered a sufficient form of support. Instead, evaluate the arguments and supporting evidence of these authorities, and include their work as support only if it directly contributes to your argument.

2. Appeal to your readers by establishing your credibility (*ethos*).

Establishing a credible ***ethos***—good character, sound knowledge, or good reputation—goes a long way toward persuading readers to have confidence in what you say. Maxine Paetro, for example, establishes her credentials before she expresses her judgments:

> As the executive recruiter for several major ad agencies, I've eyeballed more than 40,000 cover letters. Some were winners. Some should have been deleted before ever seeing the light of print.
>
> —Maxine Paetro, "Mission: Employable"
> *Mademoiselle*

As a writer, you can establish your ethos not only by offering your credentials, but also by providing readers with sound and sufficient evidence drawn from recognized authorities on the topic, thereby demonstrating your grasp of the material. By adopting a reasonable tone and treating alternative views fairly, you demonstrate that you are

FIGURE 8.5 Shrinking area of Arctic permafrost, 1979–2003 These photographs make a logical appeal: They provide factual (verifiable) evidence for global warming.

a reasonable person. By editing your prose carefully, you establish your respect for your readers.

Ethical appeals can be very effective with wavering readers. When people are undecided about an issue, they often want to learn more about it from a person of good character who has considered both sides and provides sound judgments.

More about ▶▶▶
Making a presentation, 200–08 (ch. 11)
Tone, 16–18, 143, 567, 573–74

3. Appeal to your readers' emotions (*pathos*).

Using *pathos* to support a claim means stirring the audience's emotions in an effort to elicit sympathy and, thus, agreement. Pathos often relies on examples, stories, or anecdotes to persuade readers. It also uses a tone that stimulates readers' feelings.

Visuals that appeal to the reader's emotions or beliefs (like those in Figures 8.6 and 8.7) make an emotional (or pathetic) appeal. These can be powerful motivators, but be cautious: Arguments that appeal solely to readers' emotions are ethically suspect, especially in an academic context. If backed by strong logical evidence, however, an emotional appeal can be highly effective.

Many emotional appeals make use of visuals, especially photographs, because

---

Arguing Responsibly | **Making Oral Arguments**

When you write formal arguments for college courses, rational and ethical appeals are often more appropriate to your context and genre, but when you deliver a speech, presentation, or other form of oral argument, supplement logical and ethical appeals with vivid emotional appeals that your audience will remember. But be sure to support emotional appeals with logical and ethical appeals: After telling a moving story about an individual, use statistics or an expert's opinion to show how the issue affects others. Without logical evidence and ethical appeals, an emotional appeal is merely manipulative.

FIGURE 8.6 Loss of sea ice poses a threat to the polar bear This photograph makes a strong emotional appeal—we fear for the safety and well-being of the polar bear—but it would be out of place in an academic text without statistics that show a clear relationship between dropping polar bear populations and reduced ice coverage caused by global warming.

FIGURE 8.7 Visual pathos Charitable organizations like Save the Children often use pathos to elicit donations.

Getting It Across   **Multimedia Illustrations**

Many projects are now being delivered online, which opens up the range of illustrations you can use to help convey your ideas. To enhance the *logos* of your text, consider adding an animated graphic when showing change over time. To enhance the *ethos* of your text, consider linking to video clips of experts discussing your topic. To enhance the *pathos* of your text, use images (still or video) or sound files that appeal to your audience's beliefs or emotions.

of the immediate impact they can have on the hearts of audience members. Photographs that tug on the readers' emotions are common in advertising but rare in academic or business writing, where judgments are more likely to be made on a logical basis.

EXERCISE 8.8 Assessing logos, ethos, and pathos

Examine the reasons and evidence Brent Staples offers in his editorial (pp. 125–27). Classify it as logical, ethical, or emotional. Now

connect
mhconnectcomposition.com
Online exercise: QL8108

classify the reasons and evidence in Alea Wratten's critique of the Staples editorial (pp. 137–39) in the same way. Finally, write a paragraph explaining which of these two texts you find more persuasive and why.

connect

mhconnectcomposition.com
Online exercise: QL8109

More about ▶▶▶
Sample student projects (illustrated): 106, 136, 168, 346, 389, 422, 479

➔ **EXERCISE 8.9** **Assessing visual appeals**

Write a paragraph in which you argue that illustrations in one of the student projects in this book make a logical, ethical, or emotional appeal.

⬆ Make It **Your Own**

Using the arguable thesis you developed in the Make It Your Own exercise on p. 157, devise one rational and one ethical appeal that would be appropriate to a college audience. Now devise an emotional appeal to reinforce your logical or ethical appeal.

Work **Together** ◀

In small groups, consider the emotional appeal you devised in the Make It Your Own exercise above. Would you consider it appropriate in an academic context? Why or why not?

8f **Unearthing Assumptions**

In order to persuade an audience of the truth of a claim, the writer must persuade readers to accept certain common assumptions. For Tom Hackman to convince us that colleges and universities should take the motivations for plagiarism into effect when devising academic integrity policies, we must first assume that plagiarism is a widespread problem and that it is wrong. If you do not share these basic assumptions (and most of us do), then you would not be convinced that rethinking plagiarism policies is worth the time and trouble. When Martin Luther King, Jr., said, "The nations of Asia and Africa are moving with jet-like speed toward gaining political independence, but we still creep at horse-and-buggy pace toward gaining a cup of coffee at a lunch counter," he assumed that American progress should not lag behind that of Africa and Asia. Is this assumption correct? That depends upon whether you share it. Dr. King knew that most people

▶▶▶Student sample: "Why Students Cheat," Tom Hackman, 168–74

in his audience—U.S. citizens—would. An African or Asian audience, on the other hand, might be less likely to share this assumption about American progress.

As you read and write arguments, consider carefully the assumptions, or **warrants,** that underlie the claims being made: On what common ground must both reader and writer stand before they can discuss a topic productively? What must both writer and audience agree is true without argument or evidence?

> **EXERCISE 8.10** **Identifying main claim, evidence, and assumptions**
>
> After reading the essay "An Inconvenient Truth" (pp. 76–78), identify the main claim, assess the evidence provided in support of this claim, and identify at least one underlying assumption.

connect

mhconnectcomposition.com
Online exercise: QL8110

8g Considering Alternative Viewpoints

To consider an issue in all its complexity, you must consider alternative viewpoints. When reading or writing an argument, consider the doubts you or other reasonable people might have or the objections that opponents might raise. Ask friends or colleagues to help you brainstorm alternative positions or search for alternative voices in printed and online sources. When assessing an argument, consider whether the writer has taken these alternative viewpoints into consideration and how well the writer responds to critics' concerns.

Responses to alternative viewpoints can take several approaches:

- You can provide counterevidence that refutes the opposition. Consider a supporting paragraph from Alea Wratten's response to the Bret Staples editorial on the ill effects of hip-hop music:

  > . . . While gangsta rap continues to be very popular, hip-hop includes many bands and artists who pen uplifting and socially aware lyrics. Kanye West, for instance, currently among hip-hop's biggest stars, offers a positive, spiritual message in his music, a message of which Staples would likely approve. . . . And West is not alone: Lauren Hill, Kam, KRS One, Arrested Development, Chuck D, and Public Enemy are just a few of the musicians and bands on my iPod that explore hip-hop's more socially responsible side. These artists show that the strand of hip-hop that Staples accuses of providing a "toxic diet" for listeners is just one of many.
  >
  > —Alea Wratten, Suny–Geneseo, "Reflecting on Brent Staples's Editorial"

Refutation

Counterexamples

▶▶▶Student sample essay: 137

- You can acknowledge alternative views and explain why your position is still the most reasonable *despite* this counterclaim. In the introduction to her essay, Shona Sequiera creates an appealing tension by indicating what both her counterevidence and her evidence will be:

Concession

Explanation of why opposing position is less important than the writer's

Although *Their Eyes Were Watching God* has been widely criticized for painting too romantic a picture of African American life, Hurston's heroine Janie is ultimately able to transcend oppressive stereotypes and successfully come into her own. Her journey towards self-identity and self-knowledge harbors the celebratory ethnic notion that black is not just a color but a culture as well.

—Shona Sequiera, Connecticut College, "Transcending Stereotypes in Hurston's *Their Eyes Were Watching God*"

- You can revise your thesis to include concessions, exceptions, or qualifiers such as *some* or *usually:*

Concession

Qualifier

While the media may have an effect on some young adults, bursts of violence, like those at Columbine High School, Virginia Tech, and Northern Illinois University, are far more complex and have many more underlying causes than anti–media violence activists usually acknowledge: Mental illness, alienation, availability of weapons, and defects in school security are also components of the motivation to become violent.

—Rachel Bateman, University of Kansas, "A Closer Look at the Causes of Violence"

8h   Organizing Arguments: Classical, Rogerian, and Toulmin Models

More about ▶▶▶
Organizing, 37–42
Explaining and supporting your ideas, 46–48
Purpose, 11–13
Audience, 14–16

As with any writing, an argument will be most effective when it is carefully organized. The following are three widely used models:

- *Classical:* uses deductive reasoning
- *Rogerian:* uses inductive reasoning
- *Toulmin:* uses both types of reasoning

Before choosing a structure, consider which of these models is best suited to your purpose and audience.

1. The classical model

The classical model of argumentation derives from the work of ancient Greek and Roman orators. It is composed of five parts, usually presented in this order:

1. **Introduction.** Acquaint readers with your topic, give them a sense of why it is important and why you are qualified to address it, suggest your paper's purpose, and state the essay's main claim (or thesis) in one or two sentences.
2. **Background.** Provide basic information to help your audience understand and appreciate your position. You might include a brief review of major sources on the subject or offer a chronology of relevant events.
3. **Reasons and evidence.** Explain to readers why you believe what you do, and offer logical, well-chosen examples and data as support. Appeal to readers through their intellect, their respect for you and for your sources, and their emotions (if emotional appeals can be supported logically). This is the heart of your essay, and it should be the longest section, constituting perhaps 50 percent of the whole.
4. **Counterclaims and counterevidence.** Describe and explain alternative viewpoints, treating opponents fairly.
5. **Conclusion.** Leave readers with a strong sense of why they should agree with you by suggesting solutions, calling for action, or re-emphasizing the value of your position. If your essay's argument is complex, it may also be helpful to summarize it briefly here.

The classical argument uses deductive reasoning and is well suited to traditional, persuasive arguments.

> **More about ▶▶▶**
> Deduction, 145–48

2. The Rogerian model

The purpose of Rogerian argument is to build common ground, not to "win" an argument. It was developed by Carl Rogers, a twentieth-century psychologist, who hoped this method would make discussion more productive. Like the classical model, the Rogerian model is composed of five parts:

1. **Introduction**
2. **Background**

> **3. Counterclaims and counterevidence**
> **4. Reasons and evidence**
> **5. Conclusion**

In a Rogerian argument, however, the writer works to establish a common understanding of the issue and explores the counterclaims and counterevidence *before* discussing the writer's own reasons and evidence. Instead of refuting the counterevidence, the writer explores its legitimacy first and then explains why he or she still believes the thesis afterward. Tom Hackman's essay at the end of this chapter follows the Rogerian model.

3. The Toulmin model

The model for arguments developed by philosopher Stephen Toulmin includes five parts, as do the classical and Rogerian models, but the parts in an argument in the Toulmin model are somewhat different:

> 1. **Claim:** your thesis, the central argument
> 2. **Grounds:** the reasons you believe the claim and evidence supporting your claim
> 3. **Warrants:** any assumptions that explain how the grounds support the claim
> 4. **Backing:** supporting evidence for the warrants; they require their own supporting evidence because they are themselves claims.
> 5. **Rebuttal:** counterclaims or counterevidence and your response

The Toulmin model is akin to the classical in that it presents the main claim and the reasons and evidence in support of the claim first. In this way it is a typical persuasive argument. But it also recognizes that assumptions underlie all claims and brings those assumptions to the surface, making the search for common ground easier (or at least clarifying the terms of the discussion).

More about ▶▶▶
Revising, 90–102
Claims of value,
    judgment, 154–56
Reasons and evi-
    dence, 46–48
Appeals, 158–61
Counterevidence,
    145, 163–64
Persuading and ex-
    ploring, 142–43

Quick **Reference** ➡   **Revising an Argument**

As you revise your argument, pause to consider each of these issues:

- **Claim.** Do you take an arguable position based on an opinion or be-lief on which reasonable people could disagree? Have you modified it to avoid making a stronger claim than you can effectively support? Does your introduction show why your topic is important?
- **Reasons and evidence.** Do you supply reasons and evidence in sup-port of your claim? Do you use rational, ethical, or emotional appeals that are appropriate to your topic, purpose, and audience? Where ap-propriate, do you use visuals to make or support claims?
- **Counterclaims and counterevidence.** Have you acknowledged al-ternative interpretations of your evidence? Have you explained why your position is the most reasonable despite these objections?
- **Organization.** Have you followed an appropriate model of argu-ment, such as a classical, Rogerian, or Toulmin model? Is the orga-nizational structure appropriate to your overall aim—persuasion or exploration?

▲ Make It **Your Own**

Revise a persuasive or exploratory project that you are working on (or one you have written in the past), using the revision checklist in the Quick Reference box above.

▶▶▶Student ex-amples, persuasive argument, 137, 346, 460, 465

Student Project: Exploratory Argument

In the following exploratory argument, Tom Hackman, a student at Syracuse University, first analyzes plagiarism and then uses his analy-sis as the basis of a claim that universities should take these differ-ences into consideration when devising their plagiarism policies.

Tom Hackman

Professor Howard

Writing 109

28 September 2009

Why Students Cheat: The Complexities and Oversimplifications of Plagiarism

The system of American higher education is founded on principles of honesty and academic integrity. For this reason, nearly all those invested in this system—students, instructors, and administrators—recognize that plagiarism cannot be tolerated. They also agree that a lot of plagiarism is occurring. A survey published in *Who's Who among American High School Students* (reported by Newberger) indicated that 15% of top-ranked high schoolers plagiarize. Practices among higher education students are not much better. According to research by Donald L. McCabe, a professor at Rutgers University who has done extensive work on cheating, 38% of college students admitted to committing forms of plagiarism in the previous year (Rimer 7). A recent study by Hard, Conway, and Moran showed that plagiarism was common among the 421 students who participated in their research. Fig. 1 illustrates the various forms this plagiarism took.

There is a commonly held myth about how most plagiarism occurs. Late at night, a student sits staring at a computer screen. A paper is due the following morning, and research needs to be done, notes need to be taken, and, in the end, an essay needs to be written and edited. Instead of completing this immense task, though, the student succumbs to the temptations of plagiarism—"cutting and pasting" from sources, downloading an essay from the internet, or simply buying a

Introduction: Explains why topic matters

Background: Describes extent and severity of plagiarism

Counterclaims and counter-evidence: Describes alternative perspectives

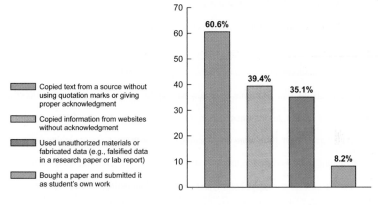

Fig. 1. Common types of plagiarism and the percentage of students who commit them. (Data and categories from Hard, Conway, and Moran 1069)

paper from another student. In this myth, students are too apathetic and slothful to complete their assignments on their own; instead, they cheat.

Concession Undeniably, some plagiarism occurs because students find it easier than simply doing the work required. The mind of a plagiarist, however, cannot be fit so easily into a single stereotype. The argument that laziness is the main cause of plagiarism is at best incomplete, and moreover it seems fed by unfair stereotypes of modern students as bored by academic rigor, more interested in video games or their *MySpace* page than the hard work of learning.

Reasons: Explains why counterclaims falter

Evidence: Reasons, expert opinions, examples In fact, some plagiarism grows from the opposite of these characteristics. High-achieving students, for example, fear what a bad grade will do to their otherwise stellar GPA. Such students treat the attainment of impressive marks as a necessity and will betray the very academic system they revere in order to sustain their average.

Other students plagiarize more from lack of interest in a particular course than general idleness. Students who view writing papers as hoops they must jump through to graduate, for instance, are more likely simply to download a paper from an online "paper mill" than write one themselves. For them, a college writing class is something to be endured, rather than an opportunity for learning. Russell Hunt, a professor at St. Thomas University in Canada, explains this attitude in point 2 of his article:

> If I wanted to learn how to play the guitar, or improve my golf swing, or write HTML, "cheating" would be the last thing that would ever occur to me. It would be utterly irrelevant to the situation. On the other hand, if I wanted a certificate saying that I could pick a jig, play a round in under 80, or produce a slick webpage (and never actually expected to perform the activity in question), I might well consider cheating. . . .

Students draw a distinction between their interests and their academic assignments. They rationalize their plagiarism as a way to escape an "unfair" academic obligation. Websites such as essaytown.com, which will write a paper to order, cater to students like these, who consider at least some aspects of academia essentially useless.

Many other instances of plagiarism are committed by students with honest intentions but who are ignorant of citation methods. Michael Gunn, a British

Quotes authority to support claim; notes qualifications of authority

student, copied quotations from internet sources in numerous papers over several years and was shocked to learn that this qualified as plagiarism (Baty). Even students who recognize the importance of citation may not know how to cite their sources correctly. A student who omits the source of a paraphrase in a paper would probably be surprised to learn that he or she is often considered as guilty of plagiarism as the student who downloads an essay.

Provides example that illustrates claim

The internet has compounded confusion with regard to citation. The internet is a place of free exchange where information moves from computer to computer with the click of a mouse. In this environment, ownership and citation become hazy. As John Leland, a reporter for the New York Times, writes, "Culture's heat now lies with the ability to cut, paste, clip, sample, quote, recycle, customize, and re-circulate." Many students find it is easy and "natural" to take text from an online source—for instance, by highlighting the text, copying it, and pasting it into a word processing document. Because it can be difficult to keep track of everything they have read, the chances of accidental plagiarism (forgetting to cite the copied text) increase. So, too, does the likelihood of "patchwriting," substituting synonyms or moving sentences around, but not fully putting the borrowed text into the writer's own words (Howard 233). Finally, some students will also be tempted to commit intentional plagiarism, choosing to leave a block of copied text uncited.

Quotes authority to corroborate claim; notes qualifications of authority

Paraphrases authority to corroborate claim

To add to the complexity of the plagiarism issue, societal norms play a significant role in students' and even scholars' views about fair use of another's work. Unlike in the West, Chinese culture largely accepts appropriating others'

Quotes and summarizes source to support claim

ideas and holds that private property is less important than the needs of the people. Professors copy from other professors, and students follow their lead. The "culture of copying" is prevalent throughout Chinese academia (Jiang A45).

Yet despite the many varieties and causes of plagiarism, college instructors and administrators too often treat the issue simply as a crime committed by the laziest of pupils. Birchard quotes a dean of Canada's Simon Fraser University, who voices a typical view: "We have a zero tolerance policy for cheating. . . . And we hope the severity of the penalties sends a strong message to other students who might be tempted to cheat or cut academic corners." Granted, there is ultimately no excuse for plagiarism, and any honest student should share the goal of eliminating it from academic life. Yet a less simplistic response to plagiarism would ultimately be more productive than the widespread law-and-order mentality that now exists.

The motivations behind plagiarism, and the situations that give rise to it, are varied. Importantly, much plagiarism occurs without the guilty student understanding that what he or she is doing represents academic dishonesty. Effectively combating plagiarism, in all its forms, requires a fuller understanding of how and why students break the rules. Academic policy writers must realize that plagiarism is not a single offense but a general term for a lack of citation, and plagiarism must be recognized as dynamic behavior, with many motivations, including social expectations, desires for high GPAs, disregard for the value of learning or intellectual property, and unawareness of citation standards. A regular user of a paper mill website has far different attitudes than a nonciting Chinese

Counterclaim

Conclusion: Restates counterclaim and rebuttal, states thesis

Concession and rebuttal

Returns to thesis

exchange student (or professor). The various categories of plagiarism threaten academia to varying extents and therefore demand a flexible response based upon the specifics of each incident. Only through this approach will plagiarism, in all its forms, be reduced.

Works Cited

Baty, Phil. "Plagiarist Student to Sue University." *Times Education Supplement*
    [London] 28 May 2004: n. pag. *TimesOnline.* Web. 15 Sept. 2009.

Birchard, Karen. "Canada's Simon Fraser U. Suspends 44 Students in Plagiarism
    Scandal." *Chronicle of Higher Education* 53.8 (2004): 46. *EbscoHost.* Web.
    21 Sept. 2009.

Hard, Stephen F., James M. Conway, and Antonia C. Moran. "Faculty and College
    Student Beliefs about the Frequency of Student Academic Misconduct."
    Journal of Higher Education 77.6 (2006): 1058–80. Print.

Howard, Rebecca Moore. "A Plagiarism *Pentimento.*" *Journal of Teaching Writing*
    11.3 (1993): 233–46. Print.

Hunt, Russell. "Four Reasons to Be Happy about Internet Plagiarism." *Teaching
    Perspectives.* Dec. 2002. St. Thomas University, Canada. Web.
    15 Sept. 2005.

Jiang, Xueqin. "Chinese Academics Consider a 'Culture of Copying.'" *Chronicle of
    Higher Education* 48.36 (2002): A45–46. *EbscoHost.* Web. 21 Sept. 2009.

Leland, John. "Beyond File Sharing: A Nation of Copiers." *New York Times*
    14 Sept. 2003, sec. 9: 1. *LexisNexis.* Web. 15 Sept. 2009.

Newberger, Eli H. "Why Do Students Cheat?" *School for Champions.* School for
    Champions, 6 Dec. 2003. Web. 16 Sept. 2009.

Rimer, Sara. "A Campus Fad That's Being Copied: Internet Plagiarism Seems on
    the Rise." *New York Times* 3 Sept. 2003: 7. *LexisNexis.* Web. 15 Sept. 2009.

Part Three

Media
Matters

9 Designing Printed and Electronic Documents

The early Peruvians wove this design to represent and honor their sun god. They used proximity to connect the head and tail to the figure's torso. They used the alignment of short yellow and red lines and the repetition of shapes (straight lines at right and left, red and yellow emblems above and below) to create the background against which the figure stands out. They used contrast of white outline against brown background to define the figure, and they inserted a rectangle in the center of the figure, which contrasts with the rest because it is filled in by color. This contrasting element attracts the eye and draws attention to the figure's core. According to renowned designer Robin Williams, these four principles—proximity, alignment, repetition, and contrast—are the pillars on which effective design rests.

9a Understanding the Four Principles of Design

Designer Robin Williams explains how the four principles work:

- *Proximity* (or nearness) suggests that content is related.
- *Alignment,* arrangement in a straight line (vertical, horizontal, or diagonal), creates connections among parts and ideas.
- *Repetition* of a design element lends unity (oneness).
- *Contrast* among design elements calls attention through difference.

In an effective design, such as that in the web page in Figure 9.1 (p. 178), these four principles work together to direct readers to the most important information and to highlight relationships among the elements on the page or screen.

EXERCISE 9.1 Analyzing a design

Find a web page, brochure, or advertisement (in print or online) that you think makes good use of words and graphics, and in two or three paragraphs, explain how it uses the four principles of design.

9b Planning Your Design Project

To figure out how best to apply the four principles of design to your project, begin with a careful consideration of your writing situation:

- **Purpose.** Is your purpose to inform, to persuade, to express yourself, or to entertain, and how should this be reflected in your design?
- **Audience.** Who will your audience be, what kind of expectations do they bring with them, and what kind of relationship do you have (or want to have) with them?
- **Context.** In what context (academic, business, public) or setting (over the internet, in person) will your project be received and how will this affect its design?
- **Genre.** What type of project is it—a résumé or business letter, an essay or lab report—and what design conventions are associated with this genre?

connect
mhconnectcomposition.com
Additional resources: QL9001

connect
mhconnectcomposition.com
Online exercise: QL9101

> *More about* ▶▶▶
Purpose, 10–13
Audience, 14–17
Context and genre, 18

Handwriting font calls attention to page title through contrast

Grayed portrait of Adams contrasts with colored background; juts out of yellow frame to call attention to subject of site

Yellow rule and white font of title contrast with dark blue background

Quotation aligns with portrait to associate the man with his words

Same color used for outline around central portion of screen and quotation to link outer and inner elements

Proximity of quotation to image associates the man with his words

Stacked links align to show similarity (all 3 are links to similar content)

Thumbnail images contrast with surrounding type to call attention to exhibition and timeline; blue and red type contrast with background and surrounding type

Tan of panel repeated in logo for the library and type below the panel

Proximity suggests similarity of information in stacked links

Proximity links thumbnail image to text (and icon)

FIGURE 9.1 A web page from the Boston Public Library's website

> **More about ▶▶▶**
> Organizing, 37–42

Next determine how the pieces of information you want to convey relate to one another:

- What information is most and least important?
- Does some of the information support a broader claim or provide evidence for this claim?
- How might you convey or reinforce your ideas visually?

connect

mhconnectcomposition.com
Online exercise: QL9102

▶ **EXERCISE 9.2 Analyzing a document**

Return to the web page, brochure, or advertisement that you used in Exercise 9.1 (p. 177). Analyze its purpose, audience, context, and genre. What categories of information (if any) did the designer use to organize the document?

▲ Make It **Your Own**

For an organization you are involved with or endorse, plan a promotional web page, brochure, or advertisement to solicit members or advertise an event. How will the purpose of your document affect its design? What audience will you appeal to? What information will they need, or what information will persuade them to join or attend an event?

9c Applying the Principles of Design

connect
mhconnectcomposition.com
Additional resources: QL9002

Once you have organized your project, you are ready to begin designing it.

1. Create an overall impression.

Start by considering the overall impression you want to give the reader: Should the design be conservative or trendy, serious or playful? Your decision will be based on your topic as well as your writing situation. Let your decision about the style of your project guide you in your choice of colors, fonts, and visuals.

More about ▶▶▶
Colors, 182
Fonts, 179–80
Visuals, 81–85,
183–84
White space, 180

2. Plan the layout.

Next consider the overall *layout,* the visual arrangement of text and images. An effective layout should use proximity, alignment, repetition, and contrast to make the relationships among the elements clear. Keep your layout simple, and use it to direct the reader's eye to the most important pieces of information. Allow for white space around elements that you wish to emphasize. Creating a sketch, or mock-up, of your layout can help you decide where to place elements on the page.

3. Format the document.

Once you have sketched your layout, you are ready to create a cohesive and attractive design by using the following elements:

Fonts Word processors give writers a wide range of fonts (or typefaces) to choose from. Selections range from **Arial** and **Courier** to **Palatino** and **Verdana**), with many choices in between. Generally, serif fonts (fonts with a little tail on the ends of letters, like **Courier** and **Palatino**) are easier to read when printed on paper, while sans serif fonts (such as **Arial** and **Verdana**) are easier to read on screen.

> ❝ When I interned at a magazine, I learned that a layout can convey a lot of information, even before someone starts reading. ❞
>
> —Betsy Smith, Barnard College

More about ▶▶▶
Using italics and un-
derlining, 846–51
(ch. 54)

In addition to selecting the font family, you can set your font in a variety of styles, including **boldface,** *italics,* underlining, or **color.** Use **color** or **boldface** for emphasis and contrast, but do so consistently and sparingly: The more they are used, the less attention they will call to themselves. Since *italics* and underlining often have a specific meaning, avoid using them except when required.

When choosing a font size, make sure it will be easy to read (especially if you are using it for the body of your project). Generally, a 10- or 12-point type will be legible to most readers, but print out a page of text to check the font size: 10-point type in one font may look larger than 12-point in another.

Writing
Responsibly

Selecting Fonts with Readers in Mind

Not all readers have perfect vision. If your audience includes members over forty (or under twelve), use a font size of at least 12 points to make the reading experience easier and more pleasant. If the visually impaired will make up a portion of your audience, increase your font size even more.

The font you choose can also add contrast, or it can group items through repetition: If most of your text is in a serif font, a sans serif font (or the same font in bold or a different color) can call attention to a heading. Use the same style, size, color, and type of font for all the headings at the same level and for all text of the same type.

Keep in mind, too, that the fonts you use (especially in headings) can reinforce the overall impression you are trying to create. A typeface such as 𝕺𝖑𝖉 𝕰𝖓𝖌𝖑𝖎𝖘𝖍, for example, might be appropriate in a poster announcing the first meeting of the Shakespeare Society. But be careful: For a text-heavy document, legibility is more important than drama. More than a few words in an ornate font like *Edwardian Script* or **Haettenschweiler** will be hard to read. Setting lengthy passages on a website in a serif font may also make the text difficult to read on screen, though such fonts can be used effectively for headings online.

connect
mhconnectcomposition.com
Additional resources: QL9003

NOTE For college writing, check the style guide for your discipline to make sure these design decisions will be acceptable.

More about ▶▶▶
Page layout:
MLA style, 340–44
(ch. 17)
APA style, 385–87
(ch. 18)
Chicago style,
420–21 (ch. 19)
CSE style, 443–45
(ch. 20)

White Space   White space (Figure 9.2) is the portion of a page or screen with no text or images—it does not literally have to be white. The margins at top, bottom, left, and right of a page provide white space, as does the extra space before a paragraph or around a heading. Extra white space above or around text or a visual groups elements into a section. Using the same amount of white space around headings at the same level or visuals of the same type lends consistency to your layout. Adding extra white space lends emphasis through contrast. Ample white space makes a page inviting and easy to read; without it, a page looks crowded, and the eye has difficulty knowing where to focus (Figure 9.3).

Lists Another strategy for grouping related items (and for adding white space) is to use lists (Figure 9.3). Keep lists succinct to allow readers to skim them for information. They can be particularly effective in web pages to summarize and break up blocks of text on the screen. When creating lists, regardless of your medium, remember to do the following:

- Keep list items parallel (use all phrases or all sentences, for example).

- Keep the number of items in a list small (four to six).

- Begin list items with a dot, diamond, or square, and align all items at left.

- Use numbered lists to indicate steps in a process and bulleted lists to group related information.

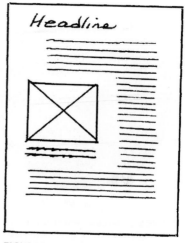

FIGURE 9.2 Using white space to group elements Adding white space above a heading or around a figure and its caption groups the information into a unit for readers.

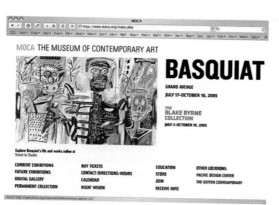

FIGURE 9.3 Formatting a web page The web page from the Museum of Contemporary Art (left) uses font size, style, color, and white space to highlight information and make the page attractive. The C-Span web page (right), crowded with information, uses colored panels, font size, style, and color, to make the page easier to navigate.

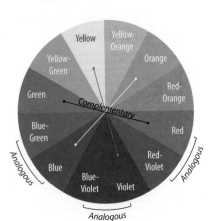

FIGURE 9.4 **The color wheel** Colors opposite each other on the color wheel are complementary; colors adjacent to each other are analogous.

While lists are common in business writing (as in résumés and *PowerPoint* presentations), they are used sparingly in most academic writing.

Color Color, through contrast, calls the reader's attention to what is important in the text: Headings; bullets or numbers in lists; boxes, charts and graphs; or illustrations often appear in color so that readers will notice them. But use color judiciously:

- Use a limited color palette. Too many colors in close proximity will create a hodgepodge effect.

- Use a pleasing color palette. Analogous colors, those adjacent to each other on a color wheel (Figure 9.4), create a softer, more harmonious look. Complementary colors, those opposite each other on the color wheel, contrast with each other, each making the other color look brighter.

- Use readable color combinations. Make sure colors contrast enough with their background that they are legible.

- Use appropriate colors. Consider the associations colors and combinations of colors carry: pastel pinks and blues for new babies, bright yellow and black for warnings, green for nature.

- Use colors consistently. The repetition of colors will group items of the same type.

Writing Responsibly   Designing for Those with Impaired Color Vision

Most of those with a color-vision impairment are unable to distinguish between red and green: Both colors appear gray. A smaller number are unable to distinguish between blue and yellow. To be sure that those with a color-vision impairment can obtain important information, avoid the red/green or blue/yellow color combination, or use labels or underlining in addition to color.

Headings Writers often use headings and subheadings to group text and guide readers. They can help readers comprehend a text's structure at a glance. The principles of repetition and contrast are crucial with headings:

- Set all headings of the same level in the same font, style, and color, and align them in the same way on the page:

First-level heading

Second-level heading

Third-level heading

- Use the same grammatical structure for all headings of the same level. For example, use all *-ing* phrases (*Containing the Economic Downturn, Bailing Out Wall Street*) or all *noun phrases* (*Economic Downturn Ahead, Wall Street Bailout*).

- Distinguish among heading levels by setting all headings of the same level in a specific font, style, or color or by placing them differently on the page (at left, centered).

4. Add visuals.

Visuals are the first thing readers will notice when they look at your text. For this reason, they are integral to documents geared toward the general public and must thus catch the eye of potential readers. Visuals are appropriate in some academic genres—in economics, for example, graphs are used frequently—but they are not customary in all academic disciplines. Ideally, any visuals you include in a document should be visually arresting. But this does not mean that you should choose images just because they will capture the reader's attention. To be effective, images must be compelling *and* must expand your readers' understanding of your text. They must also be appropriate to your writing situation.

When including visuals on a page, be sure to place them as soon as possible after the text discussion that refers to them. In academic and business

> **More about** ▶▶▶
> Parallelism, 539–48
> (ch. 27)

connect
mhconnectcomposition.com
Additional resources: QL9004

> **More about** ▶▶▶
> Visual arguments,
> 141–74 (ch. 8)
> Visuals in college
> writing assign-
> ments, 80–81

> **More about** ▶▶▶
> Incorporating
> visuals, 313–14,
> 342–44 (MLA),
> 387 (APA)
> Choosing the right
> type of visual,
> 81–85
> Revising visuals,
> 86–89
> Academic writing,
> 448–95
> Business writing,
> 496–514

Getting It Across   **Symbol Fonts and Clip Art**

Symbol fonts (such as ✹ or ♪ or ☞) and clip art (a library of generic digital drawings or graphics available online) can be inserted in texts for the general public—to ornament a website or flyer, for example—and to reinforce design principles, especially alignment, repetition, and contrast. But be wary: Symbols and clip art can confuse readers about your purpose (to entertain, or to inform or persuade?), and they can undermine the seriousness with which readers take you and your text.

Quick

Quick Reference ➤ **Including Visuals (Images and Graphics)**

	Images	**Graphics**
Type	Photographs, drawings and sketches, screenshots, film stills	Tables, flowcharts, pie charts, line and bar graphs, diagrams, timelines, maps
Purpose	Depict or explain an event, object, or process, or illustrate a concept.	Convey complex information in an easily readable form.
Audience	Use images to draw readers in.	Use graphics to help readers understand complex data, trends, processes.
Context and Genre	In academic and business contexts and genres, use images to provide evidence, to help readers grasp a point, or to provide an example. In personal and public writing, use images for these purposes, as well as to capture interest, make an argument, or reinforce a point.	In every context and genre, use graphics to help readers understand complex data quickly.

writing, include a reference to the figure or table in your text, numbered in order of appearance (such as *figure 1* or *table 2*). Provide a caption that includes this number and, wherever possible, adds information that is not included in the text. The overall effect is usually best if images are placed at the top or bottom of the page and are either centered or placed flush with the left or right margin.

connect

mhconnectcomposition.com
Online exercise: QL9103

➤ **EXERCISE 9.3 Analyzing layout**

Return once again to the design you analyzed in Exercises 9.1 (p. 177) and 9.2 (p. 178). In one or two paragraphs, analyze its layout. Consider its overall impression (trendy or conservative, playful or serious); its use of white space, lists, color, and headings to create proximity, alignment, repetition, and contrast; its use of fonts and visuals, and how the visuals function (do they reinforce product identity, provide an example, offer additional information, further the argument, demonstrate a process?). Has your assessment of the document's purpose, audience, context, and genre changed as you studied it more closely?

↑ Make It **Your Own**

Using the plan you developed for the Make It Your Own exercise on pp. 178–79, sketch the web page, brochure, or advertisement you planned. Consider the overall impression that would be most appropriate given your writing situation.

Work **Together** ←

In groups of three or four, critique the documents you produced in the Make It Your Own exercise above. How well has each designer used proximity, alignment, repetition, and contrast? How well does each design express the purpose of the group or event? How well does it appeal to the target audience?

10 Writing for Multiple Media

> AFFLUENT COLLEGE — BOUND STUDENTS FACE THE REAL PROSPECT OF DOWNWARD MOBILITY. FEELINGS OF ENTITLEMENT CLASH WITH THE AWARENESS OF IMMINENT SCARCITY. THERE IS RESENTMENT AT GROWING UP AT THE END OF AN ERA OF PLENTY COUPLED WITH REASSESSMENT OF CONVENTIONAL MEASURES OF SUCCESS.

Contemporary artists struggle to choose a medium—paint on canvas; charcoal and ink on paper; neon tubing; or, as in this work by artist Jenny Holzer above, raised lettering on a bronze plaque. They choose the medium that will best express their idea to their audience. Here, Holzer uses the contrast between her words (describing the situation of many college-bound adolescents) and a medium closely associated with commemorating historical figures. These choices enable her to challenge both her viewers (including students and faculty at the University of Chicago, where this work was shown at a gallery on campus) and the very concept of art.

Like contemporary artists, writers today have an array of media to choose from: pen and paper, email, instant message, website, blog, wiki. From these many choices, they must select the medium that will be most appropriate to their message, their purpose, and their audience. They must also choose a medium that will help them meet their responsibilities as writers. This chapter offers guidelines for matching medium to message, for deciding on the most appropriate style and tone, and for meeting your responsibilities to yourself and your readers.

10a Writing and Answering Email

Writers in many contexts have embraced email because it offers a convenient and speedy way to communicate in writing, but its very speed creates the need for special care. Before you press the Send button, consider whether you have selected and arranged your words to create the appropriate *tone*. If you have doubts, revisit your message or consider picking up the phone or paying a visit instead.

1. Writing email

Email has almost replaced the printed memo. To deal efficiently with the volume of email most of us get, even personal email should take on the characteristics of the business memo: limiting the number of recipients, providing an appropriate subject line, getting right to the point, and sticking to a single topic.

connect
mhconnectcomposition.com
Additional resources: QL10001, QL10002

▶ **More about ▶▶▶**
Tone, 16–17, 143,
567, 573–74
Business emails,
memos, 501–03
Acronyms, 565, 854

Quick Reference ➡ **Consider Your Writing Situation When Composing Email**

Purpose and Focus
In most cases, the primary purpose of an email message is to inform, so keep your message focused on a single issue, state that issue briefly in the subject line, repeat it in the first paragraph of your message, and keep the message brief.

Audience
Provide the context needed to make your message understandable, and quote or refer to earlier messages in the thread to which you are replying. Think about your tone from the reader's point of view. Before sending large files as attachments, find out if readers' email programs can accommodate them. Name and introduce attachments, so that readers can determine whether it is safe to open them.

Context
While email is generally somewhat informal, adjust your level of formality to the context in which you are writing. Unless you are writing to a close friend, avoid *emoticons*—representations of emotions on faces, such as :) (happy) and ;) (winky). Also avoid IM acronyms—LOL for "laugh out loud" or TMI for "too much information"—and nonstandard capitalization, grammar, punctuation, and spelling.

Writing Responsibly   Maintain Confidentiality in Email

You may have noticed the bcc (or "blind carbon copy") option in the header of your email messages. Any recipient you list in this line will receive a copy of your message but will not be identified to other recipients. Sending blind copies can be ethical or unethical: Use the bcc option to keep the email addresses of recipients private, as when sending a message to a group of people who do not know each other. But do not blind copy a recipient to deceive your correspondent into believing a message is confidential. If your readers might mistakenly believe they are the only recipient of a message, mention in the body of the message that it is being shared with others.

Recipients Include in the "To" line only those recipients who need to take action on the message; include in the "Cc" line anyone who must be kept informed but from whom you do not need a reply.

Subject Line Provide a short, descriptive title in the subject line of your email: "A question about tomorrow's assignment." Make sure that, even in a reply or when forwarding a message, you alter the subject line to reflect the content of the message.

Salutation An email message differs from a letter in that a formal salutation ("Dear Dr. Mansfield:") is rarely needed. Provide one only in the most formal emails, such as a letter of application, and usually only when the recipient is someone with whom you are not acquainted.

 Task-Oriented Emails Get Right to the Point In the United States, emails that are task oriented frequently dispense with formalities and personal touches and get right to the point. In some cultures, such messages would be considered rude. U.S. readers view them as efficient and timesaving.

Organization and Length State your purpose in the first paragraph, and keep the paragraphs short. If an email must be long, use numbered lists, headings, and transitions to make the organization clear and to help the recipient understand the content quickly.

Style To avoid embarrassing gaffes, treat the writing context as being slightly more formal than you think it is.

Design Some email programs allow for text styling such as boldface and italics; others allow only plain text. When you are not sure whether your recipient will see formatting, use the following conventions:

1. For book titles and other text you would normally italicize, place an underline before and after the title: _Lone Survivor_ by Marcus Luttrell.

2. For emphasis, place an asterisk before and after the word to be highlighted: *Recommendations*.

3. Place URLs on a separate line to make it easy for your readers to copy and paste them into the address bar of their web browser.

4. Avoid special characters, like dashes, that may disappear or become garbled in transmission.

More about ▶▶▶
URLs, 255–56
Block style letters, 496–99
Font types and styles, 179–80
Discussion groups, 198–99, 227

Some discussion groups require that messages be sent in plain text. In general, format paragraphs in block style, with no indention of the first line, and separate paragraphs with a blank space. Choose a standard sans serif font such as Arial or Verdana in a 10- or 12-point font size. Keep the font black.

Closing Provide a complimentary closing ("Yours truly," "Sincerely") only in the most formal emails.

Contact Information Include contact information, such as your mailing address, telephone number, fax number, or website address.

Attachments Before attaching documents to an email message, be sure to save them in a format that your recipient is likely to be able to read. Include your last name, a brief descriptive title, and a date in the file name:

connect
mhconnectcomposition.com
Additional resources: QL10003

Santos_MinimumWageEssay_Draft1_04-15-09.doc *not*

MinimumWageEssay_Draft1.doc

Because of computer viruses sent via email attachments, many people will not open attached files unless they know what it is, who it is from, and why they are receiving it. Identify attachments in your email message.

More about ▶▶▶
Spelling, 584–98
(ch. 31)
Punctuation, 782–
838 (ch. 47–52)
Capitalization,
839–845 (ch. 53)

Revision Edit for grammatical and typographical errors, check that your tone is appropriate, and check that promised files are attached. Then, pause. For important email messages, delay sending for an hour or even a day to be sure that your message is clear and reasonable. If you are tempted to send an insulting "flame" (a personal attack on someone with whom you disagree) or even a curt response, reconsider: Hostile email can establish you as an unreasonable person; it may also circulate beyond the intended recipient, doing even more harm.

Archiving Consider whether sent messages need to be preserved. You may find it helpful to establish topical archive folders for your correspondence (see Figure 10.1). Merely saving email messages in your in-box will make them difficult to find later and may use up limited storage space.

📑 Inbox	**19**
▶ 📄 Drafts	**5**
▶ ✒️ Sent	
▶ 🗑 Trash	**53**
▶ 📧 Junk	**1**
▶ 📁 Archives	**5**
📁 Eco–Cottage	
📁 Economics 240	
📁 English 201	
📁 Family	
📁 History 239	
📁 Jason	
📁 Math 313	
📁 Soccer	

FIGURE 10.1 Folders for archived email

2. Answering email

Answering email messages involves not only the issues related to writing email but also the following:

Timing Read and reply to your email every day. If replying to a particular email will take more time than you have, send an immediate reply so that the sender knows you received the message, and indicate when you will respond. If you are going to be away from email for a day or more, add an auto-reply message to alert correspondents.

Context Before answering, read all the messages that have been sent to you on that topic. If your email program allows, sort your messages by subject to be sure that you have read everything in the thread you are responding to. So that your recipient has a context for what you are saying, quote pertinent passages from the email to which you are responding, or refer your reader to an earlier message in the thread.

Writing
Responsibly **Email and Privacy**

Email is not a private medium: A confidential message to a friend may get forwarded to others (intentionally or accidentally as part of an email thread), and work sent from a company computer—even when using a web-based email program—may be read by security or by your boss, even after it has been deleted. For your own peace of mind, do not write messages that might harm your reputation or those of others.

Recipients Most people get more email than they can handle, so always consider carefully before selecting Reply All. Does everybody on the list really need to be included?

> ⟶ **EXERCISE 10.1 Analyzing an email message**
>
> Analyze an email message you wrote to a boss, an instructor, or an older family member (parent or grandparent, aunt or uncle): Is it focused on a single topic? Does it include an appropriate subject line? Is the message logically organized? Is it of an appropriate length? Is the tone appropriate given the recipient of the message? Does the message avoid errors of grammar, spelling, punctuation, and mechanics? In one or two paragraphs, explain how you would revise the message.

connect

mhconnectcomposition.com
Online exercise: QL10101

Work **Together** ⟵

A friend has just forwarded an email to you that she received from an instructor who is a native speaker of Japanese. In the forward, your friend has made some jokes about the instructor's non-idiomatic word choices. How should you respond? Discuss your options.

10b Creating a Website or Web Page

As of September 2008, *Facebook* claimed to have about 100 million active users (equal to about one-third of the total U.S. population), and in July 2008 *Google* reported that there were 1 trillion unique URLs on the Web (over 100 web addresses for every person alive today). With numbers like these, the odds that you have created (or will create) a website or web page are great. The odds that your writing will appear on a website or web page are even greater.

1. Plan your site.

Writing for the Web generally means creating a *website,* a collection of files located at a single address, or URL, on the World Wide Web. Every website begins with a **home page,** the page designed to introduce visitors to the site. Most also have additional **web pages**—documents that, like the home page itself, may include text, audio and video, still images, and database files.

Reference → Consider Your Writing Situation When Creating a Website

Purpose and Focus

Readers generally scan websites for information, so keep your sentences brief and clear and your focus tight. Images, sound files, and design should reflect your purpose and capture readers' attention.

Audience

Consider carefully the needs and expectations of your readers, and tailor your content and language appropriately. Also remember that unintended readers may also see what you post on the open Web, so avoid posting materials or using language that you or others might find embarrassing or offensive.

Context

Consider any restrictions of your host or site sponsor as you plan your site.

Genre

If you will be providing information that will remain current for a long time, create a website that you update once or twice a year; if your site requires daily or weekly updates, create a blog; if you want readers to participate in the creation of the site's content, create a wiki.

In order to make your website useful to others, plan the overall structure of the site carefully. Then create each page as a separate document (or file) on your computer, and save all the pages, with any video, image, or sound files you plan to include, in a common folder. This will save you time and trouble when you upload your files to a server.

Unlike print documents in which reading proceeds *linearly*—the document is arranged so that all readers begin at page 1 and read through to the end—most websites are *hypertextual*—users may enter the site at any page and follow their own path through the website. Just how easy it is for users to find their way around your site depends on its structure and on the navigation tools you provide.

Site Structure When creating a website, consider how the various pages will relate to one another and how users will move among them. A site that includes a home page and a handful of web pages with loosely related content may work best with a hub-and-spoke organization (Figure 10.2). If your website will offer a series of pages with related content, a hierarchical arrangement, with links from home page to lower-level pages and from page to page, may be more useful (Figure 10.3).

Navigation Tools Navigation tools include the following:

- **Menus.** Placed at the top, bottom, left, or right side of the web page, menus list main sections of your website and are consistent from page to page.

- **Breadcrumb trails.** Used to show the click-path you took to the page you are on, breadcrumb trails offer users an easy way to jump back to higher-level pages.

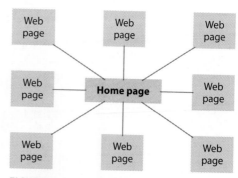

FIGURE 10.2 **A hub-and-spoke structure**

- **Hyperlinks (or links).** Used to jump from place to place on a web page or from web page to web page, links appear as highlighted words or images on a web page.

The website shown in Figure 10.4 (p. 194) offers these navigation tools.

Home Page While the contents of your home page will depend on the purpose, audience, context, and genre of your site, users will benefit from the following:

- **Title.** The home page (and each additional web page) should include a title that clearly and succinctly indicates the type of information your site will include.

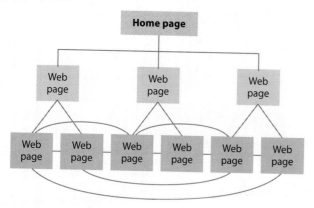

FIGURE 10.3 **A hierarchical, treelike structure, with additional links**

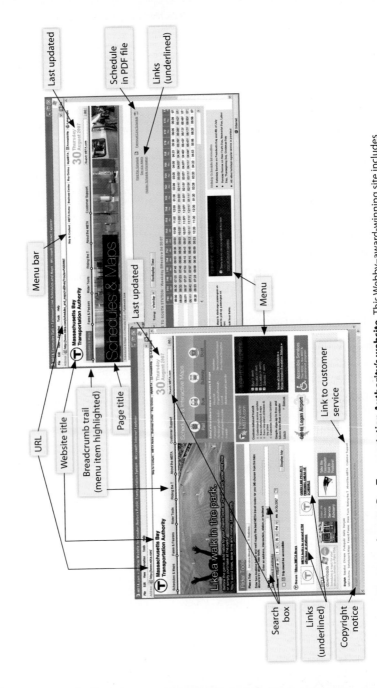

FIGURE 10.4 The Massachusetts Bay Transportation Authority's website This Webby–award-winning site includes menus, search boxes, and a breadcrumb trail that reinforces the sponsoring organization's identity by resembling a subway map. It appeals to its target audience by placing links to schedules and maps, rider tools, and subway advisories on its home page (left) and featuring a photograph of Boston's Fenway Park.

- **Date created, last updated.** Providing a copyright date or indicating when you last updated the site lets readers know how current your site is and enables users to create a complete bibliographic citation.

- **Link to a site map.** A site map is a table of contents for the site; it helps users find the information they are looking for quickly and easily.

- **Link to contact information.** Provide a link to your basic contact information, including an email address, your name, and your role. To avoid possible "cyberstalking," reveal only as much information as you are willing for the entire world to know, and establish a separate email address exclusively for correspondence from your website.

- **Copyright or Creative Commons notice.** All material published on the Web is automatically protected by copyright. Remind readers of this fact by including a copyright notice: "Copyright © 2010 Paul Jefferson." For the copyright date, use the year in which you created or last updated the page. An increasingly popular alternative notice is a Creative Commons License. Browse the Creative Commons website <www.creativecommons.com> to learn more about this project.

 Tech

Thwarting Spam

Many website owners now spell out the components of their email addresses—"jdoe AT gmail DOT com"—rather than provide the actual address (jdoe@gmail.com) in order to thwart "spambots," software programs that pick up email addresses online and deluge them with junk mail ("spam") and virus-laden messages.

connect
mhconnectcomposition.com
Additional resources: QL10004

→ **EXERCISE 10.2** **Examining the navigation tools and home page of a website**

Analyze your school's website or another website you visit regularly. In a paragraph or two, discuss the strengths and weaknesses of the site's structure and navigation tools. What tools do you use regularly, and why? Now study the website's home page. Which elements from the list on pp. 193, 195 are included? Which would you like to see added, and why?

connect
mhconnectcomposition.com
Online exercise: QL10102

❝ When I write on my website, my voice, no matter how insignificant or inane, is immediately put up for anyone to read. Sometimes I sit back and contemplate the implications that this has—on my psyche, on my writing, and in relation to the world. Other times, I simply write off the cuff. ❞

Leonard Lin, University of Southern California

2. Create your website's content.

To populate your own web pages, you can either create the content from scratch using an HTML editor or convert print-based documents.

Using an HTML Editor Creating a website from scratch entails using ***HTML*** (HyperText Markup Language), the coding system that makes the World Wide Web work. HTML tells a reader's Web ***browser*** (a software program such as *Mosaic, Internet Explorer,* and *Safari*) how to display the information on a web page and how to link to other pages.

To create a website without becoming an HTML expert, you can use an ***HTML editor*** that automatically sets up a basic page and allows you to select styles from a menu. A free HTML editor usually comes bundled with the software on a new computer—*TextEdit* on a Macintosh, *Notepad* on Windows. Or you may want a simpler-to-use visual, WYSIWYG ("what you see is what you get") editor that allows you to create a web page as easily as creating a word processing document. You may not need to buy a visual editor; often they are loaded onto the machines in your school's computer labs, or one may come bundled with your browser.

Converting Print-based Documents Texts originally prepared on a word processor can be converted into web pages or PDFs for posting online. Check the help function in your word processing program for instructions.

Incorporating Image, Sound, and Video Files Web pages more easily attract an audience when they include multimedia files—images, graphics, sound, or video. Images and graphics should do more than ornament the page, however; they should also provide useful information, set an appropriate tone, or suggest useful perspectives on the content of the page. When adding images and graphics to your site, consider how

connect

mhconnectcomposition.com
Additional resources: QL10005, QL10006, QL10007, QL10008

PDF Portable Document Format; created by Adobe, pdf format allows a document to be opened in different systems without losing its formatting

connect

mhconnectcomposition.com
Additional resources: QL10009

➤ Tech

Use a Lower Resolution to Avoid Memory-Hogging Image Files

Including high-resolution image files or a large quantity of lower-resolution image files can make loading a web page so time-consuming that visitors become exasperated and give up.

Avoid this problem by reducing the size of your images. Most image files will look fine online at 72 dots per inch.

much is enough. Just as a visually bland web page can fail to stir readers' interest, a visually cluttered page can distract them.

Since not every site visitor will actually play the files (and some may not be able to see or hear the files), provide a written description of any that are crucial to your point. A description may also pique visitors' curiosity enough for them to click the link or file you provide.

3. Design your site.

Communicating on the Web is inescapably visual, and the design of your website will influence both how clear and accessible your site is and how receptive users are to your message. To make your site visually effective, plan it carefully and apply the principles of design.

4. Revise and edit your website.

A website full of errors will undermine your credibility with readers long before they ever assess the content on your site, so check your website carefully before bringing it "live":

- Since most readers scan websites for information, make sure your prose is clear and concise.

- Check that visual and multimedia files add value and are not merely ornamental.

- Check that your design is attractive and consistent.

- Check that image and other media files open properly.

- Check all links to make sure they work.

- Ask friends to read your pages: Users with different hardware and software will run into different problems.

- Edit and proofread your site carefully for errors in spelling, grammar, punctuation, and mechanics.

More about ▶▶▶
Writing concisely,
515–25 (ch. 25)
Deciding to illustrate, 80–81
Designing printed and electronic documents,
176–85 (ch. 9)
Evaluating websites,
250–57
Editing and proofreading, 96–99,
102–4

Getting It Across — Checking Accessibility

Make sure your site is accessible to sight-impaired users by running your pages through an accessibility checker. The Assistive Technology Resource Center <http://colostate.edu/Dept/ATRC/tools.htm> provides a list of programs, some of which are free.

➤ Make It **Your Own**

Drawing on what you learned in this chapter, plan, draft, revise, and edit a website.

Work **Together** ◄

Working in groups of three or four, evaluate each group member's website (either the website created for the Make It Your Own exercise above or another website). Be sure to consider the site's structure and navigation tools as well as the writing, editing, and proofreading of the site. Provide recommendations for revising and improving the visitor's experience.

5. Maintain your website.

Once your website is up and running, check it every month or so:

- Make sure the site continues to run on different browsers.

- Delete, replace, or repair broken links.

- Make sure image files appear; if a small icon appears instead, check to make sure the image file is in your server folder and that its URL is typed correctly (including the file extension, such as *.jpg* or *.gif*).

More about ▶▶▶
Discussion lists, 227
Blogs, 227
Documenting posts
 to discussion lists,
 329 (MLA),
 381 (APA),
 416 (*Chicago*),
 442 (CSE)
Citing blogs and
 blog posts,
 330 (MLA),
 382 (APA),
 416 (*Chicago*),
 442 (CSE)

10c   **Writing in Interactive Media**

With the rapid spread of broadband access, online communication has become an increasingly familiar part of our lives: Instant messaging and chat rooms, bulletin boards and discussion groups, and wikis and blogs are now common additions to the classroom, newsroom, and living room. The very familiarity of these media can lull writers into making errors that they later regret. Many of the principles described above for email and website writing also apply to these other forms of online writing. In particular, be sure to think about your purpose and to tailor your writing style and tone to your intended audience, considering carefully how your readers might interpret your message *before* sending or posting it.

Writing Responsibly

Flaming

The quick interactivity and the anonymity of online media present a special challenge: keeping your temper. *Flaming*—writing a scathing response to someone with whom you disagree—is a great temptation, but it shuts down reasoned discourse, instead encouraging ad hominem attack. Flaming may convey a sense of power for having found a biting way to put down an opponent, but it also shuts down the possibility of anyone's listening to or being influenced by the post.

> *More about* ▶▶▶
> Ad hominem and other logical fallacies, 149–53

The goal of online discussions, as with live discussions, is to learn collaboratively through give and take; however, because participants are not physically present, the temptation to go off on a tangent may be great. To avoid this, focus on responding directly to the comments of other participants and summarizing the discussion before moving on. Your online voice can be casual, but strive to keep your comments clear and to maintain a voice that is friendly and polite, even when you disagree.

When participating in a discussion in **asynchronous media** (media that does not require participants to sign on at a specific date and time), take advantage of the opportunity to reflect on and proofread your comments before posting them. Asynchronous discussions usually require participants to make a commitment to sign on regularly and to make comments at least once a week.

In **synchronous media** such as instant messaging and chat, where communication occurs in real time, participants must make a commitment to sign on on time and to focus attention on the discussion while it is occurring. Reflection and careful proofreading are not possible, but synchronous discussions are useful for brainstorming and for developing a sense of community.

> *More about* ▶▶▶
> Collaborative writing projects, 30–32, 50–51

11 Making a Multimedia Presentation

Hurricane Katrina
August 29, 2005

Photo: NOAA

"Future generations may well have occasion to ask themselves, 'What were our parents thinking? Why didn't they wake up when they had a chance?'" So speaks Al Gore in this presentation on global warming. He has given his presentation to groups large and small across the country and around the world. It was captured in the documentary *An Inconvenient Truth,* which has been seen by thousands and thousands of viewers, both in theaters and on DVD. Very few of us ever have an opportunity to reach out to such a large audience on a topic of global importance. Still, we are often called upon to present our ideas at school, at work, and in our communities. If we can present them clearly and compellingly, using multiple media when they will help us reach listeners, we, too, can effect change.

11a Identifying Your Purpose, Audience, Context, and Genre

As with any writing project, those who are making a presentation begin by considering their *purpose*. In an academic or business context, the primary purpose is likely to be the same as for a written text: to present information or to persuade others to accept your position or to take action. Even more so than a written text, an oral presentation is likely also to have a secondary purpose: to engage the imagination or emotions of the audience so that members can more readily identify with and remember the key points.

More about ▶▶▶
Purpose, 11–13
Audience, 14–17
Context and genre, 18

A second consideration is *audience*. When addressing classmates or colleagues, you will probably have a sense of your audience's needs and expectations. When addressing an unfamiliar group, ask yourself why the group has assembled and what they hope to get out of your presentation. It may be useful to ask the event organizers what kind of audience to expect.

A third consideration is the *context* of the presentation: In how large a space will you be speaking? When addressing a small group in a college classroom, you will probably not need any special equipment. Larger settings may require a projector, a sound system, and special lighting. Consider the space in which you will be speaking and the equipment you will have access to before you design visual aids or practice your presentation. If possible, attend other presentations in the space to get a sense of what will and will not work, and discuss the context with the person who invited you to speak.

Finally, consider the *genre* of your presentation. As a college student, you are most likely to be asked to do the following:

- Contribute to or lead a class discussion
- Give a presentation in class
- Give a presentation to a student or social service organization
- Give a presentation online

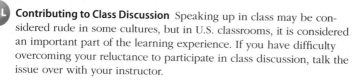 **ESL** **Contributing to Class Discussion** Speaking up in class may be considered rude in some cultures, but in U.S. classrooms, it is considered an important part of the learning experience. If you have difficulty overcoming your reluctance to participate in class discussion, talk the issue over with your instructor.

11b Devising a Topic and Thesis

More about ▶▶▶
Devising a topic, 22
Narrowing, expand-
ing a topic, 29–30
Devising a thesis,
34–35

A presentation, like a written text, begins with an appropriate topic and a well-focused thesis (or main idea). Choose a topic and an approach that will engage you and your audience and to which you can bring special insight. Craft a thesis that conveys your purpose and that will engage your audience.

11c Organizing the Presentation

People have more trouble understanding and retaining ideas presented orally than they do ideas presented in writing, so your talk must be carefully organized to help your audience hold your main points in memory while the presentation unfolds.

1. Introduction

More about ▶▶▶
Introductions, 70–72

Use your introduction (10–15 percent of your presentation) to develop a rapport with your audience and to establish the key points of your presentation. Your introduction should accomplish the following:

- Specify your topic and approach, and convey the topic's importance.

- Engage your audience: A compelling anecdote, startling statistics, or an apt quotation are all good opening gambits.

- Establish your credentials: Knowledge, experience, or the research you have conducted all give you special expertise.

- Provide a brief overview of your main points so that the audience will know in advance what they should be listening for.

2. Body

More about ▶▶▶
Organizing, 37–42,
54–58, 285–87
Explaining and
supporting ideas,
46–48, 66–70,
289–90
Using visuals as
evidence, 81–85
Finding information,
222–47 (ch. 13)

The body (75–85 percent of your presentation) should explain the points that you previewed in your introduction. It should be clearly and logically organized, so listeners know where you are going and where you have been. Ideally, you should present only three to five main supporting points, regardless of the length of your presentation. The audience might have trouble keeping track of any more.

For each claim you make, supply appropriate, relevant evidence, such as specific examples drawn from your reading or your experience. Facts and statistics can be very effective as long as you do not burden your audience with more numbers than they can process. (Presenting statistics in information graphics can help.) Engaging anecdotes or stories that use concrete, descriptive language, on the other hand, are more easily remembered.

Because listeners cannot turn back to the beginning of your speech to refresh their memories, it is crucial that the body of your presentation include signposts. Transitions such as "first," "second," and "third" are useful; so is a brief summary of the main points you made earlier ("As I explained a few minutes ago . . .") and a preview of the points you are about to discuss ("Next I will show how . . .").

More about ▶▶▶
Transitions, 61–62

3. Conclusion

Keep your conclusion brief (5–10 percent of your presentation). The conclusion should reinforce the main point of the presentation by repeating the main idea and key supporting points, by highlighting your main point with a brief but powerful statement or quotation, or by returning to the anecdote, example, or statistics you opened with.

More about ▶▶▶
Conclusions, 72–74

11d Preparing and Rehearsing the Presentation

For an oral presentation, the following methods of delivery are common:

- **Speaking off the cuff.** If you are an expert on a topic about which your audience knows little, you may be able to speak engagingly and informatively with little special preparation.

- **Reading a written presentation aloud.** If your material is highly technical or if you are anxious about speaking, reading your presentation may work. However, you will lose eye contact with the audience and risk losing their attention.

- **Speaking from your notes.** Speaking from notes will keep you organized and prevent you from forgetting important points while allowing you to make eye contact with the audience.

When making a presentation in class, check with your instructor about which method of presentation you should use. In most cases, speaking from your notes will work best.

1. Prepare a speaking outline.

To create a speaking outline, add brief notes to a topic outline about where to pause, when to increase the urgency in your voice, and when to advance to the next slide or visual aid. Add content notes too,

More about ▶▶▶
Topic outlines,
40–42, 286–87

but keep them brief, including only as much information as you need to remind yourself of the point you want to make. Be sure to print your speaking outline in a font that will be legible from arm's length, and leave ample space between lines so that you can find your place quickly.

2. Use language effectively.

Well-chosen language can help listeners understand and remember your main points. As you draft and rehearse your presentation, do the following:

> *More about* ▶▶▶
> Abstract vs. concrete
>   language, 576–77
> Eliminating wordi-
>   ness, 517–19
> Figures of speech,
>   577–78
> Parallelism, 539–48
>   (ch. 27)
> Repetition (inten-
>   tional), 559

- Use clear, familiar language.

- Choose concrete words. When abstract words are needed, support them with concrete examples.

- Eliminate wordiness.

- Keep sentences relatively short.

- Include vivid figures of speech, such as metaphors and similes, that link an unfamiliar notion to a familiar or striking one.

- Use parallelism and repetition to emphasize your main points.

3. Create visual, audio, and multimedia aids.

> *More about* ▶▶▶
> Using visuals as sup-
>   port, 81–85

Visual, audio, and multimedia aids can enhance your presentation by clarifying or providing additional information, by showing what you are describing, and by countering stage fright (directing attention away from you). When using visual or multimedia aids during a presentation, make sure the aids are relevant, that you explain them clearly and succinctly, that you do not provide so many that the audi-

Getting It Across   **Enhance Memory through Visualization**

Cognitive scientist Allan Paivio has suggested that words provide one route into memory, and images provide a second route; he calls this "dual coding." Reinforcing key points visually, by providing graphs, charts, photographs, drawings, or video clips, will ensure that your most important points are encoded in both words and images. You can also encourage listeners to create their own images by incorporating concrete descriptions as support.

ence pays attention to them rather than to you, and that you speak to your audience, not to your visual aids.

Presentation software such as Microsoft *PowerPoint* or Apple *Keynote* usefully projects visual, audio, and multimedia aids. However, overuse of presentation software or poor preparation of slides can overwhelm or distract the audience. (For advice on effective use of presentation software, see the Quick Reference box on p. 206.)

> ❝ In my speech class, I had to give many presentations in which I used photographs, charts, graphs, and maps. I think they helped a lot because none of my classmates seemed bored, and that made me feel more relaxed. ❞
>
> —Leyla Abdul-Mesih,
> Broward Community College

4. Rehearse your presentation.

Practice your presentation out loud in front of a mirror, a group of friends or family, or a video camera. Use at least two or three practice sessions to make sure of the following:

> ▶ **More about ▶▶▶**
> Visual design,
> 176–85 (ch. 9)
> Matching visual to
> information, 81–85

- You are comfortable with the content of your presentation.

- Your presentation is the right length (long enough but not too long).

- Your delivery is polished: You are familiar with the pronunciation of all words and names, you know when to pause or gesture, and you are comfortable making eye contact with the audience (or with yourself in the mirror).

- You deploy and discuss visual aids with grace.

- You have good posture and avoid nervous fidgeting and irritating mannerisms (such as the repetition of "um" or "like").

Quick Reference ➡ Overcoming Presentation Anxiety

- Get a good night's sleep the night before, and eat something an hour or two before the presentation.
- Envision your success: Picture yourself calm and relaxed at the podium; imagine your sense of accomplishment at the end of the presentation.
- Take several slow, deep breaths, or tighten and relax your muscles just before you take the podium.
- Ignore your racing heart or clammy hands. Instead, use the adrenaline surge to add energy to your presentation.
- Focus on your message: Get excited about what you have to say, and you will bring the audience with you.
- Accept the fact that you may stumble, and be prepared to go on.

Reference → Ten Steps to Using Presentation Software Effectively

1. **Review your outline to determine where slides would enhance your presentation.** Do not overwhelm your presentation by creating a slide for every moment.
2. **Begin with a title slide.** This slide should include the title of your presentation, your name, and any other useful identifying information.

3. **Keep text brief, design uniform, and contents varied.** The audience should be listening to you, not reading your slides. To make slides easy to absorb, maintain a consistent design. To enhance interest, vary the other components (images, information graphics, video clips).
4. **Add blank slides.** Go to a blank slide when no illustration is relevant.
5. **Check that slides are visually pleasing.** Keep slides uncluttered and balanced; limit your use of animations (the way text or images enter a slide).
6. **Proofread your slides.** Make sure all text is clear, and correct all misspellings and all mistakes of grammar, punctuation, and mechanics.
7. **Learn your software's commands.** Keystroke commands allow you to advance or return to slides, use the animation effects, and end the slide show.
8. **Practice your presentation with your slides in advance.** Use animations to bring information forward, and do not leave slides up after you have moved on to the next topic.
9. **Check your equipment in advance.** Make sure that cords are long enough, that you can lower the lights and cover windows, and so forth.
10. **Be prepared to give your presentation without your slides.** Murphy's Law—whenever something *can* go wrong, it *will* go wrong—applies to presentation software. If the power fails or your computer dies, you should still be able to go on with the show.

If possible, rehearse in the space where you will be making your presentation to determine how loudly you will have to speak, to test placement of visual aids or screens, and to check your equipment.

 Adjust Your Gestures to Appeal to a U.S. Audience Gestures vary from culture to culture. Pay attention to the gestures commonly made by native English speakers when presenting. How do they differ from gestures you are accustomed to? Are you aware of any gestures you should not use while speaking to a U.S. audience?

11e Delivering the Presentation

When the time comes to make your presentation, approach the podium, wait for your audience to settle down, and then begin:

- **Connect with the audience.** Introduce yourself, thank the audience for attending, and smile.

- **Maintain eye contact with the audience.** As you speak, look out at the audience, turning to the left, the right, and center, so all members of the audience feel included.

- **Control your pacing, volume, and tempo.** Speak slowly and clearly. Pause between sections of your presentation. Vary the tone of your voice. If you sense that you are losing your audience, slow your pace, increase your volume, or step closer to the audience.

connect
mhconnectcomposition.com
Additional resources: QL11001

11f Speaking Responsibly

As you prepare your presentation, keep your responsibilities as a speaker in mind:

- **Adopt a position you endorse.** Adopt a position that you believe in, one which you can offer compelling reasons and strong evidence.

- **Be truthful.** To maintain the trust of your audience, do not omit crucial information, ignore counterevidence, alter quotations unfairly, or misuse statistics. More subtly, avoid words and images that manipulate your audience or that rely on logical fallacies.

More about ▶▶▶
Biased language,
 568–71
Logical fallacies,
 149–53
Patchwriting, 271–74
Signal phrases,
 291–93,
 299–301 (MLA),
 359–60 (APA)
Revising visuals,
 86–89
Contextualizing
 sources, 291–92

Listening
↑ Responsibly   Active Listening

When attending a presentation, be fair to the speaker by listening actively:

- Give the speaker your undivided attention.
- Make an effort to understand the speaker's point of view.
- Set aside prejudices based on the speaker's appearance.
- Listen for the speaker's main points.
- Identify and assess the evidence presented.

- **Respect the time and attention of your audience.** Prepare fully for your presentation.

- **Avoid biased language.** Inclusive language draws listeners into a speech and shows that you have respect for others.

- **Treat sources fairly.** Put borrowed ideas in your own words, acknowledge them with signal phrases such as "Allison Ling's research shows . . ." and bring copies of your references for interested audience members.

- **Consider the group you are addressing.** Your appearance may be taken as an endorsement of the group's beliefs.

Work **Together**

With two to four classmates, listen to a speech posted at a website such as *American Rhetoric* <www.americanrhetoric.com>. As you listen, take notes on the main point of the speech, the organization of the speech, the transitions or other signposts the speaker used, and the speaker's language and delivery. Compare your notes. What did you notice that other group members did not (and vice versa)?

Part Four

Research
Matters

12 Planning a Research Project

To create a compelling work, an artist devises a plan, gathers the right materials, and assembles them to create a unified whole. Without the right materials, the artist cannot create the work, but it takes more than just the right materials; it takes an idea that will unify the materials and that will intrigue or engage the viewer. Similarly, a writer creating a research project must devise a plan for a project that will be of value to its readers and must gather materials that are appropriate to the topic and that readers can rely on. Besides gathering information, the writer must have a vision that will unite the materials into a text that goes beyond the pieces on which it builds to engage and even enlighten the reader. The first stage of the research process—planning—is crucial to its success.

More about ▶▶▶
Purpose, 11–12
Audience, 14–18

12a Analyzing the Assignment's Purpose, Audience, and Method of Development

Most research projects will have one of two purposes:

- **To inform:** to explain an issue, compare proposed solutions, or review the research on a specific topic
- **To persuade:** to argue for a claim

You can usually figure out the purpose of the assignment by looking closely at the words it uses:

If the assignment asks you to . . .	your purpose is likely to be . . .
describe, compare, discuss, review, analyze	informative (expository)
assess, evaluate, argue	persuasive

connect
mhconnectcomposition.com
Additional resources: QL12001

Often, college research assignments will specify the method of development to use: comparison-contrast, cause-effect, and so on. One of the most frequently used methods of development is *analysis*—the writer divides the issue, proposal, or event into its component parts; explains how the parts work together; and discusses the implications.

As a writer, you have a responsibility to shape your project with the needs and expectations of your audience in mind, so consider who that audience will be. For most college assignments, your audience will include your instructor and perhaps your fellow students, but your instructor may also expect you to write with a wider audience in mind.

Then consider what your audience will find interesting or important. Every reader wants to be engaged by a text, but each also has particular aims in reading. Your instructor, for example, may want to see not only that you understand the material covered in class, but also that you can interpret it, analyze it, synthesize ideas from multiple sources, and think creatively and critically about the material.

Finally, consider what sorts of evidence your audience will find persuasive. Idea-generating techniques such as brainstorming and clustering can help you devise both a list of topics (if your assignment requires you to generate your own topic) and the evidence you will use to support it.

More about ▶ ▶ ▶
Arguing for a claim, 153–56
Methods of development, 64–68
Interpretation, analysis, synthesis, and critique, 69, 129–35, 279–80, 289–90
Generating ideas, 22–29

> **EXERCISE 12.1 Writing with your audience in mind**
> For each of the assignments listed on the next page, determine whether the purpose is informative or persuasive. Then choose one assignment and write a paragraph about how you would approach it if you were writing for an academic audience, for the readers of your college newspaper, or for a website appealing to readers already interested in the topic.

connect
mhconnectcomposition.com
Online exercise: QL12101

1. Analyze the effect that monitoring internet searches at the library would have on patrons.
2. Argue for or against the monitoring of internet searches at libraries.
3. Evaluate the treatment options for gambling addictions—which option is most effective, and why?
4. Describe the symptoms of a gambling addiction.
5. Explain how genetic engineering is currently used to diagnose and control disease in humans.
6. Argue for or against the use of genetic engineering to control disease in humans.
7. Compare the results of homeschooling and traditional classroom education on academic success in college.
8. Evaluate the effects of homeschooling on children.
9. Define "reality television."
10. Argue for or against this statement: The nightly news is reality television.

12b Setting a Schedule

More about ▶▶▶
Setting a realistic
schedule, 20–21

Begin your research project by asking the following questions:

- When is the project due?
- How long is the project to be?
- What type of research is required?

Reference → **Questions to Ask When Planning a Research Project**

- Have you analyzed the assignment, taking its scope and purpose into consideration?
- Have you set a realistic schedule that takes your other work and activities into account?
- Have you analyzed your audience to determine what your reader will expect from you?
- Have you chosen a topic that is appropriate to your assignment and your audience?
- Have you narrowed your topic to one that can be fully explored, given the length of the assignment and the amount of time you can devote to it?

- Have you framed research questions and developed a hypothesis that will structure and focus your research project?
- Have you considered the number and type of sources that you will need to answer your research questions fully and accurately?
- Have you created a working bibliography to keep track of the information you will need for documenting your sources later?
- Have you annotated your working bibliography so that you can remember what these sources cover and how you expect to use them?

- What types of sources are required—scholarly books and articles only or a mix of scholarly and popular sources?
- How will the project be evaluated?

Check with your instructor if you do not know the answer to these questions.

→ **Tech**

Using an Assignment Calculator

To set a realistic schedule, try using an online assignment calculator like the one offered by the University of Minnesota Libraries <http://www.lib.umn.edu/help/calculator>. This tool breaks the writing process down into steps and suggests a date by which each step should be completed. The first few steps in the process are shown below.

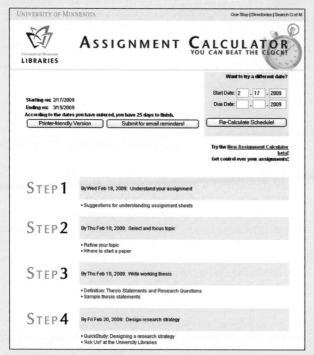

Check your own library's website to see whether a time management calculator is provided, or search for one by typing "assignment calculator" into the search box of a search engine such as *Google* or *Yahoo!*

Make It **Your Own**

For a research project you have been assigned, answer the questions in the Quick Reference box on p. 212, and then set up a schedule for each stage of your research project. Be sure to leave time for other assignments and for unexpected delays.

12c Choosing and Narrowing a Research Topic

More about ▶▶▶
Generating ideas,
22–29
Narrowing a topic,
29–30

Idea-generating techniques, such as freewriting and brainstorming, can help you devise a topic that will be of interest to your readers. These techniques can also help you narrow your topic so that you can write about it in insightful ways, given the time you have and the length of the assignment. Conducting preliminary research or reviewing class notes and reading may also help you decide on or narrow a topic.

Make It **Your Own**

Use two or more of the idea-generating techniques in chapter 2, pp. 10–32, to devise and narrow a research topic for this or another class.

▶▶▶Sample student
research essays:
"Holy Under-
ground Comics,
Batman!" Lydia
Nichols, 346–57
"The Power of
Wardrobe,"
Heather
DeGroot,
389–400

12d Drafting Research Questions and Hypotheses

Research is easiest if you know what you are looking for. After you have tentatively chosen a topic but before you begin searching for sources, list a number of questions about your topic that research might answer. These are your *research questions.* Next, write the answers you expect to find. These answers are the *hypotheses* that your research will test. Below are research questions and hypotheses for Lydia Nichols's paper on underground comics and for Heather De-Groot's paper on the effects of wardrobe on social influence.

> For class, we read Barbara Ehrenreich's *Nickel and Dimed.* I was interested in the section on Wal-Mart, so I did some preliminary research on that company and learned about the meetings where employees have to sing the company song. I was worried that focusing on Wal-Mart would be too narrow, so I focused on techniques to instill loyalty in the workplace—do they work? are they ethical?

Dave Marsteller, Syracuse University

Research question: What are the characteristics that distinguish underground comics from mainstream comics?

Hypothesis: Unlike mainstream comics, underground comics focus on topics that challenge social mores, have an author or author team that has creative control, and appeal to an adult readership.

Research question: Does the clothing a man wears influence the behavior of other men?

Hypothesis: The clothing a man wears will influence the behavior of other men when he is in a position of authority relative to the rest of the group.

As you conduct your research, you will continually revise your research questions and hypotheses; the more you learn, the more you know about what questions can be answered and what hypotheses are most plausible. You will also reduce the number of questions you are asking. Your finished project will probably answer only one of the questions you generated at the beginning of the process, and your *thesis* will probably come directly from the hypothesis that you generated to answer that question.

More about ▶▶▶
Devising a thesis, 33–35
Revising a thesis, 35–37

> **EXERCISE 12.2 Devising research questions and hypotheses**
Devise a research question for one of the assignments you analyzed in Exercise 12.1 (pp. 211–12). Then answer it to create a research hypothesis. (You may need to use the idea-generating techniques discussed in chapter 2.) If your research question cannot be readily answered through research, divide it into several more specific questions that can be.

connect
mhconnectcomposition.com
Online exercise: QL12102

Make It **Your Own**

Create three to five questions that could guide your research on the topic you devised and narrowed in the second Make It Your Own exercise on p. 214. Remember that your questions must be answerable through research. If they are too broad, divide them into more specific questions. Then turn one of your questions into a hypothesis.

Writing
↑ Responsibly   **Using Printed Sources**

With so much information available online, you might be fooled into thinking that you no longer need to consult printed materials. But many classic and scholarly books are not (yet) available digitally, and your library may not subscribe to the electronic versions of important newspapers, magazines, and scholarly journals. Dedicate yourself to finding the best information available, whether you access it through a search engine like *Google,* through an online database like *Academic Search Premier* or *Web of Science,* or through trips to your library's stacks.

12e   **Choosing Research Sources Strategically**

More about ▶▶▶
Reliability, 250–59
Scholarly vs. popular sources, 250–52
Counterevidence, 163–67
Finding online sources, 223–27
Finding articles in journals, magazines, and newspapers, 228–33
Finding specialized reference sources, 235–36
Finding books, 238–41
Finding government documents, 241–42
Finding multimedia sources, 242–43
Field research: interviews, observational studies, surveys, 244–47

The sources you use in your research project are an important factor in how well you fulfill your responsibilities to your reader, your topic, and yourself. When choosing sources, ask yourself these questions:

- Have you visited your library or your library's website to see what kinds of resources are available there (and not just through *Google*)?

- Have you chosen sources that are authoritative?

- Are your sources either up-to-date or classics that established the principles for studying the topic you are researching?

- Have you consulted sources that offer a variety of perspectives on your topic?

- Have you consulted appropriate types of sources: specialized reference works that provide overviews of the topic, scholarly books and articles that offer in-depth analysis, multimedia resources that may contribute tools for your analysis or that provide examples, government reports that provide primary data, interviews that provide expert opinion?

- When relevant, have you conducted experiments, observations, surveys, or interviews to develop information of your own?

- Have you consulted enough sources to develop a broad understanding of your topic?

- Have you consulted the best sources, even if they are not available online?

You may need help to determine whether a source is up-to-date or reliable or to locate sources online or in your library's print collection. When you do, consult a research expert—a reference librarian.

Work **Together**

Skim Lydia Nichols's "Holy Underground Comics, Batman!" (pp. 346–57) or Heather DeGroot's "The Power of Wardrobe: Male Stereotype Influences" (pp. 389–400). Then evaluate the writer's choice of sources. What types of sources were consulted? How authoritative are they? Would you suggest any strategic changes in source choices? Why or why not?

Make It **Your Own**

For the research hypothesis you devised in the Make It Your Own exercise on p. 215, make a list of sources that would allow you to uncover useful information. Write a paragraph about these sources, answering the questions on p. 216.

12f Establishing a Research Log

A **research log** is a journal in which you record research questions and hypotheses; your working thesis; your search terms; information from sources; your interpretation, analysis, synthesis, and critique of sources; and your ideas for where to go next.

1. Set up the research log.

A research log can be compiled in any of the following media:

- Index cards
- A notebook
- A computer file
- A PDA or smartphone

Before you set up your research log, consider the advantages and disadvantages of each medium: Index cards are easy to arrange in outline order or to "storyboard" when it comes time to write your paper. Notebooks are easy to carry around and more difficult to lose than

More about ▶▶▶
Keeping an idea journal or commonplace book, 22–24
Keeping a reading journal, 127–28
Annotating, 124–27
Making notes, 267–80
Avoiding "patchwriting," 271–74
Research questions and hypotheses, 214–15
Search terms (keywords), 223
Interpretation, analysis, synthesis, and critique, 129–35, 279–80, 288–90

Tech

Back Up Your Electronic Research Log

Do not be a victim of a computer crash: If you keep your research log in electronic form, be sure to back up your files after every session, and store the backup files in a separate place—on a thumb drive, for example. If you cannot save your files to a second device, print out the new material after each session or email the files to yourself.

note cards. Keeping notes on index cards or in a notebook forces you to interact with your sources, rather than just cutting and pasting information into a word processing file. Keeping a research log on a computer (especially a laptop) or a PDA or smartphone makes it possible to search your notes electronically, to rearrange them into outline order, and to copy material from your notes directly into your paper. A PDA or smartphone is likely to be with you at all times, and you can sync it with your computer.

2. Components of a research log

Divide your research log into sections for different categories of notes:

- The research assignment
- Purpose statement and audience profile
- Your research schedule
- A list of possible research questions
- Your working hypothesis
- Notes taken while reading sources
- Your own ideas
- Your working bibliography

Make It **Your Own**

Using the information you have generated in the other Make It Your Own exercises in this chapter (pp. 214, 215, 217), establish a research log.

Writing Responsibly   Avoiding Plagiarism at the Start

The ease with which you can cut and paste material from sources into a digital file makes it easy to fall into unintentional plagiarism. If you are maintaining an electronic research log, it is especially important to mark clearly what you have copied directly from a source and what you have paraphrased, summarized, or commented upon. Consider supplementing your electronic research log with a folder for printouts and photocopies, and check your text against it.

More about ▶▶▶
Taking notes to
  avoid plagiarism,
  267–68
Patchwriting, 271–74

12g   Building a Working Bibliography

After you have determined the types of sources you might need, you are ready to begin your search. While searching for sources, experienced researchers compile a ***working bibliography,*** a list of sources they may want to consult, instead of identifying and retrieving sources one by one.

1. Components of a working bibliography

A working bibliography should include information you will need to find the source and to document it. Include the following:

- The full name (if available) of the author(s) and editor(s); for a work of art, a film, a sound recording, or a website, the name of the artist, director, performer, conductor, or site sponsor

- Title and subtitle of a book or article

- Publication data, such as the name and location of the publisher for books; the title of the periodical, the volume and issue number, publication date, and the page numbers for articles in periodicals

More about ▶▶▶
Publication infor-
  mation, foldout
  following p. 297
Digital object identi-
  fiers (DOI), 370–71,
  376–77, 381,
  411–12

- Access information: for books—the call number; for online sources or sources accessed through an online database— the date you last accessed the source, the URL for the article (if freely available) or the URL for the database's home page (if available only to subscribers), and the DOI (digital object identifier) if there is one; for all sources—the medium (print, Web, DVD)

→ **Tech**

Citation Management Software

Citation management software such as *EndNote* and *RefWorks* can format the entries in your bibliography no matter what documentation style you choose. Your library may make such software available to you for free.

2. Annotate the working bibliography.

An annotated entry in a working bibliography includes not only the information you will need to document and locate the source, but also a brief note that will remind you of what the source is about and how you might use it in your project. Annotating sources will save you time later when you return to sources that looked promising or when you decide to do more research on the topic.

▶▶▶Sample student research essay, "Holy Underground Comics, Batman!" Lydia Nichols, 346–57

Below is a sample entry from a working bibliography for Lydia Nichols's research paper:

Author names	Fenty, Sean, Trena Houp, and Laurie Taylor. "Webcomics: The Influence and Continuation of the Comix Revolution." *ImageTexT* 1.2 (2004): 22 pars. Web. 18 March 2007	Article title / Medium
Publication info: –Title of journal –Volume, number, year of publication –Number of paragraphs (no page numbers)	An article in a peer-reviewed online journal. Good history of Underground Comics movement; definitions. Covers importance of comics on the internet. Compares & contrasts Underground Comics and webcomics. Mentions *The Comics Journal*—check that out.	Date accessed

↑ Make It **Your Own**

More about ▶▶▶
Finding information, 222–47 (ch. 13)
Scholarly vs. popular sources, 250–52

For the research project that you have been working on through the Make It Your Own assignments in this chapter, create a working bibliography of at least ten sources. Choose a mix of source types, including at least three books, three scholarly articles, and one or more newspaper or magazine articles, reference works, websites, pamphlets, government publications, or visual, multimedia, or audio source. Then locate and annotate the five most promising sources, recording complete publication information and taking preliminary notes on what the source covers and how it might be useful to your research project.

13 Finding Information

More about ▶▶▶
Reliability, 250–59
Scholarly vs. popular sources, 250–52

Researchers today are cursed with a wonderful gift—the internet. A simple search on *Google* or *Yahoo!* can provide ready access to a mountain of information—some excellent, much unreliable—but this mountain can collapse in an avalanche, becoming a roadblock to effective research. The inexperienced researcher, relying exclusively on popular online resources that do not require registration or payment for access, will miss out on valuable information available in scholarly sources that are accessible only to subscribers. Experienced researchers dodge the information avalanche by using advanced techniques that produce a manageable number of relevant and reliable web pages. They hold back the information onslaught by using scholarly resources—print, electronic, and multimedia—from their college library and by drawing on the knowledge of information experts—reference librarians—who help them identify useful resources.

Finding Information on the Web

connect

mhconnectcomposition.com
Additional resources: QL13001

Engines like *Google* and *Yahoo!* search billions of web pages for whatever words the user enters and then return links in order of relevance, as determined by the search engine's criteria. (*Google,* for example, ranks its results based on the number of other pages that link to a site, as well as advertising.) The results retrieved can differ based on the criteria the search engine uses to rank relevance, as well as on the web pages it indexes. For that reason, running a search on multiple engines is a good idea. A list of alternative search engines appears in the Quick Reference box below.

Before using a search engine for the first time, read about how it works. Look for links (often at the bottom of the page) called "About" or "Help" to find answers to frequently asked questions (FAQs) or for advice about how best to conduct a search on that site. Look, too, for advanced search options; these will help you focus your search.

1. Use keywords.

The most common way to begin a web search is with a simple keyword search. A search on *Google* using the term "underground comics"—the topic of Lydia Nichols's paper at the end of chapter 17—yielded more than 2 million "hits" (see Figure 13.1, p. 224).

This kind of searching is very easy, and it yields plenty of results—too many. No one could look at all 2 million results, and most are not relevant, anyway. To narrow the results to a more manageable number, and to focus more closely on sites that will be relevant to your research, you can group terms using quotation marks or use a combination of terms. A search on "underground comics" and "history," for example, reduced the number of hits from 2 million to 34,300—still too many but a definite improvement.

More about ▶▶▶
Relevance, 249

Quick Reference ➡ **Search Engines**

Alta Vista <www.altavista.com>	*Ask* <www.ask.com>
Dmoz <dmoz.org>	*Gigablast* <www.gigablast.com>
Google <www.google.com>	*HotBot* <www.hotbot.com>
Lycos <www.lycos.com>	*Yahoo!* <www.yahoo.com>

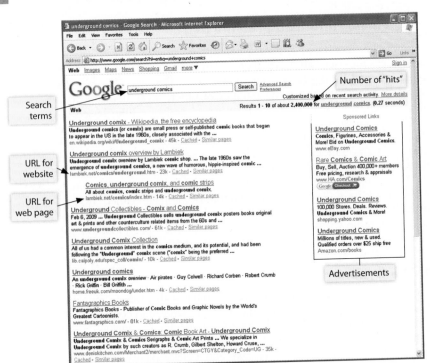

FIGURE 13.1 A simple keyword search on *Google*

2. Use advanced search options.

You can narrow search results further with advanced search options (Figure 13.2), which can limit results by language, file type (*Word,* rich text, PDF, or *Excel*), domain (.org, .gov, .edu, or .com), and other options. Limiting the search on "'underground comics' history" to sites with the domain .edu, for example, reduced the number of hits to 1,420.

3. Use metasearch engines.

Because search engines index different web pages and use different methods to rank sites, using more than one engine increases your odds of finding useful resources. To search multiple sites simultaneously, use ***metasearch engines,*** which return the top search results

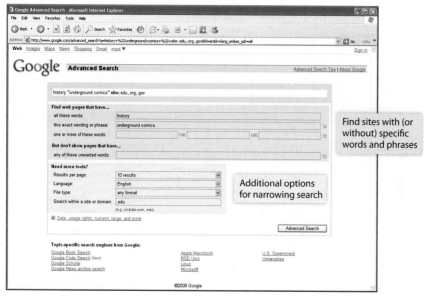

FIGURE 13.2 An advanced search on *Google*

from several search engines at once, with duplicate entries deleted. (A list of metasearch engines appears in the Quick Reference below.) Searching on the terms "underground comics" and "history" on *Dogpile,* for example, produced a manageable thirty hits.

4. Use subject directories.

Subject directories list websites by topic. Their organization—from general to specific—can provide an effective overview of a topic and

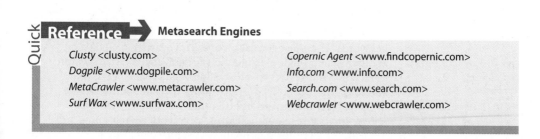

Quick **Reference** → **Metasearch Engines**

Clusty <clusty.com>
Dogpile <www.dogpile.com>
MetaCrawler <www.metacrawler.com>
Surf Wax <www.surfwax.com>

Copernic Agent <www.findcopernic.com>
Info.com <www.info.com>
Search.com <www.search.com>
Webcrawler <www.webcrawler.com>

Quick Reference → **Subject Directories**

- Academic Info <www.academicinfo.net/subject-guides>
- BUBL LINK <bubl.ac.uk/link>
- INFOMINE <infomine.ucr.edu>
- Internet Public Library <www.ipl.org>
- Librarians' Index to the Internet <www.lii.org>

More about ▶▶▶
Devising a topic,
22–29, 214
Narrowing or broad-
ening a topic,
29–30

can help you discover, narrow, or expand your topic. The Quick Reference box above lists some useful subject directories; your library may
also make subject guides available. Check your library's website or
consult a reference librarian.

NOTE Most subject directories today emphasize keyword searching
but still list websites by category.

connect
mhconnectcomposition.com
Online exercise: QL13101

→ EXERCISE 13.1 Conducting a keyword search
Using the topic you selected for Exercise 12.1 (pp. 211–12), generate three or more keywords and use them to conduct keyword
searches on two of the search engines listed in the Quick Reference box on p. 223. Write a paragraph comparing your results: Did
each search engine generate the same number of results? How do
the top ten results differ? What about the next ten?

connect
mhconnectcomposition.com
Online exercise: QL13102

→ EXERCISE 13.2 Conducting a search with a subject directory
Using the keywords you generated for Exercise 13.1, conduct a
search using one of the subject directories listed in the Quick Reference box above. Write a paragraph comparing the results from
the subject directory with those you generated in Exercise 13.1.

▲ Make It Your Own

For a research project you are developing, create a list of
keywords. Use these terms to conduct a search on *Google* or
another search engine, using the site's advanced search feature
to narrow your results to sites within the domains .edu, .gov,
and .org. Then conduct a search using the same terms in one
of the subject directories listed in the Quick Reference box
above. In your research notebook, note your search terms and
the URLs of websites that might be useful.

13b Finding Other Electronic Sources: Interactive Media

In addition to conventional websites, a variety of other electronic sources, including blogs, discussion lists, and groups on social networking sites like *Facebook,* can offer you insight into your topic. Such sources are often contributed to by experts, so they have become an important source for up-to-the-minute news.

Of course, not all blogs, discussion lists, and groups are equally authoritative. Evaluate the reliability of such sites by finding out the qualifications of the writers, and verify the information you glean from such sources by consulting additional sources.

To find a blog or discussion list on your topic, use a specialized search engine. (Some are listed in the Quick Reference box below.) You can also enter your keyword with the word *blog, listserv, newsgroup,* or *chat room* in a search engine.

News alerts and RSS feeds collect news stories on topics you specify. Registering for news alerts at sites such as *Google* <www.google.com/newsalerts> will bring daily updates on your chosen topics to your email box. As of this writing, to read RSS feeds you must first download a news reader to your computer or create a personal web page at a site like *Yahoo!* or *AOL;* then you can register at sites to have stories "clipped" and saved for you.

Sites for sharing information, whether in print or other media, are being born and expiring (or at least fading in popularity) almost every day; as this book goes to press, *YouTube, Twitter, Flickr,* and *del.icio.us* are widely used for sharing information and media files on topics of common interest, but new possibilities constantly arise.

> **More about ▶▶▶**
> Documenting a blog,
> 330 (MLA),
> 382 (APA),
> 416 (*Chicago*),
> 442 (CSE)
> Documenting a
> discussion list,
> 329 (MLA),
> 381 (APA),
> 416 (*Chicago*),
> 442 (CSE)
> Reliability, 250–59
> "Netiquette," 503

connect
mhconnectcomposition.com
Additional resources: QL13002, QL13003, QL13004, QL13005

> **EXERCISE 13.3** Researching electronic sources
> Find a blog or discussion group on the topic you explored in Exercises 13.1 and 13.2. Who are the contributors to this site? Conduct a web search to learn about contributors.

connect
mhconnectcomposition.com
Online exercise: QL13103

Quick Reference ➜ Blog Search Engines

Blog Search Engines	**Discussion List Search Engines**
Blogarama <www.blogarama.com>	*CataList* <www.lsoft.com/lists/listref.html>
Blogdigger <www.blogdigger.com>	*Google Groups* <groups.google.com>
Google Blog Search <blogsearch.google.com>	*Yahoo! Groups* <groups.yahoo.com>
Technorati <www.technorati.com>	

13c Finding Articles in Journals and Other Periodicals Using Databases and Indexes

A *periodical* is a publication, like a magazine, newspaper, or scholarly journal, that is issued at regular intervals—daily, weekly, monthly, quarterly. A search engine such as *Google* or *Ask* can point you to articles published online in magazines, newspapers, and some journals, but many articles in academic journals are not available for free on the Web, and many magazines and newspapers require subscriptions before you can access their content. For a comprehensive listing of articles published in periodicals, turn to the databases available through your college library's website. (You may be prompted to sign in.)

Library databases are organized so that you can search for articles by author, title, subject, date, and other fields. Some databases provide only an *abstract,* or summary, but many provide the complete text, either in a *PDF* file, which shows the article more or less as it would have appeared in print, or in an *HTML* file, which provides the text but not the formatting or illustrations that would have appeared in the printed text.

1. Choose an appropriate database.

❯ **More about** ▶▶▶
Writing situation,
10–18

Most college libraries provide a wide variety of databases. Most will offer an all-purpose database like *ProQuest Central, Academic Search Premier,* or *Academic OneFile* that indexes both popular magazines and scholarly journals, as well as discipline-specific databases, such as *Education FullText, PsycINFO,* and *Science Direct.* They may also offer *LexisNexis Academic,* which indexes news reports from around the world. A reference librarian can help you learn which databases available at your library will best suit your research needs.

When searching for articles, be sure to consider the types of sources that are most appropriate to your topic and writing situation. In particular, consider whether you should use popular sources, scholarly sources, or a combination of the two.

❯ ▶▶▶Sample student
research papers:
 "The Power of
 Wardrobe,"
 Heather De-
 Groot, 389–400
 "Holy Under-
 ground Comics,
 Batman!" Lydia
 Nichols, 346–57

For Heather DeGroot, writing for her psychology class, *PsycINFO* (a database that indexes articles from psychology journals) was a good starting place for her periodicals search. For Lydia Nichols, researching the characteristics of underground comics, a general database (such as *ProQuest Central* or *Academic Search Premier*), which indexes both popular and scholarly sources, was a good place to start.

→ Tech

Using *Google Scholar*

Google Scholar <scholar.google.com> allows users to search the Web for scholarly materials—articles in academic journals, theses, books, and abstracts.

More about ▶▶▶
Evaluating sources,
248–62 (ch. 14)

Pros:

- *Google Scholar* can help you locate material that you would otherwise need both your library's catalog and subscription databases to find.
- It may even link to your own library's digital holdings (see the preferences settings in *Google Scholar*).
- It indicates how many online sites have cited the source and provides links to those citations.

Cons:

- *Google* does not define "scholarly," so some hits may be to works your instructor may not consider authoritative.
- You may be shifted to sites where you will be asked to pay for full-text versions of the source. (Always check your library's holdings or try interlibrary loan—a system for borrowing from another library—before paying for access.)
- Because of *Google's* search and ranking methods, the most recent sources may not be included, or they may appear at the end of the list. (You can include a date range in Advanced Scholar Search.)
- Bibliographic data cannot be imported to citation management software such as *EndNote, RefWorks,* or *Bibliomaker.*

2. Search the database.

Searching a database is much like using a search engine such as *Google* or *Yahoo!* You type in a search term and hit Return to generate a list of articles that include your keywords. Unlike a search engine, however, the database limits its search to selected publications, so the items returned are more likely to be reliable.

To make sure the results of a database search are relevant, narrow your search by combining search terms and using the Advanced Search options the database makes available. Typing "comic books" in the search box of a database like *Academic Search Premier* generates a list of over 17,000 items—fewer than with a *Google* search but still far too many to be helpful. As with a web search engine, combining

More about ▶▶▶
Relevance, 249

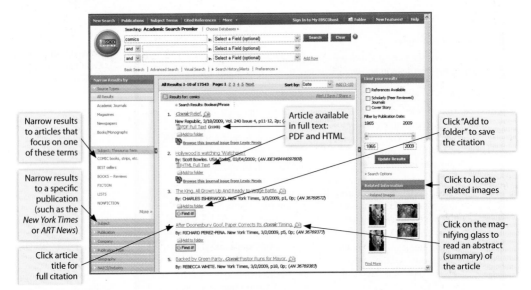

Narrow results to articles that focus on one of these terms

Narrow results to a specific publication (such as the *New York Times* or *ART News*)

Click article title for full citation

Article available in full text: PDF and HTML

Click "Add to folder" to save the citation

Click to locate related images

Click on the magnifying glass to read an abstract (summary) of the article

FIGURE 13.3 Search results for "underground comics AND genre"

terms ("comic books AND underground") narrows the search. The search could be narrowed further by using the database's search options. The menu bars on left and right in Figure 13.3 show some of the options for narrowing a search.

NOTE Databases differ from vendor to vendor and are updated frequently, so check the Help screens or ask a librarian for advice.

If narrowing your search by combining terms and using the database's narrowing options is not getting you the results you need, try the following:

- Conduct your search again with alternative or refined search terms. Check your database's subject or topics list (sometimes called *Thesaurus*) for the terms with which your topic was indexed and use those terms in your search.

- Narrow (or expand) your search using Boolean logic. (See the Quick Reference box on the next page.)

- Return to the library's database menu to run your search on other databases.

Reference ➡ Conducting a Boolean Search

Most databases (and search engines like *Yahoo!*) narrow a search with Boolean logic, which relies on the words AND, NOT, and OR to expand or narrow a search and parentheses or quotation marks to group words. Most databases also use wildcard characters (* or ?) to stand in place of letters, allowing you to search for different forms of a word at the same time. Check Help screens or consult a reference librarian to learn how to use Boolean logic in searching your library's databases.

AND   Comics AND history

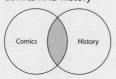

Narrows a search by retrieving items that include *both* terms.

OR   Comics OR history

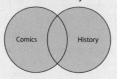

Expands a search by retrieving items that include *either* term.

NOT   Comics NOT history

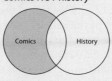

Narrows a search by retrieving items that include one term but not the other.

" "   *"graphic novel"*

Quotation marks group terms to retrieve pages with these words in this order.

( )   (*comics* OR *comix*) AND (*underground*)

Parentheses group terms so complex alternatives can be retrieved.

* / ?   *comi** (or *comi?*) to search for *comic, comics,* and *comix* simultaneously

Wildcard characters allow you to search for more than one version of a word at the same time by replacing the letters that are different in each word with an asterisk (*) or question mark (?).

→ Tech

HTML versus PDF

Articles accessed through a database are often available in both HTML and PDF versions. The HTML version will download much more quickly, but the PDF version may be a duplicate of the article as it appears in the publication, including illustrations and page numbers, which you can then include in your reference list or list of works cited.

> More about ►►►
Working bibliography, 219–20

As you find promising sources, create entries for them in your working bibliography, or follow directions on the database for emailing entries to yourself.

Just as metasearch engines allow you to send your keyword search out to several search engines simultaneously, some database vendors allow you to search simultaneously through all their databases. Increasingly, libraries are also offering "federated searching," which allows you to search across many databases simultaneously. Check your library's website to see what multiple-database searching options are available to you.

3. Find copies of articles.

Once you have generated a list of articles from your database search, you are ready to retrieve copies of the articles. Some articles you can access directly from the database search page (the first article from the search screen in Figure 13.3 is available online), and you can then print them, download them to your hard drive, or email them to yourself.

For some articles, however, only an abstract will be available through the database; in a few cases, only a bibliographic citation may be available. While it may be tempting to skip articles that you cannot have delivered instantly to your desktop, you may miss out on important sources of information, especially classics published before the internet revolution. To find articles you cannot link to from the database, follow these steps:

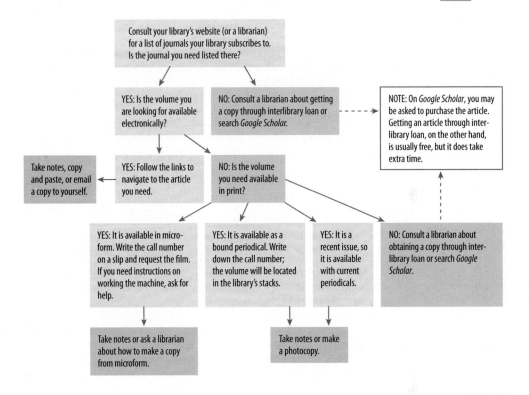

→ **EXERCISE 13.4** **Conducting a database search**
Using one or more keywords that you generated in Exercise 13.1 (p. 226), conduct a search using a general database such as *Pro-Quest Central* or *Academic Search Premier*. Now conduct the same search using an appropriate subject-specific database. (Ask your instructor or a librarian for help in determining which databases might be appropriate.) Compare the results: How many articles were returned on each search? How many of the same articles were listed on the first two pages of results?

connect
mhconnectcomposition.com
Online exercise: QL13104

→ **EXERCISE 13.5** **Locating an article**
For one of the searches you performed in Exercise 13.4, find an article that is not available as a link from the database results page. Then write a paragraph describing the steps you took to find it.

connect
mhconnectcomposition.com
Online exercise: QL13105

13d Finding Reference Works

General reference works such as dictionaries, encyclopedias, biographical sources, bibliographies, almanacs, yearbooks, and atlases can do all of the following:

- Introduce you to your topic and help you determine whether it will sustain your interest

- Provide an overview and background information

- Help you get a sense of subtopics you might want to explore

Subject-specific reference works can be even more helpful. They can:

- Introduce you to the main issues in a debate

- Provide lists of additional sources to explore

- Help you develop your list of keywords by introducing and defining the special terminology used in the discipline

> *More about* ▶▶▶
> Searching a library
> catalog, 238–41

You will find reference works listed in your library's catalog. You may also be able to link to electronic reference sources through your library's home page or databases.

Because both general and subject-specific reference works provide background information to orient you to your topic, they make a useful starting point. For a college-level research project, however, reference works are only the beginning; to fulfill your responsibilities to your topic and audience, you must go beyond these sources to find books, articles, and websites that treat your topic in depth.

1. Dictionaries and encyclopedias

> *More about* ▶▶▶
> Selecting a dictio-
> nary, 584–86
> Using a dictionary,
> 586–88

In addition to whatever online tools they may use, most writers keep a collegiate dictionary at hand to verify spellings, look up definitions, and gather additional brief information about words. An *unabridged* dictionary provides more—more words, more examples of usage, a more complete description of the word's roots in other languages. The most extensive unabridged dictionary is the *Oxford English Dictionary* (or *OED*), a multivolume work providing the entire history of English words and showing the ways in which their meanings have changed over time. Unabridged dictionaries, including the *OED,* may be available in print or online.

Quick

Reference →   **Specialized Dictionaries**

The Bedford Glossary of Critical and Literary Terms
Dictionary of American History
Dictionary of American Literary Characters
Dictionary of Art
Dictionary of 20th-Century World Politics
Public Policy Dictionary

Specialized dictionaries are written for students and scholars in specific academic fields. In addition to defining terms, subject-specific dictionaries may also provide a comprehensive introduction to the topic, as well as a list of further resources. If, for example, you want a deeper understanding of what *absolutism* means to a political scientist, you can turn to a source like the *Blackwell Dictionary of Political Science,* which offers a long paragraph explaining the term, followed by three recommended sources on the topic.

Encyclopedias such as the *Concise Columbia Electronic Encyclopedia* and *Wikipedia* are available for free online. Others, such as *The New Encyclopedia Britannica,* are available in print but may also be accessible through your library's website.

General encyclopedias provide a useful introduction to your topic, and some may offer a list of further resources. Specialized encyclopedias, on the other hand, provide not only an introduction to the topic,

Writing
Responsibly   **Using *Wikipedia***

Wikipedia <en.wikipedia.org> is an online encyclopedia created and revised by users. Because it can be updated constantly by many people, it may be more up-to-date than other encyclopedias, but it may also be more unreliable. Approach *Wikipedia* with care, and verify the information you find there. Remember, too, that while any general encyclopedia may provide a useful overview, it is useful only as an introduction to your topic. It is not an authoritative source for a college-level research project.

More about ▶▶▶
Reliability, 250–59

Quick Reference ➡ **Specialized Encyclopedias**

The Advertising Age Encyclopedia of Advertising
Cambridge Encyclopedia of the English Language
Encyclopedia of African-American Culture and History
Encyclopedia of American Cultural and Intellectual History
Encyclopedia of Bioethics
Encyclopedia of Government and Politics
Encyclopedia of Latin American History and Culture
Encyclopedia of Religion
Garland Encyclopedia of World Music
McGraw-Hill Encyclopedia of Engineering
McGraw-Hill Encyclopedia of Science and Technology
Routledge Encyclopedia of Philosophy
Women's Studies Encyclopedia

but also a sense of how scholars in the field approach the topic. They are also likely to provide a brief list of authoritative sources.

2. Almanacs and yearbooks

Almanacs and yearbooks are annual publications offering facts and statistics, such as when each phase of the moon will occur and annual per capita income of nations. The best-known general-purpose almanac is the *World Almanac and Book of Facts,* which has been published annually since 1923. Subject-specific almanacs and yearbooks, such as the *Almanac of American Politics* and the *Yearbook of Immigration Statistics,* provide a wide body of statistical and tabular data on specific topics. Today, much of the information once most readily found in an almanac or yearbook is now available online at sites such as *CIA Factbook* and the *Research Tools* page at the *Economist* magazine's website.

3. Biographical reference works

Biographical reference sources can provide you with the facts and events of people's lives (both the famous and the fairly obscure), such as their education, their accomplishments, and their current position. They can also help you understand the historical context in which the

Quick Reference → **Almanacs and Yearbooks**

Almanac of American Politics
Americana Annual
Britannica Book of the Year
Congressional Quarterly Almanac Plus
Facts on File Yearbook
Information Please Almanac
Statistical Abstract of the United States
UNESCO Statistical Yearbook

person lived or in which his or her works were produced. Numerous biographical resources are available to researchers; two of the most commonly consulted are the *American National Biography* and the *Dictionary of National Biography* (British).

4. Bibliographies

Bibliographies list sources on a particular topic, providing the information needed to locate the source. They often provide an abstract or brief summary of each source, so you can tell whether it is likely to be relevant to your research.

Quick Reference → **Biographical Reference Sources**

Baker's Biographical Dictionary of Musicians
Biographical Dictionary of American Indian History to 1900
Cambridge Biographical Encyclopedia
Cambridge Dictionary of American Biography
Fifty Major Thinkers on Education
McGraw-Hill Encyclopedia of World Biography
Mexican American Biographies: A Historical Dictionary, 1836–1987
Notable American Women: A Biographical Dictionary
Notable Black American Women
Webster's New Biographical Dictionary

Quick Reference ➡ **Bibliographical Resources**

Bibliographic Guide to Education

Bibliographic Guide to Psychology

Bibliographic Guide to the History of Computing, Computers, and the Information Processing Industry

Film Research: A Critical Bibliography

Information Sources in the Life Sciences

Information Sources of Political Science

International Bibliography of the Social Sciences

MLA International Bibliography of Books and Articles on the Modern Languages and Literatures

Sociology: A Guide to Reference and Information Sources

13e Finding Books Using Library Catalogs

While reference works can give you an overview or direct you to other sources, it is in books that you are most likely to find extensive, in-depth treatments of your topic—especially in the humanities and some social sciences. One or two well-chosen books, supplemented by a selection of journal articles and other sources, can round out your research and deepen your understanding of your topic.

> ❝ Books I've gotten out of the library generally have way more information than websites I've found on the internet. ❞
>
> —Alyssa Laferrera, University of Miami

connect

mhconnectcomposition.com
Additional resources: QL13006, QL13007, QL13008

1. Search the catalog.

Libraries index all their holdings in catalogs, which in most cases you can access through your library's website. Most library catalogs allow users to search for resources by author, title, and subject heading. Some include additional search options such as call number or keyword (see Figure 13.4). Because catalogs differ from library to library, check the Help or Search Tips screen before beginning a search.

Getting It Across   More Than Books in the Library Catalog

Many libraries list not only books but also audiocassettes, CDs, DVDs, manuscripts, maps, musical scores, and slides. Look for a list from which you can select the type of resource you need.

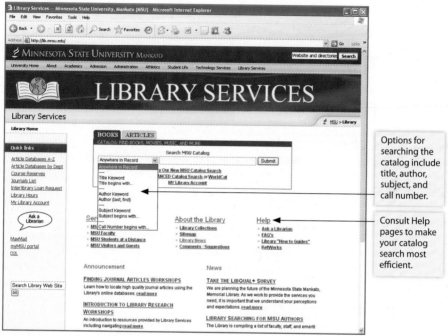

FIGURE 13.4 A library website Students at Minnesota State University, Mankato, and other colleges and universities around the country now search their library's catalog directly from their library's home page.

NOTE Some catalogs may require you to specify the category (such as author or title) in which you wish to search. If you do not, the program may default to a category you are not expecting. For example, if you are looking for books *about* Herman Melville and do not specify that you are searching by subject, your library's program may default to searching for books *by* Melville and provide you with a list of books by him as well as about him.

Search a library's catalog much as you do a search engine or a periodical database: Type a keyword or a combination of words in the search box and hit Enter. Whereas *Google* and other web search engines allow you to use any keyword related to your topic, library catalogs use a preset list of subject headings to index library books. When searching a library's catalog by subject, use these preset headings. To find the subject headings the library has used, go to a catalog

> **More about ▶▶▶**
> Keyword searching,
> 223

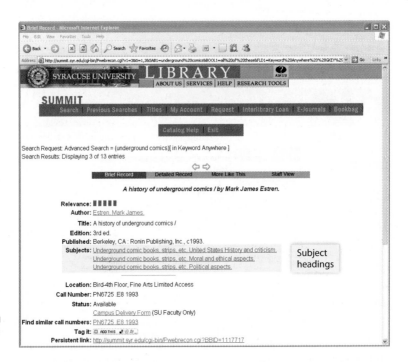

FIGURE 13.5 Finding subject headings in a library record

entry for a book on your topic that you have already identified as relevant. The book's record will list the subject headings used (see Figure 13.5). Clicking on them will bring you to a list of related subject headings and to other books catalogued using the same terms. Repeat the process with other useful books to add subject terms.

2. Browse the stacks or the catalog.

Many researchers enjoy browsing library stacks to find books on their topic: Since books on a topic all share the first part of a call number, they are all shelved close together. If you are free to wander in your library's stacks, you may also benefit from this method.

Another approach that is useful even when library stacks are closed is to browse the online catalog by call number. Once you have identified a book appropriate for your topic, look at its call number. Some library catalogs allow you to click on the call number to see other items that share the first part of the call number; others require

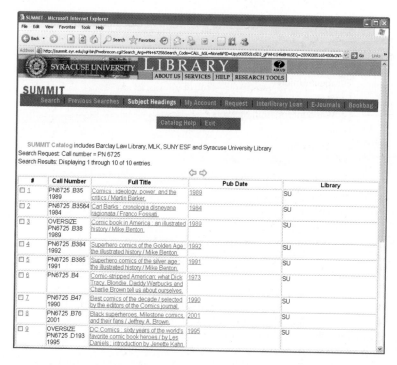

FIGURE 13.6
Browsing by call number

you to conduct a new search by call number. The search screen in Figure 13.6 shows a search for items whose call number begins with PN 6725.

 EXERCISE 13.6 Using the library catalog

Using the keywords you generated in Exercise 13.1 (226), find a book using your library's catalog. Then refine your search using the subject headings and call number.

mhconnectcomposition.com
Online exercise: QL13106

13f Finding Government Publications

Although you will usually rely on books and articles in your college research, government publications can provide you with rich resources, including congressional records, government reports, and legal documents. The federal government makes more than 300,000 documents available online, free of charge, from all three branches

Quick

Reference ➡ **Accessing Government Documents Online**

The websites for the following all provide access to government documents online:

European Union
FedStats
FedWorld Information Network
FirstGov
Library of Congress
National Institutes of Health
Organization for Economic Cooperation and Development
State and Local Government on the Net
United Nations
U.S. Census Bureau
U.S. Government Printing Office

of the government—executive, legislative, and judicial. Most state and local governments also post their documents on the Web, as do many governments around the world. If you are researching a social, legal, or political issue or if you need up-to-date statistics about almost any group, you may find valuable information in government publications. To locate government documents, conduct an advanced web search limited to the domain .gov or search databases such as *CQ Electronic Library* and *LexisNexis Congressional.*

13g Finding Multimedia Sources

Photographs, graphs, charts, and drawings have long been a staple of research papers in disciplines such as art history, film studies, history, geography, geology, political science, sociology, and psychology. With research in all disciplines now being shared through multimedia presentations and websites, the use of multimedia resources has also expanded. To find multimedia resources, start with your library's catalog. Besides the video clips you can find on *YouTube* and *Hulu,* you may also find appropriate multimedia resources online at the sites hosted by the organizations listed in the Quick Reference box on the next page.

Quick

Reference ➡️ **Multimedia Resources**

Academy of American Poets
American Rhetoric: The Power of Oratory in the United States
Library of Congress
National Aeronautics and Space Administration (NASA)
National Park Service
New York Public Library
Perry Castañeda Library Map Collection, University of Texas
Smithsonian Institution

NOTE Because you need to cite your media sources, remember to add them to your working bibliography.

More about ▶▶▶
Creating a work-
ing bibliography,
219–20

Make It **Your Own**

For a research assignment for this or another class, create a working bibliography of at least ten items. Include at least one of the following:

- Website
- Article in a scholarly journal
- Article in a newspaper
- Article in a magazine
- Subject-specific reference book
- Book
- Government publication
- Media resource

Which are available online? Which can you locate in your library?

Work **Together** ◀

In small groups or as a class, take a tour of the library. (You will need to arrange this in advance.) Come prepared with a topic, and ask a librarian for advice on how best to conduct a database search or find resources on your topic in the library's catalog. Explore the library's multimedia offerings, and check out at least one book on your topic. Finally, prepare a brief report listing at least three things you learned about the library that you did not know before your visit.

13h Conducting Field Research

Field research is often part of a research project in which the writer begins by reviewing information from secondary sources (reports of others' research) and then adds to the body of information by conducting a fresh inquiry. The most common types of field research are interviews, observational studies, and surveys.

1. Conduct an interview.

Expertise and the knowledge that comes with experience can often be gained only through an interview. Media such as email, text messaging, and even the telephone extend your range of possible interviewees, but face-to-face interviews give you an opportunity to read the other person's body language—facial expressions and bodily gestures—which can provide insight and direction for follow-up questions.

Instructors with special expertise in your subject make good subjects for an interview; government agencies, businesses, and public service organizations can also connect you with experts. When researching cultural or historical events, consider interviewing participants—the attorneys in a legal case, your soldier-cousin for her experience in Iraq, organizers of a demonstration for immigrants' rights.

Consider these tips for making the best use of your time:

Before the Interview

- Consider your purpose, and shape your questions accordingly.

- Select your interviewee with care, and contact that person for an appointment.

- Conduct background research on the topic and on the person whom you are interviewing, and develop ten to fifteen open-ended questions. (Ask "How would you rate the job the president of the student senate is doing, and why?" *not* "Is the president of the student senate doing a good job?") Avoid questions that prompt an interviewee to provide a particular answer. (Ask "How do you think the stock market will react in the coming year, and why?" *not* "How far will the stock market fall in the coming year?")

During the Interview

- Set your interviewee at ease, but remain politely neutral.

- Use your prepared questions and listen carefully to the answers; also listen for surprises and ask follow-up questions.

Writing
↑ Responsibly   **Conducting Interviews Fairly**

- Show up for the interview on time and prepared.
- Ask only for information that your expert alone could provide, not information you could easily gather on your own.
- Tell the interviewee up front how you will use the information you gather, and get her or his written consent.
- Ask for permission to record the interview, and confirm any quotations you may want to use.
- Offer the interviewee an opportunity to review your notes or your draft document. (You need not change your notes or document in response, but you should acknowledge any difference of opinion.)

- Take extensive notes or, if permitted, record the interview.
- Avoid interrupting or talking about yourself.

After the Interview

- Reflect on your notes while the interview is still fresh, recording your thoughts and any additional questions you would like to ask; then phone or email the interviewee *once* for follow-up. (Multiple follow-up calls are likely to annoy.)

- Make a transcript of the interview, and send a copy to your interviewee for comment or confirmation.

- Send a thank-you note within twenty-four hours of your interview, and send the interviewee a copy of your finished project with a note of appreciation.

2. Conduct an observational study.

Observational studies are common in the social sciences, particularly in psychology, sociology, and anthropology. Consider the following before beginning an observational study:

- **Your hypothesis.** What do you expect to learn? You can refine your hypothesis as your observations continue, but starting out with a hypothesis will help guide your observations and note taking.

❝As a writer for the college newspaper, I've learned to ask the interviewee to say something again if I miss a word or get confused. I even sometimes repeat what the interviewee has said to make sure I copied it down right.❞

—Alea Wratten, SUNY–Geneseo

> ***More about*** ►►►
> Devising a hypothesis, 214–15

Writing Responsibly

Avoiding Manipulation and Bias in Observations

- Ask permission to observe organized groups. Let the group's leader decide whether all should be informed, but reveal your purpose if asked.
- Resist manipulating the site or the community to get the results you want.
- Move around the scene to change your perspective.
- Provide groups the opportunity to read and respond to your study before

you submit it. (You need not change your report, but you should acknowledge differences of opinion.)
- Alert readers to the limitations of your study or to ways your own experiences and perspectives may have influenced your observations.

- **Your role.** Will you participate in the group, or observe the group from outside? The role you play will influence your perspective and affect your observations. Consider the steps you can take to minimize bias.

- **Your methods.** Establish categories for the observations you expect, and adjust them in response to your observations. Make notes immediately after a research session rather than during it, so your presence will be less obtrusive.

3. Conduct surveys.

Surveys are used frequently in politics and marketing but are useful in many types of research to assess beliefs, opinions, and behavior. When developing a survey, consider these issues:

- **Your hypothesis.** What do you expect to learn from your survey?

- **Your target population.** What group will you reach and how will you contact them? Strive to include a broad and representative range of respondents.

- **Your survey.** What type of questions will you ask, how many questions will you include, and how will you administer the survey?

Most surveys offer true-false, yes-no, and multiple-choice questions because these are easier to tabulate, but a few open-ended questions may deepen your sense of the respondents' feelings, and quotations can be used in your project. Whatever type of questions you ask, be sure your answer options are fair and that they offer an adequate range of choices. Because respondents are not likely to spend more than a few minutes answering questions, surveys should be brief—one to two pages is a reasonable limit.

 Tech

Online Surveys

A variety of web-based survey tools allows you to conduct surveys online. The following are among the most popular:

- *Survey Monkey*
- *Zoomerang*
- *SurveyGizmo*

Each allows users to create and send out a basic survey to a limited number of respondents for free.

connect
mhconnectcomposition.com
Additional resources: QL13009

14 Evaluating Information

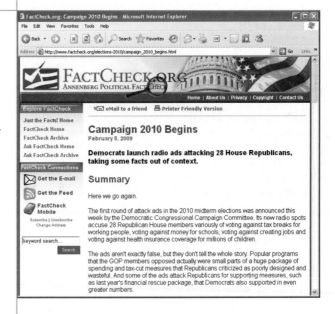

You hear an ad on the radio about a political candidate in your district who voted to "bail out big banks," but who "opposed tax breaks for 95 percent of American workers."[1] Can you take these statements at face value? The answer is no. The official might have opposed tax-cut measures for other reasons, such as cuts for the remaining 5 percent that were also included in the bill. The official might have supported a bank bailout for fear that failing banks would adversely affect citizens. If you rely merely on the sound bites from an advertisement, you

[1] FactCheck.org assessed the truthfulness of an advertisement on this theme sponsored by the Democratic Congressional Campaign Committee.

could be misled into throwing your support behind a candidate whose platform you do not endorse. Worse, you could pass along misinformation, undermining your own credibility. Whether in your personal life, your professional life, or your academic life, critically assessing sources of information is an essential skill.

14a Evaluating for Relevance and Reliability

Evaluating sources means assessing how *relevant,* or useful, a source is to your research and determining the source's *reliability*—how much you can count on it.

1. Relevance

When considering a potential source, first consider its relevance: Does the source offer information that could enrich your understanding of your topic, provide background information or evidence to support your claims, or suggest alternative perspectives? Before taking the time to read the text, determine its likely relevance by *previewing* it:

- **Check the publication date.** Recently published works are most likely to be of the greatest relevance, as they will probably provide the most up-to-date information. Be alert, though, to classics; they contain information or ideas on which researchers still rely. Classics will be cited frequently by other reliable sources; your instructor can also help you identify them.

- **Read the abstract, foreword, introduction, or lead** (first paragraph in a newspaper article). These usually provide a summary, overview, or key facts discussed in detail in the source.

- **Read the headings and subheadings.** These will provide an outline of the work.

- **Scan figures and illustrations.** These might signal important ideas and explain complex processes.

- **Read the conclusion.** The conclusion—the last few paragraphs in a journal or magazine article or the final chapter of a book—often reiterates the central idea and argument, important questions, and major findings.

- **Consult the index.** Check it for key terms in your research.

66 I do a lot of my searching for sources online, and I often find the Web very useful. The only problem I have is trying to decide whether the source is reliable or not. 99

—Stephanie Warnekros, Jefferson County Community College

connect
mhconnectcomposition.com
Additional resources: QL14001

Abstract A summary of the text's main claims and most important supporting evidence (118)

More about ▶▶▶
Previewing a text, 118
Finding the copyright date, foldout following p. 297
Primary vs. secondary sources, 452–53

Quick

Reference ➡ Judging Reliability

Scholarly work. Was the source published in a scholarly journal or book, or in a popular magazine, newspaper, or book?

Expertise. Is the author an authority on the subject?

Objectivity. Do tone, logic, quality of the evidence, and coverage of the opposition suggest that the source is unbiased?

Citations. Does the text cite sources, and is it cited in other texts?

Scrutiny. Was the text subjected to scrutiny by someone else before you saw it? For example, was it selected by the library, reviewed by another scholar, or fact-checked for accuracy?

Presentation. Is the text clearly written, well organized, and carefully edited and proofread?

Domain. Does the main portion of the URL end in *.edu* or *.org,* suggesting a noncommercial purpose, or does it end with *.com,* suggesting a commercial purpose?

Site sponsor or host. Is the site's host identified? Does the host promote a viewpoint or position that might bias the content?

2. Reliability

Judging reliability is not a simple, yes-or-no litmus test. Instead, it is a balancing act: You rate a source on a variety of criteria; the more criteria on which you can rate the source highly, the more reliable it is likely to be. Here are several criteria to consider:

- **Is the source scholarly or popular?** Scholarly texts (Figure 14.1) include articles published in academic journals and books published by scholarly presses. They are written by subject matter experts, not for profit but as a contribution to knowledge, and they are reviewed by other subject matter experts before being accepted for publication. Articles in magazines and books published by the popular press are commercial; they were selected by an editor who believes that an audience will be interested enough in the material to buy it. Popular sources may be fact-checked, but they are not reviewed by experts. Sources published in popular publications with a sophisticated or expert audience are likely to be more reliable than sources in general-audience publications, but

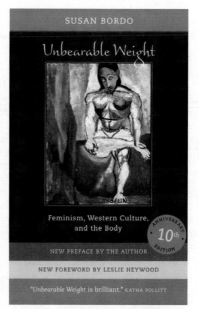

FIGURE 14.1 Popular versus scholarly books *The South Beach Diet* (Rodale) is a popular-press book aimed at a general audience: people wanting to lose weight. *Unbearable Weight: Feminism, Western Culture, and the Body* (University of California Press), on the other hand, is a scholarly book about our culture's obsession with women's weight; its target audience is scholars in fields such as women's studies and cultural studies.

those in scholarly publications are likely to be the most reliable of all.

- **Is the author an expert on the topic?** Does the author have special knowledge of or experience with the subject? You can determine this by reading about the author in a biographical reference work, by finding other works the author has published, by considering the author's academic background, and by determining whether the author has been cited in the footnotes or bibliographies of other reliable sources.

- **Does the source seem objective?** Does the author use an objective tone, make reasonable claims supported by logical reasons and solid evidence, recognize alternative perspectives, and treat opponents with respect? Or does the author use emotionally loaded language, make exaggerated claims, or support those claims with faulty logic and questionable or scanty evidence? An author may care deeply and write passionately about a subject, but if he or she characterizes groups unfairly or offensively or treats the individuals making up the group as if they are all the same, then you should suspect bias.

> **More about ▶▶▶**
> Biographical reference works,
> 236–37

connect
mhconnectcomposition.com
Additional resources: QL14002

> **More about ▶▶▶**
> Tone, 16–17, 143,
> 567, 573–75
> Opinion vs. belief,
> 154–56
> Types of evidence,
> 46–47
> Bias, 568–71

Quick **Reference** ➡ **Scholarly versus Popular Periodicals**

Scholarly

- Articles are written by scholars, specialists, researchers
- Use technical terminology
- Tend to be long
- Include citations in the text and a list of references
- Are reviewed by other scholars before publication
- Acknowledge any conflicts of interest (such as research support from a pharmaceutical company)
- Generally look serious; unlikely to include color photographs, but may include charts, graphs, and tables
- Published by professional organizations

Popular

- Articles are written by journalists or professional writers
- Avoid technical terminology
- Tend to be brief
- Do not include citations or a list of references
- May be fact-checked but not reviewed by experts
- Unlikely to acknowledge conflicts of interest
- Often published on glossy paper with color photographs
- Published by commercial companies

> ❝ When analyzing a source, I look at where and when it was published and who wrote it. If I don't know anything about the author, I do a quick Google search. Sometimes, I find out that the writer is affiliated with a certain company or political party, and this helps me uncover the writer's biases and assumptions. ❞
>
> —Mike Haxton, Oklahoma City University

■ **Does the author or publisher have a vested interest?**
Consider whether or how the author stands to benefit from
the work. Most authors will
benefit in some way: through
sales of the book or through
the prestige of publishing. But
consider whether the author or
publisher will benefit in some
other way: Is the author pro-
moting a product or process
from which she will benefit
financially? Will the author or
publisher gain adherents to a
political position? Check the
author's or publisher's website
for advertisements and to see
whether a mission statement
reveals an agenda.

> **Writing**
> **↑ Responsibly**   **Keeping an Open Mind**
>
> As a researcher, you also have a responsibility to
> avoid bias: Read sources with an open mind, use re-
> liable sources, consider evidence that undermines
> your position, avoid exaggerated claims and logical
> fallacies, and criticize unreasonable or poorly sup-
> ported conclusions but not the people who hold
> them. Unbiased research considers all sides of an
> argument, especially those that challenge the posi-
> tion the researcher holds.

■ **Does the text cite its sources?** Most scholarly articles and
books and some popular books will include a bibliography,
and some journal databases will list the article's sources in
the citation. Reputable newspapers and magazines will check
a writer's sources, though they often go unnamed, identified only as a "White House source" or a "source close to the
investigation."

■ **Do other scholars cite the text?** Also important is the number of times a source has been cited by other scholarly works.
Some journal databases indicate the number of times an article
has been cited by other articles indexed by that database (Figure 14.2, p. 254). Citation indexes such as *Web of Science* and
Google Scholar also provide this information.

■ **How did you find the source?** Sources located through your
college library are more likely to be reliable than are sources
located through a *Google* search because library sources are
selected in consultation with subject matter experts, in response to reviews, or after considering where the source was
published. A source published solely on the Web (unless in a
scholarly journal published online) is not likely to have been
subjected to the same level of scrutiny.

❯ *More about ▶▶▶*
Exploratory argu-
    ments, 142–43
Reasoning logically,
    144–48
Using evidence as
    support, 46–48,
    66–70
Citing sources,
    298–357
(MLA style, ch. 17),
    358–400 (APA
    style, ch. 18),
    401–28 (*Chicago*
    style, ch. 19),
    429–46 (CSE style,
    ch. 20)
Choosing a citation
    style, 454, 474

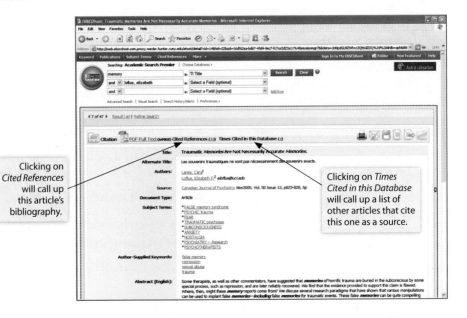

Clicking on *Cited References* will call up this article's bibliography.

Clicking on *Times Cited in this Database* will call up a list of other articles that cite this one as a source.

FIGURE 14.2 Determining reliability by assessing citations Both the number of times an article has been cited and the citations in the article itself are a useful way of determining an article's reliability.

Writing Responsibly — Online Plagiarism

The ease with which users can cut and paste information from one site into another makes it imperative that you exercise caution when using online sites for research. Unreliable sites frequently copy directly from other, more reliable sites. If you suspect plagiarism, copy a passage and paste it into a search engine's search box. The best way to avoid using material plagiarized from another site is to evaluate sites carefully for reliability.

- **Is the source well written and edited?** Has the writer approached the task with a sense of responsibility, writing, organizing, editing, and proofreading the material carefully? Is the page design easy to follow? Are the visuals appropriate to the audience and purpose and free from manipulation or distortion?

14b Evaluating Online Texts: Websites, Blogs, Wikis, and Online Discussion Forums

Anyone can create a website, post a blog, or contribute to an open wiki or discussion forum. This freedom makes the Web exciting, but it also means researchers should evaluate online sources with special

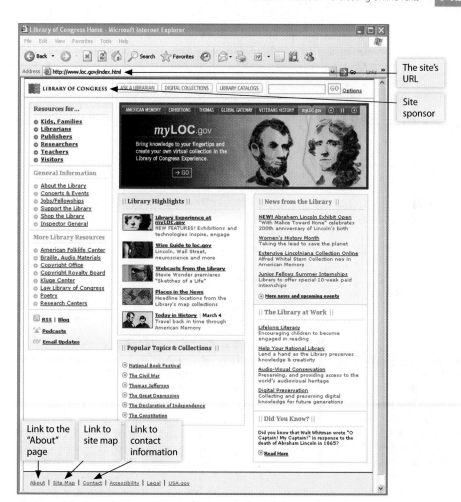

The site's URL

Site sponsor

Link to the "About" page

Link to site map

Link to contact information

FIGURE 14.3 A web page The URL appears at the top of the browser window. Note that the Library of Congress's website indicates the sponsoring organization prominently and provides links to pages providing information about the organization and site.

care. In addition to the general criteria listed above, consider these factors when evaluating websites:

URL A site's URL (short for *universal resource locator,* its web address), appears at the top of the browser window (Figure 14.3). Every item on

More about ▶▶▶
Websites, 191–98, 223–26
Interactive media, 198–99, 227

the Web has a URL, and all URLs end with an extension, or *domain,* that indicates the type of site it is. The most common domains are these:

- **.com** (commercial): sites hosted by businesses
- **.edu** (educational): sites sponsored by colleges and universities
- **.gov** (governmental): sites sponsored by some branch of federal, state, or local government
- **.net** (network): typically, sites sponsored by businesses selling internet infrastructure services (such as internet providers) but also sometimes chosen by businesses that want to appear technologically sophisticated or organizations that want to indicate that they are part of a network
- **.org** (organization): usually sites sponsored by nonprofit groups (though sometimes the nonprofit status of these groups may be questionable)

➤ Tech

Identifying Personal Websites

A URL that includes a personal name (jsmith) plus a tilde (~) or percent sign (%) or words like "users" or "members" is likely to be personal (not sponsored by a larger organization). Before using information from a personal site, investigate the author's credentials carefully.

Sites sponsored by educational, governmental, and nonprofit organizations are likely to be reliable, but your evaluation of a website should never end with its URL. Businesses usually offer information intended to sell products or services, yet commercial sites can nevertheless be highly informative. A site ending in *.edu* may just as easily have been constructed and posted by a student as by an expert, and much of the information posted on university websites is designed to entice new students and is thus a type of advertising. Nonprofit organizations are not trying to sell a product, but they are usually seeking support. Government sites, too, while often a source of highly reliable information, are unlikely to publish information that will undermine the administration's agenda. The reliability of information from all sites (indeed, all texts) must be evaluated with care.

Sponsor As with any publication, the credentials of a website's creator are an important factor in assessing reliability. You can research the owner of a blog, the contributors to a discussion list, or visitors to a chat room, and you can lurk to get a sense of the quality of a discussion. But websites frequently lack a single author. Instead, they

Lurk Read online discussions without contributing

have **sponsors**—corporations, agencies, and organizations that are responsible for creating content and making it available. To determine who sponsors a site, jump to the home page, link to pages called "About" or "Contact us," or click on the website's logo (see Figure 14.3, p. 255). If the website yields little information, try conducting a web search on the site's name. If the site is secretive about its sponsor, be especially wary of its content.

Open or Moderated? The reliability of online discussion forums depends in large part on their contributors. Sources to which anyone can contribute should be screened carefully; nonexpert enthusiasts can post inaccurate information, and people can deliberately insert distorted "truths." For example, in January 2006 *Wikipedia* had to block certain web addresses on Capitol Hill to keep congressional staffers from altering—and falsifying—the biographies of their bosses or their bosses' political opponents.

Wikis and web forums in which prospective contributors are screened by the site's owner, or *moderator,* are more likely to be reliable. The wiki *Encyclopedia of Life,* for example, promises to provide reliable information because it will be created and moderated by a consortium of highly regarded scientific institutions. Some scholars are even writing wiki textbooks to which they invite other experts to contribute.

Links An additional step in assessing the reliability of a website is to determine the number and type of sites that link to it. From the *Google* search page, you can determine the number of times a site has been linked to and review the linked sites (see Figure 14.4, p. 258): Type "link:" plus the URL in the search box and click Search or hit Return. Popularity alone does not guarantee reliability—the site may just be fun to read or authored by a celebrity—but when coupled with other criteria, it can be one indication of reliability.

14c Evaluating Visual Sources

Visual texts such as information graphics (tables, graphs, flowcharts) and photographs convey their messages powerfully yet sometimes so subtly that uncritical viewers may accept their claims without even realizing that a claim is being made. As with printed texts, researchers need to evaluate visual texts carefully to determine whether the

More about ▶▶▶
Visual arguments,
141–42, 149,
153–54, 159–61

Type "link:" plus URL in search box (no space between the colon after *link* and the URL)

Number of links to this site

Sites that link to the URL owl.english.purdue

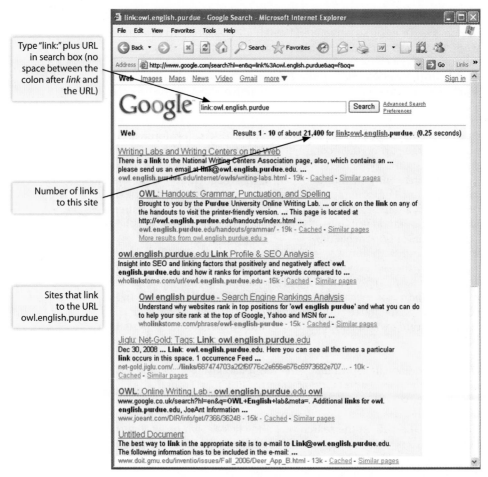

FIGURE 14.4 Using the links to a page to assess reliability

source is both relevant and reliable. To determine relevance and reliability, consider the following:

More about ▶▶▶
Purpose, 11–13
Avoiding distortion, manipulation, 87–89, 160–161

- What are the credentials of the visual's creator?
- How authoritative is the source in which the visual appeared?
- On what date was the image created or the photograph taken?

- What purpose(s) does the visual serve? Is it to entertain, to inform, or to persuade?
- Who is its intended audience?
- How accurate are the title, headings, labels, and any other text that appears with the visual? How does the text influence how you "read" the visual? How relevant is the visual to the accompanying text?
- What is in the foreground and background, and what is your eye drawn to?
- To what social, ethnic, or national groups do the subjects belong, and is this relevant?
- What emotions does the visual depict? What emotions does it elicit from you or other viewers?
- Has the visual been manipulated or cropped to omit or distort information? (See Figure 14.5.)

FIGURE 14.5 FDR in a wheelchair Although many Americans knew that President Roosevelt had been partially paralyzed by polio, only two photographs were taken of the president in a wheelchair. Were photographers protecting FDR's privacy or suppressing important information?

For graphics, also consider the following:

- What do the data represent?
- What relationships does the graphic show?
- How up-to-date is the information in the graphic?
- Are the data complete? Are there any gaps in years covered or groups represented?
- Are the data presented fairly?
- Is the source of the data unbiased?

→ EXERCISE 14.1 Evaluating reliability

Using the criteria discussed on pp. 250–54, write a paragraph in which you rate the reliability of the article excerpted below. Be sure to explain why you rated the article as you did.

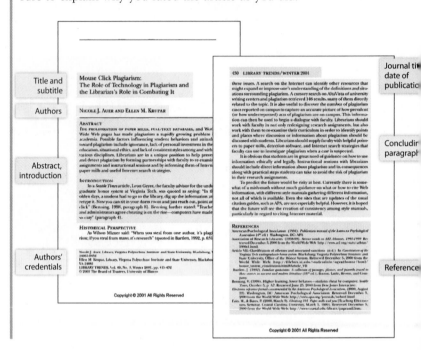

→ EXERCISE 14.2 Evaluating web pages

Using the criteria on pp. 250–57, evaluate the two web pages shown on the next page. Which would you consider the more reliable source on plagiarism, and why?

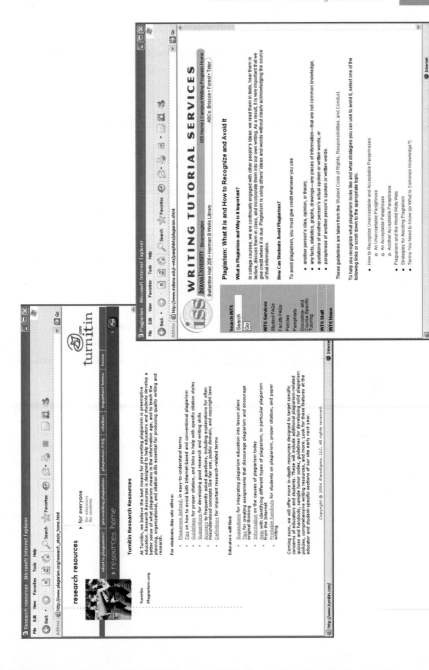

connect

mhconnectcomposition.com
Online exercise: QL14103

→ **EXERCISE 14.3 Evaluating a graph**

Using the criteria on pp. 258–59, write a paragraph evaluating the graph below. Be sure to support your assessment with specific reasons.

PINCHED FOR TIME: MORE WOMEN THAN MEN
Percentage of Americans Who Always Feel Rushed

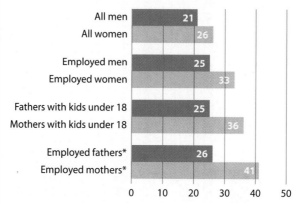

*Employed fathers, employed mothers refers to employed parents with children under age 18.
Employed does not include people who identify as retired but also work for pay.
Source: Pew Research Center

▲ Make It **Your Own**

Using the criteria in this chapter, write a paragraph evaluating three sources in the working bibliography that you began in the Make It Your Own exercise in chapter 12, pp. 220–21, or that you found for a research project in this or another class.

Work **Together** ◀

In small groups, discuss your evaluations from Exercises 14.1, 14.2, and 14.3. Where do you agree or disagree in your evaluations, and why?

15 Using Information and Avoiding Plagiarism

Louis Bloomfield

Ibrahim al-Marashi

Harold Garner

In 2001, physics professor Louis Bloomfield (University of Virginia) accused over a hundred students of plagiarism. Many were found guilty and expelled from the university.[1]

In January 2008, Mounir Errami and Harold Garner (University of Texas, Southwestern Medical Center) published a report in the journal *Nature* on duplicate articles in the *Medline* database. They tested a portion of the abstracts in *Medline* using text-matching software, coming up with some 420 potential duplicates. Of these, they found 73 that were written by different authors, leading them to suspect plagiarism. What they worry most about is the publication of plagiarized drug-safety studies, since these can give practitioners a false sense of the safety or efficacy of the drugs tested.[2]

In 2003, the British government "borrowed" information from Ibrahim

---

[1] Brian Hansen, "Combating Plagiarism: The Issues," *CQ Researcher* 13.32 (2003): 775–96. Print.
[2] Mounir Errami and Harold Garner, "Commentary: A Tale of Two Citations," *Nature* 451 (2008): 397–99. Web. 30 Mar. 2009.

connect
mhconnectcomposition.com
Additional resources: QL15001, QL15002

al-Marashi's doctoral thesis to make its case for war against Iraq—without citing the author of the thesis.[3]

Plagiarism, at least in an academic setting, involves the presentation of another person's work—a paper or story, a photograph or graphic, a speech or song, a web page or email message—without indicating that it came from a source. Buying a paper from a website or borrowing one from a fraternity's file and presenting it as one's own work would be plagiarism; so would pretending to have written someone else's song or copying material from a website without acknowledging the site's creator. College writers need to take plagiarism seriously.

Also be alert to the possibility of *patchwriting,* copying and only partially changing the language of a source. The National Council of Writing Program Administrators defines patchwriting as a misuse of sources. Sometimes, though, instructors and college policies categorize it as plagiarism. In either case, patchwriting is not good writing. It often results not from an intention to present another's words and ideas as one's own but, rather, from inaccurate note taking, misunderstanding the source, incorrect use of or omitting quotation marks, or incomplete paraphrasing.

Inform yourself in detail about what your instructor and your college (or your employer) define as ethical writing; although everyone rejects plagiarism, the definition of what constitutes plagiarism can vary subtly from one discipline or profession to another. Still, following the guidelines for writing described in this chapter (and throughout this book), you can be confident that the work you produce represents its sources responsibly.

 Plagiarism and Culture Attitudes toward and definitions of plagiarism vary from one culture to another. Individualist cultures, like that of the United States, value originality and see words and ideas as personal property that can be "stolen" by plagiarists. Collectivist cultures view information as a shared good. Whether your home culture is individualist or collectivist, when writing for a U.S. academic audience, be especially careful to mark borrowed language as quotation; to provide a citation whenever you borrow language or ideas; and to document sources fully.

---

[3] Gaby Hinsliff, Martin Bright, Peter Beaumont, and Ed Vulliamy, "First Casualties in the Propaganda Firefight," *Manchester Guardian* 9 Feb. 2003. Web. 20 Feb. 2008; "The Plagiarism Plague," *BBC News Online* 7 Feb. 2003. Web. 20 Feb. 2008.

15a Valuing Research

One of the keys to avoiding plagiarism is understanding why instructors value source acknowledgment: Seeking the truth is the heart of all academic work. To achieve this goal, academic researchers—from architects to anthropologists, psychologists to physicists—build on the work of others. They must be able to trace ideas to their source because one faulty piece of information can invalidate the whole research project. That is why failing to credit previous researchers is considered such a serious breach of academic discipline, and cheating in all its forms—from distorting an opponent's position to doctoring a quotation, manipulating an image, falsifying data, or taking credit for someone else's work—is punished so severely.

For students, conducting research and learning to write clearly and accurately has another value: It develops the intellectual, rhetorical, and ethical skills and practices needed in college, at work, and in one's community. Plagiarism averts that learning.

> In the past, I sometimes rejected a research topic because every idea I had felt influenced by what I had just read: How could I not be cheating if I wrote down those ideas? I did not see that if I recorded the ideas, documented them, and then put them in contrast with information from other sources, I could generate something new and creative.
>
> —Michael Bosomworth, Western Illinois University

15b Using Information Ethically: What You Do and Do Not Have to Acknowledge

The first step toward avoiding plagiarism is approaching your writing tasks with a clear sense of what you are and are not expected to cite and document.

1. What you *do* have to cite: quotations, paraphrases, summaries, and *un*common knowledge

You must document quotations, paraphrases, summaries, and information that is unlikely to be known by nonexperts:

- **Quotations.** Enclose short quotations in quotation marks, and indent long quotations as a block. Name the author either in a signal phrase (*Professor Jones argues*) or in a parenthetical citation, and include the page number. (In some styles, you may include this information in a footnote or endnote.) Then document the source in your bibliography, references list, or list of works cited.

More about ▶▶▶
Using quotation marks, 814–23 (ch. 50)
Block indention for long quotations, 303, 342 (MLA), 386 (APA)
Citing sources, 299–314 (MLA), 359–68 (APA), 402–21 (*Chicago*), 430–31 (CSE)
Documenting sources, 314–39 (MLA), 369–84 (APA), 402–21 (*Chicago*), 431–43 (CSE)
Using signal phrases, 291–93, 299–303, 359–60

- **Paraphrases and summaries.** Provide a citation each time you use a source, even when you are not quoting. As with quotations, cite the author and page number in the text, and include full source information in your bibliography, references list, or list of works cited.

connect
mhconnectcomposition.com
Additional resources: QL15003

- **Ideas and information.** Acknowledge the source of any information or ideas that are *not* common knowledge. As with quotations, paraphrases, and summaries, cite the author and page number in your text and provide full source information in your bibliography, references list, or list of works cited. A piece of information from the internet needs to be cited every bit as much as does a piece of information gleaned from a journal article or book.

2. What you do *not* have to cite: common knowledge (facts, dates, events, cultural knowledge)

You do *not* have to document **common knowledge** (unless it is included in a quotation)—even if you learned the information from a source. Common knowledge is general information that is available in a number of different sources and that is considered factual and incontestable. Here are some examples:

Facts

- The earth is 91 million miles from the sun.
- Labor organizer "Mother" Jones worked on behalf of the United Mine Workers of America.

Writing
↑ Responsibly   Using Illustrations and Avoiding Plagiarism

❯ **More about** ▶▶▶
Copyright, 7, 195
Creative Commons
    licensing, 195
Citing media
    illustrations,
    336–37 (MLA),
    382–83 (APA),
    417 (*Chicago*)

The web contains a variety of images, videos, and sound files that you can download to your word processor: A click of the mouse, and they are yours. Or are they? In fact, most of the materials on the Web are copyrighted or licensed in the Creative Commons. The right to reproduce them is controlled by the copyright holder, usually the person who created or published them. Be sure to keep full records of who created them, where you found them, and on what date you downloaded them so you can acknowledge them fully. If you plan to publish your project, whether in print or on the Web, you must also request permission to use them, so retain any information that will help you contact the files' owners.

Dates

- The spring equinox occurred on March 20 in 2009.
- U.S. women won the right to vote on August 26, 1920, when the Nineteenth Amendment was passed.

Events

- James Earl Ray was convicted of the assassination of civil rights leader Martin Luther King, Jr.
- Francis Crick, James Watson, and Maurice Wilkins are credited with discovering the structure of DNA.

Cultural Knowledge

- The composer Wolfgang Amadeus Mozart was a child prodigy.
- Elvis Presley made the song "Hound Dog" a smash hit, although he did not write it.

Everything outside of these categories should be cited in the text of your project and documented in a footnote or in your bibliography, references list, or list of works cited.

Getting It Across   Visuals and Common Knowledge

Images, including maps, are not considered common knowledge. You may know that the capital of Nebraska is Lincoln, but if you include a map of Nebraska (that you did not draw) in a paper, you must credit the creator of that map. Unless you made the image yourself, you must credit the source of all images that you talk about or reproduce in your paper.

15c Making Notes That Help You Avoid Plagiarizing

Inadvertent plagiarism is a growing problem for researchers today because cutting and pasting material from online sources into notes is so easy. It is easy to lose track of which material has been borrowed, and it is easy to lose track of which material came from which source. The following strategies for maintaining good research notes can help you avoid problems:

- **Keep two sets of notes—bibliography and content.** For every source you consult, create a bibliographic note in your working bibliography and create content notes in a separate section of your research log.

- **Indicate the source and page number for all content notes.** Keying your notes to a source page will help you contextualize them when you return to the notes later and will also allow you to cite the source fully.

More about ▶▶▶
Research log, 217–18
Working bibliography, 219–20

→ **Tech**

Bookmarking and Listing Favorites

If you will not always be working from a single computer, set up bookmarks on a social bookmarking site like *De.li.cious* or *Digg*, which allow you to store, tag, and share bookmarks.

connect

mhconnectcomposition.com
Additional resources: QL15004, QL15005, QL15006

- **Make a fresh card, page, or notebook section for each source.** This will help you avoid confusing one source with another.

- **Use columns or different colored cards or fonts to distinguish different types of notes.** If done consistently, using one column or color for your own comments, another for quotations, and a third for summaries and paraphrases can provide a useful visual cue for identifying source material and avoiding unintentional plagiarism.

- **Create a Favorites list or bookmark useful web pages.** If taking notes on a computer, bookmark or create a Favorites list for sites you have visited, so you can track your sources.

More about ▶▶▶
Annotation, 124–27
Summarizing,
  119–20, 269, 290
Patchwriting, 271–74
Quoting, 276–79,
  290–94
Analyzing, 129–31,
  279–80, 288–90
Interpreting, 131–32,
  279–80, 289–90
Synthesizing,
  132–34, 279–80,
  289–90
Critiquing, 134–35,
  279–80, 289–90

15d Making Research Notes That Help You Write

Research note making involves the following activities:

- Annotating sources

- Summarizing sources accurately and without patchwriting

- Paraphrasing sources accurately and without patchwriting

- Recording quotations that you may want to use later

- Analyzing sources by dividing them into their component parts

- Interpreting the meaning of sources

- Synthesizing information from one source with information from other sources

Writing
↑ Responsibly **Annotating versus Making Notes**

While annotating is a useful way to highlight important information in a source, it is not a substitute for writing your own notes about a text. Although annotations can help you mark what is important, making notes will push you to engage with a text and save you from leafing through page after annotated page, looking for a passage that you faintly recall having read. So, even though it may seem more time-consuming than annotating, making notes will actually serve you better in the long run.

- Critiquing, or evaluating, sources
- Recording source information, including the page number on which the material appears

15e Summarizing

connect

mhconnectcomposition.com
Additional resources: QL15007

An effective *summary* captures the main ideas and supporting points of a source while omitting the details. By forcing you to identify the main points and understand them well enough to state them accurately in fresh words, writing an accurate summary helps you understand a difficult text. Most of your content notes should summarize your sources.

In general, a summary should be at least 50 percent shorter than the original, but it can be as little as 10 percent of the original's length. It should be only as long as needed to capture the main point and main supporting points accurately. To summarize a source, follow these steps:

1. Read the source, underlining key terms and looking up words that you do not know. For short sources, one or two careful readings may be enough; for longer or more complex sources, you may need to reread the source several times.
2. Annotate the source. Underline or highlight the thesis or main idea of the source, and identify the main supporting ideas. For a longer source, creating an outline may be helpful.
3. Without looking at the source, write down the thesis or main idea in a sentence or two. For each group of supporting paragraphs, write a one- or two-sentence summary in your own words.
4. Combine your sentences into a paragraph, editing to omit repetition and using transitions to make logical connections between sentences clear.
5. Check your summary against the source. Have you used fresh words and sentence structures? If not, this may be a sign that you do not yet understand the source. Go back and read the material again, and revise your summary to avoid patchwriting.
6. When you incorporate your summary into your paper, credit the original source—use a signal phrase to indicate where the summary begins and a page reference (in parentheses) to indicate where it ends.

> **More about ▶▶▶**
> Transitions, 61–62
> Placing signal
>   phrases and page
>   references, 291–93,
>   301–3, 359–60

connect

mhconnectcomposition.com
Online exercise: QL15101

→ **EXERCISE 15.1 Summarizing accurately**

Write one or two sentences summarizing the following passages:

1. HAZARD, Ky.— On a rainy day in mid-January, Alan Maimon, a reporter here for the Louisville *Courier-Journal,* packed up his desktop computer, fax machine and printer in his company-owned Ford Explorer. He then drove three hours to Louisville, turned in the equipment to the newspaper and, with that, officially brought to a close *The Courier-Journal*'s storied Hazard bureau in Eastern Kentucky. . . . From the heart of coal country, the reporters used the megaphone of *The Courier-Journal*'s front page to tell the world about mining disasters and the strip mining that cut across the roller-coaster terrain here. The strip mining articles won the paper a Pulitzer Prize for public service in 1967. In 1998, its reporters wrote about the widespread doctoring of air quality tests in the mines, which left hundreds of miners breathing dangerous levels of coal dust, leading to black lung disease. And always, the paper served as a roll call for the region's dead—38 miners killed near Hyden in 1970; 15 in the Scotia mines in Whitesburg in 1976; and then, two days later, 11 more; seven in Floyd County in 1982; and so on.—Katharine Q. Seelye, "A Fabled Bureau Exits Eastern Kentucky's Coal Country"

2. Though the studies are few in number, there is some convincing evidence that children may indeed experience musical performance anxiety at least as early as sixth grade. Additionally, there is some evidence that gender may also play a role in a musician's experience of musical performance anxiety. Several studies have noted differences in the level of anxiety reported by men and women (Abel and Larkin, 1990; LeBlanc et al., 1997; Nagel, 1988; Widmer et al., 1997). In each case, females reported more performance anxiety than males. Other studies have noted physiological differences, with females experiencing higher heart rates (LeBlanc et al., 1997) and greater levels of hyperventilation (Widmer et al., 1997). In addition, men and women have shown different means of coping with musical performance anxiety. Wolfe (1990) found that women tended to use emotion-focused strategies, whereas men tended towards problem-focused strategies. The emotion-focused strategies were related to greater confidence and competence and less self-consciousness, distractibility and disruptive cogni-

tive activity than the problem-focused strategies. The evidence seems to suggest the possibility of systematic differences between the genders on the experience of musical performance anxiety.—Charlene Ryan, "Gender Differences in Children's Experience of Musical Performance Anxiety"

15f Paraphrasing without Patchwriting

connect

mhconnectcomposition.com
Additional resources: QL15008

A *paraphrase* restates someone else's ideas in fresh words and sentences. Paraphrase a source when you want to do the following:

- Understand the logic of complex passages
- Convey ideas from a source in your own words
- Mention examples and details from the source

After summarizing, paraphrasing is the technique you should use most often when making notes from sources.

 Making Notes in English As a nonnative writer of English, you may want to save time by copying passages in English into your notes word-for-word or by copying your own translation of the material into your notes. However, your English language skills will improve more quickly if you make an effort to paraphrase, and you will also be less likely to commit unintentional plagiarism.

Because you are including all of the writer's main ideas, a paraphrase is often as long as, and sometimes even longer than, the original. Like a summary, a paraphrase must not use the same language as the original (except for keywords), and the order of ideas and the sentence structures must be fresh as well. Just as you would cite the source of a quotation, you must also cite the source when you paraphrase.

Writers who are inexperienced with paraphrasing often ***patchwrite:*** They replace some terms with synonyms, delete a few words, or alter the grammar slightly, but they do not put the passage fully into fresh words and sentences.

To paraphrase *without* patchwriting, follow these steps:

1. Read the source until you feel you understand it. Think about the overall meaning of the passage you are borrowing. Figure out whether there are any key terms that must be retained in your paraphrase.

2. Close the text and walk away. Do something else for a few minutes or a few hours.

3. Come back to your desk and write what you remember. If you cannot remember anything, repeat steps 1 and 2.

4. Check your paraphrase against the source to make sure you have correctly represented what it said. If you have closely followed any of the source language (other than key terms), either copy exactly and supply quotation marks or revise your note.

When your paraphrase is complete, check to be sure that you have done *all* of the following:

- Used synonyms rather than the words of the source where possible; used key terms when no synonym is reasonable; quoted specialized terms the first time used but not thereafter.

- Rearranged the ideas of the source so that they make sense in your own text. For example, if the author presents a cause and its effects, you can present the effects first and the causes second, if that will work better in your paper.

- Provided transitions to clarify relationships among ideas.

> **More about ▶▶▶**
> Varying sentence length and structure, 550–51

- Used different sentence structures from those in the original passage. If you find yourself borrowing the sentence structures of your source, try dividing or combining sentences or varying their length and structure to alter their rhythm and blend them into your own text.

- Omitted details that are not relevant to *your* main point. The author may have included information that is relevant to a point that is different from the one you are making.

- Made sure that your deletions do not alter or distort the meaning of the source.

- Cited the source of the paraphrase in your text, usually bookending the paraphrase with a signal phrase and a page reference in parentheses.

- Documented the source in your bibliography, reference list, or list of works cited.

The following examples illustrate techniques for revising passages to avoid patchwriting:

Passage from Source

Although early speech of children consists largely of lexical or open class words, some closed class or function words also emerge early, frequently at the onset of two-word speech. (Fromkin, Victoria. *Linguistics: An Introduction to Linguistic Theory.* Malden, MA: Blackwell, 2000. 336. Print.)

Note with Patchwriting

Fromkin 336

Children's early speech consists mostly of lexical or open class words. But some closed class or function words also appear fairly early. This often happens at the onset of two-word speaking.

> Picks up language from source

> Uses synonym or word in another form

Note Revised to Avoid Patchwriting

Fromkin 336

Children's early speech ~~consists mostly of lexical or~~ *is characterized primarily by*
~~"~~ " (nouns, verbs, adjectives, and adverbs) to which
open class words ~~But some closed class or function~~
additions of "closed class words" (prepositions and determiners) may
~~words also appear fairly early. This often happens~~
readily be made, especially when children begin stringing two words together.
~~at the onset of two-word speaking.~~

The writer of the revised passage quotes "open class" and "closed class" from the source because these are specialized terms, but she defines them because doing so helps her understand the passage. She also revises to put ideas in her own words and changes the structure of the sentence.

Here is another example:

Passage from Source

Until recently, the Church was one of the least studied aspects of the Cuban revolution, almost as if it were a voiceless part of Cuban society, an institution and faith that had little impact on the course of events. (Super, John C. "Interpretations of Church and State in Cuba, 1959–1961." *The Catholic Historical Review* 89.3 [2003]: 511–529. Print.)

Note with Patchwriting

Picks up language from source

Uses synonym or word in another form

Super 511

The Catholic Church until recently was not much studied as an aspect of the Cuban revolution. It was as if the Church was voiceless in Cuban culture, as if it had little influence on events.

Note Revised to Avoid Patchwriting

Super 511

Scholarship on the Cuban revolution is only beginning
~~The Catholic Church until recently was not much studied as an aspect~~
to recognize the influential role of the Church.
~~of the Cuban revolution. It was as if the Church was voiceless in Cuban~~

~~culture, as if it had little influence on events.~~

The revised note still retains a version of a word from the source: "influence" has been changed to "influential." And of course the key words "Cuban revolution" and "Church" are in both the original passage and the revised note. But the passage no longer draws heavily on the source's sentence structure, organization, or word choices.

Writing from sources without patchwriting is an advanced skill; learning how to avoid patchwriting requires conscious, ongoing effort. You will find it hard at first, but it gets easier with practice. Remember, if you find yourself leaning heavily on the wording of the source in your first-draft paraphrases, revise them. Work for greater comprehension of the text by looking up unfamiliar words or thinking about concepts you do not understand. Then turn away from the source and write from your head rather than from the source. As long as you are looking at the source and asking yourself, "How else can I say this?" you are playing with words rather than comprehending the source.

→ **EXERCISE 15.2** **Correcting a paraphrase to avoid patchwriting**

Study the following source, as well as the first draft of a paraphrase that follows. Circle words that appear in the source, and underline synonyms or words in another form. Then revise the note to avoid the patchwriting.

connect
mhconnectcomposition.com
Online exercise: QL15102

Passage from Source

Washington has posed a special problem for *Wikipedia,* which is monitored by 800 to 1,000 active editor-volunteers. In the recent flare-up, a community of *Wikipedia* editors read a story in the *Lowell Sun* newspaper in which staffers for [Representative Marty] Meehan acknowledged replacing an entry on him [in *Wikipedia*] with more flattering verbiage. That prompted last week's Capitol Hill *Wikipedia* blackout; all computers connected to servers at the House of Representatives, identified by a numerical Web address, were denied access.

—Yuki Noguchi, "On Capitol Hill, Playing WikiPolitics,"
Washington Post

Draft Note

Noguchi A1

Wikipedia and its active editor-volunteers have a special problem with Washington. Recently the editors read a *Lowell Sun* newspaper story about Meehan's staffers having acknowledged that they had replaced an entry on him with more flattering words. That resulted in last week's *Wikipedia* blackout on Capitol Hill computers, which were denied access.

→ **EXERCISE 15.3** **Paraphrasing without patchwriting**

Using the guidelines on pp. 271–72 for paraphrasing without patchwriting, choose a key sentence from one of the passages in Exercise 15.1 and paraphrase it. Then compare your paraphrase with the original. Is your paraphrase accurate? Does it avoid patchwriting? Revise your paraphrase until it is accurate and written completely in fresh words and sentence structures.

connect
mhconnectcomposition.com
Online exercise: QL15103

▲ Make It **Your Own**

From a source for a research project (or from another college-level text), choose three sentences you consider important. Then paraphrase them following the guidelines on pp. 271–72. Bring your paraphrase and a copy of the source to class.

Work **Together**

In groups of two or three, compare the original source with the paraphrases that each group member wrote for the Make It Your Own exercise on p. 275. Did group members paraphrase accurately? Did they avoid patchwriting? Discuss any sentences that may lean too heavily on the language or sentence structure of the original source. What might the writer do to avoid patchwriting? If the paraphrase avoids patchwriting, identify the paraphrasing strategies each writer used.

15g Quoting

connect

mhconnectcomposition.com
Additional resources: QL15009

A **quotation** is someone else's words transcribed exactly, with quotation marks or block indention to signal that it is from a source. Quote from a source under the following circumstances:

- When your source uses particularly vivid or engaging language

- When you want to reproduce a subtle idea that might be difficult to paraphrase or summarize without distortion

- When your source conveys technical information that is difficult to paraphrase

> *More about* ▶▶▶
Using quotation marks, 814–23 (ch. 50)
Indention for longer quotations, 303, 342 (MLA), 386 (APA)
Deciding when to create or borrow visuals, 86
Obtaining permission, 7
Ellipses in quotations, 820–21, 835–36
Brackets in quotations, 820–21, 832
Interviews, 244–45
Surveys, 246–47
Writing about literature, 447–71 (ch. 21)

- When you want to convey ideas in an expert's own words

- When you want to analyze or highlight the specific language used in your source (as when studying a work of literature or a historical document)

- When you want to emphasize an important point

When making notes, copy quotations word-for-word, and double-check them against the source. Whether you transcribe a quotation or cut and paste it into your notes, put quotation marks around it to avoid any confusion later. In your writing project, adjust quotations to integrate them into your own sentences, using ellipses to signal cuts and brackets to indicate any words you have added or changed. In your notes, the quotation should appear exactly as it did in the source.

When working with primary sources such as interviews and surveys that you have conducted or works of literature you are studying, you are likely to use quotations extensively. In contrast, secondary sources such as newspaper articles, scholarly articles, and books are already quoting, summarizing, and paraphrasing their sources, so you should limit

Getting It
Across   Borrowing versus Creating Your Own Multimedia Resources

You must decide when to borrow and when to create your own multimedia illustrations—sound recordings, digital photographs, videos, or graphics. As you think about incorporating multimedia that someone else has created, ask yourself these questions:

- Does it contribute to the points you are making, rather than just filling up space or decorating the page?

- Will it raise readers' estimation of you as a writer?
- Will it add spark to your paper? (And is "spark" appropriate?)

If your answer to one or more of these is yes, incorporate it into your project, crediting the source. (You may also need permission from the creator.) If your answer to these questions is no, consider creating illustrations to achieve your goals.

the number of direct quotations you copy from them. Use summary and paraphrase instead.

If you find that you are copying a lot of quotations but are paraphrasing little and summarizing even less, you may not be fully comprehending what you are reading. In these situations, try the following:

- Read the source again.

- Look up words you do not understand.

- Consult reference sources that can provide background knowledge.

- Discuss the source with your instructor, classmates, or friends.

66 My first few research papers were overloaded with quotations. Now I have more confidence in my own voice, so I don't feel compelled to show due reverence by quoting. 99

—Michael Bosomworth,
Western Illinois University

Writing
Responsibly   Using Quotations Fairly

We have all seen ellipsis-laden quotations praising a new movie, and we have all wondered whether a crucial word or words might have been omitted: "This is the . . . movie of the year!" could well have been "This is the *worst* movie of the year!" in the original review. That is one reason we are skeptical when reading such advertisements. (Another is the advertiser's desire for the movie to succeed at the box office.)

In academic writing, you can adjust a quotation to bring the punctuation or grammar into line with your own text, as long as your changes are indicated with ellipses or brackets and you do not distort the author's point. Protect your credibility and be fair to your source by altering quotations accurately.

More about ▶▶▶
Evaluating sources,
248–62 (ch. 14)

Good scholarship requires that you work to understand the whole source rather than just quoting from the sections that you believe you understand or that you think sound authoritative. Understanding the difficult parts is important, for they may well change the meaning of what you thought at first you understood.

The following reading note correctly uses quotation marks to signal material taken word-for-word from the source, yet it indicates that the writer does not fully understand what she is writing about.

Draft Note

> Milne 140
>
> The "free-black community . . . of Five Points" is not reflected in "the areas of Block 160 that were excavated." "All that survived . . . were the remains of their ancestors interred in the mostly forgotten burying ground, a few intriguing and unusual items discarded in the defunct privies and cisterns, and a handful of church addresses." But "it is probable that many members of this community remained in the neighborhood, living 'off-the-grid.' . . ."

This note is merely a string of quotations, sewn together with a few of the note taker's own words. Using these notes as is would produce a research paper that would similarly be a mosaic of quotation, difficult to read and lacking the researcher's insight and critical judgment. Rereading the source in order to gain a better understanding of it enabled the writer to summarize with much less quotation. The following revision is much easier to read as well:

Revised Note

> Milne 140
>
> Very few items belonging to members of the African American population in Five Points have been excavated, most likely because members of this community were not part of mainstream society—they were "living 'off the grid'" (140)—not because they had all moved away.

> **More about** ▶▶▶
> Integrating bor-
> rowed ideas and
> words, 291–94

Other chapters in this text discuss the mechanics of using quotation marks and integrating quotations into your text. Consult these sections before you begin your research, as you make notes on sources, and as you draft and revise your text. Applying these principles will enable you to be responsible to the writers from whom you borrow, to your readers, and to yourself.

15h Using Analysis, Interpretation, Synthesis, and Critique in Your Notes

In addition to recording information from sources, the note-taking stage is also the time to start analyzing, interpreting, synthesizing, and critiquing what you read. The Quick Reference box on p. 280 lists questions to ask yourself as you read and take notes on your sources.

The following note for Lydia Nichols's research project provides a summary of the source while also including her own assessment of it:

▶▶▶ Student sample research projects: "Holy Underground Comics, Batman!" Lydia Nichols, 346–57 "The Power of Wardrobe," Heather De-Groot, 389–400

Sample Summary Note with Writer's Assessment

Heller

Provides a history of *Zap* comics from the first issue by Robert Crumb in 1968 to the most recent issue in 1994. Describes *Zap* as founding the underground "comix" movement in reaction to the superhero comics that adhered to the 1950s Comics Code and spurred on by late 1960s cultural challenges to the status quo, but doesn't go into detail or identify any comics it inspired. Identifies artists who joined forces with Crumb, and highlights their contributions. Discusses censorship battle over *Zap* #4, which was accused of violating community standards of decency. But not sure what happened: Bookstore owner was fined, but article doesn't indicate what other legal troubles it caused. Later issues continued to be sexually explicit, but they also satirized contemporary mores and included "comic documentary" similar to comic books published during World War II. Article provides a good overview of the history of *Zap* comics (including showing all 14 covers); it assumes that readers will already know a good deal about the history of comics. "Good Shall Triumph" and "Comic Book Code" provide more info. about the Comics Code Authority, but I would like to know more about early examples of documentary comics. Heller is obviously a fan of *Zap* comics (I read online that he was an art director at the *NY Times*) but I would like to know more about what motivated Crumb and the others to rebel.

Summary that includes analysis and interpretation

Critique

Synthesis

Reference ➞ Analyzing, Interpreting, Synthesizing, and Critiquing a Source

Analysis
- What is the purpose of the source?
- Who is the intended audience?
- What major claims does the source make?
- What evidence (reasons, facts, statistics, examples, expert testimony) does the source use to support these claims?

Interpretation
- What assumptions does the author make about the subject or audience, and why are such assumptions significant?
- What does the source omit (evidence, opposing views), and what might these omissions indicate?
- What conclusions can you draw about the author's attitude from the text's tone? What motives can you infer from the author's background?
- Who published this text or sponsored the research, and what influence might these sponsors have upon the way the information, arguments, or evidence is presented?
- In what context was the text written—place, time, cultural environment—and how might this context have influenced the author?

- What expertise or life experience does the author bring to the subject, and is it relevant to the topic?

Synthesis
- Do any other sources make a similar (or opposing) claim, reach a similar (or opposing) conclusion, or offer similar (or opposing) evidence?
- Do any other sources identify similar causes or effects?
- What else do you know about this topic?

Critique
- What are the aims of the source, how worthwhile are they, and how well are they achieved?
- What claims does the source make? Are you persuaded by them? Why or why not?
- How credible is the evidence? Is evidence based on verifiable facts? How relevant is the evidence?
- How logical is the source? Does the author commit any fallacies?
- How fairly does the source treat alternative viewpoints?

More about ▶▶▶
Analysis, interpretation, synthesis, and critique, 129–35, 288–90

Work **Together** ◀

Read the research project in chapter 17 (pp. 346–57) or 18 (pp. 389–400). In small groups of two or three, use the criteria in the bulleted list on p. 277 to categorize the writer's use of quotations. Has she used quotations effectively? Why or why not?

Make It **Your Own**

Create a content note on a source for an upcoming research project. First, summarize or paraphrase the source, following the instructions on pp. 269 or 271–72. Then ask yourself three or more of the questions in the Quick Reference box on p. 280 and create a note on the source. Bring it to class.

Work **Together**

In small groups of two or three, evaluate the summary or paraphrase you generated in the Make It Your Own exercise above. First, compare it with the source on which it is based. How accurate is it? Does it avoid patchwriting? (See pp. 271–72.) If not, discuss ways to revise it. Then discuss your note. Does it go beyond summary and paraphrase to analyze, interpret, synthesize, or critique the source? If the note merely summarizes, paraphrases, or quotes, discuss the passage with the group.

16 Writing the Research Project

The Hubble Space Telescope, taking pictures of the cosmos since 1990, has provided enough data to keep scores of scientists busy for years, long after the telescope stops functioning. So far, scientists have published over six thousand articles based on what they have learned from Hubble. These articles have given us a clearer idea of the age of our universe, a better understanding of how galaxies evolve, and information about what happens when stars collapse. Until these papers were published, the images from Hubble were merely pretty pictures to the rest of us. Only after scientists wrote about their findings did the new information Hubble provided become widely available.

Like the six thousand scientific articles published from the Hubble data, your college research projects are an opportunity to share what you have read and studied; they are an opportunity to provide readers with a synthesis of the information you have gleaned from a variety of sources and to present what you have learned, filtered through the lens of your understanding. They are the culmination of your research and an expression of yourself.

16a Drafting a Thesis Statement

As you began your research, you chose and defined a *topic* that would be appropriate to your purpose and of interest to your reader. You then framed *research questions* and turned them into a *hypothesis* that you tried to confirm (and undermine) through your research. Now,

Reference ➡ **Drafting the Research Paper**

- **Thesis.** Draft a one- or two-sentence thesis statement that grows out of your research questions and hypothesis. Revise your thesis as you draft your project.
- **Organization.** List and explain the reasons you believe your thesis statement or why you think it is the most reasonable way to address a difficult issue. Sort research notes into separate piles for each of your reasons. Draft an outline that organizes your material so that readers can follow your logic and maintain interest to the end.
- **Analysis, interpretation, synthesis, critique.** Divide ideas into their component parts and think about what they mean. Then combine ideas from sources with your own ideas to come up with something fresh. Decide whether sources have achieved their goals and whether their goals were worthwhile.
- **Evidence and counterevidence.** Incorporate evidence, making sure it is relevant. Use summaries, paraphrases, and a few quotations as support. Acknowledge opposing evidence and explain why your position is reasonable despite this. (If your position does *not* seem reasonable in light of counterevidence, revise your thesis.) Make sure you provide enough evidence—and the appropriate types of evidence—to persuade your readers.
- **Citation and documentation.** Cite sources in the text. Double-check that you have used quotation marks where needed and that paraphrases do not slip into patchwriting. Document sources in a list of works cited (MLA), reference list (APA, CSE), or bibliography (*Chicago*).

More about ▶▶▶
Assessing the writing situation, 10–18, 210–11
Devising a thesis, 33–37, 214–15
Choosing a topic, 22–29, 214
Using evidence, 46–48
Finding information, 222–47 (ch. 13)
Acknowledging alternative views, 163–64
Organizing, 37–43, 59–64, 164–66, 285–87
Drafting, 46–48, 288–95
Summary, paraphrase, and quotation, 269–79, 290
Avoiding patchwriting, 271–74
Relevance, 249

with research data in hand, you are ready to draft a *thesis statement* that will serve as the focus of your project.

This thesis should be a one- or two-sentence statement that grows out of your research hypothesis (or hypotheses), revised in light of what you learned through the research process. It should be a statement that you are prepared to defend, using the information you gleaned from sources and your own ideas, and it should convey your *purpose*. For illustration, read the research question, hypothesis, and thesis statement for the student research essay by Lydia Nichols:

Research question: What are the characteristics of underground comics?

Hypothesis: The characteristics of underground comics are a focus on topics that challenge social mores, an author or author team that has creative control, and an adult readership.

Thesis statement: While far less well-known than their superhero counterparts, underground comics offer an innovative and sophisticated alternative to mainstream titles.

Hypothesis answers research question by listing three distinguishing traits.

Thesis statement makes purpose clear: uses comparison of comic types to persuade readers that underground comics are more innovative and sophisticated. It transforms specifics of hypothesis into a broader, more engaging claim.

As you draft your research project, you may discover that the counterevidence is overwhelming or that the body of your draft offers a different answer to your research question than the one in your thesis. (Frequently, the true thesis takes shape in the conclusion of the first draft.) So be prepared to revisit your thesis as you draft, revising or even replacing it as necessary.

▲ Make It **Your Own**

For a research paper that you are working on, draft (or revise) a thesis statement. Does the thesis statement concisely assert your central idea? Will it appeal to your readers? Does it convey your purpose?

16b Organizing Your Ideas

The process of organizing your ideas begins with assembling the materials you will need. These include the following:

- Your research log and any other notes you have taken
- Any photocopies or printouts of sources
- A copy of your thesis statement
- Any office supplies you may need (pens, pencils, highlighters, stick-on notes, index cards, a notebook)

More about ▶▶▶
Research log, 217–18
Annotating, 124–27
Generating ideas, 22–29
Making notes, 127–28, 267–80

1. Organize your ideas and notes.

With your preliminary thesis statement drafted and necessary materials at hand, you are ready to begin organizing your ideas and notes.

1. Start by listing the reasons you believe your thesis is true. While these reasons may be derived from your research sources, they should be *your* reasons, stated in your own words. (The strategies for generating ideas can help.)
2. Review the notes you took while reading sources: Do they provide evidence that supports your reasons for believing your thesis? Organize your notes according to which of your reasons they support: Separate index cards into piles, or cut and paste notes into separate computer files for each supporting point.
3. Assess your stock of evidence: The size of a computer file or stack of index cards will indicate how much information you have collected in support of each of your reasons for believing the thesis. If a set of notes looks skimpy, find more supporting evidence, revise your thesis, or delve deeper into your reasons for believing your thesis.

Writing
▲ Responsibly Acknowledging Counterevidence

While sorting your notes, be sure to retain *counterevidence*—evidence that *undermines* your claims. If some of your research contradicts or complicates your thesis or supporting reasons, do not suppress it. Instead, revise your thesis or supporting reasons on the basis of this counter-evidence, or acknowledge the counterevidence and explain why the reasons for believing your thesis are more convincing than those that challenge it. Your readers will appreciate your presentation of multiple perspectives.

connect

mhconnectcomposition.com
Additional resources: QL16001

> **More about** ▶▶▶
> Scratch outlines, 40
> Sentence outlines,
> 40–42
> Topic outlines, 40–42

2. Outline your project.

After you have organized your ideas and notes, outline your essay to determine the most effective order for presenting your ideas. Some writers prefer a sentence outline because it aids drafting. (Each sentence in the outline becomes the topic sentence of a paragraph.) Others, eager to start writing, prefer a scratch (informal) outline that simply lists their reasons and the major supporting points in order of presentation. Still others prefer a topic outline: It is quicker to write than a sentence outline, but its formal structure of roman numerals and letters makes the structure of the draft clearer.

The topic outline below shows the structure of the first part of Lydia Nichols's research paper. Note that the roman numeral sections list Nichols's reasons; the capital letter and arabic numeral sections list the evidence in support of her reasons.

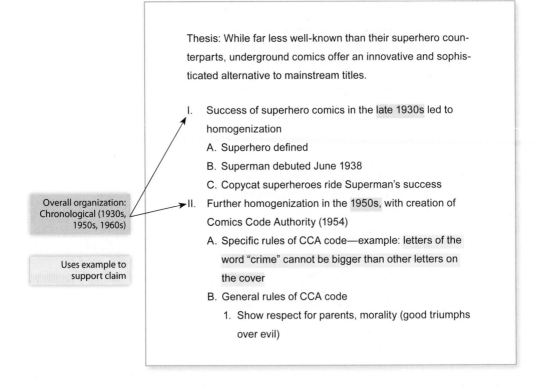

Thesis: While far less well-known than their superhero counterparts, underground comics offer an innovative and sophisticated alternative to mainstream titles.

I. Success of superhero comics in the late 1930s led to homogenization

   A. Superhero defined

   B. Superman debuted June 1938

   C. Copycat superheroes ride Superman's success

Overall organization: Chronological (1930s, 1950s, 1960s)

II. Further homogenization in the 1950s, with creation of Comics Code Authority (1954)

   A. Specific rules of CCA code—example: letters of the word "crime" cannot be bigger than other letters on the cover

Uses example to support claim

   B. General rules of CCA code

      1. Show respect for parents, morality (good triumphs over evil)

2. Portray criminals, crimes negatively

3. Religion treated respectfully

4. No profanity

C. Violators not distributed (EC Comics and others); conformers gained market share

III. Homogenization, superhero domination undermined by appearance of underground "comix" in late 1960s

A. Underground comix defined

> Uses definition to support claim

1. Not submitted to CCA for approval

2. Satirized conservative beliefs

3. Included political and sexual content (fetishism)

4. Challenged social norms

5. Offered insightful commentary on society

6. Example: Robert Crumb's *Zap,* first issue released in 1968

B. Underground comix contrasted with CCA-approved comics

1. *Amazing Fantasy* (1962) (Visual: Cover of *Amazing Fantasy* #15)

> Supports claim by showing and analyzing contrasting visuals

a. Comics Code Authority approval stamp in upper-right corner of *Amazing Fantasy*

b. Traditional superhero

c. Traditional drawing

2. *Snarf* (1976) (Visual: *Snarf* #6)

a. Not CCA-approved (no stamp)

b. Depicts regular guy fighting real problems (big oil—an important issue in the mid-1970s)

c. Takes on political issues

d. Drawing crude

⬆ Make It **Your Own**

For a research paper that you are working on:

- List reasons for believing your thesis. (Include supporting evidence and illustrations.)
- Decide on the best order in which to present your material, and make an outline (sentence, scratch, or topic) from which to work.

16c Drafting Your Research Project

When drafting your research project, your goal is to draw on information in sources to support your own ideas, weaving that information into your sentences and paragraphs so that it supports your ideas without overwhelming them. Draw on your analysis of sources, your own interpretations of what you have read, and your synthesis of ideas from sources. To support your claims, incorporate summaries, paraphrases, and quotations from your notes, using signal phrases to identify the source of borrowed ideas and to provide context for your sources.

More about ▶▶▶
Drafting, 46–48

Quick Reference ➡ Writing the First Draft

As you begin writing, keep in mind that you are composing a draft—what you write will be revised—so do not worry about whether you are saying it "right." A few writers' tricks will help you produce that first draft:

- Keep your thesis statement in front of you to help you stay focused as you write.
- Start with the sections that are easiest to write, and then organize and fill in the gaps later.
- Begin writing *without* consulting your sources. Then draw on sources for evidence to support what you have drafted on your own.
- When incorporating quotations, paraphrases, or summaries, note which source the material comes from (including the page number) to avoid having to track down this information later and, perhaps, plagiarizing inadvertently.
- Draft with a notepad next to you or another file open on your computer, so you can jot down ideas that come to you while writing another section.
- Include visuals that support your points and that help your reader understand what you are writing about.

Make It **Your Own**

For a research paper that you are working on, compose a first draft. As you write, reread the tips in the Quick Reference box on p. 288 as necessary. You will revise this draft later, so for now you can just relax.

1. Use analysis, interpretation, and synthesis to support your claims.

When you read sources and took notes, you analyzed your material to break it down into its component parts, and you interpreted what you read to determine its meaning. You also synthesized sources: You may have identified ideas in one source that were supported by information in others, described areas of agreement (or disagreement) among sources, or explained which sources were most persuasive and why. The work you have already done to analyze, interpret, and synthesize sources is what you will draw on as you draft your research project. Use it to show readers how borrowed material is relevant; do not expect readers to figure this out without your help.

▶▶▶Student sample research project: "Holy Underground Comics, Batman," Lydia Nichols, 346–57

Examine the paragraph below from Lydia Nichols's essay on underground comics to see how she uses analysis, interpretation, and synthesis to support her own claims.

Underground artists not only push the envelope in terms of content, but they also incorporate experimental visual devices, earning critical praise for breaking away from traditional comic layouts in favor of more artistic perspectives. Artists such as Daniel Clowes argue that comic art can be more evocative than film, especially in the use of nonlinear storytelling techniques (Hignite 18). *New York Times* columnist John Hodgman agrees: Discussing a moment of existential crisis in Kevin Huizenga's *Ganges* #1, he writes, "I have never seen any film . . . that gets at that frozen moment when we suddenly feel our mortality, when God is seen or denied, as effectively as a comic panel." Artist Chris Ware manipulates the borders and frames in his comics so extensively that even reading his works can feel like an art to be mastered (see fig. 3). The demands his comics place on the reader create an interaction between viewer and artist that is unheard of in the pages of superhero titles.

Sentence 1: Nichols's claim (topic sentence) offers her interpretation.

Sentences 2 and 3 synthesize information form sources to support her claim.

Sentences 4 and 5 provide her own analysis to support her claim.

Fig. 3. Cover from Chris Ware's *Jimmy Corrigan: The Smartest Kid on Earth* (New York: Pantheon, 2000). Critically acclaimed *Jimmy Corrigan* comics use visual storytelling techniques, pushing the limitations of comics and forcing the reader to work to achieve understanding.

Illustration provides an example that supports Nichols's claim, and caption offers interpretation of what the reader is seeing there.

Instead of merely stringing together material from sources, Nichols integrates her own ideas with information from sources to craft a paragraph that readers will find persuasive. She analyzes primary sources (examples of underground comics) to determine what makes them visually exciting, she interprets her sources to determine which support her claim, and she synthesizes evidence to make her case.

2. Use summary, paraphrase, and some quotations to support your claims.

More about ▶▶▶
Quoting, paraphrasing, or summarizing, 269–79
Signal phrases, 299–303, 359–60
Avoiding patchwriting, 271–74
Quotation marks, 814–23 (ch. 50)

So that your paper will not seem like a series of quotations strung together with a few words of your own, use quotations sparingly. Instead, put borrowed ideas into your own words, by either paraphrasing or summarizing, and use quotations only when the language is particularly vivid or technical, when you want to borrow the authority of the speaker, or when you are analyzing the language of the source. In the sample paragraph on pp. 289–90, Lydia Nichols uses a combination of quotation and summary to support her claims. She quotes Hodgman because the quotation is especially vivid, but she summarizes Clowes's ideas to convey his argument concisely.

NOTE When summarizing or paraphrasing, work to avoid patchwriting, and, when quoting, use quotation marks or indent longer quoted passages as a block.

Getting It Across — Incorporating Visual Evidence

Visuals can offer crucial support in college research projects as examples, explanations of processes, or presentations of factual or statistical data. When including visuals, place a figure number in the text and in the figure caption, so readers can identify immediately the visual to which you are referring. Also include the following in the figure caption:

- A title or brief description of the illustration.

- The point you are making with the visual without repeating information from the text.
- Source information, if the visual or data in the visual is borrowed.

Remember that, in academic essays, all visuals must contribute to your argument, not merely ornament the text.

3. Introduce and contextualize borrowed material with signal phrases.

To incorporate borrowed material smoothly, use a ***signal phrase*** to identify sources. A signal phrase couples the name of the writer from whom you are borrowing words or ideas with a verb that conveys your sense of the writer's intent.

In choosing a verb, consider the attitude or position of the writer you are citing. Is the writer making a claim? Is she or he agreeing or disagreeing, or even conceding a point? Or is the writer's position neutral? You will often choose a neutral verb, such as *writes, says,* or *comments.* (In the example paragraph on pp. 289–90, Nichols uses "argues" and "agrees.") Where possible, though, go beyond these neutral verbs to indicate the writer's attitude:

Oscar Wilde quipped, "A poet can survive everything but a misprint."

For the Wilde quotation above, *quipped* ("uttered a witty remark") is clearly appropriate, given the cleverness of the sentence quoted. *Snarled,* on the other hand, would not be appropriate: Wilde's quip may have an edge to it, but most would disagree that it comes up to the anger or viciousness associated with the verb *snarl.* When choosing signal verbs, avoid implying an intention that cannot clearly be determined by a dispassionate reading of the source.

To hold your audience's interest, vary the signal words you use and your placement of the signal phrase. (A list of signal verbs appears in the Quick Reference box on p. 292.) In most cases, you should also contextualize borrowed information the first time you cite a source.

Neutral signal verbs		**Signal verbs that indicate:**		
		Claim/Argument		**Concession**
analyzes	introduces			
comments	notes	argues	finds	acknowledges
compares	observes	asserts	holds	admits
concludes	records	believes	maintains	concedes
contrasts	remarks	charges	points out	grants
describes	reports	claims	proposes	
discusses	says	confirms	recommends	
explains	shows	contends	suggests	
focuses on	states	demonstrates		
illustrates	thinks			
indicates	writes	**Agreement**		**Disagreement**
		agrees	complains	questions
		concurs	contradicts	refutes
		confirms	criticizes	rejects
		supports	denies	warns
			disagrees	

Writers in literature and the other humanities generally use present tense verbs in signal phrases; writers in the sciences use the present or past tense, depending on the context.

More about ▶▶▶
Verb tense, 674–78

Establish the source's authority, especially if readers are unlikely to be familiar with the source's author, and indicate the role that the quotation, example, or statistic plays in the original, as Nichols does in the excerpt below:

Establishes source's authority

Indicates McCloud's purpose

> Artists such as Scott McCloud have changed this perception of comic books by offering a broader definition of what a comic is. According to McCloud, comics are "juxtaposed pictorial and other images in a deliberate sequence" (12). This definition includes not only what one might find in the latest Spider-Man comic, but also all the experimental work that McCloud and his underground colleagues are creating.

Establishing the authority of a source is not necessary when you are merely stating a fact.

4. Use a signal phrase and page reference to "bookend" borrowed material.

Placing a signal phrase at the beginning of a borrowed passage and a page number (in parentheses) at the end of the borrowed passage will help readers recognize where your ideas end and borrowed material begins. Notice how Nichols bookends borrowed material in the passage at the bottom of p. 292.

> ***More about*** ▶▶▶
> Bookending borrowed material, 301–3, 359–60

5. Integrate quotations smoothly into your text by adjusting the language to fit your text.

In some cases, material you want to quote may contain information that is irrelevant to your project. In the example on p. 289, Nichols deletes words from the Hodgman quotation because the words do not help her make her point. (You can often integrate a phrase from a source into your own sentence; you do not need to quote whole sentences.) As long as the meaning is not significantly changed, writers may do any of the following to fit the borrowed material more fluidly into their own sentences:

- Add or change words for clarity
- Change capitalization
- Change grammar

> ***More about*** ▶▶▶
> Using ellipses
> in quotations,
> 820–21, 835–36
> Using square brackets in quotations,
> 820–21, 832

All added or changed words should be placed in square brackets; deleted words should be marked with ellipses. The example below shows a responsible alteration of a quotation:

Quotation integrated into student text	Original quotation
Certain portions of the Comic Book Code were incredibly specific and controlling, such as the rule that forbade "[t]he letters of the word 'crime' on a comics magazine . . . [to] be appreciably greater in dimension than the other words contained in the title" (qtd. in "Good Shall Triumph over Evil").	The letters of the word "crime" on a comics magazine shall never be appreciably greater in dimension than the other words contained in the title.

A capital letter was changed to a lowercase letter, double quotation marks were changed to single, one word was added and a couple of others were omitted, but the overall meaning of the passage remains the same.

Imagine, however, that the writer had made these changes instead:

Quotation unfairly altered	Original quotation
Certain portions of the code allowed some flexibility. Consider, for example, the rule that allowed "[t]he letters of the word 'crime' on a comics magazine . . . [to] be appreciably greater in dimension than the other words contained in the title" (qtd. in "Good Shall Triumph over Evil").	The letters of the word "crime" on a comics magazine shall never be appreciably greater in dimension than the other words contained in the title.

Clearly this alteration of the quotation is not acceptable, as it changes the meaning of the passage completely.

connect

mhconnectcomposition.com
Online exercise: QL16101

→ EXERCISE 16.1   Integrating quotations

Read the passage below. Then, in the following quotations, circle the numbers for those that alter the quotation fairly, and cross through the numbers of those that change the meaning of the quotation.

> The meeting of Normans and Anglo-Saxons at Hastings was the most decisive battle of the Middle Ages and one of the determining days in the making of the West. Hastings changed Britain, which had been dominated since the end of Roman rule by invading tribes from the Continent and the North—Angles, Saxons, and Vikings. This day more than any other turned Britain away from its Scandinavian past and toward Europe. Hastings inaugurated the era of the knight, the social dominance of those who fought with lance on horseback.
>
> —Howard R. Bloch, *A Needle in the Right Hand of God*.
> New York: Random House, 2006, p. 7.

1. Bloch maintains that the Battle of Hastings "turned Britain away from its Scandinavian past" and from Europe as well (7).

2. The Battle of Hastings, notes Bloch, gave the "invading tribes from the Continent and the North" new power over Britain (7).

3. "[T]hose who fought with lance on horseback" became dominant after the Battle of Hastings, observes Bloch (7).

4. Bloch concludes that the fight between the Romans and the invading tribes from the Continent and the North was "the most decisive battle of the Middle Ages" (7).

↑ Make It **Your Own**

For a research paper you are drafting, show how you have integrated supporting evidence from sources:

1. List three sentences in which you identify source authors in a signal phrase.
2. List three sentences in which you contextualize source information.
3. List three sentences in which you incorporate quotations fairly into your own prose by adding, deleting, or changing words.

As you look at your results, think about whether you need to change or vary your methods for integrating information drawn from sources.

6. Acknowledge your sources.

Even while working on your first draft, you should acknowledge information you have borrowed from sources—quotations, paraphrases, summaries, illustrations, data, or other information—by citing them in the text and providing full documentation in a list of works cited, a reference list, or a bibliography. Both citation and documentation are necessary to support your credibility as a writer and to avoid plagiarism. No matter which citation and documentation style you use, your entries should be complete and consistent so that readers can locate your sources and enter into the conversation you have contributed to in your research project.

More about ▶▶▶
Citing sources,
   299–314 (MLA),
   359–68 (APA),
   402–19 (*Chicago*),
   430–31 (CSE)
Documenting
sources,
   314–39 (MLA),
   369–84 (APA),
   402–19 (*Chicago*),
   431–43 (CSE)

16d Revising, Proofreading, Formatting, and Publishing Your Project

Once you have composed a first draft, however rough it may be, you can begin the process of shaping and polishing it—the process of *revision.* First, attend to big-picture, or global, issues, such as clarifying your purpose, making sure your essay is cohesive and unified, and making sure your ideas are fully developed. Next, attend to local issues, such as making sure your word choices reflect your meaning and are at the appropriate level, that you have varied your sentences, and that your prose is concise.

Once revision is complete, edit your text to correct errors of grammar, punctuation, and mechanics. Then proofread carefully—remember that spell-check software can help, but it cannot replace a careful human proofreader. Finally, format your project following the requirements of your discipline.

Part Five

Documentation
Matters

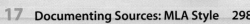

Documentation Matters

Book (Printed)

   author   title   publication information   medium

Morrison, Toni. *A Mercy*. New York: Knopf, 2008. Print.

                  place of   publisher publication
                 publication   date

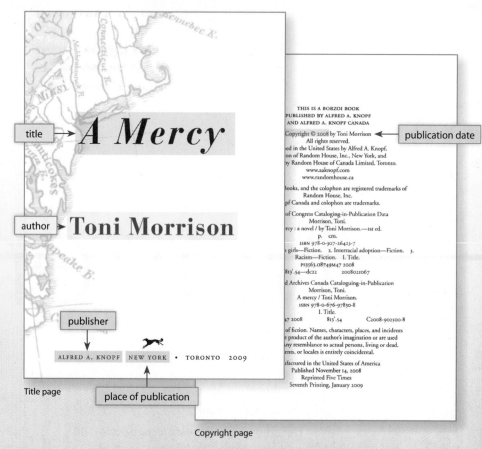

title → *A Mercy*

author → Toni Morrison

publisher → ALFRED A. KNOPF   NEW YORK • TORONTO   2009

Title page

place of publication

THIS IS A BORZOI BOOK
PUBLISHED BY ALFRED A. KNOPF
AND ALFRED A. KNOPF CANADA

Copyright © 2008 by Toni Morrison ← publication date
All rights reserved.
...ed in the United States by Alfred A. Knopf,
...on of Random House, Inc., New York, and
...y Random House of Canada Limited, Toronto.
www.aaknopf.com
www.randomhouse.ca

...Books, and the colophon are registered trademarks of
Random House, Inc.
...pf Canada and colophon are trademarks.

...of Congress Cataloging-in-Publication Data
Morrison, Toni.
...rcy : a novel / by Toni Morrison.—1st ed.
p. cm.
ISBN 978-0-307-26423-7
...h girls—Fiction. 2. Interracial adoption—Fiction. 3.
Racism—Fiction. I. Title.
PS3563.O8749M47 2008
813'.54—dc22   2008021067

...d Archives Canada Cataloguing-in-Publication
Morrison, Toni.
A mercy / Toni Morrison.
ISBN 978-0-676-97830-8
I. Title.
...47 2008   813'.54   C2008-902500-8

...of fiction. Names, characters, places, and incidents
...e product of the author's imagination or are used
...ny resemblance to actual persons, living or dead,
...ents, or locales is entirely coincidental.

...ufactured in the United States of America
Published November 14, 2008
Reprinted Five Times
Seventh Printing, January 2009

Copyright page

Look for the information you need to document a printed book on the book's title page and copyright page. If more than one location for the publisher is listed on the title page, use the first. (For more about documenting a book, see pp. 316–23.)

Documenting a Source:

Book (Printed)

authors   publication date   title and subtitle

Tavris, C., & Aronson, E. (2007). *Mistakes were made (but not by me): Why we justify*

                                   publication information

foolish beliefs, bad decisions, and hurtful acts. Orlando, FL: Harcourt.

                                     place of   publisher
                                     publication

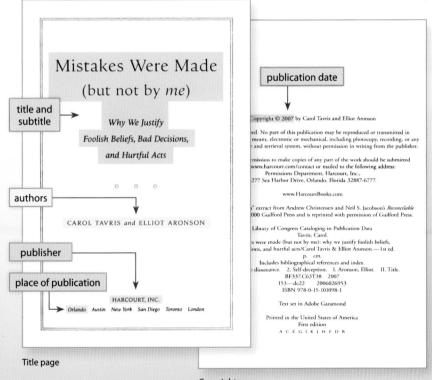

Title page

Copyright page

Look for the information you need to document a printed book on the book's title page and copyright page. If more than one location for the publisher is listed on the title page, use the first or the publisher's home office location (if indicated). (For more about documenting a book, see pp. 370–75.)

Short Work on a Website

author — web page title — website title — sponsor/publisher

Kukkonen, Karin. "The Rhetoric of Comics." *Project Narrative Weblog.* Ohio State University,

medium — access date

College of the Humanities, 4 Nov. 2008. Web. 2 Dec. 2008.

©date/last update

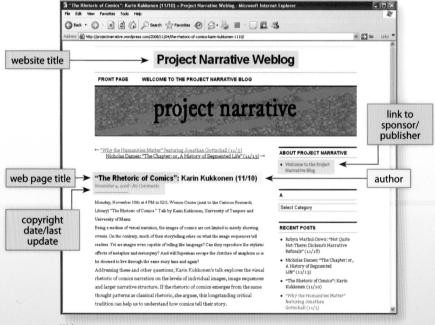

website title → **Project Narrative Weblog**

FRONT PAGE   WELCOME TO THE PROJECT NARRATIVE BLOG

project narrative

link to sponsor/publisher

← "Why the Humanities Matter" featuring Jonathan Gottschall (11/5)
Nicholas Dames: "The Chapter; or, A History of Segmented Life" (11/13)

ABOUT PROJECT NARRATIVE

• Welcome to the Project Narrative Blog

author

web page title → **"The Rhetoric of Comics": Karin Kukkonen (11/10)** ←

November 4, 2008 · No Comments

A

Select Category

copyright date/last update

Monday, November 10th at 4 PM in 021L Wexner Center (next to the Cartoon Research Library) "The Rhetoric of Comics." Talk by Karin Kukkonen, University of Tampere and University of Mainz

Being a medium of visual narration, the images of comics are not limited to merely showing events. On the contrary, much of their storytelling relies on what the image sequences tell readers. Yet are images even capable of telling like language? Can they reproduce the stylistic effects of metaphor and metonymy? And will Superman escape the clutches of anaphora or is he doomed to live through the same story time and again?

Addressing these and other questions, Karin Kukkonen's talk explores the visual rhetoric of comics narration on the levels of individual images, image sequences and larger narrative structure. If the rhetoric of comics emerges from the same thought patterns as classical rhetoric, she argues, this longstanding critical tradition can help us to understand how comics tell their story.

RECENT POSTS

• Robyn Warhol-Down: "Not Quite Not-There: Dickens's Narrative Refusals" (11/18)
• Nicholas Dames: "The Chapter; or, A History of Segmented Life" (11/13)
• "The Rhetoric of Comics": Karin Kukkonen (11/10)
• "Why the Humanities Matter" featuring Jonathan Gottschall (11/5)

Web page

Frequently, the information you need to create a complete entry in the list of works cited is missing or difficult to find on web pages. Look at the top or bottom of the web page or home page or for a link to an "About" or "Contact Us" page. If no sponsor or publisher is listed, use *n.p.*; if no publication date is available, use *n.d.* (For more about documenting online sources, see pp. 328–31.)

APA Style

Journal Article (Printed)

author   year   article title and subtitle
Fancher, R. E. 2009. Scientific cousins: The relationship between Charles Darwin and Francis Galton.

publication information
American Psychologist 64, 84–92.
journal title   volume   pages

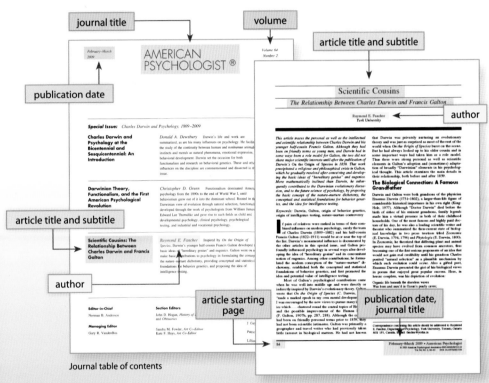

Journal table of contents   First page of article

Look for the information you need to document a journal article on the cover or table of contents of the journal and on the first and last pages of the article. (Turn to the last page of the article for the last page number.) If each issue of the journal begins with page 1, include the issue number, in parentheses, after the volume number. (For more about documenting an article from a printed or online periodical, see pp. 375–80.)

Journal Article from an Online Database

authors
Cantor, Nancy, and Steve Schomberg. "What We Want Students to Learn: Cultivating Playfulness

article title and subtitle

journal title   issue   pages   database
and Responsibility in a Liberal Education." *Change* 34.6 (2002): 47-49. *Academic Search*

medium   access date   volume   year
Premier. Web. 2 Dec. 2008.

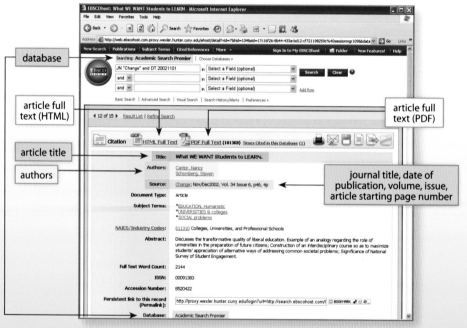

database

article full
text (HTML)

article full
text (PDF)

article title

authors

journal title, date of
publication, volume, issue,
article starting page number

Database screen: full record for article

Look for the information you need to document an article you accessed through
an online database on the search results screen, the full record of the article, or
the first and last pages of the article itself. The access date is the date you last
consulted the source; record this date in your notes. (For more about documenting
an article accessed through an online database, see pp. 324–25, 327.)

Journal Article from an Online Database

author year   article title and subtitle

Fancher, R. E. (2009). Scientific cousins: The relationship between Charles Darwin and Francis Galton.

publication information   digital object identifier

American Psychologist 64, 84–92. doi:10.1037/a0013339

journal title   volume   pages

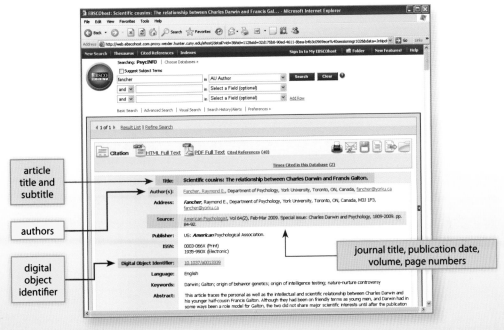

article title and subtitle

authors

digital object identifier

journal title, publication date, volume, page numbers

Database screen

Look for the information you need to document an article you accessed through an online database on the search results screen, the full record of the article, or the first and last pages of the article itself. Include a digital object identifier (DOI) if one is provided. No access date is needed. (For more about documenting an article accessed through an online database, see pp. 376–78.)

MLA Style

Journal Article (Printed)

authors | article title and subtitle
Cantor, Nancy, and Steve Schomberg. "What We Want Students to Learn: Cultivating Playfulness

journal title | issue | pages
and Responsibility in a Liberal Education." *Change* 34.6 (2002): 47-49. Print.

volume | year | medium

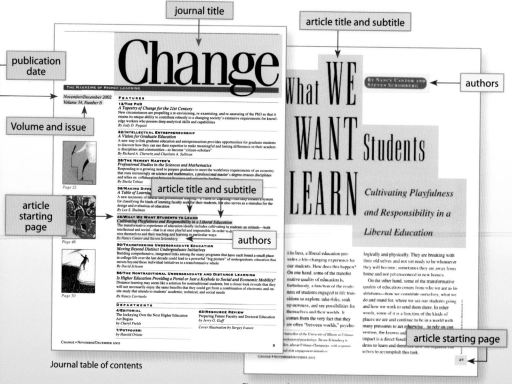

journal title

article title and subtitle

publication date

authors

Volume and issue

article title and subtitle

article starting page

article starting page

authors

Journal table of contents

First page of article

Look for the information you need to document a journal article on the cover or table of contents of the journal and on the first and last pages of the article. (Turn to the last page of the article for the last page number.) (For more about documenting an article from a printed or online periodical, see pp. 323–28.)

Short Work on a Website

corporate author/publisher ©date/last update web page title and subtitle

American Psychological Association. (2005). The fast and the furious: Psychologists figure out who

gets road rage and find ways to calm them down. Retrieved March 31, 2009, from

retrieval statement

retrieval date

URL for web page

http://www.psychologymatters.org/roadrage.html

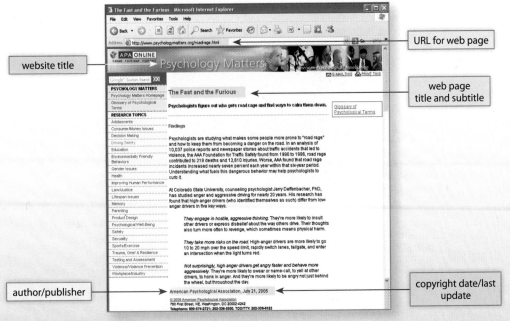

website title

URL for web page

web page title and subtitle

author/publisher

copyright date/last update

Web page

Frequently, the information you need to create a complete entry in the reference list is missing or difficult to find on web pages. Look at the top or bottom of the web page or home page or for a link to an "About" or "Contact Us" page. If no author is cited, move the title to the author position. If the web page is untitled, add a description (in brackets) in place of the title. If the page was created and published by the same group, omit the publisher name from the retrieval statement (as here); if not, add the publisher's name before the URL (*Retrieved from APA website:*). (For more about documenting online sources, see pp. 380–82.)

17 Documenting Sources: MLA Style

> **More about ▶▶▶**
> Popular academic styles per discipline, 454, 474
> APA style, 358–400 (ch. 18)
> *Chicago* style, 401–28 (ch. 19)
> CSE style, 429–46 (ch. 20)

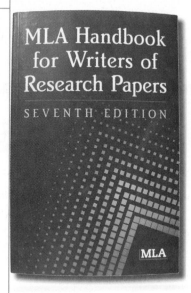

MLA Handbook for Writers of Research Papers

SEVENTH EDITION

MLA

Developed by the Modern Language Association (MLA), MLA style guidelines are used by many researchers in the humanities—especially in languages and literature—to cite and document sources and to format papers in a uniform way. The MLA requires that sources be acknowledged in two ways:

- *Citation:* Provide an in-text citation for each source used in the body of your project.

- *Documentation:* Provide a list of all works cited at the project's end.

Writing Responsibly   Citing and Documenting Sources

When you cite and document sources, you acknowledge any material that you have borrowed from a source, and you join the conversation on your topic by adding your own interpretation. Simultaneously, you give interested readers (including your instructor) a way to join the conversation: Accurate entries in the text and list of works cited allow your audience to find and read your sources so that they can evaluate your interpretation and learn more about the subject themselves. Accurate entries also demonstrate the care with which you have written your research project, and they reinforce your reputation as a sound scholar.

Quick

Reference ➡ **General Principles of In-Text Citation**

- Cite not only direct quotations but also paraphrases, summaries, and information gathered from a source.
- In most cases, include the author's surname and a page reference. You may place the name(s) in a signal phrase or a parenthetical note; the page reference should appear in parentheses.
- A signal phrase makes it easier to integrate borrowed information or the author's credentials into your own prose. A parenthetical citation is appropriate when establishing facts or citing more than one source for a piece of information.
- For one-page and unpaginated sources (such as websites), provide only the author's name.
- For two or more sources by the same author, include the title—either a complete title in the text or an abbreviated title in the parenthetical note.

More about ▶▶▶
What you need to cite, 265–66
What you do not need to cite, 266–67
Signal phrases, 291–93
Integrating borrowed material into your text, 291–94

17a Creating MLA-Style In-Text Citations

In-text citations appear in the body of your paper. They mark each use you make of a source, regardless of whether you are quoting, paraphrasing, summarizing, or drawing on an idea from the source. They also alert readers to a shift between *your* ideas and those borrowed from a source.

You can cite a source in your text by using a signal phrase, a parenthetical note, or both:

- *Signal phrase.* Include the author's name (often just the surname) and an appropriate verb in your sentence; put the page numbers from which the borrowed material comes in parentheses.

  While encouraging writers to use figurative language, journalist

  signal phrase
  Constance Hale cautions that "a metaphor has the shelf life of a fresh

  page no.
  vegetable" (224), illustrating the warning with her own lively metaphor.

  Signal phrases often make it easier for readers to determine where your ideas end and borrowed material begins. They also allow you to integrate the borrowed material into your sentence and to put the source in context by adding your own

connect
mhconnectcomposition.com
Additional resources: QL17001, QL17002

interpretation and describing the qualifications of the source author. For these reasons, most summaries, paraphrases, and quotations should be introduced by a signal phrase.

connect
mhconnectcomposition.com
Additional resources: QL17003

■ ***Parenthetical note.*** Include the author's surname plus the page number(s) from which the borrowed material comes in parentheses:

While figurative language can make a passage come alive, be aware

parenthetical note
that metaphors have "the shelf life of a fresh vegetable" (Hale 224).

Parenthetical notes are most appropriate when readers can tell from the context where borrowed material begins and ends, as in the example above. They are also useful when you are citing more than one source, when you are establishing facts, or when the author is not especially important to the point you are making.

NOTE The works-cited entry is the same whether you use a signal phrase or a parenthetical note:

author   title   publication info.   medium
Hale, Constance. *Sin and Syntax*. New York: Broadway, 2001. Print.

---

1. Include enough information to lead readers to the source in the list of works cited.

Whether using a signal phrase or a parenthetical note, provide enough information for readers to locate the source in the ***list of works cited***. In most cases, providing the author's surname and a page reference is enough to guide readers to the correct source. Occasionally, however, you may need to provide more information:

Example 6, 306–7

■ If you cite more than one source by the same author, mention the title of the work in the text or include a shortened form of the title in the in-text citation. (You may also want to mention the title of the work if it is relevant to the point you are making.)

Example 7, 307

■ If you refer to sources by two different authors with the same surname, mention the authors' first names in the text, or include the authors' first initials in the in-text citation.

➤ Tech

Page References and Web Pages

Despite the term *web page*, most websites do not have page numbers in the sense that printed books do. Your browser may number the pages when you print a web page from a website, but this numbering only appears on your printed copy. Different computers and printers break pages differently, so your printed page 5 might be someone else's page 4 or 6. For this reason, citations of most web pages include only the author's name. If a website numbers its paragraphs, provide that information instead of a page reference.

Occasionally, you may need to include less information. For example, you would omit a page number in these cases:

- When you are summarizing an entire source
- When your source is just one page long
- When your source, such as a web page, is not paginated

➤ Example 14a, 312

2. Place in-text citations so readers know where borrowed material starts and stops.

When you incorporate a quotation, paraphrase, summary, or idea from a source into your own text, carefully consider the placement of the in-text citation, keeping the following goals in mind:

- To make clear exactly which material is drawn from the source
- To avoid distracting your reader

Signal Phrase When using a signal phrase, bookend the borrowed information: Insert the author's name *before,* and the page number *after,* the cited material.

> Daniels, who has written several books about DC Comics' creations, notes that underground comix artists are not controlled by corporate interests that discourage "daring" material that might not sell (165, 180).

Parenthetical Note When using a parenthetical note, place the note at a natural pause in a sentence—at the end of a phrase, clause, or sentence—right after the borrowed material and before any punctuation.

➤ *More about* ▶▶▶
Phrases, 617–20
Clauses, 620–22
Sentences, 623–24

Following a sentence

Underground comix artists are not controlled by corporate interests that discourage "daring" material (Daniels 165, 180).

Following a clause

While underground comix artists are not constrained by the conservatism of large corporations (Daniels 165), they are beholden to a different set of standards—those of their loyal and opinionated readers, who may balk at experimental shifts in style or story.

Following a phrase

Free from the control of large corporations (Daniels 165), underground comix artists are still beholden to their readers' standards.

Multiple Sources When you use different sources for different pieces of information within a sentence, give separate citations in the appropriate places.

Example

_____from Daniels _____
Other common themes in underground comix include sex and sexual

identity, politics, and social issues (Daniels 165), as shown in Crumb's
_____from Heller_____
work, which is well known for its satirical approach to countercultural

topics (Heller).

When the information you are drawing on comes from more than one source, follow the borrowed material with a list of all relevant sources, separated by semicolons:

Example

> Jamestown was once described as a failed colony populated by failed
>
> colonists, but new findings suggest that the colonists were resourceful
>
> survivors (Howard; Lepore 43).

Block Quotations When the text you are quoting runs to more than four lines of your project, indent the borrowed material as a block, and place the parenthetical note one space *after* the closing punctuation mark.

More about ▶▶▶
Block quotations,
342

Example

> signal phrase
> Howard and Kennedy assert that parents and school officials tend to
>
> ignore hazing until an incident becomes public knowledge. They
>
> describe a concrete incident that demonstrates their claims:
>
> > In general, the Bredvik school community (parents, teachers,
> >
> > coaches, and students) condoned or ignored behaviors that
> >
> > could be called "hazing" or "sexual harassment." However,
> >
> > when the incident was formally brought to the attention of the
> >
> > larger, public audience of the community a conflict erupted in
> >
> > the community over how to frame, understand, and react to the
> >
> > event. (347-48)

3. Adjust in-text citations to different types of sources.

The exact form of an in-text citation depends on the type of source you are citing. The examples below cover the most common types. For more unusual sources, study the general principles as outlined here and in the *MLA Handbook for Writers of Research Papers,* 7th ed. (available in any library), and adapt them to your special circumstances.

MLA In-Text Citations

1. One author

a. Signal phrase

> Cahill cautions responsible historians against disparaging the Middle
>
> Ages; medieval Europe's reputation as a time of darkness, ignorance,
>
> page no.
> and blind faith is "largely (if not wholly) undeserved" (310).

b. Parenthetical note

> The Middle Ages are often unjustly characterized as a time of darkness,
>
> ignorance, and blind faith (Cahill 310).

2. Two or three authors Include the surnames of all the authors in your signal phrase or parenthetical note; use *and,* not an ampersand (&), in the parenthetical note.

> To write successfully about their families, authors must have motives—and perspective—beyond merely exposing secret histories (Miller and Paola 72).

3. More than three authors For sources with more than three authors, you may either list each author by surname (follow the order in the text) or insert the Latin phrase ***et al.*** following the first author's surname.

NOTE *al.* is an abbreviation, so it requires a period; *et* is a complete word, so it does not. There should be no punctuation between the author's name and *et al.*

> all authors in signal phrase
> Visonà, Poynor, Cole, Harris, Abiodun, and Blier stress that symbols
> used in African art are not intended to be iconic but instead to suggest a
> wide variety of meanings; the authors liken this complexity to "a
> telephone line that carries multiple messages simultaneously" (19).

> Symbols used in African art are not intended to be iconic; rather, the
> artist's goal is to suggest a complex range of meanings to different
> 1st author + et al.
> viewers (Visonà et al. 19).

Whichever you choose, do the same in your entry in the list of works cited.

MLA In-Text Citations

1. One author
2. **Two or three authors**
3. **More than three authors**
4. Group or corporate author
5. Unnamed author

---

et al. Abbreviation of the Latin phrase *et alii,* "and others"

> Example 3, 317

MLA In-Text Citations

4. Group or corporate author When a government agency, corporation, or other organization is listed as the author, use that organization's name in your in-text citation.

---

government agency as author

The Federal Emergency Management Agency indicates that Kansas

City is located in a region of frequent and intense tornado activity (4).

The MLA suggests incorporating names into your sentence in a signal phrase to avoid long parenthetical notes. If a parenthetical note makes more sense in the context, use common abbreviations ("U.S." for *United States,* "Corp." for *Corporation*) to shorten the name where you can.

5. Unnamed author If the author is unnamed and the work is alphabetized by title in the list of works cited, use the title in your in-text citation. Abbreviate long titles in parenthetical citations.

One nineteenth-century children's book vows that "when examined

by the microscope, the flea is a pleasant object," and the author's

vivid description of this sight—a body "curiously adorned with a suit of

polished armor, neatly jointed, and beset with a great number of sharp

pins almost like the quills of a porcupine"—may win readers' curiosity, if

title
not their sympathy (*Insects* 8).

Example 4, 317

If you do abbreviate the title, start your abbreviation with the word by which the title will be alphabetized in your list of works cited. Only if the author is listed specifically as "Anonymous" should you use that designation.

6. Two or more sources by the same author When you draw on two or more sources by the same author, differentiate between these sources by including titles.

book title

In her book *Nickel and Dimed,* social critic Barbara Ehrenreich

demonstrates that people cannot live on the then-current minimum

blog entry title

wage (60). Perhaps, as she notes in her blog entry "'Values' Voters

Raise Minimum Wages," they will be a little better able to hold their own

in the six states (Arizona, Colorado, Montana, Missouri, Nevada, Ohio)

that have recently raised their minimum wage.

If you use a signal phrase, use the full title; if you use a parenthetical citation, abbreviate it ("'Values' Voters").

7. Two or more authors with the same surname When your paper includes sources by two different authors with the same surname, differentiate them by including their first names (the first time you mention them in a signal phrase) or by including their first initials (in a parenthetical reference or subsequent text references).

Including citations is important not only because they give credit but

also because they "organize a field of inquiry, create order, and allow for

accountability" (S. Rose 243). This concern for acknowledging original

sources dates back to the early eighteenth century: Joseph Addison

was one of the first to argue for "the superiority of original to imitative

composition" (M. Rose 114).

8. Selection from an anthology If your source is a work included in an anthology, reader, or other collection, your citation should name the author of your source—not the editor of the anthology.

MLA In-Text Citations

> Southern fiction often explores the marked curiosity that women of
>
> *author of story*
> stature and mystery inspire in their communities. Faulkner's "A Rose for
>
> Emily," for example, describes the title character as "a tradition, a duty,
>
> and a care; a sort of hereditary obligation upon the town . . ." (79).

MLA In-Text Citations

7. Two or more authors with the same surname
8. Selection from an anthology
9. **Multivolume source**
10. **Literary source**
11. Sacred text
12. Indirect source

9. Multivolume source If you use information from more than one volume of a multivolume work, your in-text citation must indicate both the volume and page from which you are borrowing. (This information can be omitted if you use only one volume of the work, since your works-cited entry will indicate which volume you used.)

> *author*
> Tarbell writes that in 1847 Abraham Lincoln was a popular man of
>
> "simple, sincere friendliness" who was an enthusiastic—though
>
> *vol. no. pg. no.*
> awkward—bowler (1: 210).

The words *volume* and *page* (or their abbreviations) are not used.

10. Literary source Because many classics of literature—novels, poems, plays—are published in a number of editions (printed and digital) with pagination that varies widely, your citation should provide your readers with the information they will need to find the passage, regardless of which edition they are reading.

a. Novel Include the chapter number (with the abbreviation *ch.*) after the page number (or location reference for digital books) to your edition:

> Joyce shows his protagonist's dissatisfaction with family, faith, and
>
> country through the adolescent Stephen Daedalus's first dinner at
>
> the adult table, an evening filled with political and religious discord
>
> *pg. no. ch. no.*
> (274; ch. 1).

Use arabic (*2, 9, 103*), not roman (*ii, ix, ciii*), numerals, regardless of what your source uses.

If the novel has chapters grouped into parts or books, include both the part or book number and the chapter number, using the appropriate abbreviation (*pt.* for *part* or *bk.* for *book*).

MLA In-Text Citations

8. Selection from an anthology
9. Multivolume source
10. Literary source
11. Sacred text
12. Indirect source

> Even though New York society declares the Countess Olenska beyond
>
> her prime, Newland Archer sees in her a "mysterious authority of
>
> beauty" (Wharton 58; bk. 1, ch. 8).

b. Play When citing plays, use act, scene, and line numbers (in that order), not page numbers or location numbers (used in digital editions). Do not label the parts; instead, separate them with periods.

> When the ghost of Hamlet's father cries, "Adieu, adieu, adieu!
>
> remember me," Hamlet wonders if he must "remember" his father
>
> through vengeance (1.5.91).
>
> —— No spaces

c. Poem For poetry, use line numbers, rather than page or location numbers. With the first reference to line numbers, use the word *line* or *lines;* omit it thereafter.

> In Audre Lorde's poem "Hanging Fire," her fourteen-year-old frets,
>
> 1st ref.
> "What if I die / before morning" (lines 7-8), making me remember my
>
> own teenage worries of just a few years ago. Each of the three stanzas
>
> later refs.
> ends with "and momma's in the bedroom / with the door closed" (9-10,
>
> 20-21, 32-33), bringing me back to my "now": I am that mother who
>
> does not understand.

For long poems that are divided into sections (books, parts, numbered stanzas), provide that information as well, omitting the section name (or abbreviation) and separating section number from line number(s) with a period.

> David Mason's *Ludlow* (2007) begins with a description that captures
>
> Luisa's life:
>
> > Down below
> >
> > the mesa, smells of cooking rose from shacks
> >
> > in rows, and there Luisa scrubbed the pot
> >
> > as if she were some miner's wife and not
> >
> > a sapper's daughter, scrawny, barely twelve. (1.5-8)
>
> No space

MLA In-Text Citations

9. Multivolume source
10. Literary source
11. **Sacred text**
12. Indirect source
13. Dictionary or encyclopedia entry

11. Sacred text Cite sacred texts (such as the Bhagavad-Gita, the Talmud, the Qur'an, and the Bible) not by page number but by book title (abbreviated), chapter number, and verse number(s), and separate each section with a period. Do not italicize book titles or put them in quotation marks, and do not italicize the name of the sacred text, unless you are referring to a specific edition.

> sacred text
>
> In the Bible's timeless love poetry, the female speaker concludes her
>
> description of her lover with this proclamation: "This is my beloved
>
> book   ch.verse
>
> and this is my friend, / O daughters of Jerusalem" (Song Sol. 5.16).
>
> No space

> specific edition
>
> The *New Oxford Annotated Bible* offers a moving translation of the
>
> timeless love poetry in the Song of Solomon. The female speaker
>
> concludes her description of her lover with this proclamation: "This is
>
> my beloved and this is my friend, / O daughters of Jerusalem" (5.16).

12. Indirect source When you can, avoid quoting from a secondhand source. When you cannot locate the original source, mention the name of the person you are quoting in your sentence; in your parenthetical note, include *qtd. in* (for *quoted in*) plus the name of the author of the source in which you found the quote.

> Handel's stock among opera-goers rose considerably over the course
>
> of the twentieth century. In 1912, an English music critic, H. C. Colles, author quoted
>
> maintained that "it would be difficult, if not impossible, to make any one
>
> of Handel's operas tolerable to a modern audience" (qtd. in Orrey 62). source of quotation
>
> Today, however, Handel's operas are performed around the world.

In your list of works cited, include the *indirect* source (*Orrey*), not the source being quoted (*H. C. Colles*).

13. Dictionary or encyclopedia entry In the citation of a dictionary or encyclopedia entry, omit the page number on which you found the item. For a dictionary entry, place the defined word in quotation marks, followed by the abbreviation *def.;* follow this with the letter or number of the definition you wish to reference.

> Another definition of *honest* is "respectable" ("Honest," def. 6), but what,
>
> if anything, does truth have to do with respectability?

In the parenthetical note for an encyclopedia entry, include the entry's full title in quotation marks.

> The study of ethics is not limited to philosophers, as its "all-embracing
>
> practical nature" makes it an applicable or even necessary course of
>
> study in a wide variety of disciplines, from biology to business ("Ethics").

MLA In-Text Citations

11. Sacred text
12. **Indirect source**
13. **Dictionary or encyclopedia entry**
14. Website or other electronic source
15. Personal communication

More about ▶▶▶
Parts of a dictionary entry, 586–88

If you are citing two entries with the same name from different reference sources, add an abbreviated form of the reference work's title to each entry.

> While the word *ethics* is commonly understood to mean "moral principles" ("Ethics," def. 4, *Random House Webster's*), to philosophers it is "the evaluation of human conduct" ("Ethics," *Philosophical Dict.*).

14. Website or other electronic source Cite electronic sources such as websites, online articles, e-books, and emails as you would print sources, but note that many of these sources do not use page numbers.

a. Without page, paragraph, or screen numbers Unless there is another numbering system at work (such as a reference to a location or numbered paragraphs or screens), cite the author without a page reference.

> When first published in 1986, Alan Moore's *Watchmen* revolutionized the comic book; today, even its harshest critics acknowledge the
> *author only*
> book's landmark status (Shone).

You may credit your source more elegantly by mentioning the author in a signal phrase and omitting the parenthetical citation altogether.

> *signal phrase*
> Reading Alan Moore's *Watchmen* in 2005, critic Tom Shone found it "underwhelming," but he admitted that in 1985, the comic book was "unquestionably a landmark work."

b. With paragraph, screen, or slide numbers If an electronic source numbers its paragraphs, screens, or slides, you can reference these numbers as you would pages (with an appropriate identifying abbreviation—*par.* or *pars., screen* or *screens*).

> The internet has also become an outlet for direct distribution through
>
> artist websites, making independent titles not only more accessible to
>
> consumers but also more affordable for individual artists to produce and
>
> market (Fenty, Houp, and Taylor, par. 1).

c. In a PDF file Online documents offered as a PDF (portable document format) file include all the elements of the printed document, including the page number; since pages are fixed, you can and should cite page numbers.

More about ▶▶▶
PDF, 196, 228, 232

15. Personal communication As with other unpaginated sources, when citing information from a letter, email message, interview, or other personal communication, you should include the author's name in a signal phrase or parenthetical citation. Also indicate the type of source you are citing.

> Many people have asked why teachers cannot do more to prevent
> source type
> school shootings; in an email to this author, one instructor responds:
>
> "As creative writing teachers untrained in psychology, can we really
>
> determine from a student's poetry whether he or she is emotionally
> author of email
> disturbed—even a threat to others?" (Fox).

MLA In-Text
Citations

16. Table or figure If the visual you are discussing is *not* included in your paper, include the name of the artist, the work of art, and any other relevant information in the text, and include an entry in your list of works cited.

More about ▶▶▶
Examples, 47–51,
336–37

... There is no experience quite like standing in front of a full-size painting by Jackson Pollock; they have an irresistible sense of movement to them, the particular quality of which is unique to his work. This is especially evident in *One (Number 31, 1950),* which currently hangs on the fourth floor of New York's Museum of Modern Art. ...

Quick Reference ➡ MLA Works-Cited Entries

If the visual *is* included in your project, include the source information in a table's source note (see Figure 17.1), or in a figure's caption (see the figure caption on p. 349 in the model student project at the end of this chapter).

TABLE 1 | **THE DEMISE OF THE THREE-DECKER NOVEL**

Year	No. of 3-deckers published
1894	184
1895	52
1896	—
1897	4
1898	0

Source: Information from John Feather, *A History of British Publishing* (Clarendon: Crown Helm, 1988), quoted in Kelly J. Mays.

FIGURE 17.1 Table in MLA style

MLA Works-Cited Entries

1. One author
2. Two or three authors
3. More than three authors

▶▶▶Annotated visual of where to find author, title, and publication information, on foldout following p. 297

17b Preparing an MLA-Style List of Works Cited

The list of works cited, which comes at the end of your research project, includes information about the sources you have cited in your text. (A bibliography that includes sources you read but did not cite in your research project is called a list of works consulted.) Your list of works cited provides readers with the information they need for locating the material you drew on in your paper. The format of each entry depends in part on the type of source it is.

Books—Printed and Electronic

In a printed book, most or all of the information you need for creating an entry in the list of works cited appears on the title and copyright pages. In an online or e-book, print and electronic publication information often appears at the top or bottom of the first page or is available through a link.

1. One author

a. Printed The basic entry for a printed book looks like this:

Author's surname, First name. *Title: Subtitle.* Place of publication: Publisher

(shortened), date of publication. Medium of publication.

Here is an example of an actual entry in the list of works cited:

author   title   publication information   medium
Morrison, Toni. *A Mercy.* New York: Knopf, 2008. Print.
               place   pub.   date

b. Database When you are documenting a book you accessed through a database, add the name of the database and change the medium of publication from *Print* to *Web.* Also, add the date (day, month, year) on which you accessed the work.

Wharton, Edith. *The Age of Innocence.* New York: D. Appleton, 1920.
         database   date accessed
         Bartleby.com. Web. 5 July 2007.
             medium

c. E-book The citation for an electronic version of a book is the same as for a printed book except that the medium of publication changes from *Print* to the specific type of e-book file you read: Gemstar e-book file, Microsoft Reader e-book file, Kindle e-book file, and so on.

                               medium
Morrison, Toni. *A Mercy.* New York: Knopf, 2008. Kindle e-book file.

2. Two or three authors List authors in the order in which they appear on the title page. Only the first author should be listed with surname first.

author 1   author 2
Miller, Brenda, and Suzanne Paola. *Tell It Slant.* New York: McGraw,
2004. Print.

author 1   author 2   author 3
Fleming, Robert L., Jr., Dorje Tsering, and Liu Wulin. *Across the Tibetan*

Plateau: Ecosystems, Wildlife, and Conservation. New York: Norton,

2008. Print.

3. More than three authors Either list all the authors, or just list the first and add *et al.* Whichever you choose, do the same in your in-text citation.

> **More about ▶▶▶**
> *et al.,* 305

> Example 3, 305

Visonà, Monica Blackmun, et al. *A History of Art in Africa.* New York:

Abrams, 2001. Print.

Visonà, Monica Blackmun, Robin Poynor, Herbert M. Cole, Michael D.

Harris, Rowland Abiodun, and Suzanne Preston Blier. *A History of*

Art in Africa. New York: Abrams, 2001. Print.

4. Unnamed (anonymous) author Start the entry with the title.

title
Terrorist Hunter: The Extraordinary Story of a Woman Who Went

Undercover to Infiltrate the Radical Islamic Groups Operating in

America. New York: Ecco-HarperCollins, 2003. Print.

Alphabetize the entry in your list of works cited using the first significant word of the title (not an article like *a, an,* or *the*). Only if the author is listed specifically as "Anonymous" should you use that designation in the entry.

Anonymous. *Go Ask Alice.* Englewood Cliffs, NJ: Prentice Hall, 1971. Print.

5. Two or more works by the same author Alphabetize the entries by the first important word in each title. Supply the author's name only with the first entry; for subsequent works, replace the author's name with three hyphens.

> **MLA** Works-
> Cited Entries
>
> 1. One author
> **2. Two or three authors**
> **3. More than three authors**
> **4. Unnamed (anonymous) author**
> **5. Two or more works by the same author**
> 6. Group or corporate author
> 7. Author and editor or translator

Chabon, Michael. *The Final Solution: A Story of Detection*. New York:

> Fourth Estate, 2004. Print.

---. *The Yiddish Policeman's Union: A Novel*. New York: HarperCollins,

> 2007. Print.

6. Group or corporate author Treat the sponsoring organization as the author.

> corporate author
> Blackfoot Gallery Committee. *The Story of the Blackfoot People:*
>
> *Nitsitapiisinni*. Richmond Hill, ON: Firefly, 2002. Print.

7. Author and editor or translator List the author first; after the title, include the abbreviation *Ed.* or *Trans.* (as appropriate) before the editor's or translator's name.

NOTE When the abbreviation appears before the editor's or translator's name, it means *edited by* or *translated by,* so use the same abbreviation whether there is one editor or translator or many.

> Larsson, Asa. *Sun Storm*. Trans. Marlaine Delargy. New York: Delacorte.
>
> 2006. Print.

8. Edited book or anthology as a whole When citing the book as a whole, treat the editor as the author and insert the abbreviation *ed.* (or *eds.* if there is more than one editor) after the name.

> Furman, Laura, ed. *The O. Henry Prize Stories: The Best Stories of the*
>
> *Year*. New York: Anchor, 2008. Print.

> Delbanco, Nicholas, and Alan Cheuse, eds. *Literature: Craft and Voice*.
>
> New York: McGraw, 2009. Print.

9. One or more selections from an edited book or anthology If you are citing a selection from an edited book or anthology, start the entry with the selection's author and title. Include the page numbers for the entire selection (even if you used only part).

author   title (selection)
Faulkner, William. "A Rose for Emily." *Literature: Reading Fiction, Poetry,*

  and Drama. Ed. Robert DiYanni. 6th ed. New York: McGraw, 2009.
pages
  79-84. Print.

If you are citing more than one selection in the anthology or collection, include an entry for the collection as a whole. For each selection you use, include the author and title of the selection, followed by the surname of the editor and the page numbers of the selection.

> Example 8, 318

  Faulkner, William. "A Rose for Emily." DiYanni. 79-84. Print.

For a scholarly article included in an edited book, include the article's original publication information first, the abbreviation *Rpt. in* for *reprinted in,* and then the publication information for the anthology.

> Example 23 (a–c), 324–25

         original publication info.
  Stock, A. G. "Yeats and Achebe." *Journal of Commonwealth Literature*
         reprint publication info.
    5 (1968): 105-11. Rpt. in *Things Fall Apart.* By Chinua Achebe.

    Ed. Francis Abiola Irele. New York: Norton, 2008. 271-77. Print.

10. Edition other than the first Insert the edition number (*2nd ed., 3rd ed.*) or edition name (*Rev. ed.* for "revised edition") after the book's title. The edition number or name should appear on the title page.

  Rosebury, Brian. *Tolkien: A Literary Phenomenon.* 2nd ed. New York:

    Palgrave, 2004. Print.

If there is an editor or translator, insert the edition number or name after the editor or translator's name.

11. Imprint (division) of a larger publishing company Name both the imprint and publisher, separating them with a hyphen.

  Betcherman, Lita-Rose. *Court Lady and Country Wife: Two Noble*

    Sisters in Seventeenth-Century England. New York:
    imprint   publisher
    William Morrow-HarperCollins, 2005. Print.

12. Introduction, preface, foreword, or afterword Begin with the name of the person who wrote this section of the text. Then provide a

MLA Works-Cited Entries

9. One or more selections from an edited book or anthology
10. Edition other than the first
11. Imprint (division) of a larger publishing company
12. Introduction, preface, foreword, or afterword
13. Entry in a reference work
14. Multivolume work

descriptive label (such as *Introduction* or *Preface*), the title of the book, and the name of the book's author. (If the author of the section and the book are the same, use only the author's surname after the title.) Include the page numbers for the section.

author of intro.   label   title of book
Barrett, Michèle. Introduction. *The Origin of the Family, Private Property*
                                author of book
   and the State. By Friedrich Engels. New York: Penguin, 1986.

   7-30. Print.

If this section has a title, include it before the descriptive label.

                        afterword's title
Burton, Larry W. "Countering the Naysayers: Independent Writing

   Programs as Successful Experiments in American Education."
   label
   Afterword. *A Field of Dreams: Independent Writing Programs and the*

   Future of Composition Studies. Ed. Peggy O'Neill, Angela Crow, and

   Larry W. Burton. Logan: Utah State UP, 2002. 295-300. Print.

13. Entry in a reference work Format an entry in a dictionary or encyclopedia as you would a selection from an edited book or anthology. For signed articles, include the author's name. (Articles in reference works often carry the author's initials only, so you may need to cross-reference the initials with a list of contributors in the front or back of the book.) If an article is unsigned, begin with its title.

a. Printed For familiar reference works, omit publication information other than the edition and year of publication. If the entries are arranged alphabetically, omit a page reference.

   "Culture." *Oxford English Dictionary*. Compact 2nd ed. 1991. Print.

   Green, Michael. "Cultural Studies." *A Dictionary of Cultural and Critical*

   Theory. Cambridge: Blackwell, 1996. Print.

b. Online For online reference works, add the site's sponsor, change the medium of publication to *Web,* and add the date you accessed the site.

                                       sponsor
   "Culture." *Merriam-Webster Online Dictionary*. Merriam-Webster Online,
              medium access date
   2008. Web. 1 Dec. 2008.

c. CD-ROM or DVD-ROM Although CD-ROMs have largely been replaced by the internet, you may still need to use them. If the CD-ROM or DVD-ROM is published in versions rather than editions, use the abbreviation *Vers.* and include the version number after the title or editor's name. Change the medium of publication to *CD-ROM* or *DVD-ROM*.

> Cooley, Marianne. "Alphabet." *World Book Multimedia Encyclopedia.*
> <u>version</u>   <u>medium</u>
> Vers. 6.0.2. Chicago: World Book, 2002. CD-ROM.

14. Multivolume work

a. Multiple volumes Indicate the total number of volumes, followed by the abbreviation *vols.,* and indicate the span of years in which the volumes were published. Specify the volume from which you borrowed a particular passage or idea in your in-text citation.

> Example 9, 308

> <u>no. of vols.</u>
> Tarbell, Ida M. *The Life of Abraham Lincoln.* 2 vols. New York: Lincoln
> <u>pub. dates</u>
> Memorial Association, 1895-1900. Print.

b. One volume If you used only one volume, include the number of the volume you used before the publication information, and give only the publication date of that volume.

> <u>vol. used</u>
> Tarbell, Ida M. *The Life of Abraham Lincoln.* Vol. 1. New York: Lincoln
> <u>pub. date</u>
> Memorial Association, 1895. Print.

15. Book in a series
If the book you are citing is part of a series, the series title will usually be noted on the book's title page or on the page before the title page. Insert the series title (with no quotation marks or italics) after the medium of publication. If books in the series are numbered, include the number following the series title.

> Todorov, Tzvetan. *Mikhail Bakhtin: The Dialogical Principle.* Trans. Wlad
> <u>series title</u>
> Godzich. Minneapolis:U Minnesota P, 1995. Print. Theory and
> <u>no.</u>
> History of Literature 13.

16. Republished book If a book has been republished, its original date of publication will appear on the book's copyright page. If the original publication date may be of interest to your readers, include it before publication information for the version you consulted.

orig.
pub. date   repub. info.
Mallon, Thomas. *Stolen Words.* 1989. New York: Harvest, 2001. Print.

17. Title within a title Omit italics from any title that would normally be italicized when it falls within the main title of a book.

book title   title within title
Blamires, Harry. *The New Bloomsbury Book: A Guide Through* Ulysses.

3rd ed. London: Routledge, 2006. Print.

If the title within the title appears in quotation marks, retain the quotation marks and italicize both titles.

18. Sacred text Italicize the title only when you are documenting a particular edition. Editors' and translators' names generally follow the title.

The Holy Qur'an. Ed. and trans. Abdullah Yusuf Ali. 10th ed. Beltsville:

Amana, 1997. Print.

19. Missing publication information Replace missing information with an appropriate abbreviation, such as *n.d.* for *no date* or *n.p.* for *no publisher* or *no place of publication.*

Barrett, Edgar, ed. *Football West Virginia 1960.* N.p.: West Virginia

University, n.d. Print.

20. Pamphlet, brochure, or press release Follow the format for book entries. For a press release, include day and month of publication, if available.

"Family Teams Key to March for Babies." Fargo, ND: March of Dimes. 17 Jan.

2008. Print.

Examples 1–7, 316–318

If emailed or published online, document as you would a book published online.

Example 1, 316

21. Conference proceedings Include the name of the conference, the sponsoring organization, and the year the conference was held, if that information is not already conveyed by the title.

> Bizzell, Patricia, ed. *Rhetorical Agendas: Political, Ethical, Spiritual.*
> conference/sponsor   date
> Proc. of the Rhetoric Society of America, 2004. Mahwah:
>
> Erlbaum, 2005. Print.

For a paper delivered at a conference, follow the format for a lecture.

Example 46, 335

22. Dissertation Include the abbreviation *Diss.,* the school to which the dissertation was submitted (abbreviate *University* to *U*), and the year it was submitted. For published dissertations, set the title in italics.

> Agopsowicz, William Joseph. *In Praise of Fantasy: A Study of the*
>
> *Nineteenth Century American Short Story (Poe, Hawthorne, Irving,*
>
> *Melville, Bierce, James).* Diss. Arizona State U, 1992. Ann Arbor:
>
> UMI, 1992. Print.

For unpublished dissertations, put the title in quotation marks.

> Brommer, Stephanie. "We Walk with Them: South Asian Women's
>
> Organizations in Northern California Confront Domestic
>
> Abuse." Diss. U of California—Santa Barbara, 2004. Print.

Periodicals—Printed and Electronic

A periodical is a publication issued at regular intervals—newspapers are generally published every day, magazines every week or month, and scholarly journals four times a year. For all periodicals, include not only the title of the article (in quotation marks) but also the title of the periodical (in italics). The other publication information you include depends on the type of periodical you are documenting.

▶▶▶Annotated visual of where to find author, title, publication, and other information, on foldout following p. 297

23. Article in a scholarly journal The information you need to create an entry for a printed journal article is on the cover or table of contents of the journal and the first and last page of the article. For articles downloaded from a database, the information you need appears on the screen listing the articles that fit your search terms, on the first (and last) page of the file you download, or in the full record for the article you select. For articles that appear in journals published solely online, you may find the information you need on the website's home page, in the journal's table of contents, or on the first screen of the article. Access dates for online and database articles should come from your notes.

a. Printed The basic entry for an article in a printed journal looks like this:

> Surname, First name. "Article Title." *Journal Title* volume.issue (year): pages. Medium of publication.

Here is an example of an actual entry:

authors · article title
Cantor, Nancy, and Steve Schomberg. "What We Want Students to Learn:
subtitle
Cultivating Playfulness and Responsibility in a Liberal Education."
journal
title · issue · yr. · pgs. · medium
Change 34.6 (2002): 47-49. Print.
vol.

b. Accessed through a database When you document an article from a scholarly journal that you accessed through an online database, add the name of the database (in italics), change the medium of publication to *Web,* and add the date (day, month, year) on which you accessed the work.

Cantor, Nancy, and Steve Schomberg. "What We Want Students to

Learn: Cultivating Playfulness and Responsibility in a Liberal

database
Education." *Change* 34.6 (2002): 47-49. *Academic Search*
medium · access date
Premier. Web. 2 Dec. 2008.

c. Online

To document an online journal article, follow the model for a printed journal article; at the end of the entry, add the date on which you accessed the article. Although many journals that are published only online do not provide all the information that is available for printed journals, your entry should include as much of that information as possible. If the article you are documenting omits page numbers, use *n. pag.* in their place. Include the article's URL only if readers will not be able to find the article by searching for the author or title. (The parts that are different from a printed journal article are highlighted below.)

Lohnes, Sarah, and Charles Kinzer. "Questioning Assumptions about

Students' Expectations for Technology in College Classrooms."

                        medium access date

Innovate 3.5 (2007): n. pag. Web. 28 June 2007.

24. Article in a magazine

a. Printed Provide the issue's publication date (month and year or day, month, and year) and the page range for the article, but not the magazine's volume or issue number, even when they are available.

                                pub. date   pgs.

Samuels, David. "Shooting Britney." *Atlantic Monthly* Apr. 2008: 36-51.

Print.

b. Accessed through a database

Samuels, David. "Shooting Britney." *Atlantic Monthly* Apr. 2008:

                 database   medium access date

36-51. *Academic Search Premier.* Web. 25 Apr. 2008.

c. Online Very few online magazines include page or paragraph numbers; use *n. pag.* instead.

Stevenson, Seth. "Ads We Hate." *Slate* 26 Dec. 2006: n. pag. Web.

3 Jan. 2007.

MLA Works-Cited Entries

If you are documenting the online edition of a magazine that also appears in print, use the site name (usually a variation on the print title, such as *Progressive.org* or *Vanity Fair Online*).

website

Carr, Nicholas. "Is Google Making Us Stupid?" *Atlantic Online*

July/Aug. 2008. Web. 2 Dec. 2008.

25. Article in a newspaper The information you need to create an entry for a printed newspaper article is on the masthead of the newspaper (at the top of the first page) and on the first and last page of the article. For newspaper articles downloaded from a database, the information you need appears on the screen listing the articles that fit your search terms or on the first (and last) page of the article itself. Articles that appear in online versions of the newspaper usually contain all the information you need at the top of the first screen.

a. Printed For an article in a daily newspaper, include the date (day, month, year). If the paper paginates sections separately, include the section number, letter, or name immediately before the page number.

Bolanos, Enrique. "Facing Down the Sandinistas." *Washington Times*
                   date   sec. & pg.
        12 May 2005: A20. Print.

If the section number or letter is not part of the page number, add the abbreviation *sec.* and the section name, number, or letter. If the section is named, add the section name before the abbreviation *sec.* If no author is listed, begin the entry with the title of the article. If the article continues on a nonconsecutive page, add a plus sign after the first page number (*A20+*). If the newspaper's masthead specifies an edition (such as late edition or national edition), include that information after the date.

Keller, Julia. "Viral Villainy." *Chicago Tribune* 22 Mar. 2009, final ed., sec. 6:

1+. Print.

If the name of the city in which the newspaper is published does not appear in the newspaper's title, include it in brackets after the title.

Willman, David. "NIH Calls Actions of Senior Researcher 'Serious

             newspaper   city

Misconduct.'" *Plain Dealer* [Cleveland] 10 Sept. 2006: A15. Print.

MLA Works-
Cited Entries

25. Article in a
    newspaper
**26. Article on
    microform**
27. Review
28. Editorial
29. Letter to the
    editor

For well-known national newspapers (such as the *Christian Science Monitor, USA Today,* and the *Wall Street Journal*), no city or state is needed. If you are unsure whether the newspaper is well known, consult your instructor or a reference librarian.

b. Accessed through a database For a newspaper article accessed through a database, add the database name, change the medium, and add the access date.

Bolanos, Enrique. "Facing Down the Sandinistas." *Washington Times*

                database medium access date

12 May 2005: A20. *LexisNexis.* Web. 2 Dec. 2008.

c. Online For an online newspaper article, provide the title of the online publication, and include your date of access.

Woo, Elaine. "Edna Parker Dies at 115; Former Teacher Was World's

                            access date

Oldest Person." *LATimes.com* 28 Nov. 2008. Web. 2 Dec. 2008.

26. Article on microform Many libraries still store some back issues of periodicals on microform, a photograph of a periodical printed on plastic and viewed through a special microform reader. Your entry for a source stored on microform is the same as if you had accessed the source in print.

Example 23a, 324
Example 24a, 325
Example 25a, 326

    If your source is preserved on microform in a reference source such as *NewsBank,* change the medium of publication to *Microform* and add the title of the reference source and any access numbers (such as fiche and grid numbers) following the medium of publication.

27. Review Begin with the reviewer's name (if provided), followed by the title of the review (if any) and the label *Rev. of* (for *Review of*). Then include the title and author of the work being reviewed. Finally, include the title of the periodical and its publication information. If the review was accessed online, add information as shown in item 23b–c, 24b–c, or 25b–c.

MLA Works-Cited Entries

26. Article on microform
27. Review
28. Editorial
29. Letter to the editor
30. Website
31. Web page
32. Home page

Grover, Jan. "Unreliable Narrator." Rev. of *Love Works Like This: Opening*

One's Life to a Child, by Lauren Slater. *Women's Review of Books*

19.10-11 (2002): 40. Print.

28. Editorial Often editorials are unsigned; when that is the case, begin with the title of the editorial (if any). Then insert the label *Editorial* and follow with the periodical's publication information.

"Expanding the Horizon: OSU President Seeks to Give Students a New

View of Their Place in the World." Editorial. *Columbus Dispatch*

12 March 2009: A8. Print.

If the editorial was accessed online, add information as shown in item 23b–c, 24b–c, or 25b–c.

29. Letter to the editor Begin with the author's name, followed by the label *Letter* and the periodical's publication information.

Pritchett, Laura. Letter. *Poets & Writers Magazine* Jan.–Feb. 2004: 7. Print.

If the letter to the editor has a title, add it after the author's name (in quotation marks). If the letter to the editor was accessed online, add information as shown in item 23b–c, 24b–c, or 25b–c.

▶▶▶Annotated visual of where to find author, title, and publication information, on foldout following p. 297

Other Electronic Sources

While it is usually easy to find the information you need to create a complete entry for a book or an article in a periodical, websites can be a bit trickier. Most of the information you need will appear on the site's home page, usually at the bottom or top of the page, or on the web page you are documenting. Sometimes you may need to look further: Click on links such as "About us" or "More information." Frequently, websites will not provide complete information, so provide as much as you can.

30. Website The basic entry for a website looks like this:

Author's surname, First name. *Website title.* Copyright date or date last

updated. Sponsor. Medium. Access date.

Here is an example of an actual entry:

editor · title (website)
McGann, Jerome J., ed. *The Complete Writings and Pictures of Dante*
update
Gabriel Rossetti: A Hypermedia Archive. 2008. Institute for
sponsor
Advanced Technology in the Humanities, U of Virginia, and

Networked Infrastructure for Nineteenth-Century Electronic
medium · access date
Scholarship. Web. 30 Jan. 2007.

If no author or editor is listed, begin with the website's title.

31. Web page Add the title of the web page to the entry for a website.

page title
Bahri, Deepika. "Yehuda Amichai." *Postcolonial Studies.* Dept. of English,

Emory U. 13 Nov. 2002. Web. 7 Feb. 2007.

Personal websites often do not provide all the information needed to create a complete entry. If the site does not have a title, include the identifier "home page" or "website"; if the title includes the author's name, do not restate it.

32. Home page (academic)
a. Course

instructor · course title · sponsor
Gray, David. *Introduction to Ethics,* Spring 2006. Dept. of Philosophy,
medium · access date
Carnegie Mellon U. Web. 17 April 2007.

b. Department

label
English. Dept. Home page. U of CA—Santa Barbara. 2005. Web.

20 July 2007.

33. Discussion list posting Treat the subject line as the title, and include the label *Online posting,* the date of the posting (if available), and the name of the list or sponsoring group.

date
subj. line · label · posted
Tucker, Mieke Koppen. "Grammar Study." Online posting. 7 Oct. 1995.
list name
Writing Program Administration Discussion List. Web. 2 Jan. 2004.

34. Article on a wiki Since wikis are written and edited collaboratively, there is no author to cite; begin the entry with the article title.

> "The Knife of Never Letting Go." *ChildLitWiki*. Created and maintained by
>
> Mat Berman. 14 Sept. 2008. Web. 17 Sept. 2008.

35. Blog, blog posting, or comment on a blog posting
a. Blog

> blogger   blog   label   medium   access date
> Walker, Jill. *Jill/txt*. Blog. Web. 10 June 2007.

b. Blog posting

> post author   post title
> Bartow, Ann. "Why Are There So Many Academic Books Out There
>   label
> That Would Be Better as Longish Articles?" Blog entry.
>   post date
> *Sivacracy.net*. 26 Dec. 2006. Web. 30 Dec. 2006.

c. Comment on a blog posting

> comment author   title of entry commented on   label
> Bailey, Jonathan. "Content Theft / Blog Plagiarism." Comment. Ryan
>
> McCue. *Cube Games*. Blog. 18 Nov. 2004. Web. 19 Nov. 2004.

If the comment's author uses a screen name, use that; if the actual name is available and of interest to readers, provide that as well, following the screen name, in square brackets.

36. Second Life If the author/speaker uses an avatar with a different name than the writer's actual name, use the avatar's name, but if the writer's actual name is available and of interest to readers (it may lend credibility, for example), provide it in square brackets following the avatar name.

> avatar   actual name
> Reuters, Eric [Eric Krangel]. "*Second Life* on *The Daily Show*." *Second*
>   label
> *Life News Center/Reuters*. *Second Life*. 8 April 2007. Web.
>
> 10 Feb. 2008.

37. Source published in more than one medium Some sources may include multiple media; for example, a printed book may come with a supplementary website or CD-ROM. In the entry in your list of works cited, follow the entry format for the part of the source that you mainly used, but list all the media you consulted in alphabetical order.

Davis, Robert L., H. Jay Siskin, and Alicia Ramos. *Entrevistas: An*

Introduction to Language and Culture. 2nd ed. New York: McGraw,

list of media
2005. CD-ROM, print, website.

38. Computer software

release   download
title   vendor   date   date
PowerResearcher. Atlanta: Uniting Networks, 2004. 8 June 2004.

39. Video game

release
game   publisher date
Rock Band 2. Wii. Nintendo, 2008.
platform

MLA Works-
Cited Entries

36. *Second Life*
37. Source
   published in
   more than one
   medium
**38. Computer
   software**
39. Video game
40. Motion picture
41. DVD extras

Audio and Visual Sources

The information you need to create an entry for most audio and visual sources will appear on the cover, label, or program of the work or in the credits at the end of a film. The person you list in the "author" position—the director, performer, artist, or composer—will vary depending on what you have emphasized in the body of your research project. If you are writing about a director's body of work, put the director's name first; if you are writing about a performance, put the performer's name first. If it is the work itself that you are writing about, put the title of the work first. However you choose to organize the entry, indicate the role of those whom you list, using abbreviations such as *perf.* (*performer*), *dir.* (*director*), and *cond.* (*conductor*).

As with any other entry, italicize the titles of complete or longer works (such as albums, films, operas, and original works of art) and place quotation marks around the titles of shorter works or works published as part of a larger whole (such as songs on a CD or a single episode of a television show). Publication information includes the name of the distributor, production company, or network, as well as the date on which the audio or visual was created, recorded, or broadcast, and the medium through which you accessed it. If you found the audio or visual source online, also include the date on which you last accessed it.

40. Motion picture

a. Film

King of Kong. Dir. Seth Gordon. PictureHouse Entertainment, 2007. Film.

(labels above entry: title · director · distributor · release date · medium)

If other artists besides the director are relevant to your project, list them between the director and the distributor.

King of Kong. Dir. Seth Gordon. Perf. Steve Wiebe and Billy Mitchell.

PictureHouse Entertainment, 2007. Film.

(label above entry: performers)

If your project stresses the director, performer, or other contributor, place that information at the beginning of the citation.

Gordon, Seth, dir. *King of Kong*. Perf. Steve Wiebe, Billy Mitchell.

PictureHouse Entertainment, 2007. Film.

b. Video or DVD Include the original release date, when relevant, before the distributor, and include the medium you viewed.

The Lady Eve. Dir. Preston Sturges. Perf. Barbara Stanwyck and Henry
Fonda. 1941. Universal Home Entertainment, 2006. DVD.

(labels: orig. release · medium)

c. Internet download Include the date on which you accessed the film.

Juno. Screenplay by Diablo Cody. Dir. Jason Reitman. Perf. Ellen Page,

Michael Cera, Jennifer Garner, Jason Bateman, J. K. Simmons, and

Alison Janney. 2007. *iTunes,* 2008. Internet download. 19 Jan. 2009.

(label: access date)

41. DVD extras Add the title of the extra (in quotation marks).

"Making *Capote:* Concept to Script." *Capote*. Dir. Bennett Miller. Perf.

Philip Seymour Hoffman and Catherine Keener. 2005. Sony Pictures,

2006. DVD.

(label: DVD extra)

42. Television or radio broadcast In most cases, begin with the title of the series or episode. Follow that with a list of the relevant contributors and information about the local station that broadcast the

program. Because the director may change from episode to episode, other contributors, such as the creator or producer, may be more relevant. Next, include the date of the program and the medium in which you accessed it. If your project emphasizes an individual, begin with that person's name. Add any supplementary information at the end of the entry.

MLA Works-
Cited Entries

40. Motion picture
41. DVD extras
**42. Television or
radio broadcast**
43. Musical or other
audio recording
44. Live
performance

a. Series

series
Lost. Creat. and exec. prod. J. A. Abrams, Jeffrey Lieber, and Damon

Lindelof. Perf. Naveen Andrews, Matthew Fox, Jorge Garcia, Josh

Holloway, Daniel Dae Kim, Yunjun Kim, Evangeline Lilly, and Terry

city of local
network   station   broadcast dates
O'Quinn. ABC. KNXV, Phoenix, 22 Sept. 2004-29 May 2008.
medium   call letters
Television.

Bridging the Morphine Gap. Host, Mukti Jain Campion. BBC. Radio 4,

London, 3 March 2008. Radio.

b. Episode

"In Buddy's Eyes." *Desperate Housewives.* Perf. Teri Hatcher, Felicity

Huffman, Marcia Cross, Eva Longoria Parker, and Nicollette

Sheridan. ABC. KNXV, Phoenix, 20 Apr. 2008. Internet
supplementary info.
download, television. *iTunes,* 2008.

c. Single program

Persuasion. By Jane Austen. Adapt. Simon Burke. Perf. Julia Davis and

Rupert Penry-Jones. PBS. WGBH, Boston, 13 Jan. 2008. Television.

d. Podcast For a podcast, replace the original medium of publication with the word *Podcast* and the date on which you accessed the file.

"The Giant Pool of Money." Narr. Ira Glass. *This American Life.* Natl. Public
medium   access date
Radio. WBEZ, Chicago, 27 Sept. 2008. Podcast. 3 Oct. 2008.

43. Musical or other audio recording Begin with whichever part of the entry is most relevant to your project—the name of the composer or performer, or the title of the CD or song. Place the title of shorter works, such as a song, in quotation marks. Italicize the titles of longer works, such as the title of an opera, but not the titles of symphonies identified only by form, number, and key, such as Brahms's Symphony no. 1.

a. CD, LP, audiobook

Adamo, Mark. *Little Women.* Perf. Stephanie Novacek, Chad Shelton,

Margaret Lloyd, and Stacey Tappan. Houston Grand Opera. Cond.

prod. co. & release date
Patrick Summers. Ondine, 2001. CD.
medium

Brahms, Johannes. Symphony no. 1. Chicago Symphony Orchestra. Cond.

Georg Solti. Decca, 1992. CD.

b. Song or selection from a CD, LP, or audiobook

Los Campesinos. "My Year in Lists." *Hold on Now, Youngster. . . .* Arts &

Crafts, 2008. CD.

c. Compressed music file (MP3, MP4)

Los Campesinos. "My Year in Lists." *Hold on Now, Youngster. . . .*

supplementary info.   download date
Arts & Crafts, 2008. *iTunes,* 2008. MP3. 16 Dec. 2008.

d. Online sound file or clip For a sound recording accessed online, combine the format for a web page with the format for a sound recording.

Example 31, 329

author   selection title
Chaucer, Geoffrey. "'The Miller's Tale': Nicholas Seduces Alisoun."

title of work   website
Perf. Alfred David. *The Canterbury Tales.* "The Criyng and the Soun":

sponsor
The Chaucer Metapage Audio Files. VA Military Inst. Dept. of Eng.

date posted   date accessed
and Fine Arts. 11 Dec. 2006. Web. 20 July 2007.
medium

44. Live performance The entry for a performance is similar to that for a film. Instead of the distributor, year of release, and medium of publication, include the group (if any), the venue and city of the performance, the date of the performance you attended, and the word *Performance*. If your project emphasizes the composer, writer, or performer, begin the entry with that information. If the performance is untitled, include a descriptive label.

a. Ensemble

Macbeth. By William Shakespeare. Dir. Christopher Carter Sanderson.

Perf. Natasha Badillo, Ambjorn Elder, and Frances You.

_{group}   _{venue}   _{city}
Gorilla Repertory Theatre Company. Fort Tryon Park, New York.

_{perf. date}
17 May 2002. Performance.

b. Individual

_{performer}   _{label}
Stinespring, Marjorie M. Piano recital. Chicago State University.

2 Mar. 2004. Performance.

45. Musical composition To document a musical composition itself rather than a specific performance, recording, or published version of it, include only the composer and the title of the work (in italics unless the composition is identified only by form, number, and key).

_{composer}   _{titled opera}
Mozart, Wolfgang Amadeus. *Don Giovanni.*

_{composer}   _{untitled symphony}
Schumann, Robert. Symphony no. 1 in B-flat major, op. 38.

46. Lecture, speech, or debate Treat the speaker as the author; place the title in quotation marks (if there is one); and indicate the occasion and sponsoring organization (if relevant), location, date, and mode of delivery. If the lecture, speech, or debate is untitled, replace the title with a brief descriptive label.

_{speakers}   _{title}
Biden, Joseph, and Sarah Palin. "Vice Presidential Debate 2008."

_{sponsor}   _{location}   _{date}   _{medium}
Washington University, St. Louis, MO, 9 Oct. 2008. Debate.

47. Table For a table included in your paper, place a source note below the table. For a table that you are discussing but that does not appear in your paper, follow the model below:

author   title   label   medium

U.S. Senate. "Senate Salaries since 1789." Chart. 7 June 2004. Web.

access date

48. Work of art For a work of art included in your paper, place source information in the figure caption. For a work that you discuss but that does not appear in your project, follow the models below:

a. Original work

date of

artist   title   production   medium

Pollack, Jackson. *One (Number 31).* 1950. Acrylic on canvas.

location

Museum of Modern Art, New York.

b. Reproduction of a work of art

Lichtenstein, Roy. *Whaam!* 1963. Acrylic on canvas. Tate Gallery, London.

Responding to Art: Form, Content, and Context. By Robert Bersson.

New York: McGraw, 2004. Print.

49. Comic or cartoon For a cartoon reproduced in your project, provide source information in the caption. For cartoons that you discuss but that do not appear in your project, follow the models below:

a. Cartoon or comic strip

artist   title   label   publication information

Wright, Larry. "Kit 'n' Carlyle." Cartoon. *Evening Sun* [Norwich, NY] 28 Dec.

medium

2006: 8. Print.

b. Comic book or graphic novel

authors   title

Pekar, Harvey, and Joyce Brabner. *Our Cancer Year.* Illus. Frank Stack.

pub. info.   medium

Philadelphia: Running Press, 1994. Print.

50. Map or chart For a map or chart reproduced in your project, provide source information in the caption. For a map or chart discussed but not included in your project, follow the model on the next page:

MLA Works-
Cited Entries

45. Musical
composition
46. Lecture, speech,
or debate
47. Table
48. Work of art
**49. Comic or
cartoon**
50. Map or chart
51. Advertisement
52. Government
publication

"The Invasion of Sicily: Allied Advance to Messina (23 July-17 August

_{label}
1943)." Map. *The West Point Atlas of American Wars*. Ed.

Vincent J. Esposito. Vol. 2. New York: Praeger, 1959. Print.

51. Advertisement For an advertisement reproduced in your project, provide source information in the caption. For an advertisement discussed but not included in your project, follow the models below:

label
Earthlink Cable Internet. Advertisement. *Metro* 17 Apr. 2007: 11. Print.

date accessed
Infiniti. Advertisement. *Yahoo.com*. Web. 20 Apr. 2007.

date viewed
Domino's Pizza. Advertisement. Comedy Central. 2 Aug. 2006.

Television.

Miscellaneous Sources

52. Government publication If no author is listed, use the name of the governing nation and the government agency or department that produced the document as you would for a work with a corporate author. Abbreviate Government Printing Office as *GPO*.

Example 6, 318

nation   department
United States. War Department. *Advanced Map and Aerial Photograph*

Reading. Washington: GPO, 1941. Print.

For Congressional documents, include the number and session of Congress and the number and type of document. Common abbreviations in U.S. government documents include the following:

HR	House of Representatives	**Rept.**	Report
S	Senate	**Res**	Resolution
Sess.	Session	**Doc.**	Document
		GPO	Government Printing Office

a. Printed

United States. Cong. House. *Combat Bonus Act*. 110th Cong., 2nd sess.

HR 6760. Washington: GPO, 2008. Print.

MLA Works-
Cited Entries

49. Comic or
    cartoon
50. Map or chart
51. Advertisement
**52. Government
    publication**
53. Legal case
54. Letter
    (published)

b. Online

United States. Cong. House. *Combat Bonus Act.* 110th Cong., 2nd sess.

HR 6760. Web. *Thomas.gov.* Library of Congress, 31 July 2008.

16 Dec. 2008.

connect
mhconnectcomposition.com
Additional resources: QL17004

53. Legal case

legal case   case number   court   decision yr
Gideon v. Wainwright. 372 US 335. Supreme Court of the US. 1963.

website
FindLaw. Web. 16 Dec. 2008.

54. Letter (published)

a. Single letter Cite a single letter as you would a selection from an edited book or anthology but add the recipient's name, the date the letter was written, and the letter number (if there is one).

Example 9, 318

author   recipient   date written
Brooks, Phillips. "To Agnes." 24 Sept. 1882. *Children's Letters: A Collection*

of Letters Written to Children by Famous Men and Women. Ed.

Elizabeth Colson and Anna Gansevoort Chittenden. New York:

Hinds, 1905. 3-4. Print.

Example 8, 318

b. Collection of letters Cite as an edited book or anthology.

Examples 23–25, 42, 324–26, 332

55. Interview

Treat a published interview as you would an article in a periodical. Treat an interview broadcast on radio or television or podcasted as you would a broadcast. For an unpublished interview you conducted, include the name of the person interviewed, the label *Personal interview, Telephone interview,* or *Email interview,* and the date on which the interview took place.

MLA Works-Cited Entries

person interviewed   label   date
Freund, Deborah. Personal interview. 11 Feb. 2003.

56. Personal correspondence

To document personal correspondence, such as a letter or email message you received, include a descriptive label such as *Letter to the author* or *Message to the author,* as well as the medium (*MS* for "manuscript"; *Email*).

a. Letter

letter writer   label   date written
Gould, Stephen Jay. Letter to the author. 13 Nov. 1986. MS.

medium

b. Email

email author   subject line   label
Elbow, Peter. "Re: bibliography about resistance." Message to the author.
                date sent   medium
                12 Apr. 2004. Email.

A mass email or electronic memo should include a label describing recipients such as *Email to faculty and staff at Cal State—Chico* or *Email to ENG 204 students.*

c. Memorandum Very few institutions send out printed memos anymore, but if you need to document one, treat it like an email message, replacing the word *email* with the word *memo* at the end of your entry.

d. Instant message (IM)

White, Rose. Message to the author. 14 June 2007. Instant Message.

57. Diary or journal entry
a. Single entry, published Treat an entry in a published diary or journal like an article in an edited book or anthology, but include a descriptive label (*Diary entry*) and the date of composition after the entry title.

b. Single entry, unpublished

writer   title
Zook, Aaron. "Sketches for *Aesop's Foibles* (new musical)."
        label   entry date medium
        Journal entry. 1 May 2007. MS.

c. Diary or journal, published Treat a complete diary or journal as you would an edited book or anthology.

MLA Works-Cited Entries

55. Interview
56. Personal correspondence
57. Diary or journal entry

Example 9, 318

Example 8, 318

Example 9, 318

Example 8, 318

17c Using MLA Style for Content and Bibliographic Notes

In addition to in-text citations, MLA style allows for content notes and bibliographic notes. These provide information that is useful to the reader but that might be distracting if incorporated into the body of the text. The MLA recommends the use of endnotes for this purpose. Number the notes sequentially, using arabic numerals, and insert the numbers in the text, in superscript (above the line), immediately after the material they comment on. Type the notes, double spaced, on a

Sample content
note, 355

Sample biblio-
graphic note, 355

Sample student
research paper,
MLA style, 346–57

More about ▶▶▶
Choosing a typeface
and type size,
179–80

➡ Tech

Automatic Footnote/Endnote Numbering

All word processing programs can help you create correctly formatted foot- or endnotes. Find the footnote function—in Microsoft *Word,* for example, it appears on the Insert menu under Reference—and choose the appropriate settings, including arabic numerals.

new page labeled "Note" or "Notes" and insert it between the last page of your paper and your list of works cited.

Use ***content notes*** to provide information that clarifies or justifies a point in your text, but avoid notes that include interesting digressions that could distract your readers. Lydia Nichols's essay at the end of this chapter includes a content note. You can also use content notes to acknowledge the contributions of others (tutors, classmates, etc.) to the preparation of your paper.

Bibliographic notes can add information about a source or point readers to other sources on the topic. If several sources provide the same information, cite the most valuable source in your text, and list the others in a bibliographic note. Then include the full citation of all these sources in your list of works cited.

17d Formatting a Paper in MLA Style

If you are writing for English or foreign language classes (or if your instructor asks you to), format your project using MLA style. Lydia Nichols's paper, at the end of this chapter, provides a model.

1. Margins and spacing

Set one-inch margins at the top, bottom, and sides of your paper. Indent the first line of each paragraph one-half inch. Double-space the entire paper, including long quotations, the list of works cited, and any endnotes. Use a hanging indent for each entry in the list of works cited: The first line should be flush with the left margin with subsequent lines indented half an inch.

2. Typeface

Choose a standard typeface, such as Times New Roman or Arial, in a readable size (usually 12-point).

Tech

Creating a Header

Most word processing programs allow you to insert a header. In Microsoft *Word,* select "Header and Footer" under the View menu. A box for the header will appear at the top of your page, and a box for the footer at the bottom. Any information you type into these boxes will then appear on every page of your manuscript. From the menu bar, you can choose to insert page numbers into the header or footer to paginate your project automatically.

3. Header

MLA style requires that each page of the essay include a header, consisting of the student's surname and page number. Place the header in the upper right-hand corner, a half inch from the upper edge and one inch from the right edge of the page.

4. Identifying information

The following identifying information should be included in the upper left-hand corner of the first page of your research project, one inch from the top and left edges of the paper:

- Your name
- Your instructor's name
- The number of the course in which you are submitting the paper
- The date

MLA style does not require a title page, but some instructors may request one, especially if you are including additional items, such as an outline or a previous draft, with the final draft of your project. If you are required to provide a title page, Figure 17.2 provides a model.

5. Title

Center the title of your project and insert it two lines (one double-space) below the date. Do not put quotation marks around your title or set it in italics. Drop down two more lines (one double space) before beginning to type the first paragraph of your research project.

> **More about ▶▶▶**
> Crafting a title,
> 95–96

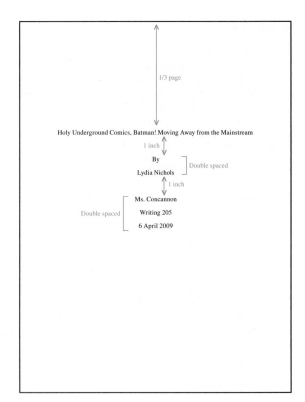

1/3 page

Holy Underground Comics, Batman! Moving Away from the Mainstream

1 inch

By

Lydia Nichols

Double spaced

1 inch

Ms. Concannon

Writing 205

6 April 2009

Double spaced

FIGURE 17.2 A sample title page Note that the title precedes the identifying information from the heading and that the title page does not include a header.

6. Long quotations

More about ▶▶▶
Block quotations, 303, 310
Example block quotation, 303, 347 (prose); 310 (poetry)

Set quotations of prose longer than four lines of your text as a block: Omit the quotation marks, and indent the quotation one inch from the left margin of your text. When quoting four or more lines of poetry, indent the lines one inch from the left margin, break lines in the same places as in the original poem, and include the line numbers of the passage quoted. If a line of the poem is too long to fit, indent the continuation by another quarter of an inch.

7. Tables and figures

Tables and figures (photographs, cartoons, graphs, and charts) will be most effective when they appear as close as possible after the text in

→ Tech

Spaces versus inches

The major style guides (MLA, APA, *Chicago*) were initially written before the widespread use of personal computers, when most writers still worked on typewriters. Indentions on a typewriter are measured by spaces—how many times the typist hits the space bar. On a computer, indentions are measured in inches and are created by using the Paragraph dialog box under the Format menu or by setting indentions on the Ruler.

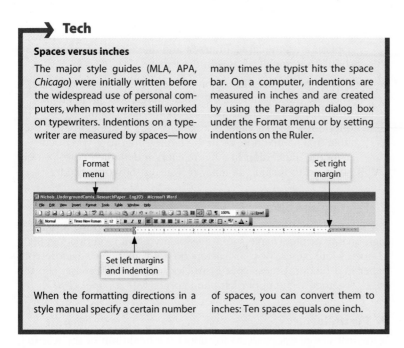

Format menu

Set right margin

Set left margins and indention

When the formatting directions in a style manual specify a certain number of spaces, you can convert them to inches: Ten spaces equals one inch.

which they are first discussed. (If placing figures and tables appropriately is awkward, consider including them in an appendix at the end of your project.) Labeling your tables and figures, both in the text and in your caption, will help readers connect your discussion with the illustration:

- Refer to the visual in your text using the word *table* or the abbreviation *fig.*, and number figures and tables in a separate sequence using arabic numerals (table 1, table 2; fig. 1, fig. 2). MLA style uses lowercase for in-text references to tables and figures unless they begin a sentence: "Table 1 presents 2005 data, and table 2 presents 2009 data."

- Accompany each illustration with the word *Table* or the abbreviation *Fig.*, the appropriate number, and a brief, explanatory title. Customarily, table numbers and titles precede the table, and figure numbers and titles follow the figure. Generally, they use the same margins as the rest of the paper.

- If additional information is needed, provide an explanatory caption after the label, number, and title. (This information should not repeat what is in the text.)

- If you borrow the illustration or borrow information needed to create the illustration, cite your source. Any photographs or drawings you create yourself should identify the subject but do not need a citation. Citations usually appear below the table in a source note or in the figure caption. If you document the illustration in a figure caption or source note, you do not need to include an entry in your list of works cited.

8. Printing and binding

If you are submitting a hard copy of your project, print it using a high-quality printer (make sure it has plenty of ink), on opaque, 8½ × 11–inch white paper. Most instructors do not want you to enclose your paper in a binder. Unless your instructor tells you otherwise, clip the pages together in the upper left-hand corner with a paper clip.

More about ▶▶▶
Portfolio, 111–12
Research log, 217–18
Working bibliography, 219
Annotated bibliography, 220
Outlining and sample outlines, 40–42, 286–87
Personal statement, 113–14

9. Portfolios

Many instructors ask students to submit the final draft of the research paper in a portfolio, which may include a research log, an outline, preliminary notes and drafts, a working or annotated bibliography, and a personal statement describing your writing process and what you have learned from the experience (Figure 17.3).

Writing
Responsibly **Of Deadlines and Paper Clips**

Instructors expect students to turn in thoughtful, carefully proofread, and neatly formatted papers on time—usually in class on the due date. Another assumption is that the writer will clip (or staple) the pages of the paper *before* it is submitted. Do justice to yourself by being fully prepared: Do not hand in a stack of loose sheets or expect your instructor to provide a paper clip.

FIGURE 17.3 Page 1 of Lydia Nichols's personal statement Nichols created a visual personal statement to explain how her interest in underground comics developed.

Student Research Project: MLA Style

In the sample student research project that follows, Lydia Nichols explores the world of underground comics. She uses comparison-contrast to support her claim that underground comics are more innovative than their mainstream cousins, and she provides a historical overview to fill in the background her readers lack. Her research draws on a variety of print and online sources, and she uses visuals to support some of her points.

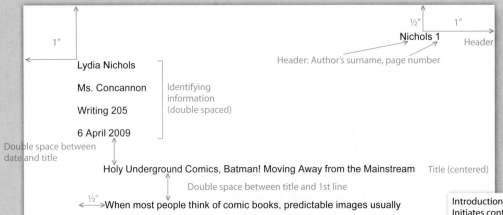

Header: Author's surname, page number

1″ ½″ 1″ Header

Lydia Nichols

Ms. Concannon

Writing 205

6 April 2009

Identifying information (double spaced)

Double space between date and title

Holy Underground Comics, Batman! Moving Away from the Mainstream — Title (centered)

Double space between title and 1st line

½″ When most people think of comic books, predictable images usually come to mind: caped heroes, maniacal villains, deeds of incredible strength, and other typical elements of super-powered adventures. Undeniably, characters like Batman, Superman, and Spider-Man are the most prominent features of the comic book landscape, in terms of both popularity and of revenue (Wright xiv). However, there is more to comic books than superpowers and secret identities. Underground comics (also known as *comix*), printed by small publishers or by individual artists, are very different from what is usually expected in the genre. While far less well-known than their superhero counterparts, underground comics often offer an innovative and more sophisticated alternative to mainstream titles.

Almost from the beginning, comic books were associated with superheroes. The first comic books appeared in the early 1930s, nearly four decades after comic strips such as *Yellow Boy* began appearing in the major newspapers. Yet comic books did not gain widespread popularity until June of 1938, when writer Jerry Siegel and artist Joe Shuster debuted their character Superman in *Action Comics* #1 (Daniels 9). Superman was an immediate success, and he quickly inspired the creation of copycat superheroes in other comic books. The

Introduction: Initiates contrast, moves from familiar to unfamiliar, concludes with thesis

In-text citation—book

Thesis: Establishes topic, purpose, and author's position

Topic sentence: Prepares reader for historical overview

Body: Begins with historical overview

1″

protagonists of these comics each had their own strengths and vulnerabilities, but the stories all shared a basic formula: individuals with extraordinary abilities battling against evil and struggling to maintain a secret identity. These superhero comics, though similar to each other, set the comic book industry on its feet, paving the way to profits and sustained success (Daniels 9). Over the decades and even today, the best-selling comics have typically been in the superhero genre.

While artists and writers over the years have certainly done inventive work in superhero comics, some similarity in mainstream titles was for many years unavoidable. This was due to the creation in 1954 of the Comics Code Authority (CCA), an organization formed by a number of the leading comic publishers to regulate the content of comics (Heller 101). It set very explicit standards, dictating what content was allowed in comic books and what content was expected. Some parts of the code are incredibly specific and controlling:

> The letters of the word "crime" on a comics magazine shall never be appreciably greater in dimension than the other words contained in the title. The word "crime" shall never appear alone on a cover. . . . Restraint in the use of the word "crime" in titles or subtitles shall be exercised.
>
> (qtd. in "Good Shall Triumph over Evil")

Other rules were more general—vague enough to allow the CCA a free hand in shaping content. One read, "Respect for parents, the moral code, and for honorable behavior shall be fostered" (qtd. in "Good Shall Triumph over Evil"). The CCA also regulated the presentation of criminals and criminal acts, themes of religion and race, and dialogue, especially profanity. While the CCA had no legal authority, major magazine distributors refused comics that did not have CCA approval. Many comic publishers, such as EC Comics (*Vault of Horror, Tales from the Crypt*), were virtually forced out of business as a result of the CCA, though the banned titles would eventually gain the appreciation of collectors and aspiring comic artists such as Art Spiegelman, author of the graphic novel *Maus* (1986) ("Comic Book Code").

Other publishers, including DC Comics, made their artists abide by CCA rules in order to continue selling to a wide audience. The result was that the comics with the largest distribution were those that conformed to the CCA's strict rules about appropriate language, subjects, and tone ("Good Shall Triumph over Evil").

In the 1960s, in contrast to mainstream CCA-approved superhero comics (fig. 1, left), alternatives (fig. 1, right) began to appear. Robert Crumb's *Zap,* first released in 1968, initiated the "underground comix revolution" (Heller 101). Crumb and other like-minded artists did not submit their comics for CCA approval. Though this limited the distribution of their work, it allowed them artistic freedom. From its first issue, *Zap* satirized mainstream, conservative beliefs and did not shy away from sexual or political content (Heller 101-2). Beneath the crude humor of *Zap* and similar comics lay insightful commentary on society and its principles, which many readers found to be a refreshing change from mainstream superhero titles.[1]

To see the contrast between these mainstream and underground comics, compare the two covers in fig. 1. The *Amazing Fantasy* cover (left) includes the Comics Code Authority approval stamp in its upper right corner, while the *Snarf* cover (right) does not. The *Snarf* cover actually pokes fun at covers like the one at left; on the *Amazing Fantasy* cover, superhero Spider-Man dangles from a high

Fig. 1. Mainstream versus Underground Comics. Spider-Man (left) extols (and exhibits) his prowess as superhero, while (right) a less conventional comic book "hero" struts his stuff. (Left: Cover from Jack Kirby & Steve Ditko, *Amazing Fantasy* #15. [New York: Marvel Comics, 1962]; right: Cover from Robert Crumb, *Snarf* #6 [Amherst: Kitchen Sink Enterprises, 1976])

building by a thread, proclaiming his "awesome might" to the world, while on the *Snarf* cover, a geeky guy in an unwieldy homemade contraption wants to save the world by fighting "the big companies"—which include oil companies (the "Gas" industry this inventor is trying to boycott) and probably DC Comics, too.

Topic sentence: Claim supported by examples

Underground comics continue to be less well-known than superhero comics, but they are also better-respected among mature readers for their bold and inventive content. Graphic novels, such as Spiegelman's *Maus* and Harvey Pekar's *Our Cancer Year* (1994), have successfully addressed some of the most highly charged and sensitive subjects in modern society. Both of these show the subtlety of and the wide range of topics that underground comics explore. Other common themes of underground comics include sex and sexual identity, politics, and social issues (Daniels 165), as shown in Crumb's work, which is well known for its satirical approach to countercultural topics (Heller).

Topic sentence: Claim supported by example, visual, quotation

Mainstream superhero comics are set on an epic scale—depicting amazing feats, heroic battles between good and evil, and the like—while underground comics tend to focus on everyday life. Adrian Tomine, for example, has been called "a master of pseudorealistic stories" due to his ability to present an ordinary situation as profoundly interesting and complex (Weiner 58; see fig. 2). Comics like Tomine's also provide a subject or situation that readers can identify with more easily than, say, Superman's battles with Brainiac.[2]

Bibliographic note

The quirky perspectives of underground artists would be impossible in mainstream comics because the structure for producing and publishing mainstream comics limits the input of the artists working on them. The modern comic book industry is a huge business, selling not only comics, but also related merchandise such as T-shirts, toys, and video games, not to mention tickets to comic book–inspired movies. Story decisions involving major characters such as Batman or the Hulk have to be made with profits in mind. Because mainstream

Fig. 2. Comic whose characters face realistic challenges—the loss of a loved one, parental guilt—that readers can easily relate to. From Adrian Tomine, *Optic Nerve* #6, p. 22. (Montreal: Drawn and Quarterly, Feb. 1999).

comic publishers often change the creative teams working on their titles (Herndon) and because teams can include dozens of members (McCloud 180), individual artists can have only so much impact on a particular character or story. Most mainstream comics are the result of work done by many different people.

Online article: no page reference

Transition   In contrast, the individual artist in the underground realm has almost total control in creating his or her comic book. The creative teams working on underground titles are usually very small, and they rarely change (Herndon).

Signal phrase Les Daniels, who has written several books about DC Comics' creations, notes that underground comic artists are not controlled by corporate interests that discourage "daring" material that might not sell (165, 180). This freedom allows for the uninhibited creativity that distinguishes underground comics from their more commercially oriented counterparts.

Information from two passages, same source

Underground artists not only push the envelope in terms of content, but they also incorporate experimental visual devices, earning critical praise for breaking away from traditional comic layouts in favor of more artistic perspectives. Artists such as Daniel Clowes argue that comic art can be more evocative than film, especially in the use of nonlinear storytelling techniques (Hignite 18). *New York Times* columnist John Hodgman agrees: Discussing a moment of existential crisis in Kevin Huizenga's *Ganges* #1, he writes, "I have never seen any film or read any prose that gets at that frozen moment when we suddenly feel our mortality, when God is seen or denied, as effectively as a comic panel." Artist Chris Ware manipulates the borders and frames in his comics so extensively that even reading his works can feel like an art to be mastered (see fig. 3). The demands his comics place on the reader create an interaction between viewer and artist that is unheard of in the pages of superhero titles.

Topic sentence: Claim supported by summary, quotation, visual example

Signal phrase with background; one-page article—no page number

While Ware and Clowes demonstrate how the page can be used to create innovative and complicated layouts, other underground artists excel at creating

Fig. 3. Cover from Chris Ware's *Jimmy Corrigan: The Smartest Kid on Earth* (New York: Pantheon, 2000).Critically acclaimed *Jimmy Corrigan* comics use visual storytelling techniques, pushing the limitations of comics and forcing the reader to work to achieve understanding.

Caption explains how visual supports claim

simple, striking visuals. Unlike mainstream comics, which depict dynamic scenes through loud, flamboyant colors, underground comics often achieve their effects through simplicity. Frequently, they are printed in black and white or with limited colors, with characters rendered in clean, bold lines. The clarity and lack of clutter in such art allows for immediate, striking storytelling (see fig. 2).

Reference to earlier figure

Obviously, most underground comics are not intended for young children. Yet, because of the childish connotations of the term "comic," most adults overlook the fascinating work that underground comic artists do. The association of comics with superheroes and children has made reading comics a source of shame or embarrassment for many adults. As Clowes comments, "I think that the average reader is far more open to a well-designed book than a standard comic book. . . . Very few would feel comfortable reading a standard comic book pamphlet" (qtd. in Hignite 17). Artists such as Scott McCloud have changed this perception of comic books by offering a broader definition of what a comic is. According to McCloud, comics are "juxtaposed pictorial and other images in a deliberate sequence" (12). This definition includes not only what one might find in the latest Spider-Man comic, but also all the experimental work that McCloud and his underground colleagues are creating.

McCloud and others have succeeded in bringing underground comics to a wider audience. Since the 1980s, comics have been finding their way into gallery and museum exhibitions, where the craftsmanship of the individual comic book artist can be better appreciated (Hignite 18). Major newspapers like the *New York Times* have begun featuring comics in their pages, including serialized graphic novels such as *George Sprott (1894-1975)* and *Watergate Sue*. The market for underground comics has also expanded through internet venues such as *eBay*, where interested readers can find not only new titles, but also classic comix otherwise available only in specialty shops. The internet has also become an outlet for direct distribution through artists' websites, making independent titles not only more accessible to consumers but also more affordable for individual artists to produce and market (Fenty, Houp, and Taylor, par. 1). While underground comics may never sell as well or be as large a part of popular culture as Superman and his ilk, their creators will likely continue to be heroes to anyone seeking courage, creativity, and artistic quality in their comics.

Side annotations:

Signal phrase and parenthetical page reference

Conclusion: Restatement of thesis—closure

Article by more than one author, paragraph no. cited

Thesis restated

Notes Heading (centered), new page

Content note: Pertinent information not central to project's claim

½"

1. According to Schnakenberg, over 2 million copies of *Zap* comix were in print by 1999.

2. For an intriguing argument that the world of classic comic book superheroes is not so different from our own—including a discussion of how comics before World War II commented on then current events—see Wright 1-28.

Bibliographic note

Works Cited Heading (centered), new page; entries alphabetized by author

"The Comic Book Code." *Culture Shock.* PBS, n.d. Web. 17 Mar. 2009. Web page: No author, no date

Daniels, Les. *Comix: A History of Comic Books in America.* New York: Outerbridge

½" and Dienstfrey, 1971. Print.

More than one author: Order of names reversed for first author Fenty, Sean, Trena Houp, and Laurie Taylor. "Webcomics: The Influence and Journal article: Published only online, paragraph numbers

Continuation of the Comix Revolution." *ImageTexT* 1.2 (2004): 22 pars. Web.

18 Mar. 2009.

Online scholarly project: No authors— alphabetized by title "'Good Shall Triumph over Evil': The Comic Book Code of 1954." *History Matters:*

The U.S. History Survey Course on the Web. George Mason University, n.d.

Web. 22 Mar. 2009.

Heller, Steven. "Zap Comics." *Print* May/June 2000: 100-105, *Academic Search*

Premier. Web. 26 Mar. 2009.

Herndon, L. Kristen. "Mainstream Culture Is in Trouble, and Superman's Not Journal article: Accessed through database

Gonna Save It. But the Simpsons Might." *Art Papers* 21 (1997): 22-25. *Art*

Index. Web. 10 Mar. 2009.

Hignite, M. Todd. "Avante-Garde and Comics: Serious Cartooning." *Art Papers* 26.1

(2002): 17-19. *Art Index.* Web. 10 Mar. 2009.

Hodgman, John. "Comics Chronicle." *New York Times* 4 June 2006, late ed., sec. Newspaper article: Accessed through database

7: 18. *LexisNexis.* Web. 19 Mar. 2009.

McCloud, Scott. *Understanding Comics, the Invisible Art.* New York: Harper Book (printed): Popular press

Perennial, 1994. Print.

Schnakenberg, Robert E. "Zap Comix." *St. James Encyclopedia of Popular Culture.*

Specialized reference work: Accessed through database 2002. *Find Articles.* Web. 17 Mar. 2009.

Weiner, Stephen. "Beyond Superheroes: Comics Get Serious." *Library Journal* 7.2

(2002): 55-58. *Academic Search Premier.* Web. 10 Mar. 2009.

Wright, Bradford W. *Comic Book Nation: The Transformation of Youth Culture in*

America. Baltimore: Johns Hopkins UP, 2001. Print.

Book (printed):
Scholarly press

18

Documenting Sources: APA Style

Sixth Edition

Publication
Manual
of the American Psychological Association

Developed by the American Psychological Association, APA style is used by researchers in psychology and many other social science disciplines, such as education, social work, and sociology. APA style requires that sources be cited in two ways:

- *Citation:* Provide an in-text citation in the body of your project for each source used.

- *Documentation:* Provide a reference list at the project's end.

Writing Responsibly — Citing and Documenting Sources

When you cite and document sources, you acknowledge any material that you have borrowed from a source, and you join the conversation on your topic by adding your own interpretation. Simultaneously, you give interested readers (including your instructor) a way to join the conversation: Accurate entries in the text and reference list allow your audience to find and read your sources so that they can evaluate your interpretation and learn more about the subject themselves. Accurate entries also demonstrate the care with which you have written your research project and reinforce your reputation as a sound scholar.

Quick Reference ➡ **General Principles of In-Text Citation**

- Cite not only direct quotations but also paraphrases, summaries, and information gathered from a source.
- Include the author's surname and the year of publication. You may place the name(s) in a signal phrase or in a parenthetical note.
- Place parenthetical citations at the end of the borrowed material; if the author is named in a signal phrase, insert the year of publication, in parentheses, immediately following the author's name and the page reference at the end of the borrowed passage.
- For works with no author, use the first few words of the title.
- For works with multiple authors, use the word *and* before the last author in a signal phrase; replace the word *and* with an ampersand (&) in a parenthetical citation.
- Include a page or paragraph number when borrowing specific information, not when summarizing an entire source.

18a Creating APA-Style In-Text Citations

connect
mhconnectcomposition.com
Additional resources: QL18001

In-text citations appear in the body of your project. They mark each use you make of a source, regardless of whether you are quoting, paraphrasing, or drawing on an idea from the source. In-text citations include just enough information for readers to locate the source in your reference list, which appears at the end of the project (followed by endnotes, if any). They also alert readers to shifts between *your* ideas and those borrowed from a source.

1. Place in-text citations so readers know where borrowed material starts and stops.

When you incorporate a quotation, paraphrase, summary, or idea from a source into your own prose, carefully consider the placement of the in-text citation, keeping the following goals in mind:

- To make clear exactly which material is drawn from the source
- To avoid distracting your reader

You can cite a source in your text in two ways:

- **Signal phrase:** Include the author's name (often just the surname) and an appropriate verb in your sentence; place the

❯ **More about** ▶▶▶
What you need to cite, 265–66
What you do not need to cite, 266–67
Signal phrases, 291–93
Integrating borrowed material into your text, 291–95

date of publication, in parentheses, immediately following the author's name.

G. H. Edwards (1992) found that beliefs regarding men and women

transcend gender. . . .

A signal phrase often makes it easier for readers to determine where your ideas end and borrowed material begins. It also allows you to integrate the borrowed material into your sentence and to put the source in context by adding your own interpretation and the qualifications of the source author. For these reasons, most of your summaries, paraphrases, and quotations should be introduced by a signal phrase.

- ***Parenthetical note:*** In parentheses, provide the author's surname, followed by a comma and the year in which the source was published. Place the note immediately after the borrowed material.

Subtypes or subcategories of beliefs emerge from within

gender categories (Edwards, 1992).

Parenthetical notes are most appropriate when citing more than one source, when establishing facts, or when emphasizing the author is not especially important to the point you are making.

NOTE The reference list entry is the same, regardless of whether you use a signal phrase or a parenthetical note:

author   pub. year   title
Edwards, G. H. (1992). The structure and content of the male gender role
                                                                      publication info.
        stereotype: An exploration of subtypes. *Sex Roles, 27,* 553–561.

Example 1, 361
Example 9, 366
Example 13, 367

Provide enough information in your in-text citation for readers to locate the source in the reference list. In most cases, the author's surname and the date of publication is sufficient. Occasionally, you may need to provide more information; when citing a specific part of a source or using a quotation, for example, you would also provide page numbers. Use paragraph numbers or section headings if no page numbers are available. When citing works by authors with the same surname, also include the authors' initials.

2. Adjust in-text citations to different types of sources.

The exact form of an in-text citation depends on the type of source you are citing. The examples that follow cover the most common types. For more unusual sources, study the general principles outlined here and adapt them to your special circumstances or consult the *Publication Manual of the American Psychological Association,* 6th ed. (available in any library).

connect
mhconnectcomposition.com
Additional resources: QL18002

1. One author
a. Signal phrase

> signal phrase
> Plummer (2001) indicates that boys begin pressuring one another to conform in childhood, telling each other to toughen up or to stop acting like a baby.

APA In-Text Citations

1. **One author**
2. Two authors
3. Three to five authors

b. Parenthetical note

> This pressure to conform to recognized masculine norms typically
>
> begins at a very young age, and boys may tell each other to toughen
>
> up or to stop acting like a baby (Plummer, 2001).

c. Specific page or section cited If you are borrowing specific language or ideas from your source, include the author's name in a signal phrase, the year of publication immediately after the author's name, and a page reference at the end of the cited passage. This not only provides source information but also makes clear what part of your text comes from the source.

> Plummer (2001) argues that an overt pressure to conform to recognized
>
> norms of masculinity typically begins at a very young age, with boys
>
> discouraging one another from being "soft" or "artistic" (p. 18).

If you cannot use a signal phrase, include all three pieces of information at the end of the passage cited.

> This overt pressure to conform to recognized norms of masculinity
>
> typically begins at a very young age, with boys discouraging each other
>
> from being "soft" or "artistic" (Plummer, 2001, p. 18).

2. Two authors List two authors by surnames in the order listed by the source; be sure to use this same order in your reference list entry. In a signal phrase, spell out the word *and* between the two surnames; in a parenthetical citation, replace the word *and* with an ampersand (&).

APA In-Text
Citations

1. One author
2. **Two authors**
3. Three to five authors
4. Six or more authors

signal phrase (*and* spelled out)
Carpenter and Readman (2006) define physical disability as "the

restriction of activity caused by impairments, for example, the loss of

a limb, involuntary movements, loss of speech or sight" (p. 131).

Medical doctors define the word *disability* as "an individual problem
parenthetical note (ampersand)
of disease, incapacity, and impairment" (Carpenter & Readman, 2006,

p. 131).

APA In-Text Citations

1. One author
2. Two authors
3. **Three to five authors**
4. Six or more authors
5. Group or corporate author

3. Three to five authors When a source has three, four, or five authors, list them all in your first in-text citation of the source.

The research of Oller, Pearson, and Cobo-Lewis (2007) suggests

that bilingual children may have a smaller vocabulary in each of their

languages than monolingual children have in their sole language.

In subsequent citations, list only the first author, representing the others with the abbreviation *et al.* In APA style, this abbreviation should not be underlined or italicized.

et al. Abbreviation of the Latin phrase *et alii,* "and others"

The bilingual children in the study were all Spanish-English speakers

(Oller et al., 2007).

NOTE *al.* is an abbreviation, so it requires a period; *et* is a complete word, so it does not. There should be no punctuation between the author's name and *et al.*

4. Six or more authors If the source has six or more authors, use only the surname of the first author plus *et al.* unless confusion will result.

> The researchers note that "there is less direct experimental evidence for
>
> effect of grazing animal species on biodiversity" (Rook et al., 2003, p. 141).

5. Group or corporate author Provide the full name of the group in your parenthetical note or signal phrase. If you are going to cite this source subsequently, use the group's name in a signal phrase and insert its acronym in parentheses. In subsequent in-text references, use only the acronym.

acronym A word
formed from the first
letters of words in a
name or phrase, such
as *NASA* from National
Aeronautics and Space
Administration (854)

> full name
> In 2003 the National Commission on Writing in America's Schools and
> acronym
> Colleges (NCWASC) demanded that "the nation's leaders . . . place
>
> writing squarely in the center of the school agenda, and [that]
>
> policymakers at the state and local levels . . . provide the resources
>
> required to improve writing" (p. 3).

APA In-Text
Citations

2. Two authors
3. Three to five
   authors
**4. Six or more
   authors**
**5. Group or
   corporate
   author**
6. Unnamed
   author
7. Two or more
   sources by the
   same author

Alternatively, include the full name in a parenthetical citation, and insert the acronym in square brackets following.

> If writing is to improve, our society "must place writing squarely in
>
> the center of the school agenda, and policymakers at the state and
>
> local levels must provide the resources required to improve writing"
> full name
> (National Commission on Writing in America's Schools and Colleges
> acronym
> [NCWASC], 2003, p. 3).

6. Unnamed author When no author is listed for a source, use the first few words of the reference list entry (usually the title) instead.

On average, smokers shave about twelve minutes off their life span for
title
every cigarette smoked ("A Fistful of Risks," 1996, pp. 82–83).

More about ▶▶▶
Quotation marks
with titles, 817–18
Italics with titles,
847–48

APA In-Text
Citations

5. Group or
corporate
author

**6. Unnamed
author**

**7. Two or more
sources by the
same author**

**8. Author
with two or
more works
published in
the same year**

9. Two or more
authors with the
same surname

Set titles of articles or parts of books in quotation marks and titles of books, periodicals, and other longer works in italics.

Only if the source lists its author as anonymous should you use that word (without italics or quotation marks) in a parenthetical citation; avoid using *anonymous* in a signal phrase.

7. Two or more sources by the same author When citing two or more sources by the same author in a single citation, name the author once but include all publication years, separating them with commas.

Wynn's work explores the ability of human infants to perform
pub.   pub.
year 1 year 2
mathematical functions, such as addition and subtraction (1992, 2000).

Human infants have shown surprising abilities to perform mathematical
pub.   pub.
year 1 year 2
functions, such as addition and subtraction (Wynn, 1992, 2000).

▶ Example 6, 372

8. Author with two or more works published in the same year When your reference list includes two or more publications by the same author in the same year, add a letter following the year (*2006a, 2006b*). Use these year-and-letter designations in your in-text citations.

The brain not only controls the senses of sight and sound, but it also

plays an important role in associating emotions such as fear with
letter assigned
particular situations (Barinaga, 1992b).

9. Two or more authors with the same surname If your reference list includes works by different authors with the same surname, include the authors' initials to differentiate them.

> Rehabilitation is a viable option for many juvenile offenders, whose
>
> immaturities and disabilities can, with institutional support and
>
> first initial + surname
> guidance, be overcome as the child matures (M. Beyer, 2006).

If more than one author is listed, include initials for the first author only.

10. Reprinted or republished work Include both dates in your in-text citation, with the original date of publication first.

> orig. year
> Danon-Boileau (2005/2006) takes a cross-disciplinary approach to the
> reprint year
> study of language disorders in children.

11. Two or more sources in one citation To cite more than one source in a single parenthetical note, list the sources in the same order in which they appear in the reference list, using a semicolon to separate them.

> When placed in well-structured rehabilitative programs, juvenile
>
> offenders—even those who commit serious crimes such as murder—
>
> can become more mature thinkers, more involved and loving members
>
> of their families, and more successful workers and learners (Beyer,
>
> 2006; Burns & Hoagwood, 2002).

12. Indirect source When you can, avoid quoting from a secondhand source (source material you have learned about through its mention in another source). When you cannot locate or translate the original source, mention the original author's name in a signal phrase. In your parenthetical note, include *as cited in* followed by the name of the author of the source in which you found the information, and conclude with the year of that source's publication.

> Choy, Fyer, and Lipsitz (as cited in King, 2008) make the distinction
>
> that people with phobias, unlike those with general anxiety, can identify
>
> specific causes for their feelings of nervousness and dread.

In the reference list, provide only the source you used: For the example above, include a reference list entry for King, not Choy, Fyer, and Lipsitz.

13. Website or other electronic source For a brief reference to an entire website that readers can retrieve, provide the URL in a parenthetical note, but do not include the source in the reference list.

> The Olympics assume great importance to the local community,
>
> as demonstrated by the website for California State University–
>
> Sacramento in the period before Olympic trials were to be held on the
>
> campus. Three out of four news bulletins on the university's home page
>
> URL
> were connected to the Olympics (http://www.csus.edu/).

APA In-Text Citations

10. Reprinted or republished work
11. Two or more sources in one citation
12. **Indirect source**
13. **Website or other electronic source**
14. Personal communication, interview, or email

Examples 20–21,
380–81

When citing a specific passage or engaging in a substantial way with an online or electronic source, cite it as you would any other source and include it in your reference list.

The website *Psychology Matters* reports that cell-phone use while

driving can impair performance as badly as drinking alcohol does: "Cell-

phone use is associated with a four-fold increase in the odds of getting

into an accident—a risk comparable to that of driving with blood alcohol

at the legal limit" ("Driven to Distraction," 2006, para. 1).

More about ▶▶▶
PDF files, 196, 228,
232

Cite specific page numbers only when they are fixed, such as in a PDF file. When no page numbers are available, use paragraph numbers or headings to guide the reader to the specific passage cited.

APA In-Text Citations

12. Indirect source
13. Website or
    other electronic
    source
14. Personal com-
    munication,
    interview, or
    email

14. Personal communication, interview, or email For sources such as personal email messages, interviews, and phone calls that your readers cannot retrieve and read, mention the communication in your text or provide a parenthetical note, but do not include an entry in the reference list.

The scientist himself was much more modest about the development

(S. J. Gould, personal communication, November 13, 1986).

Quick

Reference ➡ APA Reference List Entries

18b Preparing an APA-Style Reference List

The reference list, which comes after the body of your research project, includes the sources you have cited in your text. The format of each entry in the reference list depends in part on the type of source you are citing, such as a printed book, an article in an electronic journal or accessed through a database, or an audio recording.

Books—Printed and Electronic

In a printed book, the information you need to create a reference list entry appears on the title and copyright pages. In an online book or e-book, print and electronic publication information appears at the top or bottom of the first page or is available through a link.

▶▶▶Annotated
visual of where to
find author, title, and
publication information, on foldout
following p. 297

1. One author

a. Printed The basic entry for a printed book looks like this:

Author's surname, Initial(s). (Year of publication). *Title: Subtitle.* Place of

publication: Publisher.

Here is an example of an actual citation:

Morrison, J. R. (2007). *Diagnosis made easier: Principles and techniques*

for mental health clinicians. New York, NY: Guilford Press.

For books, only first
word of title and
subtitle (plus names)
are capitalized.

b. E-book Works published electronically or made accessible online are now frequently tagged with a digital object identifier (DOI). Unlike a URL that may change or stop working, a DOI is a permanent identifier that will not change over time or from database to database. If the e-book you are documenting is tagged with a DOI, use that identifier instead of publication information or URL; if no DOI has been assigned, replace publication information with the URL from which the electronic file can be obtained.

More about ▶▶▶
Digital object identifiers, 376–77, 381
URLs, 255–56

Carter, J. (2003). *Nasty people: How to stop being hurt by them without*

stooping to their level [Adobe Digital Editions version]. doi:

10.1036/0071410228

Includes file type in
brackets after title

Stokes, R. (n.d.) *E-marketing: The essential guide to online marketing.*

Retrieved from http://www.quirk.bix/emarketingtextbook/download

If no publication date
available, use *n.d.*

→ Tech

Citing Electronic Sources: Digital Object Identifiers (DOIs) and URLs

Because URLs change and links break, the APA now recommends using a digital object identifier (DOI), a permanent identifying code, whenever available; use a URL, or web address, only when no DOI is available. If the work was created and published by the same group, omit the publisher's name from the retrieval statement; otherwise, include the URL (*Retrieved from APA website:*). Most electronic books and articles in academic journals now include a DOI. When your citation ends with a DOI or URL, do *not* add a period after it. Break a DOI or URL (if necessary) only after a slash or before a dot or other punctuation mark.

APA Reference List Entries

1. One author
2. **Two authors**
3. **Three to seven authors**
4. **Eight or more authors**
5. **Unnamed (anonymous) author**
6. Two or more books by the same author
7. Group or corporate author

2. Two authors When there are two authors, list them in the order they appear on the title page of the source.

author 1   author 2
Tavris, C., & Aronson, E. (2007). *Mistakes were made (but not by me):*

Why we justify foolish beliefs, bad decisions, and hurtful acts.

New York, NY: Harcourt.

> Use an ampersand (&) between names.

3. Three to seven authors When the book has three to seven authors, list all their names.

Oltmanns, T. F., Neale, J. M., & Davison, G. C. (1992). *Case studies in*

abnormal psychology. New York, NY: Guilford Press.

> Use an ampersand (&) between the last two names.

4. Eight or more authors When the book has eight or more authors, list the first six authors followed by three ellipsis points and the last author's name.

Masters, R., Skrapec, C., Muscat, B., Dussich, J. P., Pincu, L., Way,

L. B., . . . Gerstenfeld, P. (2010). *Criminal justice: Realities and*

challenges. New York, NY: McGraw-Hill.

5. Unnamed (anonymous) author Start the entry with the title followed by the publication date. Alphabetize the entry in the reference list using the first significant word in the title (not an article such as *a, an,* or *the*).

And still we conquer! The diary of a Nazi Unteroffizier in the German Africa

Corps. (1968). University, AL: Confederate Publishing.

If the author is listed as "Anonymous," use that word in place of the author's name.

Anonymous. (1971). *Go ask Alice.* Englewood Cliffs, NJ: Prentice Hall.

6. Two or more books by the same author For multiple books by the same author (or authors), arrange the entries in order of publication (from least to most recent).

APA Reference List Entries

4. Eight or more authors
5. Unnamed (anonymous) author
6. Two or more books by the same author
7. Group or corporate author
8. Two authors or more with the same surname and first initial

Tonkiss, F. (2005). *Space, the city and social theory: Social relations and*

urban forms. Malden, MA: Polity.

Tonkiss, F. (2006). *Contemporary economic sociology: Globalization,*

production, inequality. New York, NY: Routledge.

When books were written by the same author(s) in the same year, alphabetize the entries by title and add the letter *a* following the publication date of the first entry, *b* following the publication date of the second entry, and so on.

Cervone, D., & Shoda, Y. (1999a). Beyond traits in the study of personality

coherence. *Current Directions in Psychological Science, 8,* 27–32.

Cervone, D., & Shoda, Y. (1999b). Social-cognitive theories and the

coherence of personality. In D. Cervone & Y. Shoda (Eds.), *The*

coherence of personality: Social-cognitive bases of consistency,

variability, and organization. New York, NY: Guilford Press.

Works written by a single author should be listed *before* sources written by that same author plus a coauthor, regardless of publication dates.

Morrison, J. R. (2007). *Diagnosis made easier: Principles and techniques*

for mental health clinicians. New York, NY: Guilford Press.

Morrison, J. R., & Anders, T. F. (1999). *Interviewing children and*

adolescents: Skills and strategies for effective DSM-IV *diagnosis.*

New York, NY: Guilford Press.

When citing multiple sources by an author and various coauthors, alphabetize entries by surname of the second author.

Clarke-Stewart, A., & Allhusen, V. D. (2005). *What we know about*

childcare. Cambridge, MA: Harvard University Press.

Clarke-Stewart, A., & Brentano, C. (2006). *Divorce: Causes and*

consequences. New Haven, CT: Yale University Press.

7. Group or corporate author List the sponsoring organization as the author of a book (or other publication) by a corporation, institution, or government agency. Use the full name, and alphabetize it in the reference list according to the name's first significant word. If the same group or corporation is also listed as the publisher, replace the name of the publisher with the word *Author.*

Fabian Society, Commission on Life Chances and Child Poverty. (2006).

Narrowing the gap: The final report of the Fabian Commission on life

chances and child poverty. London, England: Author.

8. Two authors or more with the same surname and first initial When your reference list includes sources by two different authors with the same surname and first initial, differentiate them by including their first names in brackets.

Cohen, A. [Andrew]. (1994). *Assessing language ability in the classroom.*

Boston, MA: Heinle.

Cohen, A. [Anne]. (1973). *Poor Pearl, poor girl! The murdered girl*

stereotype in ballad and newspaper. Austin: University of Texas

Press.

No state abbreviation if state included in name of press

9. Edited book or anthology as a whole Treat the editor as the author.

Ghosh, R. A. (Ed.). (2005). *CODE: Collaborative ownership and the digital*

economy. Boston, MA: Massachusetts Institute of Technology Press.

For a book with multiple editors, change the abbreviation from *Ed.* to *Eds.*

10. Selection from an edited book or anthology Begin with the selection's author, followed by the publication date of the book and the selection's title (with no quotation marks or other formatting). Then insert the word *In,* the editors' names, and the title of the book or anthology (italicized). Next include page numbers for the entire selection (even if you used only part of it). Conclude the entry with the publication information for the book in which the selection appeared.

selection author   selection title
Smither, N. (2000). Crime scene cleaner. In J. Bowe, M. Bowe, & S.

selection pg. nos.
Streeter (Eds.), *Gig: Americans talk about their jobs* (pp. 96–103).

New York, NY: Crown.

11. Edition other than the first Insert the edition number (*2nd ed., 3rd ed.*) or edition name (*Rev. ed.* for "revised edition") after the book's title. (The edition number or name should appear on the title page.)

Johnson, J. B., & Reynolds, H. T. (2005). *Political science research*

methods (5th ed.). Washington, DC: CQ Press.

12. Entry in a reference work Format an entry in a reference work as you would a selection from an edited book. For signed articles, include the author's name. (Articles in reference works often carry the author's initials only, so you may need to cross-reference the initials with a list of contributors in the front or back of the book.) If an article is unsigned, begin with its title.

a. Printed

Treffert, D. A. (2000). Savant syndrome. In A. E. Kazdin (Ed.), *Encyclopedia*

of psychology (pp. 144–148). New York, NY: Oxford.

b. Online

> Depression, reactive. (2001). In E. Reber & A. Reber, (Eds.), *Penguin*
>
> URL
> *dictionary of psychology.* Retrieved from http://www.credoreference.com

13. Doctoral dissertation or master's thesis Indicate whether the work is a doctoral dissertation or a master's thesis. If the dissertation or thesis was accessed through a database service, include the name of the database from which it was obtained and provide any identifying number. If it was obtained from a university or personal website, include the URL.

a. Published

> Song, L. Z. (2003). *Relations between optimism, stress and health in*
>
> *Chinese and American students* (Doctoral dissertation). Available
>
> from ProQuest Dissertations and Theses database. (UMI No.
>
> AAI3107041)

> Lillie, A. S. (2008). *MusicBox: Navigating the space of your music* (Master's
>
> thesis, Massachusetts Institute of Technology). Retrieved from http://
>
> thesis.flyingpudding.com/documents/Anita_FINAL_THESIS.pdf

b. Unpublished

> Luster, L. (1992). *Schooling, survival and struggle: Black women and the*
>
> *GED* (Unpublished doctoral dissertation). Stanford University, Palo
>
> Alto, CA.

c. Abstracted in DAI If you accessed the abstract in *Dissertation Abstracts International* database, include that information in the entry.

> Kelley, E. (2008). Parental depression and negative attribution bias
>
> in parent reports of child symptoms. *Dissertation Abstracts*
>
> *International: Section B. Sciences and Engineering, 69*(7), 4427.

APA Reference List Entries

11. Edition other than the first
12. Entry in a reference work
13. **Doctoral dissertation or master's thesis**
14. Article in a scholarly journal
15. Article in a magazine

Periodicals—Printed and Electronic

A periodical is a publication issued at regular intervals—newspapers are generally published every day, magazines every week or month, and scholarly journals four times a year. For periodicals, include not only the title of the article (no quotation marks or italics) but also the title of the periodical (in italics, all important words capitalized). The other of publication information you include depends on the type of periodical you are citing.

▶▶▶Annotated visual of where to find author, title, publication, and other information, on foldout following p. 297

14. Article in a scholarly journal The information needed to create a reference list entry for a printed journal article appears on the cover or table of contents of the journal and on the first and last page of the article. For articles downloaded from a database, the information appears either on the search results screen, the full record of the article, or on the first (and last) page of the downloaded file. For articles that appear in journals that are published solely online, the needed information may be on the website's home page, in the journal's table of contents, or on the first page of the article.

More about ▶▶▶
Formatting author information: examples 1–10, 370–74

a. Printed The basic citation for an article in a printed journal looks like this:

> Author's surname, Initial(s). (Year of publication). Article title. *Title of*
>
> *Journal, vol no.,* pages.

Here is an example of an actual citation:

> Fancher, R. E. (2009). Scientific cousins: The relationship between Charles
>
> Darwin and Francis Galton. *American Psychologist, 64*, 84–92.

If the article is published in a journal that starts each issue with page 1, provide the issue number after the volume number (not italicized, in parentheses).

> Sui, C. (2007, August). Giving indigenous people a voice. *Taiwan Review*
>
> *57*(8), 40.

b. Online or accessed through a database Most articles published or accessed electronically are now tagged with a digital object identifier (DOI), a permanent identifier that will not change from library to library or database to database. The DOI makes URLs unnecessary. Whenever a DOI is provided, include it at the end of your citation.

The basic citation for an article in an online journal or accessed through an online database that has a DOI is the same as for a printed journal article except that the DOI appears at the end of the citation:

More about ▶▶▶
Digital object identi-
fiers (DOI), 370,
371, 381

> Rozin, P. (2007). Exploring the landscape of modern academic psychology:
>
> Finding and filling the holes. *American Psychologist, 62*, 754–766.
>
> DOI
> doi:10.1037/1091-7527.25.4.468

For an article in an online journal that does *not* provide a DOI, include the phrase *Retrieved from* followed by the URL for the journal's home page.

> Bachner-Melman, R., Zohar, A. H., Kremer, I., & Ebstein, R. P. (2007).
>
> Psychological profiles of women with a past or present diagnosis
>
> of anorexia nervosa. *The Internet Journal of Mental Health 4*(2).
>
> Retrieved from http://www.ispub.com/journal/the_internet_journal_
>
> of_mental_health.html

15. Article in a magazine

a. Printed or accessed through a database Provide the full publication date of the issue (year, month, and day or year and month). If the volume and issue number of the magazine are available, include that information as you would for a journal article.

Example 14, 376

> Gladwell, M. (2007, November 12). Dangerous minds. *The New Yorker,*
>
> *83*(35), 36–45.

> Pelusi, N. (2009, January/February). The appeal of the bad boy.
>
> *Psychology Today, 42*(1), 58–59.

b. Online Include the URL for the magazine's home page.

> Goldberg, M. (2006, February 24). Saving the neighborhood. *Salon.*
>
> Retrieved from http://www.salon.com

If the magazine is available in a printed edition but the article is only available online, include the phrase *Supplemental material* in brackets after the article's title.

> Daniller, A. (2007, December). Psychology research done right [Supple-
>
> mental material]. *GradPSYCH*. Retrieved from http://gradpsych
>
> .apags.org/webexclusives/research.html

16. Article in a newspaper The information you need to create a reference list entry for a printed newspaper article is on the masthead of the newspaper (at the top of the first page) and on the first and last page of the article. For newspaper articles downloaded from a database, the information you need appears on the search results screen, the full record of the article, or the article itself. For articles that appear in online versions of the newspaper, the information you need is usually at the top of the first page of the article.

a. Printed or accessed through a database

> author   pub. date   title
> Friedman, R. A. (2009, January 20). Sex and depression: In the brain, if
>
>   newspaper   sec./pg. no.
> not the mind. *The New York Times*, p. D6.

If the title of a newspaper does not include its place of publication, supply the city and state, in square brackets, following the title.

> Sabo, B. (2006, July 30). Honored parents emphasize values. *The Patriot-*
>
> *News* [Harrisburg, PA], p. B4.

If the pages of the article are not continuous, provide all page numbers.

> Chen, G. (2007, May 10). Electronic baby sitter: 18% of American toddlers
>
> have a TV set in their room. *The Post-Standard* [Syracuse, NY],
>
> pp. A1, A8.

The citation for a newspaper article downloaded from a database follows the model for a printed newspaper article, but it generally omits page numbers, as they are usually not included online.

b. Online Follow the format for a printed newspaper article, but omit the page reference and include the words *Retrieved from* and the URL for the newspaper's home page.

> Friedman, R. A. (2009, January 20). Sex and depression: In the brain, if not
>
> the mind. *The New York Times.* Retrieved from http://www.nytimes.com/

17. Review Follow the model for the type of periodical in which the review appeared, and add the label *Review of the book* followed by the title and author of the reviewed work, in brackets, after the review's title.

Examples 14–16, 376–78

> review author   review title   label
> Balk, D. E. (2007). Diamonds and mummies are forever [Review of
>
> the book *Remember Me,* by L. T. Cullen]. *Death Studies, 31,* 941–947.
>
> doi:10.1080/07481180701603436

If the review is untitled, substitute the label *Review of the book,* the book's title, and the book's author in brackets.

> Schredl, M. (2008). [Review of the book *The dream experience: A*
>
> *systematic exploration,* by M. Kramer]. *Dreaming, 18,* 280–286.

18. Letter to the editor Follow the model for the type of periodical in which the letter appeared, and insert the label *Letter to the editor* in brackets following the letter's title.

> Richmond, A. (2009, May). Miracle drug? [Letter to the Editor].
>
> *The Atlantic,* 14.

If there is no letter title, substitute the label *Letter to the editor,* in brackets.

19. Abstract It is always better to read and cite the article itself. However, if you relied only on the abstract, or summary, cite only the abstract to avoid misrepresenting your source and your research.

> Loverock, D. S. (2007). Object superiority as a function of object coherence
>
> and task difficulty [Abstract]. *American Journal of Psychology, 120,*
>
> 565–591.

APA Reference List Entries

APA Reference List Entries

▶▶▶Annotated visual of where to find author, title, and publication information, on foldout following p. 297

More about ▶▶▶
Citing a website, 367

Bruce, A. S., Ray, W., & Carlson, R. A. (2007). Understanding cognitive

failures: What's dissociation got to do with it? *American Journal*

of Psychology, 120, 553–563. Abstract retrieved from http://www

.ebscohost.com.

Other Electronic Sources

While it is generally easy to find the information you need to create a complete citation for a book or an article in a periodical, websites can be a bit trickier. Most of the information you need will appear on the site's home page, usually at the bottom or top of that page, or on the web page you are citing. Sometimes, however, you may need to look further. Click on links with titles such as "About us" or "More information." Frequently, websites will not provide complete information, so include as much information in your entry as you can.

20. Website In general, when mentioning an entire website in a research project, you do not have to include an entry in your reference list. However, if you quote or paraphrase content from the site or interact with it in a substantial way, include it, following this model:

Author's surname, Initial(s). (Copyright date or date last updated). *Website*

title. Retrieved from + URL

Here is an example of an actual citation:

Gilbert, R. (2001). *Shake your shyness.* Retrieved from http://

shakeyourshyness.com

21. Web page Provide the title of the page (with no formatting), the date you last accessed the site, and the URL for the specific page you are citing.

web page title

American Psychological Association. (2008). Getting a good night's sleep

with the help of psychology. Retrieved April 23, 2007, from

URL for web page
http://www.psychologymatters.org/insomnia.html

→ **Tech**

Checking URLs and DOIs

DOIs. If your entry includes a DOI, check it before submitting your project by visiting <crossref.org> and inserting the DOI into the search box.

URLs. Just before submitting your paper, test all the URLs. Sometimes web addresses change or content is taken down. If the URL you provided no longer works, search for the work online by title or keyword; you may find it "cached" on the Web even though the owner of the original site has taken the work down. Then use the URL for the cached version in your bibliographic entry.

If the page was created and published by the same group, omit the publisher's name from the retrieval statement (as in the example above); if not, add the publisher's name before the URL (*Retrieved from APA website:*). If no author is cited, move the title to the author position. If the web page is untitled, add a description in brackets.

22. Discussion list posting Treat the subject line (or *thread*) as the title, and include the label *Message posted to.* If messages are protected by a password or unavailable to the general public (as with an email or instant message), use only an in-text citation.

             date posted   subj. line   label
Arendes, L. (2008, July 9). Objectivity [Discussion list comment]. Retrieved
                                   URL
    from news://sci.psychology.research/archived at http://groups.google

    .com/group/sci.psychology/research/

23. Article on a wiki Cite a wiki article as you would a web page. Because wikis are written and edited collaboratively, there is no author to cite; begin with the article's title. If the date of the most recent update is not noted, include the abbreviation *n.d.* in place of the date. Always include a retrieval date and direct URL.

    International relations. (n.d.). Retrieved April 22, 2008, from http://polisci

    .wikidot.com/international-relations

24. Blog posting, comment on a blog posting Include a screen name if the author's name is not provided.

a. Blog posting

post author   post date   post title

Dean, J. (2009, January 1). Gratitude enhanced by focusing on end

    of pleasurable experience [Web log message]. Retrieved from

                        URL (post)

    http://www.spring.org.uk/2009_01_01_blogarchive.php

More about ▶▶▶
Reliability, 250–51

b. Comment on a blog posting

comment author   date posted   thread title

HLVictoria. (2004, January 11). Re: Sociology of weblogs [Web log

                                  URL

    message]. Retrieved from http://blog.niceperson.org/2003/02/11/

    sociology-of-weblogs/#comment-62

Audio and Visual Sources

The information you need to create an entry for most audio and visual sources will appear on the cover, label, or program of the work or in the credits at the end of a film or television show. As with other citations, italicize the titles of longer works, such as albums and films, and do not format the titles of shorter works, such as single songs or single episodes of television programs.

APA Reference List Entries

22. Discussion list posting
23. Article on a wiki
24. Blog posting, comment on a blog posting
25. Motion picture
26. Online video or video blog (vlog)
27. Television or radio broadcast
28. Musical or other audio recording
29. Lecture, speech, or conference presentation

25. Motion picture

                                  release

Grazer, B. (Producer), & Howard, R. (Director). (2001). *A beautiful mind*

    [Motion picture]. United States: Warner Bros.

26. Online video or video blog (vlog)

    ATTC Network. (2007, July 12). Michael–Clinical psychologist [Video file].

        Retrieved from http://www.youtube.com/watch?v=4OAYT5P6xaQ

27. Television or radio broadcast

a. Series

    Garcia, R. (Executive producer). (2008–2009). *In treatment* [Television

        series]. New York, NY: HBO.

b. Episode

> Reingold, J. (Writer), & Barclay, P. (Director). (2008). Mia: Week three
>
> [Television series episode]. In R. Garcia (Executive producer), *In*
>
> *treatment*. New York, NY: HBO.

c. Podcast

> Mitchell, N. (Producer). (2008, March 15). The psyche on death row. *All in*
>
> *the mind* [Audio podcast]. Retrieved from http://www.abc.net.au/rn/
>
> allinthemind/default.htm

28. Musical or other audio recording

a. CD, LP, or audiobook

> Gore, A. (Writer), & Patton, W. (Narrator). (2007). *The assault on reason*
>
> [CD]. New York, NY: Penguin Audio.

b. Selection or song on a CD, LP, or audiobook

> writers   © date   performers
>
> Dilly, D., & Wilkin, M. (1959). The long black veil [Recorded by H. Dickens &
>
> A. Gerrard]. On *Pioneering women of bluegrass* [CD]. Washington,
>
> recording date
>
> DC: Smithsonian/Folkways Records. (1996).

29. Lecture, speech, or conference presentation

> Robinson, G. E. (2008, May 6). *Preventing violence against women.*
>
> Paper presented at the annual meeting of the American Psychiatric
>
> Association, Washington, DC.

30. Map

> U.S. Census Bureau, Geography Division. (Cartographer). (2001).
>
> Mean center of population for the United States: 1790 to 2000
>
> [Demographic map]. Retrieved from http://www.census.gov/geo/
>
> www/cenpop/meanctr.pdf

Miscellaneous Sources

31. Government publication

a. Printed

> U.S. Department of Health and Human Services, National Institutes of Health, National Institute of Mental Health. (2008). *Bipolar disorder* (NIH Publication No. 3679). Washington, DC: U.S. Government Printing Office.

Example 7, 373

> U.S. Department of Health and Human Services. (2005). *Steps to a healthier US.* Washington, DC: Author.

b. Online

> U.S. General Accounting Office. (1993, September 21). *North American Free Trade Agreement: A focus on the substantive issues* (Publication No. GAO/T-GGD-93-44). Retrieved from http://www.gpoaccess.gov/gaoreports/search.html

32. Report (nongovernmental)

> American Psychological Association, Task Force on Gender Identity and Gender Variance. (2008). *Report of the Task Force on Gender Identity and Gender Variance.* Retrieved from http://www.apa.org/pi/lgbc/transgender/2008TaskForceReport.pdf

18c Using APA Style for Notes

▶▶▶Sample content
note, 399

APA style cites sources in the body of the text rather than in footnotes or endnotes. However, it does allow for content notes and author notes. ***Content notes*** provide relevant information that is not central to the argument of the paper; ***author notes*** acknowledge any help the writer received or any possible conflicts of interest. Content notes should appear in a footnote at the bottom of the page or in a list of endnotes, on a new page following the reference list. Author notes appear on the title page.

18d Formatting a Paper in APA Style

The appearance of your paper reflects the care you have taken in writing it. If you are writing in the social sciences (or if your instructor asks you to), format your project using APA style. The following section explains how to format a student paper, and Heather DeGroot's paper at the end of this chapter provides a model.

▶▶▶Student research project (APA style): "The Power of Wardrobe," Heather De-Groot, 389–400

1. Margins and spacing

- Set margins of at least one inch at the top, bottom, and left- and right-hand sides of your paper.

- Indent the first line of each paragraph half an inch.

➜ Tech

Spaces versus inches

The major style guides (MLA, APA, *Chicago*) were initially written before the widespread use of personal computers, when most writers still worked on typewriters. Indentions on a typewriter are measured by spaces—how many times the typist hits the space bar. On a computer, indentions are measured in inches and are created by using the Paragraph dialog box under the Format menu or by setting indentions on the Ruler.

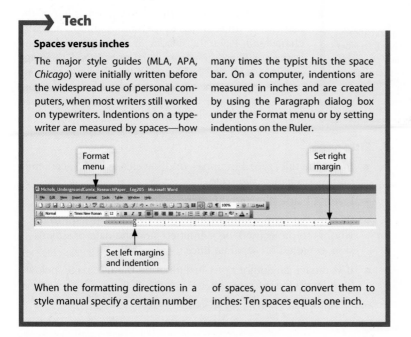

Format menu

Set right margin

Set left margins and indention

When the formatting directions in a style manual specify a certain number of spaces, you can convert them to inches: Ten spaces equals one inch.

More about ▶▶▶
Block quotations,
817

- Indent quotations of forty or more words as a block half an inch from the left margin.

- Double-space the entire paper, including the abstract, title page, block quotation, footnotes, figure captions, and the reference list. Set the text so that the right margin is uneven (ragged) and do not hyphenate words at the ends of lines. Insert two spaces after punctuation at the end of a sentence.

▶▶▶Sample refer-
ence list, 397–98

- Use a hanging indent for each reference list entry: The first line should be flush with the left margin with subsequent lines indented half an inch.

More about ▶▶▶
Choosing a typeface
and type size,
179–80

2. Typeface

Use a standard typeface such as Times New Roman or Arial in a readable size (usually 12-point).

➡ **Tech**

Creating a Header

Word processing programs allow you to insert a header automatically. In Microsoft *Word,* select "Header and Footer" under the View menu. If you have any questions about creating a header, consult the program's Help directory.

3. Header and page number

Include a header, or *running head,* consisting of the first two or three words of the title (no more than fifty characters). Place the header in the upper right-hand corner, half an inch from the upper edge; the page number should be half an inch from the top and one inch from the right edge of the page. Use your word processor's header feature to insert the running head and number the pages automatically.

More about ▶▶▶
Crafting a title,
95–96

4. Title page

- Insert the title, typed in upper- and lowercase letters, centered on the top half of the page.

- Insert a blank line and then type your name.

- Include the course number, the name of the instructor to whom the project will be submitted, and the date of submission, centered on separate lines.

- If you have an author note, include it on the title page, below the identifying information.

A sample title page appears on p. 389.

5. Abstract

The abstract generally includes a one-sentence summary of the most important points in each section:

- Introduction: Problem under investigation
- Methods: Number and characteristics of participants, research methods
- Results: Your outcomes
- Conclusions: Implications of your results

The abstract follows the title page and appears on its own page, headed with the word *Abstract* centered at the top of the page. The abstract should be no more than 150–250 words.

6. Tables and figures

- Refer to tables and figures in the text, using the word *Table* or *Figure* followed by the number of the table or figure in sequence. (The first figure is Figure 1, the second table is Table 2.) Discuss the significance of tables and figures in the text, but do not repeat the information that appears in the table or figure itself.

- Include a caption with each figure, using the word *Figure* with the number assigned in the text. The caption, which follows the figure, should describe the figure briefly but not repeat the information in your text. If you borrowed the figure or the data to create the figure, include the source information at the end of your caption.

  ▶▶▶ Sample figure captions, APA style, 400

- Include a table number (preceded by the word *Table*) and, on the next line, the table title. The table number and title should precede the table. If you borrowed the table or the data to create the table, include source information in a note below the table.

- Place tables, each on a new page, after the reference list or endnotes (if any). Place figures (photographs, drawings, cartoons, graphs, and charts), each on a new page, following the tables.

Writing
Responsibly   **Of Deadlines and Paper Clips**

Instructors expect students to turn in thoughtful, carefully proofread, and neatly formatted papers on time—usually in class on the due date. Another assumption is that the writer will clip (or staple) the pages of the paper *before* the paper is submitted. Do justice to yourself by being fully prepared: Do not hand in a stack of loose sheets or expect your instructor to provide a paper clip.

7. Printing, paper, and binding

Print your paper using a high-quality printer (make sure it has plenty of ink), on opaque, 8½ × 11–inch white paper. Most instructors do not want you to enclose your paper in a binder, but if you are in doubt, ask. If not submitted in a binder, paper-clip the pages together.

More about ▶▶▶
Writing in the sciences and social sciences, 472–86 (ch. 22)
Appendixes, 478

Student Research Project: APA Style

In the sample student research project that follows, Heather DeGroot examines the influence that gender stereotypes can have on behavior. Her paper follows the format of an APA-style research report.

Running head: Shortened title

The Power of Wardrobe:

Male Stereotype Influences

Heather DeGroot

Psychology 220

Dr. Lawrence

May 2, 2008

Identifying information (double spaced)

389

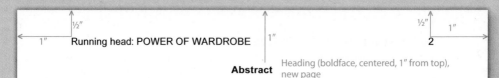

Abstract Heading (boldface, centered, 1" from top), new page

This study explores the potential influence of stereotypical appearances on male

subjects' stated opinions regarding entertainment perceived as "feminine." Results

are based on responses from 26 undergraduate males. Data were analyzed

using one-way variance tests and Tukey HSD post hoc tests. The findings show

that participants were more likely to give a favorable rating to a "chick-flick" in

the presence of a counterstereotypical male ($M = 8.67$, $SD = 1.53$) than in the

presence of a stereotypical male ($M = 5.31$, $SD = 1.97$) or control proctor ($M = 5.20$,

$SD = 1.99$). Results suggest that participants may have experienced gender role

conflict.

Abstract: Summary of problem, methods, results, discussion

The Power of Wardrobe: Male Stereotype Influences Title (boldface, centered)

¶ indent: ½"

Stereotypes—expectations placed upon people because of their gender, race, or religion—may be discouraged in their most overt forms, but they continue to flourish in the media. In contemporary American culture, this sort of bias places an exaggerated emphasis on physical appearance. Such attitudes are not isolated features of media programming; rather, they influence many interactions in everyday life—especially among adolescents and young adults, for whom clothing, personal image, and identity tend to be inextricably bound (Sontag, Peteu, & Lee, 1999).

Text: Double spaced

Summary of whole source, so no page number

Impressions of other people can be classified into two categories: stereotypes and individuating information (Kunda & Thagard, 1996). Stereotypes focus on social categories, while individuating information is the focus of other factors, including personality, actions of the individual, and so forth. The stereotype effect, as defined by Monica Biernat (2003), is "a finding that individual members (comparable in all ways except their category membership) are judged in a direction consistent with group-level expectations or stereotypes" (p. 1019). Under such circumstances, people are judged more by the category in which one can group them than by their qualities or skills as individuals. However, according to Kunda and Thagard (1996), the division of these types of judgment is not always clear. This was the influence for their impression-formation theory in which stereotypes, traits, and behaviors are all constrained by positive and negative associations. In their research, they found that appearance was crucial in this process.

Introduction (funnel): Background, definitions, hypothesis

Signal phrase with parenthetical citation for date, page number

The influential power of stereotypes is particularly interesting when gender boundaries are crossed. In a 2003 study, researchers found that while membership

1"

1"

in a socioeconomic class or "power position" tended to give participants a biased or predetermined opinion about the beliefs and behaviors (such as work ethic) by which a person in another category lived, gender exerted at least as great an influence on the manner in which people were categorized (Vescio, Snyder, & Butz). Men in power positions were likely to be viewed differently than females in the same positions (Mansfield, 2006).

Date of publication in text, so omitted from parenthetical citation

Would these findings remain consistent if only one gender were used in the study? That is to say, can we identify intra-gender roles or stereotypes that similarly affect perception and beliefs about individuals? A study by G. H. Edwards (1992) found that beliefs regarding men and women transcend gender, for subtypes or categories emerge within each sex; for example, among American men one might be perceived as businessman, athlete, family man, or loser. Typically, such seeming variations represent varying degrees of a supposed normative "masculinity," rather than truly distinct expressions of a male gender role. Rudman and Fairchild (2004) write that "for men, a lifetime of experience observing one's peers being teased or ostracized for 'effeminate' behavior may evoke strong normative pressures toward highly masculine self-presentations" (p. 160). Plummer (2001) indicates that boys begin pressuring one another to conform in childhood, telling each other to toughen up or to stop acting like a baby.

Paraphrase of whole source, so no page number included

Direct quotation from PDF; page number included

The purpose of this study is to observe whether male participants are likely to be influenced by a stereotypically "male" opinion. Are college-aged males more swayed by the "jock" or "cool guy on campus" than by those with an "average Joe" or a "metrosexual" appearance? Hypothetically, male participants should more

Hypothesis

likely be swayed by the opinions of the stereotypical male than by those of the control group ("average Joe") or the experimental group (counterstereotypical).

Methods   First-level heading (centered, boldface)

Participants   Second-level heading (left, boldface)

Twenty-six undergraduate males from a large Southeastern university, (mean age = 19) participated in this study in order to fill a course requirement in their general psychology classes.

Procedure

The participants were randomly assigned to one of three conditions in the study: the stereotypically "male" proctor group, the counterstereotypical proctor group, and the control group. The proctor was the same person in each condition, but his appearance was different in each. In the stereotypically male proctor condition, the proctor wore an outfit consisting of team sports apparel: a baseball cap, a basketball jersey, shorts, and sneakers (Figure 1a). In the counterstereotypical condition, he wore a long-sleeved, light pink button-down shirt (tucked in), creased khaki pants, and dress shoes (Figure 1b). In the control condition, the proctor wore a short-sleeved blue polo shirt (not tucked in), khaki shorts, and sneakers (Figure 1c).

Methods: How study was conducted

The participants in each condition were told at the beginning of the experiment that they were participating in a memory-recall task. They were to identify what they could remember from a clip from the movie *Pretty Woman* (Milchan, Reuther, & Marshall, 1990),[1] a stereotypical "chick-flick." During the ten-minute film clip, which was constant for each of the three conditions, the proctor read scripted lines such as

Content note: Additional information, endnote

"Oh! I love this part!" and "I'm seriously such a sap, but this film is just so good!" The script was a constant in each of the three conditions.

After the clip was viewed by all, the proctor handed out a questionnaire to conduct the "memory-recall task." The questionnaire contained diversion questions such as "What color is the dress that Vivian (Julia Roberts's character) wears in the scene?" and "What game do Edward and Vivian play after the performance?" At the end of the questionnaire, the participants rated the movie on an opinion scale from 1 to 10, with 10 being the highest overall liking.

After the experiment was over, participants in each condition were debriefed as a group and were dismissed from the study.

Results

A one-way analysis of variance (ANOVA) was conducted on the data in order to determine whether males are more influenced by a stereotypically "male" proctor in comparison to the counterstereotypical and control-group proctors. The analysis demonstrated that at least one group was significantly different from the others, $F(2, 23) = 4.08$, $p < .05$. Tukey HSD post hoc tests were performed to measure the difference between the groups individually. The Tukey HSD revealed that the participants were more likely to give a favorable movie rating under the influence of the counterstereotypically masculine proctor ($M = 8.67$, $SD = 1.53$) than the stereotypically masculine proctor ($M = 5.31$, $SD = 1.97$) or the control proctor ($M = 5.20$, $SD = 1.99$) (see Figure 2).

There were no significant differences in movie ratings between those in the stereotypically masculine proctor's group and those in the control proctor's. These

Results: Summarizes data and research findings; includes figure

results were contrary to the study's initial hypothesis, and they suggest that male participants are more likely to defy gender roles in the presence of a counter-stereotypical proctor than in the presence of a stereotypically masculine proctor.

Discussion

The study elicited something beyond stereotypical responses from the participants. In fact, the participants may have experienced gender role conflict. Instead of scoring favorably when the masculine male proctor said he enjoyed the film, the participants scored the film lower than initially expected. The presence of a highly or moderately "masculine" male, though he made favorable comments in each condition, may have caused the participants to adhere more rigidly to socialized male gender roles and thus rate the movie lower than subjects in the atypically "masculine" proctor group, who did not feel the pressure to assert masculinity in their rating of *Pretty Woman* (McCreary et al., 1996).

Certain irregularities in the study provoked questions that might be investigated in future research. Due to factors beyond the researcher's control, each condition had a different number of participants. The counterstereotypical condition, which had significant findings, had the smallest number of participants; as a result, those scores are subject to greater statistical variation due to strong individual opinion. However, one might also question whether the number of males present influences a subject's tendency to admit to a counterstereotypical opinion or value judgment. If the study were to be replicated to find for stereotype differences alone, it would be crucial for the number of participants in each

> Discussion: Author's interpretation of data, conclusions, concerns, and questions for further study

> Citations of six or more authors: First author plus *et al.*

condition to be the same. On the other hand, a separate study might use multiple viewing groups of varying individual sizes to determine the effect of group size in gender-stereotype-determined valuations.

Another issue to consider is the effect of the fictional nature of the film to which the male viewers were asked to react. A recent study reported in *Business Week* suggested that men are more willing to show empathy when they know the stories eliciting their emotional response are fictional. Jennifer Argo, one of the authors of the study, is quoted as saying that fictional works provide "an excuse to relax gender stereotypes" (as cited in Coplan, 2008, p. 17). This factor was not considered in the study reported here.

References   Heading (boldface, centered), new page; entries alphabetized by author

Biernat, M. (2003). Toward a broader view of social stereotyping. *American*

    ⟵⟶*Psychologist, 58,* 1019–1027. doi:10.1037/0003-066X.58.12.1019
   ½″

Coplan, J. H. (2008, January 28). When it's all right for guys to cry. *Business*

    Week, 4068, 17. Retrieved from http://www.businessweek.com

Edwards, G. H. (1992). The structure and content of the male gender role

    stereotype: An exploration of subtypes. *Sex Roles, 27,* 553–551.

Kunda, Z., & Thagard, P. (1996). Forming impressions from stereotypes, traits, and

    behaviors: A parallel-constraint-satisfaction theory. *Psychological Review,*

    103, 284–308.

Mansfield, H. C. (2006). *Manliness.* New Haven, CT: Yale University Press.

Milchan, A. (Producer), Reuther, S. (Producer), & Marshall, G. (Director). (1990).

    Pretty woman [DVD]. USA: Touchstone Home Video.

McCreary, D. R., Wong, F. Y., Wiener, W., Carpenter, K. M., Engle, A., & Nelson, P.

    (1996). The relationship between masculine gender role stress and

    psychological adjustment: A question of construct validity? *Sex Roles:*

    A Journal of Research, 34, 507–516.

Journal article: Accessed through database, DOI included

Magazine article: Accessed through a website—URL provided

Book: Scholarly press

Film: Medium in brackets

Plummer, D. C. (2001). The quest for modern manhood: Masculine stereotypes,

peer culture and the social significance of homophobia. *Journal of*

Adolescence, 24, 15–23.

Rudman, L. A., & Fairchild, K. (2004). Reactions to counterstereotypic behavior:

The role of backlash in cultural stereotype maintenance. *Journal of*

Personality and Social Psychology, 87, 157–176.

Sontag, M. S., Peteu, M., & Lee, J. (1999). *Clothing in the self-system of*

adolescents: Relationships among values, proximity of clothing to self,

clothing interest, anticipated outcomes and perceived quality of life.

Retrieved

April 15, 2008, from Michigan State University Extension website:

http://web1.msue.msu.edu/msue/imp/modrr/rr556098.html

Vescio, T. K., Snyder, M., & Butz, D. A. (2003). Power in stereotypically masculine

domains: A social influence strategy X stereotype match model. *Journal of*

Personality & Social Psychology, 85, 1062. doi:10.1037/0022-3514.85.6.1062

Journal article: PDF accessed through database, no DOI—page numbers included, no URL

Article on website: URL and date retrieved included; sponsor named in retrieval statement

Notes Heading (centered), new page

1. This romantic comedy starring Julia Roberts and Richard Gere (dir. Garry

Marshall) was extremely popular, grossing nearly $464 million worldwide,

according to the site Box Office Mojo (www.boxofficemojo.com/movies/?id=

prettywoman.htm). Nevertheless, participants had not seen the film before

participating in this experiment.

Content note: Relevant information not central to argument

(a) (b) (c)

Figure 1. Male proctor in three conditions: (a) stereotypical, (b) counterstereotypical, and (c) control.

Figure caption: Label *(Figure)* and number in italics; caption below illustration

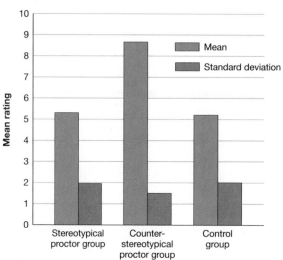

Figure 2. Tukey HSD post hoc test results for the three groups: Group with the stereotypical proctor, group with counterstereotypical proctor, and control group.

19 Documenting Sources: *Chicago* Style

THE CHICAGO MANUAL OF STYLE

The Essential Guide for Writers, Editors, and Publishers

15th edition

Written by editors at the University of Chicago Press, the *Chicago Manual of Style*, 15th ed., provides advice to help writers and editors produce clear and consistent copy for their readers. Many writers in the humanities and social sciences (in history, economics, and philosophy, for example) follow the guidelines provided by the *Chicago Manual* for citing and documenting sources. This chapter includes examples of the most common types of *Chicago*-style in-text citations and bibliography entries. For more information or for examples of less common types of sources, consult the *Chicago Manual* itself. You can also subscribe to the *Chicago Manual* online.

Editors at the University of Chicago Press recognize that readers from different disciplines may have different expectations about how in-text citations and bibliography entries should look, so the *Chicago Manual* provides an author-date system similar to that of the American Psychological Association (APA) and the Council of Science Editors (CSE) for writers in the sciences. It also provides a note and bibliography system for writers in the humanities and social sciences. If your readers (including your instructor) expect you to use the author-date system, consult the *Chicago Manual* itself or follow the style detailed in the APA and CSE chapters in this book.

▶ **More about** ▶▶▶
Popular academic documentation styles per discipline, 454–74
MLA style, 298–357 (ch. 17)
APA style, 358–400 (ch. 18)
CSE style, 429–46 (ch. 20)

Writing
↑ Responsibly   **Citing and Documenting Sources**

When you cite and document sources, you acknowledge any material from which you have quoted, paraphrased, summarized, or drawn information, and you join the conversation on your topic by adding your own interpretation. Simultaneously, you give interested readers (including your instructor) a way to join the conversation.

Accurate entries in the text and bibliography allow your audience to find and read your sources so that they can evaluate your interpretation and learn more about the subject themselves. Accurate entries also demonstrate the care with which you have written your research project and reinforce your reputation as a sound scholar.

19a   Creating *Chicago*-Style Notes and Bibliography Entries

Footnote Note that appears at the bottom of the page

Endnote Note that appears in a list of notes at the end of the project

The note system offered by the *Chicago Manual* allows you to include full bibliographic information in a footnote or endnote or to use an abbreviated footnote or endnote with a bibliography. Including abbreviated notes with a bibliography is recommended.

Examples of the *complete* form of notes and bibliography entries for different types of sources appear in the next section. An *abbreviated* note will generally include enough information for readers to recognize the work and find it in the bibliography. Generally, a shortened note will include the author's surname, a shortened version of the title that includes the title's key words in the same order as they appear on the title page, and the page number you are citing. Here is an example of an abbreviated note and a bibliography entry for the same book:

NOTE
(ABBREVIATED)

1. Vancouver, *Voyage of Discovery*, 283.

BIBLIOGRAPHY

Vancouver, George. *A Voyage of Discovery to the North Pacific Ocean and Round the World, 1791–1795*. Edited by W. Kaye Lamb. London: Hakluyt Society, 1984.

A complete bibliographic note or bibliography entry will include three parts: the author's name, the title of the work, and the publication information (print, electronic, or both). The information you include in each of these parts will differ depending on the type of source you are citing. There are many models, and every variation cannot be covered. You may have to adapt a model to your special circumstances.

Tech

Creating Footnotes and Endnotes

Most word processing programs, including Microsoft *Word* and Google *Docs,* allow you to insert footnotes and endnotes easily. This automated system for inserting footnotes will automatically renumber all the notes in your project if you add or delete one. However, the software for managing notes may not provide many formatting options, so check with your instructor in advance to make sure the software's default format is acceptable.

More about ▶▶▶
Formatting footnotes and endnotes (*Chicago* style), 420
Formatting bibliographies (*Chicago* style), 420–21

Quick Reference ➡ *Chicago* Style Note and Bibliography Entries

▶▶▶Student research project (*Chicago* style): "Exploration and Empire," Abrams Conrad, 422–28

▶▶▶Annotated visual of where to find author and publication information, on foldout following p. 297

Books—Printed and Electronic

In a printed book, the information you need to create a note and bibliography entry (with the exception of the page numbers) is on the title and copyright pages. In an online or e-book, print and electronic publication information often appears at the top or bottom of the first screen or is available through a link.

1. One author

a. Printed The basic note for a printed book looks like this:

> Ref. No. Author's first name Surname, *Title: Subtitle* (Place of
>
> Publication: Publisher, date of publication), page(s).

Here is an example of an actual note:

> 1. Michael Novak, *The Universal Hunger for Liberty: Why the Clash*
>
> *of Civilizations Is Not Inevitable* (New York: Basic Books, 2004), 96–98.

Chicago Note & Bibliography Entries

1. One author
2. Two or three authors
3. More than three authors

The basic bibliography entry for a printed book looks like this:

> Author's surname, First Name. *Title: Subtitle*. Place of publication:
>
> Publisher, date of publication.

Here is an example of an actual bibliography entry:

> Novak, Michael. *The Universal Hunger for Liberty: Why the Clash of*
>
> *Civilizations Is Not Inevitable*. New York: Basic Books, 2004.

The *Chicago Manual* allows for either full publishers' names (as above) or abbreviated versions (*Basic,* for example). Be consistent within a paper. This chapter uses full names.

b. Database

> 2. W. E. B. Du Bois, *The Souls of Black Folk* (Chicago: A. C. McClurg
>
> & Co., 1903; Bartleby.com, 1999), http://www.bartleby. com/114/.

> Du Bois, W. E. B. *The Souls of Black Folk*. Chicago: A. C. McClurg & Co.,
>
> 1903. Bartleby.com, 1999. http://www.bartleby.com/114/.

If the online book is *not* available in print or is not yet in final form and might change by the time your readers seek it out, provide your access date in parentheses following the URL.

c. E-book

3. Charles C. Mann, *1491: New Revelations of the Americas before Columbus* (New York: Knopf Publishing Group, 2005), Adobe Reader e-book.

Mann, Charles C. *1491: New Revelations of the Americas before Columbus*. New York: Knopf Publishing Group, 2005. Adobe Reader e-book.

 Tech

Guidelines for Formatting URLs

As you format notes and bibliography entries for online sources, you will find that not all URLs fit on one line. The *Chicago Manual* recommends breaking a URL (if necessary) only before a dot or other punctuation mark or after a slash (/).

2. Two or three authors

4. Peter Bernstein and Annalyn Swan, *All the Money in the World* (New York: Random House, 2008), 122.

5. Cynthia Kuhn, Scott Swartzwelder, and Wilkie Wilson, *Buzzed: The Straight Facts about the Most Used and Abused Drugs from Alcohol to Ecstasy,* 3rd ed. (New York: W. W. Norton & Co., 2008), 225.

Bernstein, Peter, and Annalyn Swan. *All the Money in the World*. New York: Random House, 2008.

Kuhn, Cynthia, Scott Swartzwelder, and Wilkie Wilson. *Buzzed: The Straight Facts about the Most Used and Abused Drugs from Alcohol to Ecstasy*. New York: W. W. Norton & Co., 2008.

3. More than three authors

6. Peter M. Senge and others, *The Necessary Revolution: How Individuals and Organizations Are Working Together to Create a Sustainable World* (New York: Random House, 2008), 83.

Chicago Note & Bibliography Entries

1. One author
2. **Two or three authors**
3. **More than three authors**
4. Unnamed (anonymous) author
5. Editor (no author)

Senge, Peter M., Bryan Smith, Nina Kruschwitz, Joe Laur, and

Sarah Schley. *The Necessary Revolution: How Individuals and*

Organizations Are Working Together to Create a Sustainable World.

New York: Random House, 2008.

4. Unnamed (anonymous) author If no author is listed, begin with the title.

7. *Terrorist Hunter: The Extraordinary Story of a Woman Who Went*

Undercover to Infiltrate the Radical Islamic Groups Operating in America

(New York: Ecco-HarperCollins, 2003), 82.

Terrorist Hunter: The Extraordinary Story of a Woman Who Went

Undercover to Infiltrate the Radical Islamic Groups Operating in

America. New York: Ecco-HarperCollins, 2003.

5. Editor (no author)

8. Susan E. Cook, ed., *Genocide in Cambodia and Rwanda: New*

Perspectives (New Haven, CT: Yale Center for International and Area

Studies, 2004), 79.

Cook, Susan E., ed. *Genocide in Cambodia and Rwanda: New*

Perspectives. New Haven, CT: Yale Center for International and

Area Studies, 2004.

For a book with multiple editors, change the abbreviation *ed.* to *eds.*

6. Author and editor or translator

9. John Locke, *The Second Treatise of Government*, ed. Thomas P.

Peardon (Indianapolis: Oxford University Press, 1990), 124.

10. Stefan Chwin, *Death in Danzig*, trans. Philip Boehm (New York: Harcourt, 2004), 24.

Locke, John. *The Second Treatise of Government*. Edited by Thomas P.

Peardon. Indianapolis: Oxford University Press, 1990.

Chwin, Stefan. *Death in Danzig*. Translated by Philip Boehm. New York:

Harcourt, 2004.

7. Selection from an edited book or anthology

selection author | selection title | title of book in which selection appears

11. Rebecca Arnold, "Fashion," in *Feminist Visual Culture*, ed. Fiona

selection pgs.

Carson and Claire Pajaczkowska 207–22 (New York: Routledge, 2001).

Arnold, Rebecca. "Fashion." In *Feminist Visual Culture*, edited by Fiona

Carson and Claire Pajaczkowska, 207–22. New York: Routledge,

2001.

8. Edition other than the first

12. James A. Herrick, *The History and Theory of Rhetoric: An*

Introduction, 3rd ed. (Boston: Allyn & Bacon, 2005), 50.

Herrick, James A. *The History and Theory of Rhetoric: An Introduction*. 3rd

ed. Boston: Allyn & Bacon, 2005.

9. Introduction, preface, foreword, or afterword by a different writer

13. Mario Andretti, Foreword to *Race to Win: How to Become a*

Complete Champion, by Derek Daly (Minneapolis: Quayside-Motorbooks,

2008), 7.

Chicago Note & Bibliography Entries

5. Editor (no author)
6. Author and editor or translator
7. **Selection from an edited book or anthology**
8. **Edition other than the first**
9. **Introduction, preface, foreword, or afterword by a different writer**
10. Entry in a reference book
11. Multivolume work

Andretti, Mario. Foreword to *Race to Win: How to Become a Complete*

intro. pgs.

Champion, by Derek Daly, 7–8. Minneapolis: Quayside-

Motorbooks, 2008.

10. Entry in a reference book For a well-known reference work such as the *American Heritage Dictionary* or the *Encyclopedia Britannica,* a bibliography entry is optional.

a. Printed

14. *The American Heritage Dictionary*, 2nd college ed., s.v.

"plagiarism."

b. Online Because online reference works are regularly updated, include an access date after the URL.

15. *Dictionary.com*, s.v. "plagiarism," http://dictionary.reference.com/

browse/plagiarism (accessed July 14, 2007).

11. Multivolume work

a. All volumes If you use information from all volumes in a multivolume work, follow the model for a bibliography entry below.

Tarbell, Ida. *The Life of Abraham Lincoln.* 2 vols. New York: Lincoln

Memorial Association, 1900.

Provide a note only when you cite a specific passage in one of the volumes; follow the model in part b below.

b. One volume

16. Ida Tarbell, *The Life of Abraham Lincoln* (New York: Lincoln

vol. pgs.

Memorial Association, 1900), 1:173.

Tarbell, Ida. *The Life of Abraham Lincoln.* Vol. 1. New York: Lincoln

Memorial Association, 1900.

---

12. Book in a series

book title

17. Oleg V. Khlevnyuk, ed. *The History of the Gulag: From*

series title

Collectivization to the Great Terror. Annals of Communism (New Haven,

CT: Yale University Press, 2004), 186–87.

Khlevnyuk, Oleg V., ed. *The History of the Gulag: From Collectivization to*

the Great Terror. Annals of Communism. New Haven: Yale University

Press, 2004.

13. Sacred text

book   lines   version

18. 1 Kings 3:23–26 (King James Version).

verse

19. Qur'an 17:1–2.

Sacred texts are usually omitted from the bibliography.

14. Dissertation For an unpublished dissertation, include the type of document (*PhD dissertation,* which can be abbreviated *PhD diss.*), the university where it was submitted, and the date of submission.

20. Jessica Davis Powers, "Patrons, Houses and Viewers in Pompeii:

Reconsidering the House of the Gilded Cupids" (PhD diss., University of

Michigan, 2006), 43–57.

Powers, Jessica Davis. "Patrons, Houses and Viewers in Pompeii:

Reconsidering the House of the Gilded Cupids." PhD diss., University

of Michigan, 2006.

For a published dissertation, format the note and bibliography entry as you would for a book.

Example 1, 404

Periodicals—Printed and Electronic

> Annotated visual of where to find author, title, and publication information, on foldout following p. 297

A periodical is a publication issued at regular intervals—newspapers are generally published every day, magazines every week or month, and scholarly journals four times a year. For periodicals, include not only the title of the article (in quotation marks) but also the title of the periodical (in italics). The type of publication information you include depends on the type of periodical you are citing.

15. Article in a scholarly journal The information you need to create a note and bibliography entry for a printed journal article appears on the cover or title page of the journal and on the first and last page of the article. For articles downloaded from a database, the information appears on the screen listing the articles that fit your search terms, on the full record of the article, or on the first (and last) page of the file you download. For articles that appear in journals published solely online, you will find the publication information on the website's home page, in the journal's table of contents, or on the first page of the article.

Chicago Note & Bibliography Entries

13. Sacred text
14. Dissertation
15. Article in a scholarly journal
16. Article in a magazine
17. Article in a newspaper (signed)

a. Printed If a journal is paginated by volume—for example, if issue 1 ends on p. 175 and issue 2 begins on p. 176—the issue number may be omitted. The basic note for an article in a printed journal paginated by volume looks like this:

Ref. No. Author's first name Surname, "Title of Article," *Title of*

Journal Vol. No. (Year of publication): Pages.

If a journal is paginated by issue—if the page numbering in each issue begins on page 1—add the issue number between the volume number and the publication date. Months (May) or seasons (Winter) may be included before the year of publication, but they are not required. Here are examples of notes and bibliography entries of journals with and without issue numbers.

Paginated by Volume (No Issue Number)

21. Jason Phillips, "The Grape Vine Telegraph: Rumors and

                                                                    vol. no.

Confederate Persistence," *Journal of Southern History* 72 (2006): 770.

Phillips, Jason. "The Grape Vine Telegraph: Rumors and Confederate

Persistence." *Journal of Southern History* 72 (2006): 753–88.

Paginated by Issue (Issue Number Included)

22. Bill McCarron, "Basilisk Puns in *Harry Potter and the Chamber*

vol. no.

of Secrets," *Notes on Contemporary Literature* 36, no. 1 (2006): 2.

issue no.

McCarron, Bill. "Basilisk Puns in *Harry Potter and the Chamber of Secrets*."

Notes on Contemporary Literature 36, no. 1 (2006): 2.

b. Accessed through a database Most researchers locate journal articles through subscription databases available through their college library. Frequently, articles indexed in such databases are also available in HTML or PDF format through the database. If the article you are citing is available in PDF format, include the page numbers you are citing in your note and the page range in your bibliography entry. If the article is available only in HTML format, add a subhead or paragraph number to your note if this will help readers locate the passage you are citing. To cite an article accessed through a subscription database, add the URL of the database's home page at the end of your entry. If the article is accessible through an open-access database, include the URL for the article itself. More and more academic journals are also adding digital object identifiers (DOIs); if the article you are citing includes a DOI, add it in place of the article's page numbers.

23. Michael J. Furlong and Sandra L. Christenson, "Engaging

Students at School and with Learning: A Relevant Construct for

DOI

All Students," *Psychology in the Schools* 45 (2008), doi: 10.1002/

database home page

pits.20302, http://www.ebscohost.com.

Furlong, Michael J., and Sandra L. Christenson. "Engaging Students at

School and with Learning: A Relevant Construct for *All* Students."

Psychology in the Schools 45 (2008), doi: 10.1002/pits.20302,

http://www.ebscohost.com.

Chicago Note & Bibliography Entries

13. Sacred text
14. Dissertation
15. **Article in a scholarly journal**
16. Article in a magazine
17. Article in a newspaper (signed)

HTML Hypertext markup language, the coding system used to create websites and web pages (196)

PDF Portable document format, a method created by Adobe for sharing documents across platforms without losing formatting (196)

DOI Digital object identifier, a permanent identifier given to electronic articles (370)

c. Online Online journals usually do not provide page numbers. Provide the issue number (if available), and include the DOI (if there is one) and the URL for the article.

24. Jeremy Adelman, "An Age of Imperial Revolutions," *American Historical Review* 113 (2008), doi: 10.1086/ahr.113.2.319, http://www.journals.uchicago.edu/doi/full/10.1086/ahr.113.2.319.

Adelman, Jeremy. "An Age of Imperial Revolutions." *American Historical Review* 113 (2008). doi: 10.1086/ahr.113.2.319, http://www.journals.uchicago.edu/doi/full/10.1086/ahr.113.2.319.

16. Article in a magazine Omit volume and issue numbers, and replace the parentheses around the publication date (month and year or month, day, and year) with commas.

a. Printed

25. Marian Smith Holmes, "The Freedom Riders," *Smithsonian,* February 2009, 72.

Holmes, Marian Smith. "The Freedom Riders." *Smithsonian,* February 2009, 70–75.

b. Accessed through a database

26. Jesse Ellison, "The Refugees Who Saved Lewiston," *Newsweek,* January 17, 2009, 69, http://www.lexisnexis.com/.

Ellison, Jesse. "The Refugees Who Saved Lewiston." *Newsweek,* January 17, 2009, 69. http://www.lexisnexis.com/.

c. Online

27. Mike Madden, "What's Love Got to Do with It?" *Salon,* January 28, 2009, http://www.salon.com/news/feature/2009/01/28/stimulus/.

Madden, Mike. "What's Love Got to Do with It?" *Salon*, January 28, 2009.

http://www.salon.com/news/feature/2009/01/28/stimulus/.

17. Article in a newspaper (signed) Because page numbers may differ from edition to edition, use edition name and section letter or number (if available) instead. Bibliography entries may be omitted.

a. Printed

28. John M. Broder, "Geography Is Dividing Democrats over Energy,"

New York Times, January 26, 2009, national edition, sec. 1.

Broder, John M. "Geography Is Dividing Democrats over Energy." *New York*

Times, January 26, 2009, national edition, sec. 1.

If the city in which the newspaper is published is not identified on the newspaper's masthead, add it in italics; if it might be unfamiliar to readers, add the state, also.

29. Jim Kenneally, "When Brockton Was Home to a Marathon,"

Brockton (MA) Enterprise, April 20, 2006, sec. 1.

Kenneally, Jim. "When Brockton Was Home to a Marathon." *Brockton (MA)*

Enterprise, April 20, 2006, sec. 1.

For well-known national newspapers (such as the *Christian Science Monitor, USA Today,* and the *Wall Street Journal*), no city or state is needed. If you are unsure whether the newspaper is well known, consult your instructor or a reference librarian.

b. Accessed through a database

30. John M. Broder, "Geography Is Dividing Democrats over

Energy," *New York Times,* January 26, 2009, late edition, sec. A,

http://lexisnexis.com.

Broder, John M. "Geography Is Dividing Democrats over Energy." *New York*

Times, January 26, 2009, late edition, sec. A. http://lexisnexis. com.

Chicago Note & Bibliography Entries

15. Article in a scholarly journal
16. Article in a magazine
17. Article in a newspaper (signed)
18. Article or editorial in a newspaper (unsigned)
19. Review

c. Online

31. Steve Chapman, "Moderating the Terror War," *Chicago Tribune,* January 25, 2009, http://www.chicagotribune.com/news/columnists/chi-oped0125chapmanjan25,0,1998584.column.

Chapman, Steve. "Moderating the Terror War." *Chicago Tribune,* January 25, 2009. http://www.chicagotribune.com/news/columnists/chi-oped0125chapmanjan25,0,1998584.column.

18. Article or editorial in a newspaper (unsigned) When no author is named, begin notes and bibliography entries with the name of the newspaper, not the title of the article.

32. *Los Angeles Times,* "Health before Ideology," January 27, 2009, sec. A.

Los Angeles Times, "Health before Ideology," January 27, 2009, sec. A.

19. Review

33. Ben Brantley, review of *Romeo and Juliet,* by William Shakespeare, directed by Michael Greif, Delacorte Theater, New York. *New York Times,* June 25, 2007, sec. E.

Brantley, Ben. Review of *Romeo and Juliet,* by William Shakespeare, directed by Michael Greif, Delacorte Theater, New York. *New York Times,* June 25, 2007, sec. E.

Other Electronic Sources

Although it is usually easy to find citation information for books and articles in periodicals, websites can be a bit trickier. Most of the information you need will appear at the bottom or top of the web page or on the site's home page. Sometimes, however, you may need to look further. Click on links such as "About us" or "More information." Frequently, websites will not provide complete information, in which case provide as much information as you can. If no author is listed, place the site's sponsor in the "author" position. If key information is missing, include a phrase describing the site, in case the URL changes.

20. Website The basic note for a website looks like this:

> Ref. No. Author, Website Title, Sponsoring Organization (if not clear
>
> from title), URL of site's home page.

Here is an example of an actual note:

> 34. Christine Roth, Victorian England: An Introduction, University of
>
> Wisconsin–Oshkosh, Department of English, http://www.english.uwosh
>
> .edu/VictorianEngland.htm.

The bibliography entry for this note looks like this:

> Roth, Christine. Victorian England: An Introduction. University of
>
> Wisconsin–Oshkosh, Department of English. http://www.english
>
> .uwosh.edu/VictorianEngland.htm.

The *Chicago Manual* indicates that access dates should be omitted except where significant updates are likely or when changes in the field can have a significant effect (as in medicine).

21. Web page or wiki article When referring to a specific page or article on a website or wiki, place that page's title in quotation marks. For a wiki article, begin with the article's title.

> 35. "Lewis and Clark County History Project," Montana History Wiki,
>
> Montana Historical Society, http://montanahistorywiki.pbwiki.com/Lewis+
>
> and+Clark+County+History+Project.

Chicago Note & Bibliography Entries

18. Article or editorial in a newspaper (unsigned)
19. Review
20. Website
21. Web page or wiki article
22. Discussion list or blog posting
23. CD-ROM

"Lewis and Clark County History Project." Montana History Wiki, Montana

Historical Society. http:// montanahistorywiki.pbwiki.com/Lewis+and+

Clark+County+History+Project.

22. Discussion list or blog posting Omit bibliography entries for electronic communications unless your instructor requires one; a mention in the text or an in-text citation (parenthetical note, footnote, or endnote) is sufficient. A note citing a blog or discussion list entry might look like this:

post author   post title   blog title

36. Francis Heaney, "The Tie Project, days 164–173," *Heaneyland,*

July 28, 2007, http://www.yarnivore.com/francis/archives/001900

.html#more.

23. CD-ROM Place the format information before publication information. City and date of publication are needed only if there is more than one version or edition of the source or if it is published periodically.

37. *History through Art: The 20th Century,* CD-ROM, Fogware

Publishing.

History through Art: The 20th Century. CD-ROM. Fogware Publishing.

Audio and Visual Sources

The information you need for creating notes and bibliography entries for most audio and visual sources will appear on the cover, label, or program, or in the credits at the end of a film or a television show. Begin with the author, director, conductor, or performer, or begin your citation with the name of the work, depending on what your project emphasizes. The *Chicago Manual* provides few models of audio-visual sources. Those below are based on the principles spelled out in *Chicago.*

24. Motion picture (film, video, DVD)

38. Jason Reitman, dir., *Juno,* DVD, written by Diablo Cody (2007;

Los Angeles: Fox Searchlight Home Entertainment, 2008).

Reitman, Jason, dir. *Juno.* DVD. Written by Diablo Cody. 2007. Los

Angeles: Fox Searchlight Home Entertainment, 2008.

25. Music or other audio recording

39. Johannes Brahms, *Piano Concerto no. 1 in D minor,*

op. 15, dir. Claudio Abbado, Berliner Philharmoniker, 1986, Philips

Classics Productions BMG D153907, compact disc.

Brahms, Johannes. *Piano Concerto no. 1 in D minor, op. 15.* Dir. Claudio

Abbado. Berliner Philharmoniker. 1986. Philips Classics Productions

BMG D153907. Compact disc.

26. Performance

40. Lauren Ambrose, *Romeo and Juliet,* dir. Michael Greif, Delacorte

Theatre, New York, July 1, 2007.

Ambrose, Lauren. *Romeo and Juliet.* Directed by Michael Greif. Delacorte

Theatre, New York, July 1, 2007.

27. Work of art If a reproduction of the work appears in your project, identify the work in a figure caption. If you discuss the work but do not show it, cite it in your notes but do not provide an entry in your bibliography.

41. Alexander Calder, *Two Acrobats,* 1929, wire sculpture, Menil

Collection, Houston.

More about ▶▶▶
Figure captions (*Chicago* style), 419

Miscellaneous Sources

28. Government publication For documents published by the U.S. Government Printing Office (or GPO), including the publisher is optional. If you omit the publisher, change the colon after the location to a period (Washington, DC.).

> 42. U.S. Department of Education, Office of Innovation and Improvement, *Charter High Schools: Closing the Achievement Gap* (Washington, DC: U.S. Government Printing Office, 2006).

> U.S. Department of Education, Office of Innovation and Improvement. *Charter High Schools: Closing the Achievement Gap.* Washington, DC: U.S. Government Printing Office, 2006.

29. Interview (published)

a. Printed or broadcast

> 43. Barack Obama, interview by Maria Bartiromo, *Closing Bell,* CNBC, March 27, 2008.

> Obama, Barack. Interview by Maria Bartiromo. *Closing Bell.* CNBC, March 27, 2008.

b. Online

> 44. Barack Obama, interview by Maria Bartiromo, *Closing Bell,* CNBC, March 27, 2008; transcript posted March 27, 2008, http://www.cnbc.com/id/23832520.

> Obama, Barack. Interview by Maria Bartiromo. *Closing Bell.* CNBC, March 27, 2008. Transcript posted March 27, 2008, http://www.cnbc.com/id/23832520.

30. Personal communication Unless your instructor requires it, no bibliography entry is required.

a. Letter

> 45. Evan Marks, letter to the author, August 13, 2005.

b. Email

> 46. Amy E. Robillard, email message to the author, March 14, 2007.

31. Indirect source

> 47. Theophrastus, *The Characters of Theophrastus,* ed. and trans. J. M. Edmonds (New York: G. P. Putnam, 1929), 48, quoted in Henry Gleitman, *Psychology* (New York: W. W. Norton & Co., 2000), 553.

> Theophrastus. *The Characters of Theophrastus,* 48. Quoted in Henry Gleitman, *Psychology* (New York: W. W. Norton & Co., 2000), 553.

19b Using *Chicago* Style for Tables and Figures

The *Chicago Manual* recommends that you number tables and figures in a separate sequence (*Table 1, Table, 2, Figure 1, Figure 2*) both in the text and in the table title or figure caption. Tables and figures should be placed as close as possible after the text reference. If you use abbreviations for such illustrations, make sure they will be clear to readers. Discuss visuals in the text, but do not repeat the information contained in the table or figure itself, or in an accompanying caption. For tables, provide a brief identifying title and place it above the table. For figures, provide a caption that includes any information about the figure that readers will need to identify it, such as the title of a work of art, the artist's name, the work's location, and a brief description. If the figure or table, or information used to create these illustrations, comes from another source, provide a source note. Source notes for tables generally appear below the table, while source information for figures appears at the end of the figure caption.

19c Using *Chicago* Style for Content Notes

Content notes offer ideas and information that clarify or justify a point in your text. They can also be used to acknowledge the contributions of others (such as tutors and classmates) in the preparation of your research project. If a paper includes both content notes and bibliographic notes, *Chicago* recommends that writers use footnotes (labeled with symbols) for content notes and endnotes (numbered sequentially) for bibliographic notes.

More about ▶▶▶
Sample content
notes, 422
MLA-style format-
ting, 340–44
Formatting college
projects, 104–05

19d Formatting a *Chicago*-Style Paper

The *Chicago Manual* provides detailed instructions about manuscript preparation for authors submitting their work for publication, but it does not offer formatting instructions for college projects. Follow the formatting instructions provided in chapter 6 or chapter 17, or consult your instructor.

The *Chicago Manual* recommends numbering bibliographic notes consecutively throughout the paper, using superscript (above-the-line) numbers in the body of the paper:

> While acknowledging that not all scholars agree, Mann observes, "If
>
> Monte Verde is correct, as most believe, people were thriving from
>
> Alaska to Chile while much of northern Europe was still empty of
>
> mankind and its works."[8]

If endnotes are used, type the heading "Notes" at the top of a new page following the end of the text, and type the notes below. (You may need to insert a page break and type the word "Notes" if your word processor has automatically created endnotes on the last page of your paper.)

To begin your list of works cited, type the heading "Bibliography" or "Works Cited" at the top of a new page. (Ask your instructor which heading is preferred.) Entries should be set with a hanging indent: The first line of each entry is set flush with the left margin, and subsequent lines are indented. Entries should also be alphabetized by the author's surname. If you used more than one source by the same author (or authors), replace the author's name with three hyphens in entries after the first:

Obama, Barack. *The Audacity of Hope: Thoughts on Reclaiming the*

American Dream. New York: Crown, 2006.

---. *Dreams from My Father: A Story of Race and Inheritance.* New York:

Crown, 1995.

Student Research Project: *Chicago* Style

The following excerpts are taken from a research project written by Abrams Conrad for a history course at American University. His formatting has been modified to show both abbreviated notes with a list of works cited and full notes without one.

> *More about* ▶▶▶
> Using abbreviated
> notes, 402

connect
mhconnectcomposition.com
Additional resources: QL19001,
QL19002

Title page model, pp. 342, 389

Abrams Conrad

History 235   Identifying information (double spaced)

Professor Burke

December 15, 2009

Title (centered)   Exploration and Empire: James Cook and the Pacific Northwest   Descriptive title

Exploration of the Pacific Northwest begins and ends with Captain James Cook, the first British explorer to reach the area, map it, and study its peoples. The men who explored and studied the area in his wake had sailed and trained under his command. While others sailed to the Pacific Northwest, their motivation was largely for trade; Cook's voyage and those of his successors were motivated as much by a desire to understand the region and its peoples as by the desire for financial gain.

Thesis at end of first paragraph to guide reader

In the late 1770s, the Pacific Northwest was the globe's last temperate coast to be explored and mapped, primarily due to its remoteness. Cook's third voyage, begun in 1778, was undertaken to discover a Northwest Passage, an inland water- way connecting the Pacific Ocean with the Atlantic that would shorten the sailing time from Europe to Asia. The Admiralty had instructed him "to search for, and to explore, such Rivers or Inlets as may appear to be of a considerable extent and pointing towards Hudsons or Baffins Bay."[1] While his findings were negative—he all but eliminated possibility of an inland passage—he was the first Briton to make contact with the area and truly to study the geography and culture of the region.*

Quotation integrated into text; source in endnote

Symbol, not number, in content footnote

*The Captain Cook Society's website <http://captaincooksociety.com/ccsu52.htm> offers a number of engravings of Pacific Northwestern peoples and their habitat based on paintings and illustrations created during Cook's voyage to the Pacific Northwest.

Cook made anchor in Nootka Sound for most of April 1778 and then ventured north along the Canadian coast, searching for a waterway northeast, until he put in at Prince William Sound.[2] He made a detailed survey of the coast, a portion of which is shown in Figure 1.

Cook's third voyage was also strategic: to thwart Spanish and Russian claims to the Pacific Northwest.[3] With the Spanish in the south and moving north, and the Russians in the north and moving south, the northwest coast, or "New Albion," was a place where the British could establish a claim and perhaps eventually a colony.[4] Another reason for Cook's exploration of the Northwest was the man

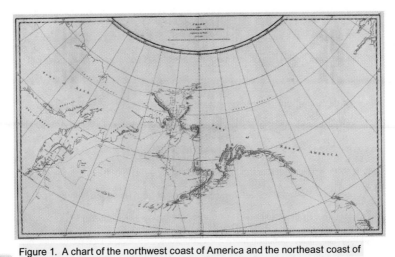

Figure 1. A chart of the northwest coast of America and the northeast coast of Asia, explored in the years 1778 and 1779. Prepared by Lieut. Henry Roberts, under the immediate inspection of Capt. Cook. (1794), David Rumsey Map Collection.

himself. Cook was the quintessential explorer; he "never missed an opportunity to chart a reef or an island," wrote Ernest Dodge of the Peabody Museum in Salem, Massachusetts.[5] Cook stood out because he was so methodical. He was exact in his measurements and never missed an opportunity to learn or write about indigenous peoples.

Cook's explorations of the Pacific Northwest ended with his death in the Hawaiian Islands in early 1779, but his explorations of the Pacific Northwest had direct consequences for traders. James King, who took over command of the expedition after Cook's death, received 800 Spanish dollars in return for twenty sea otter pelts he brought back from the Pacific Northwest—and those were the ragged ones; King received 120 dollars each for pelts in pristine condition, an immense amount of money at that time.[6] It is doubtful the price ever went that high again,[7] but this sum put the region on the map for traders and spawned a new series of voyages.

What made Cook so important to the Pacific Northwest were the explorations of the area by those who had sailed with him. In this regard, it is interesting to compare the results of those who sailed under Cook with those who did not. Some of the first voyages to the area after Cook's death were the trading voyages of James Hanna and James Strange. Hanna sailed from Macao to Nootka Sound (in what is now British Columbia) in 1784–86.[8] His voyage produced few results except those of trade, collecting more than 500 skins.[9] Strange sailed from India; his mission was to proceed to the northwest, trade at Nootka Sound and Alaska, make discoveries, and sail through the Bering Strait and Arctic Ocean, as far north as the

North Pole.[10] While his instructions stated discovery as the primary goal, his investors looked upon trade as the focus of the expedition, and Strange ended up doing neither very well. He brought back barely 600 skins, not enough to offset the costs of the voyage, and though he tried to put together another trip, was unsuccessful.[11] His voyage also proved a burden to Hanna, who returned to the Northwest for a second voyage immediately after Strange and found few furs because of Strange's expedition.[12] What the Strange voyage was notable for, other than reflecting some of the more distasteful bureaucratic aspects of the East India Company, was the growing interest in the Northwest.[13]

John Meares led a voyage in 1785 to the Gulf of Alaska, where he anticipated better trading and finer pelts. He proved ignorant both of Russian control over the area and of the harsh Alaskan climate.[14] Meares reached Cook Inlet in September and found the Russians controlling the trade in the area, so he moved east to Prince William Sound.[15] He thought wintering in the waters off what is now Alaska would be less risky than wintering in the Hawaiian Islands (then called the Sandwich Islands), where Cook had been killed six years before, yet he managed to lose twenty-three men from disease.[16] He also got his ship stuck in the ice and was released only with warm weather and the help of George Dixon and Nathanial Portlock (both had sailed with Cook), who provided aid if he promised to leave at once.[17]

Notes   Heading (centered), new page

Short form of notes used with list of works cited

"Ibid." (abbreviation of *ibidem*, Latin for "in the same place") used when source cited in note immediately above

1. Cook, *The Journals*, 220–24.

2. Ibid., 230.

3. Rose, "Captain Cook," 102–9.

4. Schwantes, *The Pacific Northwest*, 41.

5. Dodge, *Beyond the Capes*, 15.

6. Schwantes, *The Pacific Northwest*, 43.

7. Ibid.

8. Blumenthal, *The Early Exploration*, 3.

9. Dodge, *Beyond the Capes*, 43–44.

10. Gough, "India-Based Expeditions," 219.

11. Ibid., 217–19.

12. Blumenthal, *The Early Exploration*, 4.

13. Gough, "India-Based Expeditions," 219.

14. Ibid., 220.

15. Ibid.

16. Ibid.

Two citations in same footnote separated with a semicolon

Reference work; Use "s.v," *sub verbo*, "under the word" (Latin)

17. Blumenthal, *The Early Exploration*, 4; *Oxford Dictionary of National Biography*, s.v. "John Meares," http://www.oxforddnb.com/.

Works Cited

Blumenthal, Richard W., ed. *The Early Exploration of Inland Washington Waters: Journals and Logs from Six Expeditions, 1786–1792.* Jefferson, NC: McFarland, 2004.

Cook, James. *The Journals of Captain James Cook on His Voyages of Discovery.* Edited by J. C. Beaglehole. Vol. 3. Cambridge, Eng.: Cambridge University Press, 1967.

Dodge, Ernest S. *Beyond the Capes: Pacific Exploration from Captain Cook to the Challenger, 1776–1877.* Boston: Little, Brown, 1971.

Gough, Barry M. "India-Based Expeditions of Trade and Discovery in the North Pacific in the Late Eighteenth Century." *Geographical Journal* 155 (July 1989): 215–23, http://www.jstor.org/.

Rose, J. Holland. "Captain Cook and the Founding of British Power in the Pacific." *Geographical Journal* 73 (February 1929): 102–22, http://www.jstor.org/.

Schwantes, Carlos A. *The Pacific Northwest: An Interpretive History.* Lincoln: University of Nebraska Press, 1989.

Book: Editor, no author

Book: Editor and author; one volume from multivolume work; country named to avoid confusion

Journal article: Accessed through a database, URL of database home page provided

Entries alphabetical by order

Book (printed): Popular press

Book (printed): Scholarly press

Notes   *Heading (centered), new page*

1. James Cook, *The Journals of Captain James Cook on His Voyages of Discovery,* vol. 3, edited by J. C. Beaglehole (Cambridge, Eng.: Cambridge University Press, 1967), 220–24.

Book: Editor and author, one volume from multivolume work

2. Ibid., 230.

3. J. Holland Rose, "Captain Cook and the Founding of British Power in the Pacific," *Geographical Journal* 73 (1929): 102–9, http://www.jstor.org/.

Journal article: Accessed through a database, URL of database homepage provided

4. Carlos A. Schwantes, *The Pacific Northwest: An Interpretive History* (Lincoln: University of Nebraska Press, 1989), 41.

Book (printed): Scholarly press

5. Ernest S. Dodge, *Beyond the Capes: Pacific Exploration from Captain Cook to the Challenger, 1776–1877* (Boston: Little, Brown, 1971), 15.

Book (printed): Popular press

6. Schwantes, *The Pacific Northwest,* 43.

7. Ibid.

Same work, same page as note above, so only "ibid." needed

8. Richard W. Blumenthal, ed., *The Early Exploration of Inland Washington Waters: Journals and Logs from Six Expeditions, 1786–1792* (Jefferson, NC: McFarland, 2004), 3.

Book (printed): Editor but no author

9. Dodge, *Beyond the Capes,* 43–44.

10. Barry M. Gough, "India-Based Expeditions of Trade and Discovery in the North Pacific in the Late Eighteenth Century," *Geographical Journal* 155 (July 1989): 219, http://www.jstor.org/.

11. Ibid., 217–19.

Same work as above but different pages, so "ibid." plus page number needed

12. Blumenthal, *The Early Exploration,* 4.

13. Gough, "India-Based Expeditions," 219.

20 Documenting Sources: CSE Style

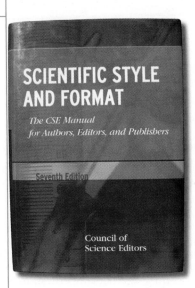

Writers in the sciences customarily use formatting and documentation guidelines from *Scientific Style and Format: The CSE Manual for Authors, Editors, and Publishers,* 7th ed., published by the Council of Science Editors (CSE). CSE style requires that sources be cited briefly in the text and documented in a reference list at the end of the project. The goal of providing in-text citations and a list of references is to allow readers to locate the sources and to distinguish the writer's ideas from those borrowed from other sources.

Writing Responsibly
Citing and Documenting Sources

When you cite and document sources, you acknowledge any material from which you have quoted, paraphrased, summarized, or drawn information, and you join the conversation on your topic by adding your own interpretation, data, methods, and results. Simultaneously, you give interested readers (including your instructor) a way to join the conversation. Accurate entries allow your audience to find and read your sources, so they can evaluate your research and learn more about the subject themselves. Accurate entries also demonstrate the care with which you have written your project and reinforce your reputation as a reliable researcher.

429

20a Creating CSE-Style In-Text Citations

In-text citations, which appear in the body of your paper, identify any material borrowed from a source, whether it is a quotation, paraphrase, summary, or idea. The CSE offers three formats for citing sources in the body of the project:

More about ▶▶▶
Popular academic
documentation
styles per discipline, 454, 474
MLA style, 298–357
(ch. 17)
APA style, 358–400
(ch. 18)
Chicago style,
401–28 (ch. 19)

- name-year
- citation-sequence
- citation-name sequence

The *name-year system* requires you to include the last name of the author and the year of publication in parentheses whenever the source is cited:

Advances have clarified the role of betalains and carotenoids in
                                          author   date
determining the color of flowers (Groteworld 2006).

Signal phrase The
author's last name
plus an appropriate
verb (291)

If you use the author's name in a *signal phrase,* include just the year of publication in parentheses:

   author   date
Christoffel (2007) argues that public health officers adopted the strategies

they did because they were facing a crisis.

More about ▶▶▶
Signal phrases,
291–93, 299–303,
359–60

The name-year system tells readers immediately how current your source is—this is particularly crucial in the sciences—and who wrote it. This system requires many rules for creating in-text citations (for example, how to create in-text citations for several authors, organizations as authors, and so on), which can make it difficult to apply the rules consistently. (For the details of creating in-text citations using the name-year system, consult the CSE style manual, *Scientific Style and Format,* 7th ed.)

The *citation-sequence* and *citation-name systems* use a superscript number (a single number for each source) to refer the reader to a list of references at the end of the report.

Place reference numbers after punctuation marks. When drawing information from multiple sources, include multiple citations, separated by commas.

Some testing of the River Invertebrate Prediction and Classification System (RIVPACS) had already been conducted.[1] Biologists in Great Britain then used environmental data to establish community type,[2] and two studies developed predictive models for testing the effects of habitat-specific sampling.[3, 4] These did not, however, account for the earlier RIVPACS research.[1]

Tech

Creating Superscript Numbers

The footnoting function in your word processing program will not work for inserting reference numbers for the citation-sequence or citation-name systems because it will only insert the reference marks in sequence (1, 2, 3, . . .), whereas the CSE system requires that you use the same super-script number for a source each time you cite it. Instead, insert superscript numbers manually, without using your word processing program's foot-note function, and type your list of references separately. (Use the *Help* function to learn about inserting su-perscript numbers.)

When using the *citation-sequence system,* arrange the sources in your reference list in order of first mention in your research report and then number them. (The first work cited is number 1, the second work cited is number 2, and so on.) When using the *citation-name system,* alphabetize sources and then number them. (The first work alphabetically is number 1, the second work alphabetically is number 2, and so on.)

The citation-sequence and citation-name systems need no rules about how to form text citations, but they do require you to renumber citations if sources are added or deleted. Since the word processor's footnoting system cannot be used, this renumbering must be done manually, which requires you to work carefully to avoid errors. Also, readers must turn to the reference list to see the name of the author and the source's date of publication.

Check with your instructor about which system to use, and use it consistently. If your instructor does not have a preference, consider the advantages and drawbacks of each system before making your choice.

connect

mhconnectcomposition.com

Additional resources: QL20001

20b Preparing a CSE-Style Reference List

A research report or project in CSE style ends with a list of cited references. How you format those references depends on which system you use.

Books—Printed and Electronic

In a printed book, you can find most or all of the information you need to create a reference list entry on the copyright and title pages. In an online or e-book, print and electronic publication information

CSE Reference List Entries

1. One author
2. Two or more authors
3. Group or corporate author

often appears at the top or bottom of the first page or is available through a link.

1. One author

a. Printed The basic format for a printed book looks like this:

Name-year system

No punctuation between surname and initials and no period or space between initials

> Author's surname First and Middle Initials. Date of publication. Title: subtitle. Place of publication: Publisher. Number of pages.

Citation-sequence and citation-name systems

Lines after the first align with the author's name, not the reference number.

> Ref. No. Author's surname First and Middle Initials. Title: subtitle. Place of publication: Publisher; date of publication. Number of pages.

NOTE Book titles are neither italicized nor underlined in CSE style.

Here are examples of actual citations:

Name-year system

Field RI. 2007. Health care regulation in America: complexity, confrontation, and compromise. New York: Oxford University Press. 336 p.

Citation-sequence and citation-name systems

1. Field RI. Health care regulation in America: complexity, confrontation, and compromise. New York: Oxford University Press; 2007. 336 p.

b. Online

Name-year system

Stroup A. 1990. A company of scientists: botany, patronage, and community at the seventeenth-century Parisian Royal Academy of
print publication information
Sciences [Internet]. Berkeley (CA): University of California Press [cited
access date   URL (permalink)
2007 Mar 10]. Available from: http://ark.cdlib.org/ark:/13030/ft587006gh/

Citation-sequence and citation-name systems

2. Stroup A. A company of scientists: botany, patronage, and community at the seventeenth-century Parisian Royal Academy of Sciences [Internet]. Berkeley (CA): University of California Press; 1990 [cited 2007 Mar 10]. Available from: http://ark.cdlib.org/ark:/13030/ft587006gh/

2. Two or more authors

Name-year system

Jamieson BGM, Dallai R, Afzelius BA. 1999. Insects: their spermatozoa and phylogeny. Enfield (NH): Science Publishers. 555 p.

Citation-sequence and citation-name systems

3. Jamieson BGM, Dallai R, Afzelius BA. Insects: their spermatozoa and phylogeny. Enfield (NH): Science Publishers; 1999. 555 p.

▶▶▶Annotated visual of where to find author, title, and publication information, on foldout following p. 297

CSE Reference List Entries

1. One author
2. **Two or more authors**
3. Group or corporate author
4. Edited book

Follow the order of authors on the title page. No *and* before last author.

If the source has more than ten authors, list the first ten; after the tenth author, insert the words *and others*.

3. Group or corporate author

Name-year system

Institute of Medicine Committee on the Use of Complementary and Alternative Medicine by the American Public. 2005. Complementary and alternative medicine in the United States. Washington, DC: National Academies Press. 337 p.

Citation-sequence and citation-name systems

4. Institute of Medicine Committee on the Use of Complementary and Alternative Medicine by the American Public. Complementary and alternative medicine in the United States. Washington, DC: National Academies Press; 2005. 337 p.

4. Edited book

Name-year system

Whelan CT, Mason NJ, editors. 2005. Electron scattering: from atoms, molecules, nuclei, and bulk matter. New York: Kluwer Academic/Plenum. 340 p.

Citation-sequence and citation-name systems

5. Whelan CT, Mason NJ, editors. Electron scattering: from atoms, molecules, nuclei, and bulk matter. New York: Kluwer Academic/Plenum; 2005. 340 p.

5. Selection from an edited book or conference proceedings

Name-year system

selection author
Berkenkotter C. 2000. Scientific writing and scientific thinking: writing the
selection title

book title
scientific habit of mind. In: Goggin MD, editor. Inventing a discipline:

CSE Reference
List Entries

1. One author
2. Two or more authors
3. **Group or corporate author**
4. **Edited book**
5. **Selection from an edited book or conference proceedings**
6. Translation
7. Multivolume work

rhetoric scholarship in honor of Richard E. Young. Urbana (IL): National

selection pages

Council of Teachers of English. p. 270–284.

Citation-sequence and citation-name systems

6. Berkenkotter C. Scientific writing and scientific thinking: writing the

scientific habit of mind. In: Goggin MD, editor. Inventing a discipline:

rhetoric scholarship in honor of Richard E. Young. Urbana (IL): National

Council of Teachers of English; 2000. p. 270–284.

To cite a paper published in the proceedings of a conference, add the number and name of the conference, the date of the conference, and the location of the conference (separated by semicolons and ending with a period) after the title of the book and before the publication information:

48th Annual American Society for Cell Biology Conference; 2008

Dec 13–17; San Francisco, CA.

6. Translation

Name-year system

Aristotle. 1939. On the heavens. Guthrie WKC, translator. Cambridge (MA):

Harvard University Press. 378 p.

Citation-sequence and citation-name systems

7. Aristotle. On the heavens. Guthrie WKC, translator. Cambridge (MA):

Harvard University Press; 1939. 378 p.

7. Multivolume work

Name-year system

Taketani M. 2001. The formation and logic of quantum mechanics.

Nagasaki M, translator. River Edge (NJ): World Scientific. 3 vol.

CSE Reference List Entries

4. Edited book
5. Selection from an edited book or conference proceedings
6. **Translation**
7. **Multivolume work**
8. Dissertation
9. Article in a scholarly journal

Citation-sequence and citation-name systems

8. Taketani M. The formation and logic of quantum mechanics. Nagasaki M, translator. River Edge (NJ): World Scientific; 2001. 3 vol.

8. Dissertation For dissertations published by University Microfilms International (UMI), include the access number.

Name-year system

Song LZ. 2003. Relations between optimism, stress and health in Chinese and American students [dissertation]. Tucson (AZ): University of Arizona.
        access information   location   access no.
107 p. Available from: UMI, Ann Arbor, MI; AAI3107041.

Citation-sequence and citation-name systems

9. Song LZ. Relations between optimism, stress and health in Chinese and American students [dissertation]. Tucson (AZ): University of Arizona; 2003. 107 p. Available from: UMI, Ann Arbor, MI; AAI3107041.

> ▶▶▶Annotated visual of where to find author, title, and publication information, on foldout following p. 297

If the location of the school is not listed on the title page of the dissertation, place square brackets around this information: [Tucson (AZ)].

Periodicals—Printed and Electronic

The information needed to document a printed journal article is on the cover or table of contents of the journal and the first and last page of the article. For articles downloaded from a database, the information you need appears on the screen listing the articles that fit your search terms, on the full record of the article, or on the first (and last) page of the file you download. For journal articles published online, the information you need appears on the website's home page, on that issue's web page, or on the first screen of the article.

9. Article in a scholarly journal

a. Printed The basic citation for an article in a scholarly journal looks like this:

CSE Reference List Entries

Name-year system

Author's surname First and Middle Initials. Year of publication. Title: subtitle.

Abbreviated Journal Title. Vol. number(Issue number):page numbers.

Citation-sequence and citation-name systems

Ref. No. Author's surname First and Middle Initials. Title:subtitle.

Abbreviated Journal Title. Year of publication;Vol. number(Issue

number):page numbers.

Here is an actual citation of each type:

Name-year system

Cox L. 2007. The community health center perspective. Behav Healthc.

27(3):20–21.

Citation-sequence and citation-name systems

10. Cox L. The community health center perspective. Behav Healthc.

2007;27(3):20–21.

Journal titles: Omit punctuation, articles (*an, the*), and prepositions (*of, on, in*), and abbreviate most words longer than 5 letters (except 1-word titles like *Science* and *Nature*).

DOI Digital object identifier, a permanent identifier assigned to electronic articles (370)

b. Accessed through a database Most researchers locate journal articles through subscription databases available through their college library. Frequently, articles indexed in such databases are available in HTML or PDF format through a link from the database. As yet, the CSE does not provide a model for an article accessed through an online database, but since most library databases are by subscription, readers will probably find the URL of the database's home page more useful than a direct link to the article itself. If a DOI is available, include it.

connect
mhconnectcomposition.com
Additional resources: QL20002

Name-year system

Borrok D, Fein JB, Tischler M, O'Loughlin E, Meyer H, Liss M,

Kemner KM. 2004. The effect of acidic solutions and growth conditions

on the adsorptive properties of bacterial surfaces. Chem Geol;

database   medium   access date
209(1–2):107–119. In Science Direct [Internet] [cited 2004 Aug 7].

URL (database home page)
Available from: http://www.sciencedirect.com doi: 10.1016/

DOI
j.chemgeo.2004.04.025

No period after URL or DOI

Citation-sequence and citation-name systems

11. Borrok D, Fein JB, Tischler M, O'Loughlin E, Meyer H, Liss M,

    Kemner KM. The effect of acidic solutions and growth conditions

    on the adsorptive properties of bacterial surfaces. Chem Geol

    2004;209(1–2):107–119. In Science Direct [Internet] [cited 2004

    Aug 7]. Available from: http://www.sciencedirect.com doi:10.1016/

    j.chemgeo.2004.04.025

c. Online Omit page numbers for online articles. When a subscription
is not required to access the article, provide a direct permalink URL to
the article; otherwise, provide the URL to the journal's home page. If
a DOI is provided, include it.

Name-year system

Patten SB, Williams HVA, Lavorato DH, Eliasziw M. 2009. Allergies and

major depression: a longitudinal community study. Biopsychosoc. Med.

[Internet] [cited 2009 Feb 5];3(3). URL (permalink) Available from: http://www.bpsmedicine

.com/content/3/1/3 DOI doi: 10.1186/1751-0759-3-3

No period after
URL or DOI

Citation-sequence and citation-name systems

12. Patten SB, Williams HVA, Lavorato DH, Eliasziw M. Allergies and major

    depression: a longitudinal community study. Biopsychosoc. Med.

    [Internet]. 2009 [cited 2009 Feb 5];3(3). Available from: http://www

    .bpsmedicine.com/content/3/1/3 doi:10.1186/1751-0759-3-3

10. Article in a magazine
a. Printed
Name-year system

Gladwell M. 2006 Oct 16. The formula. New Yorker:138–149.

Citation-sequence and citation-name systems

13. Gladwell M. The formula. New Yorker 2006 Oct 16:138–149.

b. Accessed through a database

Name-year system

Gladwell M. 2006 Oct 16. The formula. New Yorker: 138–149. In EbscoHost

[Internet] [cited 2008 Apr 23]. Available from: http:www.ebscohost.com/

Citation-sequence and citation-name systems

14. Gladwell M. The formula. New Yorker 2006 Oct 16: 138–149. In

EbscoHost [Internet] [cited 2008 Apr 23]. Available from: http://www

.ebscohost.com/

c. Online

Name-year system

Coghlan A. 2007 May 16. Bipolar children—is the US overdiagnosing?

NewScientist.com [Internet] [cited 2007 May 19]. Available from:

URL (permalink)
http://www.newscientist.com/channel/health/mg19426043.900-bipolar-

children--is-the-us-overdiagnosing.html/

Citation-sequence and citation-name systems

15. Coghlan A. Bipolar children—is the US overdiagnosing? NewScientist

.com [Internet]. 2007 May 16 [cited 2007 May 19]. Available from:

http://www.newscientist.com/channel/health/mg19426043.900-bipolar-

children--is-the-us-overdiagnosing.html/

11. Article in a newspaper
a. Printed

Name-year system

LaFraniere S. 2009 Feb 6. Scientists point to possible link between dam

edition   section   col. no.
and China quake. New York Times (Late Ed.). Sect. A:1 (col. 3).

1st pg.

CSE Reference List Entries

9. Article in a scholarly journal
10. Article in a magazine
11. **Article in a newspaper**
12. Website
13. Web page

Citation-sequence and citation-name systems

16. LaFraniere S. Scientists point to possible link between dam and China quake. New York Times (Late Ed.). 2009 Feb 6;Sect. A:1 (col. 3).

b. Accessed through a database

Name-year system

LaFraniere S. 2009 Feb 6. Scientists point to possible link between dam and China quake. New York Times. Sect. A:1. In LexisNexis [Internet] [cited 2009 Feb 28]. Available from: http://www.lexisnexis.com/

Citation-sequence and citation-name systems

17. LaFraniere S. Scientists point to possible link between dam and China quake. New York Times. 2009 Feb 6;Sect. A:1. In LexisNexis [Internet] [cited 2009 Feb 28]. Available from: http://www.lexisnexis.com/

c. Online

Name-year system

LaFee S. 2006 May 17. Light can hold fatal attraction for many nocturnal animals. San Diego Union-Tribune [Internet] [cited 2006 May 20] [about
length
11 paragraphs]. Available from: http://www.signonsandiego.com/news/
science/

Include permalink
URL if available; if not,
use URL of home page.

Citation-sequence and citation-name systems

18. LaFee S. Light can hold fatal attraction for many nocturnal animals. San Diego Union-Tribune [Internet]. 2006 May 17 [cited 2006 May 20] [about 11 paragraphs]. Available from: http://www.signonsandiego.com/ news/science/

Other Electronic and Miscellaneous Sources

The information needed to document a website or web page usually appears at the top or bottom of the home page or web page. You may also need to look for a link to a page labeled "About us" or "Contact us." Frequently, information needed for a complete reference list entry is missing, but you should provide as much information as you can.

▶▶▶Annotated visual of where to find author, title, and publication information on foldout following p. 297

12. Website
Name-year system

In the name-year system, a sample reference entry for a website looks like this:

> Author. Title of website [Medium (internet)]. Publication date [Access date].
>
> Available from: URL (home page)

Here is an example of an actual entry:

> MIT news [Internet]. 2009 Feb 9 [cited 2009 Mar 10]. Available from: http://
>
> web.mit.edu/newsoffice/index.html/

The site has no author, so the reference list entry begins with the name of the site's sponsor.

CSE Reference List Entries

10. Article in a magazine
11. Article in a newspaper
12. **Website**
13. **Web page**
14. Discussion list or blog posting
15. Email message

Citation-sequence and citation-name systems

When referencing an entire website, the only difference in the citation-sequence and citation-name systems is the addition of the reference number at the beginning of the entry.

13. Web page When documenting a web page or document on a website, provide the URL for the web page, not the site's home page.

Name-year system

> article author   article title
> Schorow, S. 2009 Feb 5. Aliens at sea: anthropologist Helmreich studies
>   website
> researchers studying ocean microbes. MIT News [Internet] [cited 2009
>   URL (web page)
> Mar 10]. Available from: http://web.mit.edu/newsoffice/2009/alien-
>
> ocean-0205.html

Citation-sequence and citation-name systems

19. Schorow, S. Aliens at sea: anthropologist Helmreich studies

researchers studying ocean microbes. MIT News [Internet] 2009 Feb 5

[cited 2009 Mar 10]. Available from: http://web.mit.edu/newsoffice/2009/

alien-ocean-0205.html

14. Discussion list or blog posting

Name-year system

date/time posted
Hall A. 2004 Aug 5, 11:33 am. Biology of deep Gulf of Mexico
disc. list   medium
shipwrecks. In: FISH-SCI [Internet discussion list]. [Lulea (Sweden):

National Higher Research and Education Network]; [cited 2005 Jan 30]

[about 4 paragraphs]. Available from: http://segate.sunet.se/archives/

fish-sci.html

Citation-sequence and citation-name systems

20. Hall A. Biology of deep Gulf of Mexico shipwrecks. In: FISH-SCI

[Internet discussion list]. [Lulea (Sweden): National Higher Research

and Education Network]; 2004 Aug 5, 11:33 am [cited 2005 Jan 30]

[about 4 paragraphs]. Available from: http://segate.sunet.se/archives/

fish-sci.html

15. Email message

Name-year system

email author   date/time sent   subject line
Martin SP. 2005 Nov 18, 3:31 pm. Revised results [Email]. Message to:
email recipient   length
Lydia Jimenez [cited 2005 Nov 20] [about 2 screens].

Citation-sequence and citation-name systems

21. Martin SP. Revised results [Email]. Message to: Lydia Jimenez.

2005 Nov 18, 3:31 pm [cited 2005 Nov 20]. [about 2 screens].

16. Government document If no author is listed, use the name of the governing nation and the government agency that produced the document, and include any identifying number.

Name-year system

> Department of Health and Human Services (US). 1985 May. Women's
>
> health. Report of the Public Health Service Task Force on Women's Health
>
> Issues. PHS:85-50206.

Citation-sequence and citation-name systems

> 22. Department of Health and Human Services (US). Women's health.
>
>   Report of the Public Health Service Task Force on Women's Health
>
>   Issues; 1985 May. PHS:85-50206.

CSE Reference
List Entries

14. Discussion list or
    blog posting
15. Email message
16. **Government
    document**

20c Formatting a CSE-Style Paper and Reference List

The CSE does not specify a format for the body of a college report, but most scientific reports include the following sections:

- Abstract
- Introduction
- Methods
- Results
- Discussion
- References

Ask your instructor for formatting guidelines, refer to the general formatting guidelines provided in chapter 6, or follow the formatting guidelines for APA style.

Start a new page for your reference list, and title it "References." CSE style does not indicate whether you should indent the lines after the first. (The manual itself shows entries both ways: aligned at left with an extra space between entries, as in the journals *Cell* and *Science,* and with the second and subsequent lines indented.) Ask your instructor which format to use.

More about ▶▶▶
Writing an abstract,
387
Writing a scientific
report, 477–78
Formatting college
papers, 104–05
Formatting a paper
in APA style,
385–88

Writing
↑ Responsibly — Of Deadlines and Paper Clips

Instructors expect students to turn in thoughtful, carefully proofread, and neatly formatted papers on time—usually in class on the due date. They also expect writers to clip (or staple) the pages of the paper *before* the paper is submitted. Do justice to yourself by being fully prepared: Do not hand in a stack of loose sheets or expect your instructor to supply a paper clip.

Name-Year System List entries in alphabetical order by author's last name or first keyword of the title (first word, omitting articles such as *the, a,* or *an*) if no author or editor is listed. Do not number the entries.

Citation-Sequence System Number your entries in order of their appearance in your paper. Each work should appear in your reference list only once, even if it is cited more than once in your report. Double-check to make sure that the numbers in your reference list match the numbers in your text.

Citation-Name System Alphabetize the entries in your reference list first, and then number them. Each work should appear in your reference list only once, even if it is cited more than once in your paper. Double-check to make sure that the numbers in your reference list match the numbers in your text.

Student Research Project: CSE Style

connect
mhconnectcomposition.com
Additional resources: QL20003

The sample reference list is taken from a laboratory report, "The Effects of Hardy-Weinberg, Natural Selection, and Allelic Frequency on *Drosophila melanogaster*" by Alicia Keefe, University of Maryland. Entries are formatted in the name-year style.

References

Geiger P. 2002. Introduction to *Drosophila melanogaster.* [Internet] Tucson (AZ): University of Arizona, General Biology Program for Teachers, Biology Department [cited 30 Apr 2008]. Available from: http://biology.arizona.edu/sciconn/lessons2/ geiger/intro.htm

Hoikkala A, Aspi J. 1993. Criteria of female mate choice in *Drosophila littoralis, D. montana,* and *D. ezoana.* Evolution 47(3):768–778. In Academic Search Premier [database on the Internet] [cited 2008 Apr 28]. Available from: http://web .ebscohost.com

Ives JD. 1921. Cross-over values in the fruit fly, *Drosophila ampelophila,* when the linked factors enter in different ways. Am Naturalist 6:571–573.

Mader, S. 2005. Lab manual. 9th ed. New York: McGraw-Hill, 528 p.

Marcillac F, Bousquet F, Alabouvette J, Savarit F, Ferveur, JF. 2005. A mutation with major effects on *Drosophila melanogaster* sex pheromones. Genetics 171(4):1617–1628. In Academic Search Premier [Internet] [cited 28 Apr 2008]. Available from: http://web.ebscohost.com doi: 10.1534/genetics.104.033159

Service PM. 1991. Laboratory evolution of longevity and reproductive fitness components in male fruit flies: mating ability. Evolution 47:387–399.

Heading (centered), new page, references alphabetized by author

Web page: Date cited and URL of web page provided

Journal article: Accessed through a database, no DOI; URL of database home page provided

Journal article: Printed, title of journal abbreviated

Journal article: Accessed through a database, with DOI

Journal article: Printed, one-word title not abbreviated

445

EXERCISE 20.1 Transforming a reference list

Using the examples in the chapter as a guide, rewrite the citations in the sample reference list on p. 445 to follow the citation-sequence or citation-name format.

Make It **Your Own**

For a paper you are writing or have written recently, format the reference list using one of the systems discussed in this chapter. (Choose a paper that includes at least three references.)

Work **Together**

Exchange drafts of the reference list you created for the Make It Your Own exercise above with a classmate. Check the citations in your partner's list of references against the citation examples in this book. Then look up three of the citations in your college library. Were the citations accurate? Were you able to find the source with the information provided? Report your findings to the class.

Part Six

Genre
Matters

Writing in and beyond College

21 Writing in Literature and the Other Humanities

There is rarely one right way to interpret or appreciate literature, art, music, or events in history. Instead, the texts studied in these humanities disciplines offer readers multiple doors to understanding. These doors may sometimes loom as opportunities for confusion, but they also offer richly rewarding opportunities to explore the many ways of being human.

21a Adopting the Approach of Literature and the Other Humanities

Whether focused solely on the text and the reader's experience of it or on its social, historical, or cultural contexts, writing in the humanities is an act of interpretation. To speak of *the* meaning of a text is to misunderstand the nature of academic studies in these disciplines. But while those who study the

> When I read for my literature classes, the material gives me a new perspective on how humans behave and function in the world. It increases my appreciation for life.
>
> —Mike Haxton, Oklahoma City University

humanities produce multiple meanings, each interpretation must be based on evidence from the text that will persuade others to accept the writer's position.

1. Read actively and reflectively.

Understanding works of literature and other texts in the humanities is not merely a matter of extracting information, but it does begin with reading to gain a basic understanding of the text. This can be fairly easy or very difficult, depending on the work. You will have greatest success if you begin by summarizing: What is its main point? In literature, this is the *theme*. A summary will help you get to the heart of the matter, but keep in mind that literary analysis must do more than repeat what the text says.

> *More about* ▶▶▶
> Summarizing,
>   119–20, 269
> Annotating, 124–27
> Reading journal,
>   127–29
> Enjoying what you
>   read, 120

Next, annotate the text or make notes in a reading journal. Some of your notes may provide perspectives on the work that you can use when writing about the text later. The notes in Figure 21.1 (p. 450), for example, show the beginnings of themes that Rita McMahan explores in her analysis of Gary Snyder's poem "Front Lines."

> ▶▶▶ Sample student
> project:
>   "My View from the
>   Sidelines," Rita
>   McMahan,
>   465–68

Finally, remember to enjoy what you are reading. If you make an effort to appreciate the language, note insights, or make connections to something in your own experience, you will get more out of your reading.

2. Analyze the text.

Understanding a historical event or work of literature, philosophy, or art involves more than just knowing what happens. It involves analysis, dividing the work or event into its component parts to see how they work together. Your analysis will begin as you study the text closely and actively.

> *More about* ▶▶▶
> Analysis, 129–31,
>   279–80, 288–90

Writing
Responsibly Reading with Study Guides

SparkNotes and similar study guides, long a staple of college bookstores and now available online, may tempt struggling students to substitute the guide for the text itself. Do not succumb! You not only deprive yourself of a learning experience, but you may also find that the study guide leaves you unprepared for the sophisticated level of un-derstanding your instructor expects. If you are having difficulty making sense of a text, discuss the work with classmates, read essays about or reviews of the work at your college library, watch a reading or a performance of the work, or seek advice from your instructor.

Battlelines? Reminds me of a Buffalo Springfield song my parents used to play—"For What It's Worth?"—from sort of the same period, I think—"Battlelines being drawn…"

FRONT LINES

Gary Snyder

The edge of the cancer   *A tumor, sickness, death…*

Yuck!   Swells against the hill—we feel   *scary*

A foul breeze—

Sounds like "stinks"   And it sinks back down.

The deer winter is here

A chainsaw growls in the gorge.   *Animal noise*

Ten wet days and the log trucks stop,   *Not real*

The trees breathe.   *breather*

Sunday the 4 wheel jeep of the

Realty Company brings in

Landseekers, lookers, they say   *Pornography?*

To the land,

Rape!? Prostitution?   Spread your legs.

The jets crack sound overhead, it's OK here;   *Hard to read this line out loud*

Rhythm   Every pulse of the rot at the heart

Heart disease?   In the sick fat veins of Amerika   *Why with a "k"?*

Edge of what? The cancer?   Pushes the edge up closer

Amerika?

A bulldozer grinding and slobbering

Sideslipping and belching on top of

Makes the bushes   The skinned-up bodies of still live bushes

seem human   In the pay of a man   *Bulldozer = mercenary*

From town.

Same rhythm   Behind is a forest that goes to the Arctic

And a desert that still belongs to the Piute

And here we must draw

Our line.   *Relates to title?*

FIGURE 21.1 **Notes from a close reading of the poem "Front Lines," by Gary Snyder**

Quick

Reference ➜ Elements of Literature

Genre. Into what broad category (or *genre*)—fiction, poetry, drama—does the work fit? Into what narrower category (mystery, sci-fi; sonnet, ode; comedy, tragedy) does the work belong? What expectations are set up by the genre, and how does the work adhere to or violate these expectations?

Plot. What happens? Does the plot unfold chronologically (from start to finish), or does the author use flashbacks or flash-forwards? Does the plot proceed as expected, or is there a surprise?

Setting. Where and when does the action occur? Is the setting identifiable? If not, what hints does the author give about the where and when? Are time and place consistent, or do elements from other times or places intrude?

Character. Who is the *protagonist*, or main character? Who are the supporting characters? How believable are the characters? Do they represent types or individuals?

Point of view. Who is telling the story—one of the characters or a separate narrator? What point of view does the narrator take—the first-person (*I*) or third-person (*she, he, it*) perspective? Does the narrator have special insight into the characters or recount events as an outsider?

Language/style. What level of diction (formal, informal, colloquial, dialect) does the author use, and why? How does the author put words together? Does the author use long, complex constructions or short direct ones? Does the author use figurative language (such as metaphor and simile), or is the writing more literal?

Theme. What is the main point of the story? If you were to phrase the story as a fable, what would its moral be?

Symbol. Do any of the characters, events, or objects represent something more than their literal meaning?

Irony. Is there a contrast between what is said and what is meant, between what the characters know and what the reader knows?

Allusion. Does the work contain references to literary and cultural classics or sacred texts?

Usually you will need to study the text again (and again) to identify the elements from which it is constructed and to determine how these parts work together. The Quick Reference box above lists some of the elements that a literary analysis should take into consideration.

> *More about* ▶▶▶
> Person, 455–56, 475–76, 646–47
> Level of diction, 16–17, 567
> Style, 515–98 (part 7, Style Matters)
> Figures of speech, 577–78

3. Adopt a critical framework.

Coming to terms with a text requires even more than comprehension and analysis. It also requires *interpretation* (determining what the elements *mean*), *synthesis* (connecting the text to what you already know and to other works you have read), and sometimes *critique* (evaluating the methods and effects of a work). You may compare two or more texts as an aid to understanding, or you may adopt a critical, theoretical approach to the work.

> *More about* ▶▶▶
> Interpretation, 131–32, 279–80, 288–90
> Synthesis, 132–34, 279–80, 288–90
> Critique, 134–35, 279–80, 288–90

Biographical approach. Focus on the author's life to understand the work. Does the work reflect the trajectory of the author's own life or perhaps depict a working out in literature of something the author was unable to work out in reality?

Deconstructionist approach. Focus on gaps, discontinuities, or inconsistencies in the text that reveal or challenge the assumptions of the dominant culture. What do these inconsistencies communicate that the author may not have intended?

Feminist approach. Focus on the power relations between men and women (or elements in the work that take on gender traits). Does the work reinforce traditional power relations or challenge them?

Marxist approach. Focus on the power relations among social classes (or among elements that take on class characteristics). Does the work reinforce the status quo or challenge it?

New historicist approach. Focus on the social-historical moment in which the work was created. How does the work reflect that historical moment?

Postcolonial approach. Focus on the power relations between colonizing and colonized peoples (or on elements in the work that reflect traditional power dynamics). Does the work reinforce or challenge those power relations?

Queer approach. Focus on the power relations between "normal" and "deviant." How differently can a text be read when the reader rejects this dichotomy?

Reader response approach. Focus not on the author's intentions or the text's meaning but on the experience of the individual reader. How does the individual reader construct meaning in the act of reading?

connect
mhconnectcomposition.com
Additional resources: QL21001

In introductory classes in literature and the other humanities, students are often expected to take a ***formalist approach,*** looking closely at the work itself to understand how it functions on its own terms. Other popular approaches are outlined in the Quick Reference box above.

Before adopting a critical framework, consider the issues you have discussed in class or in other classes you are taking. A psychology class, for example, may provide a theory that will help you explain the behavior of a character; an economics class may help you understand the market forces affecting the plot; a women's studies class may provide methods of interpretation that will help you understand historical events differently.

connect
mhconnectcomposition.com
Additional resources: QL21002

21b Using the Resources of Literature and the Other Humanities

As you prepare to write about a text, ask your instructor whether you should consult outside sources. Primary sources for studying a literary work include the work itself; they may include the author's letters or email messages, diaries, interviews, annotated manuscripts, or performances (live or recorded). To write about Gary Snyder's poem "Front Lines," Rita McMahan not only analyzed the poem but also watched a video of Snyder reading and talking about his poetry and his life, and she arranged to interview the poet via email. Primary sources in the other humanities might include any of the following:

- In film studies, a classic film like *Citizen Kane* (1941) or a popular movie like *Slumdog Millionaire* (2008); a director's annotated script; or a series of storyboards, comic-strip-like sketches showing the main characters, action, and shot sequences in a film

- In classics, a lyric poem by the ancient Greek poet Sappho; a history of ancient Rome by Livy (59 BCE–17 CE), or a vase depicting an important event in classical history

- In art history, a painting, sculpture, or other artistic production or a video of an artist at work

- In philosophy, a text like Plato's *Meno* or a lecture by a philosopher like Peter Singer

- In history, a historical document, such as the Mayflower Compact (1620), or court records detailing an event like the My Lai massacre during the Vietnam War

Secondary sources are works about the author, period, text, or critical framework you are using. Shona Sequiera used the framework provided by the documentary *Ethnic Notions,* a secondary source, to assess the main character in Zora Neale Hurston's novel *Their Eyes Were Watching God* (1937), her primary source. You can find secondary sources by searching your library's catalog, specialized databases (such as the *MLA International Bibliography, Historical Abstracts,* the *Arts and Humanities Citation Index,* or the *Philosopher's Index*), the *Book Review Digest,* and the *Literary Criticism Index.* These and other discipline-specific reference sources may be available through your college library.

21c Citing and Documenting Sources—MLA and *Chicago* Style

Whenever you borrow ideas or information or quote from a work, you must cite the source in the text and document it in a bibliography or list of works cited. While there are other style guides, most writers in literature and the other humanities use either the style detailed in the

▶▶▶Sample student project: "Transcending Stereotypes in Hurston's *Their Eyes Were Watching God,*" Shona Sequiera, 460–63

More about ▶▶▶
Finding information, 222–47 (ch. 13)

More about ▶▶▶
In-text citation (MLA), 299–315
Works-cited list (MLA), 314–39
Notes and bibliography (*Chicago*), 402–19

Quick

Reference ➡ Choosing a Style Guide

Are you writing in . . . ?	Then use . . .
Art history	Chicago
Classics	MLA
Comparative literature	MLA
English literature	MLA
Film studies	MLA
French	MLA
History	Chicago
Painting	Chicago
Philosophy	Chicago
Sculpture	Chicago
Spanish	MLA
Theater	MLA

MLA Handbook for Writers of Research Papers, 7th edition, or in the *Chicago Manual of Style,* 15th edition. The Quick Reference guide at left shows which disciplines are most likely to follow which style, but be sure to check with your instructor before beginning a research project. (Earlier chapters provide detailed instructions about citing and documenting sources in MLA and *Chicago* style.)

21d Using the Language of Literature and the Other Humanities

Each discipline uses language distinctively. Some conventions for writing in literary studies and the other humanities are discussed in the sections that follow.

1. Use the specialized vocabulary of the discipline correctly.

More about ▶▶▶
Finding subject-specific reference works, 235–36

Most academic disciplines in the humanities use specialized vocabulary. To understand sources and communicate effectively with your audience, you will need to learn that vocabulary. To master this new language, consult discipline-specific dictionaries and encyclopedias, such as the *Penguin Dictionary of Literary Terms and Literary Theory, The Columbia Dictionary of Modern Literary and Cultural Criticism,* or *The Oxford Encyclopedia of British Literature.* Consider the terms in context, and ask your instructor for help.

2. Use past and present tense correctly.

More about ▶▶▶
Tense, 674–78

Writers in the humanities, including literary studies, usually choose the present tense when writing about the work being studied (the events, characters, and setting) or the ideas of other scholars, and they use the present or past tense (as appropriate) when discussing actual events, such as the author's birth or death or a historical or cultural event from the time that the work was published. The following examples illustrate these principles:

Present Tense

These witches and ghosts are real, and often present, for Haun's characters, and "witch doctors" have busy practices fending them off. Dreams and visions are carefully noted and heeded, and the natural world is festooned with warning signs.

> Uses present tense to discuss the work studied

—Lisa Alther, "The Shadow Side of Appalachia:
Mildred Haun's Haunting Fiction"

Past Tense

Margaret Lindsey, defamed as a sorceress (incantatrix) by three men in 1435, successfully purged herself with the help of five women; her accusers were warned against making further slanders under pain of excommunication.

> Uses past tense to discuss past events

—Kathleen Kamerick, "Shaping Superstition in Late Medieval England"

3. Use first and third person correctly.

The use of the first person (*I, we*) or third person (*he, she, it, they, Elena, the conflict*) pronoun varies from one humanities discipline to another. In part, this reflects a difference in emphasis: Are writers emphasizing their arguments or the evidence on which they are based? In philosophy, the goal is often to advance one's own perspective:

More about ▶▶▶
Person, 475–76, 646–47

> I begin, in Section 1, by clarifying the kind of groups and the type of collective rights that I shall be concerned with.

> First-person (*I*)

—Steven Wall, "Collective Rights and Individual Autonomy"

In literary studies, the emphasis is on the work of literature or the reasons and evidence offered, so use the third person whenever reasonable. Compare these two versions of a sentence from Rita McMahan's essay on the poem "Front Lines":

First Person	Third Person
When I first read the poem, I thought the conflict was over property on a hillside, . . . but a closer look revealed to me that the conflict was a war between the developers (and their technology) and the hillside, or Earth, itself.	A first reading suggests a conflict over property on a hillside, . . . but a closer look reveals that the war is between the developers (and their technology) and the hillside, or Earth, itself.

The version in the third person shifts the emphasis from the writer to the poem and is thus less personal and more persuasive. (Notice also that it shifts to the present tense.)

4. Use the active voice.

More about ▶▶▶
Active vs. passive
voice, 560–61

In the humanities, writers typically use the active voice:

ACTIVE   Janie's relationship with her third husband, Tea Cake, plays a key role in transforming her concept of racial identity.

PASSIVE   A key role in transforming her concept of racial identity was played by Janie's relationship with her third husband, Tea Cake.

Use of the active voice promotes a clear, concise style and specifies who did what to whom. Of course, some circumstances may require the passive voice, as when the "who" is unknown or when you want to emphasize the action rather than the actor.

5. Use the author's full name at first mention and surname only thereafter.

In writing about the works of others, provide the author's complete name ("Zora Neale Hurston") the first time it is mentioned; subsequently, use the author's surname ("Hurston") only, unless this will cause confusion. (When writing about the Brontë sisters, for example, you may need to specify whether you are discussing Charlotte or Emily Brontë.) It is not customary to refer to an author by first name.

6. Include the work's title in your title.

More about ▶▶▶
Capitalizing titles,
843
Quotation marks
vs. italics for
titles, 817–18, 843,
847–48

When writing about a work of literature or another text (a painting or film, for example), provide the title of the work in the title or subtitle of your project and again in the first paragraph of your text. Be sure to capitalize the title correctly and to use italics or quotation marks as needed.

21e   Understanding Writing Projects in Literature and the Other Humanities

More about ▶▶▶
Analyzing assign-
ments, 19–20,
210–11, 490–91

A common assignment in the humanities is the **interpretive analysis,** which calls on the writer to study one or more elements of a text;

in literature, a writer might study a character or the setting; in philosophy, a writer might study the use of a particular word or concept (*freedom, free will*); in history, a writer might study the repercussions of a historical event. In some disciplines (such as literature, philosophy, or film), a writer might analyze a single primary source or compare one or more primary sources. Often (particularly in history and art history), students will be asked to draw on secondary as well as primary resources in addition to providing their own analysis.

Another writing assignment that is common in literature and the performing arts is the ***critique*** or review: an assessment of a work of literature or art or of a performance (a play, concert, or film). Some disciplines, such as literature or philosophy, may call on students to ***explicate*** a text, or provide a "close reading" (line by line or even word by word). Often, a close reading will focus on one or more of the elements of literature. (See the Quick Reference box on p. 451.)

Of course, many writing assignments in college will combine assignment types: Rita McMahan uses analysis to explicate a poem and draws on other primary sources for insight. Shona Sequiera uses the critical framework provided by the documentary *Ethnic Notions* to guide her analysis. To write an academic essay about a work of literature, follow the steps in the writing process discussed in part 1 (pp. 2–114) and the specific recommendations in the sections below.

▶▶▶Example interpretive analysis: "Transcending Stereotypes in Hurston's *Their Eyes Were Watching God*," Shona Sequiera, 460–63

▶▶▶ Example review: "Rash and Unadvis'd in Verona Seeks Same," Ben Brantley, 469–71

▶▶▶ Example explication: "My View from the Sidelines," Rita McMahan, 465–68

1. Devise a literary thesis.

To write effectively in any discipline, narrow your focus to an idea you can develop fully in the assigned length. To devise a topic in literature, ask yourself questions about the elements of the work:

- What are the central conflicts among or within characters?

- What aspects of the plot puzzled or surprised you, and why?

- How might the setting (time and place) have influenced the behavior of the characters?

- Did the writer use language in a distinctive (or difficult or obscure) way, and why?

- What images recurred or were especially powerful, and why?

- What other works did you think about as you were reading this one?

Then offer an answer to one or more of your questions. Your answer will become your working thesis.

More about ▶▶▶
Writing ethically, 2–9, Writing Responsibly boxes (listed on page facing inside back cover)
Planning, 10–32 (ch. 2)
Organizing and drafting, 33–51 (ch. 3)
Crafting and connecting paragraphs, 52–79 (ch. 4)
Drafting and revising visuals, 80–89 (ch. 5)
Revising, editing, proofreading, and formatting, 90–114 (ch. 6)

More about ▶▶▶
Devising a thesis,
34–37

A successful thesis for a literature project (or for a project in any of the humanities) will drive you to analyze or interpret (not merely summarize) the text, as these contrasting examples demonstrate:

SUMMARY THESIS	In this poem, Snyder shows that development destroys nature.
INTERPRETIVE/ ANALYTICAL THESIS	In this poem, Snyder uses symbolism and rhythm to urge readers to see "development" and ecological sustainability in conflict.

To satisfy the first thesis, the writer could merely report the poem's main point. To satisfy the second thesis, however, the writer must analyze the poem's symbolism and rhythm and then use that analysis to interpret the central conflict of the poem.

Make It **Your Own**

Devise a thesis for a three- to five-page paper on a work of literature you are reading or have read recently. Be sure your thesis drives you to interpret or analyze the text.

2. Support your claims with reasons and evidence from the text.

More about ▶▶▶
Idea-generating
techniques, 22–29

As with any writing project, you can use idea-generating techniques like brainstorming, freewriting, and clustering to develop reasons in support of your thesis. Then turn back to the text: What details from the work illustrate or support your reasons? These are your *evidence.* Consider this passage from Rita McMahan's essay:

Topic sentence:
States claim

Evidence: Uses quotations and summary from the poem and explains their relevance

The title, "Front Lines," implies that a battle (or perhaps multiple battles) is occurring—wars are fought on the front lines; a first reading suggests a conflict over property on a hillside between two opponents, but a closer look reveals that the war is between the developers (and their technology) and the hillside, or Earth, itself. The juxtaposition of the deer and the chainsaw in the first stanza—"The deer winter here / A chainsaw growls in the gorge" (lines 5–6)—pit them on opposite sides of this battle, as do the placement of the "log trucks" and "trees" (7–8), the "bulldozer" and "bushes" (18–20).

McMahan argues that Snyder uses the symbolism of war between the developers and nature, and she offers concrete evidence from the text—some quoted, some summarized—to support the claim. Note that McMahan does not merely drop the evidence from the poem into her essay but instead explains its relevance.

More about ▶▶▶
Incorporating evidence, 46–48, 288–95

3. Support your claims with evidence from outside the text.

Depending on your approach, you may also draw on evidence from outside the text. In the essay in the section that follows, Shona Sequiera draws her critical framework from a documentary film she watched in class. She also draws counterevidence from a secondary source, an essay in a scholarly collection.

▲ Make It **Your Own**

Draft an essay using the thesis you developed in the Make It Your Own exercise on p. 458. You may use other primary or secondary sources as support, but you should draw evidence directly from your own analysis of the work of literature.

Student Project: Writing about Fiction

The essay that follows by Shona Sequiera, a student at Connecticut College, offers an interpretation of the main character in Zora Neale Hurston's novel *Their Eyes Were Watching God* (1937). In her essay, Sequiera rebuts a common criticism of Hurston's characters—that they are "folk," simple, colorful, but not fully human. Measuring the protagonist (or main character), Janie Crawford, against the analysis of caricatured black roles described in the documentary *Ethnic Notions*, Sequiera argues that Janie develops over the course of the novel into a fully developed character who escapes stereotype.

Shona Sequiera

Professor Flood

English 342

March 9, 2009

Transcending Stereotypes in Hurston's

Their Eyes Were Watching God

Title: Includes author's surname and title of novel

Parodic images of African Americans permeated popular culture—art, film, and stage performance—from the 1820s through the 1960s, becoming deeply ingrained in the American psyche and shaping "the most gut level feelings about race" in the United States (*Ethnic Notions*). These images form a damaging visual tapestry of white-constructed black identity. As an African American writer, Zora Neale Hurston carried the burden of telling stories *of* her people and *for* her people in a manner that both protested and counteracted false representations of them in mainstream culture. Although *Their Eyes Were Watching God* (1937) has been widely criticized for painting a caricatured picture of African American life (Spencer 113–14), Hurston's heroine Janie is ultimately able to transcend oppressive stereotypes and come into her own.

Names author, includes title of work in first ¶

Thesis statement

Topic sentence

As presented in the novel, Janie Crawford is not a stereotype but a sexual, romantic, feeling woman who immerses herself in the "great fish-net" (193) of life. After her second husband Jody's death, Janie scrutinizes "her skin and features" (83) to find that "the young girl was gone but a handsome woman had taken her place" (83), a textual moment in which the heroine looks past her skin color and into the life experiences that molded and situated her within the framework of her

Page reference for quote from *Their Eyes*

Supporting evidence: Uses quotations from novel and explains relevance cultural community. Janie's setting free "the weight, the length, the glory" (83) of her "plentiful hair" (83) is a metaphorical rejection of the control Jody tried to impose upon her sexuality. While Janie may retain the self-assertiveness and independence with men of the mammy figure (*Ethnic Notions*), her physical beauty, lack of fulfillment in motherhood, and disdain for mundane domestic life separate her from that figure. Instead of a stereotypical character, Janie's taking "careful stock of herself" (83) allows her to move from under the control of men to a position of self-assertiveness and independence. By the novel's end, Janie comes to represent a positive image of black women who are not merely color-coded mammy figures (*Ethnic Notions*) but valuable contributors to and members of black culture.

> **Evidence and interpretation:** Refers to stereotype in *Ethnic Notions* and explains why stereotype does not apply

> **Topic sentence**

Like the stereotypical black comedian *Ethnic Notions* identifies as a common type, Janie acts for other people's pleasure. After Jody's death she "starched and ironed her face, forming it into just what people wanted to see" (83). Unlike those figures, however, she does not appear to be content and yet crumble with depression, humiliation, and self-hatred. She rejoices within—"She sent her face to Joe's funeral, and herself went rollicking with the springtime across the world" (88).

> **Supporting evidence:** Uses quotation as support and explains relevance

> **Topic sentence**

In particular, Janie's relationship with her third husband, Tea Cake, plays a key role in transforming her from a stereotype into a realistic black character. Over the course of the novel, Janie journeys from believing that she "wuz just like de rest" (9) of the white Washburn children to marrying the dark-complexioned Tea Cake, who teaches her to love the skin she lives in. Unlike Mrs. Turner, the mulatto who despises her own blackness, Janie learns both to value skin color as an important component of herself and her culture and to look beyond external

> **Supporting evidence:** Uses quotation, summary, and explains relevance

appearance to see that the life Tea Cake represents—a happy-go-lucky, romantic, and adventurous existence—is the one that most fulfils her.

Historically, African Americans have been called upon to be the vessels through which damaging white notions of blackness have been showcased (*Ethnic Notions*). Yet Janie Crawford transcends the stereotypical roles expected of her and proves that even though (or especially because) all three husbands are "gone from [her]" (83) upon her return to Eatonville, she values herself enough to move on with her life. Janie plays for neither a white nor a black audience but for herself. As a result, she defies white and black expectations of African American women and is able to experience the depths of love in a period when a black person must not love a thing too much (Morrison 45). In painting a romantic yet realistic portrait of Janie's joy *and* suffering, Hurston argues that the African American experience cannot be defined through distorted notions of color, but that it must be celebrated as a culture of living, fully human beings. Janie's journey toward constructing self-identity provided a model for the African American community, demonstrating how to change their notions of themselves and the ways in which they cater to the dictates of the dominant white culture. Unlike Ethel Waters, who laments in *Ethnic Notions* that "darkies never dream," Janie Crawford dares not only to dream, but to follow her dreams and defy societal guidelines that restrict people on the basis of race, class, and gender.

Conclusion: Restates thesis (in different words)

Shows importance of her analysis

Emphasizes contrast between analysis in *Ethnic Notions* and her own conclusions about Janie's character

Works Cited

Ethnic Notions. Dir. Marlon Riggs. KQED, San Francisco, 1986. Videocassette.

Hurston, Zora Neale. *Their Eyes Were Watching God.* 1937. New York:

Perennial-HarperCollins, 2000. Print.

Morrison, Toni. *Beloved.* New York: Plume-Penguin. 1987. Print.

Spencer, Stephen. "Racial Politics and the Literary Reception of Zora Neale

Hurston's *Their Eyes Were Watching God.*" *Multiethnic Literature and Canon*

Debates. Ed. Mary Jo Bona and Irma Maini. Albany: State U of New York P,

2006. 111–26. Print.

21f Writing about Poetry

While the shape of the poem on the page can be important, poetry is traditionally a spoken art form, as poetry readings and "slams" (competitions among poets reciting their work) attest. When writing about poetry, start by reading the poem aloud or listening to the poet read the work. In addition to the issues that apply to writing about literature generally, pay special attention to the sound, structure, and language of the work. (For more information on writing about poetry, see the Quick Reference box on the next page.)

More about ▶▶▶
The elements of
literature, 451
Figures of speech,
577–78
Connotation, 16–17,
575

Student Project: Writing about Poetry

The essay that begins on p. 465 was written by Rita McMahan, a student at Eastern Oregon State University. McMahan draws evidence from a close reading of the poem "Front Lines" (see Figure 21.1, p. 450) to support her claim that poet Gary Snyder uses symbolism and rhythm to persuade readers to accept his view of development. To build her case, McMahan also draws on other primary sources, including a video showing Snyder reading his poetry and information gleaned from an email correspondence with the poet.

Reference ➡ Writing about Poetry

Sound

Rhythm. Is the rhythm part of the traditional form of the poem? If not, which words are stressed, and how is this relevant to the poem's meaning?

Rhyme. Is the rhyme scheme part of the traditional form of the poem? If not, what is the purpose of the rhyme scheme? If the poem does not rhyme, are there any other sounds linking words or lines in the poem?

Alliteration/Assonance/Consonance. Does the poem use alliteration (the repetition of a consonant sound at the beginning of a stressed syllable) to link lines or words within a line? Does the poem use assonance or consonance, the repetition of a vowel or consonant sound, to link lines or words in a line? What effects do these choices have on the reader or listener?

Structure

Verse form. Is the poem written in a traditional verse form (such as the sonnet or the limerick), or is the form open, or free? Does the verse form relate to the meaning of the poem?

Line length. Are the poem's lines of regular length, or do lengths vary from line to line or from stanza to stanza? Do sentences carry over from line to line, or does each line express a complete thought? If line lengths are irregular, does length emphasize or de-emphasize a thought?

Stanzas. Are lines grouped into regular (or irregular) stanzas? If so, does the stanza convey a single unit of thought, or does an idea or sentence continue across stanzas?

Language

Imagery. What sensory "pictures" does the poem call to mind—the stultifying warmth of a July day in the Deep South? The luxuri-ant springtime riot of mountaintop flowers? What is the relationship between the images the poem calls forth and the ideas it conveys?

Figurative language. Simile (a comparison using *like* or *as*—"My love is like an ice pick"), metaphor (a comparison that does not use *like* or *as*—"My love is an ice pick"), and a host of other figures of speech create images in the reader's mind. Can you identify any figures of speech in the poem and, if so, how do they affect meaning?

Connotation. Poets choose words for their connotative (implicit) as well as for their denotative (literal) meanings. Consider the emotional difference between the verbs *gripe* and *lament*. Both mean "to complain," but, oh, the difference between the two. Note the connotations of the words in the poem you are studying and how they help create the overall effect of the poem.

Repetition. Poets may choose to repeat an important word or phrase. If a word or phrase is repeated (as is the word *and* in "The Raven"), consider its significance. How does this repetition affect your understanding and experience of the poem?

The last stanza from Edgar Allan Poe's "The Raven" (lines 103–8) demonstrates the issues of sound, structure, and language:

And the ráven, never flítting, **still is sítting,**
  still **is sítting**
On the pállid bust of Pállas just above my
  chamber door´;
And his eyes´ have all the see´ming of a
  démon's that is drea´ming,
And the lámp-light o'er him strea´ming throws
  his **shádow on the floor**´;
And my soul´ from out that **shádow** that lies
  floa´ting **on the floor**´
      Shall be lífted—nevermore´

Rita McMahan

English 110

April 17, 2009

My View from the Sidelines: Gary Snyder's "Front Lines"

Gary Snyder might be classified as not only a poet and free thinker, but also as an agent for change—a visionary. One of the Beat generation writers of San Francisco, Snyder has worked as a logger, seaman, trail crew member, and firewatcher (Maxwell); his poetry can be seen as an intersection between his alternative cultural viewpoints and his experiences in nature. In fact, many of Snyder's works focus on maintaining Earth's ecological balance, and "Front Lines," in particular, expresses his passionate feelings on the subject. In this poem, Snyder uses symbolism and rhythm to urge readers to see development and ecological sustainability in a new light.

The title, "Front Lines," implies that a battle is occurring—wars are fought on the front lines; a first reading suggests a conflict over property on a hillside between two opponents, but a closer look reveals that the war is between the developers (and their technology) and the hillside, or Earth, itself. The juxtaposition of the deer and the chainsaw in the first stanza—"The deer winter here / A chainsaw growls in the gorge" (lines 6–7)—pit them on opposite sides of this battle, similar to the placement of "log trucks" and "trees" (7–8) and "bulldozer" and "bushes" (18–20).

Snyder employs another symbol to represent the nature of this conflict: cancer. "The edge of the cancer" (1) creates fear in the reader, since cancer strikes without warning, spreading quickly and unpredictably. Likewise, Snyder implies that no one is safe from the ravages of unchecked, exploitive growth. Snyder's use

Side annotations:

- Names author, poem, in first ¶
- Introduction: Provides background on Snyder, places poem in context
- Title: Includes author's name and title of poem used in essay title
- Thesis: Calls for analysis and interpretation
- Topic sentence (begins first half of body)
- Uses quotation and summary as evidence, and explains relevance
- Topic sentence
- Explains comparison

of cancer to communicate the destruction of the environment raises what may be perceived as a benign issue—the protection of trees or deer habitat—to something more obviously dangerous, possibly fatal.

In addition to the cancer symbolism, Snyder conjures up the fearful image of rape: "To the land / Spread your legs" (12–13). This appears as a direct order, unlike any other line in the poem, and it is aggressive, not erotic. Because of its consequences to the victim, no restitution can ever be made; what is lost in the act is lost for all time. Similarly, the land can never be returned to its original state after its exploitation by developers. Like the battlefield and cancer, Snyder chooses rape as a symbol for the attack on the land, and as the images accumulate, a feeling of danger and damage overtakes the reader.

> Explains signifi-
> cance of symbol

> Connects sym-
> bolism in this
> paragraph with
> other symbols

> Topic sentence
> (begins second
> half of essay
> body)

In addition to symbolism, Snyder employs rhythm to convey this sense of danger. In a 1989 video of Snyder reading his poetry and discussing his techniques with students (*Writers Uncensored*), the way he enunciated each word and gave certain phrases special emphasis made it obvious that he wanted us to notice the sound of each syllable. Snyder explains in the video that "Sometimes driven behind the origin is the rhythm. . . . Rhythm is in a very real sense, primary" (*Writers Uncensored*). Reading "Front Lines" with this commentary in mind, one can infer that Snyder tries to make the reader *feel* "the pulse of the rot at the heart" (15–16) through the way the words themselves are chosen and arranged, with the stress on *pulse, rot,* and *heart.*

> Integrates quota-
> tion as support

> Links Snyder's
> commentary
> to poem under
> discussion

There is no single rhythmic pattern at work in the poem, but the second, fourth, and fifth stanzas all end in short choppy lines, which themselves end in one-syllable words that draw the reader's attention. Furthermore, lines 21–22 ("In the pay of a man / From town") and 25–26 ("And here we must draw / Our line") have a marching cadence, a rhythm that reinforces the battlefield symbolism. Snyder's words and lines are short and easy to read, but their rhythmic impact makes the reader sit up and take notice that something important is being communicated.

Line 14 ("The jet crack sounds overhead, it's OK here") contains a similar choppy rhythm. In an email, Snyder explained that he chose words to communicate exactness or precision. He said that the printed version of the poem is actually wrong—"jet" should be plural, and "sounds" should be singular, referring to the sound barrier. He explained that the line is meant to convey the sound of jets making sonic booms while going faster than the speed of sound. The rhythm of the line echoes the startling sounds of the sonic booms. As with Snyder's symbolism, his use of rhythm is not simply for decoration, but helps reinforce and make vivid his activist message.

Throughout the poem, Snyder uses symbolism and rhythm to compel the reader to defend the natural world, rather than to "develop" or destroy it, and his use of these techniques generates strong feelings and associations—especially if you have the chance to hear him read his own work, when his words seem even more particular and expressive. The fight to protect the environment continues, as does Snyder's advocacy. At 77, he serves as a professor emeritus at the University of California–Davis, where he continues to influence a new generation of writers and motivate readers to meet the challenges of the modern world (Maxwell).

Topic sentence

Uses information from email interview with poet as support

Topic sentence

Conclusion: Thesis restated, importance of poem's theme reiterated

Provides closure by circling back to poet

Works Cited

Maxwell, Glyn. "About Gary Snyder." *Modern American Poetry: An Online Journal and Multimedia Companion to the Anthology of Modern American Poetry (OUP, 2000).* Ed. Ian Hamilton. Dept. of English, University of Illinois at Urbana-Champaign, 2002. Web. 15 March 2009.

Snyder, Gary. "Front Lines." *No Nature: New and Selected Poems.* New York: Pantheon, 1992. 218. Print.

Snyder, Gary. Email interview. 8 Nov. 2008.

Writers Uncensored: Gary Snyder. Prod. Lewis MacAdams and John Dorr. Perf. Gary Snyder. Lannan Foundation, 1989. MPEG.

21g Writing about Drama

More about ▶▶▶
Elements of literature, 451

Like students of fiction, students of drama focus on character, plot, the language and symbols the playwright uses, and the theme (or main point) of the work. But unlike fiction, plays are written to be acted. When writing about drama, you may be asked to go beyond the words on the page, to watch a performance of a play and to critique it in a review. When writing about a performance, you will offer an assessment not only of the actors' performances and the director's staging, but also of the set, costumes, props, lighting, and sound design, to determine whether they helped to create a distinctive overall effect. Some issues to consider when critiquing a play are listed in the Quick Reference box on the next page.

Professional Project: Writing about Drama

In the review that follows, Ben Brantley of the *New York Times* says little about the play itself; the audience is expected to know the basic plot of Shakespeare's classic tragedy *Romeo and Juliet* and to accept the play as a powerful drama. Instead, he concentrates on assessing the performance—acting, direction, sets, costumes, and lighting—as a guide to potential audience members.

Quick

Reference ➡ **Writing about Drama**

Actors' performances. How well did the actors depict the characters? Did they bring something more to the character than you had recognized on the printed page? Did they build on an unspoken motive, a lie, or omission from the dialogue?

Direction. How effective was the director in shaping the overall production? Were the design elements consistent with the script and performances? Was the pacing and mood of the performance appropriate?

Stage set. Were the stage sets realistic or abstract? Did they reinforce the setting (the place and time) of the play, or were they in contrast to the conventional setting? How effective were the stage sets in reinforcing the themes of the play?

Costumes. Were the costumes appropriate to the characters? Were they appropriate to the period in which the play was set, or were they in contrast to that period? How effective were the costumes in advancing the themes?

Props. What stage properties (props) were used, and what symbolic value might they have?

Lighting and sound design. How effective was the lighting in contributing to the mood of the play? Did music underscore scene changes or contribute to the mood? Was sound used to create appropriate atmospheric effects? How effective were lighting and sound design in reinforcing the themes of the play?

Rash and Unadvis'd in Verona Seeks Same

> Playful title to appeal to general audience

By BEN BRANTLEY

Lauren Ambrose plays Juliet on a watery stage Verona in Central Park.

A battle of the elements is being pitched at the Delacorte Theater in Central Park, where "Romeo and Juliet" opened last night in a terrifically exciting new production, starring Lauren Ambrose as a Juliet truly to die for.

> Thesis: Indicates review is positive (Note: One-sentence paragraphs okay in newspapers)

On the one hand there's water, lots of it, in the form of a big, baffling pond that stretches across the stage, presumably for symbolic purposes, something to muse upon in perplexity as the actors slosh through it in rubber boots. On the other hand there's the fire that rages in the blood of every performance, a conflagration so consuming that it threatens

> Support: Examples from the production to support claim that "battle of the elements is being pitched"

to turn the show into a collective funeral pyre.

Great news: Fire wins.

Most of the advance word about this four-alarm retelling of the ultimate tragic love story, directed by Michael Greif, has centered on the body of water (70 feet round, one and a half inches deep) that has been made on the stage by the designer Mark Wendland. It looks great, reflecting twilight and moonlight as evening bleeds into night. But to be honest, it doesn't make much sense for either dramatic or poetic purposes.

For maritime Shakespearean endeavors like "The Tempest," "Twelfth Night" or even "The Comedy of Errors," turn on the taps all you want. But for "Romeo and Juliet," a play famous for its imagery of flame and lightning?

I'm not going to pretend that Mr. Greif justifies his watery conceit. But he doesn't let it bog down the real, dangerous business of the title characters' love either. . . .

In "Romeo and Juliet" all the performances are so focused and purposeful that no oversize puddle is going to deter them in their zealous course.

For what Mr. Greif and his cast have achieved, and what most productions of "Romeo and Juliet" fatally lack, is a sense of infectious, instinctive urgency. Blood is boiling in everybody's veins, whether from love or hate or an ad-

dling cocktail of the two, and it breeds impulsive action.

Led by Ms. Ambrose and Oscar Isaac as a Juliet and Romeo whose theme song would never be "You Can't Hurry Love," this production advances with hotheaded speed, even when it's standing still.

"Too rash, too unadvis'd, too sudden, too like the lightning," words with which the perceptive Juliet characterizes her newly discovered passion, apply throughout the show. It's a tempo that inevitably makes for bad ends and wonderful drama.

Mr. Greif and his designers who include Emilio Sosa (costumes) and Donald Holder (lighting) have turned Verona into a cross-cultural watering hole that suggests Venice mixed with Marrakesh and Seville, a place of open-air produce markets (convenient for food fights) and flamenco dancing (good for checking out the erotic chops of potential partners).

Quick-Temper Town would be a good nickname for this restless, bustling Verona. Mr. Greif plants storm signals even in the prologue, spoken not with the usual cosmic sadness by an anonymous narrator but in high dudgeon by Mercutio (Christopher Evan Welch), Romeo's wild and crazy best friend. . . .

It is clear in this context that when Romeo and Juliet instantly fall for each other, and then hightail it to the wedding chapel, they're just doing what comes naturally in Verona. Haste—a word that crops up a lot in the text—is the watchword for everyone's behavior. . . .

Critique: Praise for actor's performance

Mr. Isaac, last seen in the park as Proteus in "Two Gentlemen of Verona" two years ago, is sweetly and convincingly in thrall to his Juliet, a clumsy, overgrown puppy with the loyalty of a one-owner dog. But it's Ms. Ambrose who gives the production its devastatingly torn heart.

Background: Identification of actor, other roles readers may know

Best known as the petulant Claire in "Six Feet Under," Ms. Ambrose, who recently appeared on Broadway in "Awake and Sing!," makes Juliet into a compelling bundle of mixed instincts. Even at 13, she's the smartest person in Verona, capable of analyzing exactly what's happening to her. Had she lived, she might have been a Viola or Rosalind, a Shakespeare heroine to tutor brash men in the finer arts of loving.

Allusion: Other Shakespeare characters familiar to most readers

But because she is 13 (and you don't doubt it), Juliet leads not with her head but her hormones. Every line she utters is infused with equal amounts of intelligence and impetuosity. She has enough erotic life force for both herself and Romeo, but Mr. Isaac gallantly contributes his share. And without a hint of the now usually obligatory nudity, this couple can make a drawn-out kiss light up the night, as Michael Friedman's mood-enhancing (but never mood-pushing) music swells in the background.

Support: Evidence for praise of performance

Red-haired and luminously pale, this Juliet is such a brightly glowing candle that the water motif at last makes perfect sense in that final, fatal scene in the Capulet family tomb. It takes a whole lot of water to quench such a flame. But, ah my friends, before then, it gave a lovely light.

Conclusion: Returns to "two elements" theme of introduction

Allusion: Popular poem, "First Fig," by Edna St. Vincent Millay

Work **Together**

In groups of three or four, discuss the differences between the review above (pp. 469–71) and one of the student papers in this chapter (pp. 460–63, 465–68). How does the difference in purpose, audience, context, and genre affect the tone, the type of evidence provided, and the focus of the writing project?

22 Writing in the Sciences and Social Sciences

A scientist—a biologist, nurse, or physicist, for example—looking at these women playing volleyball would focus on their heart or respiration rates, or on the velocity at which the ball is traveling, because scientists focus on the characteristics, systems, and processes of the natural world, whether of people, plants, or planets. A social scientist—an anthropologist, economist, or sociologist, for example—would focus on who they are and how they work together, because social scientists focus on the behavior of people, as individuals and in groups. What unites the sciences with the social sciences, though, is a reliance on *empirical* (experimental, observational) research.

connect

mhconnectcomposition.com
Additional resources: QL22001, 22002, 22003, 22004

22a Adopting the Approach of the Sciences and Social Sciences

The search for verifiable evidence anchors the writing produced by both scientists and social scientists. Writing is integral to the work of these disciplines because it is the basic tool for keeping records and sharing results. Researchers make their notebooks and reports useful to other researchers by doing the following:

- Explaining their methods clearly and carefully so that others can repeat the experiment

- Describing data accurately and thoroughly (including the data that *disprove* the hypothesis)
- Placing their findings in the context of research conducted by others
- Offering reasonable conclusions based on those data

22b Using the Research Methods of the Sciences and Social Sciences

The research on which scientists base their reports is *primary:* They collect data by conducting tests—experiments, observational studies, and surveys, questionnaires, and interviews—to challenge their hypotheses. Scientists collect *quantitative* (numerical) data, while social scientists may collect quantitative or *qualitative* (descriptive) data.

> **More about ▶▶▶**
> Observational studies, 245–46
> Surveys, 246–47
> Interviews, 244–45

Quantitative data, which might include the temperature at which a liquid vaporizes or the number of subjects who answer a question in the same way, can be gathered through experiments, surveys, questionnaires, and interviews. For quantitative data to be meaningful, it must be based on careful measurements and observations, and it must be gathered from a sample that is both representative of the group and large enough that unusual responses will not skew the results. Any scientist who conducts the same experiment should achieve the same results.

Qualitative, or nonnumerical, data provide information about the experiences of individuals. This information may be drawn from interviews, observation, or both, and it often takes the form of a case study

Writing
⬆Responsibly   **Presenting Data Accurately**

Writing in the spring 2003 issue of the *Quarterly Journal of Medicine,* Christopher Martyn explains the importance of accurately representing research:

> Time, energy and public money are wasted when researchers follow false leads. . . . [E]very time a case of fraud hits the headlines, the reputation of scientists and scientific research

takes a knock. In biomedical research, patients may even be harmed, if conclusions are drawn from fraudulent clinical studies. (244)

When conducting an experiment, be especially careful to record data accurately. You are far more likely to receive a bad grade for falsifying data than for acknowledging that your experiment did not achieve the desired result.

or ethnography. Qualitative data might include reports on the feeling a medication induces or descriptions of a subject's behavior. For qualitative research to be useful, the data must be based on a rich understanding of the phenomenon or issues being studied and must provide great detail. Qualitative data must be organized carefully for the researcher to make sense of the information.

Quick Reference ➡ Choosing a Style Guide

Are you writing in . . . ?	Then use . . .
Anthropology	APA
Astronomy	CSE
Biology	CSE
Chemistry	CSE
Criminology	APA
Economics	Chicago
Geology	CSE
Nursing	CSE
Physics	CSE
Political science	Chicago
Psychology	APA
Sociology	APA

22c Citing and Documenting Sources—APA and CSE Style

Whenever you borrow ideas or information or quote from a work, you must cite the source. While there are a variety of style guides, many scientists use the style developed by the Council of Science Editors to document their sources, while social scientists often use the style devised by the American Psychological Association. The Quick Reference guide at left shows which disciplines are likely to follow which style, but check with your instructor before beginning your research project. All academic documentation styles require you both to cite sources in your text and to provide full bibliographic information in a reference list at the end of your project.

> *More about* ▶▶▶
> APA style, 358–400
>   (ch. 18)
> CSE style, 429–46
>   (ch. 20)

> *More about* ▶▶▶
> Figures of speech,
>   577–78
> Writing concisely,
>   516–25 (ch. 25)

connect
mhconnectcomposition.com
Additional resources: QL22005

22d Using the Language of the Sciences and Social Sciences

Since the goal of scientists and social scientists is to convey information, writers in these disciplines concentrate on making their language as clear and precise as possible. For novices, this means not only keeping sentences concise and focused, but also avoiding figures of speech and flowery descriptions. You will also need to learn the specialized vocabulary of the discipline, when to use present and past tense, when to write in the third person rather than the first, and when to use the passive rather than active voice.

1. Learn the discipline's vocabulary.

Even at the introductory level, most writing in the sciences and social sciences requires that you learn some specialized terminology and use it with precision. You can learn vocabulary from the context or from the word parts (prefixes, roots, and suffixes) that form the term. The following resources can provide comprehensive explanations:

- Discipline-specific dictionaries and encyclopedias: Since each discipline will have its own terminology, search your library's catalog for appropriate reference sources using the words *dictionary* or *encyclopedia* and the name of the discipline (such as *sociology* or *biology*). Some discipline-specific reference works may be available via your library's website.

More about ▶▶▶
Searching an online library catalog, 238–41

- Textbooks: Most textbooks in the sciences and social sciences set key terms in boldfaced or italic type and define them at first use. Check for an index or glossary at the back of the book or for a list of key terms in the margins or at the end of each chapter.

- Your instructors: Pay attention in lectures not just to what your instructors *say* but also to how they *use* words. Instructors may also define key terms or list them on slides, handouts, or the board.

The following excerpt from a student's report demonstrates both an understanding of and comfort with the specialized vocabulary of her discipline:

> The Mars Global Surveyor (MGS) magnetometer experiment was most useful due to its examination of magnetic properties present in Mars' crust. The most constructive portion was gained when the spacecraft altitude was below 200 km to as low as 101 km during the first ten minutes of periapsis (the period during which MGS was closest to the planet's surface).
>
> —Molly Patterson, Colgate University, Untitled report for Geology 105

2. Use the third person and passive voice to describe how research was conducted.

Scientists and social scientists write research reports so that other researchers can follow their procedures and produce an identical result. Since (in principle) the individual conducting the research is unimportant,

More about ▶▶▶
Person, 455–56, 646–47
Active vs. passive voice, 560–61

researchers in the sciences typically use the third person and passive voice to describe how research was conducted:

Third person

Passive voice

The materials consisted of two PsyScope computer programs run on Macintosh computers and a paper and pencil questionnaire. The participant was first assigned a room for experiment one (conditioning manipulation). The participant was then given the informed consent form, which was signed prior to the start of the experiment. The lights were turned off and the participant read the instruction. The experimenter asked if there were any questions.

—Amy M. Ehret, Illinois State University, "Effects of Stigma on Approach and Avoidance Behaviors in Social Situations"

Some social scientists use the first person (*I, we*) when discussing observations they made as a participant or the conclusions they drew from their research. Social scientists avoid the passive voice when describing the actions of participants.

> *More about* ▶▶▶
> Tense, 674–78

3. Use the past tense to discuss methods and present tense to discuss implications.

Scientists and social scientists use the past tense to discuss methods of data collection or the behavior of research participants, and they use the present tense to discuss the implications of their research. This is neatly demonstrated in the sentence below:

Past tense

Present tense

Since this study included only middle-class Caucasians, it is not representative of the population as a whole.

—Robyn Worthington, Bristol Community College, "Nature Versus Nurture: Does Birth Order Shape Personality?"

> ▶▶▶Student sample research report: "Nature Versus Nurture," Robyn Worthington, 479–86

22e Writing Assignments in the Sciences and Social Sciences

Common types of writing projects in the sciences and social sciences include the following:

- Literature review: In a literature review, writers summarize research on a specific topic, analyze and evaluate the sources and the research on which these studies were based, and synthesize sources to develop a thorough understanding of the topic.

- Research or laboratory notebook: In a research or laboratory notebook, writers record in precise detail (1) the materials (including sketches of setups if complex) in the order used; (2) a chronological list of the procedures followed; and (3) the results (raw data, clearly labeled and logically organized), including any graphs or calculations.

- Research or laboratory report: In a research or laboratory report, writers provide a detailed description of research, including methods, results, and discussion.

Unlike a humanities research paper, a research or laboratory report in the sciences and social sciences usually follows a standard format:

Title page The title page should include the following information:

- Title: Titles should accurately describe the project; titles should avoid playfulness or puns and should convey as briefly as possible the most important aspects of the report.

- Author's name

- Instructor's name and course number

- Date of submission

- Author notes

Abstract A brief summary of the report, the *abstract* usually includes a one-sentence summary of the most important points in each section of the report. The abstract should be no longer than 150–250 words.

Introduction The introduction provides necessary background, such as a brief review of other, closely related studies, indicates the purpose of conducting the research, and states the limits of what the research is intended to show.

Methods The methods section provides the following:

- Information about participants or subjects, including the number of participants and any relevant demographic information about them

- A description of the methods used to collect information (for example, face-to-face interview, online questionnaire, or telephone survey) or to conduct the experiment

connect
mhconnectcomposition.com
Additional resources: QL22006

> **More about** ▶▶▶
Summarizing,
119–20, 269
Analyzing, 129–31,
279–80, 288–90
Evaluating sources,
248–62 (ch. 14)
Synthesizing,
132–34, 279–80,
288–90

> **More about** ▶▶▶
Author notes,
384–85

- The equipment used (if any)
- The methods of recording data

The methods section must provide enough detail that others could repeat the study or experiment and achieve the same results.

More about ▶▶▶
Matching graphic to information, 81–84
Numbering figures and tables, 387 (APA)

Results The results section provides details of your outcomes. Information graphics are used to convey results succinctly.

Discussion The discussion section of the report offers readers an interpretation of the results, showing how the data collected support (or fail to support) the hypothesis. The discussion indicates the limitations of the data (what they do not indicate), and it relates the results to those of earlier researchers. (Do the data confirm, undermine, or extend earlier research?) The discussion concludes with an analysis of the implications of the research.

References The reference list includes secondary sources and begins on a new page, with the heading (the word *References*) centered at the top of the page.

More about ▶▶▶
Creating an APA-style reference list, 369–84
Creating a CSE-style reference list, 431–43

Tables and Figures Tables follow the reference list; figures follow tables. Each table or figure appears on a separate page.

Appendixes Appendixes include any figures, tables, photographs, or other materials that amplify but are not central to the discussion. Appendixes should be mentioned in the main body of the text so that readers know to consult them. Each appendix should include only one figure, set of data, and so on, but a report can include several appendixes. If more than one appendix is included, each should be assigned a letter (Appendix A, Appendix B, and so on). Arrange the appendixes in the order in which they are mentioned in the text, and give each appendix a succinct, descriptive title, such as "Appendix A: Background Questions."

Student Project: Research Report

The research report that follows describes a study on birth order and personality conducted by Robyn Worthington, a student at Bristol Community College. Worthington's study follows APA style.

Title page: Includes title that accurately reflects research topic

Nature Versus Nurture: Does Birth Order Shape Personality?

Robyn Worthington

Dr. Mary Zahm

Psychology 52

December 17, 2008

Abstract

Psychological researchers agree that the personalities of siblings differ, but there is much disagreement about the reasons for the differences. Many variables have been studied, including age range, birth order, gender, and nonshared environmental factors. This study examines the extent to which birth order affects personality and attempts to show a correlation. A revised sample of 51 participants completed a Myers-Briggs Type Indicator Test. Results show a significant relationship between birth order and introversion/extraversion, but they do not support the hypothesis fully.

Abstract: Provides summary of most important points in each section.

Introduction

Uses first person to emphasize personal observation

Shifts to third person

As the mother of three boys, I have been stunned by the differences in their personalities. Despite having the same parents and the same home environment, their personality differences are great. Researchers in psychology agree that siblings differ, but there is much disagreement about the reasons for the differences. Variables such as age range, birth order, gender, and nonshared environmental factors have been studied as possible causes. This study investigates a possible correlation between birth order and personality.

Introduction: Explains issues under consideration, offers brief review of related studies

Darwin's theory of evolution, specifically his principle of divergence, has been used as a possible explanation for the differences in sibling personality (Sulloway, 1996). Darwin theorized that "given enough time, species tend to evolve multiple forms that diverge in character, a process called adaptive radiation" (p. 85). One factor in adaptive radiation is development in different environmental niches. According to Sulloway (1996), the family environment is not a single environment, but a collection of microenvironments. The oldest child comes into an (intact) family of two; the family environment the next child experiences includes two parents and a sibling with whom the second child must compete; the third child finds a family with two parents and two siblings with each of whom the third child must compete, and so on. In short, as each child is born, the family environment changes, including the way that the parents interact with each child and the way the children interact with each other, and this difference in family environment can affect personality (Leman, 1985). By developing diverging personalities, younger siblings avoid competing with older, bigger, more experienced siblings on the same grounds (Sulloway, 1996).

Certain characteristics of personality have been associated with birth order. Oldest, or first borns, have been characterized as ambitious high achievers who are usually confident, organized, and conservative (Leman, 1985; Sulloway, 1996). Both Sulloway and Leman suggest that children born second tend to diverge as much as possible from the first born, taking on a totally different set of characteristics. They are noted as being more sociable, more cooperative, and more open to experience than their conservative older siblings, who have a tendency to relate strongly with their parents. Youngest children tend to be charming, affectionate, outgoing, and used to being the center of attention; they may also be spoiled and impatient (Leman, 1985).

Topic sentence

Support: Uses evidence from sources (Sulloway, Leman)

Gender, age range, and nonshared environment are also thought to be factors in personality differences in siblings. In a study of university psychology students, Tammy Mann (1993) predicted that nonshared environmental factors would account for personality differences more than other factors. However, the results showed that the family constellation variables of age, birth order, and gender may be more firmly associated with personality differences in siblings than the nonshared environment. In fact, 27% of the correlations between constellation variables and sibling personality differences were statistically significant (Mann, 1993).

Topic sentence

Support: Uses facts, statistics from source (Mann)

Methods

This study used Darwin's theory of evolution as well as the theory proposed by Frank Sulloway concerning birth order and personality as models. The hypothesis to be tested is that birth order would account for the differences in personality

Hypothesis

Defines key term

among siblings. Birth order was defined as either oldest, middle, youngest, or only

child. Personality was assessed by the Myers-Briggs Type Indicator (Briggs &

Myers, 1980), in the categories of extraversion/introversion, sensing/intuition,

thinking/feeling, and judging/perceiving.

Methods: Description of participants, materials; explanation of how data were collected and analyzed

The initial sample consisted of 70 randomly selected adolescents and adults

from whom 55 surveys were returned. For statistical calculations, only-children

were eliminated from the sample, as their number was too few. The revised

sample consisted of 51 people ranging in age from 14 to 90 years of age. All were

European American and considered themselves of middle-class backgrounds. Of

the 51 subjects, 16 reported being an oldest sibling, 17 reported being a middle

sibling, and 18 reported being a youngest sibling.

The Myers-Briggs Type Indicator Test was distributed to the participants

along with a background questionnaire (Appendix) on which subjects supplied

personal data, including birth order. The surveys were collected, scored, and

labeled with four letters which corresponded to the participants' personality type:

E (extraversion) or I (introversion)

N (intuitive) or S (sensing)

F (feeling) or T (thinking)

J (judging) or P (perceiving)

The information collected was statistically evaluated by establishing a null

and an alternate hypothesis for each personality trait. The scores were placed in

a contingency table, and the calculations were performed and evaluated using the

chi-square test for goodness of fit.

Results

A statistically significant relationship between birth order and personality traits

was found in one of the four areas. Calculations revealed a significant relationship

between extraversion/introversion at the .005 (0.5%) level of significance. Of the

16 oldest children, 14 preferred introversion, 10 out of 17 middle siblings showed

a preference for extraversion, and 12 out of 18 youngest siblings showed a

preference for extraversion. (See Figure 1.) In all other areas, the calculations fell

short of a reliable level of significance. In the traits of sensing/intuition, thinking/

feeling, and judging/perceiving, the test values were below 1, too low for even

a .05 (5%) level of significance.

Results: Explains outcomes (with visual representation of results) and discloses shortcomings

Discussion

While this study was able to demonstrate a significant relationship between birth

order and the traits of extraversion/introversion, the data collected do not support

the hypothesis that birth order can account for the differences in other aspects

of personality in siblings. The variables involved may be too difficult to assess

using the statistical methods of this study. Other characteristics, such as gender

and number or spacing of children, all influence the way that parents relate to

their children and the way that siblings relate to each other, so these factors, too,

are likely to affect personality. Other factors include genetics and nonshared

environmental experiences such as playgroups and nursery school/day care,

friends, teachers, and so forth—all of which may have an impact on personality.

Discussion: Interprets results

With so many variables, assessing the causes of personality differences in

siblings is extremely difficult. Based on the results of this study, I have concluded that personality development is not likely the result of any one factor but, instead,

a combination of many. Further, since this study included only middle-class

European Americans, it cannot be assumed to be representative of the population

as a whole. Future research might include a cross-sectional study of various

ethnic and socioeconomic groups as a better representation of the population.

An interesting result of the study was that, when the personality traits were divided

by gender, 24 out of 31 females demonstrated a preference for the trait of feeling

to that of thinking. Future research might include a study of the effect of gender

on personality differences or personality differences among siblings based on

gender.

Conclusion: Summarizes findings, acknowledges shortcomings, suggests new avenues for research

References

Briggs, K. C., & Myers, I. B. (1980). *Myers-Briggs Type Indicator.* Palo Alto, CA:

Consulting Psychologists Press.

Leman, K. (1985). *The birth order book.* Tappan, NJ: Revell.

Mann, T. L. (1993). A failure of nonshared environmental factors in predicting

sibling personality differences. *Journal of Psychology, 127,* 79–86. Retrieved

from http://www.heldref.org/pubs/jrl/about.html

Sulloway, F. J. (1996). *Born to rebel: Birth order, family dynamics, and creative

lives.* New York: Random House.

References: Provides full bibliographic information in APA style for all sources cited in report

Figure 1. Preference for extraversion/introversion among siblings.

Appendix: Background Questions

Date of birth:

Sex: M _____ F _____

How many siblings do you have?

Brothers _____ Sisters _____

What is your birth order? Oldest _____ Middle _____

Youngest _____ Only child _____

How many years separate you from the siblings who were born just

before and/or just after you?

A brother _____ years older

A sister _____ years older

A brother _____ years younger

A sister _____ years younger

As a young child, did you attend day care or nursery school?

Yes _____ No _____

If yes, how old were you when you first attended? _____

How many years did you attend? _____

Work **Together** ◄

In groups of three or four, discuss the differences between the research report above and one of the student projects in the previous chapter (pp. 460–63, 465–68). How do the approach, language, and structure of the two writing projects differ?

Preparing for and Taking an Essay Exam

Long before marathon runners cross the finish line, they get ready for the 26.2-mile race. They practice regularly, eat well, and learn the terrain ahead of time. They also use strategy, knowing how to pace themselves and when to turn up the heat. And they do not panic if someone else dashes ahead. Runners know that being prepared is crucial to running a good race.

Students who succeed on essay exams have many of these attributes. They prepare by reviewing their notes and answering practice questions, and they have a test-taking strategy that allows them to get to the finish line. All of this preparation—not cramming the night before—is what leads to a good grade.

487

23a Preparing for an Essay Exam

You begin to prepare for any college test by reading, taking notes, listening, and working on your assignments. An essay exam, however, requires some special preparation.

1. Take good notes and review them often.

More about ▶▶▶
Annotating, 124–27
Taking notes, 267–80
Keeping a reading
 journal, 127–28
Summarizing,
 119–20, 269
Outlining, 40–42,
 286–87

Stay up-to-date on your reading assignments, and take good notes:

- Highlight and underline important terms and concepts, but do not overdo it—highlighting everything means you must reread the whole text.

- Write down your thoughts and questions, and connect what you are reading to other ideas or situations.

- Note any statements in the text that strike you as especially crucial or interesting—or that might show up on an essay exam. A reading journal is an excellent way to generate and store notes of this type.

- For complicated texts, write outlines or summaries that will help you figure out what is going on, keep track of the development of ideas, and recall the material later on.

- When taking notes in class, focus on the major points your instructor is making—do not try to write down every detail.

As you review your notes, focus on the most important ideas and information. Using a highlighter or a pen in a new color, take notes *on* your notes, marking the big topics or drawing connections among major ideas. Reviewing your notes regularly (not just the day before an exam) will help you learn important concepts and identify material you are likely to be asked about.

Getting It Across   Study Groups

An alternative to coming up with questions on your own is to work in study groups of three to seven classmates. Each member could devise a question or an outline for the rest of the group, or members might work together to come up with questions and answers. Study groups work well when members share their ideas and learn from one another; they fail when some members rely too heavily on others to do their thinking for them.

2. Devise and answer practice questions.

After reviewing your notes, consider the terms and concepts that seem essential, and identify issues or patterns that have arisen repeatedly in readings and lectures. Then brainstorm questions based on these terms, concepts, issues, and patterns. As you brainstorm, be sure to include questions that you fear will be asked, as well as ones you hope will be on the exam. For each of the questions you develop, devise a brief outline and draft an answer while you have an opportunity to consult textbooks and notes. Spend extra time going over material on questions for which you feel least prepared.

3. Understand the parameters of the exam.

Regardless of how you study, find out from your instructor exactly what will be required of you and what will be allowed. Here are some questions you might ask:

- Is use of a dictionary, thesaurus, or writer's handbook permitted during the exam? What about electronic notebooks or laptops?

- How many questions will there be? Will different questions be worth different numbers of points, or will all questions be equally weighted?

- Is partial credit available for partial answers or for an outline of an answer?

- Are sample questions and answers available?

> " It's best to study with people that you don't know too well, because studying with friends can be distracting. "
>
> —Jeff Loken, North Dakota State University

23b Previewing the Exam

When you sit down to take an essay exam—or any test, for that matter—you may want to start writing immediately. It is a good idea, though, to take a few minutes to look over the exam, decide on a strategy, and make sure you understand the questions.

1. Read the exam, and develop a test-taking strategy.

The first step in writing a successful exam is to read through the entire exam before you write anything. As you read, develop a strategy for taking the test:

- Determine how many points are assigned to each question, and set a time limit for answering each part. (Some instructors indicate how much time to spend on each part. If yours does, try to follow those guidelines.) Give yourself more time for the questions that are worth more points: Finishing a 50-point question is more important than finishing a 10-pointer.

Quick

Quick Reference ➡ Common Verbs on Essay Exams

What Is the Question?

1. **Analyze** the architectural style of Frank Lloyd Wright.
2. **Compare and contrast** the major economic problems of the North and South during the Civil War.
3. **Define** the terms *denotation* and *connotation,* and discuss these terms in regard to the word *brother.*
4. **Describe** how bees build a hive.
5. **Evaluate** John F. Kennedy's performance as commander in chief during the Cuban Missile Crisis.
6. **Illustrate** the effects of global warming on mammals of the Arctic, including the walrus and the polar bear.
7. **List** and **explain** the four main causes of an economic recession.
8. **Summarize** Carl Rogers's humanist approach to psychology.

What Am I Supposed to Do?

1. **Critically examine** the elements of his style, and then comment on the style as a whole.
2. Explain the economic problems and tell how they were **similar and different** in the North and South.
3. Give the **main characteristics** of the terms. **Show that you understand** the definitions by applying them to *brother.*
4. Explain the process **step by step.**
5. State **what you think** of Kennedy's performance, and give specific **reasons** and concrete **evidence** for your opinion(s).
6. Give specific **examples** of the effects on the animals named and at least one additional animal.
7. **Jot down** the causes and **tell clearly** how each results in a recession.
8. Give the **main points** of his approach, and keep your answer **concise.**

- Check off the questions that you find easy and can complete quickly. You may want to start with some of those.

- Leave yourself a little time to read through your answers to add or clarify information; to correct errors of spelling, usage, and grammar; and to rewrite illegible words.

More about ▶▶▶
Analyzing the assignment, 19–20, 210–11
Writing about literature, 448–71 (ch. 21)
Writing in the sciences and social sciences, 472–86 (ch. 22)
Comparison-contrast, 68–69
Definition, 69–70
Summarizing, 119–20, 269

2. Analyze the questions: What do they ask you to do?

When you read an exam question, it is usually fairly easy to identify the topic—the plot of a Faulkner novel (for literature), the causes of schizophrenia (for psychology), the structure of DNA (for biology). Less obvious, however, may be what you are supposed to *do* with the topic. *Compare* is quite different from *define* or *summarize,* so pay close attention to the verbs and do what they tell you. (See the Quick Reference box above for sample question analyses.)

Also be on the lookout for two-part questions; make sure you answer both parts. Ask your instructor to clarify any question that is

Writing Responsibly   **Using Your Computer during an Essay Exam**

Check with your instructor in advance of an essay exam to see whether you can use your laptop to write your exam. The computer will allow you to present more readable copy: You can use cut-and-paste to revise and reorganize your answer and run a spell-check program to catch and correct the most obvious typos. But you will have to resist the temptation to consult notes or online sources.

vague or confusing. Asking for the answer (or even a hint) is inappropriate (and probably will not work), but asking your instructor to define an unfamiliar word (as long as it is not a key term) is perfectly reasonable.

23c Writing an Effective Answer: Respond to the Question, Provide Support, and Organize Logically

Writing an effective answer means answering the question you are asked, providing sufficient supporting evidence, and organizing your response clearly and logically. The following tips will help you show off what you have learned.

- Take a few minutes to create a brief scratch outline of the points you want to cover. Jot down some of the evidence you will use—for example, references to particular characters or events, details about causes and effects, or specific examples that support your argument. The most logical organization will answer question parts in the order they are asked.

- Write a thesis statement, one or two sentences that express your main point and that respond directly to the question.

- As you write, follow your outline, incorporating evidence as you go along. Be sure to connect your ideas back to your thesis and to provide transitions from one point to the next.

- Overall, devote most of your energy to supporting your thesis, but try to wrap up your answer with a concluding statement or paragraph.

- Write legibly so that your instructor does not have to struggle to read your answer.

> *More about* ▶▶▶
> Scratch (informal) outlines, 40
> Thesis statements, 33–37
> Transitions, 61–62
> Supporting your ideas, 46–48

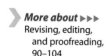

Reference ➜ **What an Effective Answer Does—and Does Not Do**

An effective answer . . .	**An effective answer does not . . .**
has a clear thesis that answers the question	answer the question you hoped would be asked
answers the question that was asked	stick in information on the topic that is unrelated to the question
provides ample and accurate supporting evidence	pad the answer by repeating what you have already said
answers the question parts in the order they were asked	make personal judgments that the question does not ask for
uses the method of development suggested by the question (such as analysis, comparison-contrast, definition)	

- Leave ample margins on each side of the page and several blank lines below each answer, in case you decide to add information later on.

23d Doing a Final Check

More about ▶▶▶
Revising, editing, and proofreading, 90–104

Although instructors do not expect an exam to be error-free, they do appreciate one that is clear and easy to read. So, in the last few minutes of the exam period, stop writing and read through your exam to make any essential corrections. Ask yourself questions like these:

- Does my thesis answer the question precisely? If not, what quick edits will make my answer respond more directly?

- Do I support all of my major points sufficiently? If not, are there one or two more reasons, facts, or examples that I can add quickly?

- Did I include any irrelevant material? If so, what should I cut?

- Did I make any mistakes of grammar or spelling? Did I use words correctly or omit any words by mistake?

- Do I need to erase (or cross out) and rewrite any illegible words?

Two Sample Answers: Effective and Ineffective

Take a close look at the essay exam topic that follows, and compare the two sample answers on pp. 493–95. The first is effective because it responds directly to the assignment and provides concrete evidence to support its claim. The second is ineffective because it does not provide a comparison or contrast as required and because it offers little concrete evidence. Note that the writer of the effective answer also underlined some key words in the question to help determine how to answer the question appropriately.

Essay Exam Question

<u>Identify</u> and <u>compare/contrast</u> the films from which the stills above are taken. Be sure to include in your discussion at least one of the <u>core concepts</u> we have discussed in class, such as genre, dialogue, film noir, etc. (30 points)

Effective Answer

Outline:
2 different heroes
   Marlowe—witty & capable
    Dude—lazy & uncomfortable
Orchid scene vs. taunting scene
2 responses to loss
   Marlowe—tough
    Dude—very passive

Answer includes scratch outline

Thesis answers question

Core concept discussed in class

Emphasizes contrast between heroes

Supports claims with details about heroes from these films

Returns to key concept and how these heroes display it

Conclusion points out shared trait: Heroes both lose but respond to loss differently

Thesis: Big Lebowski is new kind of film noir, main difference is kind of hero

Though The Big Lebowski is generally considered a parody of film noir detective stories such as The Big Sleep, it might also be categorized as a contemporary variation on the style. As the still photos show, the differences are obvious: gonzo comedy aside, Lebowski chiefly differs in the nature and quality of its hero. Instead of the occasionally superhuman wit and capability of Philip Marlowe, we have The Dude, called by the film's narrator "one of the laziest people on the planet Earth." However, though the Dude's ineptitude is largely played for laughs, much of the humor derives from discomfort and even dread; his insufficiency as a hero only heightens the sense of alienation.

At the beginning of The Big Sleep, Marlowe is made to sit in an orchid hothouse, where he proceeds to grow more physically uncomfortable with every passing moment, but he is able to speak his client's language, anticipate his interests and needs, and ultimately earn the general's quiet admiration. The Dude, in contrast, is so out of his depth that he seems incapable of scoring a single point against anyone he meets. When The Dude finds himself in a shadow-drenched room, the viewer may not feel an immediate sense of dread, but it does seem clear that the protagonist has little hope of prevailing. In a particularly revealing scene, The Dude's "client" taunts him with the failure of his generation's ideals, and our hero has no real answer.

These two scenes reveal the core of the typical noir hero: the individual who loses, over and over again, and who is compelled to absorb these defeats and continue on, often with a diminished sense of self. The hero responds by creating a persona to act as surrogate for this loss—one as the hard-boiled detective (Marlowe), and the other as the hyper-passive Dude.

Ineffective Answer

A lot of people misunderstood "The Big Lebowski" when it first came out. It bombed at the box office, and critics seemed either confused or dismissive. Nowadays it's a cult favorite. There's even a Lebowski film festival, and thousands of people show up every year dressed in costume to watch the movie, discuss it, and even present scholarly papers on its meaning. Obviously, to quote a certain political figure, the critics "misunderestimated" the film the first time around. So what went wrong? Did they not get the comedy? It's got some of the most quotable lines ever. "That rug tied the whole room together." Others thought it was just a big mess—too many different references, film styles, etc. The gonzo musical numbers may have been offputting for those who don't like movie musicals. I even talked to one person who complained that the "marmot" in the movie is actually a ferret. I told him that "marmot" sounds funnier, but he didn't seem to get it. Basically, Lebowski makes fun of lots of different movies, but especially the old black and white detective movies. But it also has a lot in common with them. Critics complained that it was too sunny and bright to be like the old detective movies, but there are a lot of scenes where the Dude is literally in the shadows. It's like the cinematography went over people's heads just because it's not in black and white. Also, the Dude doesn't get the girl, and he doesn't get the satisfaction of seeing the bad guys arrested or killed. He solves the case, but he doesn't get any kind of reward. Instead his friend dies and he goes bowling.

> Irrelevant information about the film—does not identify second film, identify a core concept, or provide a thesis that answers question

> Notes a similarity but only in general terms—no specific example

> Notes contrasts but does not discuss their importance

Work **Together**

In groups of three or four, discuss the ineffective answer above. How would you revise it to make it answer the question directly?

24

Writing in Business and as a Citizen

by Amy Rupiper Taggart

If you bought a bag of apples at the grocery store on Wednesday and discovered on Thursday that most of them were rotten, you would probably complain to the produce manager and ask for a refund. If this kind of thing happened often, you might write a letter to the store's owner. If you found something rotten in a government agency or corporation, you might write a letter to the editor to bring the problem to the attention of your community. If you found an issue that you could help resolve, you might offer a proposal for solving the problem and promote your program with a press release. Business writing, then, is more than memos or résumés and cover letters. It is something we all do, whether as employees or as citizens.

connect

mhconnectcomposition.com
Additional resources: QL24001

24a Using Business Letter Formats

Regardless of what you do after college, you will need to know how to write a good business letter. In company settings, letters are used to communicate with people outside the office—with customers, for example. While some business communications may be sent by email (letters to the editor, for example, are frequently submitted electronically), more formal communications or communications that should remain private (such as notifying employees of a salary increase) are best communicated in printed form.

In your personal life, you may need to write a business letter to request information, thank someone, or comment on a product or service. The formality of the context can serve as a guide in determining whether email or a printed letter is more appropriate.

Whether sending letters by conventional mail or email, be considerate of your reader's time and present information courteously and concisely. These guidelines can help you write an effective business letter:

- **State your purpose in the first paragraph.** Businesspeople want to see at a glance what the letter is about.

- **Be clear and specific throughout the letter.** A vague, muddled, or repetitious letter may be ignored.

- **Keep your paragraphs short.** This will help your reader grasp your major points quickly.

- **Adopt a positive yet somewhat formal tone.** Make sure the tone fits the audience and purpose.

- **Reread and edit your letter.** Clarify your points, reduce wordiness, and correct all errors. Grammatical and typographical errors may severely diminish your credibility with your reader.

1. Use a standard letter format.

Whatever the purpose of your business letter, follow one of two standard formats:

1. **Full block style.** Align all text with the left-hand margin. This is the best choice when you are writing a letter on letterhead stationery.
2. **Modified block style.** Align the following elements just to the right of the center of the page: return address, date, closing, and signature. Align everything else with the left-hand margin.

In addition to using an appropriate letter style, follow these design guidelines:

- Use 8½ × 11–inch white or off-white paper. You may also use letterhead stationery, especially if you are communicating as a representative of a company or organization.

connect
mhconnectcomposition.com
Additional resources: QL24002

connect
mhconnectcomposition.com
Additional resources: QL24003, QL24004

▶▶▶ Sample business letters:
Full block style, 500
Modified block style, 505

- Single-space your paragraphs and insert an extra line of space between them; do not indent paragraphs.

- Use a standard size (number 10) envelope, and fold the letter horizontally in thirds.

- Follow standard practice for addressing the envelope: addressee's full name, title, and address (with zip code) in the middle of the envelope; and your name and address in the upper left-hand corner. Use your computer's software to generate a neatly typed envelope or address label.

2. Include standard elements.

As you type your letter, incorporate the typical elements of a business letter:

Return Address and Date If you are using letterhead stationery with a preprinted address, add just the date. Otherwise, include your full address. Spell out the names of months.

Inside Address Give the name, title (if appropriate), and full address of the person to whom you are writing. Spell out words like *Street* or *Road,* but use the two-letter postal abbreviations for states.

Salutation In some instances, you may address a letter to a company or organization (*Dear Habitat for Humanity*) or to a job title (*Dear Shipping Department Manager*), but it is preferable to address your letter to an actual person, even if you have to contact the company to determine who that person is. Also, use appropriate titles (abbreviated before the name), such as *Mr., Ms., Dr., Gen., Prof.,* or *Rev.* Professional titles supersede gender-specific titles. For example, if you were writing to a female minister, you would address the letter to *Rev. Aldrich,* not *Ms. Aldrich.* If you have the person's name but do not know the gender, use the whole name: *Dear Pat Gonzalez.*

> *More about ▶▶▶*
> Titles before and
> after names, 854
> Abbreviating titles,
> 854

Body Type each paragraph flush with the left margin and put a line of space between paragraphs. Do not use paragraph indention.

Closing and Signature Using the formality of the letter as a guide, choose an appropriate closing phrase, such as *Sincerely, Yours truly,* or *Best regards.* Four lines (two double spaces) below the closing, type your full name, and sign in the space above.

Additional Information Below your name, include other kinds of information, such as *cc:* (*carbon copy*) if other people are receiving copies of the letter or *Enc.* (*enclosure*) if you are enclosing items with the letter.

Sample Business Letter, Block Style The letter in full-block style on the next page (Figure 24.1, p. 500) is on letterhead stationery that includes the company's address and other contact information. If this letter had been written on plain paper, a return address would be needed directly above the date. Most items and all paragraphs are separated by two lines (one double space), but below the date and below the closing, four lines of space are required.

24b Writing Business Letters

The letters you write as an employee or in your personal life will have a variety of purposes. On Monday you may be a businessperson writing a letter of apology to a customer, and on Tuesday you might be a private citizen writing a letter of complaint. It is helpful, then, to look at some guidelines for writing different kinds of business letters.

1. Letters of complaint

When writing a letter of complaint, your challenge is to exercise restraint. Be reasonable and informed, and get to the point. Effective complaint letters do not cast the recipient of the letter in a negative light. When writing a letter of complaint, follow these four steps:

connect
mhconnectcomposition.com
Additional resources: QL24006

Writing Responsibly **Letters to the Editor**

When private citizens write a letter to the editor of a newspaper or magazine, they often feel strongly about something—a previous article in the publication, a political candidate, or a local problem. If you write such a letter, keep your emotions in check. Make your point, get your facts straight, assume a courteous tone, and avoid personal attacks against the publication or writer. Most publications now accept such letters via email; read your submission over carefully and adjust the tone before hitting send.

1. Describe the problem at the outset, and include details.
2. Explain the importance of the problem and why the recipient should be involved in the solution.
3. State your hopes for the solution to the problem.
4. If you have had positive experiences with the person or organization in the past, mention that; it will help your cause.

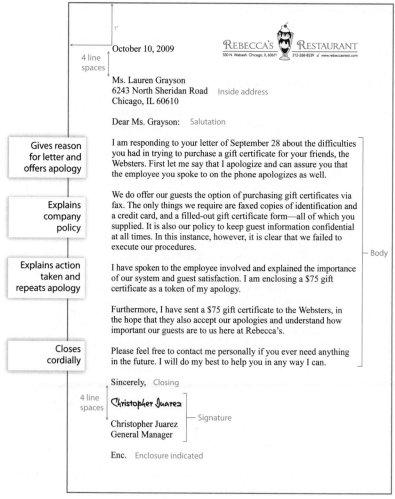

1"

October 10, 2009

REBECCA'S RESTAURANT
550 N. Wabash, Chicago, IL 60611   312-268-8539   www.rebeccasrest.com

4 line spaces

Ms. Lauren Grayson
6243 North Sheridan Road   Inside address
Chicago, IL 60610

Dear Ms. Grayson: Salutation

Gives reason for letter and offers apology

I am responding to your letter of September 28 about the difficulties you had in trying to purchase a gift certificate for your friends, the Websters. First let me say that I apologize and can assure you that the employee you spoke to on the phone apologizes as well.

Explains company policy

We do offer our guests the option of purchasing gift certificates via fax. The only things we require are faxed copies of identification and a credit card, and a filled-out gift certificate form—all of which you supplied. It is also our policy to keep guest information confidential at all times. In this instance, however, it is clear that we failed to execute our procedures.

Body

Explains action taken and repeats apology

I have spoken to the employee involved and explained the importance of our system and guest satisfaction. I am enclosing a $75 gift certificate as a token of my apology.

Furthermore, I have sent a $75 gift certificate to the Websters, in the hope that they also accept our apologies and understand how important our guests are to us here at Rebecca's.

Closes cordially

Please feel free to contact me personally if you ever need anything in the future. I will do my best to help you in any way I can.

Sincerely,   Closing

4 line spaces

Christopher Juarez

Christopher Juarez   Signature
General Manager

Enc.   Enclosure indicated

FIGURE 24.1 A letter of apology (full block style)

2. Letters of apology

In the business world, you may receive letters from customers who are complaining about the service you offer or the product you provide. In a letter of apology (Figure 24.1), your goal is to fix or make up for the problem, reassure the customer that he or she is important, and restore the reputation of your company or organization.

Follow these steps in writing a letter of apology:

1. State the problem in the first paragraph, and apologize for it.
2. Explain your company's policy (if appropriate), and admit that correct procedures were not followed.
3. Tell the customer what you have done to correct the problem within your company, and what you are doing to make things right with the customer.
4. Repeat your apology, and offer further assistance if needed.

3. Letters of rejection

When you must turn down a request, a bid on a project, or a job application, your task is not only to communicate the bad news but also to maintain goodwill with the person to whom you are writing. An effective letter of rejection will do the following:

1. Begin with a positive statement, thanking the recipient for taking the time to apply for the job, submit the proposal, or do whatever the person has done.
2. Give the reason(s) for the rejection in a clear yet kind way.
3. Conclude the letter with an expression of goodwill that is particular to the recipient.

24c Writing Business Memos

On any given workday, you may write a memo to convey information to the advertising department, to raise a question with your supervisor, or to explain a new procedure to co-workers. You may write thousands of memos during your lifetime; they are the typical communication tool people use within a company or organization. Printed memos may be distributed, but they are now most frequently sent via email (Figure 24.2, p. 502). A few tips to help you write an effective memo follow.

1. Use a standard memo format.

Insert the information in the sections of your email's header *To, From, Date,* and *Subject.* (If you are sending a printed memo, type these headings at the top of the page or use the memo template that comes with your word processing program.) All memos should include a

▶▶▶ Sample business memo (email), 502

connect
mhconnectcomposition.com
Additional resources: QL24007, QL24008

More about ▶▶▶
Writing and answering email, 187–91, 503

Recipients	

New Message

Send | Options... | HTML

To: Carter, Jane; Santos, Maria
From: Ng, Yuah
Subject: Awards for Resident Advisers
Attachment: RA of the Year--Nomination Form.doc (20 KB)

Our resident advisers are on the front line of student affairs, dealing day to day with conflicts among students, difficulties new students face in adjusting to college life, and the enforcement of college policies. So this year, in conjunction with the Student Housing Office, and the Office of Student Affairs, we are recognizing the contribution resident advisers make by conferring a Resident Adviser of the Year award.

Candidates should demonstrate the following qualities:
1. The ability to resolve conflicts among students
2. The judgment to involve the administration when necessary
3. Compassion for students struggling to adjust to life away from home
4. The ability to follow an issue through to its conclusion

The nomination form is attached.

Nominations are needed by April 15, 2010. Awards will be given out at commencement.

Thanks so much for your help in spreading the word!

Henry Washington
Director of Student Affairs
hwashington@springfieldcollege.edu

Recipients

Specific subject line

Main point stated in 1st paragraph

FIGURE 24.2
A sample memo, emailed

subject line that accurately summarizes the content of the message. If recipients are being copied, list them in the *cc* line. Attachments to emailed memos usually appear in the header; for printed memos with attachments, add *Enc.* at the end of the message.

2. Get right to the point.

Use a tone appropriate for your reader, but be clear, specific, and concise. In your first paragraph, name the issue the memo is addressing and explain briefly why you are writing. In subsequent paragraphs or in a list, add any necessary details. A numbered or bulleted list is particularly effective in memos because it helps readers "see" your points or questions clearly. Conclude on a positive note, and thank the recipient if appropriate.

Reference ➡ Email Etiquette

Following email etiquette (or *netiquette*) can make you more effective in social as well as professional settings. Here are fifteen tips for writing email:

1. **Use accurate subject lines, and focus on a single topic.** Doing so will help your recipients manage their email, and it will help you if you find your message later.
2. **Get right to the point, and keep messages brief.** Consideration for your reader's time is key.
3. **Maintain an appropriate tone.** Remain cordial and avoid *flaming* (or launching a personal attack).
4. **Include salutations (or greetings) and complimentary closings only in the most formal contexts.** Most email messages do not require a formal salutation or closing.
5. **Follow the rules of capitalization.** Avoid writing all but the most informal messages in all lowercase (or all capital) letters. (Words in all capital letters are the equivalent of shouting.)
6. **Ask permission before sharing an email message with someone to whom it was not addressed.** Sending along a message without asking permission may be unfair to the original sender.
7. **Reply promptly when your action is needed.** You may not always be able to answer swiftly, but do acknowledge receipt of the message, and let the sender know when to expect a full reply.
8. **Avoid hitting "reply all" unless every recipient will be interested in the reply.** With the quantity of email circulating today, most recipients will appreciate *not* being

included if the message is not directed toward them.

9. **Avoid "spamming" friends and colleagues.** Messages promising bad luck if you do not send the message on to five (or more) friends are commonplace on the internet, but you can choose *not* to comply.
10. **Copy portions of previous messages, or reference the email string for clarity.** If readers will need information from an earlier message, either copy and paste a portion of the message or refer the reader to a specific message.
11. **Never represent someone else's words as your own.** Acknowledge your use of any words or ideas you have borrowed from others. Usually, you need not provide a formal citation, but you should include the writer's name and any information needed to locate the source.
12. **Include your contact information with every message.** Make sure recipients know how to contact you in ways besides email: Provide a telephone number and mailing address with each message.
13. **Edit your messages.** Even readers of email deserve a text that is clear and correct.
14. **Pause before sending!** While the temptation to shoot off an angry message is sometimes great, avoid it. Treat the email recipient with courtesy, even when you are annoyed.
15. **Archive your messages.** If you are likely to need to refer to a message you have sent or received, either print it out or save an electronic copy.

> **More about ▶▶▶**
> Conciseness, 516–25 (ch. 25)
> Flaming, 199
> Tone, 16–17, 143, 567, 575
> Capitalization, 839–45 (ch. 53)

Writing
↑ **Responsibly**　**Personal Emails and IM at Work**

When you send email on computers that are the property of a business or organization, the correspondence is considered the property of the organization and is subject to search should there be a suspicion of abuse. Therefore, write responsibly at work, and assume that your email (or instant messages) may be viewed by others.

---

connect
mhconnectcomposition.com
Additional resources: QL24009

24d　Writing Job Application Letters

A letter of application (Figure 24.3) is essentially a sales letter: Your goal is to sell yourself to a prospective employer and to get an interview. To do so, your letter should be enthusiastic yet formal. Before you begin to write, learn something about the company or organization. You can then reveal a bit of your knowledge in your letter, which will show the recipient that you are serious about the job. Like other types of business correspondence, letters of application should follow some common guidelines concerning format and content:

- Use one of the two standard letter formats: block format (Figure 24.1, p. 500) or modified block format (Figure 24.3), and limit the letter's length to a single page.

- Address the letter to a specific person, even if you have to phone the company to determine who that is.

- Start by mentioning the specific job you are applying for and how you learned about it.

- In the next paragraph or two, explain why you are applying for this job, and list your specific qualifications.

- Point out the items in your résumé that are a good "fit" for this job, but do not just repeat the résumé.

- Conclude by asking for an interview and providing information about how you may be reached.

- Edit and proofread your letter carefully: A job application letter must be well written and contain no errors.

Throughout the letter, you need to walk a fine line: Do not be too modest about your accomplishments, but do not exaggerate your qualifications, either.

7716 W. Birchwood Street
Chicago, IL 60648

July 1, 2009

Mr. Aaron Gieseke
Recruitment, Human Resources
Museum of Science and Industry
57th Street and Lake Shore Drive
Chicago, IL 60637

Dear Mr. Gieseke:

I am applying for the entry-level position of assistant to the curator, which you advertised in the June 30 issue of the *Chicago Tribune*. Since childhood, I have been delighted by the museum's extraordinary exhibits, from Colleen Moore's Fairy Castle to the walk-through heart and chick hatchery. I would welcome the opportunity to put my skills and knowledge to work at your renowned institution.

Two years ago, I was fortunate to take several in-depth courses in museum curatorship at James Cook University. With European curators as teachers, I came to understand the many facets of running a museum, including preserving artifacts and tapping sources of funding. I also learned about the myriad jobs that go on behind the scenes and decided that museum life was where I wanted to be in my professional life.

This decision was reinforced many times over while I was an intern at the Smithsonian last summer. I especially enjoyed working with researchers on new interactive exhibits and using my French language skills with international visitors. Inasmuch as the Museum of Science and Industry was the first to initiate interactive exhibits and welcomes thousands of overseas travelers each year, I believe my qualifications are ideal for the job.

My résumé is enclosed. I would be delighted to meet with you for an interview at any time. You may phone me at (312) 555–1212 or email me at sonjaja@yahoo.com. I look forward to hearing from you.

Sincerely,

Sonja Jacques

Sonja Jacques

Enc.

Annotations (right margin):

- Modified block style: Return address and date align right of center
- Addresses specific person formally
- Mentions specific job and shows familiarity with museum
- Highlights educational ties to job
- Links work experience to job and shows knowledge of museum
- Asks for interview and gives contact information
- Modified block style: Closing and signature align with return address

FIGURE 24.3 Sample job application letter, modified block style

ESL **Conducting Business in the United States** Here are a few tips that may help you get a job and be successful at it:

- *Take advantage of your language skills.* Because many corporations operate globally, be sure to mention—on your résumé and in a job interview—any languages besides English in which you are fluent.

- *Do not include personal information (such as age, religion, marital status) or a photograph on your résumé.* It is not the custom in the United States to include personal information or a photograph with a job application, and U.S. employers are legally barred from assessing job qualifications on the basis of these factors.

- *Be direct and concise in your business writing.* Although your culture of origin may take a more indirect approach, follow the advice in this chapter if you are writing to a U.S. organization.

connect

mhconnectcomposition.com
Additional resources: QL24010, QL24011

24e Writing Résumés

A *résumé* is a brief document that summarizes your work and educational experience for a prospective employer. Like a job application letter, it is a tool for selling yourself and obtaining an interview. Thus, in drafting a résumé, keep your audience and purpose in mind: Who will read this résumé? What will they want to know? Especially for those new to the workforce, focus on the skills you have acquired from your work experience. For example, you might explain that you "maintained good customer relations" and "presented a positive corporate image" in your job at a fast-food restaurant. If you are changing careers—from computer programming to advertising, for example— revise your résumé accordingly.

►►►Sample résumés:
Traditional, 508
Scannable, 510

Tell the truth on your résumé, but cast the information in a positive light. Also think about what you have done that is appropriate for this particular job. You may have nearly forgotten the tutoring you did at your campus literacy center when you were a first-year student, but that experience is relevant if you are applying for a teaching position.

1. Traditional print résumés

More about ►►►
Document design,
176–85 (ch. 9)

A résumé (Figure 24.4, p. 508) arranges information in standard categories and a familiar sequence to make it easy for prospective employers to glean your qualifications quickly. This is not the place to demonstrate your flair for creative writing or flamboyant design. (The

- Leave plenty of white space; avoid a crowded look to make your résumé more readable.
- Use a slightly different design for your name and contact information to make your résumé more attractive and attention getting (see Figure 24.4).
- Use a table format for other sections, aligning items on the left and setting off headings in boldface or capitals. You may want to use the résumé template that comes with your word processing software or add

other design elements. However, be careful not to overdesign the document—keep it simple and easy to read.
- Single-space all sections, and put an extra line of space between them.
- Proofread your résumé until you are sure the document has no grammatical or typographical errors.
- Use a standard font, such as Times New Roman, and print your résumé on 8½ × 11–inch white or off-white paper. Use black ink only.

Quick Reference box above includes some basic guidelines for designing and formatting a print résumé.) Here are some tips to help you keep the content of your résumé on track:

- Arrange each section in reverse chronological order, with most recent job or degree first. If there are major gaps in your work history, or if you have changed careers, you may want to organize your résumé according to the skills that are particularly relevant to the job you are applying for. Keep in mind, however, that most employers prefer to read résumés in reverse chronological order.

- Use active verbs and parallel construction throughout. For example, if you use *managed* for the first verb, you might use *organized* and *researched* thereafter.

- Limit your résumé to one page unless your work experience is extensive. Most recent college graduates should write a one-page résumé.

More about ▶▶▶
Active vs. passive voice, 560–61
Parallelism, 539–48 (ch. 27)

Most résumes include the following sections:

Contact Information List your full name, mailing address, telephone number, and email address at the top of the résumé. If you have separate home and school addresses, give them both, but make it clear to the recipient (perhaps in your cover letter) how and when you can be contacted at each location.

Name and contact
information set
off from rest
of résumé

Sonja Jacques
7716 W. Birchwood Street
Chicago, IL 60648
(312) 555–1212

OBJECTIVE: To obtain an assistant to curator position at a museum

Education first,
as typical for
recent graduate

EDUCATION: **B.S., University of Illinois, Chicago Circle, June 2009.**
History major; International studies minor
GPA: 3.8 (on a 4-point scale)

**Summer studies in Museum Curatorship, James Cook
University, North Queensland, Australia, 2007.**
Courses in artifact preservation, program management, museum funding.

EMPLOYMENT: **Workstudy employee, UIC University Library, fall 2007–spring 2009.**
Trained workstudy employees in library policies; shelved returned books.

Intern, Smithsonian Institution, Washington DC, summer 2008.
Conducted museum tours for school groups; catalogued textual
archives; assisted researchers.

Sales clerk, Moheiser's, Park Ridge, IL, summer 2005–spring 2007.
Organized inventory; waited on customers; learned apparel business.

**SPECIAL
SKILLS AND
HONORS:**
Fluent in French.
Tutored 7th graders in French, Ebinger School, Chicago, IL, 2007–2008.
Experience with Microsoft Word, PageMaker, and Internet research.
President, Phi Kappa Phi Honor Society, UIC chapter, 2008.
Deans' list, 2008–2009.

REFERENCES: Available on request.

**FIGURE 24.4 Sample
printed résumé**

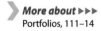 **More about ▶▶▶**
Portfolios, 111–14

Career Objective Indicate the specific position you are applying for or
your career objective. Instead of *position in publishing,* say *entry-level
editorial position in children's publishing.*

Education List the degrees you hold (college and above), the institutions that granted them, the date you received them (or anticipate
receiving them), and your major and minor. Mention any honors such
as being on the dean's list, and include your grade-point average if it
is high (say, 3.5 or above on a 4-point scale). Include certificates, such
as teaching certification.

Getting It
Across   **Applying for Jobs**

Your job application letter and résumé may get you in the door of a company, but you still need to prepare for interviews. These tips may help:

- If you have not already done so, research the company and the position. Then come up with some relevant questions to ask the potential employer. Show enthusiasm for the job and the organization.
- Think in advance about the questions you might be asked, and write out potential answers. For instance, what will you say if the employer asks about your weaknesses? Have an honest answer ready, but point out your strengths as well.
- If the employer asks for a portfolio, which is typical for writing and design positions, develop it online or on a CD or DVD so that you can hand it to the employer during the interview.

Employment History Give the names and addresses of employers, titles of jobs, primary duties, and dates of employment.

Skills, Awards, or Memberships List computer skills (such as proficiency in *PageMaker, Excel,* or *Dreamweaver*) and other skills that are relevant to the job, such as fluency in a foreign language. Include awards and memberships that are pertinent. For example, if you were applying for a job at a community organization, you would want to state that you served as a volunteer and on the board of directors of Big Brothers Big Sisters.

References Provide names, mailing addresses, phone numbers, and email addresses of three to six people who have agreed to serve as your references, or at the bottom of your résumé or say *References available on request.* In either case, be sure to obtain permission to list someone as a reference in advance.

2. Scannable or electronic résumés

Employers may request a scannable or electronic résumé (Figure 24.5, p. 510)—one that is sent within the text of an email message or as an attachment—so they can scan it to include in a database. To meet this requirement, a traditional print résumé needs to be revised and redesigned:

- Position all copy flush with the left margin. Use only capitals to set off headings. Eliminate italics, boldface, and all other design or format features.

Sonja Jacques
7716 W. Birchwood Street
Chicago, IL 60648
(312) 555–1212

> **Keywords for employer's database search**

KEYWORDS: curator, curatorship, assistant, French, museum, archives, artifact, research, researchers

OBJECTIVE
Assistant to curator at museum

> **Headings set in all capitals, flush left, with no boldface, italics, or other design features**

EDUCATION
B.S. University of Illinois, Chicago Circle, June 2009.
History major; International studies minor
GPA: 3.8 (on a 4-point scale)

Summer studies in Museum Curatorship, James Cook University,
North Queensland, Australia, 2007.
Courses in artifact preservation, program management, museum funding.

> **Nouns used instead of verbs (*trainer* not *trained*) throughout**

EMPLOYMENT
Workstudy employee, UIC University Library, fall 2007–spring 2009.
Trainer of workstudy employees in library policies; shelver of
returned books.

Intern, Smithsonian Institution, Washington, DC, summer 2008.
Conductor of museum tours for school groups; cataloguer of textual
archives; assistant to researchers.

Sales clerk, Moheiser's, Park Ridge, IL, summer 2005–spring 2007.
Inventory organization; customer service; experience with apparel business.

SPECIAL SKILLS AND HONORS
Fluent in French
Tutor of 7th graders in French, Ebinger School, Chicago, IL, 2007–2008
Experience with Microsoft Word, PageMaker, and Internet research
President, Phi Kappa Phi Honor Society, UIC chapter, 2008
Deans' list, 2008–2009

REFERENCES
Available on request

FIGURE 24.5 Sample scannable résumé

- Wherever possible, change your skills from verbs (*supervised*) to concise nouns (*supervisor of*). If you have the job description, try to use the keywords it mentions. (Employers frequently use keywords to screen out inappropriate applications.)

- Below your contact information, list keywords from your résumé, such as titles of positions you have held (*assistant*) or skills you possess (*French*).

- When your scannable résumé is complete, email it to yourself first, to make sure it is error-free and that the layout is readable.

NOTE Conventions for electronic or scannable résumés change over time and may vary from company to company. Check with your prospective employer to make sure your résumé fits the company's requirements.

↑ Make It **Your Own**

Find an appealing job ad in a local paper, or find a posting in your school's job center. Then draft a résumé for the position following the recommendations in the section above.

Work **Together** ◁

In groups of three or four, review the résumés group members drafted in the Make It Your Own exercise above. How could you rephrase the career objectives to tailor them more specifically to the job description? How might you revise the résumé to make it more appealing to the target audience?

24f   **Writing Reports and Proposals**

As a student, you may have written reports about research you have conducted. You may have written proposals as well, perhaps suggesting to your college administration that campus parking be expanded. In this case, you would have done some research on parking problems to back up your suggestions. When you write as an employee or as a volunteer, reports and proposals have these same attributes: They provide information for a specific purpose, they usually involve research and analysis, and they may suggest some kind of change. Proposals, in particular, offer solutions for problems and seek funding for the project.

Reports and proposals may vary greatly in length, from a single page to more than a hundred pages. Long reports and proposals usually follow specific formats (which are dictated by the organization you are writing for), they include a table of contents, and they are divided into sections (with subheadings) such as the following:

- **Abstract, executive summary, or overview.** A one-paragraph summary of the entire report or proposal that highlights

> *Sample research report* ▶▶▶
> "The Power of Wardrobe," Heather DeGroot, 389–400
> "Nature Versus Nurture," Robyn Worthington, 479–86

its purpose, major findings, and conclusions or recommended actions

- **Introduction or statement of the problem.** A discussion of the topic or problem that explains succinctly what is at issue and why it is important

More about ▶▶▶
Choosing the appropriate information graphic, 81–84
Revising information graphics, 86–88
Persuasive arguments, 142–43
Tone, 16–17, 143, 567, 575

- **Research methods and results.** A clear description of how you gathered information and what you discovered from your research; if appropriate, use graphs or tables to bolster your written explanation.

- **Conclusion or proposed solution.** A discussion of the relevance of your report or of the specific solution you are proposing; for a proposal, be sure to help readers see that your solution is preferable to other possible solutions and that it is feasible in terms of financing, staffing, or other potential roadblocks.

(The cover and first page of the executive summary of a report on school crime and safety appear in Figure 24.6 below.)

As you draft a report or proposal, maintain an objective tone, and include only relevant and reliable information. Keep your purpose and audience in mind. It is not unusual for reports and proposals to be read by many different people (such as managers, sales representatives, and accountants). When this is the case, think about their various concerns and the questions they will want answered. For example, if you are

FIGURE 24.6 Sample report The full report appears online at <nces.ed.gov/pubs2008/2008021.pdf>

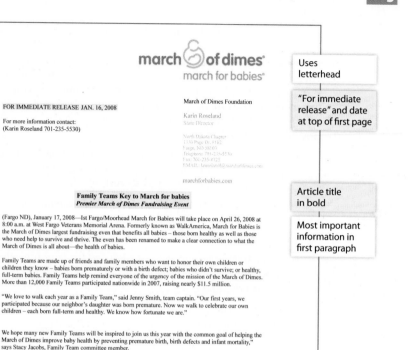

FIGURE 24.7 Sample press release (Printed with the permission of Karin Roseland, North Dakota March of Dimes)

proposing that the sales staff have larger, more expensive cars, how will you justify the extra cost to the financial experts?

24g Writing Press Releases

Press, or *media, releases,* like the one shown in Figure 24.7 above, are brief articles that announce events to newspapers, magazines, and online media outlets. If you work in the advertising or marketing department of an organization, part of your job might be writing press releases. Similarly, you could write them as a volunteer for a local charity or sporting club. Whatever organization they are written for, press releases follow a standard format because reporters and editors need to read them quickly and decide whether or not to use the information they contain. Here are some guidelines to follow when drafting a press release:

- Use your organization's letterhead, if possible, and include all pertinent contact information (address, phone number, email address, website URL, and so on).

- At the top of the first page, type *For Immediate Release* and the date.

- Include an article title in bold or capital letters.

- To enable editors to cut your release for length easily, put the most important information up front and less important details toward the end.

- Use an objective tone, and make sure the content is factual and newsworthy.

Make It **Your Own**

Draft a press release announcing a student activity on campus (real or imagined). Make sure to include the most important information in the first paragraph and to provide information that is newsworthy.

Work **Together**

With a classmate, role-play the position of editor of a local newspaper. Would you publish the press release your partner wrote in the Make It Your Own exercise above? Why or why not? Then trade roles.

Part Seven

Style
Matters

25 Writing Concisely

Young children just learning to play soccer tend to swarm around the ball, each one duplicating the effort of the others, so that they move the ball toward the goal haltingly. In practiced teams like those shown here, however, players work together efficiently to control the ball. Each player counts; none wastefully duplicates the work of another.

Wordy writing is like young children's soccer. Sentences crowded with unnecessary words compel readers to separate what matters from what does not. ***Concise*** writing, in contrast, is like the play of a practiced team. Every word counts; none duplicates the work of another. Consider an example:

Writing
Responsibly   "Concise" versus "Brief"

Effective writing should be concise, but not necessarily brief. Concise writing provides readers with all the information they need without distracting bloat, but it does not skimp on essential detail. A complex thought may be expressible only in a lengthy sentence. Don't shortchange readers—or your ideas—by omitting detail needed to convey your thoughts fully.

> **More about ▶▶▶**
> Sentence length and
> variety, 551–57

WORDY	The fact is that there is only one thing that should make us experience the emotion of fear and that is to all intents and purposes the emotion of fear itself.
CONCISE	The only thing we have to fear is fear itself.
	—Franklin Delano Roosevelt, first inaugural address

The first sentence is crowded with wordy expressions (*the fact is*), redundancies (*the emotion of fear*), and roundabout constructions (*there is only one thing*). The second, concise and direct, helped rally Americans to confront the Great Depression.

Quick **Reference** ➡   **Strategies for Writing Concisely**

- Cut wordy expressions. (517)
- Cut ineffective or unnecessary repetition. (519)
- Revise roundabout constructions. (521)
- Consolidate phrases, clauses, and sentences. (523)

Most of us write inadvertently wordy first drafts. As you revise, look for opportunities to tighten your prose. The Quick Reference box above offers some strategies.

25a Eliminating Wordy Expressions

When we begin to draft, we sometimes resort to common but wordy expressions from everyday speech. Such expressions can clutter your writing, and you should prune them as you revise.

connect
mhconnectcomposition.com
Additional resources: QL25001,
QL25002

 ESL **Conciseness** What one culture considers wordy, another may consider elegant. Not only culture but also context affects what readers expect: In literary contexts and even in some personal writing, U.S. readers sometimes appreciate rich, expansive sentences. In academic contexts, however, U.S. readers usually favor writing that is concise and to the point.

1. Empty phrases

Some wordy expressions, like *to all intents and purposes, in fact, the fact is,* and *in the process of,* carry no information, and you can delete them:

> ▶ The passengers were ~~in the process of~~ boarding the plane when
>
>   ~~in fact~~ the flight was canceled.

Similarly, intensifiers—modifiers like *absolutely, actually, definitely, really,* and *totally*—may add little meaning to the words they modify.

> ▶ The tourists were ~~absolutely~~ thrilled. None of them had ~~actually~~ seen
>
>   a polar bear before.

Phrases built around words like *aspect, character, kind, manner,* and *type* are also often mere filler.

> ▶ They ~~are the kind of people who~~ have always ~~behaved in a~~ been generous.
>
>   ~~generous manner.~~

2. Roundabout expressions

Some wordy expressions are roundabout, saying in many words what is better said with one.

Roundabout Expression	Concise Revision
at the present time	now (or delete entirely)
at that point in time	then (or delete entirely)
until such time as	until
at all times	always
at no time	never
most of the time	usually
in this day and age	today
due to the fact that	because
in spite of the fact that	although, even though
has the ability to	can
in the event that	if
in the neighborhood of	around

> ▶ ~~Due to the fact that~~ the housing market is ~~weak at this point in time,~~ Because   weak,
>
>   many homeowners are waiting to sell ~~until such time as~~ conditions
>
>   improve.

Tech

Style Checkers and Wordiness

Although they might occasionally flag an inappropriate roundabout construction, computer style checkers are generally unreliable judges of wordi- ness. Rely on readers—yourself, your instructor, writing center tutors, your friends—to help you determine what is and is not acceptable.

3. Redundant expressions

Some wordy expressions are ***redundant,*** stringing together two or more words that convey the same meaning.

Redundant Expression	Concise Revision
blue in color	blue
in close proximity	close
each and every	each (or every)
end result	result
few/many in number	few/many
final outcome	outcome
past history	history
plans for the future/ future plans	plans
repeat again	repeat
round in shape	round
sum total	total

▶ The candidate's mistakes during the campaign were ~~few in number,~~ *few,*
but they cost her the election, and she plans ~~for the future~~ never to
repeat them ~~again.~~

connect
mhconnectcomposition.com
Additional resources: QL25003, QL25004, QL25005, QL25006

25b   Eliminating Ineffective or Unnecessary Repetition

Ineffective or unnecessary repetition can dull your prose and tire your readers.

1. Repetition and redundancy

As you revise your writing, look for words repeated unnecessarily, whether exactly or in varied form.

> **More about ▶▶▶**
Transitions, 61–62
Repetition for emphasis, 559
Parallelism, 539–48
Avoiding ambiguity, 695

Getting It Across   **Intentional Repetition**

Repetition is not all bad. Writers often use it deliberately to provide clear transitions and—as the repetition of *war* in the following example illustrates—for emphasis, to maintain parallelism, and to avoid ambiguity.

> Both parties deprecated war; but one of them would make war rather than let the nation survive; and the other would accept war rather than let it perish. And the war came.
>
> —Abraham Lincoln, from his second inaugural address, March 4, 1865

DRAFT   The author's informative overview provides particularly revealing information about the Johnson administration.

REVISION   The author's informative overview is particularly revealing about the Johnson administration.

Redundancy, another form of unnecessary repetition, is not restricted to the kind of stock phrases listed in the previous section; it happens whenever one expression duplicates the meaning of another.

▶ The portrait is ~~a likeness~~ of Gertrude Stein.

A portrait *is* a likeness of a particular person.

2. Elliptical constructions

Sometimes grammatically necessary words can be omitted from a sentence when the context makes their meaning and function clear, and you can take advantage of such ***elliptical constructions*** to tighten your prose.

▶ On Saturday afternoons I went to the double feature, and on Sunday ~~mornings I went~~ *mornings,* to church.

connect
mhconnectcomposition.com
Online exercise: QL25101

EXERCISE 25.1 Eliminating wordy expressions and unnecessary repetition

Edit the following sentences to eliminate wordy expressions and unnecessary repetition.

EXAMPLE

The ~~beginning of the~~ Harry Potter books *begin with Harry's discovery* ~~start when Harry discovers the fact~~ that he has magical abilities.

1. When the seventh and final book of J. K. Rowling's popular series of books about Harry Potter, called *Harry Potter and the Deathly Hallows,* was released in July 2007, people everywhere all over the world lined up outside bookstores to buy a copy due to the fact that the series is so popular and this was the last book in the series.

2. Like the other six books, this one also recounts the really exciting adventures of Harry Potter and his wizard friends Ron and Hermione as they battle the forces of evil and try to save the world from evil.

3. Those people who read carefully and know about such things can find references in the Harry Potter series to other writers who wrote before Rowling, such as the writers Dante and George Orwell.

4. In spite of the fact that Rowling's work has the ability to impress many people and is popular, the critic Harold Bloom complained that Rowling's style is very repetitive and also complained that she used too many clichés that she did not need to use in order to tell her story.

5. Others have complained about contradictions in the books that are small but really annoying to readers, such as the fact that in spite of all of the amazing spells everyone can make, no one makes a spell to get rid of Eloise's acne.

25c Avoiding Roundabout Constructions

Certain common sentence patterns tend toward wordiness and indirection. These include *expletive constructions,* sentences in the *passive voice,* and sentences built around nouns derived from verbs.

1. Expletive constructions (*there are . . . , it is . . .*)

Expletives are an inverted construction in which *there* or *it* precedes a form of the verb *to be* and the subject follows the verb. (Do not confuse *expletive* in this sense with its other sense of *swear word* or *curse.*) Revising to eliminate expletives will often make a sentence more direct and concise.

> **More about ▶▶▶**
> Expletive constructions, 739–40

Getting It Across   Expletives

There are, of course, occasions when expletives are effective, as in this famous opening line:

It is a truth universally acknowledged, that a single man in possession of a good fortune must be in want of a wife.

—Jane Austen, *Pride and Prejudice* (1813)

DRAFT There are several measures that institutions can take to curb plagiarism.

REVISION Institutions can take several measures to curb plagiarism.

2. Passive voice

More about ▶▶▶
Passive vs. active voice, 560–61, 682–84

In an active-voice sentence, the subject performs the action of the verb. In a passive-voice sentence, the subject receives the action.

ACTIVE subj. verb
    Jared photographed the bear.

PASSIVE subj. verb
    The bear was photographed by Jared.

The passive voice often lends itself to wordiness. Removing it will usually make your sentences more concise and direct.

DRAFT A motion was proposed by the committee chair that the vote be delayed until the cost of the program could be accurately determined by the finance subcommittee.

REVISION The committee chair proposed to delay the vote until the finance subcommittee could accurately determine the program's cost.

3. Sentences built around nouns derived from verbs

As you revise, look for sentences built around nouns derived from verbs. Substituting the verb for the noun will often produce a more concise and vivid result.

DRAFT noun
    The destruction of the town by the tornado was complete.

REVISION verb
    The tornado destroyed the town.

→ **EXERCISE 25.2 Eliminating roundabout constructions**

Edit the following sentences to eliminate roundabout constructions.

connect

mhconnectcomposition.com
Online exercise: QL25102

EXAMPLE

Sleep deprivaton
~~It is sleep deprivation that~~ is a serious problem for many
       ^

college students.

1. In college, it is students who must plan their schedules and extracurricular activities carefully so they get enough sleep.

2. There are several sleep-related consequences that college students face if they do not manage their time.

3. Schoolwork is more difficult for students who are sleep deprived.

4. The reduction in the ability to concentrate as a result of inadequate sleep is serious.

5. Illness is also more frequent for sleep-deprived college students due to the fact that lack of sleep depletes the immune system.

6. The damage to the mind and body caused by lack of sleep is significant.

25d Consolidating Phrases, Clauses, and Sentences

You can often make your writing more concise by reducing **clauses** to **phrases** and clauses or phrases to single words.

> **Clause** A word group with a subject and a predicate (620–23)
> **Phrase** A group of related words that lacks a subject, predicate, or both (617–20)

DRAFT	Scientists cite glaciers, which have been retreating, and the polar ice caps, which have been shrinking, as evidence of global climate change.
REVISION	Scientists cite retreating glaciers and shrinking polar ice caps as evidence of global climate change.

Sometimes you can also combine two or more sentences into one more concise, effective sentence.

DRAFT	Scientists note that glaciers have been retreating and the polar ice caps have been shrinking. Most of them now agree that these phenomena are evidence of global climate change.

REVISION   Most scientists now agree that retreating glaciers and the shrinking polar ice caps are evidence of global climate change.

→ **EXERCISE 25.3 Combining sentences for conciseness**

Reduce clauses to phrases and phrases to words as appropriate to combine each of the following passages into a single concise sentence.

EXAMPLE

Scientists in the United States have been analyzing the results of studies that connect obesity and sleep deprivation. Scientists in the United Kingdom have also been analyzing data about sleep and obesity.

Scientists in the United States and the United Kingdom have been studying the connection between obesity and sleep deprivation.

1. Some scientists conclude from their data that lack of sleep can be the cause of weight gain. Other scientists conclude from the same data that obesity and related health problems are more likely to cause lack of sleep.

2. Scientists in the United Kingdom and scientists in the United States worked together on one study, and they found as a result of their research that there is a relationship between sleep and hormones that control appetite. In that study they compared two groups of people. In one group were people who sleep for less than five hours a night. In the other group were people who sleep for more than eight hours a night.

3. The study found that people who sleep for less than five hours a night have 15 percent more of the hormone ghrelin, which increases appetite. The study found that people who sleep for less than five hours a night also have 15 percent less of the hormone leptin, which suppresses appetite.

4. Another study was reported by Swiss scientists. They studied 496 people between twenty-seven and forty years of age. The study lasted for thirteen years. The study found that twenty-seven-year-olds who slept for only a "short duration" were much more likely to be obese than forty-year-olds who got the same amount of sleep. This study found that the connection between sleep and obesity started to diminish after age thirty-four.

5. Some people who suffer from obesity also suffer from sleep apnea. Sleep apnea is a sleep disorder associated with obesity. It causes people to wake more often and get less sleep. Some scientists argue that this can explain the correlation between obesity and shorter sleep duration in some people.

→ EXERCISE 25.4 Editing for conciseness

connect
mhconnectcomposition.com
Online exercise: QL25104

Use the strategies described in this chapter to make the following passage concise and direct.

It is a fact that citizen, or amateur, scientists have the ability to contribute to the work of professional scientists. They can be of use in many different scientific fields of endeavor. For example, in the area of biology, citizen scientists can report the observations that they make. They have the ability to report observations about bird migration, seasonal change, and other factors that they can view in the vicinity of their own backyards. The widespread, detailed data provided by amateurs can help scientists bring their studies to completion.

In the area of astronomy, discoveries that are very significant have been made by amateurs. These include the very first sightings of many comets. They also include important observations of variable stars. Variable stars are stars that change in brightness over time. There are organizations and even awards for amateur astronomers. This shows how important their work is.

↑ Make It **Your Own**

Reread a paper that you have recently written or are now working on. Which sentences could be made more concise, and how?

Work **Together** ←

Working with two or three classmates, read each other's work on a recent paper or a paper in progress. Which of your classmates' sentences could be made more concise, and how? Compare your results with those of the others in the group. Then reflect on the exercise: What have they seen that you did not, and vice versa? How might this collaborative activity help you revise your own work in the future?

26 Using Coordination and Subordination

Look up as you enter the East Wing of the National Gallery of Art in Washington, DC, and a dramatic sight confronts you. Hanging from the skylight over the building's large atrium is a giant sculpture by Alexander Calder—a 920-pound, 76-foot-long mobile made of multicolored metal rods and plates—that despite its size and weight sweeps gracefully overhead. Calder achieved this graceful effect by carefully coordinating elements of equal weight, balancing heavy elements with a series of lighter subordinate elements that descend in a branching cascade from the cable that secures the mobile to the ceiling. The subordinated and coordinated elements combine to convey Calder's visual message.

Writers can similarly use coordination and subordination to craft sentences that best convey their intended meaning. ***Coordination*** establishes the equal weight or importance of two or more sentence elements.

equal weight

▶ We entered the museum, and a dramatic sight confronted us.

equal weight

▶ The mobile is made of rods and plates.

Tech

Style Checkers and Coordination and Subordination

Using coordination and subordination requires you to figure out the logical relationships among the ideas you want to express and to decide on their relative importance, so that you can make these relationships clear to your audience. A computer style checker cannot do that for you.

Subordination establishes the supporting or modifying role of one or more sentence elements.

▸ Heavy elements balance lighter elements that descend in a branching

main idea — modifying subordinate

idea — modifying subordinate idea

cascade from the cable that secures the mobile to the ceiling.

connect
mhconnectcomposition.com
Additional resources: QL26001

26a   Coordinating Terms, Phrases, and Clauses

Coordination can link or contrast two or more equally important terms, *phrases,* or *clauses.*

1. Terms and phrases

To coordinate terms and phrases requires either a coordinating conjunction (such as *and, but, for, nor, or, so,* or *yet*) or a correlative conjunction (such as *both . . . and, either . . . or,* or *neither . . . nor*). Usually no punctuation separates two coordinated words or phrases.

▸ Both Steven Spielberg and George Romero attended the New York Film Academy.

▸ London's Theatre Royal in Drury Lane has staged performances by the Shakespearean actor Edmund Kean and by the Monty Python comedy troupe.

Commas usually separate more than two terms or phrases in a coordinated series.

▸ From John Webster's point of view in 1612, the greatest playwright might have been George Chapman, William Shakespeare, or Ben Jonson.

Phrase A group of related words that lacks a subject, a predicate, or both (617–20) **Clause** A word group with a subject and predicate (620–22). An *independent clause* can stand alone as a sentence, a *subordinate clause* cannot.

More about ▸▸▸
Coordinating and correlative conjunctions, 610

More about ▸▸▸
Punctuating terms and phrases, 688–89

2. Independent clauses

More about ▶▶▶
Punctuating coordinated independent clauses, 637–45

To coordinate two independent clauses, use a comma and a coordinating conjunction, a semicolon, or a semicolon and a conjunctive adverb such as *for example, however, in addition,* or *therefore.*

▶ Today we consider Shakespeare to be the greatest English playwright, but his contemporaries regarded him as just one among many.

▶ Norah Jones's debut CD was a huge success; it sold millions of copies.

▶ The play received glowing reviews and won a Tony award; however, it closed after only a short run.

26b Coordinating Effectively

Coordinating elements in a sentence gives them equal importance or weight. How you coordinate those elements shows your readers the relationship among them.

1. Conjunctions and their meaning

Conjunctions differ in meaning, and some can have more than one meaning depending on context (see the Quick Reference box on the next page).

A conjunction whose meaning does not match the relationship between coordinated elements might confuse readers and obscure the writer's point. In the following sentence, for example, changing *and* to *but* reveals what the writer intended to emphasize: the contrast between Einstein's youth and his accomplishments.

▶ Einstein was still young, ~~and~~ 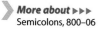 he had revolutionized physics.

More about ▶▶▶
Semicolons, 800–06

2. Independent clauses joined with a semicolon

Use a semicolon to join two independent clauses that have a logical connection to each other. The second clause can contrast with the first, provide an example of it, or give a reason for it.

CONTRAST	During the polar winter, the sun never rises; during the polar summer, it never sets.
EXAMPLE	The movie was a financial success; it set a record for opening-day box office receipts.
EXPLANATION	She wanted to be sure to have the assignment done for tomorrow; Spanish is her favorite class.

Quick Reference ➡ Conjunctions and Their Meaning

Meaning	Conjunctions	Examples
addition	*and, both . . . and*	*Both* advances in ship design *and* the introduction of the magnetic compass helped make possible the European voyages of discovery.
sequence	*and*	The lawyer turned *and* faced the jury.
cause and effect	*so, for,* sometimes *and*	The housing market has softened, *so* sellers have had to lower their prices.
choice	*or, whether . . . or, either . . . or, nor, neither . . . nor*	Tournament games can be played on neutral courts *or* home courts. *Neither* ESPN *nor* any other network wants to show empty arenas.
contrast	*but, yet*	The police raided the house, *but* the suspect had fled. The poll indicates support for the law *yet* doubt about its chance for passage.
	not just . . . but, not only . . . but also	*Not just* the NCAA *but* the teams and fans should have a voice in the decision. [In addition to contrasting the coordinated elements, these conjunctions emphasize one over the other, suggesting that the first is commonplace and expected, the second new and noteworthy.]

When you join clauses with a semicolon and a conjunctive adverb, the conjunctive adverb specifies the relationship.

▶ During the polar winter the sun never rises; in contrast, during the polar summer, it never sets.

3. Inappropriate coordination

Coordination is inappropriate when it combines elements that are not of equivalent importance or weight. The following sentence, for example, puts an incidental fact—Einstein's year of birth—on an equal footing with a statement about his early accomplishments. The revision subordinates the minor information in a modifying phrase.

INAPPROPRIATE COORDINATION	Albert Einstein was born in 1879, and by 1905 he had published four important scientific papers.
REVISED	Albert Einstein, born in 1879, had published four important scientific papers by 1905.

4. Excessive coordination

In everyday speech, people often coordinate long strings of sentences with *and* and other conjunctions. What is acceptable in speech, however, quickly becomes tedious and confusing in academic writing. As you edit, look for such *excessive coordination.*

EXCESSIVE COORDINATION	Albert Einstein was born in Germany in 1879 and graduated from the Swiss Federal Polytechnic School in Zurich in 1900, but then he was unemployed for two years before a family friend helped him secure a job at the Swiss patent office in Bern, and it was a job that left him plenty of time to pursue his scientific interests, so in 1905, known as his "miracle year," he published four papers, and they revolutionized physics.
REVISED	Albert Einstein, who was born in Germany in 1879, graduated from the Swiss Federal Polytechnic School in Zurich in 1900. He spent the next two years unemployed, until a family friend helped him secure a job at the Swiss patent office in Bern. The job left him plenty of time to pursue his scientific interests, and in 1905, his "miracle year," Einstein published four papers that revolutionized physics.

connect
mhconnectcomposition.com
Online exercise: QL26101

EXERCISE 26.1 Eliminating inappropriate and excessive coordination

Edit the following sentences to eliminate excessive or inappropriate coordination.

EXAMPLE

Your parents probably encouraged you to start the day with a good

breakfast, ~~and~~ right. The
breakfast, ~~so~~ now a five-year study suggests they were ~~right, but the~~

study found that the more likely adolescents are to eat breakfast, the

less likely they are to be overweight.

1. The study was conducted in the public schools of the Minneapolis–St. Paul area, and researchers found that there was a direct relationship between eating breakfast and body mass index (BMI), yet the more often an adolescent had breakfast, the lower was his or her BMI.

2. The adolescents studied were an average of fifteen years old at the start of the study, and those who ate breakfast consumed more carbohydrates and fiber, received fewer calories from fat, so got more exercise.

3. The relationship between breakfast eating and BMI was consistent throughout the study's entire five years, but the researchers controlled for age, sex, race, socioeconomic status, smoking, and concerns about diet and weight.

4. Girls were more likely to skip breakfast regularly, so boys were more likely to eat it.

5. The study only observed an association between breakfast-eating habits and body mass, yet it did not prove a causal relationship, and nevertheless, one of the authors said that the research provided some useful guidance for healthy eating.

6. He noted that eating a healthy breakfast would encourage healthy eating for the rest of the day, yet it might help to lessen the urge for fast food or vending-machine food, and parents could also contribute, he added, by setting a good example and having a good breakfast themselves.

26c   Distinguishing Primary from Secondary Information with Subordination

Whereas coordination allows you to link equal ideas, subordination allows you to distinguish primary claims from supporting examples, explanations, and details. Putting information in a subordinate structure de-emphasizes it.

▶ |——— main idea ———| |——— main idea ———|
   The evidence is conclusive; my client is innocent.

   Coordination gives each idea equal weight.

▶ |——— subordinated idea ———| |——— main idea ———|
   As the evidence proves conclusively, my client is innocent.

   The emphasis is on the client.

▶ |——— main idea ———| |——— subordinated idea ———|
   The evidence proves conclusively that my client is innocent.

   The emphasis is on the evidence.

Subordination can also clarify the logical relationship among a series of ideas. The revised version of the following passage clarifies the chronological relationship among the facts listed in the draft, and it emphasizes the most significant fact—that comic books did not become widely popular until 1938.

DRAFT	The first comic books appeared in the early 1920s. Nearly four decades earlier, comic strips had begun appearing in the major newspapers. Comic books did not gain widespread popularity until June 1938. Writer Jerry Siegel and artist Joe Shuster debuted their character Superman in June 1938.
REVISED	Although comic books first appeared in the 1920s, which was nearly four decades after comic strips had begun to appear in the major newspapers, they did not gain widespread popularity until June 1938, when writer Jerry Siegel and artist Joe Shuster debuted their character Superman.

1. Subordinating techniques

To subordinate information within a sentence, put it in a subordinate clause, reduce it to a modifying phrase or word, or include it in an appositive.

> **More about ▶▶▶**
> Subordinating
> conjunctions and
> relative pronouns,
> 620–22, 628–29

- **Subordinate clause.** Subordinate clauses begin with a **subordinating word,** usually either a subordinating conjunction (such as *after, although, because, before, that,* or *when*) or a relative pronoun (such as *that, what, which, who,* or *whose*).

  ▶ Hatshepsut was one of only a few women to rule ancient Egypt. *, whose reign was from 1473 to 1458 BCE,* ~~Her reign was from 1473 to 1458 BCE.~~

- **Modifying phrase or word.**

  ▶ *Enticed by months of clever advance marketing, millions* ~~Millions~~ of people bought the new multimedia smartphone within days of its release. ~~They had been enticed by months of clever advance marketing.~~

> **Appositive** A noun
> or noun phrase that
> renames a preceding
> noun or noun phrase
> (617–18)

- **Appositive.**

  ▶ The sculpture *, a giant mobile made of multicolored metal rods and plates,* sweeps gracefully overhead. ~~It is a giant mobile made of multicolored metal rods and plates.~~

Reference ➡ **Subordination and Punctuation**

In most cases, a comma follows a subordinate structure that begins an independent clause.

> After the 1965 Newport festival, fans complained about Dylan's switch from acoustic to electric guitar.

A subordinate structure that interrupts or ends an independent clause may or may not be set off with punctuation, depending on whether the information in it is **essential** (restrictive) or **nonessential** (nonrestrictive). A structure is essential if it specifically identifies the word or words it modifies. No punctuation

sets off interrupting or concluding restrictive structures.

> Athletes <u>who win Olympic gold medals</u> often earn money by endorsing products.

A structure is nonessential if the meaning or identity of the word or words it modifies is clear without it. A comma or other punctuation usually sets off interrupting or concluding nonessential structures. (See pp. 791–93.)

> Michael Phelps, <u>who won eight gold medals in 2008</u>, is a published author.

2. Choosing a subordinating term

Understanding the meaning of subordinating terms is essential to using subordination effectively (see the Quick Reference box on the next page).

Use a subordinating term whose meaning matches the relationship you intend to convey between a subordinate element and the element it modifies. The following sentence uses a term referring to cause in a context that calls for a term referring to purpose. Revising requires either changing the term or rewording the clause.

DRAFT	He ran for mayor because he could bring the town's budget under control.
REVISED	He ran for mayor so that he could bring the town's budget under control.
	or
	He ran for mayor because he wanted to bring the town's budget under control.

Be particularly careful with the subordinating conjunctions *as* and *since,* which can refer ambiguously to both cause and time.

DRAFT	As she was applying the last coat of varnish, Lisa declared the restoration complete.

Quick Reference ➡ **Subordinating Terms and Their Meaning**

Meaning	Conjunctions	Examples
time	*after, as, before, since, until, when, whenever, while*	Comics grew in popularity *after* Superman appeared in 1938.
place	*where, wherever*	Home is *where* the hearth is.
cause or effect	*as, because, since, so that*	*Because* of the water main break, traffic came to a standstill.
condition	*even if, if, provided that, since, unless*	*If* you finish the job today, you can take a vacation day tomorrow.
purpose	*in order that, so that, that*	She finished the job quickly *so that* she could have a day off.
identification	*that, when, where, which, who*	Adichie is the author *who* won the Orange Broadband Prize for fiction in 2007.
contrast or comparison	*as, although, as if, even though, though, whereas*	*Although* Einstein was still a young man, he had revolutionized physics.

REVISED   *While* she was applying the last coat of varnish, Lisa declared the restoration complete.

or

Because she was applying the last coat of varnish, Lisa declared the restoration complete.

3. Avoiding illogical subordination

State key ideas in an independent clause, and put illustrations, examples, explanations, and details in subordinate structures. Illogically subordinating a main idea to a supporting idea can confuse readers. The following sentence subordinates the idea of Einstein's accomplishments to the idea of his youth, illogically implying that he was young in spite of his accomplishments rather than accomplished in spite of his youth.

ILLOGICAL SUBORDINATION   Einstein was still young, although he had revolutionized physics.

REVISED   Although he was still young, Einstein had revolutionized physics.

4. Avoiding excessive subordination

Excessive subordination—stringing together too many subordinate structures—can make a sentence hard to read. The string of subordinate structures in the following sentence leaves readers unsure by the end where they began. The revision into two sentences clarifies the information the writer wants to convey.

EXCESSIVE SUBORDINATION	San Francisco, although generally an ideal habitat for peregrine falcons, is not entirely so, as became clear recently when rescuers had to remove falcon eggs from a nest on the Bay Bridge, despite the parents' protests, because once hatched, the fledglings would probably have drowned while learning to fly.
REVISED	San Francisco, although generally an ideal habitat for peregrine falcons, is not entirely so. Rescuers had to remove falcon eggs from a nest on the Bay Bridge recently, despite the parents' protests, because once hatched, the fledglings would probably have drowned while learning to fly.

> **EXERCISE 26.2 Eliminating excessive or illogical subordination**
>
> Edit the following passage to eliminate excessive or illogical subordination.

connect

mhconnectcomposition.com
Online exercise: QL26102

An increasing number of high school seniors, although possessing excellent grades and good prospects for gaining admittance into the colleges of their choice, are opting for another alternative called a "gap year," which involves spending the year after graduating from high school doing something other than going to college. One recent graduate said she worked so hard in high school that she felt as if she had been continually running a marathon, without enough time for her three college-level physics courses, her clarinet practice, her band competitions, and her volunteer work, all of which often left her exhausted at the end of the day. She was accepted at several colleges, although she spent her gap year teaching English in Japan. This woman, who felt so pressured by her high school schedule that she chose to postpone college, has plenty of company, which includes a young man working on a farm in Costa Rica, a man who cares for injured sled dogs in Canada, a woman who builds guitars in England, and a woman who studies ballet in New York City, all activities that, according to the man in Costa Rica, "give you a break from being a student so you can reclaim the person inside." Even if many young people feel that their gap year gives them a refreshing, stimulating, and maturing change, they are delaying their start at college.

connect
mhconnectcomposition.com
Additional resources: QL26002

More about ▸▸▸
Variety and emphasis, 549–62

26d Using Coordination and Subordination Together

Used together, coordination and subordination can add grace and variety to your writing and help readers identify the points you want to emphasize. In this passage from a paper on Shakespeare's views on war in his play *Henry V*, Jonathan Adler, a student at Syracuse University, holds readers' interest and guides them to his concluding point by using both coordination and subordination in sentences of varied length.

> Instead of glorifying war, Shakespeare shows us in *Henry V* that war is costly and that it has consequences. For his own security, however, Shakespeare had to disguise these views about war; speaking out against the government during his time was a risky thing to do. This need for disguise is where his dark comedy or satire comes in. In comedy and satire he can hide his anti-war sentiments while at the same time expressing them and mocking the entire process of going to war.
>
> —Jonathan Adler, Syracuse University

ESL **Coordination and Subordination** Mastery of subordination is considered a sign of sophistication in American academic writing, but this is not true of all languages or cultures. If academic style in your native language favors coordination over subordination, you may need to make a conscious effort to use more subordinated structures in your writing. If it favors subordination over coordination, you may have a tendency to oversubordinate your sentences in English. Your goal should be to strike a balance between both coordination and subordination.

connect
mhconnectcomposition.com
Online exercise: QL26103

> **EXERCISE 26.3 Combining sentences with coordination and subordination**
>
> Use coordination and subordination to combine sentences in the following passages in the way that seems most effective to you. Try to vary the coordination and subordination techniques you use.

1. Every holiday season, some people complain about the need to exchange gifts. Many are annoyed by the crowds, the expense, the materialism, and the overall stress of finding and buying suitable presents.

2. There are people who even refuse to take part in gift giving during the holidays. Some psychologists say that these people may be passing up an important opportunity to bond with their family and friends.

3. People's gift lists indicate who is important and unimportant in their lives, researchers note. A partner can use gift giving to show interest, strengthen a relationship, or even signal that the connection should end.

4. One researcher received a gift from her husband in a brown grocery bag. She knew her marriage was over.

5. A recent study examined gift giving by pet owners. Researchers heard from owners why they gave their pets gifts. Owners said they wanted to make the pets happy. They also wanted to improve their pets' care and make them feel more comfortable.

6. Especially noteworthy is that the pets cannot return the gifts they receive. The act of giving itself makes the pet owners feel good. Simply knowing they are taking care of their pets gives them pleasure.

→ **EXERCISE 26.4 Using coordination and subordination correctly**

Edit the following passage to correct any errors in the use of coordination and subordination.

connect

mhconnectcomposition.com
Online exercise: QL26104

It is a task almost everyone does twice a day for just about their entire lives, yet not many people do it well, for tooth brushing is supposed to take more time than nearly anyone wants to spend on it, and we usually do not do it properly. The American Dental Association is the country's foremost authority on dental hygiene, and it tells us to brush each tooth to the gum line. Although most people are too impatient to brush as long as they should, the entire process ought to take two minutes. While people have been using a form of the standard toothbrush, with bristles attached to a six-inch-long handle, for more than 5,000 years, the task has always been the same, which is to remove the leftover bits of food from our last meal, but we brush for too short a time, and we also commonly brush too hard, no matter what our dentists tell us, even though brushing too hard can cause serious harm to teeth and gums, and this damage can be expensive to repair. People's ineptitude at brushing has inspired an entire industry of toothbrush devices that are elaborate technological wonders that do the brushing for us provided that we reposition the electric toothbrushes when they beep, and we passively wait for them to do their job. Most tooth-brushing devices are made by well-known companies, and they all claim that their products are superior at cleaning teeth. Nevertheless, there are few well-controlled studies showing one brush to be better than any other. Whereas most dental experts agree that using a standard toothbrush thoroughly and gently will remove plaque from teeth as well as an electronic gadget will, an expensive tooth-cleaning machine does have one advantage, which is that people are more likely to use it than the ordinary toothbrush they get from their dentist for free.

Make It **Your Own**

On one page of a paper you recently wrote or are now writing, identify coordinate and subordinate structures. Where do they need to be revised, and why? Make those revisions, and, in the margins of the paper, note which section of this chapter explains the revision.

Work **Together**

With two or three classmates, read each other's work on a recent paper or a paper in progress. Which of your classmates' sentences could be revised for more effective coordination and subordination, and how? Compare your results with those of the others in the group. What have they seen that you did not, and vice versa? How might this collaborative activity help you revise your own work in the future?

27 Using Parallelism

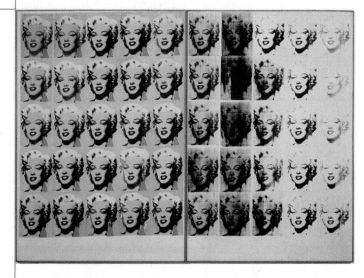

This painting by Andy Warhol, called *Marilyn Diptych* (1962), has two matching, or parallel, parts. Each part consists of twenty-five images of Marilyn Monroe, but the black-and-white panel on the right contrasts dramatically with the gaudily colored panel on the left. The images embedded within each panel are also parallel: All are copies of the same original, all are the same size, and all are equally spaced in a grid. Within this structure, however, the images differ. Those in the left panel vary subtly in color; those in the right panel vary in clarity and definition, with some smeared almost beyond recognition and others faded almost to invisibility. The overall effect suggests the transience of fame and the way image obliterates individuality.

In writing, ***parallelism*** expresses equivalent ideas in equivalent grammatical structures. As in Warhol's painting, parallel structures can be embedded one within the other—clauses within sentences, and terms, phrases, and other clauses within clauses. Used effectively, parallelism can increase the clarity of your writing and help you emphasize important points. Abraham Lincoln, for example, deployed parallelism to powerful effect as he urged his fellow citizens to persevere in the U.S. Civil War in this closing passage from the Gettysburg Address:

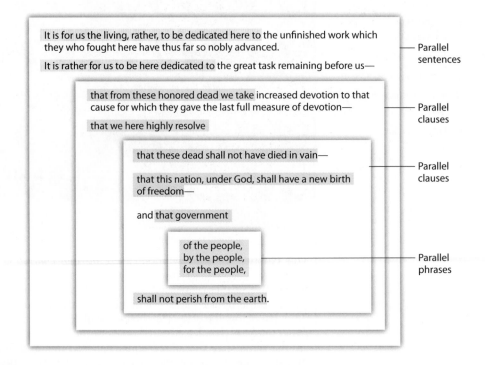

It is for us the living, rather, to be dedicated here to the unfinished work which they who fought here have thus far so nobly advanced.

It is rather for us to be here dedicated to the great task remaining before us—

— Parallel sentences

that from these honored dead we take increased devotion to that cause for which they gave the last full measure of devotion—

that we here highly resolve

— Parallel clauses

that these dead shall not have died in vain—

that this nation, under God, shall have a new birth of freedom—

and that government

— Parallel clauses

of the people,
by the people,
for the people,

— Parallel phrases

shall not perish from the earth.

connect

mhconnectcomposition.com
Additional resources: QL27001

➔ EXERCISE 27.1 Identifying parallelism

Identify and describe the parallel structures in the following passages.

connect

mhconnectcomposition.com
Online exercise: QL27101

1. It was the best of times, it was the worst of times, it was the age of wisdom, it was the age of foolishness, it was the epoch of belief, it was the epoch of incredulity, it was the season of Light, it was the season of Darkness, it was the spring of hope,

it was the winter of despair, we had everything before us, we had nothing before us, we were all going direct to heaven, we were all going direct the other way—in short, the period was so far like the present period, that some of its noisiest authorities insisted on its being received, for good or for evil, in the superlative degree of comparison only.

—Charles Dickens, *A Tale of Two Cities*

2. Those who see quickly, will resolve quickly and act quickly.

—Jane Austen, *Mansfield Park*

3. We shall not flag or fail. We shall go on to the end. We shall fight in France, we shall fight on the seas and oceans, we shall fight with growing confidence and growing strength in the air, we shall defend our island, whatever the cost may be, we shall fight on the beaches, we shall fight on the landing grounds, we shall fight in the fields and in the streets, we shall fight in the hills. We shall never surrender.

—Winston Churchill

4. We shall pay any price, bear any burden, meet any hardships, support any friend, oppose any foe to assure the survival and the success of liberty.

—John F. Kennedy

27a Using Parallelism for Paired Items and Items in a Series

For clarity and to avoid awkwardness, express paired ideas and items in a series in parallel form. Join subordinate clauses with similarly structured clauses, join phrases with similarly structured phrases, and join individual terms with other terms of the same form.

1. Items paired with a coordinating conjunction

Coordinating conjunctions include *and, but, for, nor, or, so,* and *yet.*

▶ Girls learn at a young age to be passive and ~~that they should be~~ deferential.

The original awkwardly pairs an infinitive phrase with a subordinate clause; the revision joins the adjectives *passive* and *deferential* as parallel elements in a single infinitive phrase.

connect

mhconnectcomposition.com
Additional resources: QL27002

More about ▶▶▶
Coordinating conjunctions, 610

▶ The course always covers the twentieth century through World War II
  also touches
  but sometimes ~~touching~~ on the beginning of the Cold War ~~is possible also~~.
                ^   ^

In the revision, the verbs *covers* and *touches on* are in parallel form.

> **ESL** **Deceptive Parallelism** Parallel structure is found in most languages, so the concept will probably not be unfamiliar to you. Use caution, however, to ensure that items that seem parallel are all grammatically equivalent. For example, in "He spoke only kindly and friendly about his previous professor," *kindly* and *friendly* appear parallel, but *kindly* is an adverb whereas *friendly* is an adjective. To be parallel, the sentence requires restating along these lines: "He had only kind and friendly things to say about his previous professor."

---

2. Items paired with correlative conjunctions

The correlative conjunctions include *both . . . and, either . . . or, neither . . . nor,* and *not only . . . but also.* These conjunctions can produce parallel structures that strongly equate the items they link. For items joined with correlative conjunctions to be parallel, however, the item that follows the second part of the conjunction must have the same grammatical form as the item that follows the first part.

More about ▶▶▶
Correlative conjunctions, 610

FAULTY PARALLELISM	The defense attorney not only convinced the jury that her client had no motive for committing the crime, but also was nowhere near the scene of the crime when it occurred.

This suggests that the defense attorney, not her client, was nowhere near the crime scene.

STILL FAULTY	The defense attorney convinced the jury not only that her client had no motive for committing the crime, but also was nowhere near the scene of the crime when it occurred.

A clause beginning with *that* follows *not only,* so a clause beginning with *that* should follow *but also.*

REVISED	The defense attorney convinced the jury not only that her client had no motive for committing the crime, but also that he was nowhere near the scene of the crime when it occurred.

Tech

Parallelism and Computer Style Checkers

A computer's style checker cannot identify ideas that merit parallel treat-   ment in an otherwise grammatical sentence.

3. Items in a series

Like paired items, three or more equivalent items in a series should be in parallel form.

FAULTY PARALLELISM   The detectives secured the crime scene, examined it for clues, and the witnesses were then called in for questioning.

REVISED   The detectives secured the crime scene, examined it for clues, and then called in the witnesses for questioning.

27b Maintaining Parallelism in Comparisons

When you compare two items with *than* or *as,* the items should be in the same grammatical form.

▸ Getting into debt is unfortunately much easier than to̶ g̶e̶t̲ out of it.
   getting

More about ▸▸▸
Clear comparisons, 707, 735
Including function words, 733–34

27c Including Function Words to Maintain Parallelism

Function words such as articles (*a, an, the*), conjunctions, and prepositions indicate the relationships among other words in a sentence. They should be included or repeated as needed in linked items for clarity and grammar as well as for parallelism.

▸ The trail leads over high mountain passes and d̲e̲n̲s̲e̲ forests.
   through

   Trails lead *over* passes but *through* forests.

EXERCISE 27.2 Correcting parallelism errors

Correct any errors in parallelism in the following sentences.

EXAMPLE

This spot offers a good view not only of herons but y̶o̶u̶ ̶c̶a̶n̶ also s̶e̶e̲ egrets.
   of

connect
mhconnectcomposition.com
Online exercise: QL27102

1. Many types of wading birds, some rare, are attracted to this island to rest during migration, to feed, and they nest here as well.

2. This is an ideal place for wildlife, not only shorebirds but also you can sometimes see fish, crabs, and lobsters as well.

3. Perhaps surprisingly, this habitat is located not in a national park or wildlife refuge but it is found in the middle of New York harbor.

4. The harbor contains forty-two uninhabited islands, abundant vegetation, and there are a variety of freshwater and saltwater habitats.

5. However, until ten or fifteen years ago, the area was inhospitable to wildlife because it was missing one crucial factor: not food or shelter but the presence of clean water.

6. Starting with the Clean Water Act of 1972 and accelerating within the last fifteen years with state legislation, regional planning, and as more federal funds were appropriated, the water in the harbor has become hospitable to wildlife.

7. Today, more than 2,000 pairs of shorebirds, including not only several species of herons, snowy egrets, but also great egrets, and glossy ibis nest on the different islands.

8. They must fly several miles away to feed in the marshes of New Jersey's Meadowlands, but scientists hope that as the habitat continues to improve, they will be feeding in the harbor itself.

27d Maintaining Parallelism for Items in Lists and Outlines

Each item in a list or an outline should be in the same grammatical form as the others.

1. Items in a list

Whenever you have a list of three or more items, those items should be in the same grammatical form. The following list is difficult to read in its draft form because the first and third items begin with independent clauses, whereas the other three begin with a noun followed by a bit of commentary. The revision puts them all in the noun followed by commentary form.

DRAFT LIST	REVISED
Among the top ten most healthful foods, these are my favorites:	Among the top ten most healthful foods, these are my favorites:

DRAFT LIST

1. <u>Avocados are delicious unadorned.</u> I also enjoy them sliced in half with the hole filled with a mixture of olive oil and lime juice.

2. <u>I like nuts because they are so portable.</u>

3. <u>Berries.</u> All of them are delicious, except blackberries.

4. <u>Yogurt.</u> I avoid the kind with fruit on the bottom.

5. <u>Garlic.</u> I like it, but it doesn't like me.

REVISED

1. <u>Avocados.</u> They are delicious unadorned. I also enjoy them sliced in half with the hole filled with a mixture of olive oil and lime juice.

2. <u>Nuts.</u> I like them because they are so portable.

3. <u>Berries.</u> All of them are delicious, except blackberries.

4. <u>Yogurt.</u> I avoid the kind with fruit on the bottom.

5. <u>Garlic.</u> I like it, but it doesn't like me.

2. Items in outlines

Maintain parallelism in outlines and headings by keeping all items at the same level in the same form. In the original version of the following outline, three of the top-level headings—I, II, and IV—are noun phrases whereas III is a question. Likewise, under heading I, the first subheading begins with a noun whereas the second and third are **gerund** phrases, and under heading IV, the last item is an independent clause. Revising the outline so that the headings are parallel makes it easier to understand.

> **Gerund** The *-ing* form of a verb used as a noun (619)

DRAFT OUTLINE

I. Types of literary fraud

    A. Plagiarism

    B. Forging documents

    C. Misrepresenting the facts

REVISED OUTLINE

I. Types of literary fraud

    A. Plagiarism

    B. Forgery

    C. Misrepresentation

II. Examples of literary fraud	II. Examples of literary fraud
A. Kaavya Viswanathan	A. Kaavya Viswanathan
B. The Donation of Constantine	B. The Donation of Constantine
C. James Frey	C. James Frey
III. Why do people commit literary fraud?	III. Motives for literary fraud
A. Financial gain	A. Financial gain
B. Personal glory	B. Personal glory
C. Insecurity	C. Insecurity
D. Weak writing skills	D. Weak writing skills
E. Busy schedule	E. Busy schedule
IV. Problems with literary fraud	IV. Problems with literary fraud
A. Copyright infringement	A. Copyright infringement
B. Breach of faith	B. Breach of faith
C. Readers take actions based on erroneous assumptions	C. Reader actions based on erroneous assumptions

connect

mhconnectcomposition.com
Online exercise: QL27103

→ **EXERCISE 27.3 Parallelism in lists**

Correct the parallelism errors in the following list.

Favorite Leisure Activities

1. Reading, especially contemporary novels
2. I really enjoy going to the movies with my friends.
3. To hike in the woods and to camp out
4. On the weekends, I enjoy online role-playing game marathons
5. Listening to classic rock and folk music

27e **Using Parallelism to Create Emphasis**

> **More about ▶▶▶**
> Parallelism and
> emphasis, 559

Placing ideas in parallel form highlights their differences and similarities.

▶ All the images are copies of the same original, the same size, and *all are*
they have equal space between them within a grid of rows *all are equally spaced*

and columns.

As the passage from Lincoln's Gettysburg address at the beginning of this chapter illustrates, parallelism can be a forceful tool for emphasizing important ideas. Martin Luther King, Jr., provides another example in his famous "I have a dream" speech. Notice how King's parallelisms generate an almost musical cadence that drives us toward the speech's conclusion.

> When we let freedom ring, when we let it ring from every village and every hamlet, from every state and every city, we will be able to speed up that day when all of God's children, black men and white men, Jews and Gentiles, Protestants and Catholics, will be able to join hands and sing in the words of the old Negro spiritual, "Free at last! Free at last! Thank God Almighty, we are free at last!"
>
> —Martin Luther King, Jr., from speech delivered August 28, 1963, Washington, DC

EXERCISE 27.4 Parallelism and emphasis

Use parallelism to combine and emphasize the ideas in the following groups of sentences.

connect

mhconnectcomposition.com
Online exercise: QL27104

EXAMPLE

The ancestor of the modern horse evolved in North America
                                   ago,
about 4 million years ago. It spread to Eurasia over the Bering land
bridge, and then
bridge. Horses became extinct in North America at the end of the last

Ice Age about 12,000 years ago.

1. Scientists have long debated where and when the horse was domesticated. They have also debated where and when dogs and the pig were domesticated. The time and place of the domestication of other animals, such as cattle, sheep, and goats, is much clearer.

2. Dogs were domesticated before horses. Cattle were domesticated before horses. Goats were domesticated before horses. Pigs were domesticated before horses. Sheep were domesticated before horses.

3. Scientists now believe that horses were domesticated about 6,000 years ago in Central Asia. This conclusion is based on DNA evidence. It is also based on evidence obtained from archaeological remains. It is also based on studies of contemporary nomadic peoples whose lifestyles may resemble those of the people who first domesticated the horse.

4. Initially people regarded horses as prey. They did not regard horses as domestic animals. They hunted horses as food. They also painted images of horses on cave walls.

5. All the evidence about horse domestication points to a complicated process. This process went on over a long time. This process occurred at many different places. This process was further complicated by climate changes during the last Ice Age, which altered the wild horses' habitat and forced them to migrate north.

Make It **Your Own**

Reread three pieces of your recent writing. Edit them to use parallelism more effectively.

Work **Together**

Working with a small group of classmates, identify three examples of literary parallelism from written works or speeches. Then discuss the effectiveness of the authors' use of parallelism in these texts.

28

Engaging Readers with Variety and Emphasis

In this painting, *At the Opera*, artist Mary Cassatt captures and holds our interest with a variety of visual elements, among them the large, striking figure of the woman in the foreground; the contrasting, more sketchily rendered figures in the background; the curving form of the balconies on which the figures sit; the bright points of red and white paint; and the contrasting large dark areas. Cassatt also structures the painting to emphasize certain elements over others and to direct our attention to a story unfolding within the scene. Our eyes go first to the woman in the foreground; then we follow her gaze through her opera glasses and let the curve of the balcony railing draw our attention to the upper left, where we are startled to see a male figure also looking through opera glasses. His gaze is fixed not toward the stage, however, but directly back in our direction at the woman in the foreground.

Writers also use variety and emphasis to capture and hold their readers' attention and to direct those readers to the

Quick **Reference** ➡ **Achieving Variety and Emphasis**

- Vary sentence length and structure. (550)
- Vary the placement of elements within sentences. (551)
- Choose appropriate punctuation. (557)
- Introduce questions, commands, and exclamations when appropriate. (558)
- Use strategic repetition. (559)
- Choose emphatic verbs and favor the active voice. (560)

subtleties of the story being told. Speakers use intonation, tone of voice, and timing to avoid monotony and emphasize or de-emphasize particular words or phrases. Writers use variety and emphasis to help readers "hear" the words of the text in their mind's ear.

28a Varying Sentence Length and Structure

Simple sentence One independent clause and no subordinate clauses
Compound sentence Two or more independent clauses and no subordinate clauses
Complex sentence One independent clause with at least one subordinate clause
Compound-complex sentence Two or more independent clauses with one or more subordinate clauses (623–24)

Confronting readers with page after page of sentences of uniform length—long, short, or in between—can tire them and make it hard for them to pick out important details. To hold readers' attention and direct it to the points you want to emphasize, vary the length of your sentences and include a mix of sentence structures: ***simple, compound, complex,*** and ***compound-complex.***

Short sentences deliver information concisely and dramatically. They are most emphatic, however, when they are mixed with longer sentences. In the following passage, too many short sentences in a row create a choppy effect, leaving the reader with the impression that each point is equally important. The revision combines most of the short sentences into longer sentences that clarify the relationship among the ideas the writer wants to convey. The writer's main point is now dramatically isolated in the one short sentence that remains.

DRAFT   The whole planet is at risk. We need to put a stop to the wild spread of this disease. The key is education. First, we should educate the victims. Then we should let them educate the world. They can help us win this war against AIDS. They can help other people understand that everyone is vulnerable.

REVISION   With the whole planet at risk, we need to put a stop to the wild spread of this disease. The key is education.

First, we should educate the victims; then we should let them educate the world. They can help us win this war against AIDS by helping other people understand that everyone is vulnerable.

connect
mhconnectcomposition.com
Additional resources: QL28001

➜ **EXERCISE 28.1** **Editing for varied sentence length and structure**
Revise the paragraph to create a more coherent result with a mix of sentence lengths and types.

connect
mhconnectcomposition.com
Online exercise: QL28101

Most people who are not Japanese know very little about sushi. They do know that they like it. However, they don't really know what the word *sushi* means. They think it means "fish" or perhaps "raw fish." Actually, it is a short form of the Japanese word *sumeshi*. This word means "seasoned rice." So sushi is any food whose essential ingredient is seasoned rice. The rice may have a variety of seasonings. The most common are rice vinegar, sugar, sea salt, and rice wine. Fish is not necessary to sushi. Seasoned rice is necessary, however.

28b Organizing Sentences for Variety and Emphasis

Without even being aware of it, readers have two expectations about sentence structure. First, they expect significant information in a sentence to be in the independent clause, not in modifying clauses or phrases. The following two sentences, for example, emphasize different things, although both contain the same information. (The independent clause in each is underlined.)

connect
mhconnectcomposition.com
Additional resources: QL28002

▶ <u>The museum holds an annual benefit</u> in March that raises money for new purchases.

The emphasis is on the event.

More about ▶▶▶
Independent and subordinate clauses, 531–32, 618–22

▶ <u>The museum raises money</u> for new purchases during the benefit that it holds annually in March.

The emphasis is on the money.

Second, readers look for significant information at the beginning or end of a sentence. When your sentences meet both these expectations, your readers are much more likely to understand what you intend to say.

These general principles, however, will not by themselves guarantee the kind of sentence variety that will hold your readers' attention. The strategic use and placement of modifiers and the strategic selection of sentence organization, including the occasional word-order inversion, can help keep readers engaged.

1. Modifiers

The default structure of an English sentence is S-V-O: The subject (S) comes first; then the verb (V); and then the direct object (O), if there is one. Reflecting this structure, most sentences start with the subject. However, a long string of subject-first sentences can make your text monotonous. You can avoid this problem by positioning modifying clauses and phrases not only to vary your sentence openings but also to emphasize important information.

> **Adverb** Modifies a verb, adjective, other adverb, or entire phrase or clause and specifies how, where, when, and to what extent or degree (700–09)

Adverbs and Adverbial Phrases and Clauses *Adverbs*—and phrases and clauses that function as adverbs—can be positioned in different places in a sentence. In the following examples, changing the placement of the modifier alters the rhythm of the sentence, the information it emphasizes, and, in some cases, its meaning.

ADVERBIAL SUBORDINATE CLAUSE

Commodities futures are a risky investment <u>because they are subject to large price swings.</u>

<u>Because they are subject to large price swings,</u> commodities futures are a risky investment.

Commodities futures, <u>because they are subject to large price swings,</u> are a risky investment.

ADVERBIAL PREPOSITIONAL PHRASES

World War II began <u>in Europe</u> <u>in September 1939.</u>

<u>In September 1939,</u> World War II began <u>in Europe.</u>

<u>In Europe,</u> World War II began <u>in September 1939.</u>

ADVERB

The bookstore <u>rapidly</u> depleted its stock of the new Harry Potter book.

<u>Rapidly,</u> the bookstore depleted its stock of the new Harry Potter book.

NOTE Moving an adverb can sometimes alter the meaning of a sentence. Consider these two examples:

▶   The test was <u>surprisingly</u> hard.

▶   <u>Surprisingly</u>, the test was hard

In the first, *surprisingly* modifies *hard,* suggesting that the writer found the test harder than expected; in the second, *surprisingly* modifies the whole clause that follows it, suggesting that the writer expected the test to be easy.

Adjectival Phrases The placement of **adjectives** and most adjectival phrases and clauses is less flexible than the placement of adverbs. However, participles and **participial phrases,** which act as adjectives, can often come at the beginning of a sentence as well as after the terms they modify.

> **Adjective** Modifies a noun or pronoun with descriptive or limiting information (700–09)

> **Participial phrase** A phrase in which the present or past participle acts as an adjective (619–20)

▶   New York City's subway system, <u>flooded by torrential rains,</u> shut down at the height of the morning rush hour.

▶   <u>Flooded by torrential rains,</u> New York City's subway system shut down at the height of the morning rush hour.

An adjective phrase that functions as a **subject complement** can also sometimes be repositioned at the beginning of a sentence.

> **Subject complement** An adjective, pronoun, or noun phrase that follows a linking verb and describes or refers to the sentence subject (615)

▶   The Mariana Trench is <u>almost seven miles deep,</u> making it the lowest place on the surface of the earth.

▶   <u>Almost seven miles deep,</u> the Mariana Trench is the lowest place on the surface of the earth.

Appositives and Absolute Phrases An **appositive** is a noun or noun phrase that renames another noun or noun phrase. Because they designate the same thing, the appositive and the original term can switch positions.

▶   The governor, <u>New York's highest official,</u> ordered an investigation into the subway system's failure.

▶   <u>New York's highest official,</u> the governor, ordered an investigation into the subway system's failure.

Getting It
Across **Starting a Sentence with a Coordinating Conjunction**

Should you start a sentence with a coordinating conjunction—for example, *and, but, or, yet*—as a transitional word? Some instructors discourage this usage, but it is common in both formal and informal writing. Many of the most respected writers employ it, as U.S. President John F. Kennedy did in this famous sentence from his inaugural address:

> And so, my fellow Americans, ask not what your country can do for you; ask what you can do for your country.

Judiciously placed at the beginning of a sentence to establish a connection to previous material, a coordinating conjunction can convey a sense of directness and urgency. But check with your instructor before you adopt this usage.

An ***absolute phrase,*** consisting of a noun or pronoun with a participle, modifies an entire independent clause. It can often fall either before or after the clause it modifies.

▶ The task finally completed, the workers headed for the parking lot.

▶ The workers headed for the parking lot, the task finally completed.

More about ▶▶▶
Transitional expressions, 61–62

Transitional Expressions Transitional expressions relate the information in a sentence to preceding material. Their placement affects the emphasis that falls on other parts of the sentence. The second passage below, for example, calls more attention to Superman's distinctiveness than the first does. (The transitional term is underlined.)

▶ Most comic book characters from the 1930s quickly fell into obscurity. However, Superman was not one of them.

▶ Most comic book characters from the 1930s quickly fell into obscurity. Superman, however, was not one of them.

connect
mhconnectcomposition.com
Online exercise: QL28102

⇥ EXERCISE **28.2 Varying sentence openings**

Revise the following sentences to begin with something other than the subject.

EXAMPLE

Soaring in search of food, ravens
~~Ravens~~ patrol the misty blue sky high above the valley, ~~soaring in search of food.~~

1. The Canaan Valley, one of the highest valleys east of the Mississippi, was designated a National Natural Landmark in 1974.

2. This ecosystem, with its many species of plants and animals, is an example of northern forest.

3. It seems out of place, located here in West Virginia.

4. The valley is more than 3,000 feet deep and enjoys cool summers and snowy winters.

5. The valley is likely to remain wild and natural for many years to come because it is protected by federal and state governments.

2. Cumulative and periodic sentences

A common way to organize information in longer sentences is with a cumulative or loose structure. A ***cumulative sentence*** begins with the subject and verb of an independent clause and accumulates additional information in subsequent modifying phrases and clauses.

> D. H. Lawrence's *The Rainbow* is a novel about growth and change in three generations of the Brangwen family, growth and change that takes place within the confines of a cycle, each generation developing in the pattern of the last, yet each generation straining further than the last against the confines of the cycle in search of fulfillment.

> That's the news from Lake Wobegon, where all the women are strong, all the men are good-looking, and all the children are above average.
>
> —Garrison Keillor, tag line from the radio show
> *A Prairie Home Companion*

A ***periodic sentence,*** in contrast, reserves the independent clause for the end, preceded by modifying details. The effect is to build suspense that highlights key information when it finally arrives.

> Through the center of town, up the strip, past the housing developments and shopping malls, street lights giving way to the thin streaming illumination of the headlights, trees crowding the asphalt in a black unbroken wall: that was the way to Greasy Lake.
>
> —T. Coraghessan Boyle, "Greasy Lake"

An interrupted periodic sentence begins with the subject of the independent clause but leaves the conclusion of the clause to the end, separating the two parts with modifying details. In the following example, the subject and predicate of the independent clause are underlined.

> The <u>archaeologist Howard Carter,</u> peering through the small opening to the main chamber of Tutankhamen's tomb at treasures hidden from view for more than three millennia, when asked what he saw, <u>replied "wonderful things."</u>

 Developing an Ear for Sentence Variety Many of the sentence structures that add variety to written English are uncommon in conversation and so may not come naturally to you even if you have a good grasp of conversational English. To develop an ear for sentence variety in your academic writing, try going through this chapter and imitating some of the structures it describes with examples of your own. Ask an instructor or another skilled writer of English to check your work to see if you have produced effective sentences.

connect
mhconnectcomposition.com
Online exercise: QL28103

→ **EXERCISE 28.3 Cumulative and periodic sentences**

Combine the sentences in each of the following passages into a single cumulative or periodic sentence, as specified.

EXAMPLE

Mosses generally live in shady areas. ~~In these areas~~ _{, where} they are less likely to dry out. [cumulative]

1. Business leaders must often try to predict the future. They use a variety of means. One example is prediction markets, in which employees bet on the most likely outcome of an event and win cash or other prizes for correct predictions. [cumulative]

2. I lugged the heavy sack of laundry down three flights of stairs. I loaded it into my car. I drove to the Laundromat and waited for a free washing machine. I vowed to get an apartment with its own washer-dryer someday soon. [periodic]

3. Large swathes of Earth show little evidence of human activity. Equally large areas are heavily influenced by human roads, buildings, and other structures. The human footprint is spread unevenly over the planet. [periodic]

4. I downloaded a map to Kristen's house. She lives in an isolated area. I didn't want to spend hours driving around in circles. [cumulative]

5. People who want to go green can make many small changes in their lives. One example is recycling common materials like paper, plastic, glass, and metal. They can also recycle additional materials, such as batteries, cell phones, and printer cartridges. They can use paper with as much recycled content as possible. And of course, they can replace conventional lightbulbs with compact fluorescents. [cumulative]

3. Inversions

An inversion is a sentence in which, contrary to normal English word order, the verb precedes the subject. Inverted sentences call attention to themselves. Used sparingly, they can help you emphasize a point or create a sense of dramatic tension.

> ▶ Among the director's many excellent films number a few that deserve
>   verb   subj.
>   special mention.

> ▶ Into the middle of the town rode the stranger.
>   verb   subj.

28c   Creating Emphasis with Punctuation

One way to draw your readers' attention to significant material is to place it at the end of a sentence after a colon or dash.

> ▶ According to photographer William Klein, the advertising campaign
>   for fashion designer John Galliano wasn't just influenced by Klein's
>   visual techniques—it stole them.

> ▶ The judge had two words for Galliano's use of Klein's signature visual
>   style: copyright infringement.

More about ▶▶▶
Colons, 833–34
Dashes, 828–30

You can also draw attention to nonessential phrases or clauses within an independent clause when you set them off with dashes instead of commas.

> ▶ The judge had two words—copyright infringement—for Galliano's
>   use of Klein's signature visual style.

More about ▶▶▶
Essential and nonessential modifiers,
791–93

More about ▶▶▶
Periods, 825
Semicolons, 800–06
Commas, 782–99

The punctuation between two independent clauses can affect the way readers perceive the relationship between them. A dash (as we have just seen) or a period creates a more emphatic separation than a semicolon or a comma and coordinating conjunction.

▶ The jury convicted the defendants. The judge sentenced them to life.

▶ The jury convicted the defendants; the judge sentenced them to life.

▶ The jury convicted the defendants, and the judge sentenced them to life.

28d Using Questions, Commands, and Exclamations

More about ▶▶▶
Sentence categories, 623–24

Most sentences are *declarative:* They make a statement—declare something—about their subjects. Other types of sentences include questions, commands, and exclamations. When used sparingly, these can add variety to prose and draw attention to important ideas. Overused, they sound gimmicky or childish.

Most questions in academic writing are **rhetorical;** they are meant to call attention to an issue, not to elicit an answer.

[F]or all our focus on happiness it is by no means clear that we are happier as a result. Might we not even say that our contemporary concern is something of an inauspicious sign, belying a deep anxiety and doubt about the object of our pursuit? Does the fact that we worry so much about being happy suggest that we are not?

—Darrin M. McMahon, "The Pursuit of Happiness in Perspective"

More about ▶▶▶
Person, 455–56

Commands are a type of second-person sentence: The subject of a command, even when unstated, is always *you*. The second person is best reserved for addressing the reader directly, and commands, in particular, are useful for describing a process or conveying advice.

When in doubt tell the truth.

—Mark Twain, *Following the Equator*

Exclamations are emphatic statements or expressions of strong emotion. Interjections are exclamatory words that stand alone within a sentence. Both are usually punctuated with exclamation marks, and both are rare in academic writing.

The one fact that I would cry from every housetop is this: the Good Life is waiting for us—here and now!

—B. F. Skinner, *Walden II*

28e Using Strategic Repetition

Redundancy and other forms of unnecessary repetition clutter writing and distract readers. Repetition is sometimes necessary, however, for clarity and to maintain parallelism.

Writers can also use repetition strategically for emphasis, calling attention to important ideas, as the writer Flannery O'Connor does with her repetition of the word *grotesque* in the following passage.

> I doubt if the texture of Southern life is any more grotesque than that of the rest of the nation, but it does seem evident that the Southern writer is particularly adept at recognizing the grotesque; and to recognize the grotesque, you have to have some notion of what is not grotesque and why.
>
> —Flannery O'Connor, talk delivered at Notre Dame University

Repetition for emphasis works especially well within parallel structures, as in this sentence from a paper by Syracuse University student Jessica Toro.

> *More about* ▶▶▶
> Parallelism, 539–48

> Some children are never told that they are adopted, never given the opportunity to search for their biological parents.

Toro could have used *or* instead of the second *never,* but the repetition dramatically underscores her concern about the consequences of a particular policy toward adopted children.

➔ EXERCISE 28.4 Strategic repetition

Use strategic repetition for emphasis to revise each of the following sentences.

connect
mhconnectcomposition.com
Online exercise: QL28104

EXAMPLE

What a terrible day: I forgot my gloves, *I forgot* my glasses, and *I forgot* my laptop.

1. I love you in every season of the year.

2. Everett hates all forms of exercise.

3. We are delighted that you have agreed to discuss your book idea, to visit us here in Cincinnati, and to publish your next book with us.

4. Your reasons for leaving school seem trivial, but the consequences for your future will not be.

5. The computer data that have been generated within the past twenty years now fill billions of floppy disks, CDs, and hard drives.

28f Creating Emphasis with Emphatic Verbs

Verbs that describe an action directly are often more emphatic than verbs like *be, have,* or *cause* that combine with nouns or adjectives to describe an action indirectly.

▶ Many economists ~~have a belief~~ *believe* that higher gasoline taxes would ~~be beneficial to~~ *benefit* the economy in the long run. The increased costs would ~~have a stimulating effect on~~ *stimulate* research into alternate energy sources and eventually ~~cause a reduction in~~ *reduce* both carbon emissions and our dependence on oil.

28g Choosing the Active or Passive Voice

More about ▶▶▶
Voice in verbs,
677–78
Passive voice and
wordiness, 522

In an active-voice sentence, the subject performs the action of the verb; in a passive-voice sentence, the subject receives the action of the verb. Active-voice sentences are usually more emphatic, direct, and concise than their passive-voice counterparts.

ACTIVE VOICE: EMPHATIC
Rising oil prices stimulate research into alternate energy sources.

PASSIVE VOICE: UNEMPHATIC
Research into alternate energy sources is stimulated by rising oil prices.

However, if you want to emphasize the recipient of an action over the performer, or agent, of the action, the passive voice can be an appropriate choice. In this famous sentence from his address to the nation on December 8, 1941, for example, President Franklin Delano Roosevelt used the passive voice to focus on the United States as the victim of the attack on Pearl Harbor.

▶ Yesterday, December 7th, 1941—a date which will live in infamy—the United States of America was suddenly and deliberately attacked by naval and air forces of the Empire of Japan.

Because it can allow the agent to remain unidentified, the passive voice can also be an appropriate choice when the identity of the agent is unknown or unimportant.

Writing
Responsibly   **Voice and Responsibility**

Because the passive voice allows the agent of an action to remain unnamed, it lends itself to misuse by people evading responsibility for their own or others' mistakes and misdeeds. Consider, for example, the classic dodge of the cornered politician or bureaucrat: "Mistakes were made."

Be on the lookout for this evasive use of the passive voice in the statements and writing of others and, of course, in your own. It is a usage that comes all too readily to hand when we need to convey unflattering or damaging information about ourselves or others whom we represent.

▶ According to the coroner, the victim had been murdered between 3 and 4 in the morning.

The identity of the murderer is unknown.

▶ *Harry Potter and the Philosopher's Stone,* the first book in the Harry Potter series, was published in 1997.

The focus is on the date of publication, not the specific identity of the publisher.

Similarly, in science writing, the passive voice allows the description of procedures without constant reference to the individuals who carried them out.

▶ The effects of human activities on seagrasses were studied at Sandy Neck and Centerville beaches from 31 March 2006 to 30 March 2007.

EXERCISE 28.5 Emphatic verbs, active verbs

Revise each of the following sentences, replacing indirect expressions with emphatic verbs and, when appropriate, changing verbs from passive to active voice.

connect
mhconnectcomposition.com
Online exercise: QL28105

EXAMPLE

Many people have a belief that Plymouth Colony was founded by advocates of religious freedom.

believe that the founders of Plymouth Colony advocated

1. The Pilgrims, as they came to be called, experienced persecution in England and made a decision to move to Holland.

2. In Holland, however, many members of the congregation found it a struggle to find employment and experienced economic suffering.

3. In addition, parents found the influence of Dutch language and culture on their children a source of worry and a threat to the group's survival.

4. Therefore, in 1619, a decision was made by the Pilgrims' leaders to move the entire group to the New World.

5. Although the Pilgrims wanted freedom to worship as they pleased, it was not assumed by them that religious freedom was desirable for all.

6. Rather, they were of the opinion that there was one proper way to worship and that proper way was the one observed by them.

Make It **Your Own**

Reread three pieces of your recent writing. Edit them for variety and emphasis using the strategies covered in this chapter.

Work **Together**

Working in a small group, review three examples of different types of writing—such as an advertisement, informational text, and a short story—and analyze the authors' use of the strategies covered in this chapter.

29 Choosing Appropriate Language

"We have only jobs here, Mr. Sanderson, not 'gigs.'"

During a job interview, the applicant wants to make a favorable impression while also assessing his potential boss and workplace. The interviewer wants to evaluate the applicant while accurately describing the job and presenting herself and her organization at once favorably and fairly to a potential colleague. Both have to bring to the encounter a sense of appropriate dress, appropriate demeanor, and appropriate language. Neither would be likely to show up in a bathing suit, jump up and down on a couch, use language that might offend the other, or, like the applicant in this cartoon, refer to the position casually as a *gig*. Such issues of appropriateness apply to your choice of language in every document you write.

29a Using Language in Context

A new college graduate from Brooklyn, New York, who begins working for a company in Columbus, Georgia, may find herself collaborating with colleagues in Singapore or India to write technical documents for company employees in Melbourne, Australia. As this example illustrates, English today is a multinational language that takes a variety of forms around the world. Within a country like the United States, vocabulary, usage, and even aspects of grammar vary from region to region and group to group.

We all adjust our language to suit our audience and purpose. No form of the language is intrinsically better or more correct than another, but certain forms have become standard for addressing a broad audience in an academic setting or in the workplace. In this context, using appropriate language usually means the following:

- Avoiding nonstandard dialects

- Avoiding regionalisms, colloquialisms, and slang

- Avoiding overly technical terminology (jargon and neologisms)

- Adopting a straightforward tone, one that is neither overly informal nor pompously inflated

1. Nonstandard dialects

A *dialect* is a variant of a language with its own distinctive pronunciation, vocabulary, and grammar. A linguist once quipped that the only difference between the standard form of a language and its other dialects is that the standard form has an army and a navy. The standard form, in other words, became standard because it is the dialect of the elite and powerful.

Nonstandard dialects of English are not "bad" English, as many have been taught to believe. If you speak a dialect like Appalachian English or African American Vernacular English and you are addressing an audience of peers from your community, then your home dialect *is* appropriate. If you are addressing a broader audience or writing in an academic or workplace context, however, the dialect known as Standard American English, or Edited English, is usually the appropriate choice. You need to be aware of the differences in vocabulary and grammar between your home dialect and the standard dialect, and you need to edit your writing accordingly.

> *More about* ▶▶▶
> The grammar of
> Standard American
> English, 600–25

2. Regionalisms, colloquialisms, and slang

Regionalisms are expressions that are characteristic of particular areas. Saying the car "needs washed" is acceptable in Pittsburgh but not in Boston. The expression "I might could do it" might be acceptable in Pikeville, Kentucky, but not in Des Moines, Iowa. Regionalisms can be appropriate in conversation or informal writing but are usually out of place in formal academic writing.

> ▶ Many scientists believe that we might ~~could~~ be able to slow global warming if
>
> we can reduce carbon emissions.

Colloquialisms are informal expressions common in speech but usually out of place in formal writing.

> ▶ An R rating designates a movie that is not appropriate for ~~kids~~ children
>
> under 17 who are not accompanied by ~~a grown-up.~~ an adult.

connect
mhconnectcomposition.com
Additional resources: QL29001

Used judiciously, however, the occasional colloquialism can add verve to your writing.

> ▶ The musicians were only kids, none of them more than ten years old, but they played like seasoned professionals.

Slang is the extremely informal, inventive, often colorful (and off-color) vocabulary of a particular group. People in the group may use it as a badge of membership, a way to distinguish themselves from outsiders. Slang is often ephemeral, passing rapidly in and out of fashion. Some terms endure, however, and, like *jazz,* enter the ranks of widely accepted vocabulary. In general, slang is inappropriate in formal writing, but as with colloquial language, when used sparingly and judiciously, it can enliven a sentence and help emphasize an important point.

**Writing
↑ Responsibly**   **Online Shortcuts**

Users of text messaging, instant messaging, and social networking sites have developed a host of acronyms and abbreviations—like *BTW* for "by the way" and *LOL* for "laughing out loud"—that save typing time and space on the tiny screens of mobile phones. With the possible exception of informal email, these expressions are almost never appropriate in other contexts, particularly not in academic or business writing. The same applies to emoticons like :-) and :-(and to other shortcuts such as writing entirely in lowercase without punctuation, as in *i saw her this am.*

3. Neologisms and jargon

The world changes. Technology advances, new cultural trends emerge, and new research alters our understanding of ourselves and gives rise to new fields of study. As these changes occur, people necessarily invent new words and expressions—***neologisms.*** Some neologisms gain wide currency and establish themselves as acceptable vocabulary for formal writing. The word *neologism,* for example, was itself a neologism in the eighteenth century. It would be hard to write about the effect of the internet on communication without using the word *email,* which is short for *electronic mail* and was coined in 1982. It would be similarly difficult to write about the impact of internet-based media on recent political campaigns without referring to *blogs,* a contraction of *web log* that first appeared in 1999, and *bloggers,* the people who write them.

Other neologisms, however, prove transient or never move from informal to formal usage. When you consider using a neologism, ask yourself whether a more familiar synonym might serve as well. If the neologism is necessary but you are not sure your audience will be familiar with it, define it.

▶ Some instructors use wikis as tools for teaching collaborative *, websites that allow a group of users to create and edit content collectively,*

writing.

The term ***jargon*** refers to the specialized vocabulary of a particular profession or discipline. Doctors speak of *adenomas* and *electroencephalograms.* Automobile mechanics speak of *camber angles* and *ring-and-pinion gears.* Lawyers speak of *effluxions of time* and *words of procreation.* English professors speak of *discursive historicity* and *terministic screens.* For an audience of specialists, this kind of insider vocabulary can succinctly communicate concepts that might otherwise take several sentences, even paragraphs, to explain. If you are addressing a general audience, however, it is usually inappropriate to load your writing with words your readers will not understand. In such situations, jargon becomes inappropriately technical or complicated language.

▶ The tenants lost the apartment ~~due to the effluxion of time on~~ *when their lease expired.*

~~their lease.~~

4. Appropriate formality

When you speak or write to close friends and intimates from your own age group, your language will probably—and appropriately—be relaxed and informal, sprinkled with dialect, slang, and colloquial expressions. Writing for most college courses or in the workplace, however, requires a formal tone. Addressing a broad, potentially global audience of English readers calls for clear, straightforward language free of slang and colloquialisms. Clear and straightforward, however, should not mean simpleminded or condescending. Use challenging vocabulary if it aptly expresses your meaning, but do not try to impress your readers by inflating your writing with fancy words mined from a thesaurus; the result will probably be more distractingly pompous than illuminating.

> **More about ▶▶▶**
> Using a thesaurus,
> 586

INAPPROPRIATELY INFORMAL	Tarantino is always ripping scenes from earlier flicks to use in his own.
POMPOUS	It is a characteristic stylistic mannerism of the auteur Quentin Tarantino to allusively amalgamate scenic quotations from the repertory of his cinematic forebears in his own oeuvre.
APPROPRIATE	In his movies, the director Quentin Tarantino routinely alludes to scenes from earlier movies.

Writing
⬆ Responsibly   Euphemisms and Doublespeak

We use **euphemisms** in place of words that might be offensive or emotionally painful. We speak to mourners about a relative who has *passed away,* and we excuse ourselves saying we have to go *to the bathroom* without referring to specific bodily functions. The polite or respectful use of euphemisms, however, can easily shade into a more evasive reluctance to address harsh realities. Why use *correctional institution,* for example, when what you mean is *prison* or *jail*? Why use *ill-advised* when what you mean is *foolish* or *rash*? Euphemisms that are deliberately deceptive, used to obscure bad news or sanitize an ugly truth, are called **doublespeak**. A company that announces that it is *downsizing,* not that it is about to lay off half of its workforce, is using doublespeak. *Terrorists* who call themselves *freedom fighters* are using doublespeak. When reading, ask yourself: Does this word obscure or downplay the truth? When writing, think carefully about your motives: Are you using a euphemism (or doublespeak) to avoid hurting someone's feelings, or to evade responsibility for an uncomfortable truth?

connect
mhconnectcomposition.com
Online exercise: QL29101

> **EXERCISE 29.1 Editing for language in context**

Edit the following passage to establish appropriate formality and to eliminate inappropriate regionalisms, colloquialisms, slang, and jargon.

> There are many reasons why folks are now trying essentially to effect a truncation of their consumption of meat. Some believe that having less meat will make them healthier. Some are desirous of losing weight by cutting their intake of fat. Some are doing it merely to be copycats. Regardless of the motivation, nutrition experts say that reducing meat consumption is not rocket science and can be effectuated by following some simple steps.
>
> To begin with, chill out about getting enough protein. Plants supply protein too, and some, such as spinach and lentils, proffer greater quantities of protein per calorie than a cheeseburger does. Per capita, Americans currently scarf up about a half pound of meat per day. The biggest bump in the road can be cooking more meat than you need, so start buying less meat than you usually do. When you have less meat on hand, you'll eat less of it. Have a go at planning meals with meat on the side of the plate instead of smack dab in the middle. Ramp up the amount of vegetables you buy, and dig up recipes for yummy vegetable dishes. Promulgate some rules for yourself; for example, you may want to have meatless breakfasts and lunches, and then eat whatever you like for dinners. Buckle down on this, and you'll soon find that meat plays a smaller role in your meals.

29b Avoiding Biased or Hurtful Language

Biased or **hurtful language** unfairly or offensively characterizes a particular group and, by extension, its individual members. It can be as blatant as a hatefully uttered racial, ethnic, or sexual slur, but it can also be subtle and unintentional, as in thoughtless stereotyping or an inappropriately applied label.

> **More about ▶▶▶**
Stereotyping, 153

A **stereotype** is a simplified, uncritical, and often negative generalization about an entire group of people: *Blondes are ditzy; athletes are weak students; lawyers are unscrupulous; politicians are dishonest.* Even when they seem positive, stereotypes lump people together in ways that offensively ignore their individuality. In an article in the *New York Times,* for example, Chinese American writer Vivian S. Toy remembers among her "painful experiences of being different" that a college adviser once recommended that she switch her major to biology "since Chinese are better suited for the sciences."

We label people whenever we call attention to a particular characteristic about them. ***Labeling*** is appropriate when it is relevant.

▸ **Barack Obama is the first African American president.**

Labeling is inappropriate, and usually offensive, when it is irrelevant.

▸ **President Obama, an African American, is an articulate debater.**

To appreciate how irrelevant the label "African American" is in that last sentence, consider the following:

▸ **Senator John McCain, who is of Scots-Irish and English descent, is an articulate debater.**

1. Gender bias

Gender bias can be particularly tricky to avoid because until recently it was built into standard usage and vocabulary. English has no pronouns that designate an individual person without also designating that person's gender (*she, he, her, him, hers, his, herself, himself*). This lack creates problems when a writer uses the singular to refer generically to a whole class of people or to people in general.

▸ **The sensible student is careful what [*he? she?*] posts about [*himself? herself?*] on social networking sites like *Facebook* and *MySpace*.**

connect
mhconnectcomposition.com
Additional resources: QL29002, QL29003

Until about the 1970s, the conventional solution to this problem was to use the masculine pronoun as the generic pronoun. In other words, depending on context, *he* referred either to a particular male human or to "he or she," a generic human of either gender. On the other hand, *she* always meant "female," never "she or he." Similarly, the terms *man* and *mankind* could refer generically to humanity as a whole, but *woman* and *womankind* only to women. Since the 1970s, writers have been replacing this usage—together with other vocabulary that reinforces gender stereotypes—with gender-neutral alternatives.

***Avoiding Generic* He** One way to avoid the generic *he,* and often the most graceful way, is to switch from singular to plural.

▸ ~~The sensible student is~~ careful what ~~he posts~~ about ~~himself~~ on social networking sites like *Facebook* and *MySpace*.

Sensible students are   *they post*   *themselves*

Another alternative is to use *he or she* (or *she or he*).

▶ The sensible student is careful what he or she posts on social networking sites.

Be sparing with this option, however; used many times in quick succession, it becomes awkward.

> **AWKWARD** The sensible student is careful what <u>he or she</u> posts about <u>himself or herself</u> on the social networking sites <u>he or she</u> frequents.

More about ▶▶▶
Pronoun-antecedent
agreement,
657–62

NOTE The use of *they* as a generic pronoun for singular antecedents is common in speech, and some people consider it an acceptable alternative to generic *he* in writing as well. Most readers consider this usage ungrammatical, however, so it is best avoided.

▶ ~~The sensible student is~~ *Sensible students are* careful what they post about themselves.

***Avoiding Generic* Man** Replace terms like *man, men,* and *mankind* used to represent all human beings with gender-neutral equivalents such as *humanity, humankind,* or *humans.*

▶ ~~Man is the only animal~~ *Humans are the only animals* to have ventured into space.

Replace occupational names that have the term *man* in them with gender-neutral alternatives.

▶ ~~Congressmen~~ *Members of Congress* have excellent health insurance.

Avoiding Gender Stereotypes and Inappropriate Gender Labeling Some occupations with gender-neutral names are stereotypically associated with either men or women. Avoid perpetuating those stereotypes with inappropriate gender labeling.

▶ Nursing is an ancient, honorable profession. ~~Women~~ *People* who choose it

can expect a rewarding career.

Similarly, avoid stereotyping gender roles in the home and workplace, and avoid patronizing women by addressing them in terms different from those used for men.

Quick **Reference** ➡ **Avoiding Gender-Specific Occupation Names**

Instead of	Consider
businessman	businessperson
chairman	chair, chairperson
clergyman	member of the clergy, minister, pastor, cleric
congressman	member of congress, representative
craftsman	artisan
fireman	firefighter
policeman	police officer
postman	mail carrier
salesman	salesperson, sales representative
spokesman	spokesperson
stewardess	flight attendant
workman	worker

▶ ~~Women~~ with children may want to apply to companies that offer
  job seekers

  flexible hours to working ~~mothers.~~
  parents.

▶ ~~Ladies~~ and men will be evaluated according to the same criteria.
  Women

2. Racial, ethnic, and other labels

Racial and ethnic labels are appropriate only when race or ethnicity is relevant to the topic under discussion. The same is true for references to disabilities, sexual orientation, or other personal characteristics. When you do use labels, avoid terms that may give offense; instead, call people what they want to be called. The term *African American* is now widely accepted as a designation for Americans of African descent. People from Asia are *Asians,* not *Orientals* (a term many find disparaging). *Native American* and *American Indian* (or just *Indian*), on the other hand, are generally acceptable to the people they designate. Best in all cases is to be as specific as context permits. If what you mean is *Vietnamese,* or *Japanese,* or *Inuit,* or *Lakota,* or *Catalan,* or *Sicilian,* then use those terms, not the more general *Asian,* or *Native American,* or *European.* When in doubt about appropriate labels, consult your instructor.

❝ I recently encountered a cleverly designed website intended as a manual for student tutors at a college writing center. However, many of the links that led to the various sections of the site labeled Writing Center students with terms like "clueless," "unfocused," and "disorganized." These disparaging labels encourage tutors to look down on the people who come to them for help. ❞

—Aura Whitcomb, University of Kansas

connect
mhconnectcomposition.com
Online exercise: QL29102

→ **EXERCISE 29.2 Avoiding biased or hurtful language**

Revise the following sentences to eliminate stereotypes, inappropriate labeling, or gender bias. Circle the number of sentences that are appropriate as is.

EXAMPLE

humanity
During the Neolithic Age, ~~man~~ crossed the threshold from nomadic
　　　　　　　　　　　　∧

foraging to agriculture and settled village life.

1. Over the course of history, Oriental hordes like the Huns and Mongols have periodically swept into Europe from Central Asia.

2. The nearly naked savages who greeted Christopher Columbus on the island of Hispaniola were probably members of a group known as the Tainos, who occupied many islands in the Caribbean at the time.

3. One of the reasons Senator John McCain selected Governor Sarah Palin of Alaska as his running mate in 2008 was to appeal to woman voters.

4. Governor Paterson, who is legally blind, delivered the state of the state speech last night.

5. Governor Paterson, who is legally blind, delivers his speeches from memory.

↟ Make It **Your Own**

Read one or more papers you have written or are working on to identify any passages with possibly biased or hurtful language, and then revise those passages using suggestions from this chapter.

Work **Together** ◀

Exchange your work on the Make It Your Own exercise with one or more classmates. Discuss with each other what changes you agree or disagree with and any suggestions you have for further revisions.

30 Choosing Effective Words

Describing the image in this ad as a woman in a bathing suit dancing to the music from her iPod is literally accurate, but it omits something important—the emotional associations that make the ad so effective. This image also says "sexy." It says "carefree," "ecstatic." It says "Buy an iPod, and you can be like her" (or, perhaps, "attractive to someone like her"). Like images, words have both literal meaning and emotional associations. **Diction,** or the choice of words to best convey an idea, requires attention to both.

30a Diction: Finding the Right Word

The literal meaning of a word, its dictionary definition, is its **denotation.** When you use a word, be sure its denotation

Tech

Word Choice and Grammar and Style Checkers

The grammar and style checkers in most word processing programs offer only marginal help with effective word choice. They often cannot distinguish an incorrectly used word from a correctly used one—*affect* from *effect*, for example—nor can they differentiate the emotional associations of words whose literal meaning is similar.

More about ▶▶▶
Commonly confused words, 591, G15–G21

matches your intended meaning. Be particularly careful, for example, not to misuse words that are similar in pronunciation or spelling.

> ▶ The name of the *Harry Potter* character Minerva McGonagall ~~eludes~~ *alludes*
>
> to Minerva, the Roman goddess of wisdom.
>
> To *elude* is to evade or escape; to *allude* is to make an indirect reference.

> ▶ The psychology of perception includes the study of optical ~~allusions.~~ *illusions.*
>
> An *allusion* is an indirect reference; an *illusion* is a mistaken perception.

connect
mhconnectcomposition.com
Additional resources: QL30001

Be careful, too, with words that differ in meaning even though they are otherwise closely related.

> ▶ Many people owe their lives to the ~~heroics~~ *heroism* of volunteer firefighters.
>
> *Heroics* are melodramatic, excessive acts; *heroism* is courageous, potentially self-sacrificing behavior.

connect
mhconnectcomposition.com
Online exercise: QL30101

→ EXERCISE 30.1 Denotation

Consult a dictionary, style guide, the Quick Reference box on p. 591, or the Glossary of Usage at the end of this book as needed to find and correct any misused words in the following sentences.

EXAMPLE

The reporter tried but failed to ~~illicit~~ *elicit* a simple yes or no answer from

the candidate.

1. Most scientists now except human activity as a cause of global warming.

2. Melting glaciers and rising sea levels are often sited as affects of global warming.

3. People in coastal areas may have trouble adopting to rising sea levels.

4. Another eminent result of global warming may be the breakup of ice shelves in Antarctica.

5. The strength of any one hurricane, however, cannot feasibly be attributed to global warming.

The secondary meanings of a word—the psychological or emotional associations it evokes—are its **connotations.** The word *walk,* for example, has many synonyms, including *amble, saunter, stride,* and *march.* Each of these, however, has distinctive connotations, as their effect in the following sentence suggests:

ambled
sauntered
The candidate walked   **to the podium to address her supporters.**
strode
marched

The verb *walk* in this context is emotionally neutral, but the others all have connotations that suggest something about the candidate's state of mind. *Amble* suggests a relaxed aimlessness, whereas *saunter* suggests a jaunty self-confidence. *Stride* and *march* both suggest purposefulness, but *march,* with its military associations, also carries a hint of aggressiveness.

A word's connotations can also vary from reader to reader. To some people, for example, the word *wilderness* evokes a place of great danger; to others, a place of excitement; and to still others, a treasure to be preserved.

❝ As an intern for my local police department, I once tried to spice up an incident report with the phrase 'I alighted from my vehicle.' The sergeant's response—'We don't have any [unprintable expletive] horses in this department, and no one here has ever alighted from anything'—made me realize the disparity, in both denotation and connotation, between the fancy-sounding word I had chosen and the subject and audience I was addressing. ❞

—Michael Bosomworth, Western Illinois University

➔ EXERCISE **30.2** Word choice and tone

Using a blog search engine such as *Technorati* or *Google Blog Search,* find two blogs on the same general topic (the environment or politics, for example). What is the tone of each? How do the writers' word choices create that tone? Discuss the denotation and connotations of five words in each blog that help set its tone. Which of the two blogs do you find more appealing, and why?

connect

mhconnectcomposition.com
Online exercise: QL30102

Writing
Responsibly **Word Choice and Credibility**

The denotation and connotation of the words you choose can powerfully influence the tone of your writing, the effect you have on your readers, and what your readers conclude about you. Highly charged vocabulary, as in the following examples, suggests a partisan point of view, which might lead readers to question the writer's reliability:

Hippie tree huggers are threatening the jobs of thousands of hardworking loggers.

Conscientious activists are trying to protect endangered forests from rapacious, tree-murdering logging companies.

In academic writing, you will enhance your credibility if you describe conflicting positions in even-toned language:

Environmentalists discuss their conflict with the logging industry in terms of the threat industry practices pose to a critical resource; the logging companies, contending that they are responsible forest stewards, describe the conflict in terms of their contribution to local economies.

Once you have looked at the issue fairly, nothing prevents you from then supporting one of these positions and challenging the other.

30b Choosing Compelling Words and Figures

Some words are general, some specific, and others fall between:

←—— more general ——————————— more specific —→
locomote	walk	saunter
fruit	apple	Granny Smith
mountain	California peak	Mt. Whitney

In addition, some words are concrete, designating things or qualities that can be seen, heard, felt, smelled, or touched; and others are abstract, designating concepts like *justice, capitalism,* or *democracy.*

1. Compelling words

In your writing, try to combine the general and abstract with the specific and concrete. You need general and abstract language to frame broad issues, yet specific, concrete language is usually more compelling, calling up images that can capture your readers' attention and help them see things through your eyes. Overly general and abstract language, in contrast, may tire readers and leave them on their own to fill in details in ways you may not have intended. The first of the two following descriptions of the Badwater ultramarathon lacks specific language that can tell us how long the race is, why it is challenging, or exactly where it takes place. The second fills in those details with concrete words—like "hottest spot in America," "stinking water hole," "135 miles," "Death Valley," "piney oasis," "8,300 feet up the side of Mt. Whitney," and "asphalt and road gravel." With these specifics, the writer David Ferrell evokes the challenges of the race without recourse to the abstract word "challenging."

GENERAL AND ABSTRACT   Badwater is a long, physically challenging race over a partially paved course that begins in a geological depression and ends partway up a mountain.

CONCRETE AND SPECIFIC   Badwater is a madman's march, a footrace through the summer heat of the hottest spot in America. It extends 135 miles from a stinking water hole on the floor of Death Valley to a piney oasis 8,300 feet up the side of Mt. Whitney. The course is nothing but asphalt and road gravel. Feet and knees and shins ache like they are being whacked with tire irons. Faces turn into shrink-wrap.

—David Ferrell, "Far Beyond a Mere Marathon"

2. Figures of speech

In the example above, notice how Ferrell, in addition to providing concrete specifics, also uses striking comparisons and juxtapositions to paint a vivid picture of the rigors of the race and to suggest the mindset required to compete in it. He calls the race "a madman's march," for example, and conjures up a beating with a tire iron and an image of a shrink-wrapped face to convey the physical punishment contestants endure. These are examples of ***figurative language,*** or ***figures of speech,*** the imaginative use of language to convey meaning in ways that reach beyond the literal meaning of the words involved. The Quick Reference box on the next page provides definitions and examples of some of the most common figures of speech.

Quick

Reference ➡ Figures of Speech

Figure and Definition	Examples
simile: An explicit comparison between two unlike things, usually expressed with *like* or *as*	Feet and knees and shins ache like they are being whacked with tire irons. *—David Ferrell* Only final exams, like the last lap of a long race, lay between the members of the senior class and their diplomas.
metaphor: An implied comparison between unlike things stated without *like, as,* or other comparative expressions	Faces turn into shrink-wrap. *—David Ferrell* After crossing the finish line of their last exams, seniors looked forward to that moment on the victory stand when the president of the college would bestow a diploma on them.
analogy: An extended simile or metaphor, often comparing something familiar to something unfamiliar. Well-constructed analogies can be particularly effective for explaining difficult concepts	What that means [that the universe is expanding] is that we're not at the center of the universe, after all; instead, we're like a single raisin in a vast lump of dough that is rising in an oven where all the other raisins are moving away from each other, faster and faster as the oven gets hotter and hotter. *—David Perlman, "At 12 Billion Years Old, Universe Still Growing Fast"*
personification: The attribution of human qualities to nonhuman creatures, objects, ideas, or phenomena	The plague that rampaged through Europe in the fourteenth century selected its victims indiscriminately, murdering rich and poor in equal proportion.
hyperbole: Deliberate exaggeration for emphasis	That little restaurant on Main Street makes the best pizza on the planet.
understatement: The deliberate use of less forceful language than a subject warrants	The report of my death was an exaggeration. *—Mark Twain, clearly alive and well, responding to an obituary about him in a London paper*
irony: The use of language to suggest the opposite of its literal meaning or to express an incongruity between what is expected and what occurs	I come to bury Caesar, not to praise him. *—Mark Antony, in Shakespeare's play Julius Caesar, in a speech that praises the murdered leader effusively*

→ **EXERCISE 30.3 Compelling words**

Use your imagination—and additional sentences, if need be—to flesh out the following sentences with concrete, specific words.

connect
mhconnectcomposition.com
Online exercise: QL30103

EXAMPLE

The party last night was fun because we played games and I met some people I like.

Last night's party at Jan's house was hopping until about 3 a.m., but I didn't notice the time rushing by because we played an absorbing role-playing game in which each of us tried to capture all of the others without being captured. I also met Brad, who shares my interest in composing music, and Mia, with whom I talked about anime for an hour.

1. Alexandra's apartment is rather small and plain.
2. Next year, I will study abroad at the place I've always dreamed of visiting.
3. This meal was delicious and surprisingly healthful.
4. The movie was not for squeamish people.
5. I know the exact features I want in a car.

→ **EXERCISE 30.4 Figures of speech**

Identify any figures of speech in the following passages, indicate what type of figure each is, and explain how it is used.

connect
mhconnectcomposition.com
Online exercise: QL30104

EXAMPLE

It isn't very serious. I have this tiny little tumor on the brain. (J. D. Salinger, *The Catcher in the Rye*)

This is an example of understatement. A little tumor on the brain is extremely serious.

1. The whole peninsula of Florida was weighted down with regret. Everyone had left behind a real life. —Cynthia Ozick, *Rosa*
2. Everybody lies about sex. People lie during sex. If it weren't for lies, there'd be no sex. —Jerry Seinfeld, in the *New York Times*, 18 Dec. 1998
3. Money is the mother's milk of politics. —Jesse Marvin Unruh
4. You'd be surprised how much it costs to look this cheap. —Dolly Parton

5. Pupils are more like oysters than sausages. The job of teaching is not to stuff them and then seal them up, but to help them open and reveal the riches within. There are pearls in each of us, if only we knew how to cultivate them with ardor and persistence. —Sydney J. Harris, "What True Education Should Do," 1964

6. The only monster here is the gambling monster that has enslaved your mother! I call him Gamblor, and it's time to snatch your mother from his neon claws! —Homer Simpson in *The Simpsons*

3. Inappropriate figures and mixed metaphors

Used judiciously, figures of speech can enliven and deepen your prose. Used in the wrong context or piled inconsistently one on the other in *mixed metaphors,* they can be jarring, even silly. The original simile in the following example incongruously invokes the image of a pole vaulter, an athlete who goes mostly up and down, to describe a speeding train, which travels mostly horizontally. The revision, comparing the train to a race horse, is more apt.

> ▶ The new high-speed train, like a champion ~~pole vaulter,~~ *thoroughbred,* made it from Boston to Washington in record time.

Mixed metaphors confuse readers with multiple, conflicting images for the same concept.

MIXED METAPHOR   Confronted with the tsunami of data available on the internet, researchers, like travelers caught in a blinding desert sandstorm, may have trouble finding the nuggets of valuable information buried in a mountain of otherwise worthless ore.

The sentence above, seeking to emphasize the challenges of online research, invokes tsunamis, sandstorms, mountains, and mining.

REVISED   As they mine the mountain of data available on the internet, researchers may have trouble identifying the nuggets of valuable information buried with the otherwise worthless ore they dig up.

The revision elaborates a single metaphor that compares finding useful information online to mining for precious minerals.

30c   Mastering Idioms

Idioms are expressions whose meaning does not depend on the meanings of the words that compose them. Each idiom is a unified package of meaning with its own denotations and connotations. The following sentence, for example, would make no sense if you tried to interpret it based on the literal meaning of the words *call, on,* and *carpet:*

> ▶ The directors called the CEO on the carpet for the company's poor
>
> sales in 2009.

Of course, the expression *call on the carpet* has nothing to do with calls or carpets. It is an idiom that, understood as a whole, means *to reprimand* or *scold.*

Most dictionaries list idiomatic uses of particular words. The entry for *call* in *The Merriam-Webster Online Dictionary,* for example, provides definitions for the idioms *call for, call forth, call into question, call it a day,* and *call it quits,* among others. For more detailed information on the history and meaning of particular idioms, consult a specialized dictionary such as *The American Heritage Dictionary of Idioms.*

> **More about** ▶▶▶
> Specialized dictionaries, 585–86

 Idioms, Prepositions, and Phrasal Verbs Because idioms can be understood only as a whole, you have to learn them as a whole, just as you would any unfamiliar word. Pay particular attention to the way prepositions combine with other words in idiomatic ways. A ***phrasal verb,*** for example, is a combination of a verb with one or more prepositions that has a different meaning than the verb alone.

> Raisa *saw* the flat tire on her car. [She looked at it.]
>
> Raisa *saw to* the flat tire on her car. [She had it repaired.]

> **More about** ▶▶▶
> Prepositions, 773–80
> Phrasal verbs, 756–58

30d   Avoiding Clichés

A ***cliché*** is a figure of speech, idiom, or other expression that has grown stale from overuse (see the Quick Reference box on the next page for some examples). Clichés come quickly to mind because they encapsulate common wit and wisdom in widely recognized phrases. For the same reason, they provide an easy substitute for fresh thought and expression. They may help you frame a subject in the early drafts

Reference ➡ **Dodging Deadly Clichés**

When you encounter clichés like these in your writing, delete them or replace them with fresher images of your own.

best thing since sliced bread	hit the nail on the head	smart as a whip
beyond a shadow of a doubt	a hundred and one percent	straight and narrow
cold, hard fact	in the prime of life	think outside the box
cool as a cucumber	just desserts	throw [something] to the wind
down and dirty	nip and tuck	tried and true
down the home stretch	no way, shape, or form	wallow in the mire
easier said than done	on their best behavior	without a moment's hesitation
face the music	one foot out the door	zero tolerance
faster than greased lightning	plain as the nose on your face	
green with envy	slow as molasses	

of a paper, but they can also make your writing sound trite and unimaginative. You should edit them out as you refine your ideas. As the following example indicates, writing that is loaded with clichés is often also loaded with mixed metaphors.

> **CLICHÉ LADEN** As the campaign pulled into the home stretch and the cold hard fact of the increasingly nip-and-tuck polls sank in, the candidates threw their promises to stay on their best behavior to the wind and wallowed in the mire of down-and-dirty attack ads.

> **REVISED** As Election Day neared and the polls showed the race tightening, the candidates abandoned their promises of civility and released a barrage of unscrupulous attack ads.

 What Is the Difference between an Idiom and a Cliché? The only thing that separates an idiom from a cliché is the frequency with which it is used. If you are not a native English speaker, you may not recognize an idiom as a cliché if you have not encountered it often in your reading. If you have questions about clichés and idioms, ask your instructor or consult a dictionary of idioms, such as *McGraw-Hill's Dictionary of American Idioms and Phrasal Verbs* or the *Longman American Idioms Dictionary*.

connect
mhconnectcomposition.com
Online exercise: QL30105

→ **EXERCISE 30.5 Avoiding clichés and mixed metaphors**

Edit the following sentences to eliminate clichés and mixed metaphors.

EXAMPLE

Mayor Wyndham has been reelected regularly because people feel

that she is ~~tried and true~~ and does not do anything unexpected.
      reliable

1. Her new proposal hit the town council like a ton of bricks.

2. She wanted to have the county reroute the main road to the capital smack dab through town, forcing traffic to run a gauntlet through our commercial center.

3. Store owners, who have recently seen their sales sink like a stone, thought the plan hit the nail on the head and were happy as clams.

4. However, most townspeople flooded the mayor's office with an avalanche of angry calls and emails opposing the proposal.

5. Opponents insisted that in no way, shape, or form would they take to a proposal that threatened the peace and quiet that had attracted them to the town in the first place.

▲ Make It **Your Own**

Review one of your recent writing projects to identify and revise any passages that include misused words, words with an inappropriate connotation, or words that are overly general or abstract. What effect do your changes have on your overall tone?

Work **Together** ◄

Exchange your work on the Make It Your Own exercise above with a classmate and check your classmate's writing for misused words, words with an inappropriate connotation, and words that are overly general or abstract. Then discuss possible revisions and their effect on the tone of the selection.

31 Using the Dictionary and Spelling Correctly

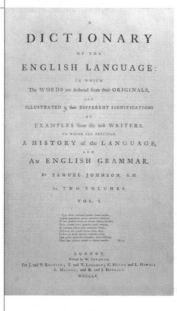

Samuel Johnson's *Dictionary of the English Language* (1755), although not the first ever published, established many of the conventions still found in dictionaries today. Johnson identified a core vocabulary of some 43,500 words; labeled each word's part of speech; briefly traced its origins; provided a concise, elegant (and sometimes humorous) definition of the word in all its senses; and accompanied each definition with an illustrative quotation. Johnson hoped to define and fix a standard of proper spelling and usage, but his dictionary, like those that have followed it, also reflects the state of the language in the time and place in which it was created.

31a Choosing a Dictionary

Dictionaries today come in a variety of forms, both printed and electronic, large and small, general purpose and specialized.

Abridged Dictionaries Sometimes referred to as "desk dictionaries," these handy volumes contain information on approximately 200,000 words. Examples include the *American Heritage College Dictionary, Merriam-Webster's Collegiate Dictionary,* the

Random House Webster's College Dictionary, and *Webster's New World College Dictionary.* The *American Heritage College Dictionary* is available online at *Yahoo! Education. Merriam-Webster's Collegiate Dictionary* is available online as the *Merriam-Webster Online Dictionary.* Most word processing programs also include a built-in dictionary with many features of an abridged dictionary.

Unabridged Dictionaries Unabridged dictionaries contain detailed entries for most words in the English language, some half a million words in total. The most comprehensive unabridged dictionary is the twenty-volume *Oxford English Dictionary* (known as the *OED*). Others include *Random House Webster's Unabridged Dictionary* and *Webster's Third New International Dictionary, Unabridged.*

Both the *OED* and *Webster's Third New International* are available online for a fee. You should be able to find an unabridged dictionary in the reference section of any library, however, and many libraries provide access to online versions.

 Dictionaries for Second-Language Learners In addition to translation dictionaries and standard abridged and unabridged dictionaries, you may also want to consult an all-English dictionary tailored for the second-language learner, such as *Heinle's Newbury House Dictionary of American English,* the *Longman Dictionary of American English,* or the *Oxford Dictionary of American English.* To understand American slang and idioms, consult a dictionary such as *McGraw-Hill's Dictionary of American Slang and Colloquial Expressions.*

Specialized Dictionaries Specialized dictionaries focus on a particular aspect of English vocabulary.

- Dictionaries of usage provide guidance about the use of particular words or phrases. Examples include the *American Heritage Book of English Usage* (available online at Bartleby .com) and *Right, Wrong, and Risky: A Dictionary of Today's American English Usage. The New Fowler's Modern English Usage* provides guidance on British usage.

- Subject-specific dictionaries explain the specialized terminology of particular fields and professions. Examples include the *Dictionary of Anthropology, Black's Law Dictionary,* and *A Dictionary of Business and Management.* For links to subject-specific dictionaries and glossaries available online, try *Glossarist* and *YourDictionary.com.*

connect
mhconnectcomposition.com
Additional resources: QL31001

> *More about* ▶▶▶
Subject-specific
dictionaries,
234–37

Writing Responsibly

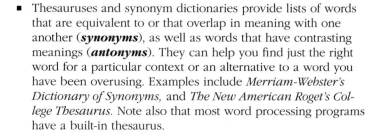

Choose Accurate Synonyms

When you consult a thesaurus, be sure you check both the meanings (*denotations*) and the associations (*connotations*) of the words you find there. A carelessly chosen synonym can distort the information you intend to convey. Suppose, for example, that you wanted to replace *intimidate* in the sentence "The professor's brilliance intimi-

dated her students." Looking in a thesaurus, you might find both *overawe* and *bludgeon* listed as synonyms. *Overawe* is an appropriate substitute, probably more precisely reflecting the effect of the professor on her students than *intimidate*. *Bludgeon*, in contrast, inaccurately conjures visions of a bloody crime scene.

> **More about ▶▶▶**
> Denotation and con-
> notation, 17–18,
> 573–75

- Thesauruses and synonym dictionaries provide lists of words that are equivalent to or that overlap in meaning with one another (***synonyms***), as well as words that have contrasting meanings (***antonyms***). They can help you find just the right word for a particular context or an alternative to a word you have been overusing. Examples include *Merriam-Webster's Dictionary of Synonyms,* and *The New American Roget's College Thesaurus.* Note also that most word processing programs have a built-in thesaurus.

> **EXERCISE 31.1 Using a thesaurus**

Look up one of the following words in a thesaurus. Choose three synonyms for that word and write a separate sentence for the original word and for each synonym that accurately reflects both its meaning and connotation.

make	problem	funny
talent	strange	fight

31b Using a Dictionary

Figure 31.1 (p. 588) shows the entry for the word *respect* in the *Merriam-Webster Online Dictionary,* the online counterpart to the eleventh edition of *Merriam-Webster's Collegiate Dictionary.* Although most online and printed abridged dictionaries present the same kinds of information, each has its own format and system of abbreviations.

Spelling, Word Division, and Pronunciation Entries begin with the word correctly spelled followed by acceptable variant spellings, if any. Dots

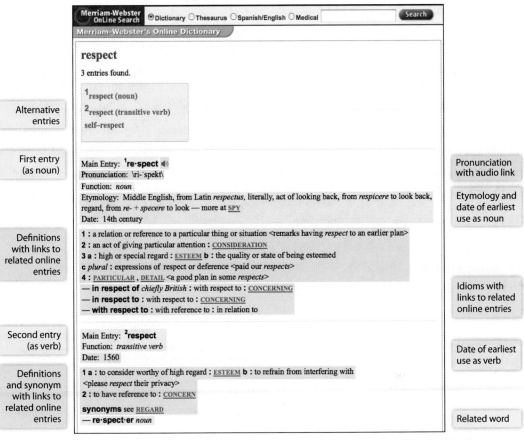

Alternative entries

First entry (as noun)

Definitions with links to related online entries

Second entry (as verb)

Definitions and synonym with links to related online entries

Pronunciation with audio link

Etymology and date of earliest use as noun

Idioms with links to related online entries

Date of earliest use as verb

Related word

FIGURE 31.1 The entry for "respect" in the *Merriam-Webster Online Dictionary*

More about ▶▶▶
Hyphenation, 826–67

More about ▶▶▶
Regular and irregular verbs, 666–69
Regular and irregular plurals, 595–96

show the division of the word into syllables, indicating where to put a hyphen if you must break the word between lines of text. Next, the pronunciation of the word is given. The print version has a key to pronunciation symbols; the online version has a link to this key, but it also gives the pronunciation in an audio link.

Grammatical Functions and Forms Labels indicate the part of speech and other grammatical aspects of a word. Most dictionaries specify the forms of irregular verbs (*draw, drew, drawn*) but not of regular verbs like *respect,* and they provide irregular plurals (*woman, women*) but not regular plurals (*dogs*). The entry shown in Figure 31.1 includes a definition of the plural form *respects* because it has a usage that does not apply to the singular form.

More about ▶▶▶
Idiomatic expressions, 581

Definitions and Examples If a word has more than one definition, each is numbered, and any additional distinctions within a definition are labeled with a letter. Several definitions in the entry for *respect* as a noun include examples of the word used in context. At the end of the entry are the definitions of several idiomatic expressions that include *respect*.

More about ▶▶▶
Usage in "A Glossary of Usage," G15–G21

Synonyms and Usage Most dictionaries list synonyms for the entry word; in online dictionaries, clicking on a synonym will take you to the full entry for that word. Usage labels offer guidance on how to use a word appropriately.

connect
mhconnectcomposition.com
Online exercise: QL31102

 EXERCISE 31.2 Using a dictionary

Look up the following words in a dictionary. Write down any alternate spellings, mark its division into syllables, and underline the stressed syllable.

permanent	develop	approximate
addition	opportunity	component

31c Avoiding Common Spelling Problems

For most people, spelling does not come easily. Even voracious readers and expert writers need to review common spelling problems, such as spelling from pronunciation, confusing homonyms, and confusing different forms of the same word.

ESL **Using a Bilingual Dictionary as an Aid to English Spelling** A bilingual or translation dictionary can help you find the spelling of English words, especially if your language, like Spanish, has a more phonetic spelling system than does English. For example, if you think "physician" begins with the letter "f," you will have a hard time finding the correct spelling in an English dictionary, but if you look up "médico" in a Spanish-English dictionary, you will immediately find the proper spelling.

1. The unreliability of pronunciation

The word *Wednesday* is pronounced without the first *d* and the second *e* ("Wensday"). The letters *ow* on *sow* are pronounced as in *cow* when *sow* is used as a noun meaning "female pig." When *sow* is used as a verb meaning "to plant seeds," however, the letters *ow* are pronounced like the *ew* in *sew*. As these examples indicate, you cannot rely on the way a word sounds to guide you to its correct spelling.

2. Homonyms and other problematic words

Many spelling errors result from confusion over homonyms and near-homonyms like those in the Quick Reference box on p. 591.

- **Homonyms** are groups of words that sound exactly alike but have different spellings and meanings, such as *to/too/two* and *cite/sight/site*.

- **Near-homonyms** are groups of words such as *personal/personnel* and *conscience/conscious* that are close but not the same in pronunciation. Near-homonyms also include groups such as *breath/breathe* and *advice/advise* that are different forms of the same word.

There is no easy formula for mastering these words. If any of them give you trouble, try to memorize their spellings and meanings, and always check for them as you proofread your writing.

> **More about ▶▶▶**
> Confusing words
> and phrases in "A
> Glossary of Usage,"
> G15–G21

 Use American Rather Than British Spelling Multilingual writers who began their study of English outside the United States may be accustomed to British spelling, which is often different from American, as the following list shows. When writing for a U.S. audience, be sure to follow American style. When in doubt, consult an American dictionary, which will give the preferred American spelling before any alternates.

American	British
airplane	aeroplane
labor/mold	labour/mould
theater	theatre
check	cheque
counseled	counselled
defense	defence
plagiarize	plagiarise
program	programme

→ EXERCISE 31.3 Using homonyms and near-homonyms

In each of the following sentences, underline the correct word from among the choices in parentheses.

EXAMPLE

In my biology (coarse, <u>course</u>), the instructor asked us to (device, <u>devise</u>) an experiment that can be completed in less (then, <u>than</u>) one class session.

1. The (plain, plane) truth is that this is a (waist, waste) of perfectly edible (meat, meet).

2. He is in such a hurry to leave that he has (all ready, already) eaten his (hole, whole) (desert, dessert).

3. Kevin's (advice, advise) is that you should be as (fair, fare) as you can and follow your (conscience, conscious).

4. This is the (forth, fourth) (complement, compliment) Ms. Johansen has received for her address to the town (council, counsel).

5. (Its, It's) (right, rite, wright) to (wear, where, were) a business suit for a job interview at a bank.

31d Remembering Spelling Rules

Mastering a few key rules—and noting their exceptions—can improve the accuracy of your spelling.

Writing
Responsibly Spelling Errors

A misspelled word is not an important issue when you are texting friends, but in other situations it may signal that you are careless about details. If you misspell *accountant* in a job-application letter to a financial firm, for example, the recipient may wonder how accurate you are about numbers. If you misspell a name, people may interpret it as a sign of indifference or disrespect.

accept (to take willingly)
except (to exclude)

advice (counsel)
advise (to offer counsel)

affect (to influence; feeling)
effect (to cause; a result)

all ready (fully prepared)
already (by this time)

allude (to mention indirectly)
elude (to avoid)

allusion (an indirect reference)
illusion (a deceptive or false
    perception)

altar (a raised structure for
    religious ritual)
alter (to change)

are (form of *be*)
our (relating to us)

ascent (upward advance)
assent (to concur)

bare (unclothed; to make
    known)
bear (an animal; to support)

board (a piece of wood; to get
    on a vehicle)
bored (uninterested)

brake (stopping mechanism)
break (to wreck; a pause)

capital (seat of government)
capitol (building for the
    legislature)

cite (to acknowledge a source)
sight (something to see)
site (a place)

complement (to complete)
compliment (an admiring
    remark)

conscience (moral awareness)
conscious (awake, mindful)

council (a governing or advi-
    sory group)
counsel (advice; to advise)

descent (downward
    movement)
dissent (disagreement)

desert (desolate area; to abandon)
dessert (a meal's last course)

device (a contrivance)
devise (to contrive)

discreet (prudent, unpretentious)
discrete (distinct)

elicit (to bring out)
illicit (illegal)

eminent (highly regarded)
imminent (about to happen)
immanent (inherent)

fair (attractive; impartial)
fare (a price for transportation)

forth (forward)
fourth (following *third*)

gorilla (a great ape)
guerrilla (a fighter in unconven-
    tional warfare)

grate (to grind or irritate)
great (large or superior)

hear (to perceive sound)
here (at this place)

hole (an opening)
whole (complete)

incidence (rate of occurrence)
incidents (occurrences)

its (possessive of *it*)
it's (*it is* or *it has*)

lead (a metal; to go ahead of)
led (past tense of *lead*)

meat (edible animal flesh)
meet (to encounter)

passed (past tense of *pass*)
past (before the present)

patience (calm persistence)
patients (people under medical
    care)

peace (tranquility)
piece (a part)

personal (private; individual)
personnel (employees)

plain (not complicated)
plane (aircraft; carpenter's tool)

presence (being in attendance)
presents (gifts)

principal (most significant;
    chief)
principle (rule or tenet)

rain (precipitation)
reign (monarch's period of rule)
rein (strap used to control an
    animal; to restrain)

raise (to lift)
raze (to demolish)

respectfully (with respect)
respectively (in the order
    given)

right (correct; opposite of *left*)
rite (ceremony or ritual)
wright (one who fashions a
    thing)
write (to form words on a
    surface)

road (street)
rode (past tense of *ride*)

stationary (immobile)
stationery (writing paper)

than (compared to)
then (at that time; therefore)

their (possessive of *they*)
there (in that place)
they're (*they are*)

to (toward)
too (also)
two (number after *one*)

waist (midriff; narrow part)
waste (garbage; to squander)

weak (not strong)
week (seven days)

wear (to have on)
where (in what direction or
    place)
were (past tense of *be*)

weather (condition of the
    atmosphere)
whether (word that introduces
    choices or alternatives)

which (what one)
witch (sorcerer)

who's (*who is* or *who has*)
whose (possessive of *who*)

your (possessive of *you*)
you're (*you are*)

1. The *ie/ei* rule

The traditional rule—"*i* before *e* except after *c* or when sounded like *ay* as in *neighbor* and *weigh*"—will help you spell words like *believe, receive,* and *sleigh* correctly.

I BEFORE *E*	diesel, piece, pier, retrieve, shield, siege
E BEFORE *I* AFTER *C*	ceiling, conceit, conceive, deceit, perceive, receipt
EI SOUNDS LIKE *AY*	beige, deign, eighteen, reindeer, sleigh, veil

Some exceptions: *feisty, forfeit, heifer, height, heir, neither, protein, sovereign, seize, their, weird.*

connect

mhconnectcomposition.com
Online exercise: QL31104

EXERCISE **31.4** Spelling *ie* and *ei* words

Correct any misspellings in the following sentences.

EXAMPLE

                  relieved   *deceive*

Superman probably would have been ~~releived~~ not to have had to ~~decieve~~

Lois Lane about his identity.

1. When Angie recieved the reciept for her rental deposit, she knew she had reached a milestone in her life.

2. It was her first apartment, and the cielings were eighteen feet high!

3. With that hieght, she could retreive her tall sculpture from her parents' backyard and install it in her apartment.

4. Of course, creating such an oversized sculpture had been a conciet, but she had always beleived that art should have no boundaries.

5. Now that fiesty conviction in the form of a huge peice of biege metal would take palpable shape in the very first home of her own.

2. Prefixes

Prefixes attach to the beginning of a root word to modify its meaning. Prefixes have no effect on the spelling of the rest of the word, even if the last letter of the prefix and the first letter of the root word are the same. For example, *re-* combines with *wind* to form *rewind, dis-* combines with *inherit* to form *disinherit,* and *mis-* combines with *statement* to form *misstatement*. In some cases, however, a hyphen separates a prefix from the rest of the word, as in *anti-inflammatory*.

More about ▶▶▶
Prefixes and hyphen-
ation, 863–64

3. Suffixes

Suffixes attach to the end of a root word to change its meaning and grammatical form. The suffix *-ly*, for example, changes the adjective *sweet* to the adverb *sweetly*. Unlike prefixes, suffixes often affect the spelling of the preceding root.

Words That End with a Silent e In most instances, drop the silent *e* if the suffix starts with a vowel:

> observe → observant   response → responsible   revoke → revoked

Retain the silent *e* if the suffix starts with a consonant:

> hope → hopeful   love → lovely   polite → politeness

Some exceptions: *advantageous, argument, duly, enforceable, judgment, serviceable.*

Words That End with y For most words that end with a consonant and *y*, change the *y* to an *i* when you add a suffix:

> apology → apologize   deny → denies
>
> heavy → heavier   merry → merriment

Retain the *y* if the suffix is *-ing*, if a vowel precedes the *y*, or if the word ending in *y* is a proper name:

> spy → spying   play → playful   McCoy → McCoys

Suffixes -cede, -ceed, and -sede To avoid confusing these three suffixes, remember these facts:

1. *Supersede* is the only English word that ends in *-sede.*
2. *Exceed, proceed,* and *succeed* are the only words that end in *-ceed.*
3. All other similar words use the suffix *-cede: accede, concede, precede, secede.*

Suffixes -ally versus -ly and -efy versus -ify When a word ends in *ic,* use the suffix *-ally.* In all other instances, use *-ly:*

> basic → basically   magic → magically
>
> brisk → briskly   confident → confidently

Only four words use the suffix -*efy*: *liquefy, putrefy, rarefy, stupefy.* All other such words use the suffix -*ify*: *beautify, certify, justify, purify.*

Words That End with a Consonant Do not double a final consonant if the suffix begins with a consonant (*commitment, fearless, kinship, poorly*). For suffixes that begin with a vowel, follow these guidelines:

- **One-syllable root words.** Double the final consonant if only one vowel precedes it:

  bit → bitten   chat → chatty   skip → skipping

  For other one-syllable words, do not double the consonant:

  chart → charted   droop → drooping   speak → speaker

- **Multisyllable words.** Double the final consonant if only one vowel precedes the final consonant and if the final syllable of the root is accented in the new word containing the suffix:

  admit → ad**mitt**ance   concur → con**curr**ent

  control → con**troll**ed

For multisyllable words that do not meet these criteria, do not double the final consonant:

  devil → devilish   parallel → parallelism

  erupt → erupted   proclaim → proclaiming

In *devilish* and *parallelism*, the accent is on the first syllable of the root word; the final *t* in *erupt* is preceded by a consonant; and the final *m* in *proclaim* is preceded by two vowels.

> 66 When editing my papers, I go through what I call the S-E-P system. The S stands for 'spell check,' which is the first thing I do. The E stands for 'every line needs your own eyes,' which translates into critically reading each line myself, because spelling checkers make mistakes. P stands for 'print and proofread.' I always proofread better when I have the actual paper in my hand. I ask a friend to read it, too. 99
> —Christina Huey, Georgia Southern University

EXERCISE 31.5 Adding suffixes

Correct any misspelled words in the following list, and circle those that are spelled correctly.

changable	truely	begining	tragicly
deploing	argueable	replys	runing
supercede	regreted	optimally	angryly
principally	soly	sponsorred	

→ Tech

Use Spelling Checkers Cautiously

Most of today's word processing programs correct some misspelled words while you type, identify other words that may be misspelled, and let you run a manual spelling check whenever you wish. Although these features are helpful, you cannot depend on them alone to guarantee error-free spelling.

- Spelling checkers do not differentiate homonyms and commonly confused words, such as *descent, dissent* or *too, two*. If you type a correctly spelled word that happens not to be correct for the context, a spelling checker will not mark it wrong.
- If you misspell a word, a spelling checker may suggest replacing it with the wrong

word. For example, if you type *retify* for *rectify,* the checker's first recommendation might be *ratify,* which is clearly the wrong word.

- A spelling checker will not catch the misspelling of most proper names unless you enter them in its dictionary.
- A spelling checker will not alert you to most errors in capitalization.

Spelling checkers, then, are a useful tool but not a replacement for a dictionary and careful proofreading. Check the spelling checker.

More about ▶▶▶
Capitalization,
839–45

31e Forming Plurals

Most English nouns form the plural by adding the suffix -*s* or -*es.* Some nouns, however, like *child* (plural *children*) and *man* (plural *men*), have irregular forms, and some compound nouns form the plural on a word that is not the last one in the compound.

1. Regular plurals

- To form the plural of most English nouns, add an -*s.*

  letter → letters   shoe → shoes   Erickson → the Ericksons

- To form the plural of nouns that end with *s, sh, ch, x,* or *z,* add -*es.*

  miss → misses   dish → dishes   latch → latches

  box → boxes   fez → fezzes   Davis → the Davises

- To form the plural of some nouns that end with *f* or *fe,* change the *f* to a *v* and add -*s* or -*es.*

  loaf → loaves   scarf → scarves   thief → thieves

  knife → knives   wife → wives

However, words that end in *ff* or *ffe* and some words that end in *f* or *fe* form the plural just with the addition of an *-s*.

bluff → bluffs   giraffe → giraffes

chief → chiefs   safe → safes

- To form the plural of nouns that end with *o*, add *-s* if the *o* is preceded by a vowel or if the word is a proper noun.

duo → duos   ratio → ratios   video → videos

Add *-es* if the *o* is preceded by a consonant.

echo → echoes   potato → potatoes   veto → vetoes

Some exceptions: *autos, ponchos, sopranos, tacos*

- To form the plural of words that end with *y*, add *-s* if the *y* is preceded by a vowel or if the word is a proper noun.

decoy → decoys   essay → essays   Hagarty → the Hagartys

Change the *y* to *i* and add *-es* if the *y* is preceded by a consonant.

berry → berries   enemy → enemies   family → families

2. Irregular plurals

The only way to learn irregular plurals is to memorize them. Many nouns have irregular plurals that have survived from earlier forms of English.

woman → women   child → children   deer → deer

foot → feet   ox → oxen   sheep → sheep

mouse → mice

Other nouns with irregular plurals were borrowed into English from languages such as Greek, Latin, and French and retain the plural form of the original language.

analysis → analyses   criterion → criteria   phenomenon → phenomena

alumna → alumnae   medium → media   tableau → tableaux

alumnus → alumni   nucleus → nuclei

For many such words, a regularized plural form is acceptable as an alternative to the irregular form: *index, indices/indexes; fungus, fungi/funguses.*

3. Plurals of compound nouns

To form the plural of compound nouns composed of separate or hyphenated words, add *-s* or *-es* to the main noun in the compound.

brigadier generals   chiefs of staff   runners-up

If there is no main noun, add *-s* or *-es* at the end: *singer-songwriters*

For compounds that are spelled as one word, add *-s* or *-es* at the end.

keyboards   spaceships   touchdowns

An exception: *passersby*

> **EXERCISE 31.6 Forming plurals**
>
> Write the plural form of each of the following singular nouns.
>
> | | | | |
> |---|---|---|---|
> | buzz | rally | half | ploy |
> | mother-in-law | domino | study | tooth |
> | handcuff | moose | studio | goose |
> | spoof | person | tomato | |

31f   Improving Your Day-to-Day Spelling

Writers who have mastered all the rules in this chapter may still misspell some words sometimes. Here are a few tips for further reducing misspellings in your work:

- If you tend to misspell the same word or types of words repeatedly, keep track of them in a vocabulary log and check for them specifically when you proofread.

- Use a dictionary often, and keep one handy next to your computer.

- Remember that pronunciation may lead you astray in your spelling. Although you may say "goverment," do not forget that *govern* is the root word, so the word is spelled "government," with an *n*.

- Use a spelling checker with caution (see the Tech box on p. 595), and proofread carefully.

▲ Make It **Your Own**

With the spelling checker on, type this sentence into a blank word processing document:

> Fore score and seven yours ago, are fathers brought fourth on this continence anew nation, conceived in liberty and dedicated to the preposition that awl men our created equal.

Now compare the sentence to the first sentence of Abraham Lincoln's Gettysburg Address <www.loc.gov/exhibits/gadd/images/Gettysburg-2.jpg>. How many errors did the spelling checker catch? Introduce two or more similar errors into other famous passages (or into passages from a textbook or a newspaper or magazine article), and see how dependably the spelling checker catches them. For famous quotations, consult a printed collection like *Bartlett's Familiar Quotations, The Yale Book of Quotations,* or *The Oxford Dictionary of Quotations.* Or consult an online source like *The Quotations Page* <www.quotationspage.com> or the quotations sections of *The Other Pages* <www.theotherpages.org/quote.html>.

Work **Together** ◀

With a classmate, exchange printouts (double-spaced) of the sentences with the errors you introduced in the Make It Your Own exercise above. Correct the sentences by hand; then check your work against the original sources.

Grammar
Matters

Common Sentence Problems

frag **Recognizing and Correcting Fragments (626–36)**

A fragment is an incomplete sentence punctuated as if it were complete.

education is

The system of American higher ~~education. It is~~ founded on principles of
^

honesty and academic integrity.

Reducing the incidence of plagiarism among college students will be difficult,

however, without

~~however. Without~~ an understanding of its causes that goes beyond simplistic explanations.
^

sv agr **Maintaining Subject-Verb Agreement (646–57)**

A verb and its subject agree when they match each other in person (first, second, or third) and number (singular or plural).

For this reason, nearly everyone invested in this system—students, instructors, and

recognizes

administrators—~~recognize~~ that plagiarism cannot be tolerated.
^

have

That plagiarism and related misconduct ~~has~~ become all too common is beyond dispute.
^

pn ag **Maintaining Pronoun-Antecedent Agreement (657–63)**

A pronoun agrees with its antecedent (the word the pronoun replaces) when they match each other in person (first, second, or third), number (singular or plural), and gender (masculine, feminine, or neuter).

students are

In this myth, ~~the student is~~ too apathetic and slothful to finish their assignments on their
^

own; instead, they cheat.

Such students may treat the attainment of impressive marks as a necessity and will betray

they revere *their*

the very academic system ~~he or she reveres~~ in order to sustain ~~his or her~~ average.
^   ^

Common Sentence Problems

shift Avoiding Confusing Shifts in Tense and Voice (710–13)

Shifts from one tense to another or from the active to the passive voice are confusing when they occur for no clear reason.

Students who view writing papers as hoops they must jump through to graduate, for

instance, ~~were~~ *are* more likely simply to ~~have downloaded~~ *download* a paper from an online "paper

mill" than to write one themselves.

Students draw a distinction between their interests and their academic assignments,

~~and plagiarism is rationalized by them~~ *and they rationalize plagiarism* as a way to escape an "unfair" academic obligation.

inc Avoiding Incomplete Constructions (733–36)

A phrase or clause is incomplete if it is missing any words required for idiomatic and grammatical clarity.

Websites such as *essaytown.com,* which will write a paper to order, cater *to* students like

these, who consider at least some aspects of academia essentially useless.

mix Avoiding Mixed Constructions (728–33)

A mixed construction is a sentence with parts that do not fit together grammatically or logically.

Even ~~recognizing~~ *students who recognize* the importance of citation may not know how to cite their sources

correctly.

ad Distinguishing Adjectives and Adverbs (700–08)

Adjectives modify nouns or pronouns; adverbs modify verbs, adjectives, other adverbs, and entire phrases and clauses.

The Internet is a place of free exchange and information ~~movement rapidly~~ *the rapid movement of* from

computer to computer.

fs Recognizing and Correcting Fused (Run-On) Sentences (637–45)

In a fused (or run-on) sentence, one independent clause incorrectly follows another with no punctuation or joining words between them.

> _better. According to_
> Practices among higher education students are not much ~~better according to~~ research by Donald
>
> L. McCabe, a professor at Rutgers University who has done extensive work on cheating, 38% of
>
> college students admitted to committing forms of plagiarism in the previous year (Rimer 7).

cs Recognizing and Correcting Comma Splices (637–45)

In a comma splice, two independent clauses are incorrectly joined by a comma alone, without a coordinating conjunction such as _and_ or _but_.

> _and_
> It is late at night, a student sits staring at a computer.

vb Using Irregular Verb Forms Correctly (664–74)

Regular verbs form the past tense and past participle by adding -ed to the base form; irregular verbs do not.

> _taken,_
> A paper is due the following morning, and research needs to be done, notes need to be ~~took,~~
>
> _written_
> and, in the end, an essay needs to be ~~wrote~~ and edited.

ref Avoiding Unclear Pronoun Reference (695–99)

Pronoun reference is clear when readers can effortlessly identify a pronoun's antecedent (the word the pronoun replaces).

> _plagiarism_ _plagiarizing_
> Undeniably, some ~~of it~~ occurs because students find ~~it~~ easier than simply doing the work required.

> _the main cause of plagiarism, however, is_
> The argument that laziness is ~~its main cause, however, is~~ at best incomplete and seems,
>
> _students_
> moreover, to be fed by unfair stereotypes of ~~them~~ as bored by academic rigor, more interested
>
> in video games or their _MySpace_ pages than the hard work of learning.

Draft of student paper with sentence problems

Why Students Cheat:
The Complexities and Oversimplifications of Plagiarism (Draft 1)

frag
sv agr
The system of American higher education. It is founded on principles of honesty and academic integrity. For this reason, nearly everyone invested in this system—students, instructors, and administrators—recognize that plagiarism cannot be tolerated. People also agree that a lot of plagiarism is occurring. Reducing the incidence of plagiarism among college students will be difficult, however. Without an

frag
sv agr
understanding of its causes that goes beyond simplistic explanations.

That plagiarism and related misconduct has become all too common is beyond dispute. A survey published in *Who's Who among American High School Students* (reported by Newberger) indicated that 15 percent of top-ranked high schoolers plagiarize. Practices among higher education students are not much better according to research *fs* by Donald L. McCabe, a professor at Rutgers University who has done extensive work on cheating, 38% of college students admitted to committing forms of plagiarism in the previous year (Rimer 7). A recent study by Hand, Conway, and Moran showed that plagiarism was common among the 411 students who participated in their research.

There is a commonly held myth about how most plagiarism occurs. It is late at night, a student sits staring at a computer. A paper is due the following morning, and *cs* research needs to be done, notes need to be took, and, in the end, an essay needs *vb* to be wrote and edited. The student, overwhelmed, succumbs to the temptations of plagiarism—"cutting and pasting" from sources, downloading an essay from the

pn agr Internet, or simply buying a paper from another student. In this myth, the student is too apathetic and slothful to finish their assignments on their own; instead, they cheat.

Undeniably, some of it occurs because students find it easier than simply doing *ref* the work required. The argument that laziness is its main cause, however, is at best *ref* incomplete and seems, moreover, to be fed by unfair stereotypes of them as bored by *ref* academic rigor, more interested in video games or their *MySpace* pages than the hard work of learning.

In fact, some plagiarism grows from the opposite of these characteristics. High-achieving students, for example, fear what a bad grade will do to their otherwise stellar GPA. Such students may treat the attainment of impressive marks as a necessity and

pn agr will betray the very academic system he or she reveres in order to sustain his or her average.

For the final draft of this paper, see page 168.

Draft of student paper with sentence problems

shift   Other students plagiarize more from lack of interest in a particular course than general idleness. Students who view writing papers as hoops they must jump through to graduate, for instance, were more likely simply to have downloaded a paper from an online "paper mill" than to write one themselves. For them, a college writing class is something to be endured rather than an opportunity for learning.

shift   Students draw a distinction between their interests and their academic assignments, and plagiarism is rationalized by them as a way to escape an "unfair" academic obligation. Websites such as *essaytown.com,* which will write a paper to

inc   order, cater students like these, who consider at least some aspects of academia essentially useless.

       Many other instances of plagiarism are committed by students whom it turns   *case* out have honest intentions but are ignorant of citation methods. Michael Gunn, a British student, copied quotations from Internet sources in numerous papers over several years and was shocked to learn that this qualified as plagiarism (Baty).

mix   Even recognizing the importance of citation may not know how to cite their sources correctly. A student who omits the source of a paraphrase in a paper would probably be surprised to learn that him or her is often considered as guilty of plagiarism as the   *case* student who downloads an essay.

       The Internet has compounded confusion with regard to citation. The Internet is a

ad   place of free exchange and information movement rapidly from computer to computer. In this environment, ownership and citation become hazy. As John Leland, a reporter for the *New York Times,* writes, "Culture's heat now lies with the ability to cut, paste, clip, sample, quote, recycle, customize, and re-circulate." Many students—for example   *mm* by highlighting it, copying it, and pasting it into a word processing document—find it easy and "natural" to take text from an online source. Having trouble keeping track of   *dm* everything they have read, however, the chances increase of students accidentally plagiarizing by forgetting to cite a copied text. So, too, does the likelihood of "patchwriting," the substitution of synonyms or the shuffling of sentences in a borrowed text without putting the information fully into the writer's own words (Howard 233). Finally, some students will also be tempted to commit intentional plagiarism, choosing to leave a block of copied text uncited.

case *He, She, Who* or *Him, Her, Whom?* Matching Pronoun Case to Function (687–95)

A case problem occurs when the form of a pronoun—subjective, objective, or possessive—does not correspond to its grammatical role in a sentence.

Many other instances of plagiarism are committed by students ~~whom it turns out~~ *who, it turns out,* have honest intentions but are ignorant of citation methods.

A student who omits the source of a paraphrase in a paper would probably be surprised to learn that ~~him or her~~ *he or she* is often considered as guilty of plagiarism as the student who downloads an essay.

mm Avoiding Misplaced Modifiers (718–24)

A misplaced modifier is an ambiguously, confusingly, or disruptively placed modifying word, phrase, or clause.

Many students ~~for~~ *find it easy and "natural" to take text from an online source—for* example by highlighting it, copying it, and pasting it into a word processing document— ~~find it easy and "natural" to take text from an online source.~~

dm Avoiding Dangling Modifiers (724–27)

A dangling modifier does not clearly modify the subject or any other part of a sentence, leaving it to the reader to infer the intended meaning.

Because students can have
~~Having~~ trouble keeping track of everything they have read, however, the chances increase ~~of students' accidentally plagiarizing~~ *that they will plagiarize accidentally* by forgetting to cite a copied text.

32

Understanding Grammar

Baseball, like any other game, has rules. These rules, which give the game meaning and structure, have become second nature to proficient players. Most rules are inflexible: A player who ran around the bases carrying the ball would not be playing baseball. Some rules vary, however. In the American League but not in the National League, teams can designate another player to bat instead of the pitcher. Rules and the style of play have changed over time, as well. The American League, for example, did not adopt the designated hitter rule until 1973.

Languages, too, have rules—*grammars*—that structure our words so they can convey meaning. Just as baseball players have internalized the rules of the game, so have we all internalized the grammar of our native language. Most rules of grammar are inflexible. Any English speaker, for example, would recognize a statement like *throw Maria ball the base first to* as ungrammatical. Some aspects of grammar, however, can vary over time, from region to region, and from group to group. There are many varieties of English around the world today, but not one of them is the same as the English of 1,000 years ago.

The form of English that is accepted today in academic settings and in the workplace in the United States is known as ***Standard American English.*** Although it is not better or more correct than other varieties, Standard American English is what readers expect to encounter in academic and business writing in the United States. This chapter reviews the rules of Standard American English grammar, and the chapters that follow it in Part 8 focus on particular aspects of grammar and usage that many writers find troublesome.

Writing
↑ Responsibly   **Why Grammar Matters**

Writers have a responsibility to use language their readers regard as grammatically correct. A shared standard of grammar eases communication, and when you follow it, you show respect for your readers. In contrast, when you use language your readers regard as grammatically incorrect, you distract and confuse them, raising doubts in their minds about your competence and reliability.

PARTS OF SPEECH

The term ***parts of speech*** refers to the functions words play in a sentence. English has eight parts of speech:

- nouns
- pronouns
- verbs
- adjectives
- adverbs
- prepositions
- conjunctions
- interjections

The same word can have more than one function, depending on the context in which it appears.

▶ Many students work to help pay for college. [*Work* is a verb.]

▶ Mastering calculus requires hard work. [*Work* is a noun.]

32a **Nouns**

Nouns name ideas (*justice*), things (*chair*), qualities (*neatness*), actions (*judgment*), people (*Albert Einstein*), and places (*Tokyo*). They fall into a variety of overlapping categories:

- ***Proper nouns*** name specific places, people, or things and are usually capitalized: *Nairobi, Hudson Bay, Laura Bush, the Taj Mahal.* All other nouns are ***common nouns,*** which name members of a class or group: *turtle, sophomore, skyscraper.*

connect

mhconnectcomposition.com
Additional resources: QL32001

Parts of Speech	Functions	Examples
Nouns	name ideas, things, qualities, actions, people, and places	Sarah usually drives her blue car to work, but, alas, it needs expensive repairs.
Pronouns	rename or take the place of nouns or noun phrases	Sarah usually drives her blue car to work, but, alas, it needs expensive repairs.
Verbs	express action, occurrence, or state of being	Sarah usually drives her blue car to work, but, alas, it needs expensive repairs.
Adjectives	modify nouns or pronouns with descriptive or limiting information, answering questions such as *What kind? Which one?* or *How many?*	Sarah usually drives her blue car to work, but, alas, it needs expensive repairs.
Adverbs	modify verbs, adjectives, and other adverbs as well as entire phrases and clauses, answering such questions as *How? Where? When?* and *To what extent or degree?*	Sarah usually drives her blue car to work, but, alas, it needs expensive repairs.
Prepositions	relate nouns or pronouns to other words in a sentence in terms of time, space, cause, and other attributes	Sarah usually drives her blue car to work, but, alas, it needs expensive repairs.
Conjunctions	join words, phrases, and clauses to other words, phrases, or clauses and specify the way the joined elements relate to each other	Sarah usually drives her blue car to work, but, alas, it needs expensive repairs.
Interjections	express strong feeling but otherwise serve no grammatical function	Sarah usually drives her blue car to work, but, alas, it needs expensive repairs.

- **Collective nouns** name a collection that can function as a single unit: *committee, administration, family.*

- **Concrete nouns** name things that can be seen, touched, heard, smelled, or tasted: *planet, liquid, symphony, skunk, pepper.* **Abstract nouns** name qualities or ideas that cannot be perceived by the senses: *mercy, fear.*

- *Countable* (or *count*) *nouns* name things or ideas that can be counted. They can be either *singular* or *plural: cat/cats, assignment/assignments, idea/ideas.*

More about ▶▶▶
Count and noncount nouns, 747–54

- *Uncountable* (or *noncount*) *nouns* name ideas or things that cannot be counted and do not have a plural form: *homework, knowledge, pollution.*

 Count and Noncount Nouns The classification of nouns as count or noncount affects the way they combine with articles and other determiners. Awareness of the effect of this aspect of nouns on sentence grammar will help you avoid errors.

Most nouns form the plural with the addition of a final *-s* or *-es: book/books, beach/beaches, country/countries.* A few have irregular plurals: *woman/women, life/lives, mouse/mice.* For some nouns, the singular and the plural forms are the same: *deer/deer, fish/fish.*

More about ▶▶▶
Noun plurals, 595–97

Nouns indicate possession with a final *s* sound, marked in writing with an apostrophe: *Rosa's idea, the students' plan.*

More about ▶▶▶
Apostrophes and possession, 808–11

32b Pronouns

Noun phrase A noun and its modifiers (617)

Pronouns rename or take the place of nouns or *noun phrases.* The noun that a pronoun replaces is called its *antecedent.* The Quick Reference box on the next page summarizes the types of pronouns and their functions.

More about ▶▶▶
Pronouns, 657–63, 686–99

EXERCISE **32.1** Identifying nouns and pronouns

Circle the nouns and underline the pronouns in the following sentences. The first sentence is marked for you as an example.

connect
mhconnectcomposition.com
Additional resources: QL32002, QL32003

1. On his way to pick up his aunt at the airport, Bradley found himself stuck in traffic.

connect
mhconnectcomposition.com
Online exercise: QL32101

2. Who could have expected such a terrible traffic jam on a Sunday afternoon?

3. Bradley was especially concerned not to be late to the airport because his aunt was the only one of his relatives who was always on time to everything.

4. Making the situation even worse, the driver behind him kept honking his horn.

Quick

Type and Function	Forms	Examples
Personal pronouns take the place of specific nouns or noun phrases.	**Singular:** *I, me, you, he, him, she, her, it* **Plural:** *we, us, you, they, them*	Yue bought the tickets for Adam, and she gave them to him before the concert.
Possessive pronouns are personal pronouns that indicate possession.	**Singular:** *my, mine, your, yours, his, her, hers, its* **Plural:** *our, ours, your, yours, their, theirs*	Adam gave one of the tickets to his roommate.
Reflexive pronouns refer back to the subject of a sentence.	**Singular:** *myself, yourself, himself, herself, itself, oneself* **Plural:** *ourselves, yourselves, themselves*	Laetitia reminded herself to return the books to the library.
Intensive pronouns rename and emphasize their antecedents.	Same as reflexive pronouns	Dr. Collins herself performed the operation.
Demonstrative pronouns rename and point to nouns or noun phrases. They can function as adjectives as well as nouns.	**Singular:** *this, that* **Plural:** *these, those*	Yameng visited the Forbidden City. That was his favorite place in China. That place was his favorite.
Relative pronouns introduce subordinate clauses that describe the pronoun's antecedent.	*who, whom, whoever, whomever, what, whose, whatever, whichever, that, which*	I. M. Pei is the architect who designed the East Wing of the National Gallery.
Interrogative pronouns introduce questions.	*who, whoever, whom, whomever, what, whatever, which, whichever, whose*	Who designed the East Wing of the National Gallery?
Indefinite pronouns do not refer to specific people or things.	**Singular:** *anybody, anyone, anything, each, either, everybody, everyone, everything, much, neither, nobody, no one, nothing, one, somebody, someone, something* **Singular or plural:** *all, any, more, most, some* **Plural:** *both, few, many, several*	Everybody talks about the weather, but nobody does anything about it. *—Attributed to Mark Twain*
Reciprocal pronouns refer to the individual parts of a plural antecedent.	*each other, one another*	The candidates debated one another many times before the primary.

5. Bradley felt his car shake a bit and realized that the driver behind him had bumped his rear fender slightly while pulling out to change lanes.

6. The other driver was out of sight by the time Bradley reminded himself to get the car's license number.

7. He arrived at the airport a few minutes late, saw that his car's fender was unharmed, scanned the monitor for information about incoming flights, and learned that many, including his aunt's, were an hour behind schedule.

32c Verbs

Verbs express action (*The quarterback throws a pass*), occurrence (*The play happened in the second half*), or state of being (*The fans are happy*). Verbs also carry information about time (tense), as well as person, number, voice, and mood.

Two kinds of verbs combine to make up a *verb phrase: main verbs* and *helping* (or *auxiliary*) *verbs.* Main verbs carry the principal meaning of a verb phrase. Almost all verb constructions other than the present and past tense, however, require a combination of one or more helping verbs with a form of the main verb. Some helping verbs (forms of *be, have,* and *do*) also function as main verbs. Others, called *modal verbs* (*can, could, may, might, must, shall, should, will, would,* and *ought to*), function only as helping verbs.

> **More about ▶▶▶**
> Verb forms, 664–74

connect
mhconnectcomposition.com
Additional resources: QL32004

ESL **Modal Auxiliaries** Modal auxiliaries can pose special problems for multilingual students. For more on their meaning and use, see pp. 763–64.

Helping verbs always precede the main verb in a verb phrase.

|———— verb phrase ————|
              main
              verb
▶ The player   **hit**   a long home run.

              helping   main
              verbs   verb
▶ The home run   **may have broken**   a distance record.

              helping   main
              verbs   verb
▶ The children   **have been being**   unusually good.

More about ▶▶▶
Verbals, 619–20

NOTE Do not confuse *verbals* with complete verbs. Verbals are verb forms functioning as nouns, adjectives, or adverbs, not as verbs within a predicate.

▶ The potters *fired* the vessels in their kiln. [*Fired* is a verb.]

▶ The *fired* clay is rock hard. [*Fired* is a verbal, in this case an adjective modifying *clay.*]

connect
mhconnectcomposition.com
Online exercise: QL32102

→ **EXERCISE 32.2 Identifying verb phrases**

Underline the verb phrases in the following sentences, and circle the main verb in each. Note that some sentences may have more than one verb phrase.

1. Rennie has been to the zoo more often this year than ever before.

2. Her twin nieces began walking recently, and since then their favorite activity has been going to the zoo with aunt Rennie.

3. This spring the twins were excited about an exhibit of newly arrived pandas.

4. For weeks, they had been begging Rennie to take them to the exhibit.

5. By the time Rennie and the twins finally saw the new exhibit, the pandas had become accustomed to visitors and chewed calmly on some bamboo.

32d Adjectives

More about ▶▶▶
Adjectives, 700–09

Adjectives modify nouns or pronouns with descriptive or limiting information. They answer questions such as *What kind? Which one?* or *How many?*

Linking verb A verb that conveys a state of being linking a subject to its complement (615)
Subject complement An adjective, pronoun, or noun phrase that follows a linking verb and describes or refers to the sentence subject (615)

	adj. noun
WHAT KIND?	a warm day
WHICH ONE?	the next speaker
HOW MANY?	twelve roses

Adjectives most commonly fall before nouns in a noun phrase and after *linking verbs* as *subject complements.*

▶ The young musicians played a rousing concert.

[adj. noun ... adj. noun]

▶ **They were enthusiastic.**
  pro-   link.   adj.
  noun   verb

Many adjectives change form to express comparison: *young, younger, youngest; enthusiastic, more/less enthusiastic, most/least enthusiastic.*

Possessive, demonstrative, and indefinite pronouns that function as adjectives—as well as the articles *a, an,* and *the*—are known as **determiners** because they specify or quantify the nouns they modify. Determiners always precede other adjectives in a noun phrase. Some, like *all* and *both,* also precede any other determiners.

  det. adj. noun   det. noun   dets. adj. noun
▶ **The new gym is in that building with all those solar panels on**
  det. noun
  the roof.

> **ESL   The Ordering of Adjectives** The ordering of adjectives in noun phrases and the use of articles and other determiners in English can be challenging for multilingual writers. For more on these topics, see pp. 767 and 748–55.

More about ▶▶▶
Comparative adjectives, 705–07

connect
mhconnectcomposition.com
Additional resources: QL32005

32e   Adverbs

Adverbs modify verbs, adjectives, and other adverbs, as well as entire phrases and clauses. They answer such questions as *How? Where? When?* and *To what extent or degree?*

HOW?	adverb verb adv. Embarrassingly, my cell phone rang loudly. The adverb *loudly* modifies the verb *rang.* The adverb *embarrassingly* modifies the whole sentence.
WHEN?	adv. adj. Dinner is finally ready. The adverb *finally* modifies the adjective *ready.*
WHERE?/ EXTENT?	verb adv. adv. Stop right there! The adverb *right* modifies the adverb *there,* which modifies the verb *stop.*

More about ▶▶▶
Adverbs, 700–09

connect ·
mhconnectcomposition.com
Additional resources: QL32006

Like adjectives, many adverbs change form to express comparison: *far, farther, farthest; frequently, more/less frequently, most/least frequently.*

More about ▶▶▶
Comparative adverbs, 705–07

Reference ➔ Common Conjunctive Adverbs

accordingly	however	otherwise
also	indeed	similarly
anyway	instead	specifically
as a result	likewise	still
besides	meanwhile	subsequently
certainly	moreover	suddenly
finally	nevertheless	then
for example	next	therefore
furthermore	nonetheless	thus
hence	now	

A ***conjunctive adverb*** is a transitional expression that can link one independent clause to another. The conjunctive adverb modifies the second clause and specifies its relationship to the first. A period or semicolon, not a comma, should separate independent clauses linked with a conjunctive adverb.

> ▶ **Writers have several options for joining independent clauses; a comma alone, however, is not one of them.**

NOTE In addition to individual words, whole phrases and clauses can function as adjectives and adverbs within sentences.

> **More about ▶▶▶**
> Adjective and
>   adverb phrases,
>   618–20
> Adjective and
>   adverb clauses,
>   621–22

connect
mhconnectcomposition.com
Online exercise: QL32103

➔ **EXERCISE 32.3 Identifying adjectives and adverbs**

Underline the adjectives and circle the adverbs in the following sentences.

1. Grace had always liked to have a tidy bedroom.

2. She had never had to live with a messy roommate.

3. Grace decided to ask Maritza gently if they could have a little chat about neatness.

4. The two were good friends as well as roommates, so they agreeably worked out a compromise.

5. They split their small room into equal halves, and each cleaned her half as thoroughly as she wished.

32f Prepositions

Prepositions relate nouns or pronouns to other words in a sentence in terms of time, space, cause, and other attributes.

connect
mhconnectcomposition.com
Additional resources: QL32007

▶ The lecture begins at noon in the auditorium.

As the Quick Reference box below indicates, prepositions can consist of more than one word.

→ EXERCISE **32.4** Identifying prepositions

Underline the prepositions in each of the following sentences.

connect
mhconnectcomposition.com
Online exercise: QL32104

1. Many people still worry about the health risks of coffee.

2. Nevertheless, over the last twenty years, research has shown that coffee is safe in moderation, and it may even offer some health benefits.

3. According to some studies, regular coffee drinkers have a lower incidence of type 2 diabetes than people who do not drink coffee.

4. However, the main ingredient in coffee, caffeine, is a mildly addictive stimulant.

5. So, as a general rule for coffee drinking, keep it moderate.

Quick Reference → Common One-Word and Multiword Prepositions

about	at	far from	near	past
above	because of	for	near to	since
according to	before	from	next to	through
across	behind	in	of	to
after	below	in addition to	off	toward
against	beneath	in case of	on	under
ahead of	beside	in front of	on account of	underneath
along	between	in place of	on behalf of	until
among	by	in spite of	on top of	up
around	by means of	inside	onto	upon
as far as	close to	inside of	out of	with
as to	down	instead of	outside	within
as well as	during	into	outside of	without
aside from	except	like	over	

connect‧
mhconnectcomposition.com
Additional resources: QL32008

32g   **Conjunctions**

Conjunctions join words, phrases, and clauses to other words, phrases, or clauses and specify the way the joined elements relate to each other.

- **Coordinating conjunctions** (*and, but, or, for, nor, yet,* and *so*) join grammatically equivalent elements, giving them each equal significance.

  ▶ Ingenious and energetic entrepreneurs can generate effective but inexpensive publicity. [The conjunction *and* pairs two adjectives; the conjunction *but* contrasts two adjectives.]

- **Correlative conjunctions** are pairs of terms that, like coordinating conjunctions, join grammatically equivalent elements. Common correlative conjunctions include *either . . . or, neither . . . nor, both . . . and, not only . . . but also,* and *whether . . . or.*

  ▶ Fred Thompson has been both an actor and a presidential candidate.

More about ▶▶▶
Independent and
subordinate
clauses, 620–23

- **Subordinating conjunctions** link subordinate clauses to the independent clauses they modify.

  ▶ The party could not begin until the guest of honor had arrived.

Quick Reference ➡ **Common Subordinating Conjunctions**

after	before	since	when
although	even if	so that	where
as	even though	though	while
as if	if	unless	
because	once	until	

> **EXERCISE 32.5   Identifying conjunctions**

connect‧
mhconnectcomposition.com
Online exercise: QL32105

Underline the conjunctions in the following sentences, and label the type of conjunction (coordinating, correlative, or subordinating) each is.

1. Photography was Randall's hobby, so he volunteered to take digital photos and interview some of the customers at the ski club's fundraising car wash.

2. He said he would send the story and photos not only to the local newspaper but also to the school's TV station.

3. After the car wash, Randall had to decide whether to download the photos to his computer or ask to use his friend Amita's computer, which was faster and had more memory than his.

4. Although he decided to ask Amita, he ended up using his own computer anyway because hers needed repairs.

5. In the end, once he had followed up his photo story submission with phone calls, both the newspaper and TV station decided to run the story.

32h Interjections

Interjections are words like *alas, bah, oh, ouch,* and *ugh* that express strong feeling—of regret, contempt, surprise, pain, or disgust, for example—but otherwise serve no grammatical function.

▶ Ugh! That's the worst coffee I ever tasted.

▶ "Bah," said Scrooge.
　　　　　　　　　—Charles Dickens, *A Christmas Carol* (1843)

SENTENCE STRUCTURE

All sentences have two basic parts: a subject and a predicate. The ***subject*** is the thing the sentence is about. The ***predicate*** states something about the subject.

▶ Digital technology transformed the music industry.

Sentences fall into one of four functional categories:

- ***Declarative sentences*** (the most common type) make a statement.

  ▶ Digital technology transformed the music industry.

- ***Imperative sentences*** give a command.

  ▶ Join the digital bandwagon to survive in today's competitive media marketplace.

- ***Interrogative sentences*** ask a question.

  ▶ Will digital technology make printed books obsolete?

- ***Exclamatory sentences*** express strong or sudden emotion.

  ▶ How I hate updating software on my computer!

32i Subjects

The ***simple subject*** of a sentence is a noun or pronoun. The ***complete subject*** consists of the simple subject plus any modifying words or phrases.

```
|— complete subject —|
            simple
            subject
```

▶ *Two robotic vehicles* have been exploring Mars since January 2004.

A ***compound subject*** contains two or more simple subjects joined by a conjunction.

```
|————————————————— compound subject ———————————————|
                    ss    conj                      ss
```

▶ *The six-wheeled, solar-powered* Spirit *and the identical* Opportunity
landed within three weeks of each other.

Quick Reference ➡ Finding the Subject

The complete subject of a sentence is the answer to the question "Who or what did the action or was in the state defined by the verb?"

```
|—complete subject —|  verb
```

▶ Two robotic vehicles landed safely on Mars in January 2004.

What landed on Mars in January 2004? Two robotic vehicles did. The subject is *two robotic vehicles.*

```
|————————— complete subject ——————————|  verb
```

▶ The scientists and engineers who designed the rovers cheered.

Who cheered? The scientists and engineers who designed the rovers did. The subject is *the scientists and engineers who designed the rovers.*

The subject usually precedes the verb, but it is not always the first element in a sentence. In the following sentence, for example, the phrase *in July 2007* modifies the rest of the sentence but is not part of the subject.

```
|————— subject ———|  verb
```

▶ In July 2007, Martian dust storms restricted the activity of the rovers.

In imperative sentences (commands), the subject, *you,* is unstated.

▸ [*You*] Learn about space exploration at www.nasa.gov.

In interrogative sentences (questions), the subject falls between a helping verb and the main verb or, if the main verb is a form of *be,* after the verb.

```
helping              main
verb  |—subject—|    verb
```

▸ **Did   the rovers   find evidence of water on Mars?**

```
verb |————— subject —————|
```

▸ **Were** *Spirit* **and** *Opportunity* **more durable than expected?**

Writers occasionally invert normal word order and place the subject after the verb for emphasis.

> ***More about*** ▸▸▸
> Word order and emphasis, 551–57

```
verb   |————— subject —————|
```

▸ **Out of the swirling dust emerged the hardy Mars rover.**

The subject also follows the verb in sentences that begin with *there* followed by a form of *be.* In these ***expletive constructions,*** the word *there* functions as a placeholder for the delayed subject.

```
v  |—subject —|
```

▸ **There are two vehicles roaming the surface of Mars.**

ESL **English Word Order** In English, word order is less flexible than in many other languages, and the position of a word often affects its grammatical function and meaning.

> ***More about*** ▸▸▸
> English word order, 738–46

32j Predicates

The ***simple predicate*** of a sentence is the main verb and any helping verbs. The ***complete predicate*** is the simple predicate together with any objects, complements, and modifiers.

```
        |——— complete predicate ———|
simple
pred.
```

▸ **Polynesian mariners** *settled the Hawaiian Islands.*

```
        |————————— complete predicate —————————|
simple pred.
```

▸ **The first settlers** *may have arrived as early as the fourth century CE.*

A ***compound predicate*** is a complete predicate with two or more simple predicates joined by a conjunction.

> ┡————————————————— complete
> simple pred.
> ▸ Polynesian mariners *navigated thousands of miles of open ocean and*
> predicate ————————————————┦
> sp
> *settled the islands of the South Pacific.*

connect
mhconnectcomposition.com
Online exercise: QL32106

→ **EXERCISE 32.6 Identifying subjects and predicates**

For each of the following sentences, underline and label the simple subject and simple predicate; then circle and label the complete subject and complete predicate.

1. Carlynn had never gone on a camping trip before.

2. Everyone else was diligently working to set up the campsite.

3. Carlynn's cousin Marilupe handed Carlynn a hatchet and told her to find some dead wood for the campfire.

4. Later, an exhausted Carlynn and a still energetic Sara stacked the wood and assembled some large rocks in a circle.

5. Then Marilupe amazed Carlynn as well as everyone else by demonstrating how to start a fire without matches.

32k Verb Types and Sentence Patterns

There are three kinds of verb, ***intransitive, linking,*** and ***transitive,*** and they combine with other elements in the predicate in five basic sentence patterns.

1. Subject → intransitive verb

Intransitive verbs require no object and can stand alone as the only element in a predicate. They are often modified, however, by adverbs and adverbial phrases and clauses.

> ┡—subj.—┦ intrans.
>   verb
> ▸ The volcano *erupted*.

> ┡—subj.—┦ intrans.
>   verb   ┡———————— adverbial modifiers ————————┦
> ▸ The volcano *erupted suddenly in a powerful blast of ash and steam.*

Reference → Five Sentence Patterns

1. subject → intransitive verb
   s   iv
   ▶ The lights dimmed.

2. subject → linking verb → subject complement
   s   lv   sc
   ▶ The audience fell silent.

3. subject → transitive verb → direct object
   s   tv   do
   ▶ The orchestra played the overture.

4. subject → transitive verb → indirect object → direct object
   s   tv   io   do
   ▶ The show gave the audience a thrill.

5. subject → transitive verb → direct object → object complement
   s   tv   do   oc
   ▶ The applause made the actors happy.

2. Subject → linking verb → subject complement

A **subject complement** is an adjective, pronoun, or noun phrase that describes or refers to the subject of a sentence. A **linking verb** connects the subject to its complement. Linking verbs express states of being rather than actions. The verb *be,* when used as a main verb, is always a linking verb. Other verbs that can function as linking verbs include *appear, become, fall, feel, grow, look, make, prove, remain, seem, smell, sound,* and *taste.*

```
                    link.
 ⊢—subj.—⊣   vb.   ⊢—subj. comp.—⊣
▶ The Oscar   is    a coveted award.

▶ The patient  felt  better.
```

3. Subject → transitive verb → direct object

Transitive verbs have two *voices:* active and passive. **Transitive verbs** in the **active voice** require a **direct object**—a pronoun or noun phrase that receives the action of the verb.

```
                        active
 ⊢——— subject ———⊣   trans. vb.   ⊢—do—⊣
▶ The undersea volcano   created   a new island.
```

The **passive voice** reverses the role of the subject, making it the recipient of the action of the verb. An active-voice sentence can usually

▷ **More about** ▶▶▶
Voice in verbs, 682–83
Voice and style choices, 560–61

be transformed into a passive-voice sentence of the same meaning. The subject of the passive-voice version is the direct object of the active-voice version.

> passive
> ├── subject ──┤ trans. verb
> ▶ A new island *was created* by the undersea volcano.

In the passive voice, the agent of the action can be left unstated.

> ▶ A new island *was created*.

NOTE Many verbs can be either transitive or intransitive.

	├────── do ──────┤
TRANSITIVE	My sister *won* the Scrabble game.
INTRANSITIVE	My sister always *wins*.

When in doubt about the usage of a verb, check a dictionary.

---

4. Subject → transitive verb → indirect object → direct object

Some transitive verbs can take an **indirect object** as well as a direct object. The indirect object, which precedes the direct object, identifies the beneficiary of the action of the verb.

> ├── s ──┤ ├─ tv ─┤ ├── io ──┤ ├──────── do ────────┤
> ▶ Juan   lent   Ileana   his notes.

> ▶ The donor   bought   the library   a new computer center.

Often, the indirect object can also be stated as a prepositional phrase that begins with *to* or *for* and follows the direct object.

> ▶ Juan lent his notes *to Ileana*.

> ▶ The donor bought a new computer center *for the library*.

Verbs that can take an indirect object include *ask, bring, buy, call, find, get, give, hand, leave, lend, offer, pass, pay, promise, read, send, show, teach, tell, throw,* and *write*.

> **More about ▶▶▶**
> Indirect objects, 742

ESL **Indirect Objects** The use of indirect objects is highly idiomatic in English. The verbs that take them are similar to others that do not. Likewise, in some situations an indirect object before the direct object is interchangeable with a prepositional phrase after it, but in others only one or the other is acceptable.

---

5. Subject → transitive verb → direct object → object complement

An ***object complement*** is an adjective or noun phrase that follows the direct object and describes the condition of the object or a change that the subject has caused it to undergo.

⊢— s —⊣	⊢— tv —⊣	⊢——— do ———⊣	⊢——— oc ———⊣
▶ The fans	considered	the umpire's call	mistaken.

▶ The manager	named	David Ortiz	designated hitter.

EXERCISE 32.7 Identifying objects and complements

In the following sentences, underline the objects and complements. Then write DO above each direct object, IO above each indirect object, SC above each subject complement, and OC above each object complement.

1. Before he died, my grandfather wrote my mother a long letter.
2. It is actually a family history in letter form.
3. In it, my grandfather describes his own parents' arduous journey from their homeland to their new home in America.
4. The story makes me grateful for their courage.

connect
mhconnectcomposition.com
Online exercise: QL32107

32l Phrases

A *phrase* is a group of related words that lacks a subject, a predicate, or both. Phrases function in various ways within sentences, but cannot function as sentences by themselves. A phrase by itself is a ***fragment,*** not a sentence.

> **Fragment** An incomplete sentence punctuated as if it were complete (626–36)

1. Noun phrases

A ***noun phrase*** consists of a noun together with any modifiers. Noun phrases function as subjects, objects, and complements within sentences.

⊢——— noun phrase/subject ———⊣
▶ *Sam's mouth-watering apple pie* emerged piping hot from the oven.

⊢——— noun phrase/direct object ———⊣
▶ The guests devoured *Sam's mouth-watering apple pie.*

⊢——— noun phrase/subj. comp. ———⊣
▶ The high point of the meal was *Sam's mouth-watering apple pie.*

connect
mhconnectcomposition.com
Additional resources: Q32009

An ***appositive phrase*** is a noun or noun phrase that renames a noun or noun phrase and is grammatically equivalent to it.

▶ The high point of the meal, *Sam's mouth-watering apple pie,* emerged piping hot from the oven.

2. Verb phrases

A ***verb phrase*** consists of a main verb and all its helping verbs. Verb phrases function as the simple predicates of sentences and clauses.

▶ By Election Day, the candidates *will have been campaigning* for almost two years.

3. Prepositional phrases

A ***prepositional phrase*** is a preposition followed by the ***object of the preposition:*** a pronoun or noun and its modifiers. Prepositional phrases function as adjectives and adverbs.

▶ The train arrives <u>in an hour</u>. [The prepositional phrase *in an hour* functions as an adverb modifying the verb *arrives*.]

▶ She recommended the book <u>about Einstein</u>. [The prepositional phrase *about Einstein* functions as an adjective modifying the noun *book.*]

connect

mhconnectcomposition.com
Online exercise: QL32108

→ EXERCISE **32.8** Identifying prepositional phrases

In the following sentences, underline each prepositional phrase, write above it the type (adjective or adverb), and circle the words it modifies.

1. Roger said he was a little nervous before he stepped into the canoe.

2. Miguel, who had been on many canoe trips before, reassured him.

3. Miguel told Roger to sit in the front of the canoe.

4. Miguel expertly steered from the canoe's back seat.

5. The trip down the river was enjoyable for both Roger and Miguel.

4. Verbal phrases

Verbals are verb forms that function as nouns, adjectives, or adverbs. Although they may have objects and complements, verbals lack the information about tense, person, and number required of a complete verb.

A *verbal phrase* consists of a verbal and any modifiers, objects, or complements. There are three kinds of verbal phrases: gerund phrases, infinitive phrases, and participial phrases.

Gerunds A *gerund* is the present participle (or *-ing* form) of a verb used as a noun; and like nouns, gerunds and gerund phrases can function as subjects, objects, and complements.

|———— gerund phrase/subject ————|
▶ *Increasing automobile fuel efficiency* will reduce carbon emissions.

|———— gerund phrase/dir. obj. ————|
▶ The mayor recommends *improving the city's mass transit system.*

Infinitives An *infinitive* is the *to* form of the verb (*to decide, to eat, to study*). Infinitives and infinitive phrases can function as adjectives and adverbs as well as nouns.

|— noun phrase/subj. comp. —|
▶ The goal of the law is *to increase fuel efficiency.*

|———— adjective phrase ————|
▶ Congress passed a law *to increase fuel efficiency.*

|———— adverb phrase ————|
▶ *To reduce traffic congestion,* the city improved its mass transit system.

ESL **Infinitive versus Gerund after the Verb** Some verbs can be followed by a gerund but not an infinitive, others by an infinitive but not a gerund, and still others by either a gerund or an infinitive.

More about ▶▶▶
Infinitive vs. gerund after verbs, 759–61

Participial phrases In a *participial phrase* the present participle or past participle of a verb acts as an adjective. The present participle ends in *-ing.* The past participle of regular verbs ends in *-ed,* but some verbs have irregular past participles.

More about ▶▶▶
Irregular past participles, 666–69

▸ *Surveying the disheveled apartment,* Grace wondered whether it would be possible to room with Maritza.

▸ *Deeply concerned,* she asked, "How long have you lived alone?"

connect

mhconnectcomposition.com
Online exercise: QL32109

⟶ **EXERCISE 32.9 Identifying verbal phrases**

In the following sentences, underline each verbal phrase. Then write above it the type (gerund, infinitive, or participial).

1. Seeking economic opportunity or freedom from political or religious repression, millions of immigrants came to the United States between the end of the Civil War and the early 1920s.

2. Many of the newcomers intended to return to their homelands.

3. Most immigrants during this period came from southern and eastern Europe, replacing the Irish and German immigrants who had predominated before the Civil War.

4. Leaving home and settling in a new environment must have been difficult.

5. Not always welcomed in their new communities, immigrants often settled together in ethnic enclaves.

5. Absolute phrases

Absolute phrases modify entire sentences rather than particular words within sentences. They usually consist of a pronoun or noun phrase followed by a participle. Set off by commas, they can often fall flexibly before, after, or within the rest of the sentence.

▸ *All our quarrels forgotten,* we sat before the fire and talked quietly.

When the participle in an absolute phrase is a form of *be,* it is often omitted as understood.

▸ *Her interview [having been] successful,* she was offered the job on the spot.

32m Independent and Subordinate Clauses

A *clause* is a word group with a subject and a predicate. An *independent* (or *main*) *clause* can stand alone as a sentence.

|⸺ independent clause ⸺|

▸ Sam's pie won first prize.

A **subordinate** (or **dependent**) clause is a clause within a clause.

```
 |————————independent clause————————|
         |———sub. clause———|
```

▶ Sam baked the pie that won first prize.

That is, a subordinate clause functions inside an independent clause (or another subordinate clause) as a noun, adjective, or adverb but cannot stand alone as a sentence. A subordinate clause by itself is a **fragment**. A subordinating word—either a **subordinating conjunction** (see the Quick Reference box on p. 610) or a **relative pronoun** (see the Quick Reference box on p. 604)—usually signals the beginning of a subordinate clause.

1. Adjective clauses

Like adjectives, **adjective clauses** (also called **relative clauses**) modify nouns or pronouns. They usually begin with a relative pronoun that immediately follows the word the clause modifies and refers back to it.

▶ Sam baked the pie *that won first prize*.

▶ The donor *who paid for the library's new computer center* is a recent graduate.

In both these examples, the relative pronoun is the subject of the subordinate clause, and the clause follows normal word order, with the subject before the verb. When the relative pronoun is the direct object, however, it still comes at the beginning of the clause, reversing normal word order.

▶ The candidate *whom we supported* lost the election.

Adjective clauses can also begin with the subordinating conjunctions *when* and *where*.

▶ Tupelo, Mississippi, is the town *where Elvis Presley was born*.

It is sometimes acceptable to omit the relative pronoun that introduces an adjective clause when the meaning of the clause is clear without it.

▶ The candidate *[whom] we supported* lost the election.

connect
mhconnectcomposition.com
Additional resources: QL32010, QL32011, QL32012

More about ▶▶▶
Subordinate clause
fragments, 633–35
Punctuating sub-
ordinate clauses,
533, 786, 791–93

More about ▶▶▶
Who vs. whom,
693–95

2. Adverb clauses

Adverb clauses usually begin with a subordinating conjunction, which specifies the relation of the clause to the term it modifies. Like adverbs, adverb clauses can modify verbs, adjectives, and adverbs as well as whole phrases and clauses.

More about ▶▶▶
The meaning of subordinating conjunctions, 534

▶ The baby boom began *as World War II ended.*

The adverb clause modifies the verb *began.*

▶ The economy grew faster *than many Americans thought it would.*

The adverb clause modifies the adverb *faster.*

▶ The 1950s were an affluent decade, *although the general prosperity did not extend to all.*

The adverb clause modifies the preceding independent clause.

3. Noun clauses

Noun clauses do not modify other parts of a sentence but instead replace noun phrases as subjects, objects, or complements within an independent clause. Noun clauses can begin with a relative pronoun as well as with certain subordinating conjunctions, including *how, if, when, whenever, where, wherever, whether,* and *why.*

├————— subject —————┤
▶ *Whoever crosses the finish line first* wins the race.

├— subject comp. —┤
▶ Home is *where the heart is.*

├————— direct object —————┤
▶ The evidence proves *that the defendant is not guilty.*

connect
mhconnectcomposition.com
Online exercise: QL32110

→ **EXERCISE 32.10 Identifying subordinate clauses**

In the following passage, underline the subordinate clauses. Then write above each clause its function (noun, adverbial, or adjectival).

Spring break is a time when most students want just to take it easy and have fun. Martin usually did just that, although he sometimes thought he should spend the time more productively.

However, he never could figure out how he could turn this desire to be useful into reality. Then he saw a flyer about the community service club's spring break project, which was to help build a home for someone in need. He decided that this was his opportunity to do something different. That he had to pay for the trip himself required Martin to spend many hours working to raise the funds. He washed cars, shoveled snow, babysat, walked dogs, and did other errands for his neighbors over the winter until he had the $600 that he needed. The bus took Martin and the other participants to the home site, which was four hundred miles from the school. The days at the construction site started earlier than the students usually liked to get up, but they all found it exciting to learn how to build a house. The construction had progressed substantially by the end of the spring break week. Martin and his fellow student home builders returned feeling as though they had used their week off doing something useful.

32n Sentence Types

Sentences fall into four types depending on the combination of independent and subordinate clauses they contain. Including a mix of types in your writing and choosing the appropriate type for the information you intend to convey can help you hold your readers' attention and emphasize important points.

> *More about* ▶▶▶
Sentence variety,
550–57

1. Simple sentences

A *simple sentence* has only one independent clause and no subordinate clauses.

connect
mhconnectcomposition.com
Additional resources: QL32013

|———————————— independent clause ————————————|
▶ **Lance Armstrong won the Tour de France seven times.**

A simple sentence need not be short or even uncomplicated. A sentence with a compound subject, a compound predicate, or both is still a simple sentence as long as it has a single complete subject, a single complete predicate, and no subordinate clauses.

|——————————————————————————————— independent
▶ **Lance Armstrong and Miguel Indurain have each won the Tour de**
   clause ———————————————————————|
   France and dominated professional cycling.

2. Compound sentences

A ***compound sentence*** has two or more independent clauses but no subordinate clauses. A comma and a coordinating conjunction, a semicolon, or a semicolon and a conjunctive adverb usually join the clauses in a compound sentence.

|———————————— independent clause ———————————|
▶ Lance Armstrong won the Tour de France seven times, and

|————————————— independent clause —————————————|
in 2002, *Sports Illustrated* named him Sportsman of the Year.

|——————— independent clause —————————| |———independent
▶ Armstrong's seven wins were in consecutive years; two other cyclists

clause ————————————————————————|
had previously won in five consecutive years.

❭ *More about* ▶▶▶
Punctuating compound sentences,
637–45

3. Complex sentences

A ***complex sentence*** consists of a single independent clause with at least one subordinate clause.

|——————— subordinate clause —————————| |———independent clause ———|
▶ After he won his seventh Tour in 2005, Armstrong retired from racing.

|——————————————————————————————————— independent
            |——————— subordinate clause ———————|
▶ The Tour de France, which is the world's longest cycling race, covers

clause ———————————————|
nearly 2,000 miles in 22 days.

4. Compound-complex sentences

A ***compound-complex sentence*** has two or more independent clauses with one or more subordinate clauses.

|——————————— independent clause ————————————————|
▶ The Tour has long been plagued by allegations of doping among

|—————————| |—————————————————————————independent
                          |————————————————— subordinate
contestants, but the 2007 race, which saw three riders disqualified for

clause ————————————————————————————————|
clause ————————————|
doping-related offenses, was particularly scandal ridden.

→ EXERCISE **32.11** Identifying sentence types

Next to each of the following sentences, write the type of sentence it is: simple, compound, complex, or compound complex.

connect

mhconnectcomposition.com
Online exercise: QL32111

1. Lindsay practices her breathing exercises every day with her husband, Larry, who coaches her enthusiastically.

2. Lindsay and Larry attend weekly childbirth classes, meet other expectant parents, learn about the stages of labor, and practice massage and relaxation techniques.

3. Lindsay and Larry will be first-time parents, but they are gaining confidence by attending classes.

4. One couple, although friendly to Lindsay and Larry, often interrupt the instructor, so Larry is sometimes annoyed by them.

5. As they attend classes, Lindsay and Larry gain confidence as prospective parents; however, the childbirth video made them nervous at first.

Make It **Your Own**

Write down five sentences from a recent reading assignment or from a newspaper or magazine article. Identify the independent and dependent clauses in each sentence, and label each sentence as simple, compound, complex, or compound-complex.

Work **Together**

Exchange your sentences and your analysis of them from the Make It Your Own exercise above with those of another student, and check each other's work. Consult your professor if you disagree about any sentences.

33 Avoiding Sentence Fragments

IN THIS CHAPTER

a. Recognizing fragments, 626

b. Correcting fragments, 630

c. Intentional fragments, 635

An open drawbridge is not a complete bridge; it is two bridge fragments, neither of which, by itself, will get travelers all the way across a river. Similarly, a ***sentence fragment*** is not a complete sentence. It may begin with a capital letter and end with a period (or a question mark or an exclamation point), but it lacks all the elements of a complete sentence. It takes readers only partway through the writer's thought, leaving them searching for the missing pieces. Although writers may use them intentionally in certain contexts, fragments are almost always out of place in academic and business writing.

> **Subject** A noun or pronoun that names the topic of a sentence (612–13)
> **Complete verb** A main verb together with any helping verbs needed to indicate tense, voice, and mood (670–71)

33a Recognizing Fragments

A sentence must have at least one ***independent clause,*** which is a group of related words that has a ***complete verb*** and a ***subject*** but does not start with a subordinating term such as *although, because, who,* or *that.* A word group punctuated like a sentence that does not satisfy these conditions is a fragment, not a sentence.

626

connect
mhconnectcomposition.com
Additional resources: QL33001,
QL33002

Quick Reference ➡ **Identifying Fragments**

To determine whether a word group is a fragment or a sentence, ask yourself these questions:

1. **Does it have a complete verb?**   If the answer is no, it is a fragment.

2. **Does it have a subject?**   If the answer is no, it is a fragment.

3. **Does it begin with a subordinating word but otherwise stand alone?**   If the answer is yes, it is a fragment.

1. No verb

A **complete verb** consists of a main verb together with any helping verbs needed to express tense, mood, and voice. If a word group lacks a complete verb, it is a **phrase,** and if that phrase is punctuated as a sentence, it is a phrase fragment.

> **More about ▶▶▶**
> Verbs, 664–85

FRAGMENT   Her beautiful new sports car.
(NO VERB)

                                subj. complete verb

SENTENCE   Her beautiful new sports car was smashed beyond repair.

Verbals are words that look like verbs—they are derived from verbs—but they lack the information about tense required of a complete verb. Instead, they function as nouns, adjectives, or adverbs. Verbals can include past participles (the *-ed* form in most verbs), present participles (the *-ing* form), and infinitives (the *to* form). Verbal phrases, by themselves, are fragments, not sentences.

> **More about ▶▶▶**
> Verbals, 619–20,
> 759–61

                  verbal   verbal

FRAGMENT   An inspired teacher making a difference in her students' lives.

                  verbal   subj.   verb

SENTENCE   An inspired teacher, she is making a difference in her students' lives.

2. No subject

The subject of a sentence is the answer to the question "Who or what did the action defined by the verb?" If a word group lacks a subject, it is a phrase. If the phrase is punctuated like a sentence, it is a phrase fragment.

> verb
FRAGMENT   Serves no purpose.

> subject   verb
SENTENCE   The breadmaker in my cupboard serves no purpose.

More about ▶▶▶
Imperatives, 680

Imperatives (*commands*) look like they do not have a subject. Actually their subject is understood to be *you,* and they are sentences, *not* fragments.

> verb
IMPERATIVE   Come here right now!
SENTENCE

ESL **Including a Stated Subject** Unlike in most other languages, all sentences in formal English except commands always require an explicitly stated subject. See Chapter 42, "Understanding English Word Order and Sentence Structure," p. 738.

More about ▶▶▶
Subordinate clauses, 620–22

3. Begins with a subordinating term

A subordinate clause and an independent clause both have a subject and verb, but a subordinate clause begins with a subordinating term, either a subordinating conjunction or a relative pronoun (see the Quick Reference box on the next page). The subordinating term links the subordinate clause to another clause, where it functions as a noun, adjective, or adverb. A subordinate clause cannot stand alone as a sentence, and if it is punctuated like a sentence, it is a subordinate clause fragment.

> subordinator
FRAGMENT   When the drawbridge closes.

> subordinator
SENTENCE   We will cross the river when the drawbridge closes.

> subordinator
FRAGMENT   Which made driving hazardous.

> subordinator
SENTENCE   The storm left a foot of snow, which made driving hazardous.

Be careful to distinguish between relative pronouns used to introduce a subordinate clause and the same words used as interrogative

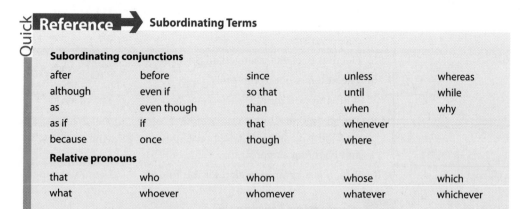

Quick **Reference** ➡ **Subordinating Terms**

Subordinating conjunctions

after	before	since	unless	whereas
although	even if	so that	until	while
as	even though	than	when	why
as if	if	that	whenever	
because	once	though	where	

Relative pronouns

that	who	whom	whose	which
what	whoever	whomever	whatever	whichever

pronouns to introduce questions. Questions beginning this way are complete sentences.

FRAGMENT	relative pronoun Who will be attending.
SENTENCE	interrogative pronoun Who will be attending?

➤ **EXERCISE 33.1 Identifying fragments**

Identify each of the following word groups as a sentence or a fragment; then further label each fragment as a phrase fragment or a subordinate clause fragment.

EXAMPLE

Which have women heads of state. [*fragment, subordinate clause*]

1. In 2006, Michelle Bachelet became the first female president of Chile.

2. Who would have predicted such a turn of events just a few years earlier?

3. Not many observers at the time.

More about ▶▶▶
Different types of pronouns, 604

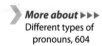
mhconnectcomposition.com
Online exercise: QL33101

4. Because Chile was for many years a bastion of gender conservatism.

5. Electing Bachelet changed all that.

6. The voters went to the polls.

7. With an open mind.

8. The people of Chile were excited.

9. Waving flags and banners, honking horns, blowing whistles, and chanting slogans.

10. Which is a promising sign for the future.

connect

mhconnectcomposition.com
Additional resources: QL33003

33b Correcting Fragments

Once you have identified a fragment, you have two options for correcting it:

1. Connect the fragment to a related independent clause.

▶ The first mission to Pluto was launched in 2006. ~~Will arrive~~ *and will arrive* in 2015.

▶ He made 5,000 songs available over the university's server. ~~Which~~ *, which* prompted the record companies to threaten legal action.

Writing Responsibly **Sentence Fragments and Context**

Although writers sometimes use them deliberately in certain contexts (see 33c), for a variety of reasons you should avoid sentence fragments in your academic or business writing. One is that fragments can create ambiguities, as in the following example:

▶ Our small town has seen many changes. Some long-time stores went out of business. <u>Because the new mall opened.</u> There are now more options for family entertainment.

Did the new mall put stores out of business, provide new entertainment options, or both? To clarify this ambiguity, the writer would need to attach the fragment to the preceding sentence or the following sentence, or rewrite these sentences in some other way.

Another reason to avoid fragments is that readers may interpret them as carelessness or a lack of competence, which would undermine your efforts to present yourself authoritatively.

2. Convert the fragment into an independent clause.

▶ The first mission to Pluto was launched in 2006. ~~Will~~ *It will* arrive in 2015.

▶ He made 5,000 songs available over the university's server. ~~Which~~ *In response,*
~~prompted~~ the record companies ~~to threaten~~ *threatened* legal action.

These options apply to both phrase fragments and subordinate clause fragments. Either option can fix a fragment; deciding on the best one is a stylistic choice that depends on the context in which the fragment occurs.

1. Phrase fragments

Phrase fragments lack a subject, a complete verb, or both. As you edit your writing, watch for fragments based on certain kinds of phrases in particular. These include prepositional phrases, verbal phrases, appositive phrases, the separate parts of compound predicates, and items in lists and examples.

> **Tech**

> **Grammar Checkers and Sentence Fragments**
>
> The grammar checkers in word processing programs may miss some fragments and, in some cases, may incorrectly flag imperatives as fragments. Although your grammar checker can help you, you will still need to edit your prose carefully for fragments.

Prepositional Phrases A ***prepositional phrase*** consists of a preposition (such as *as, at, for, from, in addition to, to,* or *until*) followed by a pronoun or noun and its modifiers. You can usually correct a prepositional phrase fragment by attaching it to an adjacent sentence.

> **More about** ▶ ▶ ▶
> Prepositions and prepositional phrases, 609, 618, 773–80

▶ The Kenyon College women won the NCAA Division III title
~~again. For~~ *for* the seventeenth consecutive year.

Verbal Phrases Although verbals are derived from verbs, verbal phrases can function as adjectives, adverbs, or nouns within a sentence but not as sentences on their own. In the following example, *stranding* is a verbal.

▶ The car had run out of ~~gas. Stranding~~ *gas, stranding* us in the middle of nowhere.

> *More about* ▶▶▶
> Appositives, 618

Noun phrase A noun together with any modifiers (617)

Appositive Phrases An ***appositive phrase*** is a noun or ***noun phrase*** that renames a preceding noun or noun phrase and is grammatically equivalent to it. Appositives become fragments when they are separated by a period from the phrases they rename.

> ▶ The diners eagerly awaited the culmination of the ~~meal. Sam's~~ meal, Sam's
>
> mouth-watering apple pie.

> *More about* ▶▶▶
> Compound predicates, 614

Compound Predicates A ***compound predicate*** consists of two or more complete verbs, together with their objects and modifiers, that are joined by a coordinating conjunction (such as *or, and,* or *but*) and that share the same subject. A fragment results when the last part of a compound predicate is punctuated as a separate sentence.

> ▶ By the end of May, the band members hated each other. ~~But~~ but still had
>
> six weeks left to tour.

Lists and Examples Lists become fragments when they are separated from the sentence to which they belong. To correct list fragments, link them to the sentence by rephrasing the passage or replacing the period with a colon or a dash.

FRAGMENT Three authors are most commonly associated with the Beat movement. Allen Ginsberg, Jack Kerouac, and William Burroughs.

> *More about* ▶▶▶
> Punctuation for lists,
> 828–30, 833

REVISED Three authors are most commonly associated with the Beat movement: Allen Ginsberg, Jack Kerouac, and William Burroughs.

or

The three authors most commonly associated with the Beat movement are Allen Ginsberg, Jack Kerouac, and William Burroughs.

Examples or explanations that begin with transitional words such as *for example, in contrast,* and *in addition* can be sentences; they are fragments, however, if they are punctuated like a sentence but lack a subject or a complete verb, or otherwise consist of only a subordinate clause. In the following example, the writer corrected a phrase fragment by rephrasing and attaching it to the preceding sentence.

▶ People today have access to many sources of news and ~~opinion. For~~ *opinion, including, for*

example, the internet and cable television as well as broadcast

television and print newspapers and magazines.

The writer of the next example corrected a subordinate clause fragment by deleting the subordinating word *that,* which turns the fragment into a sentence.

▶ Certain facts underscore the rapid growth of the internet. For

example,
~~example that~~ web browsers did not become widely available until

the mid-1990s.

→ EXERCISE **33.2** Correcting sentence fragments

Correct each sentence fragment below and write at the end what kind of fragment it is (prepositional phrase, verbal phrase, appositive phrase, compound predicate, list or example).

EXAMPLE

grandfather, Jacob
The most unforgettable character I know is my ~~grandfather. Jacob~~ Black.

[appositive phrase]

1. Even though he was only five feet four inches tall, he was a championship boxer. During high school.

2. Boxing was what many young men pursued. Back in the 1940s.

3. Later, he joined the army. Becoming a first sergeant in the quartermaster corps.

4. He was responsible for setting up army camps in Korea. Also for supervising supplies, cooking, and recreation.

5. He must have been a pretty tough guy in those days. Not the warm and loving grandpa I knew later on.

connect
mhconnectcomposition.com
Online exercise: QL33102

2. Subordinate clause fragments

A subordinate clause has a subject and a verb but begins with a subordinating word or phrase—a subordinating conjunction or a relative pronoun—and cannot stand alone as a sentence. When you correct a subordinate clause fragment, be sure to consider the relationships

▶ **More about** ▶▶▶
Subordination and subordinating conjunctions, 531–35

among the ideas you are expressing before deciding whether to transform the subordinate clause into an independent clause or to connect it to a related independent clause. Subordinating conjunctions, for example, specify the relationship between the information in a subordinate clause and the clause it modifies. If that relationship is important, you will probably want to correct the fragment by connecting it to the independent clause to which it relates.

> ▶ Blogs continue to gain popularity as a source of information. ~~Because~~ *because*
> they can publish late-breaking news as soon as it occurs.

The correction retains the subordinating conjunction *because* and with it important information about the cause-and-effect relationship between the two parts of the sentence. That information would have been obscured if the writer had simply deleted the subordinating conjunction to change the fragment into a separate sentence: *They can publish late-breaking news as soon as it occurs.*

In other cases, revising a subordinate clause fragment into a separate sentence by deleting the subordinating word can produce a clearer, less awkward result than would attaching it to another sentence.

> ▶ Horses and camels have something in common. ~~That the~~ *The* ancestors
> of both originated in the western hemisphere and migrated to the
>
> eastern hemisphere.

More about ▶▶▶
Punctuating subordinate clauses and other subordinate structures, 533, 791–93

A subordinate clause that begins with a subordinating conjunction is usually set off by a comma if it comes at the beginning of a sentence but not if it comes at the end. The punctuation of a subordinate clause that begins with a relative pronoun depends on whether the clause is **essential** (it specifically identifies the word or words it modifies) or **nonessential** (the identity of the word or words it modifies is clear without it).

connect

↱ EXERCISE 33.3 Correcting subordinate clause fragments

Correct each fragment below and write at the end whether the fragment begins with a subordinating conjunction or a relative pronoun.

EXAMPLE

springs that
Northern Florida is dotted with natural ~~springs. That~~ are direct outlets of

a huge aquifer, or groundwater source. [*relative pronoun*]

1. The springs discharge millions of gallons of cool, clean fresh water each day. Because the aquifer is very close to the surface.

2. The area contains many rivers, lakes, and ponds. That are fed from the springs.

3. Although the area still seems rural and remote. The water attracts many vacationers.

4. For many years people came to visit area tourist attractions. That included "mermaid" shows and glass-bottom boat rides.

5. Today, however, the region has gained a reputation for ecotourism. Because it abounds with state parks, water trails, and campgrounds.

33c Using Intentional Fragments Effectively and Judiciously

Writers sometimes use fragments not in error but intentionally for emphasis or to reflect how people actually speak. Exclamations and the answers to questions often fall into this category.

▶ Another loss! Ouch!

▶ What caused this debacle? The collapse of our running game.

Intentional fragments are also common in advertising copy, and many writers use them for effect when the context makes their full meaning clear.

▶ All science. No fiction.
                                            —Toyota advertisement

▶ Man is the only animal that blushes. Or needs to.
                                    —Mark Twain, *Following the Equator*

Consider your writing situation, your context and genre, and especially your audience before deciding to use a sentence fragment deliberately. If your purpose is careful reporting or analysis, you should probably avoid the intentional sentence fragment because it can create ambiguity (see the Writing Responsibly box on p. 630). In academic or business writing, where clarity of expression is highly prized, fragments are frowned upon and can undermine your authority. On the other hand, if your purpose is expressive or you are writing in an informal context or genre (for example, in a blog or for a fanzine), the occasional intentional fragment can be highly effective.

connect
mhconnectcomposition.com
Online exercise: QL33104

→ **EXERCISE 33.4 Correcting sentence fragments**

Identify and correct any sentence fragments in the following paragraph.

On January 2, miners of the morning shift reported for work. As usual beginning the descent to the coal seam deep underground. Not all had descended into the mine when the explosion happened. There were two crews. One still aboveground. The explosion occurred at 6:31 a.m. Causing a power outage throughout the mine. Which filled with smoke. And deadly carbon monoxide. A mine rescue team was called. But not until 8:04 a.m. Because it took the mine supervisors that long to ascertain what had happened. Meanwhile, the trapped miners had only a limited supply of oxygen. Distraught families gathered aboveground waiting for news. At last a shout rang out. "Alive!" A collective sigh of relief and thanksgiving was audible. As family members waited to see their loved ones once again.

Make It **Your Own**

Reread three texts you have written recently, looking for sentence fragments. How many do you find? What types of fragments do you recognize (phrases punctuated as sentences, subordinate clauses punctuated as sentences)? How would you fix them now?

Work **Together**

Exchange drafts of assignments you are working on with a classmate and analyze your classmate's writing for sentence fragments. How many do you find? How would you correct them? Then discuss your work: Which was easier to analyze— your own writing, or someone else's?

34

Avoiding Comma Splices and Fused Sentences

If not properly joined with a coupling mechanism like the one in this picture, railway cars would either pull apart when the lead car accelerated, or crash into each other when the lead car braked. Like railway cars, two independent clauses joined in a compound sentence need a proper coupling mechanism. If the clauses are incorrectly joined with a comma alone in a *comma splice,* they may seem to readers to pull apart confusingly. If the clauses crash into one another with no separating punctuation in a *fused* (or *run-on*) *sentence,* readers will not know where one ends and the other begins.

34a Correctly Joining Independent Clauses

More about ▶▶▶
Clauses, 620–23

An *independent clause* is a clause that can stand on its own as a sentence. Related independent clauses can follow one another as separate sentences, each ending in a period.

▶ Richard Harris played Dumbledore in the first two Harry ⎸———independent clause——⎸

Potter movies. Michael Gambon has played the role since ⎸———independent clause——⎸

Harris's death in 2002. ⎸——clause——⎸

637

More about ▶▶▶
Coordination,
526–31

Alternatively, you can join (or *coordinate*) independent clauses in a compound sentence with a variety of coupling mechanisms that let readers know one clause is ending and another beginning. Of these, two are the most common:

- A comma and a coordinating conjunction (*and, but, or, nor, for, so, yet*)

  ▶ Richard Harris played Dumbledore in the first two Harry Potter movies, but Michael Gambon has played the role since Harris's death in 2002.

- A semicolon

  ▶ Richard Harris played Dumbledore in the first two Harry Potter movies; Michael Gambon has played the role since Harris's death in 2002.

You can also use a colon or a dash between independent clauses when the first clause introduces the second or the second elaborates on the first. (The colon is usually more appropriate in formal writing.)

  ▶ Two actors have played Dumbledore: Michael Gambon succeeded Richard Harris in the role after Harris's death in 2002.

connect

mhconnectcomposition.com
Additional resources: QL34001,
QL34002

34b Identifying Incorrectly Joined Independent Clauses: Comma Splices and Fused Sentences

When a writer improperly joins two independent clauses with a comma alone, the result is a *comma splice*.

|————— independent clause —————| |————

COMMA SPLICE Ronald Reagan was originally an actor, he turned

independent clause ————|
to politics in the 1960s.

Writing Responsibly Clarifying Boundaries

Comma splices and fused sentences obscure the boundaries between linked ideas. If you leave them uncorrected in your writing, you burden readers with a task that should be yours: to identify where one idea ends and another begins and to specify how those ideas relate to each other.

Reference ➡ **Identifying Comma Splices and Fused Sentences**

When two independent clauses are joined by	The result is
A comma and coordinating conjunction	**Not** a comma splice or fused sentence
A semicolon	**Not** a comma splice or fused sentence
A colon or dash	**Not** a comma splice or fused sentence
A comma alone	A **comma splice—revise**
No punctuation at all	A **fused sentence—revise**

When a writer runs two independent clauses together with no punctuation between them, the result is a *fused sentence* (also called a *run-on sentence*).

FUSED
SENTENCE

├──────── independent clause ────────┤ ├──
Politics and acting have something in common they
───────── independent clause ─────────┤
both require an affinity for public performance.

34c Recognizing When Comma Splices and Fused Sentences Tend to Occur

To avoid comma splices and fused sentences in your own work, pay attention to situations in which they are particularly likely to occur:

1. When the second clause begins with a conjunctive adverb (such as *for example, however,* or *therefore*) or other transitional expression

COMMA SPLICE   In the first two Harry Potter movies, Richard Harris played Dumbledore, however, since Harris's death in 2002, Michael Gambon has played the role.

REVISED   In the first two Harry Potter movies, Richard Harris played Dumbledore; however, since Harris's death in 2002, Michael Gambon has played the role.

➡ **Tech**

Comma Splices, Fused Sentences, and Grammar Checkers

Grammar checkers in word processing programs do not reliably identify comma splices or fused sentences. They catch some, but they miss many more.

2. When the grammatical subject of the second clause is a pronoun whose antecedent is the subject of the first clause

COMMA SPLICE Ronald Reagan was originally an actor, he turned to politics in the 1960s.

REVISED Ronald Reagan was originally an actor, but he turned to politics in the 1960s.

3. When the first clause introduces the second or the second explains or elaborates on the first

FUSED SENTENCE Politics and acting have something in common they both require a willingness to perform in public.

REVISED Politics and acting have something in common: They both require a willingness to perform in public.

4. When one clause is positive and the other negative

COMMA SPLICE We were not upset that the exam was postponed, we were relieved.

REVISED We were not upset that the exam was postponed; we were relieved.

Getting It Across

Is a Comma Splice Ever Acceptable?

Comma splices often show up in compound sentences composed of two short, snappy independent clauses in parallel form, particularly when one is negative and the other positive or when both are commands. This usage is common, for example, in advertising:

Buy one, get one free.

It can crop up, too, in the work of experienced writers, who may use it deliberately because they feel a period, semicolon, or comma and coordinating conjunction would be too disruptive a separation in sentences like these:

You're not a man, you're a machine.

—George Bernard Shaw,
Arms and the Man

Go ahead, make my day.

—Joseph C. Stinson, screenplay
to *Sudden Impact*

However, this usage is best avoided in academic writing.

→ **EXERCISE 34.1 Identifying comma splices and fused sentences**

In each of the following sentences, underline the independent clauses. Then write CS after each comma splice, write FS after each fused sentence, and circle the numbers of sentences that are correct as is.

connect
mhconnectcomposition.com
Online exercise: QL34101

EXAMPLE

This is our dog her name is Dusty. [FS]

1. Dusty is a mutt, she is not a purebred dog.

2. Some people think she is a German shepherd others just ask what kind of dog she is.

3. I always say she is just a dog.

4. Dogs like Dusty are called a variety of names, mongrel is probably the most common.

5. Mutt and mixed-breed are other common names that are used for these dogs.

6. Mixed-breed dogs have fewer genetic disorders than do purebred dogs the inbreeding of purebreds has created genetic problems.

7. For example, German shepherds often have hip problems, collies often have eye diseases.

8. One type of mixed-breed is the crossbreed, a deliberate cross between two purebred strains.

9. As for Dusty, she certainly looks like a German shepherd she also looks like a Norwegian elkhound.

10. To me, she is simply the world's greatest dog, I love her very much.

34d **Correcting Comma Splices and Fused Sentences**

connect
mhconnectcomposition.com
Additional resources: QL34003

The Quick Reference box on p. 642 lists five strategies for correcting comma splices and fused sentences. The strategy you choose should depend on the logical relationship between the clauses and the meaning you intend to convey.

Quick Reference ➡ Ways to Correct Comma Splices and Fused Sentences

1. Use a period to divide the clauses into separate sentences.
2. Join the clauses correctly with a comma and coordinating conjunction.
3. Join the clauses correctly with a semicolon.
4. If appropriate, join the clauses with a colon or dash.
5. Change one independent clause into a modifying subordinate clause or phrase.

1. Separate sentences

Correcting a comma splice or fused sentence by dividing the independent clauses into separate sentences makes sense when one or both of the clauses are long or when the two clauses do not have a close logical relationship.

▶ My friends and I began our long-anticipated trip to Peru in early July **we** *. We*

arrived in Lima on Saturday morning and flew to Cuzco that same day.

Use a period also when the second clause is a new sentence that continues a quotation that begins in the first clause.

▶ "We must not be enemies," Abraham Lincoln implored the South in

his first inaugural address,⁄ *.* "Though passion may have strained, it

must not break our bonds of affection."

2. Coordinating conjunction

More about ▶▶▶
The meaning of coordinating conjunctions, 529

When you join independent clauses with a comma and a coordinating conjunction (*and, but, or, nor, for, so,* or *yet*), choose the conjunction that best fits the logical relationship between the clauses.

▶ We needed to adjust to the altitude before we began hiking in the

Andes we spent three days sightseeing in Cuzco. *, so*

3. Semicolon

More about ▶▶▶
Coordinating with a semicolon, 528–29, 802

Join two independent clauses with a semicolon when they have a clear logical relationship, either of contrast, example, or explanation.

▶ Most languages spoken in Europe belong to the Indo-European

               ;

   language family,/a few, such as Basque, Finnish, and Hungarian, do not.

           ⋀

Using a semicolon in combination with a conjunctive adverb or other transitional expression can clarify the relationship between the clauses.

▶ Most languages spoken in Europe belong to the Indo-European

               ; however,

   language family,/Basque, Finnish, and Hungarian are exceptions.

          ⋀

4. Colon or dash

You can use a colon or, less commonly, a dash to join independent clauses when the first clause introduces the second or the second explains or elaborates on the first. This usage can create a more emphatic separation between the clauses than would a semicolon.

> **More about** ▶▶▶
> Punctuating for emphasis, 557–58
> Colons, 833–35
> Dashes, 828–30

▶ The message is clear,/smoking kills.

       ⋀

▶ Don't get kicked out of school,/learn to study effectively.

         ⋀

5. Modifying subordinate clause or phrase

You can correct a comma splice or fused sentence by turning one of the independent clauses into a subordinate clause or by reducing the information in it to a modifying phrase. Note, however, that putting information in subordinate clauses and phrases usually de-emphasizes it in relation to the information in the independent clause it modifies.

> **More about** ▶▶▶
> Subordination and emphasis, 531–32

COMMA SPLICE	Spanish, like French and Italian, is a Romance language, it derives from Latin, the language of the Romans.
REVISED: SUBORDINATE CLAUSE	Spanish, like French and Italian, is a Romance language |———————— subordinate clause ————————| because it derives from Latin, the language of the Romans.
REVISED: MODIFYING PHRASE	|———————— modifying phrase ————————| Spanish, a Romance language like French and Italian, derives from Latin, the language of the Romans.

→ **EXERCISE 34.2 Correcting comma splices and fused sentences**

Choose one of the methods described above to correct each comma splice or fused sentence. Circle the numbers of any sentences that are correct as is.

EXAMPLE

Disaster films are almost as old as film itself the first was made in 1901.

1. Obviously, disasters are natural subjects for films they are dramatic and visually interesting.

2. Early disaster movies focused on natural events such as fires, floods, and earthquakes, later ones showed human-made tragedies.

3. The first modern disaster movies were made in the 1950s, they focused on airplane crashes.

4. The golden age of disaster movies was probably the 1970s, the most popular of all was *Airport,* released in 1970.

5. It was followed by numerous sequels as well as by other hugely successful examples of the genre, such as *The Towering Inferno.*

6. Since that time, the summer blockbuster has remained everyone's idea of a good time it usually includes enough romance and drama, as well as special effects, to please everyone.

7. The genre even spawned its own subgenre, the disaster spoof, represented by the hits *Airplane* and *Airplane II.*

8. With the increasing sophistication of computerized special effects in the 1990s disaster films enjoyed a huge revival they had flagged in popularity in the 1980s.

9. However, 9/11 may have changed all that how much fun is it to see a film like *The Towering Inferno* today?

10. Other disaster films that refer to real events, such as *The Day After Tomorrow,* which focused on the effects of global warming, have been successful only time will tell whether the genre will survive.

EXERCISE 34.3 Correcting comma splices and fused sentences

Revise the following passage to correct any comma splices or fused sentences.

connect
mhconnectcomposition.com
Online exercise: QL34103

Opera is an art form that combines music, lyrics, and dialogue, so is musical comedy, however. Then what is the difference between them? Perhaps it is their origins opera arose in the seventeenth century primarily in Italy as an attempt to revive classical Greek drama. Musical comedy arose in the United States in the twentieth century out of vaudeville and other plotless musical shows such as burlesque and reviews. Regardless, there is a great deal of overlap between the two forms today although the famous composer and lyricist Stephen Sondheim says that if something is performed in an opera house, it is an opera, but if it is performed in a theater, it is a musical comedy, today many works are performed in both places.

Make It **Your Own**

Choose a text you have recently written or are writing. On one page of that text, underline each independent clause; then revise the punctuation between those clauses as needed to correct any comma splices or fused sentences.

Work **Together**

Exchange your work on the Make It Your Own exercise above with a classmate and double-check each other's work. Where do you have differences of opinion? Refer back to the instruction in this chapter to resolve any differences.

35 Maintaining Agreement

In many languages, the grammatical form of some words in a sentence must match the form of other words. When the forms match, the reader can easily understand the sentence; when they do not, the effect can be like trying to force a square peg into a round hole, leaving the reader distracted or confused. In English, subjects and verbs require this kind of matchup, or **agreement,** as do pronouns and the words to which they refer.

SUBJECT-VERB AGREEMENT

A verb and its subject have to agree, or match each other, in person and number. **Person** refers to the form of a word that indicates whether it corresponds to the speaker or writer (*I, we*), the person addressed (*you*), or the people or things spoken or written about (*he, she, it, they, Alice, milkshakes*). **Number** refers to the form of a word that indicates whether it is singular, referring to one thing (*a student*), or plural, referring to more than one (*two students*).

35a Understanding How Subjects and Verbs Agree

With just a few exceptions, it is only in the present tense that verbs change form to indicate person and number. Even in the present tense, they have only two forms. One form, which ends in *-s*, is for third-person singular subjects; the other is for all other subjects.

	Singular		Plural	
	subject	verb	subject	verb
First Person	*I*	vote	*we*	vote
Second Person	*you*	vote	*you*	vote
Third Person	*he, she, it, the student*	vote**s**	*they, the students*	vote

Most nouns form the plural with the addition of an *-s* (*dog, dogs*) or *-es* (*coach, coaches*).

In other words, an *-s* on a noun makes the noun plural; an *-s* on a present-tense verb makes the verb singular:

	Noun	Verb
Singular	The dog	bark**s**
Plural	The dog**s**	bark

NOTE Nouns with irregular plurals include *woman* (plural *women*), *foot* (plural *feet*), *child* (plural *children*), and *phenomenon* (plural *phenomena*).

1. Agreement with *be* and with helping verbs

Unlike any other English verb, *be* has three present-tense forms (*am, are, is*) and two past-tense forms (*was, were*). In **verb phrases** that begin with a form of *be, have,* or *do* as a helping verb, the subject agrees with the helping verb.

→ Tech

Grammar Checkers and Subject-Verb Agreement

Grammar checkers in word processing programs can alert you to many subject-verb agreement problems, but they can also miss errors and can flag some constructions as errors that are not. Make your own informed judgment about any changes the computer might recommend.

More about ▶▶▶
The forms of regular and irregular verbs, 664–69

More about ▶▶▶
Regular and irregular plural nouns, 595–97

connect
mhconnectcomposition.com
Additional resources: QL35001

Verb phrase A *main verb* together with any *auxiliary,* or *helping, verbs.* The main verb carries the principal meaning of the phrase; the auxiliaries provide information about tense, voice, and mood. (670–71)

Writing Responsibly

Dialect Variation in Subject-Verb Agreement

The rules of subject-verb agreement are not the same in all dialects of English. In various communities in the English-speaking world, you might hear people say things like *"The cats is hungry,"* *"We was at the store,"* *"She walk to school every day,"* or *"She be walking to school."* In the contexts in which they occur, these variations are not mistakes; they reflect rules, but those rules are different from those of Standard American English. Still, the subject-verb agreement rules of Standard American English are what most readers in the United States expect to encounter.

> **More about ▸▸▸**
> Forms of *be, have,*
> and *do,* 670

			subject	verb phrase
	SINGULAR		The *price* of oil	*has* been fluctuating.
	PLURAL		Commodity *prices*	*have* been fluctuating.
	SINGULAR		The *price*	*was* fluctuating.
	PLURAL		*Prices*	*were* fluctuating.

> **More about ▸▸▸**
> Modal auxiliaries,
> 763–64

The modal auxiliaries—*can, could, may, might, must, shall, should, will, would,* and *ought to*—have only a single form; they do not take an *-s* ending for third-person singular subjects.

		subject	verb phrase
SINGULAR		The *price*	*can* change.
PLURAL		*Prices*	*can* change.

2. Subject-verb agreement pitfalls

> **More about ▸▸▸**
> Identifying sentence
> subjects, 612–13

The basic rules of subject-verb agreement may be clear, but writers (and speakers) nonetheless often trip over them. As the Quick Reference box on the next page indicates, these errors usually involve problems identifying the subject of a sentence and determining whether it is singular or plural.

35b Ignoring Words That Intervene between the Subject and the Verb

In English, the subject of a sentence is usually near the verb. As a result, writers sometimes mistakenly treat words that fall between the

Quick Reference ➡ **Avoiding Subject-Verb Agreement Pitfalls**

1. Ignore words that intervene between the subject and the verb. 648
2. Distinguish plural from singular compound subjects. 649
3. Distinguish singular from plural indefinite pronouns. 651
4. Understand collective noun subjects. 653
5. Find agreement when the subject is a measurement, a number, or the word *number*. 653
6. Recognize that some nouns that end in *-s* are singular. 654
7. Treat titles, words as words, and gerund phrases as singular. 655
8. Match the number of a relative pronoun subject (*who, which, that*) to its antecedent. 655
9. Match the verb to the subject when the subject follows the verb. 656
10. Match a linking verb with its subject, not its subject complement. 656

subject and the verb as if they were the subject. The writer of the following sentence mistook the singular noun phrase *Order of the Phoenix* for the true subject, the plural noun *members*. The revision corrects the agreement error.

connect

mhconnectcomposition.com
Additional resources: QL35002

FAULTY   The members of the Order of the Phoenix is dedicated to thwarting Voldemort.

REVISED   The members of the Order of the Phoenix are dedicated to thwarting Voldemort.

NOTE When a singular subject is followed by a phrase that begins with *as well as, in addition to, together with,* or some similar expression, the verb is singular, not plural.

▶ Harry Potter, together with the other members of the Order of the

Phoenix, ~~are~~ *is* determined to thwart Voldemort.

35c Distinguishing Plural from Singular Compound Subjects

A **compound subject** consists of two or more subjects joined by a **conjunction** (*Jack and Jill, one or another*).

> **Conjunction** Part of speech that joins words, phrases, or clauses to other words, phrases, or clauses and specifies the way the joined elements relate to each other (610–11)

1. Compounds joined by *and* or *both . . . and*

Most compound subjects joined by *and* or *both . . . and* are plural.

▶ *MySpace and Facebook **are*** two popular social networking websites.

▶ ***Both** MySpace and Facebook **allow*** users to include photos and videos in their profiles.

A compound subject joined by *and* is singular, however, if the items in the compound refer to the same person or thing.

▶ The winner *and* next president *is* the candidate with the most electoral votes.

A compound subject joined by *and* is also singular if it begins with *each* or *every*.

▶ ***Each** paper **and** exam **contributes*** to your final grade.

However, if it is followed by *each,* a compound joined by *and* is plural.

▶ The research paper *and* the final exam *each contribute* 25 percent toward your final grade.

2. Compounds joined by *or, nor, either . . . or, neither . . . nor*

When a compound subject is joined by *or, nor, either . . . or,* or *neither . . . nor,* the verb agrees with the part of the compound that is closest to the verb.

▶ ***Neither** the coach **nor** the players **were*** worried by the other team's early lead.

The second part of the compound is plural, so the verb is plural.

Applying this rule can produce an awkward result when the first item in a compound is plural and the second is singular. Reversing the order often resolves the problem.

AWKWARD   *Neither* the players *nor* the coach *is* happy about last night's loss.

REVISED   *Neither* the coach *nor* the players *are* happy about last night's loss.

connect
mhconnectcomposition.com
Additional resources: QL35003

Sometimes the result is so awkward that the only solution is to reword the sentence. This happens particularly when the subject includes the pronouns *I, we,* or *you* and the verb is a form of *be.*

AWKWARD	*Neither* Carla *nor* I *am leaving* until the job is finished.
REVISED	Carla *and* I *are not leaving* until the job is finished,
	or
	Neither Carla *nor* I *will leave* until the job is finished.

→ **EXERCISE 35.1 Making subjects and verbs agree**

Underline the subject in each of the following sentences, and then circle the verb that agrees with it.

connect

mhconnectcomposition.com
Online exercise: QL35101

> **EXAMPLE**
> Mr. Jefferson's <u>computer</u>, as well as its programs, (is/ are) out of date.

1. The participants in the panel discussion (disagrees/disagree) on nearly everything.
2. Many children today (has/have) unhealthy eating habits.
3. Both Ms. Lopez and Mr. Handler (is/are) installing energy-saving measures throughout their homes
4. Either Samantha or her parents (keeps/keep) score at our weekly card games.
5. The club's president and treasurer each (is/are) opposed to the increase in dues.

35d Distinguishing Singular and Plural Indefinite Pronouns

Indefinite pronouns (see the Quick Reference box on the next page) refer to unknown or unspecified people, quantities, or things. Most indefinite pronouns always take a singular verb:

▶ *Everybody* <u>*talks*</u> about the weather, but *nobody* <u>*does*</u> anything about it.

—Attributed to Mark Twain

Reference ➔ **Common Indefinite Pronouns**

Always singular: *another, anybody, anyone, anything, each, either, everybody, everyone, everything, much, neither, nobody, no one, nothing, one, somebody, someone, something*

Always plural: *both, few, many, others, several*
Variable: *all, any, more, most, some*

Some indefinite pronouns (*both, few, many, others, several*) always take a plural verb:

▶ *Many* of us *make* New Year's resolutions, but *few* of us *keep* them.

Some indefinite pronouns (*all, any, more, most, some*) are either singular or plural, depending on context:

connect
mhconnectcomposition.com
Additional resources: QL35004, QL35005, QL35006

▶ *Some* of these questions *are* hard.

▶ *Some* of this test *is* hard.

In the first sentence, *some* takes a plural verb because it refers to the plural noun *questions;* in the second sentence, *some* takes a singular verb because it refers to the singular noun *test.*

Getting It Across   **Can *None* Be Plural?**

Some grammarians maintain that the indefinite pronoun *none,* like *no one* or *not one,* is always singular.

▶ *None* of these questions *is* hard.

Others contend that, like *some* or *not any,* it can be either singular or plural depending on context.

▶ *None* of these questions *are* hard.
▶ *None* of this test *is* hard.

35e Understanding Collective Noun Subjects

connect
mhconnectcomposition.com
Additional resources: QL35007

A *collective noun* designates a collection, or group, of individuals: *audience, chorus, committee, faculty, family, government.* In U.S. English, a collective noun is singular when it refers to the group acting as a whole.

▶ The *faculty is* revising the general education requirements.

   The group acts as a whole.

A collective noun is plural when it refers to the members of the group acting individually.

▶ The *faculty are* unable to agree on the new requirements.

   The individual members of the group disagree among themselves.

If this usage sounds odd to you, however, you can reword the sentence with a clearly plural subject.

▶ The *members* of the faculty *are* unable to agree on the new
   requirements.

35f Finding Agreement When the Subject Is a Measurement, a Number, or the Word *Number*

connect
mhconnectcomposition.com
Additional resources: QL35008

Numbers, fractions, and units of measure take a singular verb when they refer to an undifferentiated mass or quantity.

▶ Almost *400,000,000 gallons* of gasoline *is* consumed every day in the
   United States.

▶ *One-fourth* of the world's oil *is* consumed in the United States.

▶ *Seven thousand dollars is* too high a price for that car.

Numbers, fractions, and units of measure take a plural verb when they refer to a collection of individual people or things.

▶ Recently, *more than 600,000 immigrants* annually *have become* naturalized citizens of the United States.

▶ *About a third* of the citizens naturalized in 2007 *were* from Asia.

▶ *More than 7 billion pennies were* minted in 2007.

The word *number* is plural when it appears with *a* but singular when it appears with *the*.

▶ *A number* of voters *are* in favor of the transportation bond.

▶ *The number* of voters in favor of the transportation bond *is* low.

35g Recognizing Nouns like *Measles* and *Economics* That Are Singular Even Though They End in *-s*

Some nouns that end in *-s* are singular. Examples include diseases like *diabetes* and *measles*.

▶ *Measles is* a contagious disease.

Words like *economics, mathematics,* and *physics* are singular when they refer to an entire field of study or body of knowledge.

▶ *Economics is* a popular major at many schools.

They are plural, however, when they refer to a set of individual traits related to the field of study.

▶ *The economics* of the music industry *are* changing rapidly.

35h　Treating Titles, Words as Words, and Gerund Phrases as Singular

The titles of books, articles, movies, and other works; the names of companies and institutions; the names of countries; and words treated as words are all singular even if they are plural in form.

connect
mhconnectcomposition.com
Additional resources: QL35009

▶ *Harry Potter and the Order of the Phoenix is* the fifth of J. K. Rowling's seven Harry Potter books.

▶ *The Centers for Disease Control and Prevention helps* protect the nation's health.

▶ *The United States is* one of the world's largest food exporters.

▶ *Fungi is* one of two acceptable plural forms of the word *fungus; funguses is* the other.

Gerunds and gerund phrases are also always singular.

Gerund The present participle (*-ing* form) of a verb used as a noun (619)

▶ *Conducting excavations is* just one part of an archaeologist's job.

35i　Matching a Relative Pronoun (*Who, Which,* or *That*) to Its Antecedent When the Pronoun Is the Subject of a Subordinate Clause

A relative pronoun (*who, which,* or *that*) that functions as the subject of a subordinate clause is singular if its ***antecedent*** (the word it refers to) is singular, but it is plural if its antecedent is plural.

> **More about ▶▶▶**
> Pronouns and their antecedents,
> 657–62, 695–97

▶ People *who live* in glass houses should not throw stones.

▶ The cactus is a plant *that thrives* in a hot, dry environment.

Be careful with antecedent phrases that include the expressions *one of* or *only one of.* *One of* usually signals a plural antecedent; *only one of* signals a singular antecedent.

▶ Bill Clinton is *one of several presidents* of the United States *who were elected* to two terms.

Several presidents were elected to two terms, and one of them was Clinton. The pronoun *who* refers to the plural noun *presidents.*

▶ Franklin D. Roosevelt is *the only one* of those presidents *who was elected* to more than two terms.

Only one president, Roosevelt, was elected to more than two terms. The pronoun *who* refers to that particular one and is singular.

35j Finding Agreement When the Subject Follows the Verb

More about ▶▶▶
Inverted word order, 557

If you reverse normal order and put the subject after the verb for emphasis or dramatic effect, be sure the verb agrees with the actual subject, not a different word that precedes the verb.

▶ Onto the tennis court *stride the defending champion and her challenger.*

The subject is the plural compound *the defending champion and her challenger,* not the singular term *tennis court.*

The subject also follows the verb in sentences that begin with *there* followed by a form of *be* (*there is, there are, there was, there were*).

▶ ~~There's~~ There are more people registered to vote than actually vote on Election Day.

The subject, *people,* is plural, so the verb should be plural.

35k Matching a Linking Verb with Its Subject, Not Its Subject Complement

More about ▶▶▶
Linking verbs and subject complements, 615

A *linking verb* (such as *was* or *were*) connects the subject of a sentence to a *subject complement,* which describes or refers to the subject. When either the subject or the subject complement is singular but the other is plural, make sure the verb agrees with the subject.

▶ One influential voting bloc in the election ~~were~~ young voters.
         was

The subject is the singular noun *bloc,* not the plural noun *voters.*

→ EXERCISE 35.2 Making subjects and verbs agree

Underline the subject in each of the following sentences, and then circle the verb that agrees with it.

connect
mhconnectcomposition.com
Online exercise: QL35102

EXAMPLE

The <u>orchestra</u> (is / (are)) not united behind their new conductor.

1. The number of vehicles using Reynolds Road (have/has) nearly doubled in a year.

2. Mr. Ojiba is the only one of the board members who (agree/agrees) with the proposal to cut the school budget.

3. Mumps (were/was) once a common childhood disease.

4. Working nights (seem/seems) to suit Candace well.

5. A significant number of our students (is/are) opposed to the revised dress code.

6. There (was/were) not many fans in the stands at our last soccer game.

7. The Philippines (offer/offers) many wonderful opportunities for diving.

8. Everyone (want/wants) to be rich, healthy, and good looking.

9. Currently, 90 percent of the people in my neighborhood (have/has) cats.

PRONOUN-ANTECEDENT AGREEMENT

Pronouns rename or take the place of nouns, noun phrases, or other pronouns. The word or phrase that a pronoun replaces is its **antecedent.** Pronouns and their antecedents must agree in person (first, second, or third), number (singular or plural), and gender (neuter, feminine, or masculine). The antecedent usually appears before the pronoun but sometimes follows

→ **Tech**

Grammar Checkers and Pronoun-Antecedent Agreement

Grammar checkers in word processing programs cannot identify pronoun-antecedent agreement errors.

it. The two pronouns in the following example have the same antecedent—*Emma*—which follows the first pronoun and precedes the second.

connect

mhconnectcomposition.com
Additional resources: QL35010, QL35011

▶ In *her* haste, *Emma* shut down the computer without saving *her* work.

 A Possessive Pronoun Agrees with Its Antecedent, Not the Word It Modifies In English, a possessive pronoun (such as *his, hers,* or *its*) agrees with its antecedent, not the word it modifies. In the following example, *father* is the antecedent, so the pronoun should be masculine.

▶ The father beamed joyfully at ~~her~~ *his* newborn daughter.

Quick Reference ➤ **Avoiding Pronoun-Antecedent Agreement Pitfalls**

1. Match pronouns with indefinite pronoun and generic noun antecedents. 658
2. Match pronouns with collective noun antecedents. 661
3. Match pronouns with compound antecedents. 661

As with subject-verb agreement, the basic rule of pronoun antecedent agreement—match the pronoun to its antecedent in person, number, and gender—is uncomplicated. However, writers often find themselves uncertain how to apply the rule in certain situations, as the Quick Reference box summarizes.

35l Matching Pronouns with Indefinite Pronoun and Generic Noun Antecedents

More about ▶▶▶
Singular and plural indefinite pronouns, 651–52

Antecedents that are singular but have a plural sense are among the most common sources of pronoun-antecedent confusion. These include the following:

- **Indefinite pronouns** such as *each, everybody,* and *everyone* that are singular even though they refer to groups.

- **Generic nouns**—that is, singular nouns used to designate a whole class of people or things rather than a specific individual. In this sentence, for example—*The aspiring doctor faces years of rigorous training*—the expression *aspiring doctor* generically designates all would-be doctors.

1. Singular indefinite pronoun or generic noun antecedents

A pronoun with a singular indefinite pronoun or generic noun antecedent should be singular. Do not let the plural sense of the antecedent distract you.

▶ The dog is a domesticated animal, unlike ~~their~~ *its* cousins the wolf

and coyote.

> The antecedent is the singular generic noun *dog,* so the pronoun should be singular too.

This rule creates a problem, however, when the indefinite antecedent refers to both women and men. Correct agreement requires a singular pronoun, but using *he* as a substitute for either *man* or *woman* results in gender bias.

GRAMMATICALLY CORRECT BUT GENDER-BIASED AGREEMENT

In past downturns *the affluent consumer* continued to spend, but now even *he* is cutting back.

Writers often try to avoid this conflict with a gender-neutral plural pronoun such as *they,* resulting in faulty pronoun-antecedent agreement.

UNBIASED BUT GRAMMATICALLY INCORRECT AGREEMENT

In past downturns, *the affluent consumer* continued to spend, but now even *they* are cutting back.

This usage is common in everyday speech, but it is inappropriate for formal writing (although, as the Getting It Across box below suggests, some language experts now think differently).

connect

mhconnectcomposition.com
Additional resources: QL35012

❭ **More about ▶▶▶**
Avoiding gender
bias, 568–71

Getting It
Across   **Using a Plural Pronoun with a Singular Antecedent**

The use of a plural pronoun with singular indefinite antecedents is common in everyday speech, and many language experts now maintain that it should be acceptable in formal writing, too. It is a usage, after all, that some of the finest writers in the English language have seen fit to employ:

> God send everyone their heart's desire!
>
> —Shakespeare, *Much Ado About Nothing,* 3.4

Everybody who comes to Southampton finds it either their duty or pleasure to call upon us. . . .

> —Jane Austen, from a letter

Nonetheless, many readers still find the usage grating, so it is best to avoid it when you are writing for a general audience in an academic or business context.

Quick Reference ➡ **Three Strategies for Avoiding Gender Bias with Indefinite Antecedents**

1. Make both the antecedent and the pronoun plural.
2. Rephrase the sentence without the pronoun.

3. Use *he or she, she or he,* or the appropriate variant (for example, *him or her* or *her or him*), but sparingly.

You can avoid both gender bias and faulty agreement by rephrasing according to one of these strategies:

1. Make both the antecedent and the pronoun plural.

> ▶ In past downturns, ~~the affluent consumer~~ *affluent consumers* continued to spend,
> but now even ~~he is~~ *they are* cutting back.

2. Rephrase the sentence without the pronoun.

> ▶ ~~In past downturns, the~~ *Even the* affluent consumer *, who* continued to spend
> ~~but now even~~ he is cutting back. *in past downturns,* *now*

3. Use *he or she* or the appropriate variant (for example, *him or her* or *her or him*), but sparingly.

> ▶ In past downturns, the affluent consumer continued to spend,
> but even he is *she or* now cutting back.

CAUTION Avoid overusing the phrases *he or she* and *his or her.* They can make your text sound stuffy and strained.

---

2. Plural or variable indefinite pronoun antecedents

Although most indefinite pronouns are singular, some (*both, few, many, others, several*) are always plural.

> ▶ *Both* of the candidates released *their* income tax returns.

Others (*all, any, more, most, some*) are singular or plural depending on the context.

▶ When the teacher surprised the *students* with a pop quiz, she

   discovered that *most* had not been doing *their* homework.

▶ Although some of the river's *water* is diverted for irrigation, *most*

   still makes *its* way to the sea.

35m Matching Pronouns with Collective Noun Antecedents

Collective nouns (for example, *audience, chorus, committee, faculty, family, government*) are singular when they refer to a group acting as a whole.

▶ *My family* traces *its* roots to West Africa.

Collective nouns are plural when they refer to the members of a group acting individually.

▶ *The billionaire's family* fought over *their* inheritance.

35n Matching Pronouns with Compound Antecedents

Compound antecedents joined by *and* are usually plural and take a plural pronoun.

▶ *Clinton and Obama* were the leading candidates for *their* party's nomination.

Pronouns with compound antecedents joined by *or, nor, either . . . or,* or *neither . . . nor* agree with the nearest antecedent. To avoid awkwardness when one of the antecedents is plural and the other singular, put the plural antecedent second.

▶ *Neither the coach nor the players* worried that *their* team might lose.

When the antecedents differ in gender or person, however, the results of the "nearest antecedent" rule can be so awkward that the only solution is to reword the sentence:

> **AWKWARD**　It was clear after the New Hampshire primary that either Barack Obama or Hillary Clinton would find herself the Democratic Party's nominee for president.
>
> **REVISED**　It was clear after the New Hampshire primary that either Barack Obama or Hillary Clinton would be the Democratic Party's nominee for president.

connect

mhconnectcomposition.com
Online exercise: QL35103

→ EXERCISE 35.3　Editing for pronoun-antecedent agreement

Edit the following sentences to correct errors in pronoun-antecedent agreement and avoid gender bias.

EXAMPLE

Zoe and her parents felt as though something was missing from ~~her~~ family.
_{their}

1. Nearly every home in their neighborhood had their own dog, cat, or other type of pet.

2. That is why the Conyer family was slowly walking through the animal shelter, looking over every animal as Zoe, Robert, and their parents passed his cage.

3. Neither Zoe nor her parents felt as though he or she could properly care for a rabbit, a ferret, or a piglet, but they found the dogs irresistible.

4. Robert was hesitant about getting a pet, although he was entranced by each dog frantically wagging their tail as the family passed by.

5. Some of the dogs they passed barked frantically, but others just lay idly in his or her cages.

6. The proper dog for them, thought Zoe, would hardly be able to contain their eagerness to make friends.

7. With the shelter volunteer's help, they took several male and female dogs out, one at a time, but each canine candidate pulled on their leash too aggressively for the Conyer kids to handle.

8. Zoe felt that all of the dogs they walked had his or her endearing qualities; however, she was a little afraid of most of them.

9. Then Robert pointed to a puppy enthusiastically pawing at their cage and whining to attract the family's attention.

10. That's when they found Molly, a cheerful, agreeable, and gentle dog who immediately immersed itself in the life of the Conyers family.

Make It **Your Own**

Reread several papers that you have recently written. Where have you handled agreement issues well, and where should you revise?

Work **Together**

Compare the sentences you found doing the Make It Your Own exercise above with those your classmates found. Discuss them as a group: What are the issues you will need to pay attention to in your future writing?

36 Using Verbs

Verbs are the driving force in a sentence. They specify the action (*Sylvia* <u>won</u> *the race*), occurrence (*She* <u>became</u> *a runner in high school*), or state of being (*She* <u>was</u> *worn out after the meet*) that affects the subject. Verbs also provide information about time (***tense***), the identity of the subject (***person*** and ***number***), whether the subject is acting or being acted on (***voice***), and the attitude or manner of the writer or speaker (***mood***) (see the Quick Reference box on the next page).

VERB FORMS

36a Understanding the Basic Forms of Verbs

With the exception of the verb *be,* all verbs have five forms: base, -*s* form, past tense, past participle, and present participle.

Quick Reference ➡ What Information Do Verbs Reveal?

Verbs provide information about tense, person and number, voice, and mood.

- **Tense.** When does the action occur? In the *present* (laugh/laughs), *past* (laughed), or *future* (will laugh)?
- **Person.** Does the verb form tell you that the subject is speaking (*I laugh*), spoken to (*You should laugh*), or spoken about (*He laughs*)?
- **Number.** Are the subject and its accompanying verb *singular* (He laughs) or *plural* (They laugh)?

- **Mood.** Is the verb *indicative,* stating or questioning something about the subject (*He laughs*)? Is it *imperative,* giving a command (*Douse the coach!*)? Is it *subjunctive,* expressing a possibility (*If the coach were doused again, she might lose patience with her players*)?
- **Voice.** Is the verb *active,* with the subject performing the action (*He laughs*), or *passive,* with the subject being acted upon (*The coach is doused with water by her players*)?

	Base Form	-s Form	Past Tense	Past Participle	Present Participle
Regular Verb	campaign	campaigns	campaigned	campaigned	campaigning
Irregular Verb	choose	chooses	chose	chosen	choosing

- The *base form* is what you find when you look up a verb in the dictionary. Use it with a plural noun or the pronouns *I, we, you,* or *they* to express a present or habitual action, occurrence, or state of being.

  ▶ Presidential candidates *campaign* every four years.

  ▶ I usually *choose* candidates based on their policies.

- The *-s form* is the base form plus *-s* or *-es.* Use it with a singular noun or a singular pronoun (*he, she, it*) to express present or habitual action, occurrence, or state of being.

  More about ▶▶▶
  Verb tenses, 674–79
  Voice, 682–83

  ▶ My favorite senator always *campaigns* in our town.

  ▶ She *chooses* positive messages instead of negative ones.

- The past-tense form of regular verbs such as *campaign* is the base form plus *-d* or *-ed;* the past-tense forms of irregular verbs such as *choose* vary. Use the past tense with singular or plural subjects to express past action, occurrence, or state of being.

▶ The mayor *campaigned* downtown yesterday.

▶ Some people *chose* to protest his appearance.

■ The past participle is the same as the past tense in most verbs but varies in some irregular verbs. Use the past participle in combination with forms of *have* to form the perfect tenses and with forms of *be* to form the passive voice.

▶ The candidate *has campaigned* nonstop.

▶ Our town *was chosen* by the candidate for his last campaign stop.

■ The present participle of all verbs, regular and irregular, is formed by adding *-ing* to the base form. Use the present participle with forms of *be* to form the progressive tenses.

> **More about ▶▶▶**
> Verb forms as modifiers, 619–20

▶ Senator Brown *is campaigning* here today.

▶ They *have been choosing* a running mate.

> **Verbal** A verb form that functions as a noun, adjective, or adverb (619)

NOTE Past and present participles sometimes function as ***verbals,*** not verbs. Past participles, for example, can sometimes be modifiers (*an educated public*), and present participles can be modifiers (*her opening statement*) or nouns (*campaigning is exhausting*).

➔ Tech

Grammar Checkers and Verb Problems

Grammar checkers in word processing programs will spot some errors that involve irregular or missing verbs, verb endings, and the subjunctive mood, but they will miss other errors and may suggest incorrect solutions. You must look for verb errors yourself and carefully evaluate any suggestions from a grammar checker.

36b Using Regular and Irregular Verb Forms Correctly

The vast majority of English verbs are ***regular,*** meaning that their past-tense and past-participle forms end in *-d* or *-ed:*

Base	Past Tense	Past Participle
climb	climb**ed**	climb**ed**
analyze	analyze**d**	analyze**d**
copy	copi**ed**	copi**ed**

However, about two hundred English verbs are ***irregular,*** with past-tense and past-participle forms that do not follow one set pattern:

Base	Past Tense	Past Participle
build	built	built
eat	ate	eaten
see	saw	seen

The forms of irregular verbs can easily be confused.

▶ My wool shirt ~~shrunk~~ when I washed it in hot water.
   shrank

If you are unsure whether a verb is regular or irregular or what form you should use in a particular situation, consult a dictionary or the following list. In the dictionary, you will find any irregular forms listed in the entry for the base form of a verb.

COMMON IRREGULAR VERBS

Base Form	Past Tense	Past Participle
arise	arose	arisen
be	was/were	been
bear	bore	borne, born
beat	beat	beaten
become	became	become
begin	began	begun
bid	bid	bid
bite	bit	bitten, bit
blow	blew	blown
break	broke	broken
bring	brought	brought
build	built	built
burst	burst	burst
buy	bought	bought
catch	caught	caught
choose	chose	chosen
come	came	come
cost	cost	cost
cut	cut	cut
dig	dug	dug
dive	dived, dove	dived
do	did	done
draw	drew	drawn
drink	drank	drunk
drive	drove	driven
eat	ate	eaten
fall	fell	fallen
feel	felt	felt

(continues)

COMMON IRREGULAR VERBS *(continued)*

Base Form	Past Tense	Past Participle
fight	fought	fought
find	found	found
flee	fled	fled
fly	flew	flown
forget	forgot	forgotten, forgot
freeze	froze	frozen
get	got	gotten, got
give	gave	given
go	went	gone
grow	grew	grown
hang (suspend)*	hung	hung
have	had	had
hear	heard	heard
hold	held	held
hide	hid	hidden
hit	hit	hit
keep	kept	kept
know	knew	known
lay	laid	laid
lead	led	led
leave	left	left
lend	lent	lent
let	let	let
lie (recline)†	lay	lain
lose	lost	lost
make	made	made
mean	meant	meant
pay	paid	paid
prove	proved	proved, proven
quit	quit	quit
read	read	read
ride	rode	ridden
ring	rang	rung
rise	rose	risen
run	ran	run
say	said	said
see	saw	seen
send	sent	sent
set	set	set
shake	shook	shaken
shoot	shot	shot
shrink	shrank	shrunk
sing	sang	sung
sink	sank	sunk
sit	sat	sat

Hang is regular—*hang, hanged, hanged*—when used to mean "kill by hanging."
†*Lie* is regular—*lie, lied, lied*—when used to mean "to be untruthful."

Base Form	Past Tense	Past Participle
sleep	slept	slept
slid	slid	slid
speak	spoke	spoken
spend	spent	spent
spread	spread	spread
spring	sprang, sprung	sprung
stand	stood	stood
steal	stole	stolen
strike	struck	struck, stricken
swim	swam	swum
swing	swung	swung
take	took	taken
teach	taught	taught
tear	tore	torn
tell	told	told
think	thought	thought
throw	threw	thrown
wake	woke, waked	waked, woken
wear	wore	worn
win	won	won
wind	wound	wound
write	wrote	written

> ### EXERCISE 36.1 Choosing the correct irregular verb

connect
mhconnectcomposition.com
Online exercise: QL36101

In the following sentences, fill in the blank with the correct form of the word in parentheses.

EXAMPLE

The river ___froze___ (freeze) last night. Some winters it has been ___frozen___ (freeze) for months on end.

1. The *Titanic* _____ (sink) after it _____ (strike) an iceberg.

2. After they had _____ (stand) from their chairs, the members of the chorus _____ (sing) a rousing finale.

3. Several people have now _____ (swim) the English Channel.

4. In 2007, the Boston Red Sox _____ (sweep) their World Series matchup with the Colorado Rockies. The New York Yankees have _____ (sweep) the World Series eight times.

5. The words of the Gettysburg Address are _____ (write) on a wall of the Lincoln Memorial. Lincoln _____ (write) the address in 1863.

36c **Combining Main Verbs with Helping Verbs to Form Complete Verbs**

Almost all verb constructions other than the present and past tenses require the combination of a ***main verb*** with one or more ***helping verbs*** (or ***auxiliary verbs***) in a ***verb phrase.*** The most common helping verbs are *be, have,* and *do,* all three of which can also function as main verbs (*they <u>are</u> hungry; she <u>had</u> lunch; they <u>did</u> the dishes*). *Be,* unlike any other English verb, has eight forms.

FORMS OF *BE*

Base		*be*
Present Tense	I	*am*
	we, you, they	*are*
	he, she, it	*is*
Past Tense	I, he, she, it	*was*
	we, you, they	*were*
Past Participle		*been*
Present Participle		*being*

FORMS OF *HAVE* AND *DO*

Present Tense (Base and -s Form)	I, you, we, they	*have*	*do*
	he, she, it	*has*	*does*
Past Tense		*had*	*did*
Past Participle		*had*	*done*
Present Participle		*having*	*doing*

The ***modal verbs***—*can, could, may, might, must, shall, should, will, would,* and *ought to*—function only as helping verbs. Modals indicate ability, intention, permission, possibility, desire, and suggestion. They do not change form to indicate number or tense.

More about ▶▶▶
Modals, 763–64

 Modal Verbs English modal verbs have a range of meanings and unusual grammatical characteristics that you may find challenging. For example, they do not change form to indicate number or tense:

> In a close election, one vote ~~cans~~ make a difference.
can

The main verb carries the principal meaning of the verb phrase; the helping verbs, if any, carry information about tense and voice. A **complete verb** is a verb phrase with all the elements needed to determine tense, voice, and mood. Main verbs can stand alone as complete verbs only in their present-tense and past-tense forms.

$\vdash\!\!-$ complete verb $-\!\!\dashv$
main verb

▶ The candidates   **campaigned**   until Election Day.

Main verbs in other forms (past or present participles) require helping verbs.

$\vdash\!\!-$ complete verb $-\!\!\dashv$
helping
verbs   main verb

▶ The candidates   **have been campaigning**   for almost two years.

Sometimes in informal speech you can drop needed helping verbs, and some dialects allow certain constructions as complete verbs that Standard English does not allow. Helping verbs can sometimes be contracted (*they've voted already, we'll register tomorrow*) but in formal writing should never be omitted entirely.

have
▶ The candidates been campaigning for almost two years.
     ∧

CAUTION Do not use *of* for *have* in a verb phrase with a modal. When you use informal contractions like *could've* or *might've* in speech, remember that they mean *could have* and *might have*.

36d Including *-s* or *-es, -d* or *-ed* Endings When Required

Sometimes when speaking informally, you can omit the verb endings -s, -es, -d, or -ed or blend the sound of an ending inaudibly with the initial sound of the following word. Some dialects do not always require these endings. In formal writing, include them, or not, as standard usage requires.

More about ▶▶▶
Subject-verb agreement, 646–57

says   *supposed*   *need*
▶ My dad ~~say~~ I am ~~suppose~~ to mow the lawn. I also ~~needs~~ to trim the
        ∧   ∧   ∧

moved   *used*
hedges. Before he ~~move~~ to Phoenix, my brother ~~use~~ to do the mowing.
                  ∧   ∧

> *More about* ▶▶▶
> Phrasal verbs,
> 756–59

ESL **Phrasal Verbs** Phrasal verbs, such as *ask out* and *give in,* combine a verb with one or more prepositions or adverbs known as particles. The verb and particle combination of a phrasal verb has a distinct meaning, one that is different from the stand-alone words that form it.

connect
mhconnectcomposition.com
Online exercise: QL36102

> **EXERCISE 36.2 Correcting verb endings**

In the following sentences, correct any verbs that have the wrong or missing verb endings -*s*, -*es*, -*d*, or -*ed*.

EXAMPLE

In our first year of college, many of us ~~mix~~ *mixed* studying with partying, but not one of us ~~do~~ *does* that now.

1. Eyal and Aaron wants to see the movie, but Fran and I are determine to go to the jazz concert.

2. I use to give my cat table scraps, so he immediately appear right next to me whenever I sat down to eat.

3. My roommates and I goes to our local farmer's market because we're concern about getting the freshest possible fruit and vegetables.

4. Last weekend we strip the paint on the wall down to bare wood, and then we stain it a gorgeous golden brown.

5. Because we are concern about using so many plastic bottles, we keeps a water filter in the refrigerator.

36e Distinguishing *Rise* from *Raise, Sit* from *Set, Lie* from *Lay*

The forms of *rise* and *raise, sit* and *set,* and *lie* and *lay* are easily confused. One verb in each pair (*rise, sit,* and *lie*) is **intransitive,** meaning that it does not take a direct object. The other verb in each pair (*raise, set,* and *lay*) is **transitive,** meaning that it does take a direct object (underlined in the following examples).

> *More about* ▶▶▶
> Transitive and
> intransitive verbs,
> 614–16, 682–83

- *Rise* means "to move or stand up." *Raise* means "to cause something (the direct object) to rise."

  ▶ The plane *rises* into the air. The pilot *raises* <u>the landing gear.</u>

Quick Reference ➡ Distinguishing *Rise* from *Raise*, *Sit* from *Set*, and *Lie* from *Lay*

Base form	-s form	Past tense	Past participle	Present participle
rise (to get up)	rises	rose	risen	rising
raise (to lift)	raises	raised	raised	raising
sit (to be seated)	sits	sat	sat	sitting
set (to place)	sets	set	set	setting
lie (to recline)	lies	lay	lain	lying
lay (to place)	lays	laid	laid	laying

- *Sit* means "to be seated." *Set* means "to place or put something (the direct object) on a surface."

  ▶ The passengers in coach *sit* in cramped seats. The attendants *set* drinks on their trays.

- *Lie* means "to recline." *Lay* means "to place or put something (the direct object) on a surface."

  ▶ The passengers in first class *lie* in fully reclining seats. During the landing, the pilot *lays* the plane gently on the runway.

A further difficulty with *lie* and *lay* is their confusing overlap of forms: The past tense of *lie* is *lay*, whereas the past tense of *lay* is *laid*. Changing the previous example to the past tense illustrates the issue.

  ▶ The passengers in first class ~~laid~~ ^Lay^ in fully reclining seats. During the landing, the pilot ~~lay~~ ^Laid^ the plane gently on the runway.

→ **EXERCISE 36.3** Using *rise/raise, sit/set,* and *lie/lay* correctly

In the following paragraph, correct any errors involving *rise/raise, sit/set,* and *lie/lay.*

connect
mhconnectcomposition.com
Online exercise: QL36103

Senna began her daily exercise routine as soon as she raised from bed. She seldom laid in bed long after her alarm went off. She usually set the alarm to go off at 4:30 a.m. Most of her neighbors were still laying in their beds when she was rising barbells over her head. Each time she rose a weight, she held it up for several seconds, then gently sat it down. She would also set on the floor and later lay down flat for some stretching exercises. After these warm-ups, Senna went out for a run and watched the sun raise over the lake. As she ran, she tried not to rise her knees too high, and she never let her arms lay idly at her side. Home again from her run, she would sometimes lay down again for a few minutes before beginning her workday.

TENSE

connect
mhconnectcomposition.com
Additional resources: QL36001

36f Understanding Which Verb Tense to Use

Verb *tenses* provide information about the time in which an action or event occurs—past, present, or future—about whether or not the action is ongoing or completed, and about the time of one action relative to another.

1. Simple tenses

Use the ***simple present tense*** for current or habitual actions or events and to state general truths. Accompanied by a reference to a future event, the simple present can also indicate a future occurrence (also see 36h).

CURRENT ACTION	Hernando *opens* the door to his classroom.
HABITUAL ACTION	He *enjoys* teaching second-graders.
GENERAL TRUTH	Earth *is* the third planet from the sun.
FUTURE OCCURRENCE	Winter *ends* in two weeks.

Use the ***simple past tense*** for completed actions or occurrences.

▶ The bell *rang.* Hernando *asked* his students to be quiet.

Use the ***simple future tense*** for actions that have not yet occurred.

▶ He *will give* them a spelling test this afternoon.

2. Perfect tenses

The perfect tenses generally indicate the completion of an action before a particular time. Use the ***present perfect tense*** for an action that started in the past but is now completed or for an action that started in the past but is ongoing.

Quick Reference ➡ An Overview of Verb Tenses and Their Forms

Simple Tenses

Simple present	base or -s form	I *learn* something new every day.
Simple past	past tense form	I *learned* Spanish many years ago.
Simple future	will + base form	I *will learn* to ski next winter.

Perfect Tenses

Present perfect	*has/have* + past participle	I *have learned* to water ski already.
Past perfect	*had* + past participle	I *had learned* to water ski by the time I was nine.
Future perfect	*will have* + past participle	I *will have learned* how to skydive by September.

Progressive Tenses

Present progressive	*am/is/are* + present participle	I *am learning* about Japanese food.
Past progressive	*was/were* + present participle	I *was learning* to make sushi yesterday.
Future progressive	*will be* + present participle	I *will be learning* new skills next week.
Present perfect progressive	*have/has been* + present participle	I *have been cooking* seriously since I was a teenager.
Past perfect progressive	*had been* + present participle	I *had been preparing* simple dishes even before then.
Future perfect progressive	*will have been* + present participle	I *will have been enjoying* this hobby for two decades by the end of the year.

COMPLETED ACTION	I *have read* all the Harry Potter books.
ONGOING ACTION	I *have read* books all my life.

Use the ***past perfect tense*** for actions completed by a specific time in the past or before another past action.

▶ Because the students *had studied* hard for their test, they knew most

of the spelling words.

The studying—*had studied* (past perfect)—came before the know-ing—*knew* (simple past).

Use the ***future perfect tense*** for an action that will be completed by a definite time in the future.

▶ By the time the semester ends, Hernando's students *will have improved* their spelling grades.

3. Progressive tenses

The progressive tenses indicate ongoing action. Use the ***present progressive tense*** for an action that is ongoing in the present.

▶ Matilda *is learning* Spanish.

Use the ***past progressive tense*** for an action that was ongoing in the past.

▶ Last night, Yue *was practicing* for her recital.

Use the ***future progressive tense*** for an ongoing action that will occur in the future.

▶ Elena *will be working* as a publishing company intern next summer.

Use the ***present perfect progressive tense*** for an ongoing action that began in the past.

▶ Hernando *has been working* on his master's degree in education since 2008.

Use the ***past perfect progressive tense*** for an ongoing past action that is now completed.

▶ Until this semester, he *had been taking* education courses at night.

Use the ***future perfect progressive tense*** for an ongoing action that will be finished at a definite time in the future.

▶ By the end of August, Hernando *will have been studying* education for more than six years.

ESL **Do Not Use the Progressive Tenses with All Verbs** Certain verbs, typically those that convey a mental process or a state of being, are not used in the progressive tenses. Examples include *appreciate, belong, contain, envy, fear, know, like, need, owe, own, remember, resemble, seem,* and *want.*

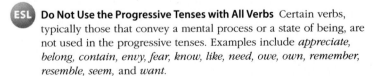

▶ She ~~is seeming~~ angry with her boyfriend. He ~~was owing~~ her an apology.
     seems   *owed*

36g Following Conventions for the Use of the Present Tense

The present tense is conventionally used for describing works of art, for describing events in literary works, and for stating scientific facts.

> ▶ In his 2007 novel *Bridge of Sighs,* Richard Russo ~~told~~ *tells* an engrossing
>
> story about the Lynch family, who ~~lived~~ *live* in a small town in upstate
>
> New York.

> ▶ Watson and Crick discovered that DNA ~~had~~ *has* a double helix structure.
>
> Although the discovery was in the past, it remains true.

In general, use the present tense to introduce a quotation, paraphrase, or summary.

> ▶ As Harriet Lerner ~~noted,~~ *notes,* "Anger is neither legitimate nor illegitimate,
>
> meaningful nor pointless. Anger simply is."

EXCEPTION The APA documentation style calls for the use of the past tense or the past perfect tense for reporting findings or introducing cited material.

> ▶ Chodoff (2002) ~~claims~~ *claimed* that in their efforts to put a diagnostic label
>
> on "all varieties and vagaries of human feelings," psychiatrists ~~risk~~ *risked*
>
> medicalizing "the human condition itself."

More about ▶▶▶
APA documentation
style, 358–400

36h Using Tense Sequence to Clarify Time Relationships

When a sentence contains two separate actions, readers need a clear idea of the time relationship between them, which writers communicate by their choice of tenses, or ***sequence of tenses.*** Change verb tenses when there is reason to do so, but do not shift tenses unnecessarily.

In a sentence with two past actions, for example, use the simple past tense for both verbs if the actions occurred simultaneously.

> ▶ When he *arrived* at the station, the train *departed.*
>
> He arrived and the train departed at the same time.

More about ▶▶▶
Inappropriate shifts
in tense, 710–11

If the actions happened at different times, use the past perfect tense for the action that occurred first.

> ▶ By the time he *arrived* at the station, the train *had departed.*

The train departed before he arrived.

1. Infinitives and tense sequence

An **infinitive** consists of *to* followed by the base form of the verb (*to listen, to go*). Use this form, the *present infinitive,* for an action that occurs after or simultaneously with the action of the main verb.

> ▶ Ivan is known to be a good student.

The knowing and the being happen together.

> ▶ Everyone expects Ivan to ace the exam.

The expectation is about Ivan's future performance on the exam.

Use the *perfect infinitive—to have* and the past participle (*to have listened, to have gone*)—for an action that happened before the action of the main verb.

> ▶ Ivan is said to have studied all weekend.

The studying took place before the talk about it.

2. Participles and tense sequence

Use the present participle (*listening, going*) to express action that happens simultaneously with the action of the main verb, regardless of the tense of the main verb.

> ▶ *Handing* her son Robbie a cup of coffee, Mona offered him some brownies.

Use the past participle (*listened, gone*) or the present perfect participle (*having listened, having gone*) to express action that happens before the action of the main verb.

> ▶ *Discouraged* by her daughter's aloofness, Mona asked her son to help.

Mona was discouraged before she asked.

> ▶ *Having mediated* their disagreements for years, Robbie refused to intervene.

Robbie mediated before he refused.

EXERCISE 36.4 Editing for verb tense

In the following paragraph, correct any errors in verb tense.

connect
mhconnectcomposition.com
Online exercise: QL36104

I was a knitter for as long as I can remember. My mother told me that, when I was about five, she has begun teaching me how to knit. All through my childhood I had always knitted whenever I had sat down to watch television. Once, when my dad had driven us from Memphis to Denver for a vacation, I knitted practically the entire way. By the time we will have arrived in Denver, I knitted most of a sweater for my brother. While I was in high school, I was starting a knitting club. At first, there were only two or three people in the club, but gradually we had recruited several new members, and it was getting to be a lot of fun. Recently, I am teaching knitting at our town's yarn shop. I had always made myself available to help beginners get started, so now I will have been doing it regularly. I find that people are appreciating it when I help them with their knitting problems. I will have even been knitting scarves, hats, mittens, and other items to sell on a crafts website. By the end of this year, I have been knitting for over fifteen years. I had been hoping that sometime in the future I will have been making a good living from my knitting, but who knows? For, as Abraham Lincoln wrote, "The best thing about the future is that it comes one day at a time."

EXERCISE 36.5 Correcting verb tense sequence

Revise each of the following sentences to achieve appropriate tense sequence.

connect
mhconnectcomposition.com
Online exercise: QL36105

EXAMPLE

Having worked
~~Working~~ on many fund-raising events in the past, Anna knew just what to do.

1. Whenever our relatives came to visit, I had escaped by taking a long bike ride.

2. Garrett expected his car to be repaired by now.

3. Susanna hopes to have gotten the lead role in the play.

4. Seeking a place to stay in the strange city, the traveler had consulted a guidebook.

5. Bursting through the doorway, Alyssa announced that she stood up to Megan's bullying and broke off their friendship.

MOOD

connect
mhconnectcomposition.com
Additional resources: QL36002

36i Understanding Verb Mood

The **mood** of a verb indicates whether a speaker or writer views what is said as a fact, a command, or a possibility. Most English sentences are in the **indicative mood,** which states facts or opinions and asks questions.

> ▶ Our research papers *are* due tomorrow morning.

> ▶ *Did* you *say* the deadline had changed?

The **imperative mood** issues commands, gives instructions, or makes requests. The subject of an imperative sentence (*you*) is usually left unstated.

> ▶ *Hand in* your papers by Friday afternoon.

> ▶ *Turn* left at the third stoplight.

> ▶ Please *pass* the salt.

The **subjunctive mood** expresses possibility (or impossibility), as in hypothetical situations, conditions known to be untrue, wishes, suggestions, and requirements.

> ▶ If I *were* finished, I could go to bed.

> ▶ The doctor suggests that he *get* more exercise.

36j Using the Subjunctive Mood Correctly

The subjunctive has three tenses: present, past, and past perfect. The present subjunctive is always the base form of the verb, regardless of the person or number of the subject: *Ramon asks that his teacher give* (not *gives*) *him an extension.* The past subjunctive of *be* is *were: I wish I were* (not *was*) *finished.* For all other verbs, the past subjunctive is identical to the past tense. Similarly, the past perfect subjunctive is identical to the past perfect indicative.

The subjunctive has been fading from everyday usage, and as a result, the indicative (*I wish I was finished*) may seem an acceptable alternative to you. Most readers, however, expect to find the subjunctive used appropriately (*I wish I were finished*) in formal writing.

Clauses with verbs in the subjunctive are always subordinate clauses. They include **conditional clauses** that begin with *if, as if,* or *as though* and describe a condition known to be untrue. Conditional clauses put forward a set of circumstances and modify a main clause that states what follows from those circumstances.

▶ If I *were* taller, I would try out for basketball.

▶ The candidate acts as though he *were* already the winner.

If the main clause includes a modal auxiliary such as *would, could,* or *should,* do not use a similar construction instead of the subjunctive in the *if* clause.

▶ If I ~~would have been~~ taller, I would try out for basketball.
 ^{were}

Verbs in the main clause that express a wish, request, recommendation, or demand also trigger the subjunctive in the subordinate clause.

▶ The hikers wished their campground ~~was~~ not so far away.
 ^{were}

▶ Citizens are demanding that the government ~~fixes~~ the economy.
 ^{fix}

▶ Senators have requested that the president ~~is~~ more responsive to the middle class.
 ^{be}

▶ Alicia's adviser recommended that she ~~takes~~ calculus.
 ^{take}

Getting It Across   Using *If* in the Indicative Mood

When an *if* clause states something that is factual or probable, use the indicative mood, not the subjunctive.

▶ If Susan *is* at the convention, she won't know about the accident.

▶ Her brother hasn't heard about the accident if he *is* on his way to Atlanta.

The indicative mood is called for in these examples because the writer knows that Susan is at a convention and that her brother is traveling to Atlanta.

▶ **EXERCISE 36.6 Using the subjunctive mood correctly**

In each of the following sentences, circle the correct verb form.

EXAMPLE

If Cally (was /(were) a morning person, she would be more alert for her 8:00 a.m. classes.

connect

mhconnectcomposition.com
Online exercise: QL36106

1. The management requests that ticketholders (be/are) on time for the beginning of the performance.

2. He took charge of the project as if it (was/were) his own.

3. If the book (were/was) lighter, I would be more inclined to bring it to class.

4. The doctor recommended that my father (gets/get) more exercise.

5. I wish I (were/was) lying on a warm, sunny beach.

VOICE

connect

mhconnectcomposition.com
Additional resources: QL36003

36k　Understanding Voice

The term *voice* refers to the role of the subject in a sentence. Only transitive verbs—verbs that take a direct object—can be in the passive voice. In the *active voice,* the subject is the actor and the direct object is acted upon.

ACTIVE

David hit the ball out of the park.

David is the subject and *the ball* is the direct object.

In the *passive voice,* the subject is acted upon. To change an active-voice sentence into the passive voice, make the direct object the subject, combine the appropriate form of *be* with the past participle of the main verb, and identify the actor in a phrase beginning with *by.*

PASSIVE

The ball was hit out of the park by David.

The passive voice also permits you to leave the actor unidentified.

PASSIVE (AGENT UNIDENTIFIED)

The ball was hit out of the park.

To change the passive voice to active, make the subject into the direct object and the actor into the subject, and change the verb from the passive form to its active form.

▶ David's ~~baseball career was enhanced by his~~ generosity off

　enhanced his baseball career.
　　the field. ✓

If the passive-voice sentence leaves the actor unidentified, you will need to supply one.

> *Americans elected the*
> ▶ ~~The~~ country's first African American president ~~was elected~~ in 2008.
> ∧

More about ▶▶▶
Style and voice,
560–61

36l   Choosing between the Active and Passive Voice

The active voice is usually preferable to the passive voice because it is the livelier and more direct of the two. The passive voice, in contrast, can deaden prose and obscure a writer's point.

In certain situations, however, the passive voice can be the appropriate choice:

- When the recipient of an action is more important than the actor or the identity of the actor is unimportant

   ▶ Hillary Clinton's appointment as secretary of state *was confirmed* by the Senate today.

   The writer wants to focus on Hillary Clinton, the receiver of the action.

   ▶ Hillary Clinton was confirmed as secretary of state on January 21, 2009.

   The focus is on the date of Clinton's confirmation, not the identity of the confirming body.

- In reports of scientific procedures

   ▶ Five hundred patients *were treated* with Cytoxan over a six-month period.

   The purpose of a scientific report is to describe what happened, not to focus on the scientists who conducted the research.

- When the actor is unknown or cannot be identified

   ▶ Our home *was burglarized* while we were on vacation.

⟶ EXERCISE 36.7 Changing passive voice to active

Revise each of the following sentences, changing the passive voice to the active voice.

EXAMPLE

Passive: The bus driver was given no authority by his supervisors to take an alternate route.

Active: *The bus driver's supervisors gave him no authority to take an alternate route.*

connect
mhconnectcomposition.com
Online exercise: QL36107

1. Taylor's performance was made more compelling than it otherwise would have been by the brilliant staging of the scene.

2. Folding chairs were brought by the maintenance crew so the unexpected attendees could sit.

3. The kitchen and bathrooms were renovated in order to increase the house's value.

4. Because Max didn't want to move to another city temporarily, an important career opportunity was squandered.

connect
mhconnectcomposition.com
Online exercise: QL36108

EXERCISE 36.8 Revising verbs

In the following paragraph, correct any verb errors.

My trip back to Chicago from vacation in San Francisco start out just fine. It was a beautiful afternoon, the plane boarding went fairly quickly, and the flight left right on schedule. I lied back in my seat for a nice nap when the pilot announced that there was some rough weather ahead, but it should not have affected our flight's arrival time. I heard this type of announcement once before on what turned out to be a horrible flight, so I should of start worrying right then. Soon there was another announcement saying that our arrival time might have been affected by the weather after all. It was actually a severe storm system covering much of the eastern half of the country. I was thinking that if I were to check the weather that morning, my flight might have been rearranged and I might have avoided this. We soon heard that the storm got so serious that all airports in the Chicago area will have been shut down. Our plane will be landing in Topeka, Kansas, instead. It was evening by the time we had gotten our luggage at Topeka's airport, where we learned that all local accommodations had already been booked. I prepared to set at the airport for the night when I had heard a few passengers sitting near me talking about renting a car. Five of us end up renting a car, and we drove all night, taking shifts at the wheel. It was rainy and windy when we arrived in Chicago, but most of the storm passed by then. As I exchanged contact information with my new friends, I told them that it has not been the arrival time I expected, but I had an adventure that could have turned out a lot worse.

Make It **Your Own**

Write a true or fictional paragraph about an event in your life that did not go according to plan. Write what you had expected to happen, why things went wrong, how it turned out, and, if you like, what you might have done differently.

Work **Together**

Exchange your work on the Make it Your Own exercise above with a classmate. How easily can you understand your classmate's paragraph? What changes in verbs might make it easier to comprehend? Explain the reasons for your recommendations.

37

Understanding Pronoun Case and Reference

© 2010 Blizzard Entertainment, Inc.

When you play an online multiplayer game like *World of Warcraft*, you may be interacting with dozens of other players who could be located almost anywhere in the world. Neither you nor they are physically present in the game. Instead, you all have virtual stand-ins—avatars—to represent you. Your avatar acts on your orders and may even change form—from human to animal, for example—depending on the way in which you want it to function in a particular environment.

Like avatars, pronouns are stand-ins. They represent other words—their ***antecedents***—from one place to another in speech or writing. Also like avatars, they sometimes change form depending on the role you want them to play within a sentence.

PRONOUN CASE

Nouns, and the pronouns that represent them, can play various roles within a sentence. They can be subjects:

	subject	
NOUN	**The Steelers** lost.	
PRONOUN	**They**	lost.

They can be objects (including direct objects, indirect objects, and objects of prepositions):

	subject		direct object
NOUN	The Bears	beat	**the Steelers.**
PRONOUN	We	beat	**them.**

They can indicate possession:

	possessive			possessive	
NOUN	**Chicago's**	team	beat	**Pittsburgh's**	team.
PRONOUN	**Our**	team	beat	**their**	team.

The term **case** refers to the different forms a noun or pronoun takes—**subjective, objective,** or **possessive**—depending on which of these roles it serves. Nouns do not change much—they have the same form as subjects that they do as objects, and they indicate possession with an *s* sound that is marked in writing with an apostrophe (*Chicago's team*). In contrast, most **personal pronouns** and some **relative** and **interrogative pronouns** are shape shifters—they have distinct forms for many of their roles:

		Subjective Case	Objective Case	Possessive Case
Personal Pronouns				
	1st person	*I*	*me*	*my, mine*
Singular	2nd person	*you*	*you*	*your, yours*
	3rd person	*he*	*him*	*his*
		she	*her*	*her, hers*
		it	*it*	*its*
	1st person	*we*	*us*	*our, ours*
Plural	2nd person	*you*	*you*	*your, yours*
	3rd person	*they*	*them*	*their, theirs*
Case-Variant Relative and		*who*	*whom*	*whose*
Interrogative Pronouns		*whoever*	*whomever*	

> **More about ▶▶▶**
> Subjects and objects,
> 612–17

> **More about ▶▶▶**
> Indicating posses-
> sion with aspostro-
> phes, 808–11

Personal pronouns
Pronouns that take the place of nouns or noun phrases
Relative pronouns
Pronouns that intro-
duce subordinate clauses that describe the pronoun's antecedent
**Interrogative pro-
nouns** Pronouns that introduce questions (602–04)

connect

mhconnectcomposition.com
Additional resources: QL37001, QL37002

Some case errors are easy to detect because they sound wrong to native speakers of English.

▶ Hermione is one of Harry's best friends, and ~~her~~ *she* often gives ~~he~~ *him* sound advice.

In many situations, however, the ear is an unreliable guide to proper case usage.

37a Using the Subjective Case for Subject Complements

A pronoun that functions as a ***subject complement*** following a form of *be* used as a main verb should be in the subjective case, not the objective case.

> **Subject complement** An adjective, pronoun, or noun phrase that follows a linking verb and describes or refers to the sentence subject (615)

▶ Asked who spilled the milk, my sister confessed that the guilty one was ~~her.~~ *she.*

If this usage sounds overly formal, try reversing the subject and subject complement.

▶ Asked who spilled the milk, my sister confessed that the guilty ~~one was her.~~ *she was* *one.*

37b *She and I* or *Her and Me*? Keeping Track of Case in Compounds

Pronouns that are part of compound subjects or subject complements should be in the subjective case.

> ┌─── compound subject ───┐
>   *I*
▶ My friends and ~~me~~ chat online while we play computer games.

Pronouns that are part of compound objects should be in the objective case.

> ┌─── compound dir. obj. ───┐
>   *me*
▶ My parents call my brothers and ~~I~~ every weekend.

Quick

Reference ➡ Editing for Case in Compounds

To determine the correct case of a pronoun in a compound, isolate the pronoun from the rest of the compound; then read the result aloud to yourself. If the pronoun sounds wrong, replace it with the one that sounds right.

| Faulty | [My friends and] me chat online while we play computer games. |
| Revised | My friends and I chat online while we play computer games. |

Me chat online is clearly wrong. Replacing the objective pronoun *me* with the subjective pronoun *I* corrects the problem.

| Faulty | My parents call [my siblings and] I every weekend. |
| Revised | My parents call my siblings and me every weekend. |

My parents call I is clearly wrong. Replacing the subjective pronoun *I* with the objective pronoun *me* corrects the problem.

| Faulty | My father often gets me [and my brother's] names confused. |
| Revised | My father often gets my and my brother's names confused. |

My father gets me names confused is clearly wrong. Replacing the objective pronoun *me* with the possessive pronoun *my* corrects the problem.

Pronouns that are part of compound possessives should be in the possessive case.

compound possessive

▶ My father often gets ~~me~~ *my* and my brother's names confused.

EXERCISE 37.1 Pronoun case in subject complements and compounds

Circle the correct pronoun from each pair in parentheses.

connect

mhconnectcomposition.com
Online exercise: QL37101

EXAMPLE

When we were about twelve, Sofia and (I/ me) were intensely interested in rocketry.

1. Actually it was (she/her) who first joined the rocketry club, and then she got me involved.

2. We got so good at building and launching model rockets that other kids would call (she or I/her or me) whenever they had problems.

3. As we got older and our interests changed, (she and I/her and me) gradually lost our fascination with rocketry.

4. Now that I'm in college, one of (me/my) and my roommate's favorite pastimes has become rocketry.

5. I'm sure this interest will again pass because our friends are continually encouraging (she and I/her and me) to try new things.

37c Keeping Track of Pronoun Case in Appositives

The case of a pronoun in an *appositive phrase* should reflect the function of the phrase the appositive renames. If the original phrase is a subject or subject complement, as in the first of the following examples, the pronoun should be in the subjective case; if it is an object, as in the second example, the pronoun should be in the objective case.

▶ The two most talented actors in our school, Valentino and ~~her,~~ she, always

   get the best roles in school productions.

▶ The director always wants the best artists, ~~she~~ her and ~~I,~~ me to work on

   the scenery.

37d Deciding between *We* and *Us* before Nouns

In expressions that combine *we* or *us* with a noun, use *we* with nouns that function as subjects or subject complements and *us* with nouns that function as objects. To decide which is which, say the sentence to yourself with the pronoun alone.

▶ ~~Us~~ We gamers live vicariously in the game world through our avatars.

   Us live vicariously is clearly wrong. The subjective pronoun *we* should replace the objective pronoun *us.*

▶ Our avatars act vicariously in the game world on behalf of ~~we~~ us gamers.

   Avatars act on behalf of we is clearly wrong. The objective pronoun *us* should replace the subjective pronoun *we.*

> **EXERCISE 37.2** **Pronoun case in appositives and before nouns**

Circle the correct pronoun or pronouns from each pair in parentheses.

connect
mhconnectcomposition.com
Online exercise: QL37102

EXAMPLE

As spring break approached, it became clear that both of us,
(Owen and I)/ Owen and me), had no ride home.

1. As a result, (we/us) non–car owners started asking all of our friends how they got home in this situation.

2. Everyone took pity on the two stranded guys, (Owen and I/ Owen and me), but nobody was able to offer us a ride.

3. Eventually, a few people who never had rides home told (we/us) increasingly nervous unfortunates how they managed.

4. The answer was that (we/us) stranded unfortunates simply had to take the bus from our small college town to the train station in the state capital.

5. This way, the two seemingly abandoned non–car owners, (Owen and I/Owen and me), became informed and even empowered commuters.

37e Using the Objective Case Both before and after an Infinitive

Both the subject and object of an *infinitive* should be in the objective case.

> **Infinitive** The *to* form of a verb (*to decide, to eat, to study*) (619)

▶ I asked *her* to recommend *me* for the job.

Both *her,* the subject of the infinitive *to recommend,* and *me,* its direct object, are in the objective case.

37f Deciding on Pronoun Case with the *-ing* Form of a Verb

In most cases, use the possessive form of a noun or pronoun with a *gerund* (the present participle, or *-ing* form of a verb used as a noun).

> **More about ▶▶▶**
> Gerunds, 619

▶ Professor Nolan, I appreciate ~~you~~ your taking time to advise me on

my résumé.

Use the objective form of a noun or pronoun, however, when the *-ing* word functions as a modifier rather than a noun.

PRONOUN IS THE MODIFIER	Margo is a Tiger Woods fan. She admires *his* playing.

PRONOUN IS MODIFIED	Margo saw *him* playing at the U.S. Open.

37g Clarifying Pronoun Case in Comparisons with *Than* or *As*

In comparisons with *than* or *as,* the choice of pronoun case can sometimes result in two otherwise identical sentences with significantly different meanings.

▸ Amy likes her new car more than I.

▸ Amy likes her new car more than me.

In the first sentence, the subjective case (*I*) signals a comparison between Amy's and the writer's fondness for Amy's car (she thinks better of it than the writer does). In the second sentence, the objective case (*me*) signals a comparison between Amy's fondness for her car and her fondness for the writer (she thinks better of her car than of the writer). To avoid confusing readers in situations like this, identify which pronoun your meaning requires by supplying any words needed to make the comparisons explicit.

▸ Amy likes her new car more than I *do.*

▸ Amy likes her new car more than *she likes* me.

connect

mhconnectcomposition.com

Online exercise: QL37103

EXERCISE 37.3 **Pronoun case with infinitives, gerunds, and comparisons**

Circle the correct pronoun from each pair in parentheses.

EXAMPLE

My uncle has put an enormous amount of time into (him /(his) gardening.

1. When he was very young, his mother taught (he/him) to help (she/her) in their backyard garden.

2. Now that he has his own backyard, it turns out that he loves gardening even more than (she/her).

3. While I certainly like to watch (him/his) gardening, I don't enjoy doing it myself.

4. Even before I could walk and talk, it was obvious that I didn't like gardening as much as (he/him).

5. I must admit, though, that I allowed (he/him) to show (I/me) how to care for a few of his fruit trees.

37h Distinguishing *Who, Whom, Whoever,* and *Whomever*

The pronouns *who, whom, whoever,* and *whomever* have two jobs. As *relative pronouns* they introduce *subordinate clauses.* As *interrogative pronouns* they introduce questions.

> **Subordinate clause**
> A word group with a subject and predicate that cannot stand alone as a sentence but instead functions within a sentence as a noun, adjective, or adverb (620–21)

- Use *who* or *whoever* for the subject of a subordinate clause or question.

      |——— subordinate clause ———|
        subj.
   ▶ Tiger Woods, *who* began playing as a toddler, has long dominated golf.

      |——— question ———|
      subj.
   ▶ *Who* began playing golf as a toddler?

- Use *whom* or *whomever* for the object of a subordinate clause or question. Notice, however, that contrary to normal word order, in which direct objects follow verbs, *whom* and *whomever* usually come at the beginning of a clause or question.

      |——— subordinate clause ———|
        dir. obj.
   ▶ Woods, *whom* many golf fans admire, was sidelined by a knee injury in 2008.

      |——— question ———|
      dir. obj.
   ▶ *Whom* do many golf fans admire?

- The case of a relative pronoun is determined by its role in a clause, not the role of the clause in the sentence. The relative pronoun in the following example is the subject of its clause and so should be in the subjective case—*whoever*—even though the clause as a whole is the object of the preposition *to*.

▶ In professional golf, the winner's prize goes to ~~whomever~~ *whoever* com-

pletes the course in the fewest strokes.

■ Match the pronoun to its verb, not to the verb of an intervening clause. In the following example, the pronoun should be the subjective case *who* because it is the subject of *was*, not the object of *know*.

▶ Thomas Edison, ~~whom~~ *who* many people know was the inventor of the

lightbulb, was also the inventor of the phonograph.

→ EXERCISE 37.4 Distinguishing *who, whom, whoever, whomever*

Circle the correct pronoun from each pair in parentheses.

EXAMPLE

Ayrton, (who / whom) grew up in southern California, was visiting New York City for the first time.

1. It was the middle of winter, and he seemed to be the only person in the city (who/whom) was not wearing heavy winter clothes.

2. (Who/Whom) wore heavy clothes in any season in southern California?

3. On one cold morning, when Ayrton slipped on some black ice and fell hard on his back, he found himself the center of atten-

tion (who/whom) everybody on the street quickly surrounded and reached down to help.

4. These were not the callous, uncaring people (who/whom) he had assumed New Yorkers were.

5. He was soon back on his feet with the help of a tough-looking but kindly old man (who/whom) Ayrton immediately invited to join him for some coffee and doughnuts.

CLEAR PRONOUN REFERENCE

connect
mhconnectcomposition.com
Additional resources: QL37003, QL37004

Pronoun reference involves the clarity of the relationship between a pronoun and its antecedent. With clear pronoun reference, readers can easily identify the antecedent of a pronoun.

▶   **Mario talked to his sister Roberta about her career plans.**

The pronoun *his* clearly refers to Mario; the pronoun *her* clearly refers to Mario's sister.

Pronoun reference is unclear when readers cannot be certain what a pronoun's antecedent is.

▶   **Mario talked to Paul about his career plans.**

Did Mario and Paul talk about Mario's career plans or Paul's? Without more information, readers will be uncertain.

37i   Avoiding Ambiguous Reference

The reference of a pronoun is ambiguous when it has two or more equally plausible antecedents.

▶   **Mario talked to Paul about his career plans.**

One way to resolve ambiguous reference is to replace the pronoun with the appropriate noun.

▶   **Mario talked to Paul about Paul's career plans.**

To avoid repeating the noun, rephrase the sentence in a way that eliminates the ambiguity.

▶   **Paul talked about his career plans with Mario.**

The position of the pronoun *his* associates the plans clearly and unambiguously with Paul, not Mario.

Getting It Across

Maintaining Clear Pronoun Reference in Paragraphs

As long as their relationship to the antecedent remains clear, pronouns can substitute for the antecedent throughout a paragraph or even through a series of paragraphs. To prevent monotony and refresh the reader's memory, however, it helps to repeat the antecedent occasionally, the way the authors of the following passage do as they narrate the story of one of the first Chinese immigrants to the United States. (The pronouns are boldfaced and the antecedent is boldfaced and underlined.)

A village fish peddler, **Fatt Hing Chin** often roamed the coast of southern China in search of fish to sell at market. One day at the wharves, **he** heard a tale of mysterious but enticing mountains of gold beckoning young Chinese to cross the ocean. At nineteen years of age, **Chin** felt restless, and **he** longed for the glittering mountains. **He** learned that he could purchase passage on a foreign ship, but **he** also needed to be cautious. **He** did not want to alarm **his** parents, nor did **he** want to draw the attention of the authorities, who were reportedly arresting individuals seeking to leave China. Eventually **he** reconciled **his** parents to his plans, and in 1849 **he** boarded a Spanish ship to sail to California and join the gold rush.

—Jerry H. Bentley and Herbert F. Ziegler, *Traditions and Encounters: A Global Perspective on the Past*, 4th ed.

37j Avoiding Confusingly Broad Reference with *It, This, That,* and *Which*

When pronouns such as *it, this, that,* and *which* refer broadly to an entire clause, sentence, or series of sentences, readers may be uncertain about what specific information the pronouns cover.

▶ Who owns Antarctica? Several countries, including Argentina, Australia, Chile, France, New Zealand, Norway, the United Kingdom, and the United States, all claim or reserve the right to claim all or part of the continent. ~~This makes it~~ *These competing claims make the question of ownership* difficult to answer.

The revision specifies what information the writer meant by *this* and *it*.

37k Avoiding Implied Reference

A pronoun should have a clearly identifiable antecedent, not an unstated, or implied, antecedent. In the following example, the only word that could serve grammatically as the antecedent to *they* is *stories,* but stories are not places. The writer's intended antecedent is implied in the adjective *small-town,* as the revision makes clear.

DRAFT   From her stories of her small-town childhood, they seem like great places to grow up.

REVISED   Her stories of her childhood make small towns seem like great places to grow up.

Similarly, in the next example, the antecedent to *he—Einstein—*is implied, confusingly, in the possessive form *Einstein's.*

▶ According to Einstein's theory of relativity, ~~he showed that~~ mass and energy are interchangeable.

37l   Reserving *You* for Directly Addressing the Reader

In formal writing, reserve the pronoun *you* (and the implied *you* of commands) to address the reader directly, as in "you, the reader." Do not use *you* as a substitute for indefinite words such as *anybody, everybody,* or *people.*

▶ Before computers and the internet, ~~you~~ got ~~your~~ news mostly from

                                             people   *their*

newspapers, radio, and television.

37m   Avoiding the Indefinite Use of *They* and *It*

In formal writing, the pronouns *they* and *it* need specific antecedents. Avoid using these pronouns to refer to unspecified people or things.

                                           students

▶ At Hogwarts School of Witchcraft and Wizardry, ~~they~~ use owls, not

email, for sending messages.

    The

▶ ~~In the~~ beginning of the chapter~~, it~~ compares pronouns to computer-

game avatars.

37n **Designating People with *Who, Whom,* and *Whose,* Not *That* and *Which***

When you are speaking, you are as likely to use *that* as you are to use *who* or *whom* to refer to people. In formal writing, however, you should usually use only *who* and *whom* to refer to people.

> ▶ According to his website, the people ~~that~~ most inspire Tiger Woods
>   ^{who}
>
>   are his parents and Nelson Mandela.

Use *that* and *which* for animals and things.

> ▶ The stray cats ~~who~~ live in the alley sometimes howl at night.
>   ^{that}

For pets and other named animals, however, *who* or *whom* is often more appropriate than *that* or *which*.

> ▶ Our cat Juniper, ~~which~~ is now twelve years old, is still healthy and spry.
>   ^{who}

The possessive pronoun *whose* is also best reserved for people but can apply to animals and things when avoiding it requires the awkward use of the phrase *of which*.

> ▶ The polar bear is an animal ~~the~~ habitat ~~of which~~ is threatened by
>   ^{whose}
>
>   global warming.

connect
mhconnectcomposition.com
Online exercise: QL37105

→ EXERCISE 37.5 Editing for pronoun reference

Edit the following passage to eliminate problems with pronoun reference.

> Everyone who knew Colin identified him as someone that loved music. When you wanted to know about a band's background, you would ask Colin, who had made a life's work of studying the histories of musicians and composers. When Sydnee Sandford, a popular host on his college's radio station, interviewed Colin about the 1960s rock musicians that she was featuring on her show, he became instantly famous on campus. That is what started it. A week later, the radio station manager told Colin that they would like to know if he wanted his own radio program. It appealed to him, but he also understood that he

was a person that was quite shy and uncomfortable with public speaking. Based on his past experiences at speaking before audiences, they caused him to avoid giving her an answer. Sensing his obvious discomfort, she pointed out that she herself was also shy and had long been terrified of public speaking. She said that her answer was that you would discuss on your show and interview others about what interested you the most: 1960s rock music. Colin remembered how easy it was to talk with her on the show because he too was a big fan of it.

The next semester, Colin's show aired at 3 to 4 a.m., and the only person the taste of which in music he used as a guide was himself. His radio show turned out to be great fun, and soon he attracted a huge listenership on campus.

Make It **Your Own**

Write a true or fictional paragraph about giving someone a birthday present. Consider writing about deciding what to give, how you found the present, and how the recipient felt about it. Use in your paragraph at least six different pronouns, and be sure to use all three pronoun cases: the subjective, objective, and possessive.

Work **Together**

Exchange your work on the Make It Your Own exercise above with a classmate. How easily can you understand your classmate's paragraph? What changes in pronouns might make it more readily comprehensible? Explain the reasons for your recommendations.

38 Using Adjectives and Adverbs

The clothing, jewelry, and hairstyles we choose—our modifiers—send a message to others about how we want them to perceive us. A flamboyant dress, a tattoo, eye-catching jewelry, and flowing hair send one impression; a tailored business suit sends another. Similarly, we send readers a message about how we want our words to be understood by our choice of adjectives and adverbs to modify them.

38a Differentiating Adjectives and Adverbs

Adjectives modify (or describe) nouns and pronouns, answering questions such as *What kind? Which one?* or *How many? Adverbs* modify verbs, adjectives, other adverbs, and entire phrases, clauses, and sentences; they answer questions such as *How? Where?* or *When?*

No hard-and-fast markers distinguish adjectives or adverbs. For example, although many adverbs end in the suffix *-ly,* many do not (*later, often, quite, seldom*), and dozens of adjectives do (*elderly, lowly, scholarly*). The only reliable way to distinguish an adjective from an adverb is not from its form but from its function (see the Quick Reference box on the next page).

connect
mhconnectcomposition.com
Additional resources: QL38001

Quick **Reference** ➔ **The Functions of Adjectives and Adverbs**

Adjectives modify:

Nouns	*sunny* day
Pronouns	someone *responsible*

Adverbs modify:

Verbs	spoke *forcefully*
Adjectives	*painfully* loud
Adverbs	*very* cautiously
Phrases	*finally* over the finish line
Clauses and sentences	*Eventually,* the story ended.

ESL **English Adjectives Never Change Form** In English, adjectives do not change form to agree with the words they modify.

Relaxing in a rocking chair, I watched ~~olds~~ movies on TV.
                                          old
                                          ︿

More about ▶▶▶
The characteristics of English adjectives, 767–68

38b **Using Adjectives, Not Adverbs, as Subject Complements after Linking Verbs**

connect
mhconnectcomposition.com
Additional resources: QL38002

Linking verbs express a state of being rather than an action or occurrence. They link the subject to a *subject complement,* which describes or refers to the subject. In other words, the subject complement modifies the subject, not the verb; it can be an adjective or a noun, but not an adverb.

The verb *be,* when used as a main verb, is always a linking verb.

▶ The *food* is *delicious.*

The adjective *delicious* modifies the subject, *food.*

Other verbs, such as *appear, become, feel, look, prove, sound,* and *taste,* may function as linking verbs in one context and action verbs in

More about ▶▶▶
Linking verbs and subject complements, 615

another. A word following one of these verbs should be an adjective if it modifies the subject and an adverb if it modifies the verb.

▶ *Maria* looked *anxious* to the dentist.

Looked is a linking verb and the adjective *anxious* is a subject complement that describes Maria's state of mind as the dentist perceived it.

▶ Maria *looked anxiously* at the dentist.

Looked is an action verb modified by the adverb *anxiously,* which describes the manner in which Maria performed the action of looking.

38c Choosing *Bad* or *Badly, Good* or *Well*

In casual speech, we commonly mingle adjectives and adverbs. In writing, however, use adjectives to modify nouns and pronouns and use adverbs to modify verbs, adjectives, or other adverbs. Do not confuse *bad* with *badly, good* with *well,* or *real* with *really.* Use the adjective form of these pairs for subject complements. Include *-ly* endings when needed, and use an adjective, not an adverb, to modify a direct object.

■ *Bad* is an adjective; *badly* is an adverb.

▶ The Patriots played ~~bad~~ badly in the fourth quarter.

Badly modifies the action verb *played.*

▶ The quarterback feels ~~badly~~ bad about the loss.

Feels is a linking verb; *bad* modifies *quarterback.*

■ The word *good* is an adjective, and *well* is its adverb counterpart. *Well* is an adjective, however, when it is used to mean "healthy."

▶ Leah did ~~good~~ well on her final exams.

The adverb *well* modifies the verb *did.*

▶ Tomás looks ~~well~~ *good* in his tuxedo.

Looks is a linking verb; the adjective *good* modifies *Tomás*.

▶ After a late-night graduation party, Leah is not feeling ~~good~~ *well*.

Well is used as an adjective because it refers to health.

- Do not confuse the adjective *real* with the adverb *really*.

▶ The actors are ~~real~~ *really* enthusiastic about tonight's performance.

NOTE Intensifiers like *really* often add little or no meaning to a sentence and can usually be dropped in the interest of conciseness.

More about ▶▶▶
Conciseness, 516–25

- Do not confuse adverbs that end in *-ly* with their adjective counterparts that do not.

▶ You should play ~~gentle~~ *gently* with small children.

The adverb *gently* modifies the verb *play*.

- Never use an adverb to modify a direct object. When a modifier follows a direct object, ask yourself, "What word is being modified?" If the answer is "the verb," then the modifier should be an adverb, but if the answer is "the direct object," then the modifier is an **object complement** and should be an adjective or noun.

More about ▶▶▶
Direct objects and
object modifiers,
614–17, 741–43

Object complement An adjective or noun phrase that follows the direct object and describes the condition of the object or a change the subject has caused it to undergo (617, 743)

▶ The divorce left *Kayla cautious* about future relationships.

The adjective *cautious* modifies the direct object *Kayla*.

▶ She *conducted* herself *cautiously* with potential new friends.

The adverb *cautiously* modifies the verb *conducted,* not the direct object *herself.*

➜ **EXERCISE 38.1 Correcting common adjective-adverb problems**

Revise the following sentences to correct any adjective or adverb errors.

EXAMPLE

                    really
Most people are ~~real~~ surprised to learn that Bennett and Raul are
                  ∧

                                 good
roommates and even ~~well~~ friends.
                    ∧

1. Raul takes unusual good care of his clothes and dresses fashionable.

2. However, Bennett feels indifferently about clothes and always dresses real sloppy.

3. Of course, Raul always keeps his side of their room awful messily.

4. Bennett, on the other hand, puts absolute everything careful in its proper place.

5. Bennett thinks neatness is healthful and says he does not feel good in a messy room.

6. Despite these stark differences, the two of them get along real good.

38d   Using Negatives Correctly

In a sentence with a *double negative,* two negative modifiers describe the same word. Because one negative cancels the other, the message becomes positive. In Standard American English, double negatives can be acceptable, but only to emphasize a positive meaning. The sentence *It is not unlikely that the attorney will be disbarred,* for example, means that the attorney's disbarment is likely. Although some dialects allow the use of double (and more) negatives to emphasize a negative meaning, and many people use them that way in casual speech, you should avoid them in formal writing. Remember that the negative word *not* is part of contractions such as *couldn't* and *shouldn't* and that words like *barely, hardly,* and *scarcely* have a negative meaning.

▶ Students ~~shouldn't~~ *should* never park in a faculty-only lot.
           ∧

▶ The children ~~can't~~ *can* hardly wait to open their presents.
              ∧

38e Avoiding Long Strings of Nouns Used as Adjectives

One noun can often function as an adjective to modify another: *government worker, traffic violation, college course.* Multiple nouns strung together this way, however, can be cumbersome and confusing.

CONFUSING	The *teacher education policy report* will be available tomorrow.
REVISED	The *policy report on teacher education* will be available tomorrow.

ESL **Order of Adjectives in a Series** When more than one adjective modifies a noun, the adjectives usually need to follow a specific order:

▶ a ~~European~~ *stunning* European racehorse

For guidance on ordering multiple adjectives, see p. 767.

38f Using Comparative and Superlative Adjectives and Adverbs

connect
mhconnectcomposition.com
Additional resources: QL38003, QL38004, QL38005

Most adjectives and adverbs have three forms for indicating the relative degree of the quality or manner they specify: positive, comparative, and superlative. The ***positive form*** is the base form—the form you find when you look the word up in the dictionary.

POSITIVE	Daryl is *tall.*

The ***comparative form*** indicates a relatively greater or lesser degree of a quality.

COMPARATIVE	Daryl is *taller* than Ivan.

The ***superlative form*** indicates the greatest or least degree of a quality.

SUPERLATIVE	Daryl is the *tallest* player on the team.

Regular adjectives and adverbs form the comparative and superlative with either the suffixes *-er* and *-est* or the addition of the words *more* and *most* or *less* and *least.* A few adjectives and adverbs have irregular comparative and superlative forms (see the Quick Reference box on p. 706). If you are not sure whether to use *-er/-est* or *more/most* for a particular adjective or adverb, look it up in a dictionary. If the entry shows *-er* and *-est* forms, use them. If no such forms are listed, use *more* or *most.*

Quick Reference ➡ **Forming Comparatives and Superlatives**

Regular forms

	Positive	Comparative	Superlative
Adjectives	bold	bolder/less bold	boldest/least bold
	helpful	more/less helpful	most/least helpful
Adverbs	far	farther	farthest
	realistically	more/less realistically	most/least realistically

Irregular forms

	Positive	Comparative	Superlative
Adjectives	bad	worse	worst
	good	better	best
	little	less (quantity)/littler (size)	least (quantity)/littlest (size)
	many	more	most
	much	more	most
	some	more	most
Adverbs	badly	worse	worst
	well	better	best

1. Comparative or superlative

Use the comparative form to compare two things, the superlative to compare three or more.

> ▶ Between Jon Stewart and Stephen Colbert, I think Colbert is the ~~funniest.~~ *funnier.*

> ▶ Of all comedians ever, I think Buster Keaton was the ~~funnier.~~ *funniest.*

2. Redundant comparisons

Do not combine the comparative words *more/most* with adjectives or adverbs that are already in comparative form with an *-er* or *-est* ending.

> ▶ Trains in Europe and Japan are ~~more~~ faster than trains in the United States.

3. Complete comparisons

Make sure your comparisons are logical and that readers have all the information they need to understand what is being compared to what.

> **More about ▶▶▶**
> Complete compari-
> sons, 735

▶ The nurses' test scores were higher. *than those of the pre-med students.*

The original makes us ask, "Higher than what?" The addition clarifies the comparison.

4. Absolute terms

Expressions like *more unique* or *most perfect* are common in everyday speech, but if you think about them, they make no sense. *Unique, perfect,* and other words such as *equal, essential, final, full, impossible, infinite,* and *unanimous* are absolutes, and absolutes are beyond compare. If something is unique, it is by definition one of a kind. If something is perfect, it cannot be improved upon. In formal writing, then, avoid using absolute terms comparatively.

▶ Last night's performance of the play was the ~~most perfect~~ *best* yet.

> **EXERCISE 38.2** **Revising errors with comparatives and superlatives**

> connect
> mhconnectcomposition.com
> Online exercise: QL38102

In the following sentences, correct any errors with the comparative or superlative forms of adjectives and adverbs.

EXAMPLE

Cameron is more ~~frugaller~~ *frugal* than even I am and may be the most ~~frugallest~~ *frugal* person I know.

1. Cameron's apartment is the most coldest of anyone's.

2. He must have the lower fuel bill in our area although his house is probably not more energy efficient.

3. Cameron feels that it is most essential for him to spend the smaller amount of money he can on anything.

4. According to him, people are more unhappy when they habitually overspend.

5. He probably uses our public library more, and whenever he takes a bus, he more often reads whatever the person next to him is reading by peeking over his or her shoulder.

6. I don't know whether I feel most admiration or disgust for Cameron's frugality, but I admit I have learned from him more useful pointers on saving money.

7. Recently, I have even been competing with him to see which of us is best at finding more free things on the internet.

connect

mhconnectcomposition.com
Online exercise: QL38103

→ **EXERCISE 38.3 Revising for problems with adjectives and adverbs**

In the following paragraphs, correct any errors in adjective or adverb usage.

It was her last year of college, and Gillian was finding life to be extreme exhilarating and real overwhelming at the same time. She had worked hardest in the previously three years to complete her required courses so that this year she could be more selective about the courses she took. That is why, although she was a chemistry major, she was taking several courses that scarcely had nothing to do with chemistry. She was furthering her study of Russian, for instance, which was more of a challenge this year. She was doing a lot of translating between Russian and English and that was terrible stressful at times. Her opera course was a purely delight, and she also loved studying European history from 1500 to 1789, although that required an immense amount of reading.

She was also enjoying her extracurricular activities, but she couldn't barely fit them all into her demanding schedule. Playing flute in the wind ensemble was fun, especially since she was the more accomplished musician in the group. However, playing in the pit band for the musical theater troupe was bad taxing because the score for the play was highly intricate. She was also a completely essential member of the Sunday afternoon role-playing game club. Life was well, and she wasn't hardly complaining.

Make It **Your Own**

Write a paragraph about your dream house, describing what it would have in it if you were fabulously rich. Use at least six adjectives and six adverbs in your descriptions of your house's features, making at least two of the adjectives or adverbs comparative or superlative.

Work **Together**

Exchange your description from the Make It Your Own exercise above with a classmate, and check each other's work for errors in adjective and adverb usage. What changes would you recommend to your classmate? What changes did your classmate recommend to you? Consult your instructor about any issues you disagree on.

39 Avoiding Confusing Shifts

When NASCAR drivers round the curves or head into the straightaway, they need to shift gears, but an expert driver shifts only when doing so will provide a clear advantage. Similarly, good writers try not to jar their readers with unnecessary shifts in style or grammar. They check their writing for consistency so that readers stay on the roadway. As you revise or edit a draft, look for unnecessary shifts in verbs (tense, mood, and voice), in nouns and pronouns (person and number), and between direct and indirect quotations and questions.

39a Avoiding Awkward Shifts in Tense

Verb tenses place events in a sentence in time. Sentences with more than one verb may require a shift in tense from one to another if the verbs refer to events that occur at different times.

More about ▶▶▶
Verb tenses, 674–79

▶ Yesterday *was* snowy, and today *is* cloudy and cold, but according to the weather report, the weekend *will be* warm and sunny.

The sentence contrasts past, present, and future weather conditions.

Shifts from one tense to another not grounded in a corresponding shift in time, however, are confusing. Avoid such inappropriate shifts, particularly when you are telling a story or describing a sequence of events.

connect

mhconnectcomposition.com
Additional resources: QL39001

▶   The guide waited until we had all reached the top of the pass; then

    led   *made*   *was*

    she ~~leads~~ the way down to the river and ~~makes~~ sure everybody ~~is~~ safe

    ^   ^   ^

    in camp.

Convention dictates the use of the present tense for writing about literary events and characters as well as about films, plays, and other similar works.

▶   In Madame Defarge, the principal villain of *A Tale of Two Cities,*

                      depicts

    Charles Dickens ~~depicted~~ the cruel ironies of the French Revolution.

                    ^

39b   Avoiding Awkward Shifts in Mood and Voice

Two other characteristics of verbs are mood and voice; as with tense, shifts in mood and voice should help make clear what the writer intends to convey.

1. Shifts in mood

English verbs have three moods: indicative, imperative, and subjunctive. Most sentences are consistently in the indicative mood, which is used to state or question facts and beliefs. You may, however, inadvertently shift inappropriately between the imperative mood—used for commands, directions, and entreaties—and the indicative mood when explaining a process or giving directions.

> **Tech**
>
> **Flagging Confusing Shifts**
>
> The grammar and style checkers in word processing programs are unreliable at differentiating appropriate and confusing shifts. One style checker, for example, had no objection to this absurd statement: "Yesterday it will rain; tomorrow it snowed two feet." On the other hand, the same style checker flags every occurrence of the passive voice, whether or not it is appropriate to the passage in which it appears.

▶   Dig a narrow hole about six inches deep, place the tulip bulb firmly at

    the bottom of the hole, and then ~~you can~~ fill the hole with dirt.

The subjunctive mood is used in certain situations to express a wish or demand or to make a statement contrary to fact. Although

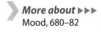

More about ▶▶▶
Mood, 680–82

many of us often replace it with the indicative in everyday speech, readers expect to encounter it in formal writing.

> ▶ If the presidential primary ~~was~~ *were* held earlier in the year, our state's
>
> voters would have a greater voice in the outcome of the race.

2. Shifts in voice

More about ▶▶▶
Voice, 682–84,
560–61

connect

mhconnectcomposition.com
Additional resources: QL39002

Avoid shifting needlessly between the active voice, in which the subject performs the action of the verb (*I wrote the paper*) and the passive voice, in which the subject receives the action (*The paper was written by me*). As originally written, the following passage started out in the active voice (*British consumed, Italians favored*) but then shifted to the passive voice for no reason:

> ▶ During the eighteenth century, the British consumed most of their
>
> carbohydrates in the form of processed sugar. The Italians favored
>
> *the French preferred*
> pasta, whereas sourdough bread ~~was preferred by the French~~.

connect

mhconnectcomposition.com
Online exercise: QL39101

➔ EXERCISE 39.1 Correcting verb shifts in tense, mood, and voice

Correct the following sentences to make the verbs consistent in tense, mood, and voice. Check for shifts both within and between sentences. If a sentence needs no revision, circle its number.

EXAMPLE

relaxed
After she mowed the lawn and pulled some weeds, Kris ~~relaxes~~ on the

was
porch until supper ~~is~~ ready.

Getting It
Across | Shifting Voice to Maintain a Consistent Subject

When you have to choose between a shift in voice and a shift in subject, sticking with a consistent subject may be the better option. Mark Twain, for example, makes *laws* the subject of the first part of both sentences in the following passage, and *customs* (or *custom*) the subject of the second part of both, even though the second sentence shifts from passive to active as a result (emphasis added).

> *Laws* are sand; *customs* are rock. *Laws* can be evaded and punishment escaped, but an openly transgressed custom brings sure punishment.
>
> —Mark Twain, *The Gorky Incident*

1. As most birdwatchers know, hummingbirds can do many things that other birds could not do.

2. With their wings being beaten an astonishing fifty times a second or more, hummingbirds sometimes fly as fast as sixty miles per hour.

3. Because hummingbirds expend so much energy, they needed to eat often, usually every twenty minutes.

4. With the highest metabolic rate of any animal, they burn energy faster than tigers, elephants, and all other birds.

5. Hummingbirds' most amazing feature, though, is their ability to fly in any direction—including upside down—something no other bird was capable of doing.

6. When birdwatchers study hummingbirds up close, the uniqueness of the species can be fully appreciated.

7. In addition, get a good view of the birds' long bills and stunning iridescent feathers.

8. Given hummingbirds' constant need for food, which they obtain from nectar and flowers, one would expect to have found them only in warm climates.

9. However, if birdwatchers are able to travel around the country, they would discover some species in chilly locales, such as the Rocky Mountains and Alaska.

10. Many hummingbirds migrate to warmer areas during winter months, but they returned to cooler areas in the spring and summer.

39c   Avoiding Shifts in Person and Number

Person refers to the identity of the subject of a sentence and the point of view of the writer. In the first person (*I, we*), the writer and subject are the same. In the second person (*you*), the reader and subject are the same. In the third person (*he, she, it, they, Marie Curie, electrons*), the subject is the writer's topic of discussion, what the writer is informing the reader about. ***Number*** refers to the quantity (singular or plural) of a noun or pronoun.

More about ▶▶▶
Person and number,
646–48

1. Shifts in person

Many situations require a shift in person. You might be telling a story in the first person, for example, but you will almost certainly have to relate some parts of it in the third person.

▶ We approached the spooky old house with trepidation. The front door creaked open. We stepped inside.

Arbitrary shifts in person, in contrast, are distracting to readers. The writer of the following passage, for example, began in the first person but shifted jarringly to the second person. The revision establishes a consistent first-person point of view.

▶ When I get together with my friends in the tech club, we usually
discuss the latest electronic devices. ~~You~~ *We* tend to forget, though,
that a garden spade and a ballpoint pen are also technological tools
and that thousands of nonelectronic items become part of ~~your~~ *our*
technological world every year.

Most academic writing is in the third person. The second person, including commands, is best reserved for addressing readers directly, telling them how to do something or giving them advice. (You have probably noticed that this handbook often addresses you, the reader, in just this way.) Be consistent, however, and avoid shifting arbitrarily between second and third person.

▶ To train your dog properly, ~~people~~ *you* need plenty of time, patience, and
dog biscuits. You should start with simple commands like "sit" and "stay."

2. Shifts in number

More about ▶▶▶
Avoiding gender
bias, 568–71,
658–60

Most inappropriate shifts in number are errors in agreement between a pronoun and its antecedent and are often the result of a writer's desire to avoid gender bias. These kinds of errors arise most commonly when the antecedent is a singular generic noun (*person, doctor*) or indefinite pronoun (*anyone, everyone*).

FAULTY   When a <u>person</u> witnesses a crime, <u>they</u> should report it to the police.

The antecedent of the plural pronoun *they* is the singular generic noun *person.*

Several options are available for revising such shifts. One is to use the plural throughout. Another is to replace the plural pronoun with *he or she* (although this expression becomes tedious when overused). A third is to rephrase the sentence to avoid the problem entirely.

REVISED: PLURAL THROUGHOUT	When people witness a crime, they should report it to the police.
REVISED: *HE OR SHE*	When a person witnesses a crime, he or she should report it to the police.
REVISED: REPHRASED	Anybody who witnesses a crime should report it to the police.

Look, too, for illogical shifts in number between two related nouns. As originally written, for example, the following sentence suggests that the passengers shared a single computer.

> *computers*
> ▶ All passengers had to open their ~~computer~~ for a security inspection.
>   ∧

> ➤ **EXERCISE 39.2 Correcting shifts in person and number**

Correct the following sentences so that they are consistent in person and number.

connect

mhconnectcomposition.com
Online exercise: QL39102

EXAMPLE

historians

Although a ~~historian~~ may understand past wars, they do not have all the
        ∧

answers to current conflicts.

1. During the nineteenth century, miners, merchants, and entrepreneurs flocked to the thriving river town of Galena, Illinois, to seek your fortune.

2. Galena was indeed "the west" in those days because you could not yet find any major cities west of the Mississippi River.

3. A Galenan can boast that their city, once the lead-mining capital of the world, was also home to Ulysses S. Grant and nine Civil War generals.

4. A Galenan is also likely to be proud of their town's renowned collection of original nineteenth-century architecture.

5. The mines are long closed, and the river resembles a meandering stream, but Galena remains a historic treasure where a visitor can step into yesterday, escape their busy life, and you can relax.

39d Avoiding Shifts in Direct and Indirect Quotations and Questions

More about ▶▶▶
Punctuating direct and indirect quotations, 814–22
Quoting sources, 276–79

Direct quotations reproduce someone's exact words and must always be enclosed in quotation marks: *My roommate announced, "The party will start at 8 p.m."* ***Indirect quotations*** report what someone has said but not in that person's exact words: *My roommate announced that the party would start at 8 p.m.*

Abrupt shifts between direct and indirect quotations, like the one in the following example, are awkward and confusing. Both of the revised versions are clearer and easier to follow than the original. In this instance, however, direct quotation is the best choice because Berra's own words express his humor most effectively.

AWKWARD SHIFT	Yogi Berra says that you should go to other people's funerals or "otherwise, they won't come to yours."
REVISED: DIRECT QUOTATION	As Yogi Berra says, "You should always go to other people's funerals. Otherwise, they won't come to yours."
REVISED: INDIRECT QUOTATION	Yogi Berra says that you should go to other people's funerals because, otherwise, they won't come to yours.

More about ▶▶▶
Punctuating direct and indirect questions, 825–26

Abrupt shifts between direct and indirect questions are likewise confusing. A ***direct question*** is stated in question (interrogative) form and ends with a question mark: *When does the library open?* An ***indirect question*** reports a question in declarative form and ends with a period: *I wonder when the library opens.*

AWKWARD SHIFT	The author asks how much longer can the world depend on fossil fuels and whether alternative sources of energy will be ready in time.
REVISED: DIRECT QUESTION	The author asks two questions: How much longer can the world depend on fossil fuels, and will alternative sources of energy be ready in time?
REVISED: INDIRECT QUESTION	The author asks how much longer the world can depend on fossil fuels and whether alternative sources of energy will be ready in time.

→ **EXERCISE 39.3 Revising confusing shifts**

Revise the following passage to eliminate confusing shifts.

connect
mhconnectcomposition.com
Online exercise: QL39103

In a blind taste test described in the *New York Times,* a cross section of the country's population sampled thousands of products in several locations, and store brands were given high marks by the testers. When the testers tried both national and store brands for such products as cereal, cream, pizza, and chicken nuggets, the researchers determine that the store brands were preferred over national brands by testers. While the testers did favor some national-brand products, such as chicken nuggets, cheese pizza, chocolate ice cream, and potatoes au gratin, the testers overwhelmingly prefer store-brand raisin bran. Store-brand frozen broccoli and chocolate chip cookies were also winners.

Although store brands have achieved a near equality with national brands in the minds of many consumers, shoppers are still careful in their choices. A shopper might ask, why shouldn't I buy a store brand if it tastes as good as a name brand? But if you find the store brand isn't good enough, you wouldn't buy it even if it was a lot cheaper.

Make It **Your Own**

Write a five- or six-sentence paragraph describing your favorite vacation, real or imaginary. Include in your paragraph as many types of awkward shifts in tense, mood, voice, person, and number as you can. You may include shifts both within and between sentences. Label this paragraph "Version A." Then rewrite your paragraph, eliminating the awkward shifts. Label this "Version B."

Work **Together**

Using the work you did on the Make It Your Own exercise above, exchange your Version A with a classmate. Eliminate the unnecessary shifts in your classmate's work. Compare your corrections with your classmate's Version B. Discuss and resolve any differences.

40 Avoiding Misplaced and Dangling Modifiers

Since 1886 the Statue of Liberty has dominated New York harbor, holding aloft a torch in the hand of her outstretched right arm. In 1876, however, while work on the rest of the statue continued in France, the arm and torch stood incongruously at the Philadelphia Centennial Exhibition, displayed there, and later in New York's Madison Square Park, to help raise funds for the construction of the statue's pedestal. This photograph of the display may strike you as strange or even funny because this huge piece of sculpture does not belong in a park; it is supposed to be attached appropriately to the rest of the statue. When you misplace modifiers in your sentences, you also may inadvertently confuse or amuse your readers.

MISPLACED MODIFIERS

A modifying word, phrase, or clause is misplaced if readers have to puzzle out what it modifies or if they stumble over it

Tech

Misplaced Modifiers and Grammar and Style Checkers

The grammar and style checkers in word processing programs usually cannot tell what a modifier is supposed to modify, so they rarely flag those that are misplaced confusingly far from their intended targets or that seem ambiguously to modify more than one term. They do flag most split infinitives and some other disruptive modifiers.

while trying to get from one part of a sentence to the next. Look for such ***misplaced modifiers*** as you revise your drafts.

40a Avoiding Confusing or Ambiguous Placement

Place modifiers so that they clearly refer to the words you intend them to modify and only those words.

1. Modifiers confusingly separated from the words they modify

We tend to associate modifiers with the words closest to them. A modifier positioned far from its intended target might appear to modify some other part of the sentence instead—and might confuse or amuse your readers.

connect
mhconnectcomposition.com
Additional resources: QL40001, QL40002, QL40003

▶ The couple moved to a bigger apartment *because they needed more space* after their first child was born ~~because they needed more space.~~

The couple's need for space did not cause the birth of their child.

▶ For more than four years, the two rovers *that landed in January 2004* have been exploring the surface of Mars ~~that landed in January 2004.~~

The rovers landed, not the surface of Mars.

EXERCISE 40.1 Confusingly placed modifiers

Revise the following sentences so that all modifiers are clearly and logically positioned.

connect
mhconnectcomposition.com
Online exercise: QL40101

EXAMPLE

Mr. Doyle walked down Main Street to Town Hall, the building that housed all the town's administrative offices, with determination.

Mr. Doyle walked with determination down Main Street to Town Hall, the building that housed all the town's administrative offices.

1. He had lived here for a long time, which was once a quiet, peaceful, and relaxing place, and he didn't like the changing atmosphere of the town.

2. Because it was so pleasant and relaxing, he realized that a lot of people had chosen to move to the town.

3. So he had decided to go to Town Hall and formally protest the installation of a traffic light in the main intersection of town, dressed in his finest suit.

4. He went straight to the main desk, walking through the large, ornate doors of the building.

5. He was there to protest the proposed traffic light, he told the receptionist, which was a direct threat to the town's long-standing harmony and tranquility.

6. The receptionist said that after holding several public meetings on the issue, he was very sorry but the Town Council had already voted for the traffic light.

2. Squinting modifiers

A *squinting modifier* confuses readers by appearing to modify both what precedes it and what follows it.

$$?\qquad\qquad ?$$

DRAFT   People who study hard <u>usually</u> will get the best grades.

Do people who make a practice of studying hard get the best grades, or do the best grades usually (but not always) go to people who study hard? The following revisions show that the sentence can be clarified in two different ways:

REVISION   People who <u>usually</u> study hard will get the best grades.

REVISION   People who study hard will <u>usually</u> get the best grades.

3. Ambiguous limiting modifiers

Limiting modifiers include qualifying words such as *almost, even, exactly, hardly, just, merely, only, scarcely,* and *simply.* Always place these words in front of the words you intend to modify. Do not place them in front of a verb unless they modify the verb. Otherwise, you risk ambiguity.

In the following example, the ambiguous placement of the limiter *just* leaves the reader with a variety of possible interpretations. If *just* is understood to modify *offers,* the sentence makes the unlikely suggestion that the only class the math department offers is Calculus III at night on Thursdays. The revisions provide three equally likely alternative readings.

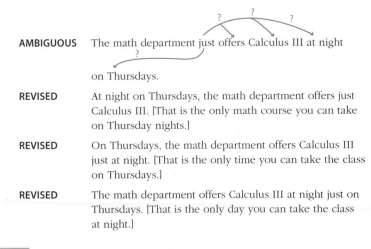

AMBIGUOUS   The math department just offers Calculus III at night

on Thursdays.

REVISED   At night on Thursdays, the math department offers just Calculus III. [That is the only math course you can take on Thursday nights.]

REVISED   On Thursdays, the math department offers Calculus III just at night. [That is the only time you can take the class on Thursdays.]

REVISED   The math department offers Calculus III at night just on Thursdays. [That is the only day you can take the class at night.]

40b Avoiding Disruptive Placement

A modifier is disruptive when it awkwardly breaks the flow among grammatically connected parts of a sentence.

1. Separation of subject from verb or verb from object

Long adverbial phrases and clauses tend to be disruptive when they fall between subjects and verbs (as in the first example below), within verb phrases (as in the second example), or between verbs and their objects (as in the third example).

▶ *The Sopranos,* ~~well after its last episode aired in June 2007,~~ continued
　　　　　　　　　well after its last episode aired in June 2007.
to elicit admiring commentary and analysis.∕
　　　　　　　　　　　　　　　　　　　∧

　If it maintains a large following, the
▶ ~~The~~ show might~~, if it maintains a large following,~~ appear in reruns for
　∧
years to come.

▶ The show often jarringly contrasts~~, leaving the viewer torn between~~

~~empathy and revulsion,~~ the mundane events of Tony's family life with
　　　　　　　　　　　, leaving the viewer torn between empathy and revulsion.
the callous brutality of the mobster's world.∕
　　　　　　　　　　　　　　　　∧

An adjective phrase or clause that modifies the subject of a sentence is not usually disruptive when it falls between subject and verb. On the contrary, it would likely be misplaced in any other location.

▶ The two Mars rovers, *which both landed in January 2004,* were designed to last only 90 days.

Writing Responsibly　　Misplaced Modifiers in the Real World

Misplaced modifiers can sometimes cause real distress. A confusing instruction like the one below from the website of the Federal Emergency Management Agency (FEMA) might bewilder a homeowner struggling to recover from a natural disaster.

> You will need your social security number, current and pre-disaster address, phone numbers, type of insurance coverage, total household annual income, and a routing and account number from your bank *if you want to have disaster assistance funds transferred directly into your bank account.* [Emphasis added.]

As written, this suggests that an applicant for relief needs all of the listed items in order to have disaster assistance deposited directly into a bank account. Here is what the writer probably meant to say:

> You will need your social security number, current and pre-disaster address, phone numbers, type of insurance coverage, total household annual income, and, *if you want to have disaster assistance funds transferred directly into your bank account,* a routing and account number from your bank.

2. Split infinitives

An infinitive consists of *to* and the base form of a verb (*to share, to jump, to remember*). An infinitive splits when a modifier is inserted between the *to* and the verb. Grammarians have traditionally considered infinitives to be indivisible units and split infinitives to be improper. Although many authorities now consider them acceptable, split infinitives can be awkward and often should be revised, particularly in formal writing.

▶ Grant's strategy was *to* ~~relentlessly~~ *attack* Lee's army despite the *relentlessly*

heavy losses the Union army suffered as a result.

Sometimes, however, a modifier is less awkward when splitting an infinitive than in any other spot in a sentence. If the adverb *relentlessly* were placed anywhere else in the following sentence, for example, it would not clearly and unambiguously modify only the word *attack*. Placed before the infinitive or at the end of the sentence, it could be understood to modify *urged;* placed after the infinitive, it could be understood to modify *retreating.*

▶ Lincoln urged his generals to *relentlessly* attack retreating enemy

forces.

➔ EXERCISE **40.2** Correcting disruptive modifiers

In the following sentences, move any disruptive modifiers, and revise any awkward split infinitives.

EXAMPLE

ever since she'd bought it.

Amber's laptop, ~~ever since she'd owned it,~~ had worked flawlessly.

1. Over the last week, however, she had been, mainly with the keyboard, having problems with it.

2. Often, when she hit the *r* key, she would see an *x* on her screen, and hitting, even when tapping gently and carefully, the *o* key gave her a *b* on the screen.

3. The technical support specialist with whom she spoke finally, after talking Amber through several troubleshooting routines, instructed her to mail the computer to a repair facility.

connect
mhconnectcomposition.com
Online exercise: QL40102

4. She worried that the repair process, leaving her to indefinitely rely on her library's computers, would take a long time.

5. When the repaired computer, two weeks later, arrived in the mail, Amber discovered that the repair staff had considerably replaced not only the laptop's keyboard, but its motherboard as well, and the computer worked better than ever.

DANGLING MODIFIERS

Consider the following sentence:

▶ While paddling the canoe toward shore, our poodle swam alongside.

Who or what is paddling the canoe? Surely not the poodle, yet that is what the sentence seems, absurdly, to suggest. The problem here is that the phrase *while paddling the canoe toward shore* does not actually modify the subject, *poodle,* or anything else in the sentence. It dangles, unattached, leaving it to the reader to infer the existence of some unnamed human paddler. Correcting this ***dangling modifier*** requires either making the paddler the subject of the sentence (as in the first revision below) or identifying the paddler in the modifier (as in the second revision).

▶ While paddling the canoe toward shore, our poodle ~~swam~~ alongside.
         I saw   swimming

▶ While ~~paddling~~ the canoe toward shore, our poodle swam alongside.
       I paddled

40c Identifying Dangling Modifiers

Dangling modifiers have the following characteristics:

- They are most often phrases that include a ***verbal*** (a gerund, infinitive, or participle) that has an implied but unstated actor.

- They occur most often at the beginnings of sentences.

- They appear to modify the subject of the sentence, so readers expect the implied actor and the subject to be the same.

- They dangle because the implied actor and the actual subject of the sentence are different.

Verbal Verb form that functions as a noun, adjective, or adverb (619–20)

> **More about ▶▶▶**
> Phrases and clauses,
> 617–23

DANGLING INFINITIVE PHRASE

To learn about new products, the company's sales meeting occurs annually in August. [Meetings do not learn.]

DANGLING PARTICIPIAL PHRASE

Hoping to boost morale, an attractive resort hotel is usually selected for the meeting. [Resorts cannot hope.]

DANGLING PREPOSITIONAL PHRASE WITH GERUND OBJECT

After traveling all day, the hotel's hot tub looked inviting to the arriving sales reps. [The sales reps traveled, not the hot tub.]

40d Correcting Dangling Modifiers

Simply moving a dangling modifier will not correct it.

connect

mhconnectcomposition.com
Additional resources: QL40004, QL40005

DANGLING To learn more about new products, the company's sales meeting occurs annually in August.

STILL DANGLING The company's sales meeting occurs annually in August to learn more about new products.

To correct a dangling modifier, first determine the identity of the modifier's unstated actor. You then have two options:

1. Rephrase to make the implied actor the subject of the sentence
2. Rephrase to include the implied actor in the modifier

Use the approach that works best given the purpose of the sentence in your draft.

MAKING THE IMPLIED ACTOR THE SUBJECT

To learn about new products, the company's sales meeting ~~occurs~~

~~annually~~ in August. [*sales reps attend* ... *annual*]

management usually selects

Hoping to boost morale, an attractive resort hotel ~~is usually selected~~ for
the meeting.

In both these cases, the implied actor—*sales reps* in the first, *manage-ment* in the second—was missing entirely from the original sentence.

INCLUDING THE IMPLIED ACTOR IN THE MODIFIER

As the sales reps arrived after

them.

~~After~~ traveling all day, the hotel's hot tub looked inviting to ~~the arriving~~

~~sales reps.~~

In this case, the implied actor, *sales reps,* appeared in the original sen-tence but needed to be repositioned.

connect

mhconnectcomposition.com
Online exercise: QL40103

→ **EXERCISE 40.3 Correcting dangling modifiers**

Revise the following sentences to eliminate dangling modifiers.

EXAMPLE

As soon as Derek stepped aboard,

~~On stepping aboard,~~ the boat began to roll back and forth.

1. Planning to enjoy a new experience, the fishing trip was eagerly anticipated.

2. Having little hope of actually catching anything, expectations for success were low.

3. To learn the basics of the sport, a few of his friends gave him fishing lessons.

4. Having dropped his line into the water, a tug indicated that he had a bite.

5. Reeling in the fish, everyone cheered because the first-timer had made the first catch.

6. After posing for a photo holding his catch, the squirming fish went back into the water.

7. To avoid seasickness in the bobbing boat, focusing on the dis-tant shoreline was a great help.

8. Catching a few more fish and not getting seasick, the trip was clearly a success.

Make It **Your Own**

Review the examples in this chapter's text and exercises. Then write one sentence each with (1) a confusingly placed modifier, (2) an ambiguous modifier, (3) a disruptive modifier, and (4) a dangling modifier. Write your four deliberately incorrect sentences on one sheet of paper and your corrected sentences on a separate sheet of paper.

Work **Together**

Exchange your incorrect sentences from the Make It Your Own exercise above with a classmate and correct each other's. Then do the same with two other classmates. Compare the results and resolve differences.

41

Avoiding Mixed and Incomplete Constructions

This disorienting image by artist M. C. Escher shows an impossible building, a mixed construction with a water channel that appears to flow horizontally but somehow ends up two stories higher than it begins, with the water cascading back to its source. As you edit your writing, look for sentences that similarly start in one direction but turn disorientingly in another, leaving readers unsure where you have taken them. Look, too, for sentences that omit words readers need to grasp fully your intended meaning.

MIXED CONSTRUCTIONS

When a sentence begins one way and then takes an unexpected turn—in grammar or logic—the result is a ***mixed construction.*** To find and correct mixed constructions in your drafts, keep your eye on the way your sentences begin, and make sure every predicate has a grammatically and logically appropriate subject.

41a **Recognizing and Correcting Grammatically Mixed Constructions**

Grammatically mixed constructions can occur when a writer treats an introductory phrase or clause that cannot function as the subject of a sentence as if it were the subject. The following example starts with a long prepositional phrase (underlined) that the writer mistakenly uses as the subject of the sentence. A prepositional phrase, although it can modify the subject or other parts of a sentence, cannot be the subject. The result is a ***sentence fragment,*** not a sentence.

MIXED   As a justification by American leaders for dropping atomic bombs on Hiroshima and Nagasaki maintained that doing so persuaded the Japanese to surrender without the need for an invasion that might have cost hundreds of thousands of casualties.

Fixing a sentence like this requires identifying a grammatical subject and isolating it from the introductory phrase. Here is one possible revision (with the subject underlined):

REVISED   As a justification for dropping atomic bombs on Hiroshima and Nagasaki, American leaders maintained that doing so persuaded the Japanese to surrender without the need for an invasion that might have cost hundreds of thousands of casualties.

Here is a more concise alternative that eliminates the introductory phrase altogether:

REVISED   American leaders maintained that dropping atomic bombs on Hiroshima and Nagasaki persuaded the Japanese to surrender without the need for an invasion that might have cost hundreds of thousands of casualties.

In the next example, the writer follows a subordinate clause (*Because the bombings had devastating effects*) with the verb *provoked,* which has no subject. The editing changes the first part of the sentence into a noun phrase subject for *provoked.*

▶   ~~Because the bombings had devastating effects~~ provoked intense

The devastating effects of the bombings

debate over the morality of the military decision.

---

connect

mhconnectcomposition.com
Additional resources: QL41001, QL41002

Sentence fragment
An incomplete sentence punctuated as if it were complete (626)

▶ *More about* ▶▶▶
Clauses, 620–23
Relating ideas with subordination, 531–36

Mixed constructions also occur when a writer treats a modifying phrase or clause as if it were the predicate of a sentence. Look for this kind of mixed construction, especially in sentences that begin with the phrase *the fact that*. The following example begins with a subject, *the fact*, followed by a long adjective *that* clause that modifies the subject but cannot at the same time be the predicate of the sentence.

> MIXED   The fact that Hiroshima and Nagasaki, which were devastated by the bomb, are once again thriving cities.

One way to revise this sentence is to add the verb *is*, making the *that* clause into a **subject complement.**

> REVISED   The fact is that Hiroshima and Nagasaki, which were devastated by the bomb, are once again thriving cities.

Better yet is simply to eliminate the phrase *the fact that*, a wordy expression that adds no information to the sentence.

> REVISED   Hiroshima and Nagasaki, which were devastated by the bomb, are once again thriving cities.

Sometimes you may find that you have written a sentence so mixed up that it resists easy revision. When this happens, step back, sort out the ideas you want to convey, and start over. If you need two sentences to express yourself clearly, use two sentences.

> MIXED   While the first atomic bomb had been successfully tested by scientists of the Manhattan Project on July 16, 1945, at Alamogordo, New Mexico, then less than one month later an American plane, after years of intensive research, dropped the bomb that destroyed Hiroshima on August 6.

> REVISED   After years of intensive research, scientists of the Manhattan Project successfully tested the first atomic bomb on July 16, 1945, at Alamogordo, New Mexico. On August 6, less than one month later, an American plane dropped the bomb that destroyed Hiroshima.

Subject complement
An adjective, pronoun, noun, or noun phrase that follows a linking verb and refers to the subject of the sentence (615)

More about ▶▶▶
Eliminating wordy expressions, 517–19

41b Recognizing and Correcting Mismatched Subjects and Predicates

The error of *faulty predication* occurs when a subject and predicate are mismatched—when they do not fit together logically. For example, the original subject of the following sentence, *recommendation,* does not work with the verb *insisted.* Recommendations cannot insist; doctors can.

▶ The ~~doctor's recommendation~~ ^{*doctor*} insisted that Joe be hospitalized immediately.

Many instances of faulty predication involve a mismatch between the subject and subject complement in sentences in which the verb is a form of *be* or other ***linking verb.***

MISMATCHED	Only students who are absent because of illness or a family emergency will be grounds for a makeup exam.
REVISED	Only students who are absent because of illness or a family emergency will be permitted to take a makeup exam.

Two forms of expression involving the verb *be* that have become commonplace in everyday speech are examples of faulty predication and should be avoided in formal writing. These are the use of *is where* or *is when* in definitions and the use of *the reason is . . . because* in explanations.

1. *Is where, is when*

Definitions with the expressions *is when* and *is where* usually result in logical mismatches because the terms defined involve neither a place (*where*) nor a time (*when*).

▶ A tornado is ~~where~~ ^{*a violent storm in which*} high winds swirl around in a funnel-shaped cloud.

A tornado is a storm, not a place.

▶ A friend is ~~when~~ ^{*who*} someone cares about you and has fun with you.

A friend is a person, not a time.

The expressions result in grammatical mismatches, too, because *where* and *when* introduce adverb clauses, which cannot function as subject complements.

2. *The reason . . . is because*

Explanations using the expression *the reason . . . is because* are similarly mismatched both logically (*the reason* and *because* are redundant) and grammatically (*because* introduces an adverb clause, which cannot function as a subject complement). The following example shows two simple ways to fix this kind of faulty predication—by changing the subject of the sentence or by substituting *that* for *because*.

▶ ~~The reason~~ I wrote this paper ~~is~~ because my instructor required it.

▶ The reason I wrote this paper is ~~because~~ my instructor required it.
　　　　　　　　　　　　　　　　　　　that

ESL **Obligatory Words and Unacceptable Repetitions in English** Unlike some languages, formal written English requires a stated subject in all sentences except commands.

More about ▶▶▶
Including a stated subject and eliminating redundant subject and object pronouns, 739–41

　　It rained
▶ ~~Rained~~ all day yesterday.

On the other hand, formal written English does not permit the use of a pronoun to emphasize an already stated subject or direct object.

▶ Maria~~, she~~ forgot to take her umbrella.

connect
mhconnectcomposition.com
Online exercise: QL41101

▶ EXERCISE **41.1** Correcting mixed constructions

Revise the following sentences to eliminate mixed constructions. Some sentences may be revised in more than one way.

EXAMPLE

While discouraging human athletes from using chemicals to improve
　　　　　　　　　　　, we ignore
performance ~~ignores~~ the reality that animals use any chemicals they can
to gain an advantage.

1. Because a hedgehog needs to avoid predators gnaws on the skin of poisonous toads.

2. The reason the hedgehog does this is because it gets the toad's toxin and then spread it over its body, making itself immune to enemies.

3. As male cardinals and house finches eat as many berries as they can in the fall unconcerned with the low nutritional value of the food.

4. Eating the berries is where the birds obtain carotenoids, the red and orange pigments that make their feathers so colorful in the spring.

5. The fact that the male *Cosmosoma myrodora* moth, which also collects steroid toxins to help attract the opposite sex.

6. The male moth's drive to lap up toxin from the leaves of certain vines stores a supply of the toxin in pouches on his abdomen.

7. When the male moth's abdominal pouches get large and heavy attracting female moths.

8. During their mating is when the male's pouches burst and spread the steroid toxins all over the female.

9. The fact is that this is how the female *Cosmosoma myrodora* moth becomes inedible to spiders.

10. By denying human athletes the use of steroids is unfair when animals use the chemicals to such great advantage?

INCOMPLETE CONSTRUCTIONS

As you draft sentences, you may unintentionally leave out grammatically or logically essential words. Sometimes these omissions result in sentence fragments. Often, however, they create seemingly minor but nonetheless distracting grammatical or idiomatic bumps. As you proofread and edit your drafts, be especially alert for such missing words in compound and other constructions and in comparisons.

41c Adding Essential Words to Compound and Other Constructions

In compound constructions, the omission of *nonessential* repetitions can often help tighten prose.

▶ Abigail needed a new dress to wear to the graduation party and [to] the wedding reception. First she shopped at Macy's and then [she shopped] at Kohl's.

Such ***elliptical constructions*** work, however, only when the stated words in one part of a compound match the omitted words in other parts. When grammar or idiom requires different words—different

More about ▶▶▶
Writing concisely,
516–25

Elliptical construction A construction in which otherwise grammatically necessary words can be omitted because their meaning is understood from the surrounding context

verb forms, different prepositions, or different articles, for example—those words should be included.

▶ The candidate claimed that she always had and always would support ^*supported*

universal health care coverage.

The word *supported* is needed because *had support* would be ungrammatical.

▶ On the campaign trail and ^*in* debates, her opponent for the nomination

insisted that his plan was better than hers.

In this situation, the word *debates* requires the preposition *in*, not *on*.

▶ A yearning for change, ^*an* unsettled economy, and ^*the* character of the

candidates themselves combined to sustain high voter turnout during

the primary season.

The word *unsettled* requires a different form of the indefinite article (*a, an*) than *yearning*, and in this situation the word *character* requires the definite article (*the*) rather than the indefinite article.

Occasionally, you may need to repeat a modifier for clarity.

▶ The candidates asked their loyal backers and ^*their* opponents to support

the winner, whoever that might be.

The repeated *their* makes clear that the adjective *loyal* applies only to *backers* and not to *opponents*.

Although you can often omit the word *that* without obscuring the meaning of a subordinate clause, sometimes you need to include it to avoid confusion.

▶ I know ^*that* Sheila, who is a sympathetic person, will not be terribly upset

about the stains on the silk shirt ~~that~~ I borrowed from her.

In the original, without the first *that, Sheila* could be understood as the object of *know* rather than the subject of the long subordinate clause that follows. On the other hand, the *that* at the end of the sentence can be eliminated because no such ambiguity affects the subject (*I*) of the clause it introduces.

41d Avoiding Incomplete or Ambiguous Comparisons

Comparisons show how two items are alike or different. For comparisons to be clear, the items they juxtapose must be logically equivalent. The original version of the following sentence confusingly compares a group of people, children, to a process, growing up. The editing makes the two sides of the comparison equivalent.

More about ▶▶▶
Comparisons,
705–08

▶ Children who grow up on farms are more active than ~~growing up in~~ ^{those who grow up in}
big cities.

To be complete, comparisons must fully specify what is being compared to what.

▶ The Log Cabin Restaurant is better. ^{than Joe's Diner.}

Be careful how you use the terms *any* and *any other* when you compare one item to others that belong to the same category.

▶ Mount Everest is higher than any ^{other} mountain in the world.

Mount Everest is a mountain in the world, so without the modifier *other,* the sentence suggests that Mount Everest is higher than itself.

▶ Huascaran, the highest mountain in South America, is higher than any ~~other~~ mountain in North America.

The sentence compares a mountain in South America to mountains in North America, not to other mountains in South America.

Be sure, also, to include any information you need to avoid ambiguity in your comparisons. In its draft form, the following comparison has two possible interpretations, as the revisions make clear.

DRAFT   Yvette is more concerned about me than my brother.

REVISED   Yvette is more concerned about me than <u>she is about</u> my brother.

REVISED   Yvette is more concerned about me than my brother <u>is</u>.

When you use the word *as* in a comparison, be sure to use it twice.

▶ Stephen King's horror stories are ^{as} scary as Edgar Allan Poe's.

→ **EXERCISE 41.2 Correcting incomplete constructions**

Revise the following sentences to eliminate incomplete constructions. Some sentences may be revised in more than one way.

EXAMPLE

                                              traveling by
Traveling by airplane was once more convenient than train.
                                                      ∧

connect
mhconnectcomposition.com
Online exercise: QL41102

1. Yuko understood, from what she heard on the news, air travel
   had become more difficult in recent years.

2. The airline Yuko chose for her trip to Los Angeles had a more
   reliable on-time record than any air carrier.

3. She thought she had been careful about her flight planning as
   she possibly could have been.

4. Unfortunately, she could not have planned for a sudden severe
   storm during her flight, resulting disruptions in the country's
   air travel system, and unexpected landing of her flight at Albu-
   querque, New Mexico, at midnight.

5. She learned that the plane would need repairs and the airline
   unable to continue the flight to Los Angeles for days.

6. Yuko knew Helen, who sat next to her on the plane, was willing to rent a car and drive the rest of the way to Los Angeles.

7. After an all-night drive, an exhausted Yuko concluded that,
   whenever available, train travel would be better.

⬆ Make It **Your Own**

Mark a sheet of paper "Page A" and write on it two sentences each
with a different type of mixed construction and two sentences each
with a different type of incomplete construction. Mark a separate
sheet of paper "Page B" and write on it your corrected sentences.

Work **Together** ◀

Using your work on the Make It Your Own exercise above,
exchange your Page A with a classmate. Make corrections to
your classmate's Page A, and then compare your results with
your classmate's Page B. Discuss and resolve any differences.

Part Nine

ESL
Matters

42 Understanding English Word Order and Sentence Structure

by Ted E. Johnston and M. E. Sokolik

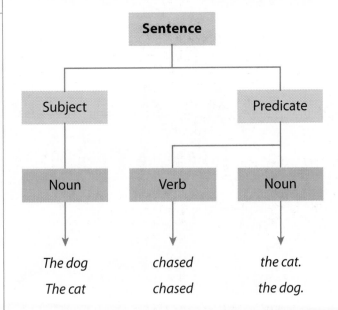

Sentence		

Subject		Predicate

Noun	Verb	Noun

| The dog | chased | the cat. |
| The cat | chased | the dog. |

English is a word-order language, which means that the position of a word in a sentence often determines its grammatical function. As a result, *The dog chased the cat* means something different from *The cat chased the dog*. This chapter describes and explains word order and related aspects of English sentence structure.

> **More about** ▶▶▶
> Sentence types, 611
> Word order in questions, 744

42a Observing Normal Word Order

In declarative sentences (as opposed to questions or commands), normal word order is subject-verb-object (or S-V-O). That is, the subject comes first, then the verb, and then the direct object, if there is one, or any other words that make up the predicate.

	v ? ?
FAULTY WORD ORDER	Chased the cat the dog.
	s v o
NORMAL WORD ORDER	The dog chased the cat.

connect
mhconnectcomposition.com
Additional resources: QL42001

42b Including a Stated Subject

Except for commands, English sentences and **clauses** require a subject to be stated, even if the identity of the subject is clear from a previous sentence or clause. In the following example, the pronoun *he,* referring to the subject of the first sentence, can serve as the subject of both clauses of the second sentence.

> He is   he
> ▶ Nico has a hard life for a ten-year-old. Is just a boy, but is expected to
> work like a man.

Similarly, a subordinate clause requires a stated subject even if its subject is a pronoun or another noun phrase that obviously refers to the same entity as the subject of the clause that precedes it.

> |— sub. clause —|
>   she
> ▶ Lucy asked for directions because was lost.

In commands, the subject is unstated but is understood to be "you."

> ▶ [you] Leave now!

42c Managing *There* and *It* Constructions

Expletives are words that are empty of content; that is, they do not refer to anything. In English, the words *there* and *it* are often used as expletives.

In *there* constructions, *there* precedes a form of *to be. There,* however, is not the subject. The subject follows the verb, and the verb is either singular or plural, depending on the subject. The expletive *it,* on the other hand, is always the singular subject of its clause. *It* constructions are often used to indicate an environmental condition or some aspect of time. The verb in expletive *it* constructions is often a form of

> **Clause** A word group with a subject and a predicate. An *independent clause* can stand alone as a sentence; a *subordinate clause* cannot. (620–23)

be, but other verbs can be used, especially those related to process (for example, *start, continue, end*). The expletives *there* and *it* cannot be omitted from such clauses, even though they do not refer to anything.

> There are
> ▶ ~~Are~~ not enough reasons to support your argument.
>   ∧

> ▶ Waiter, I am not pleased that is a fly in my soup.
>   there
>   ∧

> ▶ When was almost 3:00 p.m., started hailing really hard.
>   it   it
>   ∧   ∧

In a similar construction, the pronoun *it* is not empty, but refers to content that follows the verb. In the following sentence, for example, *it* refers to *to drive during a snowstorm.* In either case, empty or meaningful, *it* is the subject and cannot be omitted.

> It is
> ▶ ~~Is~~ dangerous to drive during a snowstorm.
>   ∧

42d Eliminating Redundant Subject and Object Pronouns

Although English requires a stated subject in all clauses except commands, the use of a pronoun to reemphasize an already stated subject is not acceptable in writing, even though such constructions often occur in informal speech.

>   │redundant subject
>   subj.   ▼
> ▶ Rosalinda, ~~she~~ left early for the airport.

Similarly, when *which* or *that* begins a clause and serves as the clause's subject or direct object, do not also add *it* to serve as the subject or direct object. In the following sentences, for example, both *which* and *it* refer redundantly to the movie *Pan's Labyrinth;* to correct the sentences requires eliminating one or the other pronoun.

>   │redundant subject
>   subj.   ▼
> ▶ Last night I saw *Pan's Labyrinth,* which ~~it~~ impressed me very much.

> or

> ▶ Last night I saw *Pan's Labyrinth,* ~~which~~ it impressed me very much.
>   ∧

dir. obj.   redundant object
                                 ↓

▶ I liked *Pan's Labyrinth,* **which** many of my friends liked ~~it~~ too.

or

▶ I liked *Pan's Labyrinth~~,~~* ~~which~~ many of my friends liked it too.
   ∧

→ EXERCISE 42.1   Using normal word order and including a subject

In the following sentences, correct word-order errors involving subjects or omissions of *it* or *there.*

connect

mhconnectcomposition.com
Online exercise: QL42101

EXAMPLE

It was
~~Was~~ obvious the students hadn't studied for the test.
 ∧

1. Without a doubt, is nothing more breathtaking than seeing a double rainbow after a storm.
2. I am excited by this letter, which I received it late yesterday.
3. Was still too early to plant the tomatoes, so died all of them.
4. We read that are several new dance clubs opening this weekend.
5. We left the office because was after five o'clock.
6. Don't you think is a little silly to argue about who is the better cook?
7. My aunt and uncle, they are both working in California as computer programmers.
8. Is completely impossible to dislike that professor!
9. This is an uplifting story because has such an optimistic ending.
10. I read a controversial article that it claims North and South America were settled much earlier than previously thought.

42e   Sentence Structure with Direct Objects, Indirect Objects, and Object Complements

Direct objects, indirect objects, and object complements can follow a transitive verb.

1. Direct and indirect objects

A **direct object** receives or carries the action of a transitive verb. Certain transitive verbs—such as *ask, find, give, order, send, show, teach, tell,* and *write*—can also take an **indirect object,** which names the recipient of the direct object. The indirect object falls between the verb and the direct object.

More about ▶▶▶
Direct and indirect
objects, 614–17

▶ She sent Michiko a book on Scandinavian cuisine.

Alternatively, the recipient of the direct object can be identified in a phrase beginning with a preposition, usually *to,* that follows the direct object.

connect
mhconnectcomposition.com
Additional resources: QL42002

▶ She sent a book on Scandinavian cuisine to Michiko.

When the direct object is a personal pronoun, the verb must be followed by a prepositional phrase, not an indirect object.

▶ She sent ~~Michiko~~ it. to Michiko.

Several common verbs do not take indirect objects even though the actions they refer to are similar to those of verbs that do. These verbs include *answer, carry, change, close, complete, deliver, describe, explain, keep, mention, open, propose, put, recommend, repair* (or *fix* when it means *repair*), and *say*. With these verbs, the function of the indirect object can be performed only by a prepositional phrase beginning with *to* (or sometimes *for*) that follows the direct object.

▶ The doctor explained ~~my father~~ the dangers of secondhand smoke. to my father.

▶ The professor opened ~~us~~ the door to understanding. for us.

2. Object complements

An **object complement** follows a direct object and describes a condition of the object or a change in the object that the subject has caused the object to undergo.

▶ Some workers here make my job impossible.

Placing an object complement before the direct object will either make a sentence ungrammatical or change its meaning. The following sentence, as originally written, was ungrammatical.

▶ The players have just elected ~~their team captain~~ Paul. *their team captain.*

The following sentences, in contrast, are both grammatical but have different meanings.

▶ We need to keep all the <u>happy</u> workers.

▶ We need to keep all the workers <u>happy</u>.

The first sentence, with the adjective *happy* before the direct object, recommends retaining the workers who are already happy, but not necessarily those who are not. The second, with *happy* in the object complement position after the direct object, recommends taking action to make sure that not one of the workers feels unhappy.

→ **EXERCISE 42.2 Using objects and object complements**

Correct any errors related to indirect objects or object complements in the following sentences. Next to sentences with an error, write IO if the problem is related to indirect objects and OC if it is related to object complements. Mark any correct sentences OK.

connect
mhconnectcomposition.com
Online exercise: QL42102

EXAMPLE

We want the ~~closed~~ door, please.   OC
closed,

1. We painted the yellow walls because yellow is a cheerful color.
2. She sent me a very informative letter.
3. I consider his inappropriate remarks and refuse to respond to them.
4. The owner described me the house in great detail.
5. The president appointed me his new assistant.
6. Frank has a build very muscular.
7. I had an extra blanket, so I gave a homeless man it.
8. We ordered the carpet baby blue, not the beige one.
9. The last treatment did to the patient more harm than good.
10. The teacher explained the students the assignment one more time.

42f Observing Word-Order Patterns in Questions

In questions, unlike declarative statements, a verb nearly always precedes the subject.

- To form a question with one-word forms of the verb *be,* simply invert subject and verb.

$$\overset{s}{\text{The}} \overset{v}{\text{grapes are ripe.}} \qquad \qquad \overset{v}{\text{Are the grapes ripe?}}^{s}$$

The grapes are ripe.   Are the grapes ripe?

- In all other cases, a question requires a helping verb as well as a main verb. The subject goes after the first helping verb in a verb phrase and before the rest of the verb phrase.

They have left for New York.   Have they left for New York?

The children can go with us.   Can the children go with us?

The painters should have finished.   Should the painters have finished?

- To form a question with one-word verbs other than forms of *be,* use the appropriate form of *do* as the helper.

The prisoner escaped.   Did the prisoner escape?

- Questions that begin with question words like *what, who,* and *why* normally follow the same word order as other questions.

What is the engineer saying about the project?

- If the question word is the subject, however, the question follows subject-before-verb word order.

Who is saying these things about the project?

42g Observing Inverted Word Order When Certain Conjunctions or Adverbs Begin a Clause

When they appear at the beginning of a sentence or clause, certain adverbs, adverb phrases, correlative conjunctions (such as *neither . . . nor* and *not only . . . but also*), and the conjunction *nor* by itself require inverted word order similar to that used in questions.

► *Neither* ~~the parents~~ have called the principal, *nor* ~~they~~ have informed

    the school board.

(the parents) *(they)*

► The twins don't bowl, *nor* they play tennis.

(do)

The adverbs *rarely, seldom, no sooner, no longer,* and similar negating or limiting expressions also require inverted word order when they start a sentence or clause. Such sentences have a formal tone.

► *Seldom* ~~the dancers~~ have had the opportunity to perform in public.

(the dancers)

Moving the adverb to the interior of the sentence cancels the inversion.

More about ►►►
Adverbs, 700–09, 769–72

► The dancers have *seldom* had the opportunity to perform in public.

Usually, this less formal, noninverted version of such sentences is preferable to the inverted version.

EXERCISE **42.3** Working with word-order inversions

In the following sentences, correct any word-order errors related to inversions. Mark any correct sentences OK.

connect
mhconnectcomposition.com
Online exercise: QL42103

    EXAMPLE

    Neither we want to go the party, nor we want to help pay for it.

(do)   *(do)*

1. Neither he takes classes at the university, nor he works.
2. Jossette has been working on her research project?
3. When Chen bought his new computer?
4. We rarely went to dinner with friends.
5. Rarely it rains in the desert.
6. Goes she often to parties?
7. Couldn't Fatima have done something sooner about the error?
8. Why smoking should be banned in bars?
9. Not only she works hard, but she also studies hard.
10. Mark neither reads French nor speaks it.

↑ Make It **Your Own**

In an issue of a newsmagazine such as *Time,* the *Economist, U.S. News and World Report,* or *Newsweek,* find two examples each of sentences with indirect objects, object complements, and inversions involving "not only," "neither/nor," or some other initial adverb or adverbial phrase. Copy the sentences and underline the components in each sentence identifying the feature. Write two examples of your own for each type of sentence patterned on the examples you found.

Work **Together** ←

In small groups, check the examples group members found and wrote on their own in the Make It Your Own activity above. Does everyone agree with the results? Why or why not? Ask your instructor if you are uncertain about any of the examples.

43 Using Nouns and Noun Determiners

by Ted E. Johnston and M. E. Sokolik

"What can I say? I was an English major."

English nouns rarely appear by themselves. Most of the time they are paired with words such as *a, an, the, my, that, each, one, ten, several, more, less,* and *fewer.* These words are known as **determiners** because they help us figure out—or determine—how a noun works and what it means when we encounter it in a sentence. As this cartoon suggests, learning to use nouns and determiners appropriately can sometimes challenge native speakers as much as it does multilingual students.

43a Understanding Different Types of Nouns

To use a noun properly, you need to know whether it is a *proper noun* or a *common noun,* and, if it is a common noun, whether it is *count* or *noncount.* A **common noun** identifies a general category and is usually not capitalized: *woman, era, bridge, corporation, mountain, war.* A **proper noun** identifies

More about ▶▶▶
Types of nouns,
601–05

someone or something specific and is usually capitalized: *Hillary Clinton, Middle Ages, Golden Gate Bridge, Burger King, Himalayas, World War II.*

    Count nouns name discrete, countable things. **Noncount nouns** (also called **noncountable** or **mass** nouns) usually name entities made of a continuous substance or of small indistinguishable particles, or they refer to a general quality. A *drop,* a *grain,* and a *suggestion,* for example, are count nouns, but *water, sand,* and *advice* are noncount nouns.

More about ▶▶▶
Forming noun
plurals, 595–97

- Count nouns can be singular (*drop*) or plural (*drops*). Most noncount nouns are singular, even those that end in *-s,* and thus should be matched with singular verbs. Noncount nouns cannot be preceded by a number or any other term that would imply countability (such as *a, an, several, another,* or *many*), nor can they be made plural if they are singular.

      ▶ Aerobics ~~help~~ helps me to relax.

connect
mhconnectcomposition.com
Additional resources: QL43001,
QL43002

Here are some examples of contrasting count and noncount nouns:

Count	Noncount
car/cars	traffic
dollar/dollars	money
noodle/noodles	spaghetti
pebble/pebbles	gravel
spoon/spoons	silverware

- Many nouns can be noncount in one context and count in another.

  ▶ While speaking of *love* [noncount], my grandmother recalled the three *loves* [count] of her life.

      In the opening phrase, *love* is an abstraction. In the main clause, *loves* refers to the people the grandmother has loved.

- All languages have count and noncount nouns, but a noun that is count in one language may be noncount in another.

43b Using Nouns with Articles (*a, an, the*) and Other Determiners

The ***articles*** *a, an,* and *the* are the most common determiners. Other determiners include possessives (*my, your, Ivan's*), numbers (*one, five,*

Reference ➡ Some Common Noncount Nouns

Although there is no hard-and-fast way to distinguish noncount from count nouns, most noncount nouns do fall into a few general categories.

Abstractions and emotions	advice, courage, happiness, hate, jealousy, information, knowledge, love, luck, maturity, patriotism, warmth
Mass substances	air, blood, dirt, gasoline, glue, sand, shampoo, water
Food items	beef, bread, corn, flour, gravy, pork, rice, salt, sugar
Collections of related items	cash, clothing, equipment, furniture, graffiti, information, jewelry, luggage, mail, traffic
Games and other activities	aerobics, baseball, checkers, homework, news, pilates, poker, pool, soccer, tennis, volleyball
Weather-related phenomena	cold, drizzle, frost, hail, heat, humidity, lightning, rain, sleet, snow, sunshine, thunder
Diseases	arthritis, chicken pox, diabetes, influenza, measles
Fields of study	botany, chemistry, mathematics, physics, sociology

a hundred), and other words that quantify (*some, many, a few*) or specify (*this, those*).

1. Articles with common nouns

The main function of the ***indefinite articles,*** *a* and *an*, is to introduce nouns that are new to the reader. The ***definite article,*** *the*, usually precedes nouns that have already been introduced or whose identity is known or clear from the context. Noncount nouns and plural count nouns also sometimes appear with no article (or the ***zero article***).

connect
mhconnectcomposition.com
Additional resources: QL43003

- Use *a* before a consonant sound (*a cat*) and *an* before a vowel sound (*an elephant*). Do not be misled by written vowels that are pronounced as consonants (*a European tour*) or written consonants that are pronounced as vowels (*an hour early*). Be especially careful with words that begin with *h* (*a* hot stove, *an* honorary degree) and *u* (*a* uniform, *an* upheaval).

- Use *a* or *an* only with singular count nouns. A singular count noun *must* be preceded by an article or some other determiner even if other modifiers come between the determiner and the noun.

  ▶ A friend of mine bought an antique car on eBay.

- Never use *a* or *an* with a noncount noun.

  > Good
  > ~~A good~~ advice is hard to find.

- Use *a* or *an* when you first introduce a singular count noun if the specific identity of the noun is not yet known to the reader or is not otherwise clear from the context. Use *the* for subsequent references to the same noun.

  ▶ A friend of mine bought an antique car on eBay. She restored the car and sold it for a tidy profit. The profit came in handy when she took a vacation.

  The is appropriate for *car* in the second sentence because it refers to the same car introduced in the first sentence. The word *profit* in the second sentence takes *a* because it is making its first appearance there. The third sentence continues the process.

- Use *the* with both count and noncount nouns whose specific identity has been previously established or is clear from the context.

  ▶ We admired the antique car that my friend bought on eBay.

  The modifying clause *that my friend bought on eBay* identifies a specific car.

  ▶ She sold it for a tidy profit and used the money for a vacation.

  The context clearly identifies the money with the profit.

  ▶ My friend is traveling around the world for three months.

  The noun *world* logically refers to the planet we live on—not, say, Mars or Venus.

❯ **More about** ▶▶▶
Superlatives, 705–07

  ▶ Vicky is the fastest runner on her team.

  The superlative *fastest* refers specifically to one person.

- No article is used to introduce noncount nouns or plural count nouns used generically—that is, to make generalizations.

  ▶ Good advice is hard to find.

  ▶ Good teachers can change lives.

- Both the definite and indefinite articles can introduce singular nouns used generically. Sometimes either is appropriate:

  ▶ **The** good teacher can change lives.

  ▶ **A** good teacher can change lives.

Sometimes the generic meaning is clear with only one or the other:

  ▶ Thomas Alva Edison invented ~~a~~ *the* lightbulb.

2. Articles with proper nouns

Proper nouns in English almost never occur with the indefinite article (*a, an*), and most occur with no article:

  ▶ **Ruby grew up in Lima, Peru, but now lives in Wichita, Kansas.**

There are many exceptions, however:

- Certain place names always occur with *the: the Bronx, the Philippines, the Northeast, the Pacific Ocean*.

- The names of ships (including airships) conventionally occur with *the: the Queen Mary, the Challenger*.

- Many product names can be used with *a* or *the* or sometimes both: *the Cheerios, an/the iPhone, a/the Toyota*.

- Many multiword proper nouns occur with *the: the United States, the Brooklyn Bridge, the Department of State, the War of 1812*. Others do not, however. The city of Chicago, for example, is home to both *the Wrigley Building* (with article) and *Wrigley Field* (no article).

- Most plural proper nouns occur with *the: the Bartons, the Chicago Cubs*.

→ EXERCISE 43.1 Using articles correctly

connect

mhconnectcomposition.com
Online exercise: QL43101

Insert *a, an, the,* or no article as appropriate in the blanks in the following paragraph.

I feel ___¹ anger whenever I see ___² poor child suffering from ___³ hunger. In ___⁴ United States, we believe that ___⁵ children need ___⁶ good breakfast every morning to do well in ___⁷ school, so schools provide ___[8] breakfast for them. I realize that ___[9] economic situation is often worse in ___[10] other countries than here, but even here, there is more hunger than ___[11] people realize. ___[12] hungriest children are found in ___[13] rural areas of our country. ___[14] boy I once knew told me that many nights he went to bed hungry after working in ___[15] fields. ___[16] boy later moved to ___[17] nearby city and his family was able to get ___[18] assistance from ___[19] various charitable organizations.

3. Nouns and other determiners

More about ▶▶▶
Order of adjectives,
767

As with articles, the use of other determiners with nouns depends on the kind of noun in question, particularly whether it is singular or plural, count or noncount. In all cases, determiners precede any other adjectives that modify a noun.

Possessive Nouns or Pronouns Use possessive nouns (*Julio's*) and possessive pronouns (*my, our, your, his, her, its, their, whose*) with any count or noncount noun.

sing. count	plural count	noncount
Ann's book	*Ann's* books	*Ann's* information
her book	*her* books	*her* information

This, that, these, those The demonstrative pronouns *this, that, these,* and *those* specify, or single out, particular instances of a noun. Use *this* and *that* only with noncount nouns and singular count nouns. Use *these* and *those* only with plural count nouns.

sing. count	plural count	noncount
this book	—	*this* information
that book	—	*that* information
—	*these* books	—
—	*those* books	—

Quantifying Words or Phrases Use numbers only with count nouns: *one shirt, two shirts.* See the Quick Reference box on p. 753 for a list of other quantifying words and how they work with different kinds of nouns in most contexts.

Few* versus *a few* and *little* versus *a little The determiners *few* and *a few* (for count nouns) and *little* and *a little* (for noncount nouns) all indicate a small quantity, but they have significant differences in meaning. *Few* means a negligible amount, whereas *a few* means a small but significant number. Likewise, *little* means *almost none,* whereas *a little* means *some.*

▶ Rhoda has *few* good friends.

  She is almost friendless.

▶ Rhoda has *a few* good friends.

  She has significant companionship.

Quick Reference ➡ **Matching Nouns with Quantifying Words and Phrases**

Quantifying Word or Phrase	Singular Count Nouns	Plural Count Nouns	Noncount Nouns	Examples
any, no	✓	✓	✓	You can read <u>any</u> book on the list.
				Have you read <u>any</u> books this summer?
				Do you have <u>any</u> information about the reading list?
another, each, every, either, neither	✓	no	no	I read <u>another</u> book last week.
the other	✓	✓	✓	<u>The other</u> book is a murder mystery.
				I haven't finished <u>the other</u> books on the reading list.
				<u>The other</u> information is the most reliable.
a couple of, a number of, both, few, a few, fewer, fewest, many, several	no	✓	no	The professor assigned <u>fewer</u> books last term.
a lot of, lots of, all, enough, more, most, other, some	no	✓	✓	<u>Some</u> books are inspiring.
				<u>Some</u> information is unreliable.
little, a little, much, a great deal of, less, least	no	no	✓	I need <u>a little</u> information about the course requirements.

▶ Pete provided *little* help before the party.

He didn't do his share.

▶ Pete gave me *a little* help after everyone left.

He made himself useful.

Indicating Extent or Amount with Noncount Nouns Because a noncount noun is always singular, do not make it plural or add a determiner that implies a plural form. For example, do not use a determiner such as *a large number of, many,* or *several* immediately before a noncount noun. Instead, use a determiner such as *a great deal of, less, little, much,* or *some*—or revise the sentence another way.

▶ The city is doing ~~researches~~ on the proposal.
  <small>some</small>

The modifier *some* is appropriate for the noncount noun *research* because it does not imply plurality.

▶ Gina bought two ~~breads~~ at the store.
  <small>loaves of</small>

In the edited version, *two* modifies the count noun *loaves.*

▶ We do not have many ~~violences~~ in our neighborhood.
  <small>incidents of violence</small>

▶ A ~~large number~~ of information is available on your topic.
  <small>great deal</small>

A large number of, which suggests plurality, cannot be used with *information,* a noncount noun.

Getting It Across   *Less* versus *fewer,* or "Do as I say, not as I do."

The quantifier *less* is properly used only with noncount nouns, not count nouns.

▶ The automobile industry sold ~~less~~ cars this year than last year.
  <small>fewer</small>

As the cartoon that opens this chapter suggests, however, many native English speakers are likely to violate this rule, particularly in everyday speech. (*Items* is a count noun.) Try not to follow their example.

→ EXERCISE 43.2 Editing for noun and determiner usage

Correct any errors resulting from the improper use of nouns and determiners in the following passage.

A great deal of students showed up at the class party this past weekend. Everyone seemed to have fairly good time despite few major problems that I am now being blamed for. However, whenever we plan this kinds of events in future, we need much more people to help. So little people actually helped that I essentially had to do all work on my own. Therefore, I refuse to take a blame for all things that went wrong. Everyone should be aware that other person (who will remain nameless) who had agreed to help me organize event didn't do his share of job. He was supposed to coordinate the individuals who had volunteered to set up and decorate hall and then to remind others who had indicated that they would provide necessary items not to forget to do so. Because he didn't call anyone, that tasks never got done, but I did best I could by myself. Not surprisingly, biggest problem we had was that there were not enough supplies. For example, we had less sodas than we needed, so some guests had to drink lot of water because it was so hot that evening. Another examples was that we didn't have as many ice as we needed, and there weren't enough plastic glasses or napkins. I had to send someone out to buy much of this items using my own moneys.

connect
mhconnectcomposition.com
Online exercise: QL43102

▲ Make It **Your Own**

Write five sentences with plural references using noncount nouns from five of the categories in the Quick Reference box on p. 749. For example, you might write, "The recipe calls for *five cups of flour*," Next, referring to the Quick Reference box on p. 753, write three sentences with count nouns and three with noncount nouns using different quantifiers. For example, you might write, "I read *a couple of* science fiction *novels* over spring break."

Work **Together** ◄

In small groups, exchange your work on the Make It Your Own exercise above. Discuss your differences, and consult your instructor if you need help arriving at a consensus.

44

Managing English Verbs

by Ted E. Johnston and M. E. Sokolik

connect

mhconnectcomposition.com
Additional resources: QL44001

Verbs can express an action or occurrence (*The dog jumps for the Frisbee*) or indicate a state of being (*The dog is frisky*). In many languages, verbs can have several forms. For example, they may change to indicate the identity of a subject or object or the time frame in which an event happens. English verbs, in contrast, have only a few forms, but these combine with other words to accomplish the same functions.

44a Using Phrasal Verbs

Phrasal verbs—sometimes called multiword verbs—consist of a verb and one or two ***particles.*** The particle takes the form of a preposition or adverb, and it combines with the verb to create a new verb with a new meaning. For example, the verb *throw* means to project something through the air. The phrasal verb *throw out* consists of the verb *throw* and the particle *out;* it means to dispose of something.

More about ▶▶▶
Verbs and verb
phrases, 664–85

phrasal vb. ⎯ particle
▶ Segundo **threw out** his old notebook.

verb
▶ Segundo **threw** his old notebook on his bed.

The meaning of a verb-and-particle combination differs from the meaning of the same words in a verb-and-preposition combination. The phrasal verb *look up,* for example, means to consult or find something in a reference work, which is different from the meaning of *look* followed by a phrase that happens to begin with the preposition *up.*

connect
mhconnectcomposition.com
Additional resources: QL44002

phrasal vb.
PHRASAL VERB Svetlana **looked up** the word in the dictionary.

verb prep.
VERB WITH PREPOSITIONS Svetlana **looked up** the steep trail and began to hike.

A transitive phrasal verb is **_separable_** if its direct object can fall either between the verb and the particle (separating them) or after the particle.

dir. obj.
▶ She **looked up** the address online.

dir. obj.
▶ She **looked** the address **up** online.

If the direct object of a separable phrasal verb is a pronoun, it must come between the verb and the particle.

it in.
I decided to hand ~~in it.~~
 ʌ

A phrasal verb is **_inseparable_** if no words can fall between the verb and the particle.

FAULTY I came an old photo across in the drawer.

REVISED I came across an old photo in the drawer.

The meaning of a phrasal verb changes when the particle changes (see the Quick Reference box on the next page). The phrasal verb *take on,* for example, means "to assume responsibility for."

▶ She **took on** the editing of the newsletter.

Quick Reference → Some Common Phrasal Verbs and Their Meanings

SEPARABLE		INSEPARABLE	
ask out	invite for a date	**add up to**	total
calm down	make calm, be-come calm	**barge in on**	interrupt unannounced
give up	surrender	**call on**	visit, or ask for a response directly
hand in	submit		
hand out	distribute	**come across**	find accidentally
look up	find something in a reference work	**drop in**	visit unannounced
		get out of	evade an obligation, exit
put back	return to original position	**give in**	surrender
put down	criticize meanly; suppress	**grow up**	mature
		hint at	suggest
take back	return; retract	**look down on**	disdain
take off	remove	**look up to**	admire
take on	assume respon-sibility for	**put up with**	tolerate
		run into	encounter; collide
take up	begin a hobby or activity	**stand in for**	substitute for
throw out	dispose of	**turn up**	show up, arrive

The phrasal verb *take back,* in contrast, means "to return" or "to retract."

▶ She took all her overdue books back to the library.

connect

mhconnectcomposition.com
Online exercise: QL44101

→ EXERCISE **44.1** Using phrasal verbs correctly

Put a check by the sentences that use verbs and phrasal verbs in-correctly, and then revise those sentences so they are correct.

EXAMPLE

After the accident, the EMT calmed down ~~him~~. *him* ✓

∧

1. I hear that Lisa is sick. Who is going to stand in for her?

2. I cannot find my glasses. Have you come them across?

3. The instructor handed the assignment out yesterday.

4. Is there any way for us to get this assignment out of?

5. If you do not understand a word, look up it.

6. That jacket looks too warm. Why don't you take off it?

7. Will you take these back to the store?

8. I ran an old friend into at the movie theater.

44b Using Gerunds and Infinitives after Verbs and Prepositions

A **gerund** is the *-ing* form of a verb used as a noun (*listening, eating*). An **infinitive** is the base form of a verb preceded by *to* (*to listen, to eat*).

1. Gerunds and infinitives after verbs

- Only gerunds can follow some verbs, and only infinitives can follow others.

  ▶ The committee recommended ~~to submit~~ *submitting* the proposal for a vote.

  ▶ Rosa Parks refused ~~sitting~~ *to sit* in the back of the bus.

- Some verbs can be followed by either gerunds or infinitives. For some of these verbs, the choice of gerund or infinitive has little effect on meaning, but for a few the difference is significant.

  SAME MEANING
  The economy *continued* to grow.
  The economy *continued* growing.

  DIFFERENT MEANINGS
  Juan *remembered* to email his paper to his professor.
  [He didn't forget to do it.]

  Juan *remembered* emailing his paper to his professor.
  [He recalled having done it already.]

- Some verbs that can be followed by an infinitive can also be followed by an infinitive after an intervening noun or pronoun.

  ▶ Yue *wanted* <u>to study</u> the violin.

  ▶ Yue's parents *wanted <u>her</u>* <u>to study</u> the violin.

Certain verbs, however, take an infinitive only after an object noun or pronoun.

  ▶ The candidate *urged <u>citizens</u>* <u>to vote</u> on Election Day.

A few verbs (for example, *feel, have, hear, let, look at,* and *see*) require an **unmarked infinitive**—the base verb alone, without *to*—after an intervening noun or pronoun.

Quick **Reference** ➡ **Gerund or Infinitive after Selected Verbs**

Some verbs that can be directly followed by a gerund but not an infinitive

admit	discuss	imagine	practice	risk
avoid	enjoy	mind	quit	suggest
consider	escape	miss	recall	tolerate
deny	finish	postpone	resist	understand

Some verbs that can be directly followed by an infinitive but not a gerund

agree	claim	hope	offer	refuse
appear	decide	manage	plan	wait
ask	expect	mean	pretend	want
beg	have	need	promise	wish

Some verbs that can be directly followed by a gerund or an infinitive with little effect on meaning

begin	hate	love	start
continue	like	prefer	

Some verbs for which choice of gerund or infinitive affects meaning

forget	remember	stop	try

Some verbs that take an infinitive only after an intervening noun or pronoun

advise	command	force	persuade	tell
allow	convince	instruct	remind	urge
cause	encourage	order	require	warn

▸ Paolo let his children ~~to go~~ *go* to the movies.

▸ Jen heard a dog ~~to bark~~ *bark* late at night.

2. Gerunds after prepositions

Only a gerund, not an infinitive, can be the object of a preposition.

▸ The article is about ~~to travel~~ *traveling* in South America.

44c Using Participles as Adjectives

Both the present participle and the past participle of a verb can function as adjectives, but they convey different meanings, especially if the base verb refers to an emotion or state of mind such as anger or boredom. The **present participle** (or *-ing* form) usually describes the cause or agent of a state of affairs. The **past participle** (the *-ed* form in regular verbs) usually describes the result of the state of affairs.

> **More about** ▸▸▸
> Regular and irregular
> verb forms, 664–69

State of Affairs	Cause	Result
verb	adj.	adj.
Physics class <u>bored</u> me today.	The class was bor<u>ing</u>.	I was bor<u>ed</u>.
verb	adj.	adj.
Dr. Sung's lecture <u>interested</u> me.	The lecture was interest<u>ing</u>.	I was interest<u>ed</u>.

connect
mhconnectcomposition.com
Additional resources: QL44003

> **EXERCISE 44.2** Using gerunds, infinitives, and participial
> adjectives

connect
mhconnectcomposition.com
Online exercise: QL44102

Use the verbs in parentheses to correctly complete each sentence. The first one is done as an example. Some may have more than one correct solution.

1. That movie was really <u>*boring*</u> (bore). I fell asleep after twenty minutes.

2. Juan was _____ (astonish) to see a rare bird in his backyard.

3. Martine advised Hugo _____ (see) the museum exhibit. Our father begged us not _____ (drive) there in the icy weather.

4. We had to postpone _____ (give) our parents an anniversary party because my mother had to work Saturday.

5. We enjoy _____ (cook) for our friends.

6. The customer inquired about _____ (purchase) a new microwave oven.

7. Nikolai admitted _____ (borrow) his roommate's computer without _____ (ask).

8. Mike continued _____ (watch) TV during dinner.

9. The sergeant commanded the advancing troops _____ (march) up the hill.

Quick Reference → Modals and Meaning

Modals	Meaning	Examples
can, could	Used to indicate ability, possibility, and willingness and to request or grant permission	Sam <u>can</u> paint wonderful watercolors. [ability]
		You <u>can</u> leave class early today. [grant permission]
		<u>Could</u> we meet at the library? [request permission]
		I'm so hungry I <u>could</u> eat a horse. [possibility]
		I <u>could</u> work your shift if you need me to. [willingness]
may, might	Used to request and grant permission and to offer suggestions. For requests, *might* has a more hesitant and polite connotation than *may*, but they are otherwise usually interchangeable.	<u>May</u> I see the comments you wrote? [request permission]
		<u>Might</u> I borrow your car this afternoon? [more polite request for permission]
		It <u>may/might</u> rain this afternoon. [possibility]
		You <u>may/might</u> want to bring an umbrella. [suggestion]
must	Expresses necessity, prohibition (in the negative), and logical probability	Passengers <u>must</u> pass through airport security before boarding. [necessity]
		Passengers <u>must not</u> leave their seats while the seatbelt sign is illuminated. [prohibition]
		We <u>must</u> be on our final approach. [logical probability]

44d Using Helping Verbs for Verb Formation

Most English verb constructions, other than the present and past tenses, consist of a main verb with one or more helping (auxiliary) verbs. The main verb carries the principal meaning, and the helping verbs carry information about time, mood, and voice. There are two kinds of helping verb: simple and modal.

More about ▶▶▶
Verb forms, 664–73
Subject-verb agreement, 646–57

- The simple helping verbs—*have, do,* and *be*—also function as main verbs, and like other main verbs, they change form to indicate person and tense.

- The modal helping verbs—including *can, could, may, might, must, ought to, shall, should, will,* and *would*—carry information about attributes of the main verb such as ability, intention, permission, possibility, desire, and suggestion (see the Quick Reference box below). Unlike the simple auxiliaries,

Modals	Meaning	Examples
shall, should, ought to	*Should* and *ought to* express advisability and expectation, usually interchangeably. *Shall* expresses intention as well as advisability, but in American English it usually appears only in questions.	Shall/Should we eat in or go out for dinner tonight? [advisability] We should/ought to eat out less to save money. [advisability] The pizza should/ought to arrive in 20 minutes or so. [expectation]
will, would	*Will* expresses intention, willingness, and expectation. *Would* expresses intention, willingness, typical or repeated action, and logical assumption, and it is also used for polite requests.	I will finish the laundry if you want. [willingness] I will apply to graduate school next year. [intention] The bus will arrive soon. [expectation] Would you mind opening the window? [request] Amalia decided she would apply to graduate school. [intention] When preparing dinner, he would always clean up as he cooked. [repeated action] That alarm you're hearing would be the monthly test of the emergency system. [logical probability]

the modal auxiliaries do not change form to indicate number or tense.

▶ All the contestants at the Olympics can swim fast, but Michael

           can
Phelps ~~cans~~ swim faster than any of the others.
       ∧

                                   should have worked
▶ William should work all day today, and he ~~shoulded work~~
                                          ∧

yesterday too.

NOTE When you hear such contractions as *should've* or *could've* in speech (or similar contractions with other modals), remember that the contracted word is *have* (*should have, could have*), not *of.*

———————

■ In a verb phrase, auxiliaries almost always precede the main verb, and modals precede any other auxiliaries.

                  auxiliaries   main verb
             modal   simple
▶ In June, Chen **will**   **have been**   living in Seattle for ten years.

■ When forming verbs, include needed auxiliaries.

        is
▶ Demetrio taking six courses this semester.
      ∧

             have
▶ My grandparents been visiting Scotland every year.
           ∧

■ In general, never follow a modal with another modal, and always follow a modal with the base form of a simple auxiliary or main verb.

                 be able to
▶ Tomás should ~~can~~ finish his calculus homework before the
              ∧

movie starts.

▶ Yuki must ~~to~~ take three more courses to graduate.

➔ **EXERCISE 44.3 Using modal auxiliaries**

The following email message has six errors in the use of modals and auxiliaries. Edit the message to correct these errors. The first error has been found for you.

Hi Mario,

I hope everything is going well. I~am~ writing to ask you a favor. We want to organize an auction for the baseball team. If you might could contribute a little time, that would to be great! We need someone who cans contact potential donors, assign starting bids for items, and mail out publicity. We think we might raise as much as $10,000 for team uniforms if we can get enough volunteers. I really hope you will to help us out. Do you think you come on Saturday for a short meeting?

Thanks in advance!

Bill

Make It **Your Own**

Review a recent piece of writing you completed for one of your classes. Print a new copy and circle all the verbs, gerunds, infinitives, and participial adjectives. Note any that you find confusing or that were marked by your instructor as incorrectly used. Make notes about their correct use by consulting this book, your instructor, or your college writing center.

Work **Together**

The use of modals affects how polite (or impolite) a piece of writing is considered to be. Working with a partner, consider the following pairs of sentences. Decide which in each pair is more polite, and discuss why. Does it depend on your audience? Be prepared to discuss your conclusions with your class.

1. a. Can you open the window?
   b. Would you mind opening the window?
2. a. Might I have a bite of your cake? It looks delicious.
   b. Could I have a bite of your cake?
3. a. Can I get a letter of recommendation from you?
   b. May I ask you to write me a letter of recommendation?

45 Managing Adjectives and Adverbs

by Ted E. Johnston and M. E. Sokolik

connect

mhconnectcomposition.com
Additional resources: QL45001

Just as a coat of paint can change our perception of the surface it covers, adjectives and adverbs color our understanding of the words they modify. **Adjectives** modify nouns and pronouns. **Adverbs** modify verbs, adjectives, other adverbs, and entire phrases, clauses, and sentences. This chapter will help you use adjectives and adverbs correctly and place them appropriately in your sentences.

45a Placing Adjectives in the Proper Order

Linking verbs *Be* and other verbs that express a state of being rather than an action and connect a subject to its subject complement (615)

- Most English adjectives have only one form, regardless of whether the noun they modify is singular or plural.

  ▶ Serena wants a <u>white</u> dress, but many of these <u>white</u> dresses are not to her liking.

- English adjectives usually come before a noun (*Serena has a white dress*) or after a **linking verb** (*Serena's dress is white*).

More about ▶▶▶
Articles and other determiners, 748–54
Cumulative vs. coordinate adjectives, 789–90

- When multiple adjectives cumulatively modify the same noun, the kind of information they convey determines their proper order (see the Quick Reference box below).

Quick Reference ➡️ **Putting Cumulative Adjectives in Standard Order**

Article or other determiner	Overall evaluation or opinion	Size	Shape or other intrinsic aspect	Age	Color	Essence: nationality, material, or purpose	Noun
two		big			red	rubber	balls
an	exciting			new		mystery	novel
my		tiny	helpless	newborn			kitten
those	funny			old	black and white		sitcoms
the	delicious		round			French	pastry

45b Choosing the Correct Prepositions with Adjectives

On a particular day, you might be excited *by* a lecture, mad *at* a friend, or happy *about* the election in Pakistan. As these phrases reveal, you need to be careful when combining adjectives and prepositions. When in doubt, consult a dictionary to make sure you are using the proper idiom. The editing in

Getting It Across **Avoid Too Many Adjectives in Front of a Noun**

More than three adjectives in a sequence can be awkward. Instead, vary your sentences to distribute the adjectives without confusing your readers.

More about ▶▶▶
Prepositions, 773–80

the following paragraph gives additional examples of correct idiomatic usage:

with
Ally is delighted ~~in~~ her midterm grades. She had been nervous *about* ~~of~~ flunk-

to
ing biochemistry. Ally is grateful ~~at~~ her instructors. When she struggled,

in *of*
they were not disappointed ~~at~~ her, and they were proud ~~about~~ her when

to
she succeeded. She is dedicated ~~with~~ completing her nursing degree.

> **EXERCISE 45.1 Using adjectives correctly**

Correct problems with adjective order or prepositions used after adjectives in the following sentences. (The Quick Reference box on p. 767 will help you with some of these.) If a sentence has no problems, circle its number.

EXAMPLE

new
The ~~new~~ ridiculous parking regulations are hurting students financially.

connect
mhconnectcomposition.com
Online exercise: QL45101

1. In our old cozy kitchen, we had a blue round table.

2. The professor gave a historical lengthy overview World War II.

3. The mayor is devoted for eliminating gang violence in our city.

4. There used to be a beige big leather sofa in the waiting room.

5. The lawyer's final pathetic defense of his client was embarrassing.

6. Everyone should be alarmed with global warming.

7. My economical new hybrid car helps me cope with the price of gas.

8. The witness said he saw a green old van leave the scene of the crime.

9. That gray-haired wise doctor still maintains a practice private.

10. The residents are worried from the possibility of another hurricane.

45c   Placing Adverbs Correctly

- An adverb cannot be located between a verb and its object.

connect
mhconnectcomposition.com
Additional resources: QL45002

  ▶ Susan plays ~~beautifully~~ the piano. *beautifully.*

  In this sentence, *beautifully* fits correctly only at the end, after *piano,* the direct object.

- Many adverbs, primarily those related to time (such as *often* and *frequently*), may be placed either before the subject or verb or after the direct object.

  ▶ *Recently,* Susan learned ~~recently~~ a new concerto.

  ▶ Susan learned ~~recently~~ *recently* a new concerto.

  ▶ Susan learned ~~recently~~ a new concerto. *recently.*

- When a main verb has no helping verbs, the adverb should precede it. When the main verb has helping verbs, the adverb should usually be placed between the first helper and the main verb.

  ▶ Carla <u>carelessly</u> *wasted* gas by leaving the motor running.

  ▶ Carla ~~carelessly~~ *has been wasting* gas by leaving the motor running. *carelessly*

  Some adverbs (but not all) can be placed between the second helper and the main verb.

  ▶ Carla ~~carelessly~~ has been wasting gas by leaving the motor running. *carelessly*

- In most instances, place an adverb first if it modifies the entire sentence.

  ▶ <u>Surprisingly,</u> she has decided to change her major to psychology.

- When certain negative adverbs or adverb phrases begin a sentence, they require a change in the standard subject-verb

More about ▶▶▶
Inverted word
  order when certain
  negative adverbs
  start a sentence,
  744–45

order. Included in this group are *not only, at no time, never, rarely,* and *seldom.*

▶ Seldom I ~~have~~ $\overset{have}{\wedge}$ been so proud of my brother.

EXERCISE 45.2 Putting adverbs in the right place

Correct any adverb placement problems in the following sentences. Circle the number of any sentences that are already correct.

connect
mhconnectcomposition.com
Online exercise: QL45102

EXAMPLE

$\overset{unintentionally}{}$
The doctor gave me ~~unintentionally~~ the wrong information.
$\wedge$

1. The children played fast and furiously the game and then fell instantly asleep.

2. Sam is doing well in math now that he is doing diligently the homework.

3. Seldom does the manager promote new employees so quickly.

4. We should consider always the suggestions of our employees rather than implementing suddenly changes.

5. Not only Tom works on Saturday, but also on Sunday.

6. Little Ralph has sadly never learned to read.

7. The judge soon should make his decision.

8. Do you really think that Ivan treats Martha unfairly?

45d Dealing with Confusing Adverbs

Certain English adverbs seem similar but actually have significantly different connotations and functions. Often-confused words include *too* with *so, too* with *either, not* with *no, hard* with *hardly,* and *such* with *so.*

1. *Too* and *so*

To give an adjective a negative or more negative meaning, use *too* in most instances. To intensify any adjective, use *so* or *very* or a similar adverb.

▶ The professor realized her first test had been ~~so~~ ^{too} difficult and was
surpriosed to find us still ~~too~~ ^{so} excited about the class.

2. *Too* and *either*

When following up a statement about one subject's action with a statement about another subject's doing likewise, use *either* after a verb that is grammatically negative (as with *not* or *never* or *won't* or *hasn't*), and use *too* after a verb that is grammatically positive. Remember that unless verbs such as *avoided* or *refused* are used with a negative adverb (such as *not*), they are grammatically positive, even though by themselves they have negative meanings.

▶ Floyd <u>didn't join</u> the fraternity, and I <u>didn't, either</u>.
Neither one joined.

▶ Floyd <u>joined</u> the fraternity, and I <u>did, too</u>.
Both joined.

▶ Floyd <u>refused to join</u>, and I <u>did, too</u>.
Neither one joined.

▶ Floyd <u>didn't refuse to join</u>, and I <u>didn't, either</u>.
Both were willing to join.

3. *Not* and *no*

Because *no* is an adjective, it can only modify a noun. The adverb *not*, however, can modify an adjective, a verb, or another adverb. The expression *not a* (*an*) can replace the adjective *no* in front of a noun.

▶ Keith is ~~no~~ ^{not} friendly. Because he will ~~no~~ ^{not} talk to me, he is ~~not~~ ^{no (or not a)} friend
of mine.

4. *Hard* and *hardly*

The word *hard* can be either an adjective or an adverb. As an adverb, it means *intensely* or *with great effort*. The adverb *hardly* means *just a little* or *almost not at all*.

▶ Juan got an A after he studied <u>hard</u> for the exam. Laura got a D
because she <u>hardly</u> looked at her notes.

5. *Such* and *so*

Such a (an), *such,* or *so* can emphasize a type or a quality. Use *such a (an)* before an adjective that precedes a concrete noun: *She is such a wise person.* Use *such* by itself directly in front of an abstract noun: *Such wisdom is rare.* To intensify any freestanding adjective, as in the case of a subject complement, use *so: She is so wise.*

> ### EXERCISE **45.3 Correcting easily confused adverbs**
> Correct any adverb errors in the following sentences, and circle the number of those sentences that have no errors.

EXAMPLE

either.

Jack didn't go to the party, and I didn't too.
                                            ∧

1. We worked hardly on this project, and all we got was a C.
2. We don't feel guilty about this decision, and you shouldn't, too.
3. The waiters here are so slow; we may never get our food.
4. Mark is not millionaire, but he is so generous person.
5. I really admire that she helps her elderly parents too much.
6. We have come so far to give up now.

▲ Make It **Your Own**

Review a text that you were assigned to read in one of your classes, and find examples of cumulative adjectives used before a noun. Look for strings of two, three, or more adjectives not separated from one another by commas, being sure to include any noun determiners. Use the Quick Reference box on p. 767 to account for the order in which the adjectives appear. Do any examples violate the usual order?

Work **Together** ◀

Join with several other students and compare the examples of cumulative adjectives you analyzed in the Make It Your Own exercise above. Consult your instructor if your group disagrees about the analysis of any of the examples.

46

Using Prepositions

by Ted E. Johnston and M. E. Sokolik

OVER

AERIAL AND UNDERWATER PHOTOGRAPHS BY LOUIS HELBIG AND RIC FRAZIER

UNDER

Prepositions are words that specify a relationship between other words or phrases. They usually combine with nouns, pronouns, or noun phrases to form *prepositional phrases.* In the sentence "I found my socks under the washing machine," for example, *under the washing machine* is a prepositional phrase introduced by the preposition *under.*

To help you learn to use prepositions correctly, this chapter explains how to identify prepositions (46a), how to determine the function they serve (46b), and how to use them correctly (46c and d).

46a Recognizing Prepositions

Although there are fewer than one hundred single-word prepositions in use in English, many additional multiword prepositions function in similar ways. The Quick Reference box on the next page lists some of the most common of both.

→ EXERCISE 46.1 Recognizing prepositions

Identify the prepositional phrases in the following sentences. Underline the prepositional phrase, and circle each preposition.

connect

mhconnectcomposition.com
Online exercise: QL46101

EXAMPLE

A small air carrier might assume responsibility (for) the freight (from) the customer.

1. The Dehkhoda Institute, which is devoted to the teaching of Farsi, was founded in 1945.

2. The black-backed jackal is an African canine with a foxlike appearance.

3. The first cricket test match was played in 1877 between Australia and England.

4. In November, snow fell on the coast, which is rare so early in the season.

5. The citywide depression lasted for two centuries, through famine and war, until the 1990s.

Quick **Reference** → **Common Single-Word and Multiword Prepositions**

Single-Word Prepositions

about	beneath	like	to
above	beside	near	toward
across	between	of	under
after	by	off	underneath
against	down	on	until
along	during	onto	up
among	except	out	upon
around	for	outside	with
at	from	over	within
before	in	past	without
behind	inside	since	
below	into	through	

Multiword Prepositions

according to	by means of	in front of	on account of
ahead of	close to	in place of	on behalf of
as far as	due to	in spite of	on top of
as to	far from	inside of	out of
as well as	in accordance with	instead of	outside of
aside from	in addition to	near to	
because of	in case of	next to	

46b The Functions of Prepositions

Every preposition has multiple possible functions depending on the context in which it occurs. As a result, it is often easier to understand prepositions in terms of their function than to try to memorize what each one means.

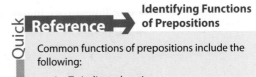

Quick Reference → Identifying Functions of Prepositions

Common functions of prepositions include the following:

1. To indicate *location*
2. To indicate *time*
3. To indicate *condition* or *degree*
4. To specify *cause* or *reason*
5. To designate *possession, attribute,* or *origin*

The most basic use for a preposition is to indicate *location.* Other important functions are to indicate *time,* to indicate *condition* or *degree,* to specify *cause* or *reason,* and to designate *possession, attribute,* or *origin.*

1. Location

The most basic prepositions for indicating the location of things are *at, on,* and *in.*

- *At* specifies a general point of orientation.

  ▶ Meet me at the station.

- *On* specifies contact between two things.

  ▶ The book is on the table.
  ▶ The clipboard hangs on the wall.

- *In* specifies that one thing is contained within another.

  ▶ The solution is in the beaker.
  ▶ Liz is in San Francisco.

NOTE Many locations operate like *surfaces* or *containers.* Generally, use *in* for locations that seem like containers and *on* for locations that seem like surfaces.

CONTAINER	He sat in his car. [**Not:** *He sat on his car,* which would mean he was on top of it.]
SURFACE	He sat on the bus. [Buses, trains, and airplanes are usually considered surfaces because people can walk around on them.]
CONTAINER	We walked in the hallway.
SURFACE	We walked on the sidewalk.

2. Time

The most common prepositions for relating things to a moment in or period of time are *at, in, on,* and *by.*

- *At* designates a particular point in time.
  - ▶ Let's meet at 4:00.
  - ▶ The party ended at midnight.

- *In* can designate either a future time or a particular period.
  - ▶ I'll leave in 10 minutes.
  - ▶ We'll finish the job in April.

- *On* designates a particular day or date.
  - ▶ His birthday is on Friday.
  - ▶ Her birthday is on the twelfth.

- *By* indicates *no later than.*
  - ▶ Turn in your essay by 3:00 p.m.
  - ▶ They decided to leave by 5:00 a.m. to avoid rush hour.

3. Condition / Degree

Prepositions of condition or degree indicate the state of the object. Some common prepositions in this category are *of, on, in, about,* and *around.*

- *In* or *on* can specify a condition. These uses are often idiomatic.
  - ▶ The house is on fire.
  - ▶ She is on vacation.
  - ▶ Charlie is not in trouble.
  - ▶ Darlene left her desk in perfect order.

- *Of* is used in phrases indicating fractions or portions.
  - ▶ Three of the books are required for the course.
  - ▶ One of those coats is mine.

- *Around* or *about* can indicate approximation.
  - ▶ That book costs around twenty dollars.
  - ▶ I walked about ten miles.

4. Cause / Reason

Prepositions showing cause include *from, of, for,* and *because of.*

- *From* indicates cause or explains a condition.
  - ▶ We were wet from the rain.
  - ▶ We were tired from walking all day.

- *For* often indicates a cause and answers the question *Why?*

  ▶ Oregon is famous for its forests.
  ▶ He got an award for selling more cars than anyone else.

- *Of* and *because of* both show a reason.

  ▶ The patient died of pneumonia.
  ▶ I sneezed because of my cold.

5. Possession / Attribute / Origin

The most common prepositions showing possession, attribute, or origin are *of, from,* and *with.*

- Possession is typically shown with *of.*

  ▶ That song is one of Wilco's.
  ▶ The composer of the song is Jay Bennett.

- An attribute can be indicated by *with.*

  ▶ He was a man with real talent.
  ▶ He is the one with the red beard.

- *From* can show origin.

  ▶ Bennet was from Illinois.
  ▶ The CD came from a website.

NOTE Indicating possession with *of* instead of *'s* or *s'* is often awkward.

AWKWARD   the bike of Bob

PREFERRED   Bob's bike

> EXERCISE **46.2** Determining the function of a preposition

Write in the function of the underlined preposition in the space to the right of each sentence. Choose from *Location, Time, Condition/ Degree, Cause/Reason,* or *Possession/Attribute/Origin.*

connect
mhconnectcomposition.com
Online exercise: QL46102

EXAMPLE
She bought the car <u>with</u> greater fuel efficiency. <u>attribute</u>

1. The construction will be completed <u>in</u> 2012. _____
2. In 1946, Margolin moved <u>to</u> Lebanon. _____
3. Bellatrix is described as a tall woman <u>with</u> pale skin. _____
4. Let's meet <u>at</u> the library to study tonight. _____
5. We were dying <u>of</u> thirst. _____

6. He's having a birthday party <u>in</u> July. _____

7. Hearing loss is estimated to begin <u>at</u> age 30. _____

8. There are no students <u>from</u> Japan here. _____

46c Using Prepositions Correctly

Certain verbs or nouns will suggest the use of particular prepositions. It may help to memorize these phrases:

▶ *give* something <u>*to*</u> someone

▶ *take* something <u>*from*</u> someone

▶ *sell* something <u>*to*</u> someone

▶ *buy* something <u>*from*</u> someone

▶ *lend* something <u>*to*</u> someone

▶ *borrow* something <u>*from*</u> someone

▶ get *married* or *engaged* <u>*to*</u> someone

▶ *fill* something <u>*with*</u> something

▶ *shout* <u>*to*</u> someone (in greeting)

▶ *shout* <u>*at*</u> someone (in anger)

> **More about ▶▶▶**
> Passive voice,
> 560–61, 682–83
> Direct and indirect
> objects, 616,
> 741–43

In addition, some prepositions serve a particular grammatical function. For example, in passive constructions, the preposition *by* identifies who or what did something.

▶ The car was repaired by Pat.

Similarly, indirect objects, when placed after rather than before a direct object, are usually preceded by *to:*

▶ Theo gave the present to his father.

connect
mhconnectcomposition.com
Online exercise: QL46103

→ **EXERCISE 46.3** Using prepositions correctly

Insert the correct preposition into the blanks below. In some cases, more than one preposition may be acceptable.

EXAMPLE

He came *from* a small village *in* the middle *of* the country.

1. Our sense ___ identity—___ who we are and what we have done—is tied ___ our memories.

2. *The Big Knife* is a 1955 film directed and produced ___ Robert Aldrich and based ___ the play ___ Clifford Odets.

3. Ronald and Reginald Kray were identical twin brothers and the foremost organized crime leaders ___ London ___ the 1950s and 1960s.

4. The original manuscripts ___ Oscar Wilde today are found ___ many collections, but ___ far the largest collection is found ___ the William Andrews Clark Memorial Library ___ UCLA.

5. Tortell is a Catalan pastry stuffed ___ marzipan, which ___ some special occasions is topped ___ glazed fruit. It is traditionally eaten ___ January 6.

46d Necessary and Unnecessary Prepositions

Unfortunately, there is no rule of grammar to tell when a preposition is needed. Consider these examples:

▶ I like to listen ^to^ music.

▶ She was looking ^at^ the book.

Similarly, there is no rule to tell when one is not needed:

▶ ~~In~~ ^One^ ~~one~~ block from the school, there is a coffee shop.

▶ We were discussing ~~about~~ climate change in class.

To make things more complicated, sometimes a phrase is acceptable with or without a preposition.

▶ I've lived here for six years.

▶ I've lived here six years.

One strategy for mastering these usages, some of them idiomatic, is to notice in your reading when you encounter unfamiliar constructions involving prepositions. Some students keep a grammar log or other notebook to help them remember these constructions.

connect
mhconnectcomposition.com
Online exercise: QL46104

→ **EXERCISE 46.4 Distinguishing between necessary and unnecessary prepositions**

Correct the following passage for preposition usage. Cross out any prepositions that are not needed, insert any that are missing, and leave unchanged any that are correctly used. There are thirteen preposition errors in the passage, not including the one in the example.

EXAMPLE

Flip the Frog is an animated cartoon character created ~~by~~ an American

cartoonist, Ub Iwerks, who also helped ~~with~~ ^to create another famous

character—Mickey Mouse.

Flip starred a series cartoons distributed by MGM from 1930 to 1933. Apart Flip, the series had many other characters, including Flip's dog and a mule named of Orace.

Flip's first appearance was in a cartoon called by *Night*. Iwerks animated this short feature while working his friend Walt Disney in 1930. After a number disagreements between them, Iwerks left Disney and went on to accept an offer to open a cartoon studio his own a salary of $300 a week. Disney at the time couldn't match with this offer. The first cartoon series Iwerks was expected to create featured on a character called Tony the Frog, but Iwerks didn't like the name and had it changed Flip.

▲ Make It **Your Own**

In a paper you have recently written or are now writing, look for preposition errors. How many do you find? What functions of these prepositions do you recognize (location, time, etc.)? How would you fix the errors?

Work **Together** ◀

For a paper you have recently written or are now writing, exchange texts with a classmate and analyze your classmate's writing for prepositional errors. How many do you find? How would you correct them? (If your partner is a native speaker of English, you may find very few errors. If this is the case, note any preposition usages that are unfamiliar to you and discuss their meaning with your partner.) Be prepared to discuss what you gained from this exercise.

Part Ten

Detail
Matters

Punctuation and Mechanics

47

Using Commas

Commas function as dividers within—but not between—sentences: Think of each sentence as a room. If the periods are walls between these rooms, then the commas are screens used to make subdivisions within them. As a screen might set off a dressing area from a larger bedroom, so a comma sets off information within the main sentence. As a screen might divide a work space into offices, so commas mark divisions between independent clauses. Problems with commas can be caused not only by omitting them but also by inserting them where they are *not* needed: Imagine having a screen in your kitchen between your stove and refrigerator.

The rules for comma placement are fairly straightforward. A list of the rules writers use most often appears in the Quick Reference box on the next page.

Quick **Reference** ➡ **Common Comma Do's and Don'ts**

Do use a comma . . .

. . . to separate independent clauses joined by a coordinating conjunction. 784

              independent clause   coord.
                                     conj.   independent clause

▶ Hip-hop music was born in the 1970s, but it continues to flourish.

. . . to set off introductory elements from an independent clause. 785

          subordinate clause   independent clause

▶ Although it was born in New York City, rap has become popular around the world.

. . . to separate three or more items in a series. 788

                                          ①   ②

▶ Some early hip-hop artists include Afrika Bambaataa, Grandmaster Flash,
   ③   ④
Run DMC, and LL Cool J.

. . . to separate coordinate (but not cumulative) adjectives. 789

                          coordinate adjectives

▶ Hip-hop soon grew to have a huge, enthusiastic audience outside the New York club scene.

. . . to set off nonessential elements. 791

                          nonessential clause

▶ Afrika Bambaataa, who adopted the name of a Zulu chieftain, formed Zulu Nation to attract kids toward hip-hop and away from gangs.

Do *not* use a comma . . .

. . . following a coordinating or subordinating conjunction. 784, 786

▶ Run DMC is popular enough to be featured on the game *Guitar Hero,*
   sub. conj.
although, the songs the group plays are by the band Aerosmith.

. . . to separate paired elements. 784

▶ Even scholars are writing about hip-hop music, and culture.

. . . to separate independent clauses not joined by a coordinating conjunction. 784

▶ LL Cool J's 1985 *Radio* was perhaps the first mainstream rap hit, it went platinum within five months.

. . . preceding the first item or following the last item in a series. 788

                                          ①   ②   ③

▶ Hip-hop has also merged with musical styles such as, hip house, nu soul, reggaetón,
   ④
and merenrap, to create exciting sounds.

. . . between a subject and its verb or a verb and its object or complement. 797

          subj   verb   direct obj.

▶ LL Cool J, has had, eight platinum records in a row since then.

Writing Responsibly   **Commas and Clarity**

Like Alice in Wonderland, most of us aim to say what we mean and mean what we say. But sometimes in writing an incorrect use of commas can have us saying something we do not mean (or meaning something we do not say). Consider this example, with and without commas:

This sentence . . .	*means . . .*
Writing to my mother is a terrible chore.	I find writing to my mother a real pain!
Writing, to my mother, is a terrible chore.	My mother finds writing a real pain!

You have a responsibility to your reader to look carefully at your use of commas when editing a document; ask yourself, "Do I mean what I say and say what I mean?" If not, correct your use of commas.

47a   Using Commas in Compound Sentences

Quick Reference →

The Seven Coordinating Conjunctions

and	but	or	nor
for	so	yet	

Compound sentence Two or more independent clauses linked by a comma and a coordinating conjunction or a semicolon (624)

Independent clause A word group that includes a subject and a predicate that can stand alone as a sentence (620)

In a ***compound sentence*** a comma and ***coordinating conjunction*** work together: The comma marks the break between the two ***independent clauses,*** and the coordinating conjunction joins them into a single sentence. When a coordinating conjunction combines two independent clauses, place a comma *before* it (not *after* it):

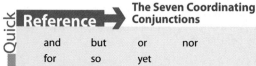

 ▶ My heart is in San Francisco, but my body is in New York.

NOTE Unless readers will be confused, the comma can be omitted when the two independent clauses are very short:

 ▶ I sing in Italian but I speak only English.

Do not use a comma before the conjunction if both parts cannot stand on their own as sentences:

>   independent clause   verb phrase
 ▶ My accountant left the country, and took my bank balance

with him.

Paired items should not be separated by a comma:

> Both my purse, and my bank account are empty.

pairs (above "purse, and")

More about ▶▶▶
Comma splices,
637–45 (ch. 34)
Semicolons,
800–06 (ch. 48)

When the clauses are long and punctuated with commas already, readers might find the sentence clearer if you replace the comma before the coordinating conjunction with a semicolon:

> Comic books are gradually becoming more respectable as works of
> serious fiction, with graphic novels such as *Maus* and *Watchmen*
> earning tremendous critical acclaim; yet many people, including my
> girlfriend, refuse to take them seriously.

NOTE Without a coordinating conjunction, a comma between two independent clauses creates a ***comma splice.***

EXERCISE 47.1 Commas in compound sentences

Correct the sentences below by adding or deleting commas. (Some may already be correct!)

connect
mhconnectcomposition.com
Online exercise: QL47101

> EXAMPLE
>
> The dollar has dropped against the euro, so tourists have flocked to
>
> the United States to shop.

1. The U.S. dollar continues to be weak against both the euro, and the pound.

2. The yen remains strong against the U.S. dollar but it fell against the Australian dollar as markets opened this morning.

3. The yen, and the yuan are strengthening.

4. The currencies of Latin America continue to be weak relative to the euro, but they are holding their own against the U.S. dollar.

5. Japanese, and American travelers who visit Europe this summer will feel the pinch, but Australian, and Chinese visitors should find Europe a bargain.

47b Using a Comma after Introductory Elements

A word, phrase, or subordinate clause introducing an independent clause is usually followed by a comma. There are two exceptions:

- In an inverted sentence, where an introductory word group immediately precedes the verb

  introductory word group   verb
  ▶ **Into the deep, dark jungle marched** Dr. Livingston.

- Following an introductory word group that acts as the subject of the sentence

  subject   verb
  ▶ **Exploring deep, dark jungles is** what he does.

When the introductory element is very brief, some writers omit the comma. If readers might be confused, even for a moment, include it:

▶ Before eating ˏthe missionaries said grace.

1. Insert a comma after introductory clauses.

When a ***subordinate,*** or dependent, clause introduces an independent clause, place a comma between the two.

subordinate clause
▶ **Although Boythorn prided himself on his gruff demeanor,** he doted on his pet bird.

subordinate clause
▶ **Because his theories addressed the Great Depression,** John Maynard Keynes became the most influential economist of the 1930s.

2. Insert a comma after introductory phrases.

Insert a comma following an introductory ***phrase*** to signal the start of the main clause:

participial phrase
▶ **Lacking Mozart's natural abilities,** Salieri formed an obsessive hatred for his rival.

prepositional phrase
▶ **In an unguarded moment,** the politician muttered an unprintable phrase into the live microphone.

absolute phrase
▶ **A vegetarian for many years,** he suddenly craved bacon.

Subordinate clause
A word group that lacks a subject or predicate or that begins with a subordinating word or phrase; a word group that cannot stand alone as a sentence (621)

Phrase A group of related words that lacks a subject, predicate, or both; it cannot stand alone as a sentence, but it can function *in* a sentence as a noun, a verb, or a modifier (617)

> *More about* ▶▶▶
Participial phrases, 619–20
Prepositional phrases, 618
Absolute phrases, 620

connect
mhconnectcomposition.com
Online exercise: QL47102

> **EXERCISE 47.2 Commas after introductory elements**

Supply a comma as needed after introductory elements in the sentences below. (You will not need to add a comma in every sentence.)

EXAMPLE

With infection rates continuing to rise, developing nations in
southern Africa and around the world face shrinking populations.

1. With the advent of the AIDS epidemic around 1990 the rate of population growth in southern Africa has decreased substantially.

2. According to the U.S. Census Bureau population growth rates in Zimbabwe and South Africa are expected to drop 75 percent or more by 2010.

3. In fact life expectancies in Zimbabwe have already fallen by twenty-six years.

4. In the next decade, the population of southern Africa is expected to be smaller by 71 million people than it would have been without the AIDS epidemic.

5. Developing countries like Haiti and Cambodia sadly are also experiencing AIDS-related drops in population growth rates.

47c Using Commas to Set Off Conjunctive Adverbs and Most Transitional Phrases

Transitional expressions and *conjunctive adverbs* are usually set off by commas.

> The basking shark, in fact, consumes only zooplankton and small fish. It may end up as dinner for an orca or tiger shark, however.

When the transitional expression or conjunctive adverb is used to link independent clauses, place a semicolon before it.

> The whale shark is the largest fish in today's oceans; nevertheless, it presents no threat to humans.

Transitional expressions Words and phrases that show the relationship between sentences (61–62)
Conjunctive adverb A transitional expression that can link one independent clause to another; it modifies the second clause and specifies its relationship to the first (608)

47d Inserting Commas to Set Off Interjections, Contrasting Information, Expressions of Direct Address, Parenthetical and Conversational Expressions, and Tag Questions

interjection
▶ Wow‸ that wind farm is gorgeous!

interjection
▶ Some people‸ sadly‸ think the industrial look of a wind farm is ugly.

contrasting information
▶ The current energy situation requires us to revise‸ not cling to‸ traditional notions of beauty.

direct address
▶ Professor Kinney‸ how much do you know about offshore wind farming?

parenthetical
▶ The first U.S. offshore wind farm‸ it turns out‸ is on Nantucket Sound.

conversational
expression
▶ No‸ it isn't a single-handed solution to our energy problems.

tag
▶ Wind farms will make a big contribution‸ won't they?

connect
mhconnectcomposition.com
Additional resources: QL47001

47e Using Commas to Separate Items in a Series

Place a comma between items in a series of three or more.

▶ Our new house will feature solar panels‸ a hilltop windmill‸ and rainwater conversion.

Getting It Across

To Use or Not to Use the Serial Comma

British writers have more or less dispensed with the serial comma (except to avoid confusion), while Americans (except for journalists) continue to use it. When writing for a U.S. audience, use the serial comma.

Some writers omit the comma before the coordinating conjunction (*and* in this example) in a series, but readers may find the final comma helpful in distinguishing paired and unpaired elements. The managing editor of the *Chicago Manual of Style* likes to quote this hypothetical dedication, which highlights the potential problems that can be caused by omitting the serial comma:

▶ I dedicate this book to my parents, Mother Teresa and the Pope.

When the items in the series are long or contain internal commas, substituting semicolons for commas can make the sentence easier to read:

More about ▶▶▶
Using semicolons in
a series, 803–04

▶ Phillis Wheatley was born in Senegal in 1753, was sold into slavery

to a Boston, Massachusetts, family, studied Greek, Latin, and English,

and became the first published African American writer.

EXERCISE 47.3 Commas with conjunctive adverbs, transitional phrases, interrupting words and phrases, and items in a series

Supply commas as needed in the sentences below. (You will not need to add a comma in every sentence.)

connect
mhconnectcomposition.com
Online exercise: QL47103

EXAMPLE

My goodness, did I have a horrible cold last week!

1. I originally thought my sneezing was due to an allergy; however my doctor pointed out the difference between symptoms from an allergy and a cold.

2. A telltale sign for example is how quickly the symptoms develop.

3. Allergy symptoms start immediately, but cold symptoms, on the other hand, take a day or longer to develop and gradually worsen.

4. Allergies nearly always cause itchiness in the eyes nose and throat, while a cold usually does not.

5. My obvious cold symptoms according to my doctor were fever aches and chest congestion.

47f Using Commas to Separate Coordinate, Not Cumulative, Adjectives

Coordinate adjectives each modify the noun or pronoun they precede and are of equal weight; **cumulative adjectives,** on the other hand, modify not only the noun or pronoun they precede but also the next adjective in the series. Hence, the order of coordinate adjectives does not matter, but the order of cumulative adjectives does.

Reference ➡ **Testing for Coordinate and Cumulative Adjectives**

To determine whether two or more adjectives should be separated by a comma, try these two tests:

1. **Reverse the order.** If the meaning remains the same no matter what order they appear in, then the adjectives are coordinate, and you should insert a comma between them:

   Yes: sexy, exciting boyfriend =
        exciting, sexy boyfriend
   No: enormous shoulder bag ≠
        shoulder enormous bag

2. **Place the word *and* between the two adjectives.** If the phrase still makes sense, then the adjectives are coordinate, and you should put a comma between them:

   Yes: sexy and exciting boyfriend
   No: enormous and shoulder bag

Consider the example below:

coordinate adjectives

▶ The girl struggled to hide her brooding, moody nature from the

More about ▶▶▶
Adjective order, 767

coordinate adjectives

sympathetic, insightful child psychologist she visited weekly.

cumulative adjectives

While you could reverse *brooding* and *moody* or *insightful* and *sympathetic,* you could not reverse *insightful* and *child:* a *child insightful psychologist* does not make sense.

→ **EXERCISE 47.4 Commas with coordinate and cumulative adjectives**

Add commas as needed in the sentences below.

EXAMPLE

How likely is it that a curious, adventurous sixth grader will take up

smoking?

1. As part of a revealing new study, researchers interviewed 1,195 sixth graders and then spoke to them several times over the next four years.

2. The study suggested that two characteristics indicate a heightened identifiable risk level for becoming a smoker.

3. The clearest key indication for future smoking is that it is easy to get cigarettes.

4. The other demonstrated major characteristic is that young people tend to become smokers if they have friends who smoke.

5. Furthermore, combining these two characteristics is a strong indicative risk factor.

47g Using Commas to Set Off Nonessential Appositives, Phrases, and Clauses

Words, phrases, or clauses that add information to a sentence but do not identify the person, place, or thing being described are **nonessential** (or *nonrestrictive*) **elements** and are set off by commas from the rest of the sentence. Elements that identify the person, place, or thing being described are **essential** (or *restrictive*) and are *not* set off by commas. Consider the following sentence:

More about ▶▶▶
Essential and non-
essential elements,
634

essential   nonessential
▶ My co-worker Philip, whom I had never seen without a tie, arrived at the office this morning wearing a toga.

Philip picks out one co-worker from among the rest, so that element is essential. The nonessential clause—*whom I had never seen without a tie*—provides important information about Philip, but it does not identify him from among the writer's colleagues, so it is nonessential.

Compare the sentence above to this sentence:

nonessential
▶ My co-worker, Philip, showed up at work this morning wearing a toga.

In this sentence, *Philip* is set off by commas, suggesting that the writer has only one colleague, so identifying him by name is not essential.

1. Use commas with nonessential appositives.

An **appositive** renames a preceding noun phrase. When it identifies, or specifies, the noun phrase, it is essential and is not set off by commas:

Appositive A noun or noun phrase that renames the noun, pronoun, or noun phrase that precedes it (618)

noun phrase   essential
              appositive
▶ The Roman emperor Claudius suffered from an ailment that caused him to limp and to stammer uncontrollably.

In this case, *Claudius* distinguishes this Roman emperor from all the other Roman emperors, so it is essential and should not be set off by commas.

When the appositive adds information but does not identify, it is nonessential and is set off by commas.

> noun phrase   nonessential appositive
> ▶ The fourth Roman Emperor, Claudius, suffered from an ailment that caused him to limp and to stammer uncontrollably.

Because there was only one *fourth Roman emperor,* the name *Claudius* is nonessential.

2. Use commas with nonessential phrases.

A phrase that acts like an adjective, modifying a noun, pronoun, or noun phrase, can also be essential or nonessential: If it identifies what it is describing, then it is essential and should *not* be set off by commas; if it does not identify, then it is nonessential and *should* be set off by commas.

> noun   essential phrase
> ▶ Bismarck the master statesman has been replaced in some
>   noun   essential phrase
> history books by Bismarck the lucky diplomat.

> noun   nonessential phrase
> ▶ Otto von Bismarck, the Prussian statesman, successfully unified the German principalities into a single state.

3. Use commas with nonessential clauses.

A subordinate (or dependent) clause can also act like an adjective, modifying a noun, pronoun, or noun phrase. When it identifies the noun, pronoun, or noun phrase, it is essential and is *not* set off by commas; when it does not, it is nonessential and *is* set off by commas.

Adverb Clauses The placement of an adverb clause indicates whether it is essential or nonessential: If it appears at the beginning of the sentence, it is generally nonessential and set off by a comma; if it appears in the middle of the sentence, it is generally essential and is not set off by commas:

> nonessential adv. clause
> ▶ Because he found the politics required to win an Academy Award
>   noun
> demeaning, George C. Scott refused to accept an Oscar for his performance in the movie *Patton.*

noun
▶ George C. Scott refused to accept an Academy Award for his performance

essential adv. clause
in the movie *Patton* **because** he found the politics required to win an

Oscar demeaning.

That *Clauses versus* Which *Clauses* Subordinate clauses beginning with the word *that* are always essential and thus never set off by commas.

essential clause
▶ Produce **that has been genetically modified** differs from its non–GM

counterpart by a human-made alteration to its DNA.

The word *which,* on the other hand, is used today to introduce both essential and nonessential clauses:

nonessential clause
▶ Genetically modified produce, **which is sold in grocery stores**

throughout the United States, is still looked on with suspicion by

many consumers.

NOTE Some writers (and instructors), especially in the United States, believe *which* should be used exclusively with nonessential clauses.

EXERCISE 47.5 Commas with appositives, phrases, and clauses
Correct the errors in the following sentences by inserting or deleting commas as necessary.

connect
mhconnectcomposition.com
Online exercise: QL47105

EXAMPLE

Lyme Disease, a bacterial infection, was named for the town in

Connecticut where it was first identified.

1. The malady, Lyme Disease, is transmitted by deer ticks.

2. A person can become infected by deer ticks, that wait among tall grass for someone or something to latch onto.

3. When someone gets Lyme Disease he or she will sometimes develop a reddish rash that looks like a spreading bull's-eye.

4. Lyme Disease is difficult to diagnose because many people, who have it, do not remember getting bitten by a tick.

5. There is a good protective measure completely covering the arms and legs whenever walking in tall grass that can help a person avoid deer ticks and the Lyme Disease that they carry.

47h Using Commas with Quotations

> **Direct quotation** The exact words someone has used; direct quotations must be placed in quotation marks to avoid plagiarism (815)
>
> **Signal phrase** A noun or pronoun plus an appropriate verb identifying the writer from whom you are borrowing words or ideas (291)

In most cases, separate a **direct quotation** from a **signal phrase** with a comma:

> signal phrase
> ▶ After learning that he had been appointed poet laureate, **Charles Simic exclaimed,** "I'm almost afraid to get out of bed—too much good luck in one week."

Exceptions

- When the quotation begins the sentence and ends with a question mark or exclamation point, no comma should be added.

  > ▶ "When shall we three meet again, in thunder, lightning, and in rain?" asks the first witch in Shakespeare's *Macbeth*.

- When the quotation is integrated into your own sentence, omit the comma:

  > ▶ Friar Lawrence warns Romeo that "these violent delights have violent ends."

- When the signal phrase is incorporated into a complete sentence that makes sense without the quotation, use a colon before the quotation:

  > ▶ Hamlet exits the graveyard scene with a veiled threat: "The cat will mew and dog will have his day."

> **Indirect quotation** A quotation that has been paraphrased (put into the writer's own words), instead of taken word-for-word from the source (816)

Indirect quotations should *not* be set off by commas.

> ▶ New poet laureate Charles Simic confessed that, having so much good luck worried him.

47i Using Commas with Numbers, Names and Titles, Place Names and Addresses, and Dates

Numbers, names and titles, place names and addresses, and dates are each punctuated according to specialized conventions, some of which vary from one community or discipline to another.

1. In numbers

The following conventions are standard in most American English usage:

More about ▶▶▶
Numbers, 858–61
(ch. 56)

- In four-digit numbers, using a comma to mark divisions of hundreds is optional, except with years, when no comma should be included:

  ▶ The company paid $9347 for those supplies in 2007.

  ▶ The company paid $9,347 for those supplies in 2007.

- In five-digit numbers, a comma is used to mark divisions of hundreds.

  ▶ Workers have filed 93,471 unemployment claims since January.

2. Between personal names and titles

Use a comma to separate a personal name from a title that follows it:

▶ Send the request to Janet Woodcock, director of the Center for Drug Evaluation and Research.

Use no comma when a title precedes the name or when the "title" consists of Roman numerals:

▶ Send the request to Doctor Janet Woodcock.

▶ My son will be named Albert Farnsworth IV.

The titles Jr. and Sr. may appear with or without commas:

▶ Ken Griffey, Jr., appears in the *Simpsons* episode "Homer at the Bat."

▶ Ken Griffey Jr. appears in the *Simpsons* episode "Homer at the Bat."

3. In place names and addresses

Use a comma to separate names of cities from states, provinces, regions, or countries:

▶ Boston, Massachusetts, was the birthplace of Benjamin Franklin. Famous as an American patriot, Franklin also lived for several years in London, England, and Paris, France. He died at age eighty-four in Philadelphia, Pennsylvania.

Do *not* place a comma between the name of a state and the zip code:

▶ The Franklin Institute, founded to honor Benjamin Franklin, is located at 222 North 20th Street, Philadelphia, Pennsylvania◯19103.

4. In dates

Use commas to set off dates in which the day follows the month and when dates include the time of day or the day of the week:

▶ I will never forget that my son was born at 5:17 a.m.◯Tuesday◯March 17, 2009.

No comma is needed in dates when only the month and year are used or when the day *precedes* the month:

▶ My niece was born in February◯2000.

▶ Her exact birth date is 13 February 2000.

connect

mhconnectcomposition.com

Online exercise: QL47106

→ EXERCISE **47.6** **Using commas with numbers, names, places, and dates**

In the following sentences, add commas as necessary to mark numbers, names and titles, place names and addresses, and dates. (Not all sentences will need correction.)

EXAMPLE

The board of directors met on Thursday⌄June 5, 2008⌄at 3:00 p.m.⌄in the institute's new offices in Swansea⌄Massachusetts.

1. Yvonne Gesinghaus, MD, disagrees with the board's decision.

2. According to Dr. Gesinghaus "We should spend the $10500 on research, not on a party in San Antonio Texas."

3. Nevertheless, she requests that we send an invitation to William Green Sr. 217 Adamson Parkway Seattle WA 90107.

4. His invitation must go out by 7 October 2009.

5. The next meeting of the board of directors has been rescheduled to Monday January 10 2010.

6. The finance officer told Dr. Gesinghaus that, the meeting on Monday will start promptly at 5 p.m.

7. Also, please change your records to reflect her new job title: Yvonne Gesinghaus Director of Research and Development.

8. The foundation she now works for is located in a suburb of Fall River Massachusetts.

9. The new director's annual salary will be $165000.

10. The increase will take effect in January 2010.

47j Using Commas to Avoid Ambiguity

A comma can separate ideas that might otherwise be misinterpreted, and it can also mark places where words have been deleted.

1. To separate ideas

When two ideas could be misread as a single unit, add a comma to separate the two:

▶ My friends who can afford to, take taxis frequently.

2. To replace omitted words and avoid repetition

Replace a repeated word with a comma after its first use:

▶ I vacationed in the Adirondacks, my brother, ~~vacationed~~ in British Columbia.

47k Avoiding Commas between Subjects and Verbs, Verbs and Objects

A single comma should not separate a subject from its verb or a verb from its object unless another rule calls for it:

▶ The Senate finance committee, is the focus of much attention.
              subject   *verb*

▶ The committee must explain, its decision to a nervous public.
           verb   *object*

➔ EXERCISE **47.7** Using commas to resolve ambiguity

Correct the following sentences by inserting or deleting commas as necessary. (Not all sentences will need correction.)

connect

mhconnectcomposition.com
Online exercise: QL47107

EXAMPLE

The members who want to‚ contribute their time to painting the club's
meeting hall.
‸

1. Fiona is painting a wall, and Helen the baseboards.

2. Those who can stay and keep painting through the second shift.

3. Although most members never help, those who do devote a great deal of their spare time to it.

4. Jason worked ten hours this week, Alika eight, and Jesse fifteen.

5. The members who do enjoy a sense of satisfaction that they have made a difference.

➔ **EXERCISE 47.8 Avoiding unnecessary commas**

Delete any unnecessary commas from the following sentences.

EXAMPLE

Current treatments for multiple myeloma include͵⁄ chemotherapy,
radiation, and stem-cell transplantation, but͵⁄ other treatments are
under development.

1. In April 2007, researchers at the Mayo Clinic, discovered that a by-product of wood mold, chaetocin, kills multiple, myeloma, cells more effectively than current treatments, such as thalidomide, or stem-cell transplantation.

2. The doctor, who led the study told reporters, that the team had found chaetocin to cause myeloma cell, death in mice and, that it had also provided new avenues for research.

3. This cancer of the bone marrow cells, is currently incurable, but this new research on chaetocin holds, promise for a cure.

4. Chaetocin kills myeloma cells in mice by, accumulating in the cancer cells, slowing the growth of myeloma cells, and causing biological changes in cancer cells that led to, their death.

5. Dr. Bible, who led the team of researchers, noted that treatments are still several years off, but expects that his team's discovery will help patients in the future.

connect
mhconnectcomposition.com
Online exercise: QL47109

→ **EXERCISE 47.9 Using commas correctly**

Add or delete commas as needed in the paragraph below.

EXAMPLE

Americans, instead of losing their spirit of creativity, seem to be
getting more inventive, than ever.

The United States Patent Office, is so overwhelmed that it now has a backlog of 700000 applications and its average review time is now thirty-one months. In an attempt to deal with the flood of applications the office has proposed new rules. The new rules would make inventors provide more information than they now do; in addition the agency would also allow expanded public review of applications. What's more and this may be of greater concern to inventors the office is now approving a smaller percentage of applications. In 2007 it approved approximately 50 percent of applications which is down from 72 percent in 2000. To improve the chances of approval inventors, need to be sure that their inventions are both new, and useful. The description of an invention whether it is simple, or highly complex should also be understandable, and written clearly. Today American inventiveness is not only thriving but it is also more competitive than ever before.

▲ Make It **Your Own**

Review your use of commas in a recent writing project of two or more pages. Add commas where needed and cross through unnecessary ones. Then analyze the impact these changes would have on your reader. (Refer to the sections in this chapter as needed.)

Work **Together** ◄

Exchange your work on Exercise 47.9 with a partner. Check your classmate's use of commas. Did he or she make any errors? If so, explain the effect these errors had on you as a reader. (Be specific.)

48 Using Semicolons

'I think Lassie is trying to tell us something, ma.'

Although there are other uses of the semicolon, its main function is to link two independent clauses into a single sentence. The comma and a coordinating conjunction also play this role, so what makes the semicolon useful? It is the signal the semicolon sends to the reader; it tells the reader that the clause that follows will specify consequences, restate meaning, or introduce a contrast.

A list of the most important rules for using semicolons appears in the Quick Reference box on the next page.

Reference → Common Semicolon Do's and Don'ts

Do use a semicolon . . .

. . . to link two closely related independent clauses when the second clause specifies the consequence of the first, restates its meaning, or introduces a contrast. 802

▶ In 1911, Italian nationalist Vincenzo Peruggia stole the *Mona Lisa* from the Louvre in France; he believed fervently that da Vinci's painting should be displayed in Italy.

. . . when a conjunctive adverb or transitional phrase links them. 803

▶ Peruggia was arrested while trying to sell the painting to a Florence art gallery; however, his mission was not entirely in vain.

. . . to distinguish items in a series with internal commas. 803

▶ Before arresting Peruggia, authorities questioned Guillaume Apollinaire, a French poet; Pablo Picasso, a Spanish painter and founder of cubism; and various Louvre employees.

. . . to repair a comma splice. 804

▶ Before the *Mona Lisa* was restored to Paris, it was exhibited in museums across Italy; as a result, Peruggia was hailed as a national hero and served only a brief prison term.

Do *not* use a semicolon . . .

. . . to link an independent clause to anything except another, related independent clause. 802

▶ During his trial, Peruggia leapt to his feet ; ~~independent clause~~ , ~~phrase~~ raging at the prosecutor, the judge, and even his own lawyer.

▶ Peruggia claimed he was motivated only by patriotism ; ~~independent clause~~ , ~~subordinate clause~~ even though he had demanded a "reward" of half a million lire.

. . . to introduce a list. 803

▶ Despite an outcry, the *Mona Lisa* was returned to France after visiting the following Italian cities ; : ~~list~~ Naples, Rome, Florence, Venice, and Milan.

Writing Responsibly

Sending a Signal with Semicolons

Writers who do not understand the role of the semicolon may use it to connect independent clauses randomly, and this can lead readers to see a connection between ideas that the writer did not intend or cannot defend. Consider this sentence: *Angelina is working in New York; Brad* *has a headache.* The semicolon here suggests that there is a logical relationship between the two clauses, that one is the cause or effect of the other, when, in fact, the two may reflect mere coincidence. Avoid conveying more than you meant; use the semicolon with care.

Independent (or main) clause A word group that contains a subject and a main verb and that does not begin with a subordinating conjunction, relative pronoun, or relative adverb (620)

> **More about ▶▶▶**
> Parallelism, 539–48 (ch. 27)
> Commas, 782–99 (ch. 47)
> End punctuation, 824–27 (ch. 51)
> Dashes, 828–30
> Colons, 833–35
> Coordinating conjunctions (list), 784

48a Using a Semicolon to Link Independent Clauses

When two ***independent clauses*** are closely related and balanced, a semicolon emphasizes their relationship.

|————————— independent clause 1 —————————| |–independent
▶ Adjusting to life in a new country does not come easily; I learned that
clause 2 —|
firsthand.

A semicolon replaces a comma and coordinating conjunction:

                    coord. conj.
▶ Summer traffic to Jones Beach can be slow, so you might want to take
the train instead.

▶ Summer traffic to Jones Beach can be slow; you might want to take
the train instead.

A semicolon is often used when the second clause emphasizes the consequences of the first, restates the first, or offers a contrast with the first:

              emphasize consequences
▶ My mother's taste is always changing; just when I think I know what
she likes, she proves me wrong.

▶ When the French arrived, this area was very different from what it has
              restates
become; Detroit was once a deep forest.

▶ People think of Franklin Delano Roosevelt as the architect of the
           contrasts
New Deal; he actually designed buildings, too.

Do not use a semicolon to link a phrase or a subordinate clause to an independent clause:

Getting It Across — Choosing the Semicolon

The semicolon is very seldom the only option. You can almost always combine independent clauses with a comma and coordinating conjunction, use a period to create two separate sentences, or re-

vise to make one of the independent clauses subordinate. What the semicolon does that the other options do not is stress the equal importance of the two clauses.

▶ The new Harry Potter film proved successful; grossing $22 million in
phrase

the first night.

48b Using a Semicolon before a Conjunctive Adverb or Transitional Phrase Linking Two Independent Clauses

When a conjunctive adverb (such as *therefore, however,* and *furthermore*) or a transitional phrase such as *on the other hand* or *for example* comes between two independent clauses, precede it with a semicolon (and follow it with a comma).

> **More about ▶▶▶**
> Conjunctive adverbs (list), 608
> Transitional words and phrases (list), 62

▶ *Shakespeare in Love* introduced the playwright to a new
    semi. + conj. adv. + comma
generation of moviegoers; moreover, it was an entertaining film.

When the conjunctive adverb or transitional phrase is placed within one of the independent clauses rather than between them, retain the semicolon between the clauses and insert a comma before and after the conjunctive adverb or transitional phrase:

        semi.   *comma + trans. + comma*
▶ Film is a popular form of entertainment; it can be, in addition, a means

of exploring literature's classic themes in contemporary contexts.

48c Using a Semicolon to Mark a Series with Internal Commas

Ordinarily, commas are used to mark items in a series:

▶ You can create an off-grid home by building with straw bales, using solar
power, and generating additional energy with windmills on the property.

However, when the items are especially long or complex or when an item in the series has internal punctuation, use semicolons. Do not use a semicolon to introduce a list.

▶ The architectural firm of Hanover, Harvey, and Witkins recommends creating an off-grid home by building with straw bales; packing them tightly, which makes them flame-resistant; utilizing solar power; and generating additional energy through windmills on the property.

▶ I used the following in my "green" home; straw bales, solar panels, and water-conserving fixtures.

48d Repairing a Comma Splice

Comma splice Two independent clauses joined by a comma alone (638)

One way to repair a **comma splice** is to replace the comma between the two independent clauses with a semicolon.

▶ Reporters without Borders fights restrictions placed on journalists; the group also raises awareness about this increasingly important issue.

Sometimes a comma splice occurs because a comma is placed before a conjunctive adverb or transitional phrase that links two independent clauses. To correct it, replace the comma with a semicolon:

▶ Most people don't think of babies as prospective employees; however, in Hollywood infants can become working actors at fifteen days old.

48e Avoiding Overuse

More about ▶▶▶
Sentence variety, 550–57

Compound sentence
Two or more independent clauses linked by a semicolon or a comma plus a coordinating conjunction (624)
Complex sentence
One or more subordinate clauses linked to an independent clause (624)

Use semicolons sparingly to avoid suggesting that everything in the passage is of equal importance. Overusing semicolons can also be a sign that you need to vary your sentence structures. You can turn some independent clauses into phrases, replace two independent clauses linked by a semicolon with a **compound sentence,** or create **complex sentences** by turning some of your independent clauses into subordinate clauses.

DRAFT

According to the *Los Angeles Times,* the earliest known gunshot victim in the Americas died in 1536; archaeological exploration in Peru has uncovered a pierced skull. The Inca warrior was shot by Spanish

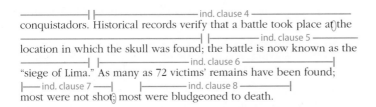

———————————| |——————————— ind. clause 4 ———————————
conquistadors. Historical records verify that a battle took place at the
———————————————| |——————————— ind. clause 5 ———————
location in which the skull was found; the battle is now known as the
———————————| |——————————— ind. clause 6 ———————————|
"siege of Lima." As many as 72 victims' remains have been found;
|—— ind. clause 7 ——| |——————— ind. clause 8 ———————|
most were not shot; most were bludgeoned to death.

REVISION

According to the *Los Angeles Times*, the earliest known gunshot victim in

the Americas died in 1536. Archaeological exploration in Peru has
|——————— sub. clause ———————|
uncovered the pierced skull of an Inca warrior who was shot by Spanish
———————————|
conquistadors. Historical records verify that the skull was found at the site
|——————————— phrase ———————————|
of a battle now known as the "siege of Lima." As many as 72 victims'
|——— phrase ———|
remains have been found. Most were not shot but were instead
———————————————|
bludgeoned to death.

> Combines indepen-
> dent clauses 2 and 3;
> clause 3 becomes a
> subordinate clause
> introduced by the rela-
> tive pronoun *who.*

> Combines indepen-
> dent clauses 4 and 5;
> clause 5 becomes a
> phrase.

> Combines indepen-
> dent clauses 7 and 8;
> clause 8 becomes a
> phrase.

→ EXERCISE 48.1 Correcting the use of semicolons

Add or delete semicolons or replace them with a different punctuation mark to correct or improve the sentences below. (Some sentences may be correct.)

EXAMPLE

About 10 percent of Americans are dyslexic; they have a learning

disability that causes them to have difficulty with written language,

particularly reading and spelling.

1. Very few corporate managers are dyslexic; and this is understandable, since corporate management requires strong reading
   and writing skills.

2. Their disability does seem to exclude dyslexics from participating in this major business sector, however, according to a
   recent study, dyslexics are well represented as entrepreneurs or
   small-business owners.

3. About 35 percent of the entrepreneurs surveyed identified themselves as dyslexic apparently, it is common for dyslexics to develop important strengths precisely because of their weakness.

connect
mhconnectcomposition.com
Online exercise: QL48101

4. The study concluded that dyslexics were more likely than non-dyslexics to be willing to delegate authority, to be especially adept at key business skills, such as oral communication and problem solving, and to be owners of two or more businesses.

5. Researchers noted that dyslexics' willingness to delegate authority gives them a specific advantage over nondyslexic entrepreneurs; the ability to focus on what they do best.

connect

mhconnectcomposition.com
Online exercise: QL48102

→ **EXERCISE 48.2 Using semicolons correctly**

Add or delete semicolons or replace them with a different punctuation mark to correct or improve the paragraph below.

EXAMPLE

Many elderly people worry that they may lose certain mental abilities,

such as memory,/ recently, researchers have uncovered some potentially

useful methods of maintaining mental sharpness.

In general, the idea is for the aging to get plenty of mental and physical stimulation just as physical exercise strengthens muscles, mental exercise strengthens the brain. The brain needs novelty; new challenges; and continued stresses to maintain or increase its strength, this type of stimulation creates new nerve cells and connections between them. It is common for some cells of an elderly person's brain to deteriorate, however; the newly developed brain tissue may compensate for the lost brain cells. So those who knit should try ever more complicated patterns, those who like listening to opera should try to learn the libretto, and those who like crossword puzzles should try new kinds of puzzles; such as Sudoku and double crostics. Also important for keeping mentally sharp is to pursue stimulating activities with other people, these can include taking classes; playing bridge; or participating in a reading group.

Work **Together** ◄

Exchange Exercise 48.2 with a partner. Check your classmate's use of semicolons. Did he or she make any errors? If so, explain the effect these errors had on you as a reader. (Be specific.)

49 Using Apostrophes

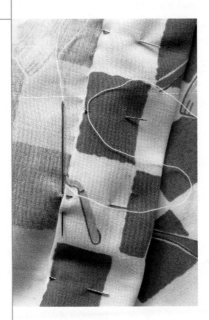

Apostrophes, like pins, replace something that is missing: Pins replace stitches; apostrophes replace letters in contractions (*can't*, *ma'am*). Apostrophes also make nouns and indefinite pronouns possessive (*Edward's* or *somebody's horse*). Centuries ago, English speakers indicated possession with a pronoun (*Edward his horse*), so, in fact, today's possessive form (*Edward's horse*) is also an age-old contraction. A list of the most important rules for using apostrophes appears in the Quick Reference box on the next page.

Writing Responsibly   Contractions in Formal Writing

Contractions and other abbreviations provide useful shortcuts in speech and informal writing, and they are finding their way into more formal academic and business writing. They are still not fully accepted, however. To determine whether contractions will be acceptable to your readers, check with your instructor, look for contractions in academic journals in your field, or consult reports or business letters written by other company employees. If you are in any doubt, spell the words out.

Reference ➡ **Common Apostrophe Do's and Don'ts**

Do use an apostrophe . . .

. . . to indicate possession (with singular and plural nouns and indefinite pronouns) **808**

▶ The book's cover promised "a thrilling read," but we were skeptical.

▶ Everyone's taste is different.

▶ Most books' covers are beautifully designed.

▶ She borrowed Socrates' book, not Jess's.

. . . to form a contraction or abbreviate a year 811

▶ Didn't you forget your anniversary last year?

▶ You only got married in '08!

Do not use an apostrophe . . .

. . . with possessive pronouns, especially *its* 809

▶ Now that they've played their CD, I want to play our's.

▶ Sadly, it's sales are lagging.

. . . with plurals 810

▶ I've got load's of song's in my brain just itching to get out.

. . . with dates, letters, and numbers 811

▶ The members of her club were born in the 1950's.

. . . with verbs ending in -s 810

▶ My mom still hope's to sell downloads to members of her book club.

49a Using an Apostrophe to Indicate Possession

In English, you can indicate possession (ownership) in nouns and indefinite pronouns by using the preposition *of:*

➡ **Tech**

Apostrophes and Spelling or Grammar Checkers

Be wary of apostrophe-related "errors" identified by your word processor's spelling or grammar checker. These programs may mistake *its* for *it's* (or vice versa). Pay attention to the program's suggestions, but always double-check them for accuracy.

▶ Many admired the commitment of the students. But the involvement of everybody is needed to make real progress.

You can also do so by adding an apostrophe, with or without an *-s:*

▶ Many admired the students' commitment. But everybody's involvement is needed to make real progress.

1. With singular nouns and indefinite pronouns (but not personal pronouns)

Singular **nouns** and **indefinite pronouns** add an apostrophe and an -s to indicate possession:

▶ The factory's smokestacks belched thick, black smoke.

▶ No one's health was unaffected.

Even for most singular nouns that already end in -s, add an -'s:

▶ Dolores's asthma was particularly aggravated.

Add an apostrophe alone to a singular noun or pronoun only when adding an -'s would make the word difficult to pronounce:

▶ Socrates' pneumonia became so serious he had to be hospitalized.

Personal pronouns are *never* made possessive by adding an apostrophe. Be sure to use the possessive form, *not* a contraction.

▶ We regret that ~~you're~~ _{your} new power plant will have to close, but ~~they're~~ _{their} health is more important.

Be especially careful with *its:*

■ *It's* (*it is*) is a contraction like *don't* (*do not*) and *can't* (*cannot*).

■ *Its* is a **possessive pronoun** like *his* and *hers*.

If you tend to confuse *it's* and *its*, remember that the contraction *always* takes an apostrophe, but the personal pronoun *never* does:

▶ Buca Di Becco serves Italian cuisine at its best, so it's a good idea to call ahead for reservations.

2. With plural nouns

To make plural nouns possessive, first form the plural and then the possessive. When the plural form ends in -s, just add an apostrophe; when it does not end in -s, add an apostrophe and -s.

Singular	Plural	Possessive
lady	ladies	ladies'
person	people	people's

Noun A word that names ideas, things, qualities, actions, people, and places (601)

Indefinite pronouns Pronouns that do not refer to specific people or things, such as *all, anybody, either, everybody, few, many, either, no one, some-one* (604)

Personal pronouns Pronouns that replace specific nouns or noun phrases, such as *I, me, he, him, she, her, it, we, us, you, they, them* (604)

Possessive pronouns Pronouns that indicate ownership, such as *my, his, yours, mine,* and *theirs* (604)

> ▶ By midnight, the ladies⁀ maids were exhausted.

> ▶ I'm often amazed by people⁀s consideration for the well-being of others.

This rule applies to family names that end in -s, too: Make the name plural and then possessive.

> *Williamses'*
> ▶ The ~~William's~~ parties always ended at dawn.
>   ∧

NOTE Just because a word ends with an -s does not mean that it needs an apostrophe. Delete apostrophes from plural nouns and singular verbs:

>   noun (plu.)   verb (sing.)
> ▶ Your dog⁀s bark wildly, but my cat remain⁀s placid.

3. To indicate joint or individual ownership or possession

First, decide whether the apostrophe indicates *joint* or *individual* ownership. When the nouns share possession, make only the last noun possessive:

> ▶ Giorgione and Titian⁀s painting *Portrait of a Venetian Gentleman*
>
> (c. 1510) is on view at the National Gallery of Art in Washington, DC.
>
> Giorgione and Titian painted the portrait collaboratively.

When the nouns each possess the same object, quality, or event, make each noun possessive:

> ▶ Giorgione's and Titian's paintings of Venus are important milestones
>
> in the art of the High Renaissance.
>
> Each produced paintings of Venus that are important milestones.

4. With compound nouns

While number (singular or plural) is usually attached to the core noun in a compound noun, the possessive is attached to the last noun:

>   core (plural)
> ▶ Jeremiah is driving his <u>sisters-in-law</u> crazy.
>
> Jeremiah has more than one sister-in-law, and he is driving them all crazy. Attach number to the core noun, *sister.*
>
>   last
> ▶ Jeremiah is driving his <u>sister-in-law⁀s</u> car.
>
> Jeremiah is using the car belonging to his sister-in-law; attach possession to the last noun, *law.*

▶ Jeremiah has his <u>sisters-in-law(s)</u> unwavering support.

   core (plural) last

Jeremiah has more than one sister-in-law, and he has their unwavering support; attach the plural to the core noun (*sisters*) and possession to the last noun (*law's*).

49b Using Apostrophes in Contractions and Abbreviated Years

An apostrophe can stand in place of missing letters or numbers in a contraction or in an abbreviated year.

▶ I am	I'm	▶ Cannot	Can't
▶ He is, she is	He's, she's	▶ Could/ would not	Couldn't/ wouldn't
▶ It is/has	It's	▶ Let us	Let's
▶ They are	They're	▶ Who is	Who's
▶ You are	You're	▶ 2009	'09

49c Moving Away from Using Apostrophes to Form Plurals of Abbreviations, Dates, Numbers, and Words or Letters Used as Words

Only a few years ago, -*'s* was a common way of creating the plural for abbreviations, dates, and words or characters used as words. These practices are now in flux, but using apostrophes for this purpose seems to be falling out of fashion. Unless the style guide you use instructs otherwise, do not use apostrophes to form these plurals.

▶ My brother has stayed in more YMCA's than anyone else I know.

▶ He spent the 1990's traveling around the United States playing music.

▶ Now he minds the *p's* and *q's* of students in composition classes.

▶ His students give him 5's on his evaluations.

NOTE The Modern Language Association (MLA) still recommends the use of an apostrophe with the plurals of letters:

Now he minds the *p*'s and *q*'s of students in composition classes.

Getting It Across   **Apostrophes and Plural Letters**

Use an apostrophe to form a plural letter if its absence might cause confusion.

	may be misread as *is*
CONFUSING	You've dotted your *t*s and crossed your *i*s.
CLEAR	You've dotted your *t*'s and crossed your *i*'s.

Add the apostrophe to *t*'s for consistency's sake.

connect

mhconnectcomposition.com
Online exercise: QL49101

→ EXERCISE **49.1** Correcting apostrophes

Supply or delete apostrophes as appropriate. (Some sentences may be correct.)

EXAMPLE

The sopranos voice crack's whenever she thinks about PhD's in

musicology assessing her performance.

1. It was one of her biggest crowd's since the 1990's.

2. Many of the audience member's were fans who gave the performance 10's.

3. The auditorium resounded with they're *bravo*'s and *more*'s.

4. Personally, I think singer's who can't hit the high notes should issue IOU's with each performance.

5. This singer's high *C*'s are always flat, and she deserve's *F*'s for how she manage's the tempo of her concerts.

6. My two sisters and brothers-in-laws applause was among the most enthusiastic of the entire audience.

7. At our' dinner after the concert, my sister's were in agreement over their appreciation of the soprano, and Suzie's and Amber's praise for the soprano was fervent and wholehearted.

8. I didn't want to hurt Suzies and Ambers feelings, so I kept my criticisms about the soprano to myself' during dinner.

9. On the way to our's car I tugged my husband Marks arms and I told him how shocked I was at my sisters's not noticing the soprano's lack of professionalism.

10. Mark smiled and said, "Your wise to let you're sisters' savor the performance, but I think you should be honest but tactful at next weeks concert when we sit in the Jones' special box at the opera house."

EXERCISE **49.2** Using apostrophes correctly

In the following paragraph, add or delete apostrophes as necessary.

connect

mhconnectcomposition.com
Online exercise: QL49102

One of Adam Smiths contributions to modern economic's is the distinction between use value and exchange value. Writing in the 1700's, Smith defined *use value* as the ability to satisfy peoples wants. In Smiths analysis, *exchange value* is the amount of good's or service's that people are willing to pay for something. His economics can help us understand our's. Smiths pointing out the difference between use value and exchange value can help contemporary economist's understand that value doesnt just derive from price. Jeremy Reiss essay clearly reflects this understanding.

Work **Together** ⟵

Exchange Exercise 49.2 with a partner. Check your classmate's use of apostrophes. Did he or she make any errors? If so, explain the effect these errors had on you as a reader. (Be specific.)

50 Using Quotation Marks

Indicating who said what is an important use of quotation marks. When we fail to indicate that words were spoken or written by others—whether accidentally or on purpose—we open ourselves up to charges of plagiarism. Misusing quotation marks can also confuse or annoy your readers. (Think how much better the couple in the cartoon would get along if the man would learn to use quotation marks correctly!) Learning when to use—and when *not* to use—quotation marks is an important part of a writer's responsibilities. A list of the most important rules for using quotation marks appears in the Quick Reference box on the next page.

Quick Reference ➡ Common Quotation Mark Do's and Don'ts

Do use quotation marks ...

... to set off direct quotations. 815

▶ Eisenhower once said that any person "who wants to be president is either an egomaniac or crazy."

... to indicate irony (use sparingly). 818

▶ After an unsuccessful stint as president of Columbia University, Eisenhower let himself be "persuaded" to run for the U.S. presidency.

... to refer to words as words. 818

▶ "Popular" is an adjective often attached to Eisenhower's presidency.

(Italics are also widely used for this purpose.)

Do *not* use quotation marks ...

... to set off indirect quotations (paraphrases). 816

▶ Eisenhower once said that "lunatics or narcissists are the only people who would desire the presidency."

... for emphasis. 819

▶ Eisenhower was a five-star general and "Supreme" Commander of Allied forces in Europe during World War II.

... with slang or clichés. 819

▶ "Snafus" occur regularly in the army, but Eisenhower generally avoided them through careful planning.

In formal contexts, consider recasting to avoid slang. Clichés are rarely appropriate; rewrite to avoid them.

50a Setting Off Direct Quotations

Double quotation marks (" ") indicate the beginning and end of direct quotations (someone's exact words, whether written or spoken):

▶ Of grappling with the unknown, Albert Einstein wrote this: "The most beautiful thing we can experience is the mysterious. It is the source of all true art and all science."

More about ▶▶▶
Plagiarism, 263–81
Patchwriting, 271–74

Writing Responsibly   Using Quotations Fairly

You have a responsibility to your reader and other writers to supply quotation marks whenever you borrow language from a source. Omitting quotation marks when needed can undermine your reputation as a writer to be trusted.

Single quotation marks (' ') indicate quotations within quotations:

▶ Barbara Jordan, the first black woman to represent a southern state in Congress, felt that when the Constitution was written she "was not included in that 'We, the people.'"

ESL Quotation Marks in American English Use of quotation marks varies from place to place and culture to culture. In contemporary American English, double quotation marks signal a quotation, and single quotation marks signal a quotation within a quotation. British usage is the opposite:

▶ John complained, 'For the third time this month, Mary asked me for "a few bucks to tide me over till payday." And it's only June 15!'

More about ▶▶▶
Paraphrasing,
271–74

Indirect quotations, which paraphrase someone's words, do *not* use quotation marks:

▶ Albert Einstein said that the unknown inspires scientists as well as artists.

▶ Barbara Jordan felt that she was excluded by the founding fathers when they drafted the U.S. Constitution.

1. In dialogue

When quoting dialogue, start a new paragraph each time the speaker changes, and put all spoken words in quotation marks:

▶ "Have you brought women here before?" He smiled and kept chewing, so I said, "Do you always use the same tricks?"

　　—"What tricks?" He looked at me like he didn't understand.

　　　　　　　　　　　　　　　　—Leslie Marmon Silko, "Yellow Woman"

Tech

Smart Quotes versus Straight Quotes

Word processing programs usually default to *smart,* or curly, quotation marks ("/"). Smart quotes may look more professional than straight quotes ("/"), but they often turn to gibberish when they are pasted into an online document or uploaded to a web page. If you plan to email or post content that includes quotation marks, change your program's preferences to straight quotation marks. Use the Help function to locate this option.

If one speaker continues for more than a paragraph, use quotation marks at the beginning of each paragraph, but omit closing quotation marks until the end of the speech.

2. With long quotations

For lengthy quotations, omit quotation marks, and indent quotations in a block from the left margin:

> ▶ Lucio Guerrero examines how local Goths feel about their lifestyle's mass-market appeal:
>
> > For some, that suburbanization of Goth may be what saves the subculture. "If someone who identifies as Goth doesn't have easy access to the fashion or accouterments that they feel drawn to, but they do have access to a store like Hot Topic, then it's a positive thing," said Scary Lady Sarah, a local DJ and supporter of Chicago's Goth community.
> >
> > —Lucio Guerrero, "Like a GOTH," *Chicago Sun-Times*

Generally, introduce block quotations with a complete sentence plus a colon.

In block quotations, use double quotation marks for quotations within a quotation.

3. With quotations from poetry

When quoting one to three lines of poetry, use quotation marks and run the lines into your text. Indicate the end of each line by inserting a slash, with a space on each side:

> ▶ Furthermore, lines 21–22 ("In the pay of a man / From town") and 25–26 ("And here we must draw / Our line") have a marching cadence, a rhythm that reinforces the battlefield symbolism.

When quoting four or more lines, omit quotation marks, set the poetry as a block, and retain the original line breaks:

> ▶ Gary Snyder's "Front Lines" begins powerfully:
> > The edge of the cancer
> > Swells against the hill—we feel
> > A foul breeze—
> > And it sinks back down. (lines 1–5)

More about ▶▶▶
Formatting block quotations, 303, 342 (MLA style), 386 (APA style)

50b Indicating Titles of Short Works

Most American style guides suggest placing titles of short works in quotation marks and titles of long works in italics:

> ■ Lahiri's short story "Year's End" appeared in the collection *Unaccustomed Earth*.

More about ▶▶▶
Italicizing titles of longer works, 847–48

- "Front Lines," a poem by Gary Snyder, is from his book *No Nature.*

- Ben Brantley's review of *Romeo and Juliet,* "Rash and Unadvis'd Seeks Same," ran in the *New York Times.*

- *Grey's Anatomy* is my guilty pleasure; "I Am a Tree" is my favorite episode.

- The podcast "Of Two Minds, One Consciousness" from the *Scientific American* website uses results from split-brain studies to explore thought.

- "Bleeding Love," from Leona Lewis's album *Spirit,* reached the top of the Billboard charts.

More about ▶▶▶
Citing and documenting sources
298–357 (MLA style, ch. 17),
358–400 (APA style, ch. 18),
401–28 (*Chicago* style, ch. 19),
429–46 (CSE style, ch. 20)

In APA, CSE, and the *Chicago Manual of Style* parenthetical style, omit quotation marks from the titles of short works in bibliographic entries.

50c Indicating Words Used in a Special Sense

Quotation marks can call attention to words used in a special sense. When talking *about* a word, enclose it in quotation marks to avoid confusion:

▶ Many people confuse "lay" and "lie."

Italics can also be used for this purpose.

To signal that you are using a word ironically or sarcastically, place it in quotation marks:

▶ I didn't know that the Indian "problem" on the plains began in the 1860s. . . .

—James Welch, *Killing Custer*

Use quotation marks sparingly for indicating irony. Overuse can annoy readers. Your words should usually be able to convey irony on their own.

Set a term to be defined in italics and the definition in quotation marks:

▶ Many writers don't realize that *e.g.* stands for "for example" in Latin.

50d Misusing Quotation Marks

It is important to use quotation marks where needed; it is also important to omit them where they are not needed.

1. *Not* for emphasis

More about ▶▶▶
Using italics for
emphasis, 848

▶ Paul Potts's debut album was ⸢amazing,⸢ selling 130,000 copies in its
first week alone.

Let your words and the rhythms of your sentences create emphasis.
On the rare occasion when something more is needed, use *italics,* not
quotation marks.

2. *Not* with slang

If slang is acceptable in the context, use it without the apology that
quotation marks represent; if it is not (as in business or academic writing), choose a more appropriate word or phrase:

▶ Daniel Radcliffe "beat out" hundreds of competitors to win the role

      bested
          ∧

of Harry Potter.

3. *Not* with clichés

Clichés are rarely appropriate; instead of attempting to justify them
with quotation marks, revise the sentence to avoid them altogether:

                          drinks were served.

▶ I left the party before the "sun was over the yardarm."

                             ∧

50e Punctuating Quotations

Whether punctuation appears before or after the closing quotation
mark depends on the punctuation mark.

More about ▶▶▶
Periods, 825
Commas, 782–99
  (ch. 47)
Question marks, 825
Exclamation points,
  826
Dashes, 828–30

1. With periods and commas

In American English, commas and periods go *inside* the closing quotation mark, except when a citation follows the quotation:

▶ "Sacred cows," said the sixties radical Abbie Hoffman, "make the tastiest hamburger."

▶ According to sixties radical Abbie Hoffman, "sacred cows make the
tastiest hamburger" (qtd. in Albert 43).

More about ▶▶▶
Citing indirect
  sources, 311 (MLA),
  367 (APA)

Commas and Periods with Quotation Marks In Britain as well as in many other countries that use the Roman alphabet, commas and periods follow the closing quotation mark. Be sure to adjust your usage to meet readers' expectations.

2. With question marks, exclamation points, and dashes

Question marks, exclamation points, and dashes go *inside* the closing quotation mark when they are part of the quotation:

▶ In *The Graduate* (1967), a family friend offers Benjamin career advice: "I just want to say one word to you . . . plastics!"

They go *outside* the closing quotation mark when they are not:

▶ Why does Robert Duvall's character in *Apocalypse Now* (1979) say "I love the smell of napalm in the morning"? He explains that "it smells like victory"!

3. With colons and semicolons

Colons and semicolons go outside the closing quotation mark:

▶ "Love means never having to say you're sorry"; so wrote Erich Segal in *Love Story*.

▶ "Lions and tigers and bears": These are the only problems Dorothy doesn't encounter on her yellow-brick road to self-knowledge.

▶▶▶Student project "My View from the Sidelines," 465–68

50f Altering Quotations with Ellipses and Square Brackets

To fit a quotation into your own sentence, you may alter the wording (but not the meaning) by adding, changing, or deleting words. You have a responsibility, though, to alert your readers to your changes: Enclose additions or changes in brackets, and replace deleted words with ellipses:

Original: "Sometimes driven behind the origin is the rhythm, and the rhythm, as it comes out, causes the rest of the poem to follow. Rhythm is, in a very real sense, primary."

changed letter in brackets

▶ Snyder explains in the video that "[s]ometimes driven behind the

deletion marked by ellipses

origin is the rhythm . . . Rhythm is, in a very real sense, primary"

(*Gary Snyder*).

—Rita McMahan, "My View from the Sidelines"

Remember, too, it is unethical to distort the meaning of the original text by altering a quotation or taking a quotation out of context.

More about ▶▶▶
Altering quotations
fairly, 832, 835–36

NOTE In MLA style, if you must change a capital to a lowercase letter (or vice versa), place brackets around the letter to alert readers to the change.

50g Introducing and Identifying Quotations

Use a colon to introduce a quotation if the clause preceding the quotation could stand on its own as a sentence and could make sense without the quotation:

More about ▶▶▶
Clauses, 620–22

▶ Darwin's own words clarify the issue: "It is not the strongest of the species that survive . . . but the ones most responsive to change."

Use a comma with signal phrases such as "Darwin said" or "she wrote":

signal phrase
▶ Charles Darwin said, "It is not the strongest of the species that survive . . . but the ones most responsive to change."

More about ▶▶▶
Using signal phrases,
291–93, 299–303,
359–60

Use no punctuation if the quotation is needed to complete the sentence (as when the word *that* precedes it), and do not capitalize the first word in the quotation:

▶ Darwin asserts that "[i]t is not the strongest of species that survive . . . but the ones most responsive to change."

If a signal phrase interrupts the quotation, insert a comma before the closing quotation mark and after the signal phrase:

signal phrase
▶ "It is not the strongest of species that survive," Darwin asserts, ". . . but the ones most responsive to change."

↪ **EXERCISE 50.1** Correcting problems with quotation marks and other punctuation

Edit the sentences below as needed to correct problems with quotation marks and other punctuation.

connect
mhconnectcomposition.com
Online exercise: QL50101

EXAMPLE

Ashley said that "~~Our~~ *our* library research would go a lot faster if we did

it ~~together~~, *together,"* and I said ~~why not.~~ *, "Why not?"*

1. On our way to the library, I said You're right. Some sources just aren't available online.

2. In fact, didn't Professor Fass say "Only one-third of your sources may be online?" asked Ashley.

3. "Yes," I said, but that depends on what the word online means; "I pointed to a copy of the *New York Times* that I found lying on a table."

4. Opening it to an article titled Resisting the Rush to a World of No Cash, I said that "I found this in the library, but why can't I get it online and simply pretend that I got it from the periodicals room"?

5. Ashley smiled and said What you call "pretending" is what some might call cheating.

6. In any case, she added, "I don't think I could find this copy of Michael Chabon's short story, The Little Knife, online, and she pointed out that at the library she could also thumb through the magazine in which it originally appeared for more information."

7. "I actually knew you were right," I said, because I needed to go to the library to do this: I was looking through the "Oxford English Dictionary" for the derivation of the word turncoat.

8. Then I noted that "in my paper on Vidkun Quisling, I'd like to go beyond the standard definition of turncoat: One who traitorously switches allegiance".

9. Ashley asked Can you work into your paper the quote from the *Godfather* trilogy, "Keep your friends close, but your enemies closer?"

10. As I searched the library's catalog, I said that "I'd try, but I thought I'd find so much useful material in the library that I might not be able to fit it in."

→ **EXERCISE 50.2** Correcting errors with quotation marks

Edit the passage below to correct problems with quotation marks and other punctuation.

connect

mhconnectcomposition.com
Online exercise: QL50102

EXAMPLE

Ross said that "he came across this quote attributed to Albert

Einstein": Only two things are infinite, the universe and the stupidity
                ^

of people, and I'm not so sure about the universe."
                                              ^

These, said Ross, are from the collection of references I found during research but did not use. He showed us a copy of a book by Abbie Hoffman titled, "*Steal This Book*," noting that 'it is hard to find even in libraries because many people followed the title's advice.' Then he said, I was researching what people sell when I opened a copy of the newspaper "*The Rock Ridge Record*" to the want ads in the back". He pointed to a want ad that offered the following. Used tombstone: Perfect for someone named Hancock Arnold Henry Field. One only. Then Ross continued, 'Here is one of several quotes I've collected by Woody Allen': "Why does man kill? He kills for food. And not only food: frequently there must be a beverage." Ross added that "Woody Allen also wrote one of his favorite short stories," which was titled, Notes from the Overfed: After reading Dostoevsky and the new "*Weight Watchers*" magazine on the same plane trip. "Finally", said Ross, "for an English essay, I found this play on the word "strip" by Groucho Marx: If you want to see a comic strip, you should see me in the shower."

Work **Together** ←

Exchange Exercise 50.2 with a partner. Check your classmate's use of quotation marks. Did he or she make any errors? If so, explain the effect these errors had on you as a reader. (Be specific.)

51

Using End Punctuation

Periods, Question Marks, and Exclamation Points

Imagine that each of the people in these photographs has just uttered the words "you're here." Just by looking at their faces, can you guess who was perplexed, thrilled, or neutral? In face-to-face encounters, sight and sound play a huge role in how we interpret tone and meaning, but in a written text, we depend on words and punctuation—especially the punctuation ending the sentence—to signal mood. Think of the question mark as a raised eyebrow, the exclamation point as wide eyes and an open mouth, and the period as the neutral expression we usually wear.

51a Using Periods to End Statements and Mild Commands

Periods mark the end of most sentences, including statements (or *declarative sentences*), *indirect* (or reported) *questions,* and mild commands:

STATEMENT	Our library has survived a flood and two fires.
MILD COMMAND/ INSTRUCTION	Please urge the council to situate the new library building on higher ground.
INDIRECT QUESTION	She wondered whether the water had ever risen so fast before.

> **More about ▶▶▶**
> Using periods with
> abbreviations, 852

Periods are also used with some, but not all, abbreviations.

51b Using Question Marks to End Direct (Not Indirect) Questions

Most writers do not need a handbook to tell them to use a question mark to end a *direct question:*

▶ When did Uzbekistan declare its independence?

▶ Did you know that the median age in Uzbekistan is only 23.2 years?

Use a period, not a question mark, to punctuate *indirect* questions, that is, questions that are reported, not asked directly:

▶ Dr. Wilson asked why the median age in Uzbekistan is so low.

Use a period, not a question mark, in requests phrased as questions to soften the tone:

▶ Would you please find out the life expectancy in Uzbekistan.

A question mark in parentheses can also suggest doubt about a date, number, or word.

Life expectancy at birth in Uzbekistan is 67 (?).

You may also punctuate a series of questions with question marks, even when they are part of the same sentence:

▶ Do you know what Uzbekistan's primary crop is? what language the majority speaks? what countries surround this landlocked nation?

> Note that capital letters are optional if each question is not a complete sentence.

Getting It
Across   Question Marks and Exclamation Points

In an email to a friend, you might use a series of question marks or exclamation points to convey surprise or lend emphasis:

▶ Isn't it about time Joey got rid of the goatee???!

But such techniques are not appropriate in more formal contexts, such as an email to an instructor:

▶ I look forward to studying Indiana government with you next term.!!!!

51c **Using Exclamation Points with Strong Commands or to Express Excitement or Surprise**

➤ Tech

Using Exclamation Points in Email Messages

Because warmth can be difficult to convey in email, writers often use exclamation points to soften the tone. Compare:

▶ We look forward to seeing you next week.

▶ We look forward to seeing you next week!

When giving an emphatic command or expressing sudden excitement or surprise, use an exclamation point to end the sentence:

▶ Don't go there!

▶ "Mom is coming!"

The same sentence, when ended with a period, conveys much less urgency:

▶ Don't go there.

▶ "Mom is coming."

NOTE Overusing exclamation points, especially in more formal contexts, may undermine your credibility with readers.

---

connect
mhconnectcomposition.com
Online exercise: QL51101

➤ EXERCISE **51.1** Using end punctuation

Write six sentences modeled on the examples above that use periods, question marks, and exclamation points appropriately. The context for this exercise is academic.

EXERCISE 51.2 Editing end punctuation

Insert end punctuation—periods, question marks, and exclamation points—as needed. If multiple end punctuation is appropriate, explain why you chose the punctuation mark you did.

connect
mhconnectcomposition.com
Online exercise: QL51102

EXAMPLE

"Could you repeat the question?" That's the most common response law
                               ∧
professor David Cole gets when he calls on disengaged students during

class at Georgetown University.
                              ∧

The laptop—the favorite in-class tool for college and university students across the country—is coming unplugged When used responsibly—for taking notes or quickly accessing research—a laptop provides valuable educational support But when used irresponsibly—for watching YouTube, surfing the Web, emailing, IM-ing, playing games, checking sports scores, and shopping for shoes instead of engaging in class—laptops become the scourge of professors, some of whom are now banning them, especially in law schools
. . . Herzog banned all laptops from his classes for a day, and was so "stunned by how much better the class was," that he has vowed to make the embargo permanent in the fall

—Kathy McManus, "Class Action: Laptops Not Allowed,"
Responsibility Project

Work **Together** ⬅

Exchange Exercise 51.2 with a classmate. Check your partner's use of end punctuation. Did he or she make any errors? If so, explain the effect these errors had on you as a reader. (Be specific.)

52

Using Other Punctuation

Dashes, Parentheses, Brackets, Colons, Ellipses, Slashes

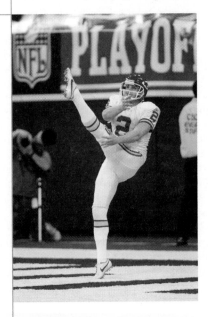

Writers thinking about punctuation typically focus on the comma, the semicolon, the period, and maybe the quotation mark—the star players of the punctuation team. But dashes, parentheses, brackets, colons, ellipses, and slashes also play key roles. Think of these other marks as the special teams of punctuation: While you may call on them in only a limited number of situations, when needed, there is no better punctuation mark for the job. The Quick Reference box on the next page summarizes how these punctuation marks are used.

52a Using Dashes

Dashes can be used singly, when the information to be set off falls at the end of the sentence, or in pairs, when it falls in the middle. They are used to lend emphasis and to mark examples, explanations, and appositives:

▶ In almost every era of Western culture, women's clothing has

been decidedly restrictive and uncomfortable—and the gar-

example

ments of the mid-nineteenth century are a prime example.

Reference → What These Punctuation Marks Do

Dashes lend emphasis and set off examples, explanations, appositives, contrasts, definitions, series items, interruptions, and shifts.

Parentheses set off information of lesser importance.

Brackets set off a writer's insertions in a quoted passage or replace parentheses within parentheses.

Colons link introductory independent clauses to examples, explanations, appositives; they introduce lists (when the intro-

ductory clause does *not* include the words *including, like,* or *such as*); and they introduce quotations (when the introductory clause can stand on its own and make sense without the quotation).

Ellipses indicate an omission or a delay for dramatic effect.

Slashes divide lines of poetry, fractions, and URLs. In formal writing, slashes are not used to separate alternatives (*and/or, he/she*) or parts of dates (*10/23/09*).

▶ To be fashionable, women had to wear clothing that hampered their mobility—cumbersome petticoats and long dresses dragged in puddles and snagged on stairways, turning even a short walk into a navigational challenge.

explanation

▶ In the 1870s another torture device—the bustle—was introduced.

appositive

→ **Tech**

Typing a Dash

Keyboards do not have a single key for dashes, but you can usually create them with a special series of keystrokes or from the Insert menu. If you cannot find your word processor's combination for typing a dash, type two hyphens (--) instead.

Dashes also emphasize contrasts, definitions, and items in a list:

▶ The bustle, which emphasized a woman's backside, was considered erotic in its day—but from a modern perspective, it is quite modest.

contrast

▶ For both daytime and evening wear, women were strapped into corsets—close-fitting undergarments that laced tightly around the torso.

definition

▶ The trappings of mid-nineteenth-century dress—six petticoats, a long hem, a bulky bustle, and a tight corset—guaranteed women's discomfort.

list

More about ▶▶▶
Apostrophes,
807–13 (ch. 49)

Dashes can also be used to indicate a break in thought, speech, or tone:

▶ Women's dress today ranges from the prim to the promiscuous—
  break (tone)
  anything goes!

CAUTION If you use dashes more than once or twice over several pages, consider replacing one or more with commas: As with antibiotics, overuse of dashes undermines their effectiveness.

52b　Using Parentheses

Use parentheses to set off supplementary information (such as examples, dates, abbreviations, or citations) to avoid distracting readers from the main point. Parentheses also enclose letters or numbers delineating items in a list.

▶ The English word for a trifling flaw or offense (*example* *peccadillo*) comes
  from the Spanish word for a small sin, but many other borrowings
  from Spanish (*examples* *barbecue, chocolate, hammock, potato, tomato*)
  actually originated in languages of the peoples whom the Spanish
  conquered in the Caribbean, Mexico, and South America.

▶ In 1991, the Spanish government founded the Instituto Cervantes (IC), *abbrev.*
  named for Miguel de Cervantes (1547–1616), the author of *Don Quixote* *dates*
  (1605, 1615). *dates*

> Unless a complete sentence is enclosed, punctuation goes outside closing parenthesis.

Getting It Across　Dashes, Parentheses, or Commas?

Compare these three versions of the same sentence and consider the effect the punctuation has on you as a reader:

- Echinacea is reputed—despite many scientists' skepticism—to prevent and relieve colds.
- Echinacea is reputed (despite many scientists' skepticism) to prevent and relieve colds.
- Echinacea is reputed, despite many scientists' skepticism, to prevent and relieve colds.

The dashes lend emphasis—sometimes even a touch of drama—to the material they enclose, while the parentheses downplay that material. The comma is the most neutral mark. Select the punctuation mark best suited to the effect you want your words to have on your readers.

list item 1

▶ The goals of the IC are (1) to promote the study of Spanish worldwide,

list item 2

(2) to improve the methods of teaching Spanish as a second language,

list item 3

and (3) to advance understanding of Spanish and Latin American

cultures.

▶ The proverb "Make hay while the sun shines" first appeared in *Don*

citation

Quixote (vol. 1, ch. 11).

EXERCISE **52.1** Dashes or Parentheses?

connect

mhconnectcomposition.com
Online exercise: QL52101

Edit the sentences below to add dashes or parentheses as needed. If either is possible, explain why you chose one over the other.

EXAMPLE

Getting old does not necessarily mean getting frail spending decades

in pain, being stooped over, and having to use a walker for many people

are now in good mental and physical health well into their nineties.

I used dashes here to emphasize the description of "getting frail."

1. People over 85 constitute the fastest-growing segment of our population, and by 2050 researchers project that a substantial number of Americans 800,000 will be over 100 years old.

2. Many studies predicting the length of people's lives indicate that about 35 percent of the factors are determined by genes that we cannot control which leaves about 65 percent that we may be able to influence.

3. One particular long-term study it tracked elderly men for 25 years pointed out that the men who lived to at least age 90 were primarily the ones who did not smoke; prevented diabetes, obesity, and high blood pressure; and exercised regularly.

4. A key indicator for many of the "young-elderly" 70-year-olds is eating healthily limiting calories, saturated fat, and sugar as well as getting high-quality protein and whole grains with plenty of fiber.

5. In addition, several long-term studies have shown that exercise for both women and men is the strongest predictor of healthy longevity.

More about ▸▸▸
Altering quotations
with ellipses and
brackets, 820-21

Capital replaced to fit
quotation into writer's
sentence.

Gutenberg replaces
he in source for clarity.

Freshwater added to
explain an antiquated
meaning of "sweet."

Writer uses *[sic]* to
point out subject-verb
agreement error (*are*
should be *is*).

52c Using Brackets

Square brackets have two primary uses—to indicate additions or changes to a quotation and to replace parentheses within parentheses:

▸ Ramo and Burke explain that "[i]n 1456, when the first Bible rolled off [Gutenberg's] press, there were fewer than 30,000 books in Europe."

▸ Only four years after Gutenberg printed his first book, the Spanish explorer Vincente Yanez Pinzón reached the mouth of the Amazon, which he called Río Santa María de la Mar Dulce ("River St. Mary of the Sweet [Freshwater] Sea").

Square brackets are also used to enclose the Latin word *sic,* which means *thus* or *so.* It is inserted into a quotation following an error to make clear that it was the original writer, not the person using the quotation, who made the mistake:

▸ The most compelling review noted that "each of these blockbusters are [sic] flawed in a different, and interesting, way."

NOTE The Modern Language Association (MLA) and the Council of Science Editors (CSE) do not recommend underlining or italicizing *sic*; the *Chicago Manual of Style* and the American Psychological Association (APA), on the other hand, do recommend setting this Latin word in italics.

Writing
Responsibly Using *[sic]*

Use *[sic]* cautiously: Calling attention to an error simply to point out another writer's mistake can make you look impolite or even condescending and might undermine your reputation (or *ethos*) as a respectful writer. When you come across a simple typographical error in a passage you want to quote (the writer typed *teh* instead of *the,* for example), either paraphrase or simply correct the error.

52d Using Colons

A colon is usually used after an independent (or main) clause to introduce and call attention to what follows. Colons are also used to separate titles from subtitles and in other conventional ways.

More about ▶▶▶
Independent clauses, 620–21, 637–39

1. To introduce an example, explanation, appositive, or list

Use a colon following an independent (or main) clause to introduce an example, an explanation, an appositive, or a list:

> examples
> ▶ Cervantes was unlucky : At the battle of Lepanto, he lost the use of his left hand, and on the return journey, he was captured by Algerian pirates.

> ▶ Writing *Don Quixote* gave its impoverished author something more
> appositive
> than just satisfaction : the opportunity to make some money.

> ▶ A number of important writers died on April 23 : Rupert Brooke,
> list
> William Wordsworth, Miguel de Cervantes, and William Shakespeare.

A dash can substitute for a colon in these cases, but a colon is more appropriate in formal writing.

Colons are also used to introduce a list that is preceded by the phrases *as follows* or *the following:*

> list
> ▶ **The following** writers all died on April 23 : William Wordsworth, Miguel de Cervantes, and William Shakespeare.

Do not introduce a list with a colon when the introductory clause concludes with *like, such as,* or *including:*

> ▶ A number of important writers all died on April 23, including : William Wordsworth, Miguel de Cervantes, and William Shakespeare.

More about ▶▶▶
Using commas in quotations, 794

2. To introduce a quotation

Use a colon to introduce a quotation only when it is preceded by an independent clause that would make sense without it, but not when the quotation is introduced by a signal phrase such as *she said* or *Hughes asks.*

                    ind. clause makes sense without quotation

COLON   In 1918, William Strunk, Jr., gave writers a piece of time-

              less advice: "Omit needless words."

             signal phrase needs quotation to make sense

COMMA   In 1918, William Strunk, Jr., said, "Omit needless words."

3. Other conventional uses

- Between title and subtitle and between publication date and page numbers (for periodicals) and location and publisher (for books) in bibliographic citations for some documentation styles

More about ▶▶▶
MLA style, 298–357
(ch. 17), *Chicago*
style, 401–28
(ch. 19), CSE style,
429–46 (ch. 20)

                  title   subtitle

Langford, David. "Hogwarts Proctology Class: Probing the End of Harry

    Potter." *New York Review of Science Fiction* 20.2 (2007): 1, 8–11. Print.

            title   subtitle   city   publisher

Satrapi, Marjane. *Persepolis 2: The Story of a Return.* New York: Pantheon,

    2004. Print.

More about ▶▶▶
Business letter
formats, 497–99

- Following the salutation and following *cc* in formal business correspondence

  ▶ Dear Professor Howard:

  ▶ cc: KM

- Between chapter and verse in scripture; between hours, minutes, and seconds; in ratios:

  ▶ Song of Solomon 3:1–11

  ▶ 4:30 p.m.

  ▶ Women outnumber men in college 2:1.

4. Avoid common mistakes with colons.

- Do not insert a colon between a verb and its complement or object.

               verb   object

  ▶ Young readers clamored: for the next volume in Stephenie

    Meyer's vampire love saga.

- Do not insert a colon between a preposition and its object.

  prep.   object
  ▸ *Vogue* announced a return to: hippie-style clothing.

EXERCISE 52.2 Using colons in a sentence

Write two sentences using colons, one to introduce an example or explanation and the other to introduce an appositive, list, or quotation. (See the section above for examples.)

connect

mhconnectcomposition.com
Online exercise: QL52102

52e Using Ellipses

Ellipses are a set of three periods, or *ellipsis points,* with a space between each. They are most often used to replace words removed from quotations, but they are also sometimes used to create a dramatic pause or to suggest that the writer is unable or unwilling to say something.

1. To indicate deletions from quotations

Although it is not acceptable to alter the meaning of a quotation, writers can and do omit words from quotations as needed to delete irrelevant information or to make a quotation fit into their own sentence. The ellipses alert readers that a change has been made:

comma + ellipses
▸ *Don Quixote* begins like a fable: "In a village of La Mancha, . . . there
comma + ellipses
lived not long since one of those gentlemen that keep a lance, . . . a
comma + ellipses   period + ellipses
lean hack, . . . and an old greyhound for coursing. . . ."

> Use four dots—a period plus the ellipses—if a deletion occurs at the end of the sentence.

With a parenthetical citation, insert the ellipses before the closing quotation marks and the period after the citation.

ellipses + close quote
▸ "They will have it his surname was Quixada . . ." (1).
citation + period

When only a few words are quoted or when the quotation begins with a lowercase letter, it is obvious that words have been omitted from the quotation, so no ellipses are needed:

▸ That Don Quixote keeps "a lean hack" suggests that he is no romantic hero, but instead minor, rather poor, country gentry.

Writing Responsibly

Altering Quotations

Exercise care when changing quotations: Never make a change that might distort the original or that might mislead readers, and always use ellipses and brackets to indicate an alteration.

More about ▶▶▶
Altering quotations,
293–94, 820–21,
832

NOTE If you are quoting a complete sentence, no ellipses are needed to indicate that the sentence comes from within a longer passage.

---

2. To indicate the omission of a line (or lines) of poetry

Use not a single ellipsis mark (three dots) but a whole line of dots to replace a missing line of poetry:

> ▶ One of the most famous lines in Robert Frost's poem "Mending Wall" is "Good fences make good neighbors," but the speaker's meaning is lost when this line is taken out of context:
>
> There where it is we do not need the wall:
>
> . . . .
>
> My apple trees will never get across
> And eat the cones under his pines, I tell him.
> He only says, "Good fences make good neighbors." (lines 23–27)

3. To indicate a dramatic pause or interruption in dialogue

An ellipsis can indicate an incomplete thought, a dramatic pause, or an interruption in speech:

> ▶ The disgruntled writer muttered, "The only word to describe my editor is . . . unprintable."

connect

mhconnectcomposition.com
Online exercise: QL52103

> **More about ▶▶▶**
> Signal phrases,
> 291–93, 299–303,
> 359–60

> **EXERCISE 52.3 Using brackets and ellipses with quotations**

Write a paragraph in which you quote a passage from another text, marking deletions with ellipses and enclosing additions in brackets. Your paragraph must include at least one addition and two deletions. Be sure to identify the quoted passage by using a signal phrase and parenthetical page number.

52f Using Slashes

The slash (or *virgule*) is used to mark the ends of lines in poetry when the poetry is run into a sentence:

▶ *Don Quixote* opens with some "commendatory verses" that warn the writer "Whoso indites frivolities, / Will but by simpletons be sought" (lines 62–63).

Slashes are also used in fractions and URLs:

▶ 1/2   1/3   3/4

▶ http://www.epcc.edu/Student/Tutorial/Writingcenter/handouts.html

In informal contexts, the slash is sometimes used to indicate that either term is applicable:

▶ I've got so many courses this semester that I decided to take Spanish pass/fail.

In more formal contexts (such as academic or business writing), replace the slash with the word *or,* or rewrite the sentence:

DRAFT   An effective writer revises his/her work.

BETTER   An effective writer revises his or her work.

BEST   Effective writers revise their work.

Slashes are also used in dates, but only in informal or technical contexts or in tables where space is at a premium.

TECHNICAL OR INFORMAL   6/26/09

FORMAL   June 26, 2009 or 26 June 2009

connect

mhconnectcomposition.com
Online exercise: QL52104

→ **EXERCISE 52.4** **Editing dashes, parentheses, brackets, colons, ellipses, and slashes**

In the following paragraph, add or delete dashes, parentheses, brackets, colons, ellipses, and slashes as necessary.

The Welsh poet Dylan Thomas 1914–1954 wrote many memorable poems but is perhaps most famous for one "Do not go gentle into that good night." Thomas's poem attempts to arouse his dying father a robust and vigorous man throughout most of his life to avoid leaving life weakly. The poem states its plea in its first two lines "Do not go gentle into that good night, Old age should burn and rave at close of day." The poem's second stanza begins: "Though wise men at their end know dark is right," pointing out that people often are aware "at the end know" of the finality of death. However, the stanza ends with "Do not go gentle into that good night." Stanzas 2 through 5 of the poem where Thomas shows it's only fitting to fight death to the very end explain that wise men, good men, wild men, and grave men do not leave life softly. The poem's last two lines demonstrate (as well as plead) "Do not go gentle into that good night. Rage, rage against the dying of the light." Perhaps the most moving line [in the poem] is also in the last stanza "Curse, bless, me now with your fierce tears, I pray." Here, Thomas's words they become increasingly stirring when one repeats them aloud express how his father's "fierce tears" would be both a misfortune and a mercy.

Work **Together**

Exchange Exercise 52.4 with a classmate. Check your partner's use of punctuation. Did he or she make any errors? If so, explain the effect these errors had on you as a reader. (Be specific.)

53 Capitalizing

Like a spire soaring over surrounding rooftops, a capital letter beckons the reader, calling attention to the word it adorns. But just as architecture varies from place to place, so the rules of capitalization vary from language to language.

ESL **Capitalization** For the non-native writer, English capitalization can be confusing. In Spanish, French, and German, the first-person singular pronoun is lowercase (*yo, je, ich*), but in English it is capitalized (*I*), although the other personal pronouns are not. In Spanish and French, the names of months and days of the week are lowercased, but not in English. In German, all nouns are capitalized, but in English only proper nouns are. Languages such as Arabic and Korean have no capital letters at all. Proofread your work carefully to adhere to the conventions of capitalization in the language in which you are writing, referring to this chapter and a good college dictionary as needed.

In English, capital letters are used to call the reader's attention in a variety of contexts. The Quick Reference box on the next page outlines the most important rules of capitalization in English. For cases not covered here, or when you are not sure,

839

Reference ➡ **Common Capitalization Do's and Don'ts**

Do capitalize . . .

   . . . the first word of a sentence. 840

     ▶ The day broke gray and dull.—Somerset Maugham, *Of Human Bondage*

   . . . proper nouns and proper adjectives. 842

     ▶ Aunt Julia, Beijing, Dad (used as a name), Band-Aid, Shakespearean, Texan

   . . . the first, last, and important words in titles and subtitles. 843

     ▶ *Harry Potter and the Order of the Phoenix*

   . . . the first-person pronoun *I*. 843

     ▶ I think; therefore, I am. —René Descartes

   . . . abbreviations and acronyms. 844

     ▶ Eng. Dept., UCLA, NYPD

Do *not* capitalize . . .

   . . . common nouns. 842

     ▶ dog, cat, aunt, city, my dad, bandage

   . . . compass directions. 842

     ▶ north, south, northwest, southeast

   . . . seasons or academic years and terms. 842

     ▶ spring, freshman, intersession

More about ▶▶▶
Nouns, 601–3
Adjectives, 606–7
Titles and sub-
  titles, 817–18, 843,
  847–48
Pronouns, 603–4

consult a dictionary. Your readers will think better of you if you avoid overcapitalizing.

53a Capitalizing the First Word of a Sentence

Capitalize the first letter of the first word of every sentence:

   ▶ (In response to Franklin Roosevelt's long tenure, the U.S. Congress passed an amendment limiting a president to two terms.

This rule applies even to sentences in parentheses, unless they are incorporated into another sentence:

More about ▶▶▶
Parentheses, 830–31

   ▶ His vice president, Harry S. Truman, decided not to run for reelection, although the amendment did not apply to him. (The sitting president was exempted.)

▶ Although the amendment did not apply to him (the sitting president was exempted), Truman decided not to run for reelection.

Capitalize the first word of a sentence you are quoting, even when it is incorporated into your own sentence:

▶ In response to a question about the amendment, President Eisenhower said, "By and large, the United States ought to be able to choose for its president anybody that it wants, regardless of the number of terms he has served."

Do not capitalize the first word when you are quoting only a phrase:

phrase
▶ President Eisenhower's "faith in the long-term common sense of the American people" made him feel the amendment was unnecessary.

When interrupting a quoted sentence, do not capitalize the first word of the second part:

▶ "By and large," Eisenhower said, "the United States ought to be able to choose for its president anybody that it wants, regardless of the number of terms he has served."

NOTE In MLA style, if you must change a capital to a lowercase letter (or vice versa) to incorporate a quotation into your sentence, place brackets around the letter to alert readers to the change.

> ***More about*** ▶▶▶
> Brackets, 832
> Altering quotations,
> 293–94, 820–21,
> 832, 835–36

If a colon links two ***independent clauses,*** capitalizing the first word following the colon is optional, but be consistent:

▶ Before Franklin Roosevelt, no U.S. president had held office for more than two terms: That precedent was broken with Roosevelt's third inauguration.

or

▶ Before Franklin Roosevelt, no U.S. president had held office for more than two terms: that precedent was broken with Roosevelt's third inauguration.

> **Independent (or main) clause** A word group that contains a subject and a main verb and that does not begin with a subordinating conjunction, relative pronoun, or relative adverb (620)

53b Capitalizing Proper Nouns and Proper Adjectives

Capitalize the first letter of ***proper nouns*** (the names of specific people, places, and things) and the adjectives derived from them. Do not capitalize common nouns (names for general groups of people, places, and things). The Quick Reference guide below provides examples of words in each group.

Quick Reference ➡ **Capitalize Proper Nouns and Proper Adjectives, but Not Common Nouns**

Proper Nouns and Proper Adjectives	Common Nouns
ACADEMIC DEPARTMENTS AND DISCIPLINES	
Political Science Department, Linguistics 377	political science, linguistics
PEOPLE	
Senator Robert C. Byrd, Mom (used as a name), Dickensian	the senator, my mother, novelistic
PLACES	
Yosemite National Park, Neptune, the Midwest	the park, that planet, midwestern
TIME PERIODS AND HOLIDAYS	
Tuesday, June, Memorial Day	a weekday, this summer, spring break
HISTORICAL EVENTS, PERIODS, AND DOCUMENTS	
Korean War, Roaring Twenties, the Emancipation Proclamation	the war, the twenties, the proclamation
ORGANIZATIONS, OFFICES, COMPANIES	
National Wildlife Federation, General Accounting Office, National Broadcasting Corporation	a conservation group, the legislative branch, the network, the corporation
TRADE NAMES	
Coke, Kleenex, Xerox	a soda, a tissue, a photocopy
NATIONS, ETHNIC GROUPS, RACES, AND LANGUAGES	
Pakistan, Pakistani, African American, Caucasian, Swahili	her country, his nationality, their language
RELIGIONS, RELIGIOUS DOCUMENTS, AND RELIGIOUS TERMS	
Buddhism, Jewish, Vedas, Bible, Allah, God	your religion, a religious group, a sacred text, biblical, the deity
TRANSPORTATION	
Greyhound, Amtrak, U.S.S. *Constitution*	a bus, the train, this battleship

53c   Capitalizing Titles and Subtitles

In general, capitalize the first and last words of titles and subtitles, as well as any other important words: nouns (*Pride, Persuasion*), verbs (*Is, Ran*), pronouns (*It, Their*), adjectives (*Green, Starry*), and adverbs (*Slow, Extremely*). Do not capitalize prepositions (*in, at, to, by*), co-ordinating conjunctions (*and, but, for, nor, or, so, yet*), *to* in infinitive verbs, or articles (*a, an, the*) unless they begin or end the title or subtitle.

Extremely Loud and Incredibly Close: A Novel	"I Kissed a Girl" (song)
"In the Basement of the Ivory Tower" (article)	*The Dark Knight* (movie)
Pokéman XD: Gale of Darkness (game)	*Flying Popcorn* (software)

NOTE Style guides may recommend different capitalization for titles and subtitles in reference lists and bibliographies. Check the style guide you are using and follow the rules described there.

> **More about ▶▶▶**
> MLA style, 298–357 (ch. 17)
> APA style, 358–400 (ch. 18)
> *Chicago* style, 401–28 (ch. 19)
> CSE style, 429–46 (ch. 20)

53d   Capitalizing the First-Person Pronoun *I* and the Interjection *O*

In all formal contexts, capitalize the first-person singular pronoun *I:*

▶ I wish I could meet myself in twenty years.

Although rarely used in contemporary prose, the interjection *O* should always be capitalized:

▶ Awake, O north wind, and come, O south wind! —Song of Solomon 4.16

However, the word *oh* should be capitalized only when it begins a sentence:

▶ "Oh literature, oh the glorious art, how it preys upon the marrow in our bones." —D. H. Lawrence

Writing
Responsibly | Capitalizing in Email and IM

In general, the rules of capitalization are the same online as they are in print. But while in print a writer may sometimes type a word in all capital letters for emphasis, in email or other online contexts, words typed in all capital letters are interpreted as shouting. When formatting is available, use italics (or bold-face type) for emphasis in online writing; when such formatting is unavailable, place an asterisk before and after the word you want to emphasize. Also, although omitting capital letters in email and instant messages may be acceptable in informal contexts, you should follow the rules of capitalization when texting or emailing in business or academic settings.

> **More about** ▶▶▶
> Abbreviations,
> 852–57 (ch. 55)

Acronym Words formed from the first letter of each major word in a name (854)

53e Capitalizing Abbreviations and Acronyms

Abbreviations of proper nouns should be capitalized, and acronyms should be typed in all capital letters:

| ABBREVIATIONS | U. of Mich., Anthro. Dept. |
| ACRONYMS | RADAR, NASA, OPEC |

→ **EXERCISE 53.1 Correcting capitalization**

The following sentences have been typed entirely in lowercase letters. Supply correct capitalization.

EXAMPLE

~~when~~ i moved into my first apartment this ~~september~~, i quickly

When I   *September I*

realized that i had to watch my pennies at ~~stop~~ and ~~shop~~.

I   *Stop*   *Shop*

connect
mhconnectcomposition.com
Online exercise: QL53101

1. when i went shopping with my friend jason, he called me a dumb shopper.

2. my cart was filled with products with names like kellogg's, maxwell house, and tide, but his cart had mostly store brands.

3. i told him that my mom would ask me, "why do you always have to have levi's? aren't the sears jeans just as good?" now that it was my own money, i understood.

4. on monday, I saw jason in the english class we have together, and as we opened up our books to a short story titled "king of the bingo game," i whispered to him, "thanks to you i saved fifteen dollars at the supermarket yesterday."

5. as we walked out of tyler hall and headed west to our history class, he said, "you'll have more money to spend on fashion if you spend less on detergent and ketchup."

Work **Together**

The rules of capitalization have not always been in place for writers of English. In groups of two or three, revise the passage below to follow today's rules of capitalization in English. Refer to this chapter or to a good dictionary to settle any disputes.

I do here in the Name of all the Learned and Polite Persons of the Nation, complain to your Lordship, as First Minister, that our Language is extremely imperfect; that its daily Improvements are by no means in proportion to its daily Corruptions; and the Pretenders to polish and refine it, have chiefly multiplied Abuses and Absurdities; and, that in many Instances, it offends against every Part of Grammar.

—Jonathan Swift, *Proposal for Correcting, Improving, and Ascertaining the English Tongue* (1712)

54 Italics and Underlining

Before the desktop computer, writers typed on typewriters and used underlining to emphasize words; set off the titles of longer works; distinguish words, letters, and numbers used as words; set off unfamiliar non-English words; and call out the names of ships, airplanes, spacecraft, and other vehicles. Now most writers type on computers and use italics for these purposes. Just about the only time underlining is used is to denote links to web pages and websites on the internet—something writers could not have imagined when they were typing on their Olivettis and Smith Coronas. The Quick Reference box on the next page outlines the most important rules for using italics and underlining.

Quick Reference ➡ **Common Italics Do's and Don'ts**

***Do* use italics . . .**

. . . with titles of longer works. 847

▶ We will be discussing the novel *Wuthering Heights* for the next two weeks. By the way, the novel's main character has nothing to do with the comic strip *Heathcliff.*

. . . for emphasis. 848

▶ I ask you *not* to read beyond the first chapter until we have discussed it in class.

(Use italics for emphasis sparingly in academic prose.)

. . . with words, letters, and numbers used as words. 849

▶ You will notice that several of the characters' names begin with the letter *h;* this can be confusing.

***Do not* use italics . . .**

. . . with titles of short works. 847

              "Girl"
▶ Jamaica Kincaid's story ~~*Girl*~~ is only one page long.
                ^

. . . with historical documents and religious works. 848

     Declaration of Independence   Bible
▶ The ~~*Declaration of Independence*~~ and the ~~*Bible*~~ take pride of place on my
           ^   ^
grandmother's bookshelf.

. . . with links to websites and web pages; underline links instead. 849

▶ If you do not want to buy the book, you can download it from *Project Gutenberg* <www.gutenberg.org/etext/768>.

54a Italicizing Titles of Longer Works

Use italics (or underlining) for titles of longer works, such as books, periodicals (magazines, journals, and newspapers), films, CDs, television series, and websites; use quotation marks for shorter works, such as stories, articles, songs, television episodes, and web pages:

▶ Annie Proulx's collection *Close Range: Wyoming Stories* includes the story "Brokeback Mountain," which originally appeared in the *New Yorker* magazine. Kenneth Turan, critic for the *Los Angeles Times,* called the 2005 film *Brokeback Mountain* "groundbreaking," and Roger Ebert of the *Chicago Sun-Times* gave it two thumbs up. The

More about ▶▶▶
Using quotation marks with titles of shorter works, 817–18

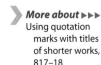
mhconnectcomposition.com
Additional resources: QL54001

Brokeback Mountain soundtrack on CD includes songs like "He Was a Friend of Mine" by Willie Nelson and "The Devil's Right Hand" by Steve Earle.

In addition, stand-alone items like court cases and works of art (paintings and sculptures) are italicized:

- ▶ *Bowers v. Hardwick*
- ▶ *Mona Lisa*
- ▶ *The Bronco Buster*

In contrast, the titles of major historical documents and religious works are not italicized:

- ▶ Magna Carta, Mayflower Compact, Kyoto Protocol
- ▶ Bible, Qu'ran, Vedas

54b Italicizing for Emphasis

Italics are sometimes used for emphasis:

- ▶ Rowling wants readers to *identify* with Harry, not merely to *sympathize* with him.

In the sentence above, the italics heighten attention to the contrast. To be effective, use italics sparingly for emphasis. Using italics haphazardly or overusing them can annoy or even confuse readers:

- ▶ He wanted *readers* to know *his* characters, not *merely* to observe them.

Writing Responsibly
Using Italics for Emphasis

When using italics for emphasis, consider your reader. Sometimes italics can help convey the writer's feelings, but will readers be interested? In a personal context, the use of italics in the sentence below might be acceptable:

- ▶ Should *I* call *him*, or should I wait for *him* to call *me*?

But such emphasis on the writer's emotions is usually inappropriate in a business or academic context.

54c Italicizing Names of Vehicles

The names of individual trains, ships, aircraft, and spacecraft are all italicized:

Titanic, Spirit of St. Louis, Challenger

However, vehicles referred to by company, brand, or model names are not:

Corvette, Boeing 747

54d Italicizing Words, Letters, or Numbers Used as Words

When referring to words, letters, or numbers used as words, set them off from the rest of the sentence with italics:

▶ My chemistry teacher used the word *interesting* to describe the results I got on my last lab. He told me to be more careful next time, to dot all my *i*'s and cross all my *t*'s.

54e Italicizing Unfamiliar Non-English Words and Latin Genus and Species

More about ▶▶▶
Plurals of letters, 811

English is an opportunistic language; when encountering new things or ideas, English speakers often adopt words already used in other languages. The word *raccoon,* for example, comes from Algonquin and the word *sushi* from Japanese. Once they are fully absorbed, they are typed with no special formatting. Until then, borrowings should be italicized:

▶ The review provides a good example of *diegesis* in that it describes the film without making a judgment about it.

To determine whether a non-English word warrants italics, check your dictionary: Words familiar enough to be found in a college dictionary should not be set in italics.

Latin genus and species names are also set in italics:

▶ *Acer saccharum* are the Latin genus and species for the sugar maple.

54f Underlining Hyperlinks

In recent years, underlining has taken on a new, specialized meaning: It is used (along with color) to indicate hyperlinks in both printed and online documents (Figure 54.1, p. 850). Because many documents today will ultimately appear online, writers are increasingly reserving underlining for hyperlinks and using italics for all the other purposes outlined in this chapter.

FIGURE 54.1 Hyperlinks The hyperlinks on many web pages (including the *Google News* page shown here) are set in bright-blue type and underlined to set them off from the surrounding text.

connect

mhconnectcomposition.com
Online exercise: QL54101

→ **EXERCISE 54.1 Correcting underlining and italics**

Cross through words or phrases that should not be italicized or underlined, and circle any words or phrases that should be.

EXAMPLE

The 1960s television show ⟨Hogan's Heroes⟩ depicted ~~Nazism~~ as a joke, and the show ⟨F Troop⟩ falsified the relationship between ~~Native Americans~~ and the military.

1. In a review of the book "Hot, Flat, and Crowded," by Thomas Friedman, David Victor reminds readers that the Soviet Union's 1957 launch of the spacecraft Sputnik galvanized the United States's space program and calls Friedman's book "a plea for a new Sputnik moment."

2. The film The Matrix makes references to Plato's *Cave Allegory* from the book "The Republic" and is also indebted to Buddhist philosophy in that it considers the world *maya,* or illusion, a concept expressed in the Buddhist religious works the *Tripitaka.*

3. Thomas Jefferson's motto while writing the Declaration of Independence might have been "novus ordo seclorum," a new order of the ages, for with that document a new nation was born.

4. In 1992, Vice President Dan Quayle mistakenly told a sixth grader that the student had spelled the word potato incorrectly and that the word should not end with an o but with an additional e.

5. Articles on these and other topics appear in Wikipedia, http://en.wikipedia.org, but remember that Wikipedia is often more *comprehensive* than *reliable.*

EXERCISE **54.2** Adding italics and underlining

Underline any words in the passage below that should be set in italics or underlined, and add quotation marks where needed.

A study reported in the journal Archives of General Psychiatry this month linked the father's age with the likelihood that his children will develop bipolar disorder. The study, called Advancing Paternal Age and Bipolar Disorder by Emma M. Frans et al., looked for a link between paternal, not maternal, age, although a slight correlation with maternal age was also found. The suspected cause is a type of random mutation among sperm cells called de novo mutations. An article called Advancing Paternal Age and Autism, published two years ago, also found a link between the likelihood of having an autistic child and paternal age. Both articles can be found at the Archives of General Psychiatry website: http://archpsyc.ama-assn.org/.

connect
mhconnectcomposition.com
Online exercise: QL54102

> *More about* ▶▶▶
> Using quotation
> marks, 814–23
> (ch. 50)

Work **Together** ◀

Exchange Exercise 54.2 with a partner. Check your classmate's use of italics and underlining. Did your partner make any errors? If so, explain the effect these errors had on you as a reader. (Be specific.)

55 Using Abbreviations

▶ **More about** ▶▶▶
MLA style, 298–357 (ch. 17)
APA style, 358–400 (ch. 18)
Chicago style, 401–28 (ch. 19)
CSE style, 429–46 (ch. 20)

When you see this familiar symbol, you know at a glance that the object it adorns was made from recycled materials. When they are familiar to the audience, icons like this one communicate information briefly and quickly. Abbreviations accomplish a similar goal in writing: They convey information rapidly, but they work only when readers know what they stand for.

While used frequently in business, scientific, and technical contexts, abbreviations are used sparingly in writing in the humanities and for a general audience, except in tables (where space is at a premium) and in bibliographic citations.

When you do abbreviate, use a period with a person's initials and with most abbreviations that end in lowercase letters:

▶ J. K. Rowling   Martin Luther King, Jr.   St. John

▶ St.   Blvd.   Ave.

Use a period after each letter with abbreviations of more than one word:

▶ i.e.   e.g.   a.m.   p.m.

Most abbreviations made up of all capital letters no longer use periods:

▶ BS   MA   DVD   UN

Reference ➡ **Common Abbreviation Do's and Don'ts**

Do use abbreviations . . .

. . . of titles before or after names. 854

▶ Dr. Martin Luther King, Jr. *or* Martin Luther King, Jr., PhD

. . . when they are familiar to readers. 854

▶ The role of the CIA has changed dramatically since 2001.

. . . with specific numerals and dates. 855

▶ My class on ancient Rome meets at 8:30 a.m. to study the period from 509 BCE to 476 CE. The book for that class costs $87.50.

. . . in names of businesses when they are part of the official name. 856

▶ Warner Bros. Entertainment Inc.   Spindletop Oil & Gas Co.

Do *not* use abbreviations . . .

. . . of titles not used with a proper name. 854

    doctor   *colonel*

▶ My ~~dr.~~ is married to a ~~col.~~ in the Marines.

. . . of popular online terms in formal prose. 855

Too much information

▶ ~~TMI~~ with very little focus makes this work a data parade without a point.

. . . of names, words, courses, parts of books, states and countries, days and months, holidays, and units of measurement in formal prose. 855

    brothers William Joseph   *feet*

▶ My ~~bros.~~ ~~Wm.~~ and ~~Jos.,~~ even though they are both now over six ~~ft.~~ tall, still

                morning Christmas

love waking up early in the ~~a.m.~~ on ~~Xmas.~~

. . . of Latin terms. 856

(Replace with English equivalents in prose.)

        for example

▶ Leafy green vegetables, ~~e.g.,~~ arugula, kale, and spinach, can reduce the risk of heart disease.

The Quick Reference box above outlines the most important rules for using abbreviations.

connect
mhconnectcomposition.com
Additional resources: QL55001

55a **Abbreviating Titles before and after Names**

▶ Mr. Tony Carter   Christopher Aviles, PhD

▶ Ms. Aoife Shaughnessy   Namazi Hamid, DDS

▶ Dr. Jonnelle Price   Robert Min, MD

▶ Rev. Jane Genung   Frederick C. Copelston, SJ

In most cases, avoid abbreviating titles when they are not used with a proper name:

▶ I'm hoping my English ~~prof.~~ *professor* will write me a letter of recommendation.

Academic degrees are an exception:

▶ My auto mechanic comes from a highly educated family: His father has an MS, his mother has an MLS, and his sister has a PhD.

Never use a title both before and after a name: Change *Dr. Hazel L. Cunningham, PhD* to either *Dr. Hazel L. Cunningham* or *Hazel L. Cunningham, PhD*.

connect
mhconnectcomposition.com
Additional resources: QL55002,
QL55003

55b **Using Familiar Abbreviations: Acronyms and Initialisms**

Acronyms and initialisms are abbreviations made of all capital letters formed from the first letters of a series of words. Acronyms are pronounced as words (*AIDS, CARE, NASA, NATO, OPEC*), while initialisms are pronounced as a series of letters (*DNA, HBO, JFK, USA*). Familiar acronyms and initialisms are acceptable in any context:

▶ Myanmar democracy advocate Aung San Suu Kyi failed to meet with UN envoy Ibrahim Gambari on Wednesday.

However, if the abbreviation is likely to be unfamiliar to readers, spell out the term on first use and follow it with the abbreviation in parentheses. Subsequently, just use the abbreviation:

▶ The International Olympic Committee (IOC) failed to take action following the arrest of two elderly Chinese women who had applied for permission to protest in the designated protest areas during the Beijing Olympics. A spokesperson claimed that the IOC has no control over the protest areas.

Writing
↑ Responsibly   **Using Online Abbreviations Appropriately**

connect
mhconnectcomposition.com
Additional resources: QL55004

A new breed of initialism has emerged in online discourse. Here are some examples:

BFN (bye for now)   LOL (laughing out loud)

OIC (oh, I see!)   ROTFL (rolling on the floor, laughing)

OMG (oh, my God!)   TMI (too much information!)

OTOH (on the other hand)

The irreverence of some of these initialisms corresponds with the freewheeling characteristics of online discourse. Use them in text messages or on informal networking sites, but avoid them in college and professional writing, including most emails. While they might establish your online savvy, they might also annoy readers in more formal contexts, undermining your ethos (or credibility).

> **More about ▶▶▶**
> Ethos, 159–60

55c   Using Abbreviations with Specific Years (BC, BCE, AD, CE), Hours (a.m., p.m.), Numbers (no.), Dollars ($)

▶ The emperor Augustus ruled Rome from 27 **BCE** until his death in 14 **CE**.

▶ The Roman historian Titus Livius (known as Livy) lived from 59 **BC** until **AD** 17.

> AD precedes the number; BC, BCE, and CE follow the number.

▶ I didn't get home until 11:45 p.m., because the no. 27 bus was so late.

▶ I owe my sister $27.32, and she won't let me forget it.

connect
mhconnectcomposition.com
Additional resources: QL55005, QL55006

NOTE The abbreviations BCE (for *before the common era*) and CE (for *common era*) are now generally preferred over BC (*before Christ*) and AD (*anno domini*, "the year of the Lord" in Latin).

55d   Avoiding Abbreviations of Names, Words, Courses, Parts of Books, States and Countries, Days and Months, Holidays, and Units of Measurement in Prose

connect
mhconnectcomposition.com
Additional resources: QL55007, QL55008

      France   Christmas January
▶ In ~~Fr.,~~ people receive gifts not on ~~Xmas~~ but on ~~Jan.~~ 6.
    ^   ^   ^

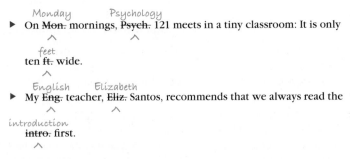

▶ On ~~Mon.~~ mornings, ~~Psych.~~ 121 meets in a tiny classroom: It is only
    Monday ⌃   *Psychology* ⌃

    feet
ten ~~ft.~~ wide.
   ⌃

▶ My ~~Eng.~~ teacher, ~~Eliz.~~ Santos, recommends that we always read the
    English ⌃   *Elizabeth* ⌃

    introduction
~~intro.~~ first.
 ⌃

An exception is the names of businesses, when the abbreviation is part of the official name:

▶   Dun & Bradstreet, Inc., was ~~inc.~~ in New York **&** is still located there.
                           incorporated ⌃   *and* ⌃

connect
mhconnectcomposition.com
Additional resources: QL55009

55e Replacing Latin Abbreviations with English Equivalents in Formal Prose

Latin abbreviations, like those below, are generally avoided in formal writing (except in bibliographies).

▶ e.g.	for example	▶ cf.	compare
▶ i.e.	in other words	▶ et al.	and others
▶ etc.	and so forth	▶ N.B.	note especially

NOTE Both *etc.* and *and so forth* are best avoided in formal prose. Instead, include all the items or precede a partial list with *such as* or *for example*. Follow *e.g.* and *i.e.* with a comma if you use them in tables or parenthetical material. Common Latin abbreviations are not italicized or underlined.

connect
mhconnectcomposition.com
Online exercise: QL55101

→ **EXERCISE 55.1 Correcting abbreviations**

Correct the use of abbreviations, in the following sentences, which were written for an academic reader in the humanities.

EXAMPLE

    spring   *Astronomy*   *History Astronomy*
This ~~spr.~~ I am taking ~~Astro.~~ 121, the ~~Hist.~~ of ~~Astro.~~
     ⌃   ⌃   ⌃   ⌃

1. My prof. (Dr. Wm. Irvine, PhD.) assigned a fascinating book on Ptolemy (83–168 A.D.), a Gr. astron. and astrol. who lived in Egypt.

2. Ptol. wrote his great treatise on astron., the *Almagest,* in 147 A.D.

3. In addition to the *Almagest,* Ptol. wrote other works, e.g., *Tetrabiblios, Harmonics,* and *Optics,* that are important in their fields.

4. The National Aeronautics and Space Administration has a good website, and one of its pages mentions Ptol.'s model for predicting eclipses, but it says he developed it in about BC 150, which I think is a mistake.

5. The final for this class is scheduled for Jan. 5, after Xmas, so I'm hoping Santa will bring me a copy of the *Almagest,* trans. by GJ Toomer.

6. I would buy a copy of it for myself but, OMG, it costs over 67.50 dollars.

7. To understand Ptol. more fully, I read ch. 2 from Seilik's book, which explains Ptol.'s geocentric model of the universe.

8. Cf. that with Evans's discussion in ch. 1 of *The Hist. and Pract. of Ancient Astro.*

9. I would major in astro. except that all the classes are held in a bldg. on a noisy blvd.

10. Instead, I will major in accounting, get a job with Deloitte & Touche or Kraft Bros., and study astro. on the side.

⬆ Make It **Your Own**

Rewrite a recent text message to avoid abbreviations. Then write a paragraph explaining how this change affects the tone of the message. (If you do not have such a text message, write one using at least two of the abbreviations in the Writing Responsibly box on p. 855.)

Work **Together** ◀

In groups of two or three, craft a text message using as many abbreviations and initialisms as you can. Then trade messages with another group and translate.

56 Using Numbers

Are we "number one" or "#1"? It depends on the context. At a football game, while dressed in your team's colors, you would probably use the numeral: The context is informal and, besides, the word *one* might not fit as well on the giant hand! But just as you would not attend an interview with your face painted orange and white, in many formal contexts spelling out the number is more appropriate.

More about ▶▶▶
Appropriate language, 563–72 (ch. 29)
Ethos, 159–60

Writing Responsibly   Ethos and Convention

Using numbers and symbols in conventional ways does not normally affect meaning. Yet conventional usage is important, especially in formal contexts like school or the workplace, because it lends support to your *ethos*, or credibility. As a marker of appropriateness, it can subtly affect the way your audience perceives you and how seriously they take what you have to say.

Rules for deciding whether to use numerals or to spell out numbers vary widely according to context. In business and the news, single-digit numbers are usually spelled out, while numerals are used for numbers over ten. In the humanities, numbers that can be written in one or two words are usually spelled out, while numerals are used for larger numbers. In the sciences, numerals are customarily used for all numbers. The best practice is to choose a style that will make sense to your audience, and then be consistent in its use. The rules below are appropriate to an academic audience in the humanities.

56a Spelling Out Numbers When They Can Be Expressed in One or Two Words

Spell out numbers under a hundred and round numbers—numbers that can be expressed in one or two words:

▶ Satchel Paige pitched sixty-four scoreless innings and won twenty-one games in a row.

If your text uses a combination of numbers—some that can be expressed in one or two words and others that cannot—use numerals throughout for consistency's sake:

▶ Satchel Paige pitched an estimated ~~two thousand~~ 2,000 baseball games during his career. At his first game, 78,383 fans were in attendance, and at his first game as a starter, 72,434 spectators looked on.

Avoid beginning a sentence with numerals. Instead, spell out the number or revise your sentence:

▶ ~~78,000~~ Seventy-eight thousand people attended Satchel Paige's first game as a pitcher.

▶ Satchel Paige's first game as a pitcher drew 78,000 fans.

Numbers over a million are often best expressed as a combination of words and numerals:

▶ Over 10 million fans attended Negro League baseball games in 1930.

56b **Following Conventions for Dates, Times, Addresses, Specific Amounts of Money and Other Quantitative Information, and Divisions of Literary Works**

- **Dates:** May 4, 2010   the fourth of May   429 BCE
  1066 CE   AD 1066

- **Times, years:** 4:15 p.m.   seven o'clock   1990s
  the nineties   1999–2009   from 1999 to 2009

Getting It
Across   **Exceptions to the Rule**

In some places—such as New York City—avenue numbers are spelled out: *Fifth Avenue.*

- **Phone numbers, addresses:** (800) 624-5789
  26 Peachtree Lane   221 W. 34th Street
  Atlanta, GA 30303   New York, NY 10001

- **Exact sums of money:** $10.95 $579.89
  $24 million

- **Decimals and fractions:** half   ½
  three-quarters   ¾   4⅝   3.95

NOTE MLA style generally recommends using the percent symbol (%) with numerals. The *Chicago Manual* recommends using the word *percent* with numerals in writing for the humanities and the symbol % with numerals in writing for the sciences.

- **Scores, statistics, and percentages:** 5 to 4   42–28
  13.3 percent (or 13.3%)   3 out of 10

- **Measurements:** 55 mph   90–100 rpm   135 pounds   5 feet
  9 liters   41°F

- **Divisions of books, plays, poems:** part 3   book 7
  chapter 15   page 419 or p. 419   act 1   scene 3   lines 4–19

 Punctuating Numbers in American English Conventions for punctuating numbers differ across cultures. In the United States, use a comma to mark divisions of hundreds and a period to separate whole numbers from decimal fractions:

▶ 2,541   94.7

connect
mhconnectcomposition.com
Online exercise: QL56101

→ **EXERCISE 56.1** **Correcting numbers: Spelling out numbers or using numerals**

Revise the following sentences according to the rules for using numerals or spelling out numbers discussed above.

EXAMPLE

                6:30
At about ~~six thirty~~ a.m., the planet Venus is visible low on the horizon;
thirty   ∧
~~30~~ minutes before that, you can also see Jupiter.
∧

1. 1965 saw the first probe reach Mars; it took 22 close-up pictures of the planet and 2 pictures of its moons.

2. The *Mars Pathfinder* was launched on December four, nineteen ninety-six and landed seven months later, on July four, nineteen ninety-seven.

3. *Pathfinder* collected over 16,000 images and conducted 20 tests of the soil.

4. In all, *Pathfinder* collected over two billion bits of data.

5. Mars has a mountain that is seventy-eight thousand feet tall and a canyon that is six to seven times as deep as the Grand Canyon.

6. A Martian day is forty-five minutes longer than an Earth day.

7. Mars is about fifty percent smaller in diameter than Earth: Its diameter is about 4,200 miles, whereas Earth's is about eight thousand miles.

8. Venus, the 6th largest planet, is roughly the size of Earth, at about seven thousand seven hundred miles in diameter.

9. The 2nd closest planet to the sun, its surface can heat up to 900 degrees F.

10. I love to study the night sky, but living at 253 6th Avenue, New York, NY, I can see it only when I travel.

Work **Together** ←

Read the student paper in chapter 18 (pp. 389–400). In groups of two or three, discuss whether Heather DeGroot has followed the rules for using numbers laid out in this chapter. What effect does context have on following the rules? What effect would changing her treatment of numbers have on her intended audience?

57 Using Hyphens

More about ▶▶▶
Using a dictionary,
586–88

Just as glue can hold pieces of paper, plastic, wood, and glass together, hyphens can bind pieces of a word into a single whole. They join parts of a compound adjective or number, link some prefixes and suffixes to the root word, connect numbers in a fraction, and link word parts that split at the end of a line.

Keep in mind, though, that while some words, like *cross-purposes* or *cross-examination,* use a hyphen, not all compounds need that glue: Some are so closely bound by usage that they have become a single unit (*crosscurrent*), while others are linked merely by placement (*cross hairs*). Consult a dictionary to determine how the parts of a compound should be connected, and if a compound word is not in the dictionary, follow the rules below.

57a Using Hyphens to Form Compounds

1. Hyphenate compound adjectives before the noun but not after.

Hyphenate compound modifiers when they precede the noun but not when they follow it:

Writing Responsibly

Hyphenating with Readers in Mind

Correct hyphenation can make reading easier for your audience, but over-hyphenating may drive readers crazy. When editing your paper, check a dictionary to make sure not only that all compounds are hyphenated correctly but also that you have not added hyphens where they are not needed. Keep a particularly close eye on phrasal (or multiword) verbs and subject complements, which do not need hyphens:

phrasal verb
▶ The police knocked on our door after Fred turned up the volume on the stereo.

subject complement
▶ Sometimes Fred seems like a thirteen year old.

More about ▶▶▶
Phrasal verbs,
756–58
Subject complements, 615

noun
▶ The well-intentioned efforts by the International Olympic Committee

(IOC) to allow peaceful protests were thwarted by the Chinese government.

noun
▶ The efforts of the IOC to allow peaceful protests were

well-intentioned but ill-conceived.

When an adverb ending in *-ly* is part of a compound adjective, no hyphen is necessary:

▶ In China, politically-sensitive websites are blocked by the

government.

When two or more parallel compound adjectives share the same base word, avoid repetition by putting a space after the first hyphen and stating the base word only once:

Class- and race-based analyses of *To Kill a Mockingbird* show that
Harper Lee was not completely able to rise above her social background.

2. Use a hyphen to link certain prefixes and suffixes to the root word.

In general, hyphens are not needed to attach prefixes and suffixes to the root word:

*de*compress   *pre*test   *re*define   *sub*category

But the prefixes *all-*, *ex-*, and *self-* and the suffix *-elect* are always attached to the root word with a hyphen:

> ▶ *all*-star   *ex*-boyfriend   *self*-absorbed   president-*elect*

When *all, elect, self,* and even *ex* (a word in Latin, meaning *from*) are freestanding words, they do not need a hyphen:

> ▶ *all* the participants in the game   ▶ to *elect* the candidates
>
> ▶ her sense of *self*   ▶ an *ex* officio member

In most cases, to avoid double or triple letter combinations, add a hyphen:

> ▶ *anti*-inflationary   *multi*-institutional   *re*-education   ball-*like*
>
> ▶ Exceptions: override   cooperate

If the prefix will be attached to a numeral or to a root that begins with a capital letter, insert a hyphen:

> ▶ post-1914   pre-1945   anti-Semite   un-American

Finally, if the prefix-plus-root combination could be misread as another word, add a hyphen to avoid confusion:

> ▶ He finally recovered from a bout of the flu.
>
> ▶ We re-covered the sofa with a floral fabric.

3. Use a hyphen in compound numbers under one hundred, between scores (in sports), and between numbers (to replace *from . . . to*).

Numbers over twenty and under one hundred are hyphenated when written out:

> ▶ Workaholics would work twenty-four hours a day, seven days a week, fifty-two weeks a year if their bodies would cooperate.

In sports scores, use a hyphen between numbers instead of *to*.

> ▶ The Vikings lost to the Bengals 23-17.

A hyphen can replace the words *from* and *to* with dates:

▶ The years from 1919 to 1938 offered a brief respite between the two world wars.

or

▶ The years 1919-1938 offered a brief respite between the two world wars.

But do not combine methods:

▶ from 1919~~/~~1938 to   or   ~~from~~ 1919-1938

57b   Using Hyphens to Break Words at the Ends of Lines

Word processing programs generally "wrap" text (that is, they move a too-long word at the end of a line to the beginning of the next line). Still, you may occasionally need to break words manually. If you do, follow these rules:

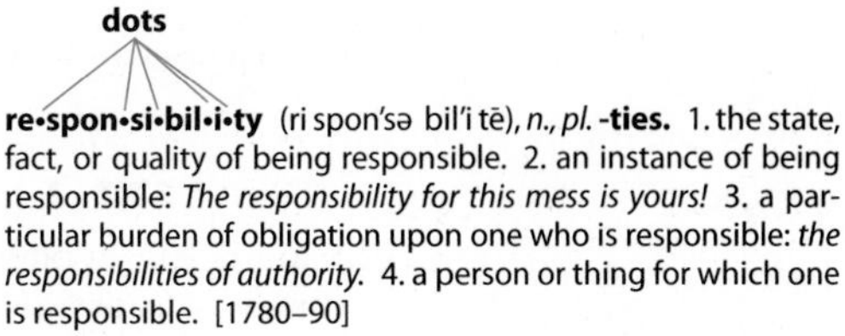

- Break words between syllables. (Check your dictionary for syllable breaks.)

  ▶ CIA operatives in the Middle East have found it impossible to ~~infiltr~~ infil- ~~trate~~ ate al Qaeda.

- Break compound words between parts or after hyphens.

  ▶ Washington DC's long-standing handgun ban was ~~overturn~~ over- ~~turned~~ ed in 2008 by the Supreme Court.

- Do not break one-syllable words or contractions.

  ▶ To determine surface area, multiply the ~~wid~~ width ~~th~~ of a room by its length.

dots

re·spon·si·bil·i·ty (ri spon'sə bil'i tē), *n., pl.* **-ties.** 1. the state, fact, or quality of being responsible. 2. an instance of being responsible: *The responsibility for this mess is yours!* 3. a particular burden of obligation upon one who is responsible: *the responsibilities of authority.* 4. a person or thing for which one is responsible. [1780–90]

FIGURE 57.1 Syllable breaks in the dictionary Dictionaries indicate syllabification by placing dots between syllables.

Tech

Breaking URLs and Email Addresses

Most word processing programs offer automatic hyphenation of words. However, you must break URLs or email addresses manually. If you are following MLA or CSE style guidelines, break URLs only after a slash. If you are following *Chicago Manual* guidelines, break a URL or email address before a period or other punctuation, or after the @ symbol, a single or double slash, or a colon. Do *not* insert a hyphen.

- Break words so that at least two letters remain at the end of a line and at least three letters move down to the beginning of the next line.

   ▶ Increases in the cost of gas and food have ~~reduc-~~ *re-*
   duced
   ~~ed~~ discretionary spending.
   ^

connect

mhconnectcomposition.com
Online exercise: QL57101

→ **EXERCISE 57.1 Adding and deleting hyphens**

Add and delete hyphens as needed in the following sentences. (You may consult a dictionary.)

EXAMPLE

The Deadhead phenomenon began in the mid-1960s, when the
^
Grateful Dead became active in the Haight-Ashbury music scene.
^

1. In 1971, a long time friend of the Grateful Dead took on a self assigned project to put together a mailing list to keep fans informed of upcoming shows.

2. Clearly, there were more than just fifty or seventy five people on this list, because city to city caravans of tie dye wearing Deadheads soon sprang up.

3. Their long distance travel was motivated by changes night to night in the songs the musicians played.

4. Shows sold out for the long lived and well loved band, and a true blue community of Deadheads was created.

5. Although the band is now defunct, well and long proven loyalty is still highly-visible in thruway rest stops, where large
groups of slack jawed fans, exhausted from concerts by Grateful Dead spinoff bands like RatDog and Phil Lesh and Friends,
still congregate.

→ **EXERCISE 57.2 Correcting hyphens**

connect

mhconnectcomposition.com
Online exercise: QL57102

Using a dictionary, correct the passage below, adding and deleting
hyphens or revising as needed:

Attention Deficit Hyperactivity Disorder (ADHD) was first described in a children's book called "The Story of Fidgety Philip"
(1845), written for the author's three year old son. Today, the
National Institute of Mental Health estimates that from 3-5 percent of children have ADHD. But diagnosis is difficult because
loss of self control and attention is common. To be diagnosed,
children must have difficulties in two or more of the following areas: school-, social-, community-, home-, or playground-
behavior. Other causes of inattention or hyperactivity include
middle-ear infections that cause hearing loss, seizure disorders,
and learning disabilities. Baby-sitters and class-room teachers frequently notice problems and recommend testing, but
well-qualified and highly-experienced clinicians are best able
to diagnose the disorder and recommend treatment.

Work **Together** ←

Exchange Exercise 57.2 with a classmate. Check your partner's
use of hyphens. Did he or she make any errors? If so, explain
the effect these errors had on you as a reader. (Be specific.)

Glossary of Key Terms

A

absolute phrase (620) A phrase consisting of a noun or pronoun followed by a participle (the *-ing* or *-ed* form of a verb) that modifies an entire clause or sentence: *Our spirits rising, we began our vacation.*

abstract (118) Overview of a text, with a summary of its main claims and most important supporting points.

abstract noun (621) See *noun.*

acronym (854) An abbreviation formed from the first letters of a series of words and pronounced as a word (*AIDS, NASA*). Compare *initialism.*

active voice (682–84) See *voice.*

adjective (606–07, 700–08) A word that modifies a noun or pronoun with descriptive or limiting information, answering questions such as *what kind, which one,* or *how many: a happy camper, the tall building.*

adjective clause (621) A subordinate clause, usually beginning with a relative pronoun (such as *who, whom, which,* or *that*), that modifies a noun or pronoun: *Sam baked the pie that won first prize.* Adjective clauses can also begin with the subordinating conjunctions *when* and *where.*

adverb (607–08, 700–08) A word that modifies a verb, adjective, other adverb, or entire phrase or clause, answering questions such as *how? where? when?* and *to what extent or degree? The door opened abruptly.*

adverb clause (622) A subordinate clause, usually introduced by a subordinating conjunction such as *although, because,* or *until,* that functions as an adverb within a

sentence: *I walk to work because I need the exercise.*

agreement (646–63) The matching of form between one word and another. Verbs must agree with, or match, their subjects in person and number (subject-verb agreement), and pronouns must agree in person, number, and gender with their antecedents (pronoun-antecedent agreement). See also *antecedent, gender, number, person.*

alignment (177) Arrangement in a straight line (vertical, horizontal, or diagonal) of elements on a page or screen to create connections among parts and ideas.

alternating method (68) A method of organizing a comparison-contrast paragraph or essay by discussing each common or divergent trait of both items before moving on to the next trait. See also *block method.*

analogy (578) An extended comparison of something familiar with something unfamiliar. (See also *figurative language, simile, metaphor.*) An analogy becomes a false analogy (150) when the items being compared have no significant shared traits.

analysis (69, 129–30) The process of dividing an entity, concept, or text into its component parts to study its meaning and function. Analysis is central to critical reading and is a common strategy for developing paragraphs and essays in academic writing. Also called *classification, division.*

annotation (124) The process of taking notes on a text, including writing down definitions, identifying key concepts, highlighting unfamiliar vocabulary and words that reveal tone, and making

connections or noting personal responses.

antecedent (657) The noun or noun phrase to which a pronoun refers. In the sentence *The pitcher caught the ball and threw it to first base,* the noun *ball* is the antecedent to the pronoun *it.*

antonyms (586) Words with opposite meanings—for example, *good* and *bad.* Compare *synonyms.*

APA style (358–400) The citation and documentation style of the American Psychological Association, used frequently in the social sciences.

appeals (158) Efforts to engage the reader. Emotional appeals (**pathos**) engage the reader's feelings; intellectual appeals (**logos**) engage the reader's rational faculties; ethical appeals (**ethos**) engage the reader's sense of fairness and respect for good character.

appositive (618) A noun or noun phrase that renames a preceding noun or noun phrase and is grammatically equivalent to it: *Miguel, my roommate, avoids early morning classes.*

arguable claim (142) A claim on which reasonable people might hold differing opinions and that can be supported by reasons and evidence.

argument (142) An attempt to persuade others to accept your opinion by providing logical reasons and compelling supporting evidence. See also *persuasive argument, purpose.*

article (606, 748–51) The words *a, an,* and *the. A* and *an* are the **indefinite articles;** *the* is the **definite article.** The **zero article** refers to nouns that appear with no article.

G1

asynchronous media (199) Communication media such as email and discussion lists that allow users to participate at their own convenience. Compare *synchronous media; see also discussion list.*

audience (10–17) The intended readers for a writing project or listeners for a presentation.

author note (385) In APA style, a note that occurs on the first page of an article to identify the author, provide contact information, and acknowledge support and conflicts of interest; student projects usually omit author notes.

authority (134, 150) An expert on a topic. An authority becomes a false authority when the person from whom the writer draws evidence is not truly an expert on the topic.

B

bar graph (83) An information graphic that compares data in two or more categories using bars of different heights or lengths.

belief (153–55) A conviction based on values.

biased or hurtful language (568–72) Language that unfairly or offensively characterizes a particular group and, by extension, the individual members of that group.

bibliographic notes (340) Notes that add information or point readers to other sources on the topic.

block method (68) A method of organizing a comparison-contrast paragraph or essay by discussing all the traits of the first item before moving on to traits of the second item. See also *alternating method.*

block quotations (342, 386, 817) Exact quotations of longer than four lines (MLA style) or forty words (APA style) in which quotation marks are omitted and the quotation is indented as a block from the left margin of the text.

block-style letter (497) A format for business letters in which all text is flush with the left margin and a line space is inserted before paragraphs. In **modified block style,** all text begins flush left except for the return address, date, closing, and signature.

blog (or **weblog**) (192) An online journal that chronicles thoughts, opinions, and information often on a single topic. See also *asynchronous media.*

body (39) The portion of a text or presentation that develops and supports the thesis.

Boolean operator (231) The terms *AND, NOT,* and *OR* used in databases and search engines for refining keyword searches.

brainstorming or **listing** (25) A technique for generating ideas by listing all the ideas that come to you during a fixed amount of time; brainstorming can also take place in groups.

breadcrumb trail (193) A navigation tool for websites that shows the click path the user took to get to the page.

C

case (686–95) The form of a noun or pronoun that corresponds to its grammatical role in a sentence. Many pronouns have three cases: **subjective** (for example, *I, we, he, she, they, who*), **objective** (for example, *me, us, him, her, them, whom*), and **possessive** (for example, *mine, ours, his, hers, theirs, whose*). Nouns change form only to indicate possession.

cause and effect (69) A method of paragraph or essay development that explains why something happened or what its consequences were or will be.

***Chicago* style** (401–28) The citation and documentation style recommended in the *Chicago Manual of Style,* used frequently in the humanities.

chronological organization (39) A pattern of organization in which events are discussed in the order in which they occurred; chronological organization is used when telling a story (narrative) or explaining a process (process analysis).

citation (295, 298, 358) The acknowledgment of sources in the body of a research project, usually tagged to a bibliography, works-cited list, or reference list. See also *in-text citation, parenthetical citation, signal phrase.*

citation-name system (430–31) In CSE style, a system of acknowledgment for research projects that provides a superscript number in the text and a list of references, numbered in alphabetical order (usually by author's surname) at the end of the project.

citation-sequence system (430–31) In CSE style, a system of acknowledgment for research projects that provides a superscript number in the text and a list of references, numbered in order of appearance, at the end of the project.

claim (153–56) An assertion that is supported by reasons and evidence. A *claim of fact* asserts a verifiable piece of information; it can be a central claim in an informative writing project but not in an argumentative writing project. A *claim of causation* asserts the causes or effects of a problem; a *claim of policy* asserts how best to resolve a problem or what is the best course of action to take; a *claim of value* asserts that one's personal beliefs or convictions should be embraced. Claims of causation, policy, and value are all appropriate central claims in argumentative writing projects.

classical model (164–65) A model for organizing an argument composed of five parts: introduction, background, reasons and evidence, counterclaims and counterevidence, and conclusion.

Compare *Rogerian* and *Toulmin* models.

classification See *analysis*.

clause (620–24) A word group with a subject and a predicate. An **independent clause** can stand on its own as a sentence. A **subordinate** (or **dependent) clause** functions within a sentence as a noun, adjective, or adverb but cannot stand as a sentence on its own. See also *sentence*.

cliché (581–82) A figure of speech, idiom, or other expression that has grown stale from overuse. See also *figurative language, idiom*.

climactic organization (39) A pattern of organization that orders supporting paragraphs from least to most engaging or compelling.

clustering or **mapping** (26–27) An idea-generating technique for organizing, developing, or discovering connections among ideas by writing a topic in the center of the page, adding related topics and subtopics around the central topic, and connecting them to show relationships.

coherence (42, 59–64) The quality of a writing project in which sentences and paragraphs are organized logically and clearly so that readers can move from idea to idea without having to puzzle out the relationships among parts.

collaborative learning (30–32, 50–51) A process by which classmates or colleagues enhance understanding by studying together and reviewing one another's writing.

collective noun (602) See *noun*.

colloquialism (565) An informal expression common in speech but usually out of place in formal writing.

comma splice (637–45) The incorrect joining of two independent clauses with a comma alone—without a coordinating conjunction.

common knowledge (266) General information that is available from a number of different sources and that is considered factual and incontestable. Common knowledge does not require documentation.

common noun (601) See *noun*.

commonplace book (22–24) A written record (quotations, summaries, paraphrases) of the ideas of others and your own reactions to those ideas, preserved in a notebook or online document.

comparative form (705–07) See *comparison of adjectives and adverbs*.

comparison and contrast (68–69) A pattern of paragraph or essay development in which the writer points out the similarities and differences among items. See also *alternating method, block method*.

comparison of adjectives and adverbs (705–707) The form of an adjective or adverb that indicates the relative degree of the quality or manner it specifies. The **positive form** is the base form of the adjective (for example, *brave*) or adverb (for example, *bravely*). The **comparative form** indicates a relatively greater or lesser degree (*braver, more bravely*). The **superlative form** indicates the greatest or least degree (*bravest, most bravely*).

complement (614–17) See *subject complement, object complement*.

complete predicate (613) See *predicate*.

complete subject (612) See *subject*.

complete verb (627, 670–71) A main verb together with any helping verbs needed to express tense, mood, and voice.

complex sentence (624) See *sentence*.

compound-complex sentence (624) See *sentence*.

compound predicate (614) See *predicate*.

compound sentence (624) See *sentence*.

compound subject (612) See *subject*.

conciseness (516) The statement of something in the fewest and most effective words needed for clarity and full understanding.

conclusion (72–74) The closing paragraph or section in an essay or other writing project. An effective conclusion provides readers with a sense of closure.

concrete noun (602) See *noun*.

conditional clause (680–81) A subordinate clause that begins with *if* and describes a set of circumstances (*conditions*) and that modifies an independent clause that describes what follows from those circumstances.

conjunction (529, 534, 610) A word that joins a word, phrase, or clause to other words, phrases, or clauses and specifies the way the joined elements relate to one another. **Coordinating conjunctions** (*and, but, or, for, nor, yet,* and *so*) join grammatically equivalent elements, giving them each equal significance: *Jack and Jill went up the hill.* **Correlative conjunctions** are pairs of terms (such as *either . . . or, neither. . . nor,* and *both . . . and*) that join grammatically equivalent elements: *Both Jack and Jill fell down.* **Subordinating conjunctions** link subordinate clauses to the clauses they modify. *After Jack and Jill went up the hill, they both fell down.*

conjunctive adverb (608) A transitional expression (such as *for example, however,* and *therefore*) that can relate one independent clause to a preceding independent clause.

connotation (16, 575) The emotional resonance of a word. Compare *denotation*.

content notes (339–40, 384–85) Footnotes or endnotes that clarify or justify a point in your text or that acknowledge the contributions of others in the preparation of your project.

context (18) The social, rhetorical, and historical setting in which a text is produced or read. The context in which Lincoln's Gettysburg

Address was produced is different from the context in which it may be read today, but both are important for fully understanding the text.

contrast (177) In design, differences that call attention to and highlight one element among others.

coordinate adjectives (789–90) Two or more adjectives that separately and equally modify the noun they precede. Coordinate adjectives should be separated by a comma: *an innovative, exciting vocal group.*

coordinating conjunction (529, 610) See *conjunction.*

coordination (526–31) The joining of elements of equal weight or importance in a sentence. See also *subordination.*

correlative conjunction (610) See *conjunction.*

counterevidence (145, 163–67) Evidence that undermines your claim.

count noun (or **countable noun**) (603, 748) See *noun.*

critical reading and thinking (116–40) A thoughtful, systematic approach to a text or idea, going below the surface to uncover meaning and draw conclusions. Critical reading and thinking begins with reading actively; it requires analysis, interpretation, synthesis, and critique.

critique (134) An evaluation based on evidence accumulated through careful reading, analysis, interpretation, and synthesis. It may be positive, negative, or a bit of both.

CSE style (429–46) The citation and documentation style recommended in *Scientific Style and Format: The CSE Manual for Authors, Editors, and Publishers,* used frequently in the sciences.

cumulative adjectives (789–90) Two or more adjectives that modify not only the noun or pronoun they precede but also the next adjective in the series. Cumulative adjectives should not

be separated by commas: *A great American rock band.*

cumulative sentence (555) A sentence that begins with the subject and verb of an independent clause and accumulates additional information in subsequent modifying phrases and clauses: *The mountaineers set off, anticipating the view from the peak but wary of the dangers they faced to get there.*

D

dangling modifier (724–26) A word, phrase, or clause that erroneously does not actually modify the subject or anything else in a sentence, leaving it to the reader to infer the intended meaning. In the sentence "As your parent, you should put on a sweater when it is cold," the phrase "as your parent" dangles; it appears illogically to modify the subject, "you," but actually refers to the speaker, as in "As your parent, I recommend that you put on a sweater when it is cold."

database (228) A collection of data, now usually available in digital form. In research, databases provide citations to articles in academic journals, magazines, and newspapers.

declarative sentence (611) See *sentence.*

deductive reasoning (144–46) A form of reasoning that moves from a general principle to a specific case to draw a conclusion; if the premises are true, the conclusion must be true. Compare *inductive reasoning;* see also *syllogism.*

definite article (749) See *article.*

definition (70) An explanation of the meaning of a word or concept made by including it in a larger class and then providing the characteristics that distinguish it from other members of that class: In the definition *People are reasoning animals, people* is the term to be defined, *animals* is

the larger class to which people belong, and *reasoning* is the trait that distinguishes people from other animals. Also, a pattern of development in which the writer explains the special meaning of a term by explaining what the term includes and excludes.

degree (705–07) See *comparison of adjectives and adverbs.*

demonstrative pronouns (604) The pronouns *this, that, these,* and *those* used as nouns or adjectives to rename and point to nouns or noun phrases: *These are interesting times we live in.*

denotation (573–75) The literal meaning of a word; its dictionary definition. Compare *connotation.*

dependent clause (621) A subordinate clause. See *clause.*

description (66–67) In writing, a pattern of paragraph or essay development that draws on specific, concrete details to depict a scene or object in terms of the senses: seeing, hearing, smelling, touching, tasting.

determiner (607, 748–54) An article (*a, an,* or *the*) or a possessive, demonstrative, or indefinite pronoun that functions as an adjective to specify or quantify the noun it modifies: *a cat, some cats, that cat, her cat.*

development (46–48, 66–70, 288–90) The depth at which a topic or idea is explored.

dialect (564) A variant of a language with its own distinctive pronunciation, vocabulary, and grammar.

diction (573) The choice of words to best convey an idea.

direct object (615) See *object.*

direct question (716, 825) A sentence that asks a question and ends with a question mark. Compare *indirect question.*

direct quotation (716, 815–16) A copy of the exact words that someone has written or spoken, enclosed in quotation marks or, for longer quotations, indented as a block. Compare *direct quotation.*

discussion list (198–99, 277) An electronic mailing list that enables a group of people to participate in email conversations on a specific topic. See also *asynchronous media*.

division (69) See *analysis*.

documentation (295, 298, 358) Information in a bibliography, reference list, or list of works cited that allows readers to locate a source cited in the text. See also *citation*.

document design (176–84) The arranging and formatting of text elements on a page or screen using proximity (nearness), alignment, repetition, and contrast to indicate their relative importance and their relation to each other.

DOI (376, 411, 437) Digital object identifier, a permanent identifier assigned to electronic publications.

domain (255–56) The ending of the main portion of a URL; the most common domains are *.com* (commercial), *.edu* (educational), *.gov* (governmental), and *.net* (network).

double-entry reading journal (127) An online or printed journal with one column for passages from sources (quotations, summaries, or paraphrases) and another column for the writer's response to the passage.

doublespeak (576) Euphemisms that are deliberately deceptive, used to obscure bad news or sanitize an ugly truth.

drafting (43, 46–48, 288–90) The stage of the writing process in which the writer puts ideas on paper in complete sentences and paragraphs.

E

editing (96–99) The stage of the writing process in which the writer fine-tunes the draft by correcting words and sentences and revises them to enhance clarity and power.

ellipses (835–36) A set of three periods, or *ellipsis points,* with a space between each. Ellipses are used to replace words deleted from quotations; they are also sometimes used to create a dramatic pause or to suggest that the writer is unable or unwilling to say something.

elliptical construction (520, 733) A construction in which grammatically necessary words can be omitted as understood because their meaning and function are otherwise clear from the context: *The movie [that] we saw last night is excellent.*

entertaining text (11) See *purpose*.

essential (or restrictive) element (791–93) A word, phrase, or clause that provides essential information about the word or words it modifies. Essential elements are not set off by commas: *The train that she is on has been delayed.* See also *nonessential element*.

et al. (305, 363) Abbreviation of the Latin phrase *et alia,* "and others."

ethos (158) See *appeals*.

euphemism (567) An inoffensive word or expression used in place of one that might be offensive or emotionally painful.

evaluation (249–59) In research, assessment of sources to determine their relevance and reliability.

evidence (46–48) The facts, examples, statistics, expert opinions, and other information writers use to support their claims.

excessive coordination (530) The joining of tediously long strings of independent clauses with *and* and other conjunctions.

excessive subordination (535) The stringing together of too many subordinate structures.

exclamatory sentence (611) See *sentence*.

exemplification (67–68) A pattern of paragraph or essay development that explains by example or illustration.

expletive construction (521) A kind of inverted construction in which *there* or *it* precedes a form of the verb *to be* and the subject follows the verb: *There are seven days in a week.*

explicate (457) To read a text closely, analyzing it line by line or even word by word; explications of a text are common in literary analysis.

exploratory argument (142) An argument in which the author considers a wide range of evidence before arriving at the most plausible position; in exploratory arguments, the thesis is often offered at the conclusion of the writing project. See also *argument, persuasive argument, purpose*.

expressive text (11) See *purpose*.

F

fact (154) A piece of information that can be verified.

fallacy (149–53) A mistake in reasoning.

familiar to unfamiliar (39) A method of organization that begins with material that is known by the audience and moves toward material that the audience will not know.

faulty predication (731–32) A logical or grammatical mismatch between subject and predicate.

field research (244–47) The gathering of research data in person rather than from sources. Field research includes interviews, observational studies, and surveys. See also *primary source*.

figurative language or **figures of speech** (577–78) The imaginative use of language to convey meaning in ways that reach beyond the literal meaning of the words involved. See *analogy, hyperbole, irony, metaphor, personification, simile, understatement*.

flaming (199) Writing a scathing, often ad hominem, response to someone with whom the writer disagrees, usually in email or on internet forums.

focused freewriting (24–25) See *freewriting.*

font (179–80) Typeface; fonts may be serif (such as Times Roman) or sans serif (such as Arial), may be set in boldface, italics, or underlining, and may be in a larger or smaller size (the most common sizes are 10 point and 12 point).

formal outline (40–42) See *outline.*

formalist approach (452) An approach to literature and art that focuses on the work itself rather than on the author's life or other theoretical approaches.

format (179–84) The look of a document created by choice of font and color and use of white space, lists, headings, and visuals. See also *layout.*

fragment (626–36) An incomplete sentence punctuated as if it were complete, beginning with a capital letter and ending with a period, question mark, or exclamation point.

freewriting (24–25) An idea-generating technique that requires writing nonstop for a fixed period of time (often ten to fifteen minutes); in *focused freewriting,* the writer writes nonstop about a specific topic or idea.

function word A word that indicates the relationship among other words in a sentence. Examples include **articles, conjunctions,** and **prepositions.**

funnel introduction (70–72) An essay introduction that begins with broad statements and narrows in focus to conclude with the thesis statement. See also *introduction.*

fused sentence or **run-on sentence** (637–45) A sentence in which one independent clause improperly follows another with no punctuation or joining words between them.

future perfect progressive tense (676) See *tense.*

future perfect tense (676) See *tense.*

future progressive tense (676) See *tense.*

future tense (674) See *tense.*

G

gender (657) The classification of nouns and pronouns as feminine (*woman, mother, she*), masculine (*man, father, he*), or neuter (*table, book, it, they*).

general to specific (38–39) A method of organization that begins with a general statement (the **thesis statement** or **topic sentence**) and proceeds to provide specific supporting reasons and evidence.

generalization (149–50) A broad statement. If not supported by specific details, a generalization becomes a hasty generalization (jumping to conclusions) or a sweeping generalization (application of a claim to all cases when it applies only to a few).

generic noun (658) A noun used to designate a whole class of people or things rather than a specific individual or individuals: *the average child.*

genre (18) A category or type of writing; in literature, genres include poetry, fiction, and drama; in college writing, genres may include analytical essays, case studies, or observational reports.

gerund (619) The present participle of a verb (the *-ing* form) used as a noun: *Walking is good exercise.*

grammar (600) The rules of a language that structure words so they can convey meaning.

grounds (166) In an argument, the reasons or evidence that support the claim. See *Toulmin model.*

H

helping verb or **auxiliary verb** (605, 670–71, 763–64) A verb that combines with a main verb to provide information about tense, voice, mood, and manner. Helping verbs include forms of *be, have,* and *do* and the modal verbs *can, could, may, might, must, shall, should, will, would,* and *ought to.*

home page (191, 193, 195) On a website, the page designed to introduce visitors to the site.

homonyms (589) Words that sound exactly alike but have different spellings and meanings: *their, there, they're.*

HTML (196) Hypertext Markup Language, a coding system used to format texts for the Web.

hyperbole (578) Deliberate exaggeration for emphasis: *That restaurant makes the best pizza in the universe.* See *figurative language.*

hyperlink (193) A navigation tool that allows users to jump from place to place on a web page or from web page to web page; hyperlinks (or links) appear as highlighted words or images on a web page.

hypertext (192) An online text that provides links to other online files, texts, images, audio files, and video files, allowing readers to jump to other related sites rather than reading *linearly.*

hypothesis (214–15) A proposed answer to a research question that is subject to testing and modification during the research process.

I

idea journal (22–23) An online or printed record of your thoughts that you can draw on to develop or explore a topic.

idiom (581) A customary expression whose meaning cannot be determined from the literal meaning of the words that compose it: *They struggled to make ends meet.*

imperative (680) See *mood, sentence.*

indefinite article (606, 748–51) See *article.*

indefinite pronoun (604, 651–52, 658–59) A pronoun such as *anybody, anyone, somebody, some,* or *several* that does not refer to a specific person or thing.

independent clause (620) See *clause.*

indicative (680) See *mood.*

indirect object (616, 742) See *object.*

indirect question (716, 825) A sentence that reports a question and ends with a period: My teacher asked us *if we texted each other even when we're in the same room.* Compare *direct question.*

indirect quotation (716, 816) A sentence that reports what someone has said rather than quoting word-for-word. Compare *paraphrase, direct quotation.*

inductive reasoning (144–45) A form of reasoning that draws conclusions based on specific examples or facts. Compare *deductive reasoning.*

infinitive (619, 759–61) A verbal formed by combining *to* with the base form of the verb (*to decide, to eat, to study*). Infinitives can function as adjectives and adverbs as well as nouns. See *verbal.*

informal (scratch) outline (40) See *outline.*

information graphics (81–84) Graphics that convey and depict relationships among data; information graphics include tables, bar graphs, line graphs, and pie charts.

informative (or **expository**) **report** (12, 477–78) A text in which the main purpose is to explain a concept or report information. See also *purpose.*

initialism (854) Abbreviation formed from the first letters of a series of words and pronounced as letters (*DNA, HBO*). Compare *acronym.*

intensive pronoun (604) A pronoun that renames and emphasizes its antecedent: *Dr. Collins herself performed the operation.*

interjection (611) Words like *alas* and *ugh* that express strong feeling but otherwise serve no grammatical function.

interpret (131–32, 279–80, 288–90) Explain the meaning or significance of a text, artwork, or event.

interpretive analysis (451) Writing that studies in detail the meaning or significance of literary texts, cultural works, political events, and so on.

interrogative pronoun (604) A pronoun such as *who, whom, whose, what,* or *which* used to introduce a question: *What did she say?*

interrogative sentence (611) See *sentence.*

in-text citation (299–314, 359–68, 401–02, 430–31) A citation that appears in the body of the research project. See also *parenthetical citation, signal phrase.*

intransitive verb (614) A verb that does not require a direct object: *The child smiled.*

introduction (38, 70–72) The opening paragraph or section of an essay or other writing project. An effective introduction should identify your topic and your stance toward the topic, establish your purpose, and engage your readers. See also *funnel introduction.*

invention techniques (22–29) Prewriting strategies that help you generate and explore ideas. See *brainstorming, freewriting.*

inverted-funnel conclusion (73) A conclusion that begins with a restatement of the thesis (in different words) and broadens out to discuss implications, next steps, or possible solutions. See also *conclusion.*

irony (451, 578) The use of language to suggest the opposite of its literal meaning or to express an incongruity between what is expected and what occurs. See *figurative language.*

irregular verb (666–69) A verb that does not form the past tense or past participle by adding *-ed* to the base form.

J

jargon (566) The specialized vocabulary of a particular profession or discipline; inappropriately technical language.

journal (22, 127–28) A place to record observations and ideas in writing. Also, a periodical that publishes scholarly articles. See also *periodical.*

journalists' questions (plus two) (27) Questions that ask *who, what, where, when, why,* and *how* to help you explore a topic. In college writing, also ask yourself about the significance of your topic (*Is it important?*) and its consequences (*What are its effects?*).

K

keyword (223–24) A term entered into an internet search engine, online database, or library catalog to find sources of information.

L

layout (179) The visual arrangement of text and images using proximity (nearness), alignment, repetition, and contrast. See also *format.*

level of diction (16) The choice of words to convey a tone (formal or informal) appropriate to the audience. See *tone, connotation.*

linear text (192) A document, such as a novel or magazine article, that is arranged so that readers begin at page 1 and read through to the end. Compare *hypertext.*

line graphs (84) A type of information graphic that uses lines and points on a graph to show changes over time.

link (193) See *hyperlink.*

linking verb (615) A verb that expresses a state of being rather than an action and connects the subject to its subject complement.

The verb *be,* when used as a main verb, is always a linking verb. *They are excited.* See also *subject complement.*

logical fallacy (149–53) See *fallacy.*

logos (158) See *appeals.*

lurk (256) Read online discussions without contributing.

M

main verb (605, 670) The part of a verb phrase that carries its principal meaning. See *verb phrase.*

mechanics (839–67) Conventions controlling capitalization, italics, abbreviation, numbers, and hyphenation.

menu (193) A list of the main sections of a website.

metaphor (578) An implied comparison between unlike things stated without *like, as,* or other comparative expressions: *Her mind buzzed with original ideas.* See *figurative language, simile.*

metasearch engine (224–25) Internet search engines that return the top search results from several search engines at once, with duplicate entries deleted.

misplaced modifier (718–24) An ambiguously, confusingly, or disruptively placed modifying word, phrase, or clause.

mixed construction (728–32) A sentence with parts that do not fit together grammatically or logically.

mixed metaphor (580) A combination of multiple conflicting figures of speech for the same concept. See *figurative language.*

MLA style (297–357) The citation and documentation style of the Modern Language Association, used frequently in literature and languages.

modal verb (605, 670, 762–64) See *helping verb.*

modified block-style letter (497) See *block-style letter.*

modifier A word, phrase, or clause that functions as an adjective or adverb to qualify or describe another word, phrase, or clause.

mood (680–82) The form of a verb that indicates how the writer or speaker views what is written or said. The **indicative mood** states facts or opinions and asks questions: *I finished my paper.* The **imperative mood** issues commands, gives instructions, or makes requests: *Hand in your papers by Friday.* The **subjunctive mood** expresses possibility, as in hypothetical situations or wishes: *If I were finished, I could go to bed.*

N

name-year system (430) In CSE style, a system of acknowledgment for research projects that includes the last name of the author and the year of publication in parentheses in the text; is accompanied by an alphabetical list of references at the end of the project.

narration (67) A pattern of paragraph or essay development that tells a story, usually in chronological (time) order. See also *chronological organization.*

near-homonyms (589) Words that are close but not the same in pronunciation (*moral, morale*) or are different forms of the same word (*breath, breathe*).

neologism (566) A newly coined word or expression.

netiquette (503) A word composed of parts of the words *internet* and *etiquette* that refers to conventions of politeness in online contexts.

noncount noun (or uncountable or mass noun) (603, 748) See *noun.*

nonessential (or nonrestrictive) element (791–93) A modifying word, phrase, or clause that adds information to the element it modifies but does not identify it. Commas should set off nonessential elements from the rest of the sentence. *My grandfather, who*

recently retired, worked for the same company for forty-five years.

noun (601–03) A word that names an idea (*justice*), thing (*chair*), quality (*neatness*), action (*judgment*), person (*Albert Einstein*), or place (*Tokyo*). **Proper nouns** name specific places, people, or things and are usually capitalized: *Nairobi, Laura Bush.* **Common nouns** name members of a class or group: *turtle, skyscraper.* **Collective nouns** name a collection that can function as a single unit: *committee, family.* **Concrete nouns** name things that can be seen, touched, heard, smelled, or tasted: *planet, symphony, skunk.* **Abstract nouns** name qualities or ideas that cannot be perceived by the senses: *mercy, fear.* **Count (or countable) nouns** name countable things and can be either singular or plural: *cat/cats, idea/ideas.* **Noncount (or uncountable or mass) nouns** name ideas or things that cannot be counted and do not have a plural form: *knowledge, pollution.*

noun clause (622) A subordinate clause that functions as a noun. See *clause.*

noun phrase (617–18) A noun and its modifiers.

number (646) The form of a word that indicates whether it is singular, referring to one thing (*a student*), or plural, referring to more than one (*two students*).

O

object (615–18, 741–42) A noun or pronoun (or a noun phrase or noun clause) that receives or benefits from the action of a transitive verb or that follows a preposition. A **direct object** receives the action of the verb: *My friend wrote a letter.* An **indirect object** benefits from the action of the verb: *My friend wrote me a letter.* The **object of a preposition** usually follows a preposition to form a prepositional phrase. *She sent the letter by mail.*

object complement (617, 742–43) An adjective or noun phrase that follows the direct object and describes the condition of the object or a change that the subject has caused it to undergo: *The candidate declared his opponent incompetent.*

objective case (686–95) See *case.*

object of a preposition (618) See *object.*

opinion (155) The most plausible answer for now, based on an evaluation of the available facts. Opinions are subject to revision in light of new evidence and are often the basis of argumentation.

outline (40–42, 286–87) A method of classifying information into main points, supporting points, and specific details. An **informal** (or **scratch**) **outline** arranges ideas in order of presentation; a **formal outline** uses roman and arabic numerals, upper- and lowercase letters, and indentions to classify information into main points, supporting points, and specific details; a **sentence outline** writes out main points, supporting points, and specific details in complete sentences; a **topic outline** uses words and phrases to indicate the ideas to be discussed.

P

paragraph (52–79) A group of sentences that focus on a single topic or example, often organized around a *topic sentence.*

parallelism (539–48) In writing, the expression of equivalent ideas in equivalent grammatical structures. In an outline, the use of the same pattern or form for headings at each level.

paraphrase (118–19, 271–74) The statement of the ideas of others in one's own words and sentence structures, rather than using the words and sentence structures of the source.

parenthetical citation (300–68) A citation to a source that appears in parentheses in the body of a research paper. Compare *signal phrase;* see also *in-text citation.*

participial phrase (619–20, 761) A phrase in which the present or past participle of a verb acts as an adjective: *the writing assignment, the written word.*

participles (619–20, 664–66) Forms of a verb that combine with helping verbs to form certain tenses and that, as verbals, can function as adjectives. The **present participle** is the *-ing* form of the verb. The **past participle** is the *-ed* form in regular verbs (the same as the past tense) but takes various forms in irregular verbs. See *participial phrase, tense, verbal.*

particle (756–57) A preposition or adverb that combines with a verb to create a new verb with a meaning that differs from the verb's meaning on its own—for example, *throw away* versus *throw.*

parts of speech (601–11) The categories in which words can be classified according to the role they play in a sentence. English has eight parts of speech: *noun, pronoun, verb, adjective, adverb, preposition, conjunction,* and *interjection.*

passive voice (682–84) See *voice.*

past participle (664–69) See *participle.*

past perfect progressive tense (674–79) See *tense.*

past perfect tense (674–79) See *tense.*

past progressive tense (674–79) See *tense.*

past tense (674–79) See *tense.*

patchwriting (271–74) A faulty paraphrase that relies too heavily on the language or sentence structure of the source text. Patch-written texts may replace some terms from the source passage with synonyms, add or delete a few words, or alter the sentence structure slightly, but they do not put the passage fully into fresh words and sentences.

pathos (158) See *appeals.*

patterns of development (66–70) See *analysis, cause and effect, comparison and contrast, definition, description, exemplification, narration,* and *process analysis.*

PDF (Portable Document Format) (196, 228) A file format developed by Adobe Systems that allows documents to be opened in different systems without altering their formatting.

peer revising (100–101) A revising strategy in which the writer solicits feedback on a text from classmates, colleagues, or friends. See also *revising.*

perfect progressive tense (674–79) See *tense.*

perfect tenses (674–79) See *tense.*

periodical (228) A publication, such as a magazine, newspaper, or scholarly journal, that is issued at regular intervals—daily, weekly, monthly, quarterly. See also *journal.*

periodic sentence (555–56) A sentence that reserves the independent clause for the end, building suspense that highlights key information when it finally arrives.

person (646) The form of a word that indicates whether it corresponds to the speaker or writer (*I, we*), the person addressed (*you*), or the people or things spoken or written about (*he, she, it, they, Marta, milkshakes*).

persona (8) The personality of the writer as reflected in tone and style.

personal pronoun (604, 687) The pronouns *I, me, you, he, him, she, her, it, we, us, they, them,* which take the place of specific nouns or noun phrases.

personal statement (112–14) In a portfolio, the writer's description of the contents and explanation for the choice and arrangement of selections. See also *portfolio*.

personification (578)   The attribution of human qualities to nonhuman creatures, objects, ideas, or phenomena: *The tornado swallowed the house.* See *figurative language*.

persuasive argument (142)   An argument that advocates for a claim. The writer's purpose is to convince readers to agree with or at least to respect a position on a debatable issue. See also *argument, exploratory argument, purpose*.

phrasal verb (756–59)   A verb combined with one or two particles that together create a new verb with a meaning different from that of the original verb alone. See *particle*.

phrase (617–20)   A group of related words that lacks a subject, predicate, or both. A phrase cannot stand alone as a sentence, but it can function *in* a sentence as a noun, a verb, or a modifier.

pie chart (82–83)   An information graphic that depicts the relationship of the parts to the whole; its sections must add up to 100 percent.

plagiarism (263–80)   Presenting a work or a portion of a work of any kind—a paper, a photograph, a speech, a web page—by someone else as if it were one's own. At some colleges and universities, *patchwriting* is considered plagiarism.

plain text (189)   A computer text format that does not allow for styling such as boldface and italics.

plural (646–47)   Referring to more than one thing. See *number*.

point of view (451)   The perspective of the narrator in a work of literature.

portfolio (111–14)   A printed or online collection of a writer's work. A portfolio may contain the writer's best work, a range of types

of writing (a proposal, a report, a set of instructions), or a collection of texts from a single project (prewriting, outline, first draft, revised draft). A portfolio usually also includes a table of contents and a personal statement. See also *personal statement*.

positive form (705–07)   See *comparison of adjectives and adverbs*.

possessive case (687–95)   See *case*.

possessive pronoun (604)   The pronouns *my, mine, your, yours, his, hers, its, our, ours, your, yours, their,* and *theirs,* which indicate possession.

predicate (613–14)   The part of a sentence or clause that states (*predicates*) something about the subject. The **simple predicate** consists of a main verb together with any helping verbs: *Marta is writing her parents a long email.* The **complete predicate** consists of the simple predicate together with any objects, complements, and modifiers: *Marta is writing her parents a long email.* A **compound predicate** is a complete predicate with two or more simple predicates joined with a conjunction: *Marta wrote the email but decided not to send it.*

prefix (592)   A group of letters that attaches to the beginning of a root word to modify its meaning: *act, react.*

prejudice (155)   Ascribing qualities to an individual based on generalities about a group, generalities that are often inaccurate. See also *stereotype*.

premise (145–48)   A claim or assumption on which the conclusion of an argument is based. See *syllogism*.

preposition (609, 773–80)   A word or term that relates nouns or pronouns to other words in a sentence in terms of time, space, cause, and other attributes.

prepositional phrase (618)   A preposition followed by its object—a noun or pronoun

and its modifiers. Prepositional phrases function as adjectives and adverbs: *the cat with gray fur.*

present participle (664–66)   See *participle*.

present perfect progressive tense (674–79)   See *tense*.

present perfect tense (674–79)   See *tense*.

present progressive tense (674–79)   See *tense*.

present tense (674–79)   See *tense*.

press, or **media, releases** (513–14)   Brief articles that announce events to newspapers, magazines, and online media outlets.

previewing (118–19)   Scanning the title, subtitle, abstract, introduction, conclusion, sidebars, key terms, headings, subheadings, figures, and illustrations of a text to get a sense of its content, organization, and emphases before reading it in full.

primary source (244–47, 276–77)   Firsthand information, such as an eyewitness account, a research report, a recorded interview, or a work of literature or art. See also *field research*.

process analysis (67)   A pattern of paragraph or essay development that explains a process step by step.

progressive tenses (674–79)   See *tense*.

pronoun (603–04, 657–62, 686–99)   A word that renames or takes the place of a noun or noun phrase.

pronoun reference (695–99)   The relationship between a pronoun and its antecedent (the word it replaces). Pronoun reference is clear when readers can tell effortlessly what a pronoun's antecedent is.

proofreading (103–04)   Reading a text to identify and correct spelling and typographical mistakes as well as punctuation and mechanical errors.

proper noun (601)   See *noun*.

proximity (177)   In design, the arrangement of content to show relationships. Material that is related should be placed close together; material that is unrelated should be placed at a distance.

purpose (11–13)   Your main reason for writing: to express your feelings or impressions or to entertain, inform, or persuade your audience.

Q

quantifier (752, 753)   An adjective such as *some, many, much, less,* or *few* that indicates the amount of a noun.

quotation (276–79, 815–17)   A restatement of what someone else has said or written, either in a *direct quotation* (word for word) or an *indirect quotation* (a report of what was said or written). See *direct quotation, indirect quotation.*

R

reading journal (127–28)   An online or printed record of a reader's reactions to, analysis of, or critique of a text.

reciprocal pronoun (603–04)   A pronoun that refers to the individual parts of a plural antecedent: *The candidates debated one another.*

redundancy (519–20)   Unnecessary repetition: *It was a cloudy, overcast day.*

reference list (370, 386, 429, 443–44)   In APA and CSE style, a section at the end of a writing project in which the writer provides full bibliographic information for all sources cited in the text.

reference work (234–38)   Sources, such as dictionaries, encyclopedias, bibliographies, almanacs, and atlases, that provide overview and background information on a word or topic. Specialized reference works may be appropriate sources for college projects, but general reference works are not.

reflection (124–28)   The process of thinking about, annotating, and

writing about a text in a reading journal; reflection is a necessary step for coming fully to terms with the text. See also *annotation, reading journal.*

reflexive pronoun (603–04)   A pronoun that refers back to the subject of a sentence: *She helped herself to the buffet.*

regionalism (565)   Nonstandard usage characteristic of people in a particular locality.

regular verbs (666–69)   Verbs whose past-tense and past-participle forms end in *-d* or *-ed.*

relative clause (621)   An adjective clause introduced by a relative pronoun such as *who, whom,* or *that.* See *adjective clause.*

relative pronouns (603–04)   Pronouns such as *who, whom, whose, that,* and *which* used to introduce a subordinate clause that describes the pronoun's antecedent: *The apartment that I rented is small.*

relevance (53, 249)   The extent to which supporting evidence not only addresses the general topic of a text but also contributes to the reader's understanding of or belief in the text's main idea (the *thesis*). A relevant source offers information that will enrich understanding, provide background information or evidence to support claims, or suggest alternative perspectives.

reliability (250–59)   The extent to which a source is accurate and trustworthy.

research hypothesis (214–15)   A tentative assertion of what the writer expects the research to prove.

research log (217–18)   A journal in which a researcher records research questions and hypotheses; a working thesis; information gathered from sources; interpretation, analysis, synthesis, and critique of sources; and ideas for next steps.

research questions (214–15)   Questions about a topic that research might answer, devised to help guide the search for sources.

restrictive element (791–93)   See *essential element.*

résumé (506–11)   A brief summary of an applicant's qualifications and experience.

revising (90–102)   The stage of the writing process in which the writer assesses global issues such as whether the text fulfills its purpose, addresses its intended audience, is fully developed, and is organized clearly and logically; also the stage in which the writer assesses local issues such as word choice, sentence variety and emphasis, and wordiness. See also *conciseness, peer revising.*

rhetorical question (558)   A question that is meant to call attention to an issue, not to elicit an answer.

Rogerian model (164–66)   A model for organizing an exploratory argument that discusses evidence and counterevidence before drawing a conclusion. Compare *classical* and *Toulmin models.*

roundabout expression (518)   A wordy expression that should be more concise.

S

s.v. (408)   Abbreviation of the Latin phrase *sub verbo,* "under the word."

scholarly sources (250–52)   Peer-reviewed journal articles and books by experts, often published by university presses.

scratch (informal) outline (40)   See *outline.*

search engine (223–33, 238–41)   Computer software that retrieves information from the internet, online databases, and library catalogs.

secondary sources (276–77)   Sources that describe, evaluate, or interpret primary sources or other secondary sources. A textbook is a secondary source.

sentence (610–25, 626–36)   A word group with a subject and predicate that does not begin with a subordinating expression. A **declarative sentence** makes a statement: *The phone rang.* An **imperative sentence** gives a command: *Answer the phone.* An **interrogative sentence** asks a question: *Did the phone ring?* An **exclamatory sentence** expresses strong or sudden emotion: *How I hate annoying ring tones!* A **simple sentence** has only one independent clause and no subordinate clauses: *The phone rang.* A **compound sentence** has two or more independent clauses but no subordinate clauses: *The phone rang, and I answered it.* A **complex sentence** consists of a single independent clause with at least one subordinate clause: *My cell phone rang while I was in the elevator.* A **compound-complex sentence** has two or more independent clauses with one or more subordinate clauses: *My cell phone rang, but I didn't answer it because I was in a crowded elevator.*

sentence outline (41–42)   See *outline.*

sequence of tenses (677–79)   The choice of tenses that best reflect the time relationship among the events described in the clauses of a sentence.

server (192)   A computer that links other computers into a network.

setting (451)   In works of literature, where and when the action occurs.

signal phrase (291–93, 299–303, 359–60)   A phrase that names the person being cited: *"How do I know what I think," E. M. Forster asked, "until I see what I say?"*

simile (578)   An explicit comparison between two unlike things,

usually expressed with *like* or *as: run like the wind* (see also *figurative language, metaphor*).

simple future tense (674)   See *tense.*

simple past tense (674)   See *tense.*

simple predicate (613)   See *predicate.*

simple present tense (674)   See *tense.*

simple sentence (623)   See *sentence.*

simple subject (612)   See *subject.*

simple tenses (674)   See *tense.*

singular (646)   Referring to one thing.

site map (195)   A list of a website's contents.

slang (565)   The informal, inventive, often colorful (and off color) vocabulary of a particular group. Slang is usually inappropriate in formal writing.

spam (195)   Unsolicited advertising sent to email or social software accounts such as *Twitter.*

spatial organization (39)   An organizational strategy that structures a description visually, from left to right, from inside to outside, from top to bottom, and so on.

sponsors (256–57)   Corporations, agencies, and organizations that are responsible for creating and making available a website's content.

squinting modifier (720)   A modifier that appears confusingly to modify both what precedes it and what follows it.

Standard American English (601) The dialect of English that prevails in academic and business settings in the United States.

stereotype (155, 568)   A simplified, uncritical, and often negative generalization about an entire group of people. See also *prejudice.*

subject (612–13)   The part of a sentence that identifies what the predicate is making a statement about. The **simple subject** is a noun or pronoun: *The cat hissed at the dog.* The **complete subject**

is the simple subject with any modifying words or phrases: *The excitable gray cat chased the dog.* A **compound subject** is a complete subject with two or more simple subjects joined with a conjunction: *The cat and the dog usually get along.*

subject complement (615)   An adjective, pronoun, or noun phrase that follows a linking verb and describes or refers to the sentence subject: *This food is delicious.*

subject directory (29, 225–26)   A collection of websites organized into groups by topic and arranged hierarchically from most general to most specific.

subjective case (686–95)   See *case.*

subjunctive mood (680–82)   See *mood.*

subordinate clause, or **dependent clause** (620–22)   See *clause.*

subordinating conjunction (533–34, 610)   See *conjunction.*

subordination (527, 531–35)   The incorporation of secondary or modifying elements into a sentence or clause: *Although he got a late start, he arrived on time.*

suffix (593–94)   A group of letters that attaches to the end of a root word to change its meaning and grammatical form: *act, action.*

summary (119–20, 269)   A passage restating the main idea and major supporting points of a text in the reader's own words and sentence structures. A summary should be at least 50 percent shorter than the text it restates.

superlative form (705–07)   See *comparison of adjectives and adverbs.*

superstition (154)   A belief with no basis in fact: *A wish made on a falling star will come true.*

syllogism (145–48)   A form of deductive reasoning in which the conclusion follows logically from the premises: If the premises are true, the conclusion must be true. For example: Socrates is human. Since all humans are mortal, and

Socrates is human, then Socrates is mortal. See also *deductive reasoning*.

symbolism (451)   The use of a character, event, or object to represent something more than its literal meaning.

synchronous media (199)   Communication media such as instant messaging and online chat in which participants discuss topics in real time. Compare *asynchronous media*.

synonyms (586)   Words with similar meanings—for example, *wrong* and *incorrect*. Compare *antonyms*.

synthesis (132–34, 279–80, 288–90)   The process of making connections among ideas in a text, ideas in other texts, and the writer's own ideas and experiences. Synthesis is an important component in critical thinking and reading and is central to much successful college writing.

T

table (82)   An information graphic that organizes data into rows and columns.

tense (674–79)   The form of a verb that indicates the time in which an action or event occurs, when it occurred relative to other events, and whether it is ongoing or completed. The three **simple tenses** are the simple present (*I practice*), the simple past (*I practiced*), and the simple future (*I will practice*). The **perfect tenses** generally indicate the completion of an action before a particular time. They include the present perfect (*I have practiced*), the past perfect (*I had practiced*), and the future perfect (*I will have practiced*). The **progressive tenses** indicate ongoing action. They include the present progressive (*I am practicing*), the past progressive (*I was practicing*), the future progressive (*I will be practicing*), the present perfect

progressive (*I have been practicing*), the past perfect progressive (*I had been practicing*), and the future perfect progressive (*I will have been practicing*).

tense sequence (677–78)   See *sequence of tenses*.

theme (451)   The main point of a work of literature.

thesis statement (33–37, 283–84)   A brief statement (one or two sentences) of the writing project's main idea.

tone (16–17, 573–76)   The attitude of the writer toward the audience, the topic, and the writer her- or himself as conveyed through word choice, style, and content.

topic (22, 214)   The subject of a writing project.

topic outline (41–42, 286–87)   See *outline*.

topic sentence (54–57)   A sentence (sometimes two) that states a paragraph's main idea.

Toulmin model (164–66)   A model for organizing an argument based on *claims* (or assertions), *grounds* (or reasons and evidence), and *warrants* (or assumptions linking claims to grounds). Compare *classical* and *Rogerian models*.

transitional expressions (61–62)   Words and phrases, such as *in addition, however,* and *since,* that show the relationship between sentences.

transitive verb (614–17)   A verb that takes a direct object.

tree diagram (38)   A way to depict the relationships among topics and subtopics visually by placing the main idea at the top of the page and letting topics and subtopics branch off below it.

U

understatement (578)   The deliberate use of less forceful language than a subject warrants. *An A average is pretty good.* See *figurative language*.

unfamiliar to familiar (39)   An organization pattern that presents surprising ideas, examples, or information first, before moving on to familiar ground.

unity (42, 54–59)   A quality of a writing project in which all the examples, reasons, and evidence support the paragraph's topic sentence and in which each of the supporting paragraphs supports the project's thesis statement.

unmarked infinitive (760)   The base verb alone, without *to*.

URL (255–56)   Universal resource locator, a website's internet address.

V

verb (605–06, 664–85)   A word that expresses action (*The quarterback throws a pass*), occurrence (*The play happened in the second half*), or state of being (*The fans are happy*). Verbs also carry information about time (tense), as well as person, number, voice, and mood.

verbal (619)   A verb form that functions as a noun, adjective, or adverb. Verbals may have objects and complements, but they lack the information about tense required of a complete verb.

verb phrase (618, 670–71)   A main verb with any helping (or auxiliary) verbs.

verbal phrase (619)   A verbal and any modifiers, objects, or complements.

voice (682–84)   In grammar, the form of a transitive verb that indicates whether the subject is acting or acted upon. In the **active voice,** the subject performs the action of the verb: *The dog chased the cat.* In the **passive voice,** the subject receives the action of the verb: *The cat was chased by the dog.* Also, in writing, the sense of the writer's personality as conveyed through the writer's word, style, and content choices. See also *persona, tone*.

W

warrant (166)   An unstated assumption that underlies an argument's main claim. See *Toulmin model*.

web browser (196)   The software program that interprets HTML code, making it possible for users to view websites and web pages.

weblog (or **blog**) (227)   See *blog*.

web pages (191)   Files on a website in addition to the home page; web pages may include text, audio, video, still images, and database files.

website (191)   A collection of files located at a single address (URL) on the World Wide Web.

white space (180–81)   The portion of a page or screen with no text, graphics, or images.

wiki (192)   A website designed for collaborative writing and editing.

working bibliography (219–20)   A list of sources a researcher compiles before and during the research process.

works-cited list (298, 316, 340)   In MLA style, a section at the end of a research project in which the writer provides full bibliographic information for all sources cited in the text.

writing process (10–114)   The process a writer engages in to produce a writing project. The writing process includes analyzing the assignment, planning the project, generating ideas, drafting, revising, editing, designing, proofreading, and publishing.

writing situation (10–18)   The characteristics of a writing project, including its purpose, audience, context, and genre, as well as its length, due date, and format.

Z

zero article (749)   See *article*.

Glossary of Usage

This usage glossary includes words that writers often confuse (*infer, imply*) or misuse (*disinterested, uninterested*) and expressions that are nonstandard and sometimes even pretentious. As a responsible writer, strive to avoid words and expressions that will confuse or distract your readers or that will undermine their confidence in you. Of course, not all words and expressions that cause writers problems are listed here; if a word or expression with which you have trouble is *not* included here, check the index, review chapters 29 and 30 ("Choosing Appropriate Language" and "Choosing Effective Words"), review the list of homonyms and near homonyms on p. 591, consult the usage notes in a dictionary, or consult another usage guide, such as *Fowler's Modern English Usage, The New York Times Manual of Style and Usage, 100 Words Almost Everyone Confuses and Misuses,* or *The American Heritage Book of English Usage.*

A

a, an *A* and *an* are indefinite articles. Use *a* before a word that begins with a consonant sound: *a car, a hill, a one-way street.* Use *an* before a word that begins with a vowel sound: *an appointment, an hour, an X-ray.*

accept, except *Accept* is a verb meaning "agree to receive": *I accept the nomination. Except* is a preposition that means "but": *Everyone voted for me except Paul.*

adapt, adopt *Adapt* means "to adjust": *Instead of migrating, the park's ducks adapt to the changing climate. Adopt* means "to take as one's own": *I adopted a cat from the shelter.*

adverse, averse *Adverse* means "unfavorable" or "hostile"; *averse* means "opposed": *She was averse to buying a ticket to a play that had received such adverse criticism.*

advice, advise The noun *advice* means "guidance"; the verb *advise* means "to suggest": *I advised her to get some sleep. She took my advice and went to bed early.*

affect, effect As a verb, *affect* means "to influence" or "to cause a change": *Study habits affect one's grades.* As a noun, *affect* means "feeling or emotion": *The defendant responded without affect to the guilty verdict.* As a noun, *effect* means "result": *The decreased financial aid budget is an effect of the recession.* As a verb, *effect* means "to bring about or accomplish": *Submitting the petition effected a change in the school's policy.*

aggravate, irritate *Aggravate* means "to intensify" or "worsen": *Dancing until dawn aggravated Giorgio's bad back. Irritate* means "to annoy": *He was irritated that his chiropractor could not see him until Tuesday.* Colloquially, *aggravate* is often used to mean *annoy,* but this colloquial usage is inappropriate in formal contexts.

agree to, agree with *Agree to* means "to consent to": *Chris agreed to host the party. Agree with* means "be in accord with": *Anne agreed with Chris that a party was just what everyone needed.*

ain't *Ain't* is a nonstandard contraction for *am not, are not,* or *is not* and should not be used in formal writing.

all ready, already *All ready* means "completely prepared"; *already* means "previously": *They were all ready to catch the bus, but it had already left.*

all right, alright *All right* is the standard spelling; *alright* is nonstandard.

all together, altogether *All together* means "as a group": *When Noah's family gathered for his graduation, it was the first time they had been all together in years. Altogether* means "completely": *Noah was altogether overwhelmed by the attention.*

allude, elude, refer to *Allude* means "to refer to indirectly"; *Elude* means "to avoid" or "to escape": *He eluded further questioning by alluding to his troubled past.* Do not use *allude* to mean "refer directly"; use *refer to* instead: *The speaker referred to [not alluded to] slide six of her PowerPoint presentation.*

allusion, illusion An *allusion* is an indirect reference: *I almost missed the author's allusion to Macbeth.* An *illusion* is a false appearance or belief: *The many literary quotations he drops into his speeches give the illusion that he is well read.*

almost, most *Almost* means "nearly;" *most* means "the majority of": *My roommate will tell me almost [not most] anything, but I talk to my sister about most of my own problems.*

a lot, alot *Alot* is nonstandard; always spell *a lot* as two words.

among, amongst *Amongst* is a British alternative to *among;* in American English, *among* is preferred.

among, between Use *among* with three or more nouns or with words that stand for a group composed of three or more members; use *between* with two or more

G15

nouns: *I'm double majoring because I could not decide between biology and English. Italian, art history, and calculus are among my other favorites.*

amoral, immoral   *Amoral* means "neither moral nor immoral" or "indifferent to moral standards"; *immoral* means "violating moral standards": *While secularists believe that nature is amoral, religionists often view natural disasters as punishments for immoral behavior.*

amount, number   Use *amount* with items that cannot be counted (noncount or mass nouns); use *number* with items that can be counted (count nouns): *The dining hall prepares the right amount of food based on the number of people who eat there.*

an   See *a, an.*

and/or   *And/or* is shorthand for "one or the other or both." It is acceptable in technical and business writing, but it should be avoided in most academic writing.

ante-, anti-   The prefix *ante-* means "before," as in *antebellum,* or "before the war"; the prefix *anti-* means "against," as in *antibiotic* ("against bacteria").

anxious, eager   *Anxious* means "uneasy": *Dan was anxious about writing his first twenty-page paper. Eager* indicates strong interest or enthusiasm: *He was eager to finish his first draft before spring break.*

anybody, any body; anyone, any one   *Anybody* and *anyone* are singular indefinite pronouns: *Does anybody [*or *anyone] have an extra pen? Any body* and *any one* are a noun and pronoun (respectively) modified by the adjective *any: She was not fired for making any one mistake but, rather, for making many mistakes over a number of years.*

anymore, any more   *Anymore* means "from now on": *She does not write letters anymore. Any more* means "additional": *I do not*

need *any more stamps.* Both are used only in negative contexts, for example, with *not* or other negative terms such as *hardly* or *scarcely.*

anyplace   *Anyplace* is an informal way of saying *anywhere. Anywhere* is preferable in formal writing.

anyways, anywheres   *Anyways* and *anywheres* are nonstandard; use *anyway* and *anywhere* instead.

as   *As* should not be used in place of *because, since,* or *when* if ambiguity will result: *As people were lining up to use the elliptical machine, the management posted a waiting list.* Does this sentence mean that management posted the sign *while* people were lining up, or does it mean that the management posted the sign *because* there was such demand for the machine?

as, as if, like   Use *as,* or *as if,* not *like,* as a conjunction in formal writing: *The president spoke as if [*not *like] he were possessed by the spirit of Abraham Lincoln. Like* is acceptable, however, as a preposition that introduces a comparison: *The president spoke like a true leader.*

at   *At* is not necessary to complete *where* questions: *Where is Waldo?* not *Where is Waldo at?*

averse, adverse   See *adverse, averse.*

awful, awfully   In formal writing, use *awful* and *awfully* to suggest the emotion of fear or wonder, not as a synonym for *bad* or to mean *very.* The high priest gave forth an *awful* cry before casting the captive from the top of the pyramid toward the crowd below.

awhile, a while   *Awhile* is an adverb: *They talked awhile before going to dinner. A while* is an article and a noun, and should always follow a preposition: *Rest for a while between eating and exercising.*

B

bad, badly   In formal writing, use the adjective *bad* to modify nouns and pronouns and after linking verbs (as a subject complement): *Because I had a bad day, my husband feels bad.* Use the adverb *badly* to modify verbs, adjectives, and adverbs: *Todd's day went badly from start to finish.*

being as, being that   *Being as* and *being that* are nonstandard substitutes for *because: Because [*not *being as] Marcus did well as a teaching assistant, he was asked to teach a class of his own the next year.* Avoid them.

beside, besides   *Beside* is a preposition that means "next to" or "along side of": *You will always find my glasses beside the bed. Besides* is an adverb meaning "furthermore" or a preposition meaning "in addition to": *Besides, it will soon be finals. Besides chemistry, I have exams in art history and statistics.*

between, among   See *among, between.*

bring, take   Use *bring* when something is coming toward the speaker and *take* when it is moving away: *When the waiter brought our entrees, he took our bread.*

burst, bursted; bust, busted   *Burst* is a verb meaning to break apart violently; the past tense of *burst* is also *burst,* not *bursted. Bust* is slang for *to burst* or *to break* and should be avoided in formal writing: *The boiler burst [*not *bursted* or *busted] in a deadly explosion.*

C

can, may   Use *can* when discussing ability: *I know she can quit smoking.* Use *may* when discussing permission: *The server told her that she may not smoke anywhere in the restaurant.*

capital, capitol   *Capital,* a noun, can mean "funds," or it can mean "the city that is the seat of government": *The student council did not have enough capital to travel to Harrisburg, Pennsylvania's capital.* The word *capitol* means "the building where lawmakers meet": *The state's capitol is adorned with a golden dome.* When capitalized, *Capitol* refers to the building in Washington, DC, where the U.S. Congress meets.

censor, censure *Censor* means both "to delete objectionable material" (a verb) and "one who deletes objectionable material" (a noun): *The bedroom scenes, but not the battle scenes, were heavily censored. Clearly, the censors object more to sex than to violence. Censure* means both "to reprimand officially" (verb) and "an official reprimand" (noun): *The ethics committee censured the governor for lying under oath. Members of his party were relieved that a censure was all he suffered.*

cite, sight, site *Cite,* a verb, means "to quote" or "mention": *Cite your sources according to MLA format. Sight,* a noun, means "view" or "scene": *The sight of a field of daffodils makes me think of Wordsworth. Site,* a noun, means "location" or "place" (even online): *That site has the best recipes on the internet.*

climactic, climatic *Climactic* is an adjective derived from the noun *climax* and means "culminating" or "most intense"; *climatic* is an adjective derived from the noun *climate: The climactic moment of a thunderstorm occurs when the center of the storm is overhead. Tornados are violent climatic phenomena associated with thunderstorms.*

complement, compliment *Complement* is a noun meaning "that which completes or perfects something else"; it can also be used as a verb meaning "the process of completing or making perfect." *Compliment* means either "a flattering comment" or

"the act of giving a compliment": *My husband complements me and makes me whole; still, it annoys me that he rarely compliments me on my appearance.*

conscience, conscious *Conscience* is a noun meaning "sense of right and wrong": *Skipping class weighed heavily on Sunil's conscience. Conscious* is an adjective that means "aware" or "awake": *Maria made a conscious decision to skip class.*

continual(ly), continuous(ly) *Continual* means "repeated frequently": *The continual request for contributions undermined her resolve to be more charitable. Continuous* means "uninterrupted": *The continuous stream of bad news forced her to shut off the television.*

could care less *Could care less* is an illogical, and nonstandard, substitute for *could not care less:* If one *could* care less, then one must care, at least a little, and yet this is not the intended meaning.

could of, must of, should of, would of These are misspellings of *could have, must have, should have,* and *would have.*

criteria, criterion *Criteria* is the plural form of the noun *criterion,* Latin for "standard": *His criteria for grading may be vague, but I know I fulfilled at least one criterion by submitting my paper on time.*

D

data, media, phenomena *Data, media,* and *phenomena* are plural nouns (*datum, medium,* and *phenomenon* are their singular forms): *The data suggest that the economy will rebound by the time you graduate. The news media raise the alarm about public corruption, but it is the voters who must take action. The Aurora Borealis is one of many amazing natural phenomena.* (*Data* is increasingly used as a singular

noun, but continuing to use it as a plural is never wrong.)

differ from, differ with *Differ from* means "to lack similarity": *Renaissance art differs greatly from art of the Middle Ages. Differ with* means to disagree: *Martin Luther's forty-nine articles spelled out the ways in which he differed with the Catholic Church.*

discreet, discrete *Discreet,* an adjective, means "tactful" or "judicious": *Please be discreet— don't announce that you saw Ada crying in the bathroom. Discrete* means "distinct" or "separate": *The study revealed two discrete groups, those who can keep a secret and those who cannot.*

disinterested, uninterested *Disinterested* means "impartial": *A judge who cannot be disinterested should recuse him- or herself from the case. Uninterested* means "indifferent": *The book seems well-written, but I am uninterested in the topic.*

don't, doesn't *Don't* is a contraction of *do not;* it is used with *I, you, we, they,* and plural nouns: *I don't want to drive, but the trains don't run very often. Doesn't* is a contraction of *does not;* it is used with *he, she, it,* and singular nouns: *It doesn't matter whether you're a little late; Fred doesn't mind waiting.*

E

each and every *Each and every* is a wordy substitute for *each* or *every;* use one or the other but not both.

eager, anxious See *anxious, eager.*

effect, affect See *affect, effect.*

e.g., i.e. *E.g.* is an abbreviation of a Latin phrase meaning "for example" or "for instance"; *i.e.* is an abbreviation of a Latin phrase meaning "that is." In formal writing, use the English equivalents rather than the Latin abbreviations; the Latin abbreviations are acceptable in tables, footnotes, and other places where space is at a premium.

elicit, illicit   *Elicit,* a verb, means "to draw out": *Every week,* American Idol *contestants try to elicit enough support to avoid elimination.* Illicit, an adjective, means "illegal" or "impermissible": *In 2003,* American Idol *contestant Frenchie Davis was disqualified for posing in illicit photos.*

elude, allude, refer to   See *allude, elude, refer to.*

emigrate from, immigrate to   *Emigrate from* means "to leave one's country and settle in another": *Jake's grandmother emigrated from Poland in 1919. Immigrate to* means "to move to and settle in a new country": *Jake's grandmother immigrated to the United States in 1919.*

eminent, imminent, immanent   *Eminent* means "renowned": *The university hosts lectures by many eminent scientists. Imminent* means "about to happen" or "looming": *In the last year of the Bush administration, many felt that a recession was imminent. Immanent* means "inherent" or "pervasive throughout the world": *Many religions teach that God's presence is immanent.*

enthused   *Enthused* is a colloquial adjective meaning "enthusiastic." In formal writing, use *enthusiastic: Because of the team's excellent record, Eric was enthusiastic [not enthused] about joining.*

etc.   *Etc.* is an abbreviation of the Latin phrase *et cetera,* meaning "and others." Because *et* means "and," adding the word *and* before *etc.* is redundant. In a series, include a comma before *etc.: A great deal of online media are used in classes today: blogs, wikis,* Blackboard, Facebook, *etc.* In most formal writing, concluding with a final example or *and so on* (the English equivalet of *etc.*) is preferable.

everybody, everyone; every body, every one   *Everybody* and *everyone* are interchangeable singular indefinite pronouns: *Everybody [or everyone] who went to the concert got a free T-shirt. Every body* and *every one* are a noun and a pronoun (respectively) modified by the adjective *every: Coroners must treat every body they examine with respect.*

except, accept   See *accept, except.*

expect, suppose   *Expect* means "to anticipate": *I expect to be home when she arrives. Suppose* means "to presume": *I suppose she should have a key just in case.*

explicit, implicit   *Explicit,* an adjective, means "overt" or "stated outright": *The rules are explicit: "No running." Implicit* is an adjective that means "implied": *Implicit in the rules is a prohibition against skipping.*

F

farther, further   Use *farther* with distances: *I'd like to drive a hundred miles farther before we pull over for dinner.* Use *further* to mean "more" or "in addition": *I have nothing further to add.*

fewer, less   Use *fewer* with items that can be counted (count nouns). Use *less* with items that cannot be counted (noncount or mass nouns): *This semester, I am taking three fewer classes than I took in the fall, but because I have a job now, I have less time to study.*

first, firstly   *Firstly* is used in Britain, but it sounds overly formal in the United States. *First* (and *second* and *third*) is the standard form in the United States.

flaunt, flout   *Flaunt* means "to parade" or "show off"; *Ivan flaunted his muscular torso on the quad. Flout* means "to disobey" or "ignore": *He flouted school policy by parading about without his shirt on.*

further, farther   See *farther, further.*

G

get   Many colloquial expressions with *get* should not be used in formal writing. Avoid expressions such as *get with the program, get your act together, get lost,* and so on.

good, well   *Good* is an adjective; *well* is an adverb: *Playing well in the tournament made Lee feel good.* In references to health, however, *well* is an adjective: *She had a cold, but now she is well and back at work.*

H

hanged, hung   Use the past-tense verb *hanged* only to describe a person executed by hanging. Use the past-tense verb *hung* to describe anything else (pictures, clothing) that can be suspended.

hardly   Use *can hardly* instead of *can't hardly,* a double negative: *I can hardly keep my eyes open.*

he, she; he/she; s/he   Historically, the pronoun *he* was used generically to mean *he or she;* in informal contexts, writers avoid bias by writing *he/she* or *s/he.* In formal writing, however, revise your sentence to avoid a gendered pronoun: *Sensible students are careful what they post on social networking sites [not The sensible student is careful what he posts about himself on social networking sites].*

hisself   *Hisself* is a nonstandard substitute for *himself.* Avoid it.

I

i.e., e.g.   See *e.g., i.e.*

if, whether   Use *whether* not *if* when alternatives are offered: *If I must go out, I insist that we go to a decent restaurant. I do not care whether we eat Chinese food or Italian, but I refuse to eat at Joe's.*

illicit, elicit   See *elicit, illicit.*

illusion, allusion   See *allusion, illusion.*

immigrate to, emigrate from   See *emigrate from, immigrate to.*

imminent, eminent, immanent See *eminent, imminent, immanent.*

immoral, amoral See *amoral, immoral.*

implicit, explicit See *explicit, implicit.*

imply, infer *Imply* means "to suggest indirectly": *The circles under Phillip's eyes implied that he had not slept much. Infer* means "to conclude": *From the way he devoured his dinner, I inferred that Raymond was famished.*

incredible, incredulous *Incredible* means "unbelievable": *Debbie told an incredible story about meeting the Dalai Lama. Incredulous* means "unbelieving": *I am incredulous of everything that the tabloids print.*

infer, imply See *imply, infer.*

in regards to *In regards to* is nonstandard. Use *in regard to, as regards,* or *regarding* instead.

irregardless *Irregardless* is nonstandard; use *regardless* instead.

irritate, aggravate See *aggravate, irritate.*

is when, is where Avoid these phrases in definitions: *An oligarchy is a system of government in which the many are ruled by a few,* or *Oligarchy is government of the many by the few* [not *An oligarchy is when the many are ruled by a few*].

it's, its *It's* is a contraction of "it is" or "it has," and *its* is a possessive pronoun: *It's been a long time since the ailing pigeon flapped its wings in flight.* One trick for distinguishing the two is to recall that contractions such as *it's* are often avoided in formal writing, while possessive pronouns like *its* are perfectly acceptable.

K

kind, kinds *Kind* is a singular noun: *This kind of weather is bad for asthmatics. Kinds* (a plural noun) is used only to denote more than one kind: *Many kinds of pollen can adversely affect breathing.*

kind of, sort of *Kind of* and *sort of* are colloquial; in formal writing, use "somewhat" or "a little" instead: *Julia was somewhat* [not *kind of*] *pleased to be going back to school.* Use *kind of* and *sort of* in formal writing only to mean "type of": *E.E. Cummings's poetry creates a new kind of grammar.*

L

lay, lie *Lay* means "to place"; it requires a direct object. Its main forms are *lay, laid,* and *laid: She laid her paper on the professor's desk. Lie* means "to recline"; it does not take a direct object. Its main forms are *lie, lay,* and *lain: She fell asleep as soon as she lay down.*

leave, let *Leave* means "to go away"; *let* means "to allow." *If I leave early, will you let me know what happens?*

less, fewer See *fewer, less.*

like, as, as if See *as, as if, like.*

loose, lose The adjective *loose* means "baggy" or "not securely attached": *I have to be careful with my glasses because one of the screws is loose.* The verb *lose* means "to misplace": *I am afraid I will lose the screw and have to attach the earpiece with duct tape.*

lots, lots of *Lots* and *lots of* are colloquial and should be avoided in academic writing; use terms like *much, many,* and *very* instead.

M

may, can See *can, may.*

maybe, may be The adverb *maybe* means "possibly" or "perhaps": *Maybe I'll apply for an internship next semester, but if I wait too long all of the positions may be filled.*

may of, might of *May of* and *might of* are misspellings of *may have* and *might have.*

media See *data, media, phenomena.*

moral, morale *Moral* means "ethical lesson": *Aesop's fables each have a moral, such as "don't judge others by their appearance." Morale* means "attitude" or "spirits": *April's warm weather significantly raised student morale.*

most, almost See *almost, most.*

must of See *could of, must of, should of, would of.*

myself, himself, herself, etc. Use pronouns that end with *-self* to refer to or intensify other words: *Obama himself made an appearance.* Do not use them when you are unsure whether to use a pronoun in the nominative case (*I, she, he, we, they*) or the objective case (*me, her, him, us, them*): *This conversation is between him and me* [not *himself and myself*].

N

nohow, nowheres *Nohow* and *nowheres* are nonstandard forms of *anyway, in any way, in any place, in no place,* and *nowhere.* Avoid them.

number, amount See *amount, number.*

O

off of Omit *of: Sarah took the pin off* [not *off of*] *her coat.*

OK, O.K., okay These are all acceptable spellings, but the term is inappropriate in formal writing. Choose a more specific word instead: *Food served in the dining hall is mediocre* [not *okay*].

P

phenomena See *data, media, phenomena.*

plus Avoid using *plus* as a substitute for the coordinating conjunction *and* or the transition *moreover.*

precede, proceed   *Precede* means "come before"; *proceed* means "continue": *Despite warnings from those who preceded me, I proceeded to take six classes in one semester.*

principal, principle   *Principal*, a noun, refers to the leader of an organization. *Principal*, used as an adjective, means "main." *Principle*, used as a noun, means "belief" or "standard": *The school principal's principal concern is the well-being of her students. She runs the school on the principle that fairness is essential.*

proceed, precede   See *precede, proceed.*

R

raise, rise   The verb *raise* means "lift up" or "move up" and takes a direct object: *Joseph raised the blinds.* The verb *rise* means "to go upward" and does not take a direct object: *We could see the steam rise as the solution started to boil.*

real, really   Do not use *real* or *really* as a synonym for *very*: *Spring break went very [not real or really] fast.*

reason is because, reason why   To avoid redundancy and faulty predication, choose either *the reason is that* or *because*: *The reason Chris fell is that he is uncoordinated. It is not because his shoe was untied.*

refer to, allude, elude   See *allude, elude, refer to.*

relation, relationship   Use *relation* to refer to a connection between things: *There is a relation between the amount one sleeps and one's overall health.* Use *relationship* to refer to a connection between people: *Tony has always had a close relationship with his grand-father.*

respectfully, respectively   *Respect-fully* means "with respect": *Ben treats his parents respectfully.*

Respectively means "in the given order": *My mother and father are 54 and 56, respectively.*

rise, raise   See *raise, rise.*

S

set, sit   The verb *set* means "to place" or "to establish," and it takes a direct object. *The professor set the book on the desk.* The verb *sit* means "to assume a sitting position," and it does not take a direct object: *You can sit in the waiting room until the doctor is ready.*

shall, will   In the past, *shall* was used as a helping verb with *I* and *we*, and *will* was used with *he, she, it,* and *they: I shall go on dancing,* and *they will go home.* Now *will* is generally used with all persons: *I will go on singing, and they will all cover their ears. Shall* is used mainly with polite questions (*Shall we invite your mother?*) and in rules and regula-tions (*No person shall enter these premises after dusk.*).

should of   See *could of, must of, should of, would of.*

since   *Since* can mean "because" or "from that time," so use it only when there is no chance that readers will infer the wrong meaning. In the sentence that follows, either meaning makes sense: *Since I moved to the coun-try, I have had no trouble sleep-ing.* Revise to make your mean-ing clear: *Since January, when I moved to the country . . .* or *Be-cause I moved to the country, . . .*

sit, set   See *set, sit.*

site, sight, cite   See *cite, sight, site.*

somebody, someone   *Somebody* and *someone* are interchangeable singular indefinite pronouns: *Someone [or somebody] is at the door.*

sometime, sometimes   *Sometime* is an adverb meaning "at an indefi-nite time"; *sometimes* is an adverb meaning "on occasion," "now and

then": *Sometimes I wish my future would come sometime soon.*

somewheres   *Somewheres* is non-standard; use *somewhere* instead.

stationary, stationery   *Stationary* means "not moving"; *stationery* means "writing paper." (Thinking of the *e* in "stationery" as standing for *envelope* may help.)

supposed to, used to   *Supposed to* means *should; used to* means "did regularly in the past." In speech, the final *-d* is often dropped, but in writing, it is required: *I was supposed [not suppose] to practice piano daily; instead, I used [not use] to play hockey.*

sure and, sure to; try and, try to   *Sure to* and *try to* are standard; *sure and* and *try and* are not.

T

take, bring   See *bring, take.*

than, then   *Than* is a conjunc-tion used in comparisons; *then* is an adverb of time. *If Betsy is already taller than I, then I will be impressed.*

that, which   In formal writing, *that* is generally used with essential (or restrictive) clauses and *which* with nonessential (nonrestrictive) clauses: *The project that I am working on now is due on Mon-day, which is why I really have to finish it this weekend.*

that, who   In formal writing, use *who* or *whom*, not *that*, to refer to people: *I. M. Pei is the architect who [not that] designed this building.*

their, there, they're   *Their* is a possessive pronoun, *there* is an adverb of place, and *they're* is a contraction of "they are": *They're always leaving their dishes in the sink. Why must they leave them there instead of putting them in the dishwasher?*

theirself, theirselves, them-self   *Theirself, theirselves,* and *themself* are nonstandard. Use *themselves* instead.

them In colloquial speech, the pronoun *them* is sometimes used in place of the demonstrative adjective *those;* avoid this nonstandard usage: *Those [not them] are the books I need for class.*

then, than See *than, then.*

this here, these here, that there, them there *This here, these here, that there,* and *them there* are nonstandard for *this, these, that,* and *them.*

to, too, two *To* is a preposition, *too* is an adverb, and *two* is a number: *To send two dozen roses to your girlfriend for Valentine's Day is too expensive.*

try and, try to See *sure and, sure to; try and, try to.*

U

uninterested, disinterested See *disinterested, uninterested.*

unique *Unique* means "the one and only thing of its kind," so it is illogical to modify it with words like *somewhat* or *very* that suggest degrees: *Your approach to the issue is unique [not somewhat unique].*

usage, use The noun *usage,* which means a "customary manner, approach," should not be used in place of the noun *use: The use [not usage] of cell phones in this restaurant will not be tolerated.*

use, utilize The verb *utilize,* which means "to use purposefully," should not be used in place of *use: Students must use [not utilize] parking lots D, E, and F, not those parking lots reserved for faculty and staff.*

W

wait for, wait on Although *wait on* is sometimes used colloquially as a substitute for "wait for," it is nonstandard. Use *wait on* to mean "serve" and *wait for* to mean "await": *I am waiting for [not waiting on] my mother, who is always late.*

ways *Ways* is sometimes used colloquially as a substitute for "distance." Avoid this usage in formal writing: *We still have quite a distance [not ways] to go before we get to a rest area.*

weather, whether *Weather,* a noun, means "the state of the atmosphere"; *whether,* a conjunction, indicates a choice between alternatives: *It does not matter whether you prefer rain or snow; the weather will be what it will be.*

well, good See *good, well.*

whether, if See *if, whether.*

which, that See *that, which.*

who, that See *that, who.*

who, whom Use *who* for the subject of clauses; use *whom* for the object of clauses: *Who will be coming to the party? Whom did you ask to bring the cake?*

who's, whose *Who's* is a contraction of "who is" or "who has"; *whose* is a possessive pronoun: *Who's at the door? Whose coat is this?*

will, shall See *shall, will.*

would of See *could of, must of, should of, would of.*

Y

you *You* (the second-person singular pronoun) should be used only to refer to the reader, not to refer to people in an indefinite sense (to replace *one*): *In medieval society, subjects [not you] had to swear an oath of allegiance to the king.*

your, you're *Your* is a possessive pronoun; *you're* is a contraction of "you are": *You're as stubborn as your brother.*

Credits

Text Credits

343 Microsoft Word toolbar for setting margins. Microsoft Office Word. **351 SSE 19.3** Adrian Tomine, 8-panel cartoon "Optic Nerve #6," p. 22, from *Drawn and Quarterly,* February 1999. © 1999 by Adrian Tomine. Reproduced by permission. **385** Microsoft toolbars showing margins & indentation. Created with Microsoft Office software.

PART 6: Fig. 21.1, p. 450 Gary Snyder, "Front Lines," from *Turtle Island,* copyright © 1974 by Gary Snyder. Reprinted by permission of New Directions Publishing Corp. **469–471** Ben Brantley, "Rash and Unadvis'd in Verona Seeks Same" (review of "Romeo and Juliet") *New York Times,* 25 June 2007, pp. E1, E7. <http://theater2.nytimes.com/2007/06/25/theater/reviews/25bran.html?scp=1&sq=%22Romeo%20and%20Juliet%22%202007&st=cse>. © 2007 The New York Times. All rights reserved. Used by permission and protected by the Copyright laws of the United States. The printing, copying, and redistribution, or retransmission of the Material without express written permission is prohibited. **Fig. 24.2** Sample Microsoft Outlook screen shot of an emailed memo. Created with Microsoft Outlook. **Fig. 24.7** Sample Press Release, "Family Teams Key to March for Babies," March of Dimes, North Dakota Chapter, January 1, 2008. Reprinted with the permission of Karin Roseland, State Director, March of Dimes North Dakota Chapter.

PART 7: 541 Winston Churchill, speech to House of Commons, 4 June 1940. Copyright © Winston S. Churchill. Reproduced with permission of Curtis Brown Ltd, London on behalf of The Estate of Winston Churchill. **547** Martin Luther King Jr., speech, Washington, DC, August 26, 1963. Copyright 1963 Dr. Martin Luther King Jr.; copyright renewed 1991 Coretta Scott King. Reprinted by arrangement with The Heirs to the Estate of Martin Luther King Jr., c/o Writers

House as agent for the proprietor, New York, NY. **558** Darrin M. McMahon, "The Pursuit of Happiness in Perspective," April 8, 2007, *Cato Unbound* <www.cato-unbound.org/2007/04/08/darrin-m-mcmahon/the-pursuit-of-happiness-in-perspective>. All Rights Reserved, ©2008 Cato Institute. **559** Flannery O'Connor, talk delivered at Notre Dame University, 1957, published in *Mystery and Manners: Occasional Prose* by Flannery O'Connor. Selected and edited by Sally Fitzgerald and Robert Fitzgerald. New York: Farrar, Straus and Giroux, 1969. Reprinted by permission of Farrar, Straus & Giroux and the Harold Matson Company, Inc. © 1957 by Flannery O'Connor. © Renewed 1985 by Regina Cline O'Connor. Reprinted by permission of the Mary Flannery O'Connor Charitable Trust via Harold Matson, Inc. **563** *The New Yorker,* July 8, 1996. © The New Yorker Collection 1996 Mick Stevens from cartoonbank.com. All Rights Reserved. **577** David Ferrell, "Far Beyond a Mere Marathon; Ultra-race from Death Valley to Mt. Whitney—135 miles—tortures the body and mind." *Los Angeles Times,* Home Edition, August 23, 1997, p. 1, Part A, Metro Desk. © 1997 Los Angeles Times. Reprinted by permission. **588** Merriam-Webster's Online Dictionary, entry for "respect." <http://www.merriam-webster.com/dictionary/respect[1]>. By permission. From the *Merriam-Webster Online Dictionary* © 2009 by Merriam-Webster, Incorporated (www.Merriam-Webster.com).

PART 10: 747 *The New Yorker,* July 28, 2008. © The New Yorker Collection 2008 J. C. Duffy from cartoonbank.com. All Rights Reserved. **800** CartoonStock.com. By Gerard Whyman, reproduced by permission from www.CartoonStock.com. **814** © 2003 Stivers. 11/19/03. © 2003 www.markstivers.com. Reproduced by permission. **817** Lucio Guerrero, "Like a GOTH," *Chicago Sun-Times,* Sept. 16, 2005, p. 53. Courtesy of the Chicago Sun-Times; Gary Snyder, "Front Lines," from *Turtle Island,* copyright © 1974 by Gary

Snyder. Reprinted by permission of New Directions Publishing Corp. **827** Kathy McManus, "Class Action: Laptops Not Allowed," Liberty Mutual's www.responsibilityproject.com, Aug. 14, 2008. <www.responsibilityproject.com/blog/>. Used by permission. **838** Dylan Thomas, "Do not go gentle into that good night," from *The Poems of Dylan Thomas,* published by New Directions. Copyright © 1952 by Dylan Thomas. Reprinted by permission of New Directions Publishing Corp. **Fig. 54.1, p. 850** Google News screen shot showing a list of hyperlinks. © 2009 Google. **Fig. 57.1** dictionary definition of "responsibility" from Random House Webster's College Dictionary, © 1995. Reprinted with permission from *Random House Webster's College Dictionary,* © 1995, published by Random House, Inc.

Documentation Foldout:
Verso book page—front Toni Morrison, *A Mercy* (Alfred A. Knopf, 2008). Copyright © 2008 by Toni Morrison. Used by permission of Alfred A. Knopf, a division of Random House, Inc.

Page 1 Table of Contents, *Change,* November–December 2002, Vol. 34, No. 6, p. 3. Reprinted with permission of the Helen Dwight Reid Educational Foundation. Published by Heldref Publications, 1319 Eighteenth St., NW, Washington, DC 20036-1802. Copyright © 2002; Nancy Cantor and Steven Schomberg, "What We Want Students to Learn: Cultivating Playfulness and Responsibility in a Liberal Education," *Change* 34.6 (2002), 46–49; p. 46. Reprinted with permission of the Helen Dwight Reid Educational Foundation. Published by Heldref Publications, 1319 Eighteenth St., NW, Washington, DC 20036-1802. Copyright © 2002.
Page 2 front EBSCO Host Academic Search Premier page showing listing and abstract of Nancy Cantor and Steven Schomberg, "What We Want Students to Learn: Cultivating Playfulness and Responsibility in a Liberal Education," *Change* 34.6 (2002), 46–49. Reproduced by permission of

Photo Credits

Index

ESL Index

ESL Notes

Getting It Across and Tech Boxes

Quick Reference and Writing Responsibly Boxes

Writing Responsibly Boxes